The United States and Africa

THE UNITED STATES AND AFRICA

A HISTORY

PETER DUIGNAN AND L. H. GANN

Senior Fellows
Hoover Institution

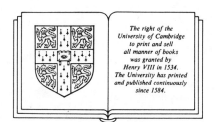

The right of the
University of Cambridge
to print and sell
all manner of books
was granted by
Henry VIII in 1534.
The University has printed
and published continuously
since 1584.

CAMBRIDGE UNIVERSITY PRESS

CAMBRIDGE

LONDON   NEW YORK   NEW ROCHELLE

MELBOURNE   SYDNEY

AND

HOOVER INSTITUTION

Published by the Press Syndicate of the University of Cambridge
The Pitt Building, Trumpington Street, Cambridge CB2 1RP
32 East 57th Street, New York, NY 10022, USA
296 Beaconsfield Parade, Middle Park, Melbourne 3206, Australia

First published 1984

Printed in the United States of America

Library of Congress Cataloging in Publication Data
Duignan, Peter.
The United States and Africa.
Bibliography: p.
Includes index.
1. Africa – Relations – United States.   2. United
States – Relations – Africa.   3. Slave-trade – United
States.   4. Slave-trade – Africa.   I. Gann, Lewis H.
1924–   .   II. Title.
DT38.D85   1984   303.4'8273'06   84–9552
ISBN 0 521 26202 X

IN MEMORY OF CLARENCE CLENDENEN,
SOLDIER, HORSEMAN, TEACHER, SCHOLAR,
AND FRIEND

Contents

Contents

Illustrations and maps

Illustrations

Maps

Preface

Contacts between Africa and the United States are of ancient origin. They are closer perhaps than those that exist between Africa and any European country. The literature on the subject is considerable, but most of it consists of specialized monographs that are neither accessible nor of interest to the ordinary reader. There is only one general survey, Edward W. Chester's study *Clash of Titans: Africa and U.S. Foreign Policy* (Maryknoll, N.Y.: Orbis Books, 1974), but this has now gone out of print. Our present work attempts to describe America's ties with Africa from the beginnings of the United States to the present. Our work incorporates three earlier monographs long since out of print, expanding them to cover the period since 1900.[1] Clarence Clendenen and Robert Collins collaborated with us on these earlier studies, and before Clendenen's death, he and Peter Duignan had sketched out chapters for the period 1900 to 1939. We have now revised and completed the history of American involvement with Africa.

Our work is addressed to Americanists as much as to Africanists. Our purpose has been to set down in broad strokes a general picture of U.S. activity in the African continent. This is above all a history of Americans; we have concentrated on the American aspect of African affairs and have said little about African reactions to American merchants, missionaries, and explorers – a field that needs to be further explored. Our work does not pretend to give equal coverage to every aspect of Afro-American relations; had we tried to be more comprehensive, we should have had to write a multivolume work. Instead we have concentrated on certain major aspects, including such themes as American involvement in the suppression of the slave trade, on which relatively little work has been done by others. This study is based largely on primary and secondary printed sources, on many doctoral dissertations, and on the private papers of a number of men; it represents a synthesis of historical scholarship. Much of the information has derived from American memoirs and autobiographies, missionary reports, journals, and government dispatches. We now hope that others will be encouraged to work in this field, since much remains to be done. Because we have primarily dealt with American activities in Africa, we have left to others the equally important task of assessing in detail Africa's impact on the United States. We made no attempt to consider in detail such wider questions as the United States and the disposal of the German colonies after World War I; those have already been elucidated by other scholars to whose work we refer in the notes.

Many friends and colleagues read and criticized various versions of the manuscript: Thomas Bailey, professor emeritus from Stanford University, Dr. Alan Booth of Ohio University, Dr. George Brooks of Indiana University, Dr. Norman Bennett of Boston University, Dr. John Peterson and Dr. David K. Patterson of the

University of North Carolina, and Professor George Shepperson of Edinburgh. A special thanks to Katherine Duignan Peck for checking legions of footnotes and quotations and to Dr. J. C. St. Clair Drake, professor emeritus from Stanford University, for his extensive comments on the entire manuscript.

The authors take full responsibility for any errors that remain, and the opinions and judgments expressed here are theirs alone.

Peter Duignan
L. H. Gann

I

The Slave Trade

Bartering for slaves on the Gold Coast. Courtesy Hoover Institution Archives.

Audience in Liberia for Commodore Perry's officers, ca. 1845. Courtesy Hoover Institution Archives.

The African squadron, 1843. Courtesy Hoover Institution Archives.

Slave captures. Courtesy Hoover Institution Archives.

Slave caravan. Courtesy Hoover Institution Archives.

How slaves were stowed on a slave ship. Courtesy Hoover Institution Archives.

CHAPTER I

The transatlantic slave trade

An overview

America's first permanent link to Africa derives from the slave trade. The origins of slavery in Africa date from remote antiquity. Ancient Egyptians brought slaves from Nubia; the Carthaginians used captives from the Sudan to work on the North African plantations and fight in their armies. In more recent times, long before the transatlantic slave trade came into being, East Africa had become an important supplier of captives for Asia. Human merchandise from East Africa passed to Turkey, Arabia, Persia, India, Indonesia, and even China. Records of this trade are scattered in different parts of the world and are uneven in quality, but occasionally some of the documents are revealing; for instance, a great revolt of African slaves in ninth-century Persia continued for fifteen years. The Arab invasion of North Africa and the subsequent Arabic conquests inland occasioned a substantial increase in the trans-Saharan slave trade, a traffic that gave considerable wealth to many of the medieval kingdoms and empires of West Africa and also accounted in part for the growth and prosperity of the Hausa city-states.

On the whole, however, neither the Arabs nor the Afro-Islamic societies of Africa developed huge plantations with an unlimited demand for unskilled manpower. There were occasional exceptions: Nineteenth-century Zanzibaris, for instance, profited from clove plantations worked by servile hands. But Muslim slavery in general depended on the requirements of small-scale craft industries, on the need for soldiers and domestic servants, on the desire for conspicuous consumption and the luxuries of the harem. The rich men of Bornu, for example, bought slaves not only as field hands but also as concubines, as eunuchs for their harems, as palace retainers, as wrestlers, and as craftsmen. They did not, however, employ labor gangs on a huge scale to work large estates dependent on export industries.

Slavery also existed among many of non-Muslim African societies. Free men could lose their liberty by being captured in war, by being convicted for crimes, or by becoming the victims of political intrigue. There were even certain voluntary kinds of slavery; among the Ibo, for instance, a man might pawn his person for debt or offer himself as a cult slave to a local deity.[1] Captives or criminals might even be sacrificed to the gods. The fortunes of a slave were subject to immense variations. In some societies his fate might be of the harshest; in others, the slave was practically absorbed into the owner's family. Among the coastal communities of Nigeria, for example, slaves were usually assigned to the house of a polygamous owner's wife; this woman became the "mother" of the slaves and treated them with kindness. The "house" system welded slaves and freemen into closely knit trading corporations in which slaves had opportunities to acquire wealth and improve their social status.[2]

Some African slaves came to be employed on the land. Thus John Matthews, an

English naval officer sent to Sierra Leone in 1785, noted that Mandingo notables in the highlands often owned from seven hundred to a thousand slaves apiece. Many of these bondsmen had to work in the fields. Among the Mandingo (as among West Indian and American slaves) the farm laborers suffered more brutal treatment than the domestic servants, and there were even rural insurrections. In early nineteenth-century Dahomey, the foreign demand for palm oil caused Dahomeans to employ slaves on estates. Prisoners not required for this purpose were sold abroad. West Africa, however, never developed an indigenous plantation economy on a large scale. Backward methods of production and transport and lack of technical knowledge and capital probably prevented the West African notables from building up plantation economies on anything remotely resembling the transatlantic scale.

Africans in the more remote parts of the continent found themselves in even greater difficulties. Wherever they came in contact with foreign traders, they increasingly became accustomed to the use of imported cloth, knives, hatchets, beads, guns, and the like. All too often such commodities either could not be made as cheaply or as well as foreign manufactures. It is likely that the industrial revolution in Europe, especially in Great Britain, may have further stimulated Africa's demand for inexpensive foreign goods. These imports, however, had to be paid for. To some extent, Africans were able to meet their obligations by selling ivory or gold, but the riches of nature were not inexhaustible. Elephants might be exterminated in the ruthless search for tusks. Alluvial gold supplies were liable to be worked out. Any number of impediments stood in the way of expanding agricultural exports. Many African communities thus were beset by what one might call a perennial balance-of-payments problem. Accordingly, they were encouraged to sell human beings, their most precious asset, and the slave traffic in time became Africa's most extensive export industry.

The growth of the transatlantic slave economies

The pioneers of the Christian slave trade in Africa were the Portuguese, and during the latter part of the fifteenth and the early portion of the sixteenth centuries there was a considerable rise in the export of slaves. But in all likelihood the Muslims remained the main slave dealers in Africa. From the seventeenth century onward, however, crucial changes took place in the extent and organization of maritime slave traffic. The northern European powers, especially the Dutch, forced their way into the slaving business. Moreover, the overseas commerce of Europe experienced profound modifications. The purchase of luxury goods for the few was replaced by the importation of consumption goods for an increasingly large number of customers. The reasons for this transformation are complex, and can be alluded to only briefly in this chapter. Improvements in agricultural techniques, for instance, allowed more European housewives to buy fresh meat all the year round and thus diminished the importance of spices. Western Europe built up new industries; living standards went up; and Europeans began to buy tropical plantation products on a much larger scale. Commerce with the tropics thus grew both in bulk and in value.

Tobacco importing, for example, received a tremendous impetus as the habits of smoking and taking snuff spread to all classes. Coffee, tea, and chocolate began to be widely drunk. The consumption of these beverages in turn stimulated the demand for cane sugar and led to what some historians have called the "sugar revolution." Molasses or sugar could also be distilled into rum, and this heavy liquor proved as popular with American Indian braves and Benin warriors as with British tars. Similarly, the growing British and French textile industries depended on large-scale imports of cotton and of dyes such as indigo, brazilwood, and cochineal – all indispensable to manufacturers before the advent of chemical dyes.[3]

These commodities were supplied by plantations in what might be called Europe's agricultural periphery in the New World. Before the days of mechanized farming, these plantations required a vast army of cheap and preferably docile laborers inured to the heat of the tropics. The plantation owners increasingly came to rely on the manpower reservoir of sub-Saharan Africa. The far-flung partnership among European shippers, merchants and manufacturers, transatlantic landowners, and African slave-trading chiefs produced one of the most extensive and brutal systems of forced labor known to history. Reduced to its simplest dimensions, this system depended on a triangle of trade in which European workshops shipped their products to West Africa; Africans sold their captives to the plantations of the New World, north and south; and the plantations in turn dispatched their crops to Europe. Hence, from a cold economic point of view, the history of transatlantic slavery can be written in terms of sugar, tobacco, cotton, rum, and similar commodities.

The main beneficiaries of this trade were not – as is sometimes assumed – the territories that now constitute the United States. The thirteen colonies imported few slaves before the eighteenth century. Even thereafter, between 1700 and the American Revolution, they received only about 20 percent of the British slave trade. Philip Curtin, an outstanding modern historian, has reassessed past estimates of the traffic in a pioneer study.[4] The Old World was but little affected by the huge *Völkerwanderung* brought about by the commerce in slaves; only some 1.8 percent of all the captives were taken to Europe. North America received no more than 6.8 percent of all the slaves, 4.5 percent of them being sent into the territory of what is now the United States. Subtropical and tropical America, extending from Brazil to the Caribbean, employed about 90 percent of all the Africans taken to the New World. Important as slavery became in the history of North America, the main development of plantation slavery took place in the West Indies and in Latin America; the statistical facts have been obscured by the high growth rate of the Afro-American population in the United States as against the low survival rate of slaves in Brazil. These figures cast doubt on the theory propounded by some scholars that Mediterranean-derived institutions helped to protect the slaves against their masters.

Speaking in general terms, these plantation systems usually had a proclivity toward expansion. The growing demand for sugar and other tropical crops caused entrepreneurs to step up production. Increasingly monoculture production with unskilled and unwilling workers, generally based on methods ill designed to preserve the fertility of the land, commonly led to soil erosion. The planters opened up new acres, on which they raised more crops, which in turn furnished the profits to purchase additional slaves. By and large, however, the supply of servile labor born in the West Indies did not keep pace with the demand. The planters were, therefore, often under pressure to overwork their laborers. Overwork, poor living conditions, and ill treatment of field hands caused heavy mortality rates, which gave yet another stimulus to the Atlantic slave trade.

In the subtropical regions of North America, large-scale slavery became an established institution only after a considerable time lag. In 1619 the North American colonies received their first consignment of African slaves. During the rest of the seventeenth century, however, the increase in slaves was small. For a variety of economic and geographical reasons, the plantation economy of the South grew at a slow pace; the colonists preferred to use white indentured laborers who were ultimately assimilated into the community. Most early Americans at first opposed the introduction of Africans, and colonial legislatures passed a series of acts designed to prevent or hinder the importation of blacks.

The appearance of rice and indigo culture in South Carolina and the concurrent expansion of tobacco production in Virginia from about 1680 onward led, however, to an economic and social revolution of vast consequences. By the early eighteenth century the days of a largely self-sufficient agriculture were at an end. South Carolina planters began to make large profits from rice and indigo grown in the marshy lands of the seacoast and along the rivers. In Virginia the cultivation of tobacco expanded, and the small independent farms gave way to the lordly proprietors of hundreds, even thousands, of acres. Virginia and Maryland became the tobacco colonies. South Carolina and, later, Georgia were the rice colonies. Their labor requirements could not be met, even partially, by white redemptioners and convicts. The southern colonies became increasingly dependent on African labor, South Carolina and Virginia remaining the major customers. Large-scale slavery, broadly speaking, found its limit at the borders of the temperate zones, where the cultivation of tropical crops proved impracticable. But the slave trade was also important to the economy of the northern colonies, whose mercantile houses, shipping firms, and incipient manufacturing establishments likewise participated in it.[5]

Slavery in North America received yet another stimulus with the invention of the cotton gin in 1793. By this time British textile manufactures were being increasingly mechanized, and British factory owners cried out for more raw material. The cotton gin allowed American planters to meet this demand. Previously the customary process of seeding cotton lint by hand had been so slow as to prevent cotton from becoming a great American export. The cotton gin, however, enabled unskilled black workers to seed lint on a vastly expanded scale, and the new device changed a by-product of Southern agriculture into a staple crop, raised the price of slaves, increased the size of plantations, and convinced Southern landowners that slaves were indispensable for raising cotton. Plantation slavery, therefore, formed the backbone of the transatlantic slave trade and profoundly affected the fortunes of the African continent.[6]

The middlemen

The development of the plantation economy of the Americas gave tremendous opportunites to European and African merchants alike. But after the Dutch had broken the supremacy of the Portuguese on the African west coast during the seventeenth century, no European state was able to attain a monopoly of the African commerce. Americans, Dutchmen, Englishmen, Frenchmen, Portuguese, and Brazilians all took part in the West African slave trade, but no single power was able to dominate the region. The direct influence of the Europeans did not extend much beyond the range of the guns mounted on their forts and their men-of-war. Throughout the seventeenth century, moreover, the greater part of the West African shore remained innocent of European trade. There were permanent posts from the Senegal River down to the Sherbro, on the Gold Coast, and in Angola. But except on the Gold Coast, where the factories of European powers jostled in profusion, such settlements were few and far between. The influence a European power could wield in West Africa depended, when the crunch came, not on brick and mortar, but on the number of warships it could allocate to the region. There was a good deal of fighting among local white competitors; but gradually a policy of live and let live came to prevail among the white powers, so that even a number of smaller powers, including Sweden, Denmark, Brandenburg, and Courland, were able to obtain more or less temporary footholds.

In addition, Americans participated in the traffic. New Englanders, for instance, would ship foodstuffs, lumber, and manufactured products to the West Indies in exchange for rum. The captains proceeded to Africa, bartered their liquor for slaves, and then transported the latter to the West Indies. In exchange, Americans bought sugar and molasses, which were carried to New England to be distilled into rum. Alternatively, Yankee mariners would take rum, trinkets, bar iron, beads, and cloth directly to Africa, where they bought blacks with the proceeds.

No one will ever know how many people were abducted or killed through the slave trade. All we can say is that the number was very high. Anthony Benezet, an eighteenth-century abolitionist, calculated that during the middle of the century – when the traffic was at its height – British slavers brought something like 100,000 blacks a year from Africa to the New World. Other European nations shared their burden of responsibility, especially the French, the Portuguese, and the Dutch.[7] The figures varied considerably from year to year, and the evidence is contradictory. According to the calculations of Robert Kuczynski, one of the world's most prominent population experts, some 15 million people were taken from Africa to the New World between the sixteenth and the nineteenth centuries, though the total may well have been larger.[8] Basil Davidson, another British writer, opts for an even higher figure. Bearing in mind the loss of life caused by slave wars as well as slave sales, he concludes that "before and after embarcation, the Atlantic slave trade must have cost Africa at least 50,000,000 souls" over several centuries.[9]

Recent research into the subject has seriously modified these figures. Present investigations suggest that the numbers customarily accepted owe more to abolitionist passion than to statistical knowledge. Philip Curtin suggests that the total number of slaves shipped across the Atlantic during the four centuries of the trade did not exceed some 9 million, and that the figure may well have been rather less. Curtin doubts whether the Europeans had enough shipping space to transport more people over such huge distances. He also considers that the losses incurred by the captives en route could not have amounted to more than about 16 percent. This would still be a high figure, equivalent to that suffered by an army in battle; nevertheless, if his estimates are correct, the total number of men and women taken from Africa during the entire period of the slave trade could not have exceeded about 11 million. The numbers game has continued to preoccupy scholars ever since. Subsequent research summarized in James A. Rawley's standard work, *The Transatlantic Slave Trade*, suggests that the total may have somewhat exceeded 11 million. J. F. Ade Ajayi and J. E. Inikori, two prominent African scholars, opt for an even higher figure – their estimates more or less agree with Kuczynski's – but no investigator can ever be quite sure.[10]

For all its bloody inhumanity, the traffic in West Africa as a whole presumably did not diminish the total number of people. Even during its eighteenth-century peak, the trade merely tended to check the natural population growth. For the other centuries, the effects of the trade would have been relatively slight. Densely populated regions like the Akan states and the Yoruba and Benin kingdoms were most deeply implicated in the trade. In the New World, on the other hand, many black communities must have increased their numbers by natural growth rather than by forcible transplantation; the black people in the United States, notably, have experienced a phenomenal expansion of their numbers from the end of the eighteenth century to the present.

In the absence of truly reliable statistics, these questions can never be fully resolved. All we can say for certain is that the slave trade – for all the abolitionists' exaggerations – occasioned human misery on an unimaginable scale, and that it must have been very destructive of human life. Certain areas suffered severely; others were little affected, or even derived economic benefit from the growing commerce. The traffic cannot, moreover, be understood in isolation; it went with a more extensive process of African state building. The trade partly Africanized portions of the New World; it permitted the rise of tropical plantation economies and brought about a transatlantic variety of hereditary serfdoms in which bondsmen came to be distinguished by the color of their skin. The transatlantic traffic represented the greatest forcible transplantation of human beings known to history before the mass deportations and expulsions initiated by totalitarian regimes of the twentieth century. Muslim traders in North and East Africa played their part in the traffic, together with their African associates. But the main culprits were the kings and merchants, the slavers, and their Afro-European partners who supplied the slave owners' insatiable demand for cheap manpower.

The impact of the slave trade was enormous. The commerce was part of a great transatlantic system that involved the export of manufactured goods from Britain to Africa, the shipment of African slaves to the plantations of the New World, and the sale of American-grown crops to northwestern Europe (see Map 1). The slave trade did not merely help to create the plantation economies of the Deep South; it also played a major part in the economy of the northern colonies. In Rhode Island, for instance, the economic benefits of the African trade extended to the large number of artisans employed to the owners and sailors of small boats delivering materials, and to the distilleries. New England fishermen were concerned with salt and with dried fish; these were important articles of commerce with the West Indies and the Southern colonies because they were used as food for the slaves. Landowners were likely to profit from the sale of timber from their woodlots or forest lands, and so on. Indeed, "the financial ramifications of the trade with Africa extended deeply into all elements of American society."[11]

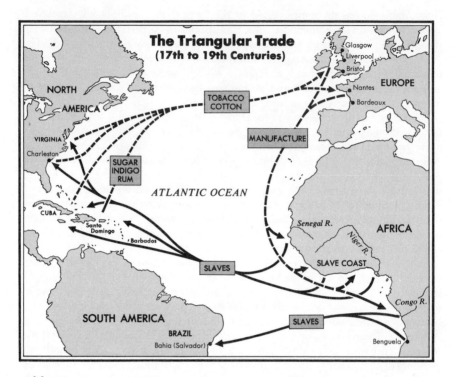

Map 1

The complexities of the traffic were such that no one will ever be able to draw up an exact balance sheet of profits and losses. The difficulty of striking a balance is increased by the fact that the commerce in human beings was so inextricably intertwined with "legitimate" trade in commodities that the various trends of the triangular trade can hardly be disentangled. There is not the slightest doubt that slavery played a great role. Without this massive importation of labor the plantation economies of the New World could not have developed in the way they did. Sugar, tobacco, and similar crops could all have been grown by free workers or by indentured white laborers. But during the seventeenth and eighteenth centuries, before the extensive development of agricultural machinery, small farmers could never have rivaled the immense production figures obtained on slave-run plantations. There is no doubt that American, Brazilian, and West Indian planters owed their very existence to the transatlantic slave trade. Similarly, the traffic gave a stimulus to European trade and manufacturers.

But the tale of unlimited profits can easily be exaggerated, and recent research has done much to modify the reputation of the African trade for immense gain. The commerce in slaves was subject to serious internal weaknesses that subsequently played an important part in bringing about its abolition. It involved little capital outlay to African slave-hunters and middlemen who supplied the human "raw material," but European participants had to invest an immense amount of capital to make their businesses pay. They had to outfit vessels for long journeys. They had to meet the cost of cargoes made up of goods as varied as cloth, firearms, gunpowder, knives, brass and iron ware, pewter, and rum. They had to supply food and drink to their crews and garrisons, pay salaries, maintain forts and factories, and incur all manner of miscellaneous expenditure. They stood to suffer immense losses from fire, tempests, or pirates. A great concern such as the Royal African Company thus failed to make ends meet and finally had to be wound up. Smaller independent traders subsequently seem to have done better, but for them too the slave trade represented a gamble. As K. G. Davies, the historian of the Royal African Company, puts it:

> While all seaborne trade in the eighteenth century was risky, the slave trade must have been among the riskiest. The alternations of war and peace in some remote African kingdom could determine the scarcity or glut of Negroes. The local demand for European goods in Africa was liable to fluctuate sharply from year to year and from region to region. Sudden changes in world prices for sugar or rum could make or mar a whole voyage. An outbreak of disease on the dreaded "Middle Passage" could wipe out a fortune in a few days.[12]

And there was the ever-present threat from competition.

Lastly, it is difficult to separate the money made in the slave trade from the gains obtained through the purchase of such other African goods as gold, ivory, beeswax, and pepper. In crediting all receipts from sales of the inward cargo to the sale of slaves, many abolitionist writers in the nineteenth century tended to exaggerate the profits from the slave trade. S. Daniel Neumark, an economist, thus concludes that "probably, on balance, the direct returns to the European economy that can be credited to the slave trade *alone* were barely sufficient to cover all costs."[13] Similarly, the importance of the colonial trade to the Western economies as a whole can easily be overestimated. Overseas trade accounted for but a fraction of Britain's total commerce. During the eighteenth century, when the slave trade – a highly speculative enterprise – had reached its zenith, the bulk of British trade was carried on with Europe, especially with the countries geographically closest to the British Isles. "Compared with this, the traffic with India, the West Indies and North America was small, and that with Africa insignificant."[14]

Economic historians have therefore modified older interpretations of the slave trade that credit the commerce in human beings with providing much of the capital that set off the industrial revolution in northern Europe. Some industries undoubtedly benefited from the trade – especially sugar refining and the manufacture of textiles, hardware, and cheap guns. But the contribution of the slave trade to manufacturing was specific and limited. The formation of industrial capital was more complex than the operation of the slave trade; the profits of the commerce were too small and uncertain to create entirely new forms of economic enterprise.

Another misconception concerns the African share in the slave trade. Earlier accounts, written in a patronizing spirit common to Victorian historiography, suggested that slaves were obtained through unequal bartering between clever whites and unsophisticated blacks. The trade in fact rested on an Afro-European partnership: Africans supplied the "raw material" in the shape of condemned criminals or captives taken in war. The black traders in their operations displayed a high degree of sophistication; they took care to retain sovereignty over forts and factories; as Rawley points out, they collected customs duties and business fees;[15] they organized complex systems of supply and marketing; they showed profound economic sense in choosing those commodities that they would accept in exchange for slaves.

In purely economic terms, the slave trade of course appears a roundabout way of producing tropical crops. Why did Europeans or Africans not use land in West Africa itself to grow sugar or similar commodities? Such attempts were actually made. Compared with the West Indies or the American South, however, West Africa suffered from many economic disadvantages. The West African climate was more deadly for whites at a time when Europeans and Americans had no means of defending themselves against tropical diseases; West Africa did not have the trade winds required to power windmills at a time when steam-driven machinery was unknown; West African soils posed special difficulties of drainage and salinity.

To North America the importance of the slave trade was enormous. The traffic did more, perhaps, than any single other form of early enterprise to shape modern American society. The economies of Great Britain's colonies in the American South came to be dominated by the production of "money crops" on large plantations. The South therefore had to import most necessities – including labor. New England was in a good position to help meet these needs, for its scanty resources prompted the rapid development of shipping.[16] Since a large part of the carrying trade of New England was with the Southern and West Indian colonies, New England merchants almost inevitably became involved in the slave trade.

CHAPTER 2

The legal slave trade in North America

The American slave trade is of early origin. The first documented sale of black captives dates from 1619, when twenty Africans arrived on a Dutch ship. During the remainder of the seventeenth century, however, the traffic in human beings grew but slowly, owing to the presence of European indentured servants and the scanty progress made by the plantation economy of the South. American slavers usually obtained slaves in the West Indies, where blacks were shipped for resale until it was found that profits could be increased by eliminating the West Indian middlemen. Colonial ships loading in the Mediterranean, at Madeira, or at the Canaries often had space left for human merchandise. When such was the case, they might visit the African coast and add a few profitable black slaves to their cargoes of wine and salt. In the seventeenth century, slaves thus acquired were ordinarily brought to the West Indies rather than to the continental colonies.

The first American slave ship of which there is any record was the *Desire*, built in 1636 at Marblehead in the Massachusetts Bay Colony. It sailed from Salem to the West Indies in 1637 with miscellaneous New England products and several Pequot Indian prisoners of war for sale wherever a buyer might be found, and returned the next year with Africans as part of its cargo.[1] The first American ship to take blacks directly from the coast of Africa was the *Rainbow* in 1654. For most of the seventeenth century, however, direct trade and intercourse between the American colonies and Africa did not flourish. The slave trade was distinctly a part-time enterprise.[2]

Many, if not most, of the colonists were at first opposed to the introduction of Africans, and colonial legislatures passed a series of acts intended to prevent or to hinder their importation.[3] Such laws were eventually disallowed by the British crown, but the numbers of blacks imported into the continental colonies remained negligible between 1619 and 1690 in spite of the crown's interference in favor of the trade. Virginia, for example, had only twenty-three slaves in 1625. Thirty years later there were a mere three hundred; the number of Africans in Virginia did not begin to increase sharply until about 1700.[4] Governor Simon Bradstreet of Massachusetts reported in 1680 that "no company of blacks or slaves" had been brought into the colony for more than half a century except for the forty or fifty from Madagascar delivered by one small vessel in 1678.[5]

In South Carolina the first African slaves were procured by Sir John Yeamans from Barbados in 1671 to clear his new plantation on the Ashley River.[6] Although few blacks were brought into the colony – only twenty-four were imported in 1706, for example – the importation was steady. The governor, Sir Nathaniel Johnson, reported to the lords proprietor in 1708 that the colony's black and white populations were almost exactly equal in number, a little more than four thousand each.[7]

The introduction of rice and indigo culture in South Carolina and the concurrent expansion of tobacco production in Virginia around 1680 converted slavery, and the consequent enforced migration of Africans to America, into a fixed institution. By the early eighteenth century the days of subsistence agriculture had passed. In South Carolina it was found that rice and indigo would yield richly paying crops in the marshy lands of the seacoast and along the rivers. In Virginia the cultivation of tobacco expanded, and the small independent farmer gave way to the lordly proprietor of hundreds, even thousands, of acres. The labor requirements of the new agriculture could not be met, even partially, by redemptioners and convicts. The white man, it was believed, could not easily sustain long hours of labor in the rice and indigo fields. The result was an impetus to the slave trade and a stimulus to the plantations, merchants, shipowners, and incipient manufacturing establishments of the South and New England.

The North American colonies became increasingly dependent upon African labor for their economic expansion. Although Virginia had 300 slaves in 1659, by 1683 the number had increased to 3,000, and by 1708 there were no fewer than 12,000 black slaves in the Old Dominion. Almost 3,000 newly imported blacks were sold each year in Virginia after 1752. From a mere 24 Africans imported into South Carolina in 1706, the number shot up to 734 in 1724, and this was only the beginning.[8] In 1726 Samuel Wragg, a prominent Charleston merchant, testified to the Board of Trade in London that South Carolina then had 40,000 Africans and imported about 1,000 annually. Throughout the remainder of the colonial period the number of blacks imported into South Carolina continued to mount, until in 1765 Lieutenant Governor William Bull reported to the Board of Trade that more than 8,000 had been brought into the colony that year.[9]

Although South Carolina and Virginia were the major continental customers for African slaves, the black populations of all the other North American colonies showed parallel, though smaller, increases throughout the colonial period. Despite occasional recessions, the agricultural economy of the Southern colonies continued to expand, and the expansion was entirely dependent upon the cheap and seemingly limitless manpower of Africa. But the slave trade was also important in the economy of the Northern colonies; indeed, it is probably not an exaggeration to say that the slave trade was the lubricating oil that kept the machinery of the colonial economy moving smoothly. For this reason, the trade was as vital to New England as to the South.

The merchants and shipowners of Massachusetts started dabbling in the slave trade almost with their first overseas commercial ventures, and they continued to deal in Africa's major export throughout the colonial period. Up to 1750 Boston and Salem were among the chief slavery ports of New England; direct participation in the slave trade, however, seems never to have become the business of any considerable number of the Bay Colony's leading merchants.[10]

It was otherwise in the neighboring colony of Rhode Island and Providence plantations. During the eighteenth century the cities of Newport and Bristol became the centers of American activity in the African trade. Rhode Island had initially displayed strong convictions against enforced servitude. On May 19, 1652, the General Court passed an act providing "that no blacke mankind or white being [be] forced by convenant bond, or otherwise, to serve any man . . . longer than ten yeares, or untill they come to bee twentie four yeares of age, if they bee taken in under fourteen, from the time of their cominge within the liberties of this Collonie."[11] Although Rhode Island's convictions about chattel slavery gradually died out, the number of slaves in the colony did not greatly increase, nor did Rhode Island merchants and shippers engage extensively in the slave trade until well into the eighteenth century. In 1708 Governor Samuel Cranston, responding to inquiries from the Board of Trade, reported "that from . . . 1698 to . . . 1707, we have not had any negroes imported into this colony from the coast of Africa, neither on the account of the Royal African Company, or by any of the separate traders."[12] But in 1700 three small vessels from Rhode Island voyaged to the coast of Africa and sold their black cargo at Barbados, in violation of the act of Parliament that gave a monopoly of the slave trade to the Royal African Company.

The venture of these three "bootleggers" may be cited as the beginning of Rhode Island's interest and participation in the African trade. The Royal African Company's monopoly, which had always been impossible to enforce, was opposed by influential bodies of merchants in Great Britain as well as by the planters and merchants in all the colonies. It was finally abolished by Parliament in 1712. With restrictions removed, and under the stimulation of the profits that would be obtained, Rhode Islanders soon were among the foremost voyagers to Africa, the West Indies, and the Spanish colonies. Between 1725 and 1728 eight ships left Newport for the African coast or returned from there to Newport. Between 1731 and 1739 the number was twenty, and between 1747 and 1755, thirty-seven.[13] These numbers are not, at first glance, indicative of an extensive trade, but they include only vessels sailing directly for, or directly from, the African coast.

Not included are vessels sailing to or from intermediate ports, and the intermediate voyage was an essential part of a slaving expedition. The reasons for making the intermediate voyage have been succinctly explained by Lorenzo Johnston Greene:

> From New England's many ports, trim, sturdy ships, built from her own forests, carried to the West Indies much needed food and other commodities, such as surplus beans, peas, hay, corn, staves, lumber, low-grade fish, horses, dairy products, and a miscellaneous assortment of goods. When the captains of these vessels were able to exchange their cargoes for rum, they would next proceed directly to Africa. There they bartered their rum for slaves whom they transported to the West Indies where they disposed of them for rum, sugar, molasses and other tropical products or for bills of exchange . . . The sugar and molasses were carried to New England, distilled into rum, and along with trinkets, bar iron, beads and light-colored cloth taken to Africa and exchanged for Negroes.[14]

This was why most of the vessels entering Virginia and South Carolina ports carrying slaves directly from Africa were from English rather than colonial ports. Commercial necessity forced the colonial trader to deal with the West Indies, since at first the products of the continental colonies had no exchange value in Africa.[15]

The economic situation in Rhode Island gave its citizens special advantages in competing for the wealth afforded by the increasing demand for slaves in the early part of the eighteenth century. The minuscule colony, almost barren of natural resources, had gradually shifted from an agricultural to a commercial economy.

Governor Peleg Sanford had reported to London in 1680 that the colony's population included no merchants or "men of substance," and that the only shipping was carried on by a few small sloops. But by the end of the century Rhode Islanders developed two skills that transformed the colony: They became excellent shipbuilders, and they ranked among the foremost distillers of rum.

Rhode Island-built vessels in fact became so well known that the shipyards of Providence and Newport turned out ships for English as well as colonial owners.[16] As for the manufacture of rum, the colony informed the Board of Trade in 1764 that there were "upwards of thirty distill houses" in active operation.[17] The steady business of Rhode Island shipyards demonstrated that the African trade was indirectly giving employment to large numbers of colonial artisans and laborers— woodsmen, blacksmiths, and cord- and sailmakers, to name only a few. The economic benefits of the trade extended as well to the owners and sailors of small coasting boats that delivered materials to Rhode Island and, of course, also to the distilleries that bottled veritable seas of strong drink to be exchanged on the African coast for men and women.

The benefits of the Africa trade filtered from Rhode Island and other slaving colonies throughout New England, as a glance at the lading of almost any vessel engaged in slaving will illustrate. The invoice of the cargo carried from Newport to the African coast by the ship *Success* in 1749 shows 130 hogsheads of rum (14,147 gallons), 5 barrels of sugar, 14 barrels of pork, 5 half-barrels of pork, 31 barrels of beef, 19 barrels of flour, 30 barrels of tar, 2 barrels of menhaden, and 156 rolls of tobacco. All these items, except the sugar and tobacco, were of New England production and represented income for New England farmers and workmen. The manifest of the *Sierra Leone,* which sailed from Newport for the African coast in 1754, is even more illustrative of the economic activity stimulated by the slave trade. Its cargo included "Thirty four hogsheads, Tenn Terces, Eight barrils and Six halfe barrils Rum, one barril Sugar, Sixty Musketts, Six halfe barrils Powder, one box beads, Three boxes Snuff, Two barrils Tallow, Twenty-One barrils Beefe Pork and Mutton, . . . 22 lbs. bread, One barril mackrell, Six Shirts, five Jacketts, one piece blew Callico, one piece Chex, one mill, shackles and Hand Cuffs etc."[18]

Although all sorts of trade goods were exchanged for slaves on the African coast, the principal medium of barter was rum. The quantities shown in the cargoes of the *Success* and *Sierra Leone* were typical. In 1759 Captain William Ellery sailed from Newport directly for Africa with a cargo including 82 barrels, 6 hogsheads, and 6 tierces of New England rum, 33 barrels of the "best Jamaica spirits," and 33 barrels of Barbados rum.[19] The quantities of rum needed for the trade with Africa ran to fantastic amounts. To supply them, more than thirty distilleries operated in Rhode Island, as we have seen, and in neighboring Massachusetts there were more than sixty. Although huge amounts of rum were consumed in the colonies, the greater part of this liquor production was probably dispensed on the coast of Africa.[20]

Prices of slaves rose and fell, as with any other merchandise, but the accounts of Caleb Godfrey, who made a slaving voyage in the *Hare* in 1755, show that one dealer on the coast sold him four men, three women, three girls, and one boy for 799 gallons of rum, 2 barrels of beef, 1 barrel of pork, and some smaller items. From another dealer he was able to obtain two men, one woman, one girl, and four boys for a smaller price—only 416 gallons of rum.[21] In 1767 Captain William

Taylor, submitting his accounts to his employers, Richard Brew and Company, noted that male slaves had cost 130 gallons apiece; women, 110 gallons each; and young girls, 80 gallons.[22]

Rum, the ordinary medium of exchange in the slave trade, was by no means the only commodity acceptable. Many slaves were purchased from American and European traders already on the coast, and these people needed other articles in addition to the rum that was so attractive to African leaders. For example, the cargo of the *Whydah*, which sailed from Newport in 1762, included wine, coffee, sugar, tea, tobacco, turpentine, beef, pork, onions, tar, flour, and bread.[23] These articles were in addition to thirty-five hogsheads and tierces of New England rum. Other manifests show pickles, butter, sperm candles, clothing, beans, barrel staves and hoops, and scores of other items. Bars of iron and colored beads were currency almost as acceptable and as widely used as rum.[24]

Until 1775 Americans who engaged in the slave trade participated as British subjects. When they exchanged rum, bar iron, or cotton goods for Africans at Cape Coast Castle or Luanda, vessels from Newport, Boston, or Charleston flew the British flag, carried British papers, and were under the protection of the Royal Navy. But the events of the spring of 1775 brought about a sudden change. Vessels from colonial ports were seized as lawful prizes by the British, and the few American ships that reached the coast of Africa had to skulk from harbor to harbor, hoping that word of their presence in African waters would not reach British officials.[25] For a few years, at least, ships from continental North America ceased to appear. When they came again, they no longer flew the Red Ensign but sported a flag never before seen in African waters.

Whether or not the war in America was the cause, for one captain it took almost a year on the African coast to gather a cargo of slaves.[26] The importation of Africans into the rebellious colonies ceased until after the Revolutionary War had ended. The Liverpool and London merchants who had provided the vast majority of slaves sold in the colonies sent their cargoes to the West Indies or to the colonies of Spain and Portugal.[27] The American revolt thus interrupted the movement of Africans to North America, but it is doubtful that it had any marked effect upon the international slave trade as a whole.[28] After the war the merchants, shipowners, and planters of the new republic lost little time in endeavoring to make up for the lean years. The plantations of the Carolinas and Georgia needed field hands; for almost eight years no new labor had been imported. Slavers from New England and New York once again sailed to the African coast and discharged their living cargoes at Charleston and Savannah and in the West Indies.

Although the greater part of the slaves imported into the United States continued to be transported by British ships and sold for British slave dealers, the slave trade speedily regained its important role in the New England economy. But a new element was introduced, an element that was a direct outcome of the Revolutionary War and of the social and political ideals that it had fostered.

From early colonial times there had been some opposition of slavery and the slave trade, but it had been of little effect against the accepted mores of the time and the rich profits resulting from the trade. When the colonies gained their independence after basing their claims upon inalienable human rights, the idealists—in England as well as in America—gained a new and effective weapon. Condemnation of the slave trade became open and vocal, especially in New England, and within a few years attained a power that spelled the doom of the legal slave trade.

The abolitionist movement was not led only by Englishmen like Granville Sharp and William Wilberforce; the Quakers of the United States also played an important role. By 1787 Quakers were no longer slaveholders. They had always been against the traffic in human beings, and they were especially numerous and influential in Pennsylvania and in Rhode Island, the latter the state that had profited most from the slave trade.[29] In 1761 the Quakers of Pennsylvania had the Assembly place a duty on every imported slave. This step ended the trade in Pennsylvania.[30] Virginia closed its ports to the importation of slaves in 1778, and Maryland followed suit in 1783. North Carolina placed prohibitory duties on imported slaves in 1786, and even South Carolina, the major market for cargoes from Africa, placed restrictions on the traffic in 1787 and prohibited it completely in 1792.[31] Because of Quaker pressure, the Rhode Island legislature passed an act in 1787 forbidding citizens of the state to engage in the slave trade "either as master, factor, or owner of any vessel, [or to] ... import or transport, buy or sell, or receive on board [as slaves] any of the natives or inhabitants of any state or kingdom in that part of the world called Africa."[32] Rhode Island's lead was quickly followed by Connecticut, New York, Massachusetts, and Pennsylvania.

The major effect of the laws to stop the traffic in African human beings was, however, to cut down competition, increase profits, and thereby make the trade even more attractive. Although public sentiment against the trade must have been strong for such measures to pass, the merchants, shipowners, and planters who profited from it were not greatly handicapped in their operations; they merely sought new markets or resorted to smuggling.

Prohibitory laws would have been difficult to enforce, even had the states possessed adequate maritime police forces. In all the states, and particularly in New England, large numbers of otherwise respectable and law-abiding people saw nothing reprehensible in smuggling. The post-revolutionary generation had been raised in an atmosphere in which smuggling was deemed a necessary and defensible practice. As a result of the royal government's attempts in the early 1770s to enforce the Sugar Acts and other unpopular restrictive laws, the whole commercial atmosphere of the colonies was surcharged with illicit trade in one form or another.[33] Furthermore, many respectable people saw nothing immoral in the African slave trade, and the commerce in blacks continued.[34] In fact, it flourished. Respectable merchants and shipowners amassed fortunes,[35] and thousands of Africans, laboring for respectable planters, contributed to the expanding cotton economy of the South. Indeed, slaves were smuggled into South Carolina in such numbers that the state soon abandoned all attempts to enforce its legal ban on the trade.[36]

By the end of the eighteenth century, however, the commerce seemed to decline. The Northern members of the newly independent United States all abolished slavery within their own borders, and even in the plantation states of the South sentiment against slavery was widespread and vocal. The Constitutional Convention, drawing up the articles of government for the new country, passed the provision for abolition of the slave trade at a specified time without any serious opposition. As the ideals and aspirations of the evangelical revival, the American Revolution, and the French Revolution transformed the way people thought, slavery seemed to be on the way out.

CHAPTER 3

Ending the slave trade

Serfdom or slavery, for untold centuries, seemed part of the natural order in most parts of the world and was accepted as such. To give an example: In the early part of the eighteenth century Job ben Solomon, a Fula prince, was tricked into slavery and sold to a Maryland tobacco farmer who put him to rigorous field work. After attempting to escape, Job, a Muslim who could write Arabic, succeeded in contacting some distinguished philanthropists in England. He was redeemed, invited to London, and lionized in British high society before being shipped back to his native Gambia.

Job's story now seems strange. There is an incongruous element in the tale of an ex-slave who mingled on terms of social equality with the governor of the Royal Africa Company, the duke of Montagu, and was presented at the Court of St. James as a distinguished stranger. But the story did not strike either Job or his hosts in this fashion. Both parties believed in the mysterious working of divine Providence. Muslim Fula and most Christian Englishmen considered slavery or some other variety of servile status a normal part of human existence. Job himself did not deplore slavery as such; on the contrary, he dealt in slaves himself. British patriots extolled their country as freedom's chosen bastion, but they saw nothing wrong in press-ganging white sailors into the Royal Navy under conditions scarcely better than slavery, in purchasing mercenaries from petty German princelings, or in flogging their own soldiers with incredible brutality.

In the latter part of the eighteenth century, however, there was a slow and gradual change in what might be called the European climate of opinion. The institution of slavery especially came increasingly under intellectual attack. Blacks in the West Indies manfully strove against their fate. There was widespread resistance in Jamaica. In Haiti black liberation forces threw off the French yoke and destroyed slavery as an institution. The antislavery campaign, moreover, was part of a wider European upsurge against hereditary class and kin privileges that affected the whole of Western Europe and many parts of Central and Eastern Europe and also had profound consequence for the West Indies and Africa. Slave traders, plantation owners, and many great landed *seigneurs* in Europe all had stakes in a social order that allotted a subordinate hereditary status to certain groups of farm workers, white or black. Whether field hands were treated well or badly, they could not escape from their station in life without their masters' consent. Even if they did, their social mobility remained extremely limited.

From the end of the eighteenth century onward, however, the whole of Western and Central Europe was shaken by a profound social transformation in which old seignorial claims were suppressed, serfdom disappeared in all of its many forms, and labor became free to seek its own price. French Jacobins, British Methodists,

German Free Masons might differ on a great variety of issues, religious, political, and philosophical. But they all looked to the end of society divided into hereditary status groups, differentiated by hereditary privileges specific to particular social groups or localities, and articulated through a complex system of exemptions and franchises. The reformers anticipated the creation of a new society whose members would be entitled to individual rights, inalienable, universal, and founded upon reason.

The French Revolutionary governments played an essential part in the social transformation of Europe. Quite independently of the French example, however, major reforms were also pioneered by minor powers. These included Denmark, a small kingdom but the first country in the world to abolish the slave trade. Denmark thereby had an influence on world history quite out of proportion to the size of the country.

Denmark enjoyed a favorable geographical situation between the Baltic and the North Sea. In the eighteenth century Danish entrepreneurs made good their opportunities and greatly expanded their country's trade and banking while Danish agriculturists multiplied their crops and their cattle. The kingdom's economic development, however, placed an intolerable strain on the traditional institution of villenage and resulted in bitter political conflict. In the end, the innovators won the day, and in 1788 the great Danish statesman Count Reventlow (1748–1827) abolished the *Stavnsbaand,* the instrument that set out the terms of Danish serfdom. Further reforms followed, and in 1799 a royal ordinance put an end to all remaining labor obligations of the feudal kind. Denmark experienced a peaceful land reform: Many peasants received plots of their own, and the nation successfully moved from villenage to a system of fairly widespread freehold ownership.

The campaign against Danish feudal privileges spilled over into the colonies. In 1792, four years after the suppression of the *Stavnsbaand,* the Danish king issued an edict prohibiting the traffic in slaves. This prohibition came into force in 1803 and thus left time for Danish colonists in the West Indies to purchase sufficient workers for their needs. Danish reformers were also fortunate in that they did not have to contend with a powerful colonial lobby. The Danish possessions were small. Danish plantation owners could no longer expand their acreage. The local black population in the Danish possessions was gaining in numbers, owing to relatively good treatment and a high birthrate, so Danish estate owners could make do without large additional imports, and the reformers did not have to battle against a powerful but desperate pressure group. Neither was there much to fear from Danish shipping interests. Denmark was mainly an agricultural country; Danish Guinea merchants thus found considerable difficulty in competing against British traders with their cheap manufactures. Despite state aid, the Danish Baltic and Guinean Trading Company kept incurring losses, and the abolition of the slave trade was accomplished without serious internal friction.

The Danish initiative had far-reaching consequences. The slave traders' front broke at its weakest link. By the end of the eighteenth century the Danish slave trade was open to the flags of all nations. Foreign – especially British – merchants managed to gain the lion's share of the Danish traffic. Denmark's prohibition of the commerce in slaves delivered a serious blow to the British slave trade by destroying Britain's best foreign market for black captives. The British faced a major decision. Their policy, backed by the country's overwhelming naval might, would decide the course of Europe and the world at large.

The British political climate had by this time become increasingly favorable to the abolitionists' cause. In the early part of the eighteenth century abolitionism had been advocated primarily by a few negrophile intellectuals, but missionary and other ecclesiastical groups later began to play their part in the abolitionist campaign. Toward the latter part of the century the abolitionists formed political groups that transcended sectarian boundaries. Finally, the abolitionists, many of them Quakers, began to exert pressure on Parliament itself. Their cause became a major political issue.

At the same time there was a profound transformation within the structure of British politics. The "West India Interest," powerfully represented in the House of Commons before the Reform Bill of 1832, largely rested on the strength of the great sugar producers in the Caribbean. These great landowners continued to remain powerful; nevertheless, by the end of the eighteenth century, they began to encounter new difficulties. Much of the good land in the British West Indies had been exhausted by wasteful methods of production. There was competition from Santo Domingo. New competitors arose in the East Indies, where the British East India Company took up sugar production in 1789. (Yet another rival appeared on the scene later when European tillers learned how to grow beet sugar.) In addition, the American War of Independence delivered a smashing blow to the colonial system. Trade between independent America and Great Britain rapidly increased, helping to discredit accustomed mercantilist orthodoxies.

The war also brought political changes. The British faced renewed unrest in Ireland, and in 1800 the British Parliament passed an Act for the Union of Great Britain and Ireland in order to cement the imperial structure. British abolitionists at Westminster then obtained an unforeseen but welcome advantage in the shape of Irish members who lacked a direct economic stake in the traffic. Finally, the abolitionists benefited from internal political change in Great Britain itself. In 1806 Lord Grenville and Charles James Fox, an enthusiastic advocate of freedom for black slaves and one of the fathers of British parliamentarian radicalism, formed the short-lived "Ministry of All the Talents." In that year the new government put on the statute books the Slave Importation Restriction Act which forbade British subjects from participating in the foreign slave trade. A year later in 1807, shortly after Fox's death, the British legislature finally passed the momentous Act for the Abolition of the Slave Trade.

Once the British had put a stop to their own traffic, they had a natural interest in preventing foreigners from engaging in a trade that they themselves had forsaken and that went counter to the aspirations of British and foreign humanitarians alike. British statesmen became the foremost adovcates of abolitionism on the international plane. Great Britain used its enormous naval, financial, and diplomatic resources to wipe out the commerce altogether.

Historical debate over the profounder causes that led to the abolition of the slave trade has continued ever since. Victorian scholars stressed the role of religion and humanitarian sentiment. They were succeeded by men such as Sir Eric Williams, a West Indian scholar-statesman, who linked abolition to the dictates of industrial capitalism. According to these interpretations, the British West Indies were already in a state of economic decline at the time of abolition; maintenance of the slave traffic moreover conflicted with a free-trade economy of the kind desired by British entrepreneurs. In fact, the British slave system continued to expand until it was outlawed. In purely economic terms the British could have chosen to create new plantations in West Indian territories captured during the French Revolutionary Wars. Furthermore, the traffic in slaves and free trade were not incompatible. Despite the economic difficulties that we have mentioned, the West Indies as a whole were not in a state of economic decline during the abolitionist period.

The end of the slave trade had instead wider sociological implications. It was linked to a revolutionary transformation that steadily disrupted many social distinctions and seignorial and caste privileges in Central and Western Europe. There was a new social consciousness, and a new abolitionist international imbued with a new sense of social justice, and new convictions concerning the proper aims of society. As Heinrich Heine, one of Germany's greatest poets, and a man of profound intuitive sense, put the matter at the time, "What is the great task of our age? It is emancipation. Not only the emancipation of Irishmen and Greeks, of Frankfort Jews and West Indian Blacks, but the emancipation of the entire world, especially of Europe . . . which breaks away from the iron leading strings of the privileged."[1]

The British and American campaigns against the slave trade had much in common. Within a few days after the British had outlawed the commerce, the U.S. Congress also enacted a law making it illegal.[2] Nevertheless, a long struggle lay ahead. The British law was backed by the world's mightiest navy, whereas the Americans lacked the means to enforce their legislation. Moreover, the demand for captives suddenly began to rise. As a result of the industrial revolution in Great Britain, cotton had begun to supersede the traditional wool and linen in fabrics for daily use. Great Britain had to import cotton from warmer countries, and the available supply was strictly limited by the difficulties of separating the fiber from the seed. No one had devised a successful or practicable machine for the purpose, and a man working all day could separate by hand only a little more than a pound of cotton fiber.

The impasse was broken by a young Yankee schoolteacher in Georgia. Eli Whitney, something of a mechanical genius, in April 1793 designed and built in a few days a machine by which a laborer could prepare more than fifty pounds per day – a revolutionary invention that at once stimulated the agriculture of the South. England's capacity to consume cotton seemed limitless. Overnight the dying institution of slavery received a new lease on life as Southern economy and organization shifted to the production of a new staple, one that could be profitably produced by slave labor. And increased numbers of slaves called for corresponding increases in the materials and products useful to a society based on slave labor: ships, rum, trinkets, salt fish, lumber, firearms, and scores of other items.

Thus Whitney's invention of the cotton gin suddenly made slavery profitable again.[3] Great numbers of slaves were imported before Congress formally abolished the trade in 1808. After that year there can be no doubt that contraband slaves continued to come into the country, but the extent of that illegal trade is controversial. Some estimates indicate that between ten and twenty thousand slaves a year were smuggled into the United States after 1810, but such a figure is highly doubtful. The various estimates seem to have been based as much upon the prejudice of the estimator as on any reliable evidence. The best available sources seem to indicate that no large number of contraband Africans were imported into the United States between 1808 and 1861 and that the major markets for African slaves lay in Brazil and Cuba.

Philip Curtin's monograph on the African slave trade concludes that 9,566,000 slaves were brought into Europe and the Americas. Of these, only about 427,000, or 4.5 percent, came to North America during the period of the slave trade. Up to 1808 about 345,000 slaves had come into the United States; between 1808 and 1861 about 1,000 a year were imported clandestinely, for a total of 399,000. Slaves brought into French and Spanish Louisiana after 1807 accounted for 28,000, to give the total figure of 427,000.[4]

Efforts to end the commerce in slaves were to involve the United States in a long and bitter debate with Great Britain over American rights on the high seas and to expose the United States to charges of indifference to the evils of slaving. On the positive side, humanitarian interest in ending slavery and the slave trade was linked closely with the founding of Liberia as a home for freed American blacks as well as a refuge for slaves liberated from captured slave ships. The American Colonization Society was founded in 1817, and settlements in Liberia began to be established from 1820 onward.

Although the United States government at least sought to mitigate the effects of the slave trade by sponsoring Liberia as a colony for rescued slaves and allowing the Colonization Society to send freed slaves there, the major responsibility for putting an end to the slave trade was first assumed by the British navy, backed by an aroused British public and Parliament. During the French Revolution, Great Britain used belligerent's rights to seize slavers and suspected slavers wherever they were found.[5] Promises to forbid the slave trade seem to have been conditions attached to the subsidies and aid granted to Great Britain's allies in the struggle, and a clause by which France agreed to abolish the trade in five years was appended to the peace treaty negotiated with the restored Bourbon monarchy in 1814.[6] At the Congress of Vienna, the British representatives strove to obtain consent for some form of action against slavers, and succeeded in having a condemnatory clause included in the final settlement.[7] The Treaty of Ghent in 1814, which ended the War of 1812 between the United States and Great Britain, stated:

> Whereas the Traffic in Slaves is irreconcilable with the principles of humanity and justice, and whereas both his Majesty and the United States are desirous of continuing their efforts to promote its entire abolition, it is hereby agreed that both the contracting parties shall use their best endeavors to accomplish so desirable an object.[8]

The British government then began a long series of attempts to gain U.S. support for British efforts to suppress the slave trade. John Quincy Adams, who became minister to the Court of St. James immediately after negotiating the Treaty of Ghent, recorded in his diary one of his early interviews with Castlereagh:

> He passed immediately to . . . the slave-trade, which he said was now carrying on to a very great extent, and in a shocking manner; that a great number of vessels for it had been fitted out in our Southern States and that the

barbarities of the trade were even more atrocious than they had been before the abolition of it had been attempted. The vessels sailed under the flags of the nations which were still allowed the trade, Spain and Portugal.[9]

Two years later, in 1818, Castlereagh proposed to the United States the establishment by treaty of a reciprocal right of search as a measure that would finally abolish the trade. But in the United States, even among people who had no sympathy with slavery or the slave trade, there existed bitter memories of the right of search as a major cause of the War of 1812. Because of this feeling, and for some other constitutional reasons, the reply penned by Adams, then secretary of state, was a categorical refusal.[10]

In spite of the Monroe administration's strong stand against search, there was considerable popular support in the United States for the British proposals. In 1821 and 1822 the House Committee on the Slave Trade recommended conceding the right of search, and in 1823 the House, by a vote of 131 to 9, passed a resolution calling on the president to negotiate with other maritime powers for the abolition of the slave trade and the denunciation of slaving as piracy.[11] But such resolutions were not binding upon the executive branch, and John Quincy Adams, unconvinced of the purity of British intentions, had the president's ear.

After lengthy discussions in the cabinet, Adams himself finally drafted a convention that would have permitted the search of American slavers without conceding the principle: Suspected slavers could be searched as pirates, not as slavers, for the right to investigate and capture pirates was well recognized in international law. Great Britain ratified the convention at once, and Parliament quickly enacted a law declaring slave trading to be piracy, but in the United States the convention became inextricably mixed up with the issue of domestic slavery and failed to win ratification in the Senate.[12]

There the matter rested for several years. No further attempt was made to settle the problem of American ships in the illegal slave trade until the Webster–Ashburton Treaty of 1842. That is not to say, however, that there were no problems growing out of the African trade, for a great share of Washington's attention was directed toward incidents – usually disagreeable – occurring on the African coast and involving the American flag.

Because of the determination of U.S. statesmen to forbid British interference with American shipping, the Stars and Stripes protected slavers. While negotiating with the United States, Great Britain had approached other maritime powers with regard to a reciprocal right of search. Spain, Brazil, Portugal,[13] and the Netherlands consented very early, and by the end of the 1830s France, Denmark, the Hanseatic cities, and several minor powers had added their agreement. The result was that a ship flying the American flag was almost the only one that the Royal Navy was not permitted to stop and search – and seize if it was found to be a slaver.[14]

Since the slave trade was illegal, the extent of American participation in it between the War of 1812 and the Civil War cannot be determined, even approximately. Probably there were far fewer people actively engaged in the African trade than before the passage of the prohibitory act, but the fantastic profits to be made would still have attracted plenty of men who felt no qualms at taking part in it. For several years the port of Bristol, Rhode Island, seems to have occupied the first place in the commerce, as shown by a letter from an unidentified correspondent to Obadiah Brown in August 1816: "The impunity with which prohibited traffic is carried on from this Place has for some time past rendered it the resort of many violators of commercial law . . . The African slave trade is the one of this description now most successsfully and extensively prosecuted."[15]

Although the slave trade was not a matter of deep concern to most Americans, the U.S. government was interested in fulfilling its obligations and enforcing the law. Its basic difficulties lay in having to deal with other, more pressing issues and in the lack of a naval force adequate to police the African coast and the slave-trade routes. A small American naval force sailed for Africa in 1820 with multiple missions, only one of which was to seize American slavers. The force displayed the American flag along the coast, captured a few slave ships, and precipitated a sudden diplomatic embarrassment. Knowing that slavers frequently disguised themselves under the flag of some country that had not yet forbidden the trade, Lieutenant Robert Stockton, commanding the *Alligator,* seized four vessels flying the French flag. He put prize crews aboard and sent the ships to Boston, convinced by various items of evidence that they were actually American craft.

France was as touchy as the United States about the sanctity of its flag, and an immediate outcry was raised. This incident, coupled with the seizure of some French vessels accused of piratical practices on the Grand Banks of Newfoundland, caused the French government to take a rather belligerent stand. On November 25, 1821, the French minister, Baron Hyde de Neuville, created a stormy scene in the office of Secretary of State Adams:

> In a loud and peremptory tone, rising from his seat and with vehement gesture, [he] said, "Well, sir, since you think proper to report to the President what I came here to say in confidential conversation with you, I desire you to tell him from me, as my individual opinion, that if satisfaction is not made to France . . . La France doit leur déclarer la guerre."
>
> These last words he spoke in a manner nearly frantic, dwelling upon the word *guerre* with a long and virulent emphasis, and, without waiting for a reply, rushed out of the room (forgetting his overcoat in his hurry).[16]

Because of the slow communications of the time, Stockton probably did not know of the crisis he had caused, and he again brought himself to diplomatic attention by sending another prize to Boston – this time a Portuguese slaver that had committed the mistake of firing upon him first. Portugal did not openly threaten war, but the Portuguese chargé d'affaires filed a protest.[17]

For months afterward the French minister lost no opportunity to complain to the secretary of state about Stockton, referring to him as a pirate and practically demanding his punishment for publishing a statement in the *National Intelligencer* in defense of himself – all this even though the president had given assurances that the whole affair was a mistake and that positive orders had been issued to forbid American naval vessels from capturing any ship that flew a foreign flag.[18] The immediate effect was, of course, that American naval vessels were as thoroughly handicapped as were those of the British navy, who could not seize slavers flying the Stars and Stripes.

Although American naval vessels cruised the African coast only occasionally and

British ships were not supposed to molest or even investigate any ship under the American flag, a considerable number of American slave ships were seized. To stimulate interest and activity, the U.S. government had authorized, under an act of 1819, the payment of a bounty of twenty-five dollars for each African liberated from a captured ship and turned over to government agents as provided for in the same law.[19] But the stimulus of a reward (and the additional prize money from the condemnation of captured vessels) was soon offset by a series of judicial decisions.

Various courts decided that the only acceptable proof of a vessel's character as a slaver was the actual presence of slaves on board. No amount of obvious preparation to receive and transport slaves was considered sufficient evidence: The presence of manacles, special slave decks, cooking equipment, quantities of special foodstuffs – none of these proved a ship to be a slaver. Such decisions added to the difficulty of convicting a captured slaver and consequently gave new vigor to the trade. Not only was the actual presence of slaves on board held to be the only acceptable proof that a vessel was a slaver, but it was further decided by the courts that an American vessel carrying supplies and equipment for a slave depot was engaged in legitimate business as long as it did not transport any slaves. Nor was it ruled illegal for an American citizen to take a ship to the African coast and there sell it to known slavers, as long as he did not know specifically that the buyers intended to use it in the slave trade.

There can be no denial that the enthusiasm of officers and men of the U.S. Navy, sweltering in the African heat, was dampened by judicial hairsplitting. But the fact that some slave ships were captured and condemned in spite of adverse court decisions, so that more than a few American shipmasters found themselves behind prison bars, argues well for the devotion to duty of the handicapped officers of the scanty American naval forces on the African, Brazilian, and Cuban coasts.

For all the growth of legitimate commerce with Africa, the slave trade remained an ugly reality until 1862. Few American citizens may have given it much thought, but some startling incident occasionally brought home to the average person that Africans were still being brought across the Atlantic for sale as so much merchandise. Such an incident occurred on August 26, 1839, when Captain Gedney of the USS *Washington*, surveying the waters of Long Island Sound, investigated a suspicious schooner at anchor near Culloden Point, thinking it to be a smuggler. An armed boarding party led by Lieutenant Richard W. Meade and Midshipman David D. Porter (who later gained fame as an admiral in the Civil War) found on board two terrified Spaniards and fifty-three blacks. The vessel was the *Amistad*, a fast, Baltimore-built schooner owned in Havana and under Spanish registry. In June, two months earlier, it had sailed from Havana for eastern Cuba, having on board some newly imported Africans. On the night of June 30, led by one of their number called Cinqué, the blacks rose; they killed the captain and another white man, sent the crew ashore, and held as hostages and navigators the two Spaniards whom the Americans found on board. Threatening them with death if they did not comply, Cinqué ordered the hostages to sail the ship to Africa. Instead, by covertly altering their course, the Spaniards slowly approached the U.S. coast, hoping to be captured.

The Africans were jailed at New London pending decision of the case, and the Spanish minister in Washington at once demanded that the ship and the live merchandise be turned over to him in accordance with the treaty of 1795 between Spain and the United States. Officials in Washington were perfectly willing to comply with this demand, but the matter had got out of their hands. The plight of the unfortunate Africans aroused the pity of numerous philanthropists, and the case was fought in the courts until finally, after two years, it reached the Supreme Court. The legal issue was whether Cinqué and his group were lawful slaves. It was clearly proved that the *Amistad*'s papers describing them as *ladinos* – that is, black slaves and natives of Cuba – were fraudulent; not even under Spanish law, which formally forbade the importation of Africans, were they legal slaves. John Quincy Adams was persuaded to represent the blacks before the Supreme Court. On March 9, 1841, Justice Story delivered the verdict of the Court:

> The very language of the treaty of 1795 requires the proprietor to make
> due and sufficient proof of his property. And how can that proof be
> deemed either due or sufficient which is but a connected and stained tissue
> of fraud? Upon the whole, our opinion is ... that the said negroes be
> declared free, and be dismissed from the custody of the court.[20]

Concurrently with the *Amistad* case, another incident reminded the people of the United States that the slave trade still existed and that Americans were deeply involved in it. On June 12, 1839, the American public and government officials were astonished when HMS *Buzzard* sailed into New York harbor escorting two captured American ships, the brig *Eagle* and the schooner *Clara*. They had been taken, with blacks on board, on the African coast. Two weeks later the schooner *Wyoming* arrived, manned by a prize crew from HMS *Harlequin*. Since there seemed to be no American naval vessels on the coast of Africa at that time, the local British authorities, irked by the way American slavers openly flouted attempts to stop the trade, decided to force the issue. The U.S. government had stiffly and continuously maintained the principle that American ships were not subject to seizure by the Royal Navy and that they could not be judged and condemned in British prize courts. So the British had brought the American slavers into a U.S. port as captives.

A tempest raged. British motives in suppressing the slave trade were regarded in some quarters with a considerable degree of suspicion; it was charged that, under the guise of eliminating slavers, the British were also eliminating competitors in legitimate trade. When the British apprehended American ships, it was widely (and wildly) charged that they were arrogating to themselves the right to police the seas – and did the United States not fight for the freedom of the seas in 1812? The city of Baltimore in particular was indignant, because some of the vessels captured had been built in Baltimore.[21]

Nor were these the only ships that were proved by the British navy to be engaged in the slave trade. The Baltimore-built *Catherine*, when nearing the African coast, was overhauled by HMS *Dolphin*. The *Catherine* hoisted American colors, supposed to be certain protection, but the British captain was unconvinced. His suspicions were heightened when he found cooking arrangements for 300 people, planks cut and numbered for the speedy installation of a slave deck, almost 600 wooden spoons, and 350 pairs of handcuffs. If this evidence were not enough, the American captain had on his person written instructions from the ship's owners advising him how to convince boarding officers that the Spaniards and Portuguese aboard were passengers only and that the handful of Americans was the whole crew.[22]

Few apologists for the slave trade could be found in the United States, even among the most ardent believers in slavery. The government's failure to take adequate measures to enforce the law, and its opposition to British attempts to obtain consent to search American ships, grew rather from failure to regard the problem as a serious one. Even to an antislavery statesman of the stature of John Quincy Adams, possible British interference with American rights upon the seas was a matter of more pressing importance than suppression of the slave trade. But the *Amistad* affair – and the issue squarely presented by the British navy's enforcing American law upon American citizens because their own government was not doing so – brought the problem into the open.

To the enemies of the slave trade it seemed high time for some action to be taken. The intransigent attitude of the U.S. government, together with the lack of American naval forces in African waters, had made the American flag an almost sure protection for slavers. This had been the case to some extent for several years; but an Anglo-Spanish treaty of 1835, which gave the Royal Navy the right to search and seize Spanish slavers, increased the number of Spaniards who found it convenient to disguise their operations under the American flag either by changing the registry or, better still, by purchasing American vessels without bothering to change the registry.

Under the terms of their treaty of 1835, Great Britain and Spain established a joint commission at Havana for the suppression of the trade. The commission reported in 1836 that a recent declaration by the president of the United States "not to make the United States a party to any convention on the subject of the Slave Trade" would encourage a large number of Americans to embark in it and would facilitate the use of the American flag by foreigners.[23] It was reported to Parliament, in fact, that in 1837 the number of American ships in the slave trade was eleven, but in 1838 the number was found to be nineteen. A Lieutenant Reeve wrote to the secretary of the Admiralty on April 2, 1839, that unless steps were taken to prevent the use of the American flag by slavers, the efforts of Her Majesty's navy would be utterly wasted and British ships might as well be withdrawn.[24]

Not only did American policy operate to encourage slavers to use the American flag, but the United States was instrumental in killing an attempt by the British government to obtain international agreement on the right of search. In 1841 the Melbourne ministry negotiated the Quintuple Treaty with France, Russia, Prussia, and Austria, outlawing the slave trade and providing that war vessels of the contracting nations might search and seize vessels belonging to any one of them. The American minister in Paris, Lewis Cass, a veteran of the War of 1812, scented danger in the words "right of search" and persuaded the French to withdraw from the treaty, an action that effectively killed it.[25]

Since the American slavers of the period did not seek publicity and did not hesitate to falsify or destroy records, the extent to which Americans were involved in the trade and the number of Africans imported illegally into the United States are matters of conjecture. We can surmise that a fair number of unscrupulous Americans may have profited hugely from the forbidden traffic, and there is little doubt that at least small numbers of blacks were surreptitiously introduced into the plantations of the South, particularly those in the Gulf states.[26]

Since the extent of American participation in the slave trade can only be estimated, it is difficult to say how many other American businesses and trades were affected. One feature, however, can be evaluated: The shipbuilders of Baltimore and all the allied trades enjoyed great prosperity for several years. By the middle of the century Baltimore had become famous for its fast and seaworthy clippers. Ships built at Baltimore were seen on every one of the seven seas and in ports from Canton to St. Petersburg. And in no part of the world, it seems, were they better known than on the coast of Africa, for the speed that the Baltimore shipwrights were able to build into their craft was exactly what the slaver needed. There were few men-of-war, even those powered by steam, that could overhaul a Baltimore clipper. The designers of Baltimore studied their market diligently and reaped a golden harvest – but not without resort to sharp practices and even violence:

> It must be said . . . that the builders of slavers resorted to highly unprincipled actions in order to get their vessels into the slave trader's hands. Shanghaied crews, bribed officials, and murder were not uncommon; and as most of the Baltimore Clippers built for the slave trade were built on speculation, it follows that these builders were, usually, the guilty parties, as well as the owners.[27]

Chief Justice Roger Brooke Taney suddenly ended the legal subterfuges and connivance of public officials by which Baltimore citizens were prospering in the African trade. Taney was a citizen of Maryland, a slave owner, and an outspoken believer in the institution of slavery within the United States; but he was also a member of the American Colonization Society and was no friend of the African slave trade. When the case of the Baltimore-built and Baltimore-owned schooner *Butterfly* came before the Supreme Court for adjudication in 1840, Taney refused to allow any legal technicalities to obscure the issues, and in his decision he excoriated the practices that had brought disgrace upon the American flag and the city of Baltimore.[28]

CHAPTER 4

The U.S. Navy and the antislavery campaign

No matter what the lawgivers might say, Americans continued to participate extensively in the slave trade. Cuban and Brazilian plantations provided some of their best markets. British diplomatic pressure, reinforced by British demands for the right of search and by humanitarian and missionary lobbies within the United States, finally persuaded Washington to become active in suppressing the traffic. Under article 8 of the Webster–Ashburton Treaty concluded with Great Britain in 1842, the United States agreed to set up a permanent naval force on the African coast in order to "enforce, separately and respectively, the laws, rights, and obligations, of each of the two countries, for the suppression of the slave trade."[1] The two naval forces were completely independent. The governments agreed that the commanders should consult with each other, keep each other fully informed, and act in concert, but the United States still refused to concede to Great Britain the right to interfere at any time with a ship displaying the American flag. The first squadron dispatched, under the command of Commodore Matthew C. Perry, consisted of four ships: the frigate *Macedonian;* two sloops, the *Decatur* and the *Saratoga;* and the brig *Porpoise.*[2]

Perry arrived on the African coast early in August 1843. Before commencing operations, he established a base at Porto Praia in the Cape Verde Islands where his crews could rest and recuperate and where the fresh water and stores could be obtained. The Cape Verde Islands were distant from his theater of operations, but they were far enough from the fever and disease zone to allow his crews to recover from the ills they were certain to contract in the Gulf of Guinea and the Bight of Benin. Although the long voyage to and from Porto Praia took time from patrolling, at that point the loss of time was accepted as inevitable if the squadron was to be able to operate at all.

The initial business for the new American squadron on the African coast, before it took steps against the slave trade, was to impress Africans with the fact that Americans must be respected. Since legitimate African commerce was looming large in American business, Perry's instructions from Washington made its promotion an important part of his mission; possibly it was his primary mission, with suppression of the slave trade being purely secondary and incidental. Washington, moreover, was still suspicious of British motives and of the right of search. Succeeding Perry in command of the African squadron, Commodore Charles Skinner received categorical orders from the secretary of the navy to make suppression of the slave trade a distinctly secondary mission: "The rights of our citizens engaged in lawful commerce are under the protection of our flag. *And it is the chief purpose, as well as the chief duty of our naval power,* to see that those rights are not improperly abridged."[3]

Most authorities consider that the American naval squadron on the African coast, which was maintained until the Civil War, was unsuccessful in either capturing slavers or lessening appreciably American participation in the slave trade. The reasons advanced vary from the time lost in the voyages between Porto Praia and the coast to allegations that the Americans deliberately sought not to capture slavers. Some writers even asserted that Southern officers in command of ships on the patrol intentionally avoided areas in which slave ships might be encountered and that the government in Washington handicapped the squadron in various ways so as to avoid irritating slave-owning interests in the United States.[4] Commodore Perry has been accused by some historians of indifference toward suppressing the slave trade;[5] the handful of ships under his command captured only one slaver in his two years as commander of the squadron. Perry appeared to hold the protection of commerce as his primary responsibility.

The accomplishments of the American squadron, however, clearly indicate that its unspectacular performance as a captor of slavers was not due to lack of effort by most of the squadron's officers.[6] Nor were instructions given to the successive commanders deliberately intended to prevent interference with the slave trade. Washington did not, as has been alleged, purposely send to Africa men-of-war that were manifestly unsuitable for the duty, leaving suitable ships in American waters or sending such ships to the West Indies or Asia. On the few ships the United States could spare for African service, the officers and crews – in spite of official and geographical handicaps – made a conscientious effort to comply with their orders. The U.S. Navy of the early and middle nineteenth century did not have a large number of ships, and the American public would never have stood for the expense of constructing ships especially for African service.[7] But the government lived up to the terms of the Webster–Ashburton Treaty: It maintained on the African patrol as high a proportion of its available ships of war as did Great Britain.[8] Though one study of the slave trade states that the African squadron took only nine slave ships between 1842 and 1853,[9] records in the National Archives show that the U.S. Navy and port authorities formally libeled and made naval prizes of twenty-six such ships in those years.[10]

In charging that the government in Washington was deliberately indifferent to its treaty obligations, one writer says categorically, "It is clear that there was a deliberate attempt on the part of the Navy Department to comply only technically with the Treaty" by sending a small number of heavily overgunned ships to the African coast, and that the United States rarely had more than five ships as compared with some twenty-five maintained there by the British and French. This writer says further that frequently the ships sent to Africa were the culls of the U.S. fleet and were wholly unsuited to their task.[11]

Admittedly, the U.S. naval ships sent to Africa were unsuited to chasing slavers; in some instances, they were so old as to be unseaworthy. But only a casual glance is needed to show that the naval authorities were limited by what they actually had. Such criticism fails to take into account the fact that the United States of the 1840s was not a great naval power. In 1843, the year in which the African squadron came into being, the entire strength of the U.S. Navy consisted of 76 vessels of all sizes, classes, and descriptions. Of these, 11 (several of them uncompleted but nevertheless carried on the list) were ponderous ships of the line that no one would have considered sending to Africa. There were 15 frigates, almost equally inappropriate. Ten vessels were storeships or were in use as receiving ships at various ports. Of the 5 small steamers, one was permanently landlocked in the Great Lakes and the others were unfit for a transatlantic voyage. In 1843 the available ships were spread over the whole world: 9 in American waters, 4 or 5 in Africa, 5 in the Mediterranean, 5 on the Brazilian coast, 6 in the Pacific, 2 in the East Indies (with replacements en route), and most of the remainder either "in mothballs" (as were nearly all the large vessels) or under repair and refit.[12] The Royal Navy, on the other hand, included over 250 vessels in active commission, not counting those that were laid up or unmanned.[13]

The inability of the United States to proceed more actively on the African coast was summarized succinctly by Lord Napier, then British minister to Washington, in a dispatch to Lord Aberdeen on April 19, 1858: "The American navy is ill supplied with light vessels, and it may be doubted whether Congress would sanction any pecuniary appropriation for the purpose indicated."[14] A moment of mental arithmetic will show that the U.S. Navy, proportionally, made as heavy a contribution as the Royal Navy.[15]

The more serious allegations that Southern officers avoided capturing slavers and that their instructions were so framed by Southern secretaries of the navy that it would be impossible for them to make such captures are not borne out by the records or by the instructions themselves. The two most effective slave-ship catchers were both Southerners: Lieutenant William McBlair of the *Dale* was from Florida, and Lieutenant Thomas W. Brent of the *Marion* was a Virginian. These men, in the late 1850s, when the slavery controversy at home was at its bitterest, were a scourge to American slavers in African waters.[16] Although instructions to the African squadron stressed that American ships were to protect lawful American commerce and to use all means to promote and further it, nowhere was it either stated or implied that they were to neglect paying due attention to the slave trade. On the contrary, instructions were specific and so definite as to leave no room for doubt. It might be added that even among proslavery Southerners there was no considerable body of opinion favoring the slave trade, in spite of the vehemence of a few extremists in the late 1850s.[17] The handful of ships, all that were available from year to year, cruised continually in areas where slavers might be encountered. To complain that they were ineffective ignores the fact that criminals take care not to practice their profession when a law enforcer is in the vicinity.

As for orders to the squadron that made suppression of the slave trade secondary to protection and promotion of American commerce, it should be remembered that Great Britain's motives for urging the right of search and for wanting to suppress the slave trade were distrusted. Commodore Skinner, Perry's successor in command of the African squadron, wrote to Secretary of the Navy Bancroft in November 1845: "Under the pretense of suppressing the slave trade, I have not a doubt that it is the intention of both England and France to make as many settlements on the Coast as they can for the purpose of monopolizing the trade of the continent."[18]

In spite of the fundamental disagreement between the American and the British governments, and in spite of the suspicions entertained by a few senior American officers, with few exceptions Americans and Englishmen cooperated in performing their duties regarding the disagreeable African situation.[19] In 1840 – before the establishment of the American squadron and when only an occasional American man-of-war visited the African coast – Lieutenant John S. Paine, commanding the USS *Grampus,* made a working agreement with Commander William Tucker of HMS *Wolverine* that each would investigate any and all suspicious craft; any vessel claiming to be American intercepted by the *Wolverine* would be held for the *Grampus,* and any non-American ship intercepted by the *Grampus* would be held until the *Wolverine* could arrive and take charge. Under this arrangement several ships were seized. In Washington, however, Paine's agreement with Tucker aroused indignation and was promptly disavowed, for it involved authorizing a British officer to investigate and hold ships displaying the American flag, a possible opening for the right of search.

Late in the 1840s the USS *Dolphin* held under surveillance the American vessel *Chancellor,* observed to be trading with a shore establishment occupied by a notorious slaver, Theodore Canot. The *Chancellor* was nominally a legitimate trader, but there was little doubt about its real business; in any case, the goods being landed at Canot's place could be used in the slave trade. The commander of HMS *Favourite,* lying nearby at Cape Mount, suggested to the local chiefs that their treaty with Great Britain obliged them to do everything possible to impede the slave trade. Taking the hint, the Africans promptly raided, looted, and destroyed Canot's establishment, carrying away with them a large consignment of goods he had just received from New York. This was probably the only instance of an attack upon a foreign trader being made with the full approval – and even the connivance – of the British and American navies.[20]

Cooperation between the two navies was sometimes very direct. In 1845 Commander Bruce of the USS *Truxtun* sent a landing party to assist a force from HMS *Ardent* in a raid on the slave depots along the Pongo River. In spite of his orders to prevent any interference with American ships, Bruce made no objection when the *Ardent* fired on an American ship to bring it to, the *Truxtun* being well out of range. The *Ardent,* a steamer, later towed the *Truxtun* and two prizes to Sierra Leone. British naval officers never objected to American use of the white ensign to disguise U.S. ships, nor to American officers' boarding ships flying the British flag. If responsible officials in Washington could have seen eye to eye with the relatively subordinate naval officers whose responsibility was actually to capture slavers, the frequent diplomatic clashes would never have arisen.

The African squadron and the various secretaries of the navy appear to have been reasonably competent and conscientious in enforcing the law, though apathy in Congress and among the American public left legal loopholes unfilled. There were some incompetent officers, but not many; some squadrons did not cruise long enough or far enough, and some took too many pleasure cruises to Madeira. Porto Praia in the Cape Verde Islands was a poorly situated base, too far from areas where slavers operated – especially in the 1840s and 1850s, when most slave ships were working the area around the Congo and Angola. Naval officers suggested bases at St. Helena or near the Congo River, but nothing was done until 1858, when the Buchanan administration began a vigorous drive against slave ships flying the American flag. The African squadron was strengthened, a base was established at Luanda, and captures increased dramatically.

Between 1837 and 1862, thirty-eight slave ships were captured by the African squadron, and more than a few American shipmasters spent some time behind bars.[21] But too often the courts freed the slavers. This outcome dampened the zeal of the officers and men of the squadron; their enthusiasm was lowered further by damage suits entered in the federal courts against the capturing officers.[22] Added to such morale-destroying factors were the deadly African climate and the monotony of cruising for months on end.[23] "On the whole, however, they [the African squadron] did a good job with what they had. Lack of numbers and adverse court decisions . . . crippled their efforts."[24] The suit for false arrest brought by a libeled slaver against two U.S. officers in 1847 led to an inglorious episode in American naval history, "a mass shirking of assigned duties carefully concealed from the American public."[25] Until a favorable legal decision was rendered in 1849, the officers on the African squadron avoided the waters south of the equator where most of the slaving was going on.

The African squadron did reasonably well for such a small force, but it hardly was able to limit the large American involvement in the slave trade. As noted previously, the flag of the United States was used as a flag of convenience by a great number of slavers. Only in the 1850s and 1860s did the squadron become effective. Between 1837 and 1862 American courts libeled 107 slavers, 4 of them captured by the British. Of the 103 seized by American authorities, 50 were taken in U.S. waters by customs agents or U.S. marshals and 53 were captured by the U.S. Navy, 15 of them by the Brazilian or Cuban squadrons. Of the 38 captures made by the African squadron, 20 were taken between 1857 and 1861, when the patrol was most effective (with more ships and a better base); from 1840 to 1856 only 18 were detained.

Still, the failure to stop the slave trade by ships flying the American flag cannot in all fairness be attributed to the African squadron, Southern officers or secretaries of the navy, or even Congress. The blame was more general:

> The crux of the matter is that if the Government and people of the United States had sincerely wished to end the slave trade, they could have easily done so at any time by making full use of the Freetown naval base (which they were invited to do) and by providing a naval squadron strong enough to carry out the system of joint cruising. Stationing a squadron of five or six ships at the Cape Verde islands was merely playing with the problem.[26]

This is a harsh judgment, perhaps, but essentially a correct one. We must conclude that Congress failed to act because the American public was not very interested in the problems of ending the slave trade.

The African squadron did not sail in East African waters. Although most American commercial ventures in East Africa after 1819 were legitimate, some Americans – a small number of merchants and shipowners – were there as active slavers. After 1807 some slavers tried East Africa in order to avoid British patrols, and the British complained that American slavers worked along the East African coast each year loading their human cargoes.[27] Not until 1820 did the British undertake naval patrolling there, and it was 1842 before the patrol became effective. British efforts to limit the slave trade in the Indian Ocean were handicapped by the fact that the "Arabs" (most of the Swahili-speaking Muslims) had no inhibitions about the trade and saw no reason why it was not as lawful as any other activity. Cargoes of African tribesmen were carried regularly from East Africa to Arabia and other places where slavery was taken for granted. In spite of the prohibition of the trade by most of the nations of Europe and by the United States, there were, unfortunately, plenty of men – Arab, European, and American – for whom the huge profits of the slave trade outweighed considerations of humanity, decency, or law. The Mozambique and Zanzibar slave trade was therefore active, and American ships were involved in it, although the extent of that involvement is not known.[28]

Slaving and ivory often went together in East Africa. During the nineteenth century elephant ivory became important to the expanding European luxury industries for piano keys, billiard balls, ornaments, and fans. When elephants were depleted along the coast, the Arabs pushed inland; by 1840 they were on Lake Tanganyika. The heavy tusks had to be carried by manpower from the interior to the coast; in addition to employing professional carriers, dealers also captured and kidnapped porters, and sold them , along with the ivory, on reaching salt water. As one observer noted, "Ivory and slaves, . . . these two are one."[29] Not all of those miserable porters of ivory went to Arabia; many may have gone to Brazil or Cuba. But few could have come to the United States after 1808, since it was no longer a major slave market.

Although there were never as many American slavers on the East Coast of Africa as on the West Coast, there were enough of them to cause a great deal of irritation to the British officials and naval officers who were trying to extirpate the trade.[30] Taking over a practice already common in the Atlantic, American slavers sailing the Indian Ocean disguised themselves under Spanish colors and carried false papers.[31] The British consul, General Christopher P. Rigby, reported in 1858 that several large American ships, under Spanish colors, shipped Africans for conveyance to Cuba from the ports of Mozambique. The following year he rendered a similar report about another American ship, and in August 1860 he reported the capture by HMS *Brisk* of a large American ship with 846 slaves aboard.[32]

The establishment of a permanent American naval force on the West African coast did not end British efforts to persuade the United States to agree to a reciprocal right of search, nor did it put a stop to the search and occasional seizure of American ships.[33]

General Lewis Cass, a stalwart veteran of the War of 1812 to whom Great Britain's right of search was anathema, in 1857 became secretary of state in President Buchanan's cabinet. While minister to France in 1842, he had, on his own initiative, persuaded the French authorities to reject the Quintuple Treaty because it seemed to revive – or to give international sanction to – the right of search. Not even to suppress the slave trade would Cass concede to Great Britain the right to search ships of other nations. In his mind, the right of search was inextricably involved with the impressment of seamen, and to concede the one would be to admit the propriety of the other. To a British philanthropist who attempted to convince him of the necessity and desirability of permitting the British navy to search suspected slavers, Cass replied that "having a right to enter, for the purpose of ascertaining the character of a vessel, or of searching for contraband articles, when once on board for a lawful purpose, they then might look round them with other objects."[34] This conversation occurred when Cass was on a visit to Great

Britain while he was American minister to the court of King Louis Philippe of France. When he became secretary of state in 1857, the intervening years had not changed his belief that under no circumstances could the British be trusted with the privilege of being allowed to search vessels flying the American flag.

British naval vessels continued to stop and search American ships nonetheless, in spite of formal protests from the United States and previous Admiralty orders forbidding the practice.[35] As long as such interferences with American shipping were confined to the African coast, they attracted little popular attention in the United States. In 1858, however, for a variety of reasons, Her Majesty's Government decided to attack the slave trade at both ends: to charge the British West Indian squadron with antislavery duties as well as the African squadron. The principal slave market in the Caribbean was Cuba, and the seizure of slave ships near the end of their voyage would have a depressing effect upon all slavers. Several American ships were seized as a result, and more were "visited" in areas where such occurrences were previously unknown, areas that Americans had come to regard as their own territorial waters.

Unhappily, these incidents occurred at a time when relations between Great Britain and the United States were somewhat strained because of conflicting interests in Central America. The American public had not been greatly excited by what happened to American ships on the African coast, but seizure of American ships in the Gulf of Mexico aroused a furor. In Congress, oddly, the most belligerent expressions came from Northerners, while the senators and congressmen who were in favor of calmness and consideration were mostly from the South.

Secretary of State Cass responded vehemently to the challenge. The British government promptly disavowed the action of its naval commanders in the Caribbean and issued sharp orders forbidding them to interfere with American ships. In numerous conversations between Cass and Lord Napier, the British minister in Washington, Cass showed no intention of yielding an inch; he stubbornly refused to recognize the slightest difference between "visit" and "search."[36] The result was a diplomatic victory for Cass and the United States – and for American slavers. The British government formally and openly recognized the correctness of the U.S. legal position. The visiting and seizure of ships under the American flag did not again cloud relations between the two countries, and the right of search was not revived until, under vastly changed circumstances, the U.S. government itself made the suggestion.[37]

The increased safety thus afforded to slave ships by the American flag caused more and more slave dealers to take cover beneath it. And since the profits from the illegal commerce were probably enormous, increasing amounts of investment capital must have been poured into the trade. The 1850s saw a revival of the slave trade, although its extent is not known. Slaving seems to have been carefully organized and planned during this period. It has been said that fattening farms, where slaves could be conditioned for sale after the long voyage from Africa, were maintained in out-of-the-way places in the Caribbean and on the Gulf of Mexico.[38] Slaves were landed secretly in Southern ports and sold in small batches so as not to alert the abolitionists,[39] but in the 1850s "black ivory" was big business, requiring an investment far beyond the capabilities of the small trader. New York, already the financial capital of the country, became the financial center of the trade. A speculative member of the prominent Lamar family in Georgia calculated the cost of an expedition that he attempted to promote at $300,000; if successful, its net profit would have been almost $500,000. Such earnings on investment were likely to arouse the interest of even the most conservative businessmen.[40]

The extent to which New York merchants and bankers were involved in the unlawful slave trade is necessarily obscure, but of the suspected ships seized by the U.S. authorities in home ports over a period of several years, by far the greatest number were taken in New York.[41] In June 1858 the British navy reported that of twenty-two vessels captured with blacks on board during the preceding year, all but one were American, and the greater number hailed from New York, Boston, or New Orleans.[42] As late as 1862, when the energies of the nation were being poured into a war the basic cause of which was African slavery, the ship *Reindeer,* outfitted and supplied for a slaving voyage, was apprehended as it was about to sail from New York.[43]

The year 1862 marked a turning point in American relations with Africa and an abrupt about-face in the American attitude toward the seizure or detention of American vessels by the British navy. With the North engaged in a life-and-death struggle with the slaveholding South, and with an administration whose members held no personal memories of the War of 1812, a change in policy was easily effected. Withdrawal of the vessels of the African squadron to home waters became necessary to strengthen the blockade of the Confederate States. Concurring fully in the necessity of continual efforts to suppress the trade at its source, Secretary of State Seward (probably to the surprise of Her Majesty's Government) took the initiative in 1862 by suggesting a treaty authorizing the British navy to search and seize American slavers on both the African and the Cuban coasts. The treaty, which was readily accepted by Britain, further provided for mixed courts to be established at Freetown, the Cape of Good Hope, and New York.[44]

Seward's treaty of 1862 marks the end of American involvement in the slave trade. The first American appointed to the court at Sierra Leone finally resigned because he could not conscientiously continue to draw his salary while doing nothing at all. For several years the court did not try a single case, and in 1870–1 the mixed courts were closed.

Historians still differ in their assessment of the part played by the United States in ending the African slave trade. As already noted, some argue that the government deliberately ignored its treaty obligations or that Southern naval officers turned a blind eye toward slave ships. Yet the American record in suppressing the African slave trade is far from negative. The vigor with which the African squadron carried out its duties varied with its commanding officers, but that is true of any military force in any military situation. The U.S. Navy at that time included a considerable proportion of older officers who by law could not be retired and whose seniority was so high that their claims to command could not be ignored. But they were in the minority, and the presence of young officers with energy and determination guaranteed that the laws against slaving were enforced some of the time.[45] The placement of the base in the Cape Verde Islands, however, was a major handicap to effective patrolling.

Considering the small number and the types of American naval vessels available for service in the African squadron, the number of slavers captured is not insignificant.[46] In 1867, when the trade was dead, the American Colonization Society reported that the United States had sent 5,722 recaptured African natives to Liberia alone.[47] (Not all such slaves were sent to Liberia; the majority, in fact, seem to have been unloaded at British colonial ports, especially at Freetown.) Even the critical British showed a degree of approval when they noted that American gunboats based at Luanda, Angola, had liberated 4,200 black captives in 1860.[48] The total number of slaves retaken by the U.S. Navy is unknown.

But more than the African squadron was involved in ending the slave trade. As noted, customs officials along the U.S. coast and U.S. marshals sought to make captures, and the Brazilian and Cuban squadrons also captured slavers and libeled them in the courts. Total American efforts to destroy the slave trade thus resulted, as previously noted, in 107 ships being seized and libeled as slavers. Overall, the United States made a substantial effort to end the transmaritime commerce in slaves.

CHAPTER 5

The effects of the slave trade

From early colonial times until 1862, Africa had served as a reservoir of labor for the New World. The English colonies and the United States took a prominent part in exploiting African manpower, but they were not the major customers for the human commodity shipped out from the African coast. The United States received approximately 4.5 percent, or 427,000 out of an estimated 9,566,000 slaves shipped from Africa. Because of the slave trade, American relations with Europe, particularly with Great Britain, were complicated and even rendered acrimonious at times.

The history of the slave trade is a tale of misery, exceeded in horror only by the record of the Gulag Archipelago in the Soviet Union and by the Holocaust. There are indications that slave mortality may have diminished during the nineteenth century.[1] Even so, the annals of this commerce make one of the blackest pages in history. The traffic, however, must be put into historical perspective. The commerce in slaves did not depend solely on white men's greed. Slavery existed in Africa before the Europeans came, and it was the Arabs and the Africans who collected and sold the slaves. African traders and African chiefs supplied the human merchandise that was shipped to the New World.[2] Long after Western European nations condemned the slave trade and sought to restrict it, Africans and Arabs continued to sell their fellows. In the end, once humanitarian feelings gained wide acceptance, it was above all the Europeans and Americans who stopped the traffic.

Nor can the slave trade be seen only as an example of European and American abuse of people of color. The slave trade and slavery were racist institutions, but they were not the only exploitative ones. Whites mistreated whites in harsh and freewheeling eighteenth- and nineteenth-century Europe. The treatment of African slaves was probably not much worse than that endured by Russian serfs or Irish peasants. Whereas the evils of the slave ships and of the industrial towns of Lille, Manchester, and Liverpool have long been exposed, the exploitation and foul living conditions of immigrants have only recently been recorded.[3] The "Middle Passage" from Africa to the West Indies was grim, but so was the northern route from Liverpool to Boston or New York. The European immigrants traveled on small, overcrowded ships; they had to supply their own food and protect themselves and their families; they were usually kept below deck for the whole voyage; they were cheated and abused by the shipowners; the women were preyed on by the sailors; thefts, quarrels, and disease were common. Before 1860 mortality on such voyages averaged 10 to 20 percent (sometimes higher than the death rate on slave ships). Cholera, dysentery, smallpox, and ship fever, as well as starvation and malnutrition, took their toll. The Irish were even worse off: They sometimes sailed to Canada on open lumber ships, and when, in 1847 eighty-four lumber ships were held at Grosse Isle below Quebec, ten thousand Irish immigrants died in the winter's cold as a result of the delay in landing.[4]

Societies only slowly become sensitive to suffering. It took time to improve the conditions of factory workers and the Irish peasantry, as it took time to awaken the public conscience to oppose the slave trade and then to enforce the laws against it. We cannot with justice apply the standards of our day to previous centuries. History shows only the slow growth of our concern for our fellows and the gradual creation of institutions and values which insist that men and women be treated in a more humane fashion.

The slave trade and Africa

"Our common goods here for a prime slave . . . up the river Shabrow in the year 1755 . . . stands thus," recorded an English slave dealer in his journal, "4 guns, 2 kegs powder, 1 piece blew baft [a coarse cotton material from the East Indies], 1 kettle, 2 brass pans, 1 duzn. knives, 2 basons, 2 iron bars, 1 head beads, 50 flints, 1 silk handk."[5] Commodities such as these were imported into Africa in large quantities and helped to occasion considerable changes in many indigenous economies. Guns and gunpowder were of value not only in war but in the chase. Hunters equipped with adequate firearms could kill "for the pot" more easily than their ancestors had been able to do with bows and lances. In regions where elephants were liable to trample over the crops, villagers with guns could drive away these great animals with less peril and trouble than could neighbors who depended on fiery torches and spears. Knives and hatchets proved a boon to artisans and cultivators alike. Textiles were valuable in everyday use. Iron bars supplied smiths with the raw material for their craft. Imported salt was indispensable in cookery. In many parts of Africa the indigenous people were therefore enmeshed – however tenuously – in a worldwide network of trade. Many of the so-called traditional economies, which anthropologists described in later generations, had for a long time been affected by foreign intercourse and had benefited to some extent from international exchange and the operation of the market.

The wider effects of the traffic are hard to trace, and we can deal only in outline with a subject that is still a source of dispute among historians of Africa. Despite the barbarities of the commerce in human beings, its effects were not all negative. Foreign contacts, for example, enriched the African's larder. West Africa was not well supplied with native fruits and green vegetables. The European garrisons stationed in West Africa had to fill these deficiencies, and every fort maintained a large garden to grow European salad plants, cabbages, and cauliflowers from imported seed, and fruit trees introduced mainly from tropical Asia and America. Many of these crops can first be traced to the Portuguese, although some appear to have been introduced later, chiefly by the Dutch. Among the earliest plants were the lemon, the sugar cane, and melons from the Mediterranean, probably brought to Africa via the Portuguese-owned islands of Madeira and São Tomé. The orange, tamarind, banana, and coconut came from the Indian Ocean. The pineapple, pawpaw (papaya), and guava were brought from the Americas. Europeans acclimatized these crops in their gardens and helped to pass them on to their African neighbors.[6]

Some Europeans, especially the Danes, deliberately attempted to create agricultural plantations in their West African possessions. In this respect the Danes appear to have been more successful than either the British, farther west on the Gold Coast, or the French in Senegal. In 1809 Christian Schionning, a Dane, had forty thousand coffee shrubs on his estate at the foot of the Akwapim Scarp and a further hundred thousand plants in an adjoining nursery.[7] The dissemination of such crops was a slow process, as may be inferred from the fact that in 1692 a coconut grove near Accra formed a landmark to seamen who called it the "Spanish cavalry." Palms also seem to have been rare on other parts of the coast now fringed with them. The mango, avocado, and other fruits that have become quite common also seem to have been unknown until the nineteenth century.[8]

The Europeans (and also the Arabs) likewise carried essential staple crops to Africa, most of them in the European case, of American Indian origin. These included maize, now an article of major importance to the Africans though it did not quickly become a popular food. As late as 1784 the Fanti grew it only for sale to Europeans or to Africans living near the forts. In contrast, the groundnut or peanut, of American derivation, soon became widespread. Cassava or manioc, the present staple food of many African communities, was probably introduced to Africa by the Portuguese, who brought it from Brazil to their African stations, ranging from Elmina in present-day Ghana to Mogadishu in Somalia. The plant was first acclimatized around the mouth of the Congo, and from there it spread all over Central Africa. Manioc was probably taken to the upper Guinea coast when it was taken to the Congo, but it became established in indigenous agriculture there much more slowly than in the south. It was almost certainly brought to the Portuguese stations in East Africa at a later time than to the west.[9] Other plants owing their spread to the transoceanic trade include the prickly pear or Indian fig, sisal, and aloe, as well as tobacco; all these were first developed in America and formed part of the great agricultural heritage that the Indians bequeathed to the rest of the world.

These gains were bought at a terrible price, and no balance sheet can ever present the full debt account of the slave trade. Some historians have ascribed the relative cultural backwardness of sub-Saharan Africa to the ravages of the traffic. The commerce, according to their argument, deprived Africa of countless able-bodied workers; it perverted or disrupted indigenous societies; it also created an atmosphere of violence, debauchery, and uncertainty that militated against all economic progress.[10] This interpretation contains some truth. But not all African areas were equally affected. The chief sufferers were the weaker and more scattered communities, often those not yet supplied with muskets. As the gunpowder frontier gradually moved inland, the erstwhile victims would acquire firearms and prey on their neighbors in turn, so that the impact of the traffic was very uneven. The slave trade may have helped to strengthen the great West African states such as Oyo and Dahomey. Indeed, the most impressive development of the seventeenth and eighteenth centuries was the growth of African states just inland from the coastlands and the shift of West Africa's economic center of gravity away from the Sudan toward the Atlantic shore.[11]

Africa sustained vast biological losses as a result of the transatlantic slave trade. But the total social effects of these casualties are not easy to assess. The ravages of the transatlantic commerce extended over some four centuries. Their incidence was uneven, and they did not lead to wholesale depopulation. As J. D. Fage points out, nearly 80 percent of the slaves exported in the 1790s were taken from the region between the Gold Coast and the Cameroons. If the Atlantic slave trade had caused serious depopulation, the loss of manpower should have been most clearly evident in this region, but the available figures do not show any such results. On the contrary, these West African lands are as thickly settled as any in Africa.[12]

Economists have reached similar conclusions. S. Daniel Neumark calculates that even if the population of West Africa amounted to no more than twenty million at the height of the traffic – a very conservative estimate – the average annual loss was at the most 0.5 percent. The slave trade must have reduced population densities in some areas, but it is still not certain that a higher level of economic development would have been attained in the absence of the traffic. What may be an optimum population under one set of technological and economic conditions may be either above or below the optimum under another. Migration, one might add, does not necessarily impede development. During the nineteenth century, for instance, some nineteen million people left Great Britain, but this was a period of unparalleled economic growth in the United Kingdom. In Africa population densities may also have been kept down by unfavorable geographical and climatic conditions, as well as by political instability that had nothing to do with the commerce and that also plagued regions unaffected by the trade. Some authorities have even speculated whether the ghastly commerce did not at times play the role of more peaceful migration to happier lands, relieving pressure on scanty means of subsistence for those who remained.

Such theorizing is highly problematical. But we can be certain that the *absence* of the traffic did not necessarily make for a greater degree of economic development or cultural maturity. The kingdom of the Barotse (Lozi) in what is now Zambia was not much involved in the slave trade. The Lozi were geographically far removed from the main centers of the trade, and they were anxious to bring people into the fertile Zambezi Valley rather than to export their manpower. But Barotseland's cultural attainments were inferior to those of the great West African kingdoms that played such a dominant part in the commerce. Similarly, the Ndebele (Matabele) of southern Africa did not deal in slaves. They raided their neighbors but preferred to assimilate their captives within their own community rather than sell them abroad. Yet the Ndebele did not succeed in progressing beyond a fairly simple pastoral economy, while their victims suffered as much as or more than they would have done had they been exposed to the depredations of slave commerce.

The damage from the slave trade varied from area to area. Slaving seems to have been, for instance, less disruptive of the social structures of Guinea than of Angola. Guinea probably benefited economically from the trade, for exchange with Europe brought in wealth. But even in Angola the slave trade has been credited with introducing American plants and fruits. "From a demographic point of view it might be argued that the loss of slaves was compensated by the introduction of these crops."[13] In areas where the population was thin, however, a small loss of manpower in a subsistence economy could be disastrous.[14]

Foreign trade also had far-reaching political effects. Commerce supplied rulers with new revenue. Many African potentates thus took part in the traffic directly or benefited from it through levies, customs, duties and other imposts. Local dignitaries on the West African coast also charged rent from white men for the right to trade. This income provided black lords with a means to increase their power, and the black monarchs remained "distributor kings." They might control the wealth of their respective countries, but they could not accumulate riches to any very great extent. By and large, they continued to give their surplus to their followers: They invested their revenue in political power rather than in more productive enterprises.

The slave trade did not, therefore, give rise to new methods of production in Africa. African craftsmen could not easily compete with European factory workers, and African technicians could not rival the skills of their more advanced contemporaries in Europe. African smiths could not outsell goods made in Birmingham, England, nor could African weavers undercut the cost of cotton goods of Lancashire. Indeed, the only West African communities that exported manufactures on any considerable scale were the cities of Hausaland on the western flank of Bornu. The artisans of Katsina, Kano, and Zaria, for instance, were renowned for their skills in weaving, dyeing, leatherwork, glassmaking, and metal fashioning. The Sudanic towns, however, looked northward to the great caravan routes that radiated across the Sahara to Tripoli and Ghadames and then on to Tunis. They exerted but little influence on the black states of the southern forest belt. Indeed, the slave trade, as we have seen, helped to shift West Africa's center of economic gravity from the Sudanic interior to the littoral, and the transatlantic commerce possibly helped to diminish the relative importance of traditional craft industries.

The states of the woodland belt involved in the Christian slave trade developed what might be called a proto–middle class, including African slave vendors as well as indigenous agents of European firms (many of them mulattoes). Nevertheless, there was no bourgeoisie in the European sense. Wealth meant the ownership of consumer goods. Slaves were generally the most profitable form of investment, and all they bought in return were more consumer goods. Chiefs and wealthy commoners alike used their riches in conspicuous consumption or as a means to gain more clients and added status. Hence there was no capital formation in the Western meaning of the term.

The political impact of the slave trade on the indigenous states of Africa remains a matter of dispute.[15] One school of historians attributes tremendous importance to this traffic in the creation of the great forest states of West Africa. According to their interpretation, the arms and revenue derived from the trade enabled Benin and Dahomey to expand at their neighbors' expense and to build up powerful empires. Similarly, the destruction of these states is ascribed to moral decay from within and to the ending of the slave trade by pressure from without.

Other historians recently have challenged some of these conclusions.[16] They have rightly argued that the widespread but little-documented exchange of food among hunters, cultivators, and fishermen was of greater importance to African economic history than the more spectacular long-distance traffic in slaves and gold. Some also believe that the effects of slave wars have been exaggerated by European missionary and humanitarian opinion, that European imperialists had a natural interest in painting a dark picture of precolonial Africa, and that conflicts such as the Yoruba wars of the nineteenth century did not produce a general holocaust.

Wars between African states, moreover, did not necessarily derive from disputes about commerce, though such disagreements may have further envenomed diplomatic relations between hostile communities.

Even insofar as the slave trade nourished wars by providing soldiers with imported guns and ammunition, the commerce in human merchandise did not by itself necessarily raise the political issues that had created the desire for foreign-made weapons in the first place. In all probability, the traffic in guns allowed traditional chiefs, or even upstart warlords, to arm their retinues with more effective weapons and thus to gain considerable advantages over the ordinary villagers. Common peasants could still fashion their own bows and lances, but they could not manufacture muskets to rival the weapons of more professional soldiers. Among the Yoruba, for example, military specialization was encouraged not only by the challenge of troubled times but by the changing nature of warfare. From an army consisting of mounted men and levies armed with homemade arms, the Yoruba forces gradually turned into infantry armed mainly with muskets. Cavalry declined as Fulani conquerors in the savannah belt cut off the supply of horses from the north. The Yoruba warriors learned how to fire their guns accurately; they developed new tactics of war; and they taught these skills to young recruits through a process of apprenticeship. Every successful war chief built up his own clientage of followers in search of booty and fame. The war leaders became increasingly important in Yoruba politics and often clashed with the traditional civil authorities. The importation of firearms thus gave an impetus to military specialization of labor, whereby rulers with an adequate surplus surrounded themselves with a professional or semiprofessional class of privileged warriors. The musket did not, however, initiate this process, which seems to have begun in many of the more advanced African states long before the introduction of the pistol and the blunderbuss.

On the basis of existing literature, we may surmise that the slave trade tended to benefit the strong and to injure the weak, and that it always accelerated existing social trends. Kingdoms already in the ascendant thus derived further benefit from foreign commerce. States suffering from internal discussions were wrecked, and their people were left prey to new conquerors.

The slave trade and the United States

The effects of the slave trade on the New World were so profound that we can only allude to them in a fairly cursory fashion. As noted, the financial ramifications extended deeply into all elements of American society. Any landowner was likely to profit from the sale of timber from his woodlot or forestland: Timber went into ships, barrel staves, and lumber, all of which had their place in the lucrative trade with Africa.[17] The New England fisherman was concerned with salt and dried fish; these were important articles of commerce with the West Indies and the Southern colonies because they were used as food for slaves. And, of course, the Southern plantation economy depended largely on a plentiful supply of cheap black labor.

The dependence of the North American colonies upon slavery for a large measure of their material progress and development makes sad reading, but the historical facts cannot be controverted. From approximately 1619 on, English settlements on the North American continent were largely dependent upon Africa for their economic success. Without slaves, the agricultural colonies would probably have languished in a largely subsistence economy, and the New England colonies could have had considerable difficulty in finding any other means of heightening the value of their colonial products through commercial exchange. Northern slaves worked on farms or in rural industries – tanneries, saltworks, iron foundries. A substantial number of slaves dwelt in the cities, where they were widely employed as house servants; they were also used in maritime trades as sailors and shipyard workers and in sail factories. They thereby made a valuable, though little-recognized, contribution to Northern life.

The great African migration also affected American culture in other ways. Whites and blacks alike developed contradictory attitudes that have profoundly affected American life to this day. The growth of the aristocratic or pseudo-aristocratic tradition of the South is directly – if partly – attributable to the existence of slavery and the presence of large numbers of slaves. The distrust that the colonists felt toward Africans sprang naturally from being surrounded by people of a strange race who were regarded as primitive savages. All colonial legislatures passed laws imposing severe restrictions upon blacks, laws seemingly justified by the frequent uprisings on slave ships and the number of slave insurrections in several colonies. The slave trade with Africa brought into the North American colonies a substantial population that was feared and that could not easily be assimilated.

The Southern colonies in particular lived under constant fear of slave uprisings. South Carolina and, later, Georgia were especially sensitive to such a danger, partly because the whites were outnumbered by the blacks, and partly because it was suspected that the Spanish authorities in Florida were continually plotting and encouraging slave revolts against their English neighbors.

Not the least important effect of the African trade was the cultural interchange. African settlement in the New World helped to produce a host of syncretic cultures that differed widely, not merely from one country to the next, but within different regions of the same territory. In North America, for instance, a black's life on the rice plantations of the Carolina coast or in the cotton country of Alabama was very different from the existence of a black employed in a turpentine factory or on a small upland farm.[18]

The rate of acculturation differed in a similar fashion. A field hand on a large plantation usually led a harsh life (though not necessarily a worse one than that of, say, a white redemptioner or a white sailor press-ganged into the British navy). Field hands had little opportunity to learn new skills; in this respect there was no difference between a serf exploited on a great estate in Brazil and a slave on a similar establishment in the American South. (Modern research has modified the once widely held belief that slavery in Brazil was essentially milder in nature than elsewhere, and that Portuguese people in general were more tolerant of slaves than northern Europeans.) But in Brazil, where white women were scarce, miscegenation took place on an even greater scale that it did in the French, Spanish, and English colonies, and miscegenation entailed a considerable degree of cultural reciprocity: African influences made a deeper impact on the social and economic institutions of Brazil than on those of English-speaking North America, where blacks remained a minority and had to compete with a considerable class of white artisans and small white farmers. But whatever their nationality, all groups of European colonists used both skilled and unskilled African labor in their tropical and subtropical possessions.

The whites made extensive use of the blacks' experience. Their intimate knowledge of natural conditions in subtropical lowlands stood the transplanted Africans in good stead in many parts of the South. Ira Berlin, a modern historian, has described this process well:

> Since the geography, climate, and topography of the low country more
> closely resembled the West African than the English countryside, African,
> not European technology and agronomy often guided lowland develop-
> ment. From the first, whites depended on blacks to identify useful flora and
> fauna, and to identify the appropriate methods of production. Blacks,
> adapting African techniques to the circumstances of the Carolina wilder-
> ness, shaped the lowland cattle industry and played a central role in the
> introduction of the region's leading staple. In short, transplanted English-
> men learned as much or more from transplanted Africans as did the former
> Africans from them.[19]

Acculturation was thus not a one-way street; the master was influenced by the slave, as well as the slave by the master. As Berlin points out, blacks were particularly influential in farming. Colonial planters used African skills in rice cultivation and cattle raising. In the Carolinas and Virginia African slaves became the pioneers, the craftsmen, the watermen, and the woodsmen to settle the Southern wilds.

Blacks also learned from the Indians and taught them medicinal herbs; African folktales became common among the Creek, Cherokee, and Seminole. Escaped slaves often settled among the Indians and intermarried with them.

The whites likewise passed on some of their own culture to the slaves, especially to men and women who had managed to learn English and who had succeeded in improving their lot by becoming craftsmen, supervisors, or sometimes even independent traders. All transatlantic colonies, English as well as Portuguese and Spanish, gradually acquired a class of free blacks, former redemptioners whose contracts had expired, blacks legally manumitted by their masters, or even free immigrants from other territories. This group varied greatly in number, attainments, and pursuits, depending on local circumstances. Some became soldiers or frontiersmen; some acquired estates and even slaves of their own. Others became traders, artisans, or members of the liberal professions. Many of them proved highly adaptable, and their life stories reveal a great deal of personal initiative. Olaudah Equiano, an Ibo enslaved in Africa at a tender age during the eighteenth century and subsequently freed in the New World, became proficient in all manner of jobs. He knew something of seamanship; he could work as a barber; he knew how to distill liquor and run a store. He acquired an excellent command of English and compiled what is still a highly readable autobiography in his adopted tongue. He also became a convinced abolitionist and helped to interpret the cultural heritage of his own people for the benefit of his English readers.

The less tangible effects of the African's forcible transplantation into the New World are harder to assess. Discussion is bedeviled by two opposing stereotypes.

The old-fashioned view sees the black immigrants as a mass of faceless people, stripped of all tradition or individuality, mere human raw material to be shaped at the will of their masters. A more recent school of thought tries to make up for these failings by putting special stress on the blacks' personalities. In doing so, it sometimes – though not always – descends into a mixture of philanthropy and romanticism. A history of limitless suffering, an age-old aboriginal contact with nature, and a special sense for the numinous and for the deeper rhythms of life have supposedly given black people a more intuitive understanding of nature than is available to whites bred in the materialistic and mechanistic tradition of the West. This interpretation sometimes also assumes that blacks have a richer sexuality and a deeper feeling for the rhythm of life than have white people.

We disagree with both interpretations. We regard the "faceless person" school of slavery, according to which black captives were like so many bricks to be placed into a white-designed structure, as a piece of fantasy. We equally disagree with the folk-soul interpretation, which reminds us of nothing so much as the musings of many German romantics in the nineteenth and twentieth centuries. But we are fully persuaded that black cultures did indeed make their impact on the New World. This impact differed greatly in intensity, being greatest in Brazil and the West Indies, but it was found wherever Africans were forced to settle.

Africans, for instance, considerably enriched the diet of the New World. Edible plants such as the kidney bean, the banana, and the okra were transferred from Africa to America. Black cooks taught their masters how to prepare all kinds of new dishes; they also introduced palm oil and malaguetta pepper to the Americas. American English to this day reflects the impact of the African migration across the Atlantic in African-descended words for foods, such as "goober" (peanut), "gumbo" (okra), "yam" (sweet potato), and so forth.

The Africans also brought with them their music. Music, like dancing, easily crosses linguistic boundaries, and African strains have had a profound impact on the musical heritage of the world. Brazilian music today – the simple, short melodic line, the repetition of phrases – derives in large part from the chants in the religious rituals of the Sudanese and from the songs of every occasion of daily life that were so much a part of the African tradition. Brazilian composers have drawn heavily on African themes; Brazilian musicians have adapted African percussion instruments to their use. The African cultural heritage had an equally profound effect on the music of North America. American spirituals probably came into being through a blending of European Protestant and African music. Jazz, the most distinctive North American contribution to the world's music, derives its inspiration from the rhythm of African drums, with its vigor and infinite variety.

African slaves likewise carried their dances across the Atlantic. The samba, the national dance of Brazil, derives from the *quizomba,* a wedding dance from Angola, and from the Angolan-Congolese dance called the *batuque.* The Cuban rumba is African in its spirit; so are many other Latin American and North American dances, such as the Charleston, the Black Bottom, the Buzzard Lope, and the ring shout, some of which are used in present-day gospel movements. Even a well-known American song like Stephen Foster's "Camp-Town Races" has been traced back to a Yoruba tune.

Blacks also left their mark on the literature and folklore of the New World. The popular tales and legends of Brazil are, in large part, of African origin. Most North American children are familiar with the tales concerning Uncle Remus or Brer Rabbit, whose French West Indian cousin goes by the name of *Pé Lapin*. An account of either the folk literature or the more sophisticated literary works produced by Afro-American writers in English, French, Spanish, or Portuguese would fill many volumes. So would an account of black influence on the European languages spoken in the New World. Such a survey would have to range all the way from the creation of independent French and English patois in the West Indies to the infiltration into English of individual words like "tote" (to carry) or "juke" (as in "juke box"). The musical quality, the tonality, the cadence of American black speech is reflected in Southern white dialects. The African influence on Southern American English was apparently of much greater significance than the Bantu impact on Afrikaans in South Africa.

Finally, Africans brought their religious beliefs into the New World, where they blended with white Protestant revivalist strains. Clearly, the white impact was bound to be greater in North America, where the blacks were in a minority, than, say, in Haiti, where Africans came to form the great majority of the population. According to Roger Bastide, a French scholar, the impact of Catholic Christianity was also somewhat different in kind.[20] Afro-Catholicism emphasized ritual and collective participation more than mystic beliefs; the inculcation of Christian doctrines was, on the whole, more superficial than in Protestant countries. The slaves in North America, on the other hand, acquired a much greater familiarity with the Bible than did their brethren in the Latin countries; the blacks were quick to see real or assumed parallels between their own situation and that of the Jews in the Old Testament, as demonstrated by their spirituals. The details of this cultural and religious interchange remain to be elaborated. It is, however, clear that cultural assimilation operated in two directions and that African strains have decidedly influenced many of the emergent cultures of the New World.

II

Commerce, Christianity, and colonization societies
up to 1865

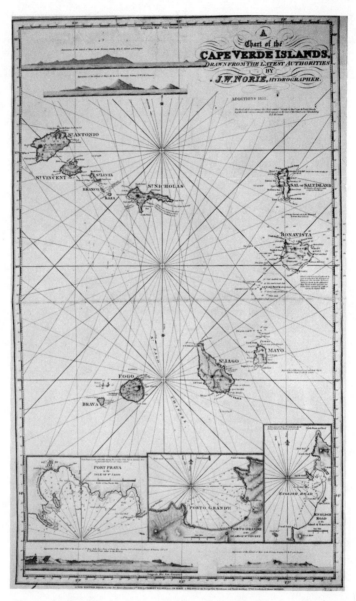

Chart of Cape Verde. By permission of the Whaling Museum, New Bedford, Mass.

The whaling ship *Maria*, Nantucket. Reprinted, by permission of the Whaling Museum, New Bedford, Mass., from Edouard A. Stackpole, *Whales and Destiny: The Rivalry between America, France, and Britain for Control of the Southern Whale Fishery, 1785–1825* (Amherst: University of Massachusetts Press, 1972).

Panorama of New Bedford harbor. Reprinted, by permission of the Whaling Museum, New Bedford, Mass., from Stackpole, *Whales and Destiny*.

Ships anchored off Table Mountain, Cape Town, South Africa. Courtesy Zimbabwe Archives.

Joseph J. Roberts, first president of Liberia, 1847. Courtesy Library of Congress.

Early mine on the Rand, South Africa. Courtesy Hoover Institution Archives.

Major Frederick Russell Burnham. Courtesy Hoover Institution Archives.

CHAPTER 6

American traders and whalers

The eighteenth century was the era of the slave trade. But the traffic in human beings, from its inception, was linked to what later became known as "legitimate" enterprise: the commerce in tools, textiles, and consumption goods. Many of the ships that sailed to Africa from Europe or America during the seventeenth and eighteenth centuries went in search of slaves, but available records indicate that vessels bound for the African coast usually carried general trade goods as well as rum, brandy, and tobacco, the recognized instruments of barter for slaves. Whaling ships in large numbers also went to Africa after 1770. Ships returning to America or Europe from Africa generally carried other products in addition to human chattels: gum; spices; hides; gold dust; whale oil, sperm, and bones; and other merchandise.

Initially, this traffic was proportionately small. The commerce largely centered on a single New England community: American trade with Africa was a near monopoly of Salem, though whaling ships sailed primarily from Nantucket and New Bedford. Salem merchants, a small and tightly knit group, simultaneously developed American trade with the west and east coasts of Africa. In many particulars, the commerce of the two Africa coasts differed considerably. Moreover, the geographical areas involved were so vast that, for clarity of discussion, we shall draw an arbitrary distinction between American dealings with West Africa, on the one hand, and the exchange of goods with eastern and southern Africa, on the other.

West Africa

Direct commercial relations between America and Africa seem to have developed first on the west coast, where the close union between the slave trade and legitimate commerce in the colonial era is illustrated by a venture undertaken by the Beekmans, a prominent merchant family of New York, in 1748. Late in that year they dispatched their brig *Revenge* on a speculative voyage to Gambia and loaded it with the usual quantities of rum, along with "musketts," brass pans and basins, and other odds and ends. Months later, when the owners had almost given up the *Revenge* as lost, the ship sailed into New York bay, badly battered but still afloat and carrying, in addition to forty-five slaves, seventy-nine ounces of gold dust and three and a half tons of dyewood. The *Revenge* had arrived at the African coast at a time when the market was glutted. Consequently, most of its cargo was untouched, but the slaves, the gold dust, and the dyewood together prevented the Beekmans from suffering a ruinous loss.[1]

The whalers. Probably the first American vessels to arrive in African waters without any interest in slaves were the whaling ships. Whalers are known to have reached the Guinea coast as early as 1763 and were in Walvis Bay before 1770. Edmund Burke, in his famous 1775 speech "Conciliation with the Colonies," declaimed: "Look at the manner in which the people of New England have of late carried on the whale fishers . . . We know that whilst some of them draw the line and strike the harpoon on the coast of Africa, others run the longitude and pursue their gigantic game along the coast of Brazil."[2] Although whalers were not engaged in commerce in the usual sense of that term, there can be little doubt that they hired Africans as sailors, purchased provisions, refilled their water butts, and bought small amounts of African wares when they touched land.

Nantucket pioneered the southern whale fishery, devoted to the capture of the great sperm whale, whose oil was worth twice that of the "black oil" of the Arctic white whale. No British-based vessels engaged in this type of whaling until the Revolutionary War, when some Nantucketers went over to England and sailed for British merchants.[3] New Bedford replaced Nantucket for a time as the leading whaling port and rewon control of the southern whale fishery for the United States in the 1790s. Nantucket then revived and became once again the leading whaling port, dominating, for example, the whaling in the Walvis Bay area (South Africa).

The War of 1812 decimated whalers, but from 1815 on the United States controlled the best whaling regions. After 1825 England ceased to be a competitor. In 1840 seven hundred whaling ships sailed from the American ports of Nantucket, New Bedford, Newport, and New London. They stopped often in African ports, especially Cape Town, homeward bound from the east or outward bound to the Indies and Australia.

As noted, Africans engaged in substantial economic and social activity with the whalemen, for they were employed either to work aboard the vessels while they were in port or to sail as foremasthands. They were usually paid in cash or in such goods as cloth, tobacco, bread and meat, or rum. The Africans sometimes provided feasts and dancing, and the whalers gave parties on their ships. There was also a great deal of informal associating in local bars, brothels, and restaurants. Drinking and whoring led often to jail in the larger European-controlled ports. Whalers were not usually welcome visitors. Long months at sea and pent-up emotions led to heavy drinking and fighting: The whaler was known wherever he sailed for his violence, abusiveness, and drunkenness.

The whalers left Nantucket or New Bedford, sailed south to the West Indies and on to South America, and then across to Africa on trade winds. In addition, St. Helena, Walvis Bay, the Cape Verde Islands, and the Azores were major bases and resupply stations for American whalers.[4] Cape Verdeans and Azoreans were good sailors and signed on as crewmen. Hundreds of Cape Verdeans (a mixture of Portuguese and African peoples) wound up living in New Bedford and parts of Massachusetts, Connecticut, and Rhode Island (see "Africans in the United States" in Chapter 24).

The influence of the whalers was minimal in larger ports like Cape Town, but they were a major factor in island ports such as St. Helena, Cape Verde, and the Azores in the Atlantic and the Comoros and Seychelles in the Indian Ocean. Evidently islands were much preferred by whaling captains because of lower prices

and their free wood and water, but especially because islands did not lend themselves as havens for runaway seamen.[5] In 1788, of 202 foreign vessels stopping in
the Cape Verde port of Praia, 74 were American. They came for sailors, salt, and
fresh fruit and vegetables – and for drink and women. Many ships returning from
Europe without cargo stopped at Cape Verde to load salt; the historian George
Brooks suggests that they may have learned of trading opportunities in Africa
while they were there.[6]

The Azores (islands in the north Atlantic nine hundred miles west of Portugal)
figured importantly in the whaling enterprise of the United States. Practically all
American whalers leaving to fish the southern waters called there, outward bound
as well as homeward bound, for the islands provided a convenient port for trans-
shipping oil and for hiring a ready supply of cheap labor. The Azores were also
used for food resupply, especially for water and cheap agricultural produce. The
local economy benefited mostly from the sale of food; port charges and entertainment added something also; and wages for the Azorean sailors (again, a mixture of
Portuguese and African peoples) contributed to the local wealth. The whalers'
money, in fact, was of vital importance to the prosperity of the main island.

Finally, the islands were a source of rest and recreation for the crews. But the
whalers also brought trouble. Rioting, drinking, and whoring were widely reported.[7] Venereal diseases were widespread. The U.S. consul in 1870 wanted to
import two healthy prostitutes to serve the whalers, but the State Department
refused his request.

By the middle of the nineteenth century, Americans dominated the world's whaling industry. They – and the British – had revolutionized its techniques; they had
invented and applied the use of bombs and grenades, going as far as to combine
the two in single shots. In 1853, during a typical year in the golden era of whaling,
ships brought home 3,298,464 gallons of sperm oil, 8,332,648 gallons of whale
oil, and 5,632,300 pounds of whalebone. The value of this catch stood at $11
million, a large sum in those days.

American whaling influence in the Azores and along the African coast ended in
the 1870s, when whale oil was replaced by cheaper petroleum oil and when bone
whales became more valuable than sperm whales. The growing cities of New York,
Boston, Philadelphia, and Baltimore had been lucrative markets for whale oil (for
lighting) and sperm candles. Industry used the oil for paints, for lubrication, and for
tanning hides, and the oil was also used to fuel lighthouses and beacons.[8] Whalebone
was made into umbrella ribs, buggy whips, canes, corset stays, and hoops for skirts.
The growth of domestic manufacturers and the opening of the West caused domestic
wages to rise; henceforth a skilled man could earn on shore two to three times what
he made by doing the rough and dangerous work of a whaler.

The traders. American legitimate trade with Africa began after the Revolutionary
War. The period following the war was an era in which the American merchants
and shipowners, freed from the restrictions of British mercantilism, were feeling
their way over the world, searching for markets (U.S. ships were excluded from the
British West Indies after 1783), hunting for cargoes and salable commodities. In
the summer of 1783 Moses Brown, a wealthy Quaker merchant and shipowner of
Providence, Rhode Island, and (unlike some members of his family) an uncompro-

mising enemy of the slave trade, heard rumors that the prominent firm of Clark and Nightingale was fitting a ship for a slaving voyage to the Guinea coast. Brown protested vigorously and was informed that the objective of the voyage was not slaves but "ivory, wax and gold dust." Although there is some indication that Clark and Nightingale were actually concealing their real purposes, the incident is significant as showing that commodities other than slaves attracted the attention of the American merchants.[9]

The establishment of the British colony for free blacks (including black soldiers who had fought for the king in the American War of Independence) in Sierra Leone in 1787 marked the beginning of a significant change in the economy of West Africa. Sierra Leone became both a colony for freed slaves and, after 1807, a base for the Royal Navy's operations against the slave trade; it was also a center of legitimate trade. Such American trade goods as rum and tobacco, once used almost exclusively for the purchase of human beings, became items of exchange for palm oil, dyewoods, and, after 1830, the peanut.

American commercial opportunities on the African coast were greatly increased by the long series of wars that started with the French Revolution and lasted until 1815. With shipping from France and other Continental countries driven from the seas, with British shipping preempted by the government or harassed by French privateers, the European stations and factories on the African coast became virtually dependent upon American merchants and U.S. shipping for both necessities and luxuries.[10] European traders were unable to do business with African customers unless they could offer trade goods, which they could purchase only from the Yankees. Americans were able to obtain cloth from India and the products of the East Indies, as well as commodities from North Africa. In 1809 Governor Thompson of Sierra Leone reported regretfully to Lord Castlereagh: "I have the honour to represent to your Lordship that this Colony has hitherto been in a great measure supplied with the articles of trade with the Natives by the Americans, particularly with cotton cloths." A year later he morosely reported again: "The cargoes of the Americans consisted in a great measure of India Cloths of the kind principally used in bartering with the Natives." Because of unfavorable financial regulations, he added, the Americans could supply these goods at much lower prices than the East India Company. The governor lamented that Sierra Leone was becoming an American colony.[11]

This condition continued in spite of interruptions caused by President Jefferson's embargo (1807–9) and the Royal Navy's flagrant disregard of neutral rights on the African coast, as well as in European and North American waters.[12] Between 1793 and 1812 American rum, beef, flour, tobacco, and lumber became necessities in West Africa, especially in Sierra Leone. The colony was almost isolated from Europe, and colonists and officials found themselves unable to subsist upon local products—especially with no European trade goods to exchange. Except for American ships and traders, Europeans in Africa would have been in acute discomfort, if not actual hardship. This condition was accentuated in Sierra Leone by the fact that many of the colonists were Americans or the offspring of Americans who had a distinct taste for things American.[13] The War of 1812, however, interrupted American activities on the African coast and brought considerable discomfort to the scanty European population, then cut off from practically all sources of supply.

With the restoration of peace in 1815, American ships and traders returned to Africa at once, but conditions had changed. After years of war, the merchants and shipowners of London, Liverpool, and Paris were hungry for business and profits and were not disposed to look kindly upon interlopers from across the Atlantic. The government officials of Great Britain and France felt the same; in the capitals, the old mercantilistic theories had not lost their vitality, and the governing classes believed that they must, by any and all means, promote the trade of their own countries and exclude competitors. Immediately after the close of the wars, by various expedients ranging from preferential duties to outright prohibition of trade with foreigners, the British and French governments attempted to close their African bases to Americans. Within a short time only the small Dutch and Danish factories remained officially open to international trade.

Attempts to keep out American and other competition were foredoomed to failure. Many traders in Africa, whether European or native, were unimpressed by restrictionist arguments; they saw no reason to confine their trade to Europeans when Americans supplied what they wanted at a substantially lower price than was demanded in England or France and would give a higher price for whatever the trader had to sell. And the Americans had no qualms about smuggling when necessary. Consequently, even in the face of duties intended to be prohibitive and despite the efforts of conscientious officials, American trade with West Africa flourished. In 1822, for example, the British merchants of Sierra Leone, in a petition to Governor MacCarthy by which they hoped to check the alarming increase in American trade, stated that although the British trade with the Gold Coast was worth £118,636, American trade had reached £40,000.[14]

It would be profitless to go into the details of the European powers' rather slow and uneven abandonment of restrictionist theories and practices in Africa. The change was, of course, closely linked with the rise of free-trade theories in Europe, and particularly in Great Britain. Nevertheless, the uninhibited Yankee shipmaster and trader had something to do with convincing the authorities of the utter futility of trying to enforce restrictions and maintain national monopolies.

In Sierra Leone and on the Gold Coast, efforts to eliminate Americans and make the areas complete British commercial monopolies were largely the work of a single official, Charles MacCarthy, a soldier by profession. In 1814 Governor Maxwell of Sierra Leone returned to England. MacCarthy, who was in command of the British garrison in Senegal, became acting governor, and a year later he was confirmed as permanent governor of the colony. Able, conscientious, and conservative, he was guided by an almost fanatical devotion to the British monarchy. He had served in the British army in Canada, and to his dislike of American republicanism seems to have been added a thorough distrust of American expansionist proclivities. When such a man received a royal command to enforce the Navigation Laws and exclude American shipping, the order would be enforced rigidly and without deviation. Consequently, American ships were soon forbidden to land their cargoes in Sierra Leone except under extraordinary circumstances that seldom arose. MacCarthy was also suspicious of the first steps of the American Colonization Society to establish a base in what was to become Liberia, believing that the society was merely a cloak for American schemes to plant a colony that would endanger British interests; he urgently pleaded for permission to seize the island of Sherbro and forestall the American peril. The British government refused, however, believing that the possibility of trouble with the United States outweighed any vague and unproved threat to Sierra Leone's revenues.[15]

Closing the port to American ships did not keep American goods from finding their way to Sierra Leone. Shut out of Freetown, American traders resorted to smuggling (with the tacit approval and the wholehearted cooperation of local merchants and traders) and established themselves at the Los Islands. From there they undercut British trade in the Scarcies, Pongo, Nuñez, Grande, and Sherbro rivers. Goods brought to Africa in American ships, upon which no duties were ever paid, continued to flow into British territory in spite of MacCarthy. The actual smuggling of American goods to the rivers seem to have been done by British merchants already established in the Los Islands. To eliminate this nuisance and cut off the supply of American goods, MacCarthy seized the islands in 1818. The Americans, deprived of their island base, transferred their operations to the rivers, thus eliminating the British middlemen. In this way the rivers (particularly the Nuñez), which had been slaving centers, became assembly and trading places for legitimate commerce in such products as ivory, dyewoods, and hides, even though the unhealthy river areas were still deadly places for white men through a large part of the year.[16] By the 1820s New England shoe factories provided a major market for West African hides.[17] In the 1830s and 1840s whale oil, hides, and peanuts were the major U.S. imports from Africa.

Sierra Leone was finally opened to American shipping in 1831, but even then there was little legal American trade for a number of years. Because the duties on rum and tobacco, the two major American products, were prohibitive, American ships usually bypassed Freetown for more obscure places. Their goods still found their way into Sierra Leone, but by devious routes through the bush. Nevertheless, American trade seems to have been continuously prominent in the economic life of the colony, and it increased sharply after 1841. In 1849, with Great Britain's final adoption of free-trade principles, the ancient Navigation Laws were repealed; American trade then became so important on the west coast that finally, in 1852, an Order in Council made American money legal tender, along with British coinage.[18] American commercial enterprise in other parts of West Africa in the early nineteenth century followed a similar pattern.

Closely associated with Sierra Leone was the small British colony on the Gambia River. Great Britain had been forced to abandon Gambia during the long period of wars with France and did not immediately move to reoccupy it at the end of the wars. Meanwhile, slavers, particularly Americans operating under the Spanish flag, were taking full advantage of the Gambia River as a favorable location for their activities, so in 1816 Governor MacCarthy led a force from Sierra Leone and hoisted the Union Jack over the island of Banjol at the mouth of the river.[19] American shipping was speedily excluded. But, as in Sierra Leone, legitimate American traders merely became illegal traders. Using the Cape Verde Islands as their base, they sold their illegal cargoes and took on, in increasing amounts, equally illegal African products. One American in particular, Samuel Hodges, Jr. (from Massachusetts, as were nearly all American traders in Africa), built a trading post on São Tiago Island in 1818 and from there supplied Gambia and the neighboring coastal areas with everything that was wanted.[20]

The British were finally forced by the demands of their own merchants to open Gambia to American tobacco and lumber in 1824 so that the competition of the French merchants at Albreda could be met. American shipping and other American products were excluded until 1835, when such restrictions were abolished. From that time forward, legitimate and open American trade was important to the economic life of the colony. The volume of American business became so large that an American consul was assigned to Bathurst in 1834, and in 1851 Lieutenant Commander E. R. Thompson of the USS *Porpoise* reported that from thirty to forty American vessels touched there annually. In 1858 Daniel R. B. Upson, an American trader at Bathurst, informed the State Department that during the preceding year thirty-one American ships had entered the port. Of the total imports of the colony ($569,728), more than $70,000 worth was in American goods.[21]

In the West African areas claimed by France, the story was quite similar to that of the British colonies: a tale of futile efforts to enforce the old restrictions and to maintain a monopoly of both transportation and goods. The French government and its officials also found themselves unable to prevent a constant influx of American rum, lumber, tobacco, and cotton goods. The French, however, began to view the situation realistically somewhat in advance of the British, and in 1822 a port in Senegal, Gorée, was opened to the ships and products of all nations. An attempt was made to favor French ships by lowering the duties on goods carried in French holds, but this step did not stop smuggling, and in 1852 Gorée was designated a free port. Other ports, such as Saint-Louis in Senegal, were opened later, and mercantilism appeared to be dead on the African coast. For a number of years American traders and skippers seem almost to have dominated the commercial scene in West Africa.[22]

The outlines of American trade on the African coast south of Cape Palmas are quite similar to what has been described, with certain noteworthy differences. On the windward coast north of Cape Palmas, trade was largely centered in a few places and carried on by a small number of merchants and traders. It was decentralized on the Ivory Coast, the Gold Coast, the Slave Coast, in the Gulf of Guinea, and southward, with small quantities of goods at each trading point. A vessel would pick up a single tusk of ivory at one village, a few pieces of dyewood at another, a few measures of African pepper or a few hides at still another. A trader might taken months in disposing of his cargo and accumulating a new one for his return voyage. This system led to a commercial practice that seems to have been confined almost entirely to Americans: To save time, the Yankee trader would leave a quantity of trade goods at a coastal village, then sail to the next one, where more goods would be deposited. When the entire cargo had been landed he retraced his route, picking up whatever had been left in trade at each village.[23]

As the British extended their control over most of the coastal areas on the Bight of Benin, they endeavored to apply the restrictions that they had used in Sierra Leone. They enjoyed even less success, for there were no natural ports—no funnels—through which commerce had to flow and which could be watched and guarded with relative ease. Trading took place wherever a village lay within reach of the sea and the native boatmen could get through the surf. The geographical conditions that made this area a favored hunting ground for slaves also made it a profitable area for the trader with a small, handy vessel. The American trader became a familiar figure from Cape Palmas to Angola, with an occasional American ship going to Principle and São Tomé for coffee, dyewood, and palm oil.[24] Commanders Joel Abbott of the USS *Decatur,* Thomas Miller and William Tucker of the Royal Navy, and John Carroll Brent of the USS *Jamestown* all gave reports of numerous American vessels trading up and down the coast, and the missionaries of the American Board of Commissioners for Foreign Missions, establishing a mission at the mouth of the Gabon River in the early 1840s, were heartened by the frequent visits of American ships.[25]

When mercantilism was abandoned and free trade was introduced, American traders were able to push their wares and press their own interests with even greater ease. They had learned to cater to the tastes and needs of their African customers; they had a wide variety of goods to offer, usually at a lower price than that demanded by European competitors; their ships were reputed to load and unload faster than others. In the period from 1850 to the outbreak of the Civil War it seemed likely that Americans would dominate African commerce. European merchants and officials regarded them with dislike and apprehension, and many believed that American trade was the forerunner of annexation. An early instance was MacCarthy's suspicion of the settlement of Liberia. In the 1840s there was considerable fear in British circles that if the Gold Coast were abandoned (as the government in London contemplated at one time), the Americans would step in and assume control. American competition in trade, therefore, may have been one factor that led the British and French to pursue annexationist policies in parts of West and South Africa.

Although African commerce was a small part of U.S. commerce as a whole (less than 1 percent for the entire period between 1840 and 1870), it was sufficiently important to receive special attention from the national government, which sought to foster it by all possible means. Beginning with the appointment of a consul at Cape Town in 1799, American consulates and commercial agencies were established at points along the length of the West African coast. A consulate was established at Gambia in 1834; Angola gained a consulate and commercial agency in the 1850s; and a commercial agent was appointed at Bissau in the same decade. Similar offices were established in other parts of Africa, until by 1862 twenty-five consuls and agents watched over American interests in Africa.[26]

The American naval squadron stationed in West African waters from the early 1840s to the Civil War to aid in suppressing the slave trade had another and almost equally important mission – the protection and furtherance of American commerce. The instructions of the secretary of the navy to Commodore Charles Skinner are illustrative: "The rights of our citizens engaged in lawful commerce are under the protection of our flag. And it is the chief purpose as well as the chief duty of our naval power to see that those rights are not improperly abridged or [violated]."[27] American naval officers acted on such instructions with the utmost seriousness.

Commodore Matthew C. Perry, who commanded the first American squadron stationed in West African waters (a result of the Webster–Ashburton Treaty of 1842), after forcibly breaking a boycott against American traders in certain native villages, devoted considerable thought and attention to promoting American trade. As a result, he forwarded a lengthy letter to Washington suggesting items to compose the cargo that could be profitably traded on the African coast. His list included the usual tobacco and cotton goods – he omitted rum – and such things as brown sugar, hams, cheese, crockery, tin buckets, ladies' shoes, gloves, paint, palm-leaf hats, brass kettles, paper and ink, ribbons for bonnets, silk stockings, sperm candles, and even "5 dozen cotton umbrellas."[28]

Eastern and southern Africa

As American trade grew on Africa's west coast, the ubiquitous and enterprising Yankee trader became even more prominent on the eastern side of the continent. In fact, for a time the Yankee dominated the commerce and traffic of the western Indian Ocean.

Although there was no regular trade between America and the east coast of Africa during the colonial period, Americans were not complete strangers to the waters east of the Cape of Good Hope. One of the first recorded cargoes of slaves was brought to Massachusetts from Mozambique about 1680, and there were occasional cargoes from Madagascar; the slave trade from East Africa, however, never became particularly important. In addition to the possible whalers, slavers, and traders during the colonial era, numerous freebooters and pirates sailed from American ports in the seventeenth century for lawless strongholds in Madagascar and on the offshore islands of East Africa to prey on the rich trade of the Arabian Gulf and Red Sea.[29] Everyone who in youth reveled in pirate stories will recall that Captain Kidd sailed from New York. In 1698 the earl of Bellomont, royal governor of New York, reported to the Lords of Trade and Plantations: "I find that those Pyrates that have given the greatest disturbance in the East Indies and Red Sea have either been fitted from New York or Rhode Island, and manned from New York."[30]

During the Revolutionary War an adventurer calling himself Mauritius Augustus, count de Benyowski, established a kingdom for himself in Madagascar. Driven out because of his brutal excesses, he went to Paris, where he favorably impressed no less a person than Benjamin Franklin. Benyowski then came to America to enlist aid and finally returned to Madagascar in an American vessel. In 1786 the governor of the Ile de France (Mauritius) sent an expedition against him, and the adventurer was killed while resisting. Benyowski's following probably included at least a few Americans.[31]

Beyond doubt, the Americans who ventured into the Indian Ocean and along the eastern coast of Africa in pre-Revolutionary times included a due proportion of respectable traders. Unfortunately for the American historian, they sailed under the British flag and, unlike the freebooters and cutthroats, did not attract the special attention of the authorities. They consequently left no records. Early American voyages to the waters and lands east of the Cape of Good Hope were only occasional and sporadic, but after the Revolutionary War those areas became of direct interest and importance. Excluded from the West Indies, their major market in colonial times, American merchants and shipowners began searching the world for other and better markets. Robert Morris, the so-called financier of the Revolution, wrote to John Jay in 1783: "I am sending some ships to China in order to encourage in others the adventurous pursuit of commerce."[32] On Washington's birthday in 1784 the 360-ton *Empress of China,* sponsored by Morris and some other businessmen, slipped past Sandy Hook bearing a cargo intended to open the spice and silk lands of the Far East to the American merchant.

Morris was not alone in his hopes. While he was planning the voyage to China, several other merchants and shipowners were planning similar projects. In 1784 Christopher Champlin of Newport fitted a ship for an exploratory voyage to India, and Elias Hasket Derby of Salem dispatched one of his vessels on a similar mission to the Cape of Good Hope and the Guinea coast, and thence to the West Indies.[33] And in that same commercially eventful year of 1784, on the day after Christmas, a ship flying a flag never before seen in Indian waters dropped anchor at Pondicherry. This was the *United States,* sailing from Philadelphia just a month after the *Empress of China* had left New York. Although the merchants and shipowners of Philadelphia have not attained the historical fame of their New England counterparts, in this instance they moved ahead of them and reached the goal first.

An unexpected development of these early voyages of commercial exploration was the sudden growth of American commerce with the Ile de France and the neighboring islands of the Mascarene group. The islands produced rich crops of such tropical products as coffee, but did not grow sufficient food stuffs for their fairly large European populations. Moreover, during a long series of wars, French privateers in the Indian Ocean and East Indies usually sent their prizes to the Ile de France for condemnation and sale. The market was often glutted, and captors and prize courts were glad to sell their prizes for anything they would bring. Such a situation was meat and drink to the Yankee trader, who took full advantage of it.

The commercial possibilities of the Ile de France were first discovered by Derby, whose *Grand Turk* dropped anchor there in April 1786, two years after its voyage to West Africa. The cargo was quickly sold, and the ship was chartered by a French merchant for a voyage to Canton. Other American merchants followed Derby's lead, and the Admiralty records of the island show that eighty-seven American ships anchored there between 1786 and 1793. An American merchant colony became an element in the population; the U.S. government established a consulate in 1794, several years before an American consulate was established anywhere on the African continent. There were periods when relations were somewhat strained, as during the quasi war between the United States and France, but even that unhappy situation did not completely interrupt the commerce or exclude the Yankee shipmaster-trader. Until the British captured the Ile de France in 1810 and added it to the empire, it was important in American foreign commerce and served admirably as an American commercial base in the Indian Ocean.[34]

Because Indian trade was supposedly a tight monopoly of the East India Company, the Americans approached the shores of India with some misgivings; but their doubts were quickly dispelled. They were received hospitably, even by the company's officials. In 1788 the governor of Bengal, Lord Cornwallis (who had surrendered to Washington at Yorktown), commanded that American vessels should be treated as the "most favoured foreigners" at all of the company's settlements. One of the earliest American arrivals, in fact—the *Chesapeake* of Baltimore—was granted exemption from customs duties by the Supreme Council of Bengal.[35]

With this somewhat unexpected encouragement and with the profits accruing from the China trade, American shipping into the Indian Ocean increased rapidly. The trade was further stimulated by the Jay Treaty of 1794 – a "Treaty of Amity, Commerce, and Navigation" – whereby commerce between the United States and India became entirely legal. The speed of the relatively small and handy American vessels, the safety to cargoes and passengers resulting from neutral status during the Napoleonic Wars, the shipmasters' willingness to connive at breaking certain British laws, and their role as brokers for seized and confiscated goods – all operated to the advantage of the American trade.[36]

After the first American ship anchored at the Cape of Good Hope in 1784, the number stopping there increased annually. Between 1795 and 1800 no less than 124 vessels flying the American flag paid port charges at Cape Town. And this figure does not include American ships that avoided port charges by filling their water butts and buying fresh provisions at obscure and out-of-the-way places along the coast.[37]

South Africa quickly became an important point in U.S. trade with the Far East and in the Indian Ocean. Many vessels stopped at Cape Town for water and provisions. What was more natural and logical than to include in the cargo materials that were salable in South Africa and thus increase the profits of the voyage? William Milburn, in his survey published in 1813, noted that "American ships frequently stop at the Cape on their outward voyage to China, to dispose of a part of their cargoes, consisting generally of lumber, for which they receive bills on India, or Spanish dollars." On the return voyage the shipmaster could top off his Chinese or Indian cargo with such South African products as wines (well known even then), ivory, hides, ostrich feathers, salt meats, or a score of items that commanded a ready sale in Europe or the West Indies.[38]

American shipping to the Far East and Africa was interrupted by the War of 1812, during which American ships, except for privateers and a few war vessels, vanished from the seas. But the traffic was resumed immediately after the Treaty of Ghent (1814) – not merely resumed, but expanded with almost explosive violence. On the east coast of Africa, as on the west, the American trader and the American ship came almost invariably from New England, more often than not from the little port of Salem.

Boston took the lead in traffic with the Orient, but Salem was not far behind. Boston ships often went around Cape Horn to the northwest coast of North America, where they loaded furs; thence they proceeded to China, and came home through the Indian Ocean. The Salem ships went out via the Cape of Good Hope, often avoiding Table Bay for fear of being windbound, touched at Madagascar or the Mascarenes, and then sailed on to Arabia and the East Indies. They returned by the same route, sometimes converging with ships from Boston.

Soon the Yankee trader was a familiar sight from the Cape of Good Hope to Cape Guardafui and at Madagascar and the offshore islands. Nathaniel Isaacs, an enterprising Anglo-Jewish trader, explorer, adventurer, and inadvertent empire builder, said in commenting upon a visit to an obscure port in 1831:

> The post of Lamoo [Lamu, Kenya] is free to all nations, but few have
> visited it, except the enterprising Americans, whose star-spangled banner
> may be seen streaming in the wind, where other nations, not even my own

country, would not deign to traffic. America is the forerunner of commerce in new countries, and she enjoys the sweets which they afford.[39]

The same keen observer, while at his home at St. Helena recovering from illness contracted in Africa, "became accidentally acquainted with an American captain, who commanded the ship *Francis*." The American plied everyone with questions about East Africa and spoke openly of his intention of making a trading voyage to that coast. Isaacs, irked by the supercilious treatment he had received from British officialdom, answered him freely. "I cannot conceal that I felt this desire from the insufferable indifference we met with." But being a loyal British subject, Isaacs appealed strongly to his compatriots to annex Natal to the British Empire immediately so that British traders could enter into "an advantageous traffic with those nations and tribes between Point Natal and the entrance to the Red Sea, with the islands in the Mozambique Channel, and with the Western Coast of Madagascar, *now almost exclusively enjoyed by the Americans*."[40]

Possibly even before American traders arrived on the East African coast, American whalers passed the Cape of Good Hope on their way into the Indian Ocean. They had ranged the west coast since before the Revolution, and a few years after the war they discovered that the waters surrounding Madagascar teemed with whales.[41] In 1795 Commodore Blankett of the Royal Navy reported the presence of American whalers along the South African coast; in the same year, to the consternation of the Portuguese officials, a number of American whaling ships anchored in Delagoa Bay. By 1813 American whalers needing repairs were heaving down at a natural pier formed by the rocks at Saldanha Bay, not far from Cape Town.[42] In the early 1830s Captain William T. Owen of the Royal Navy, a noted explorer and indefatigable extender of the British Empire, reported that Delagoa Bay was "very much frequented" by both British and American whalers.[43] Nathaniel Isaacs, upon one of his visits to the same place, saw "no less than eight American and one English whaling ships lying there, as well as an English brig and an American brigantine."[44]

As may be inferred from Isaacs's remarks about American enterprise and practical monopoly of the trade of the eastern coast of Africa, there was a certain degree of jealousy among the British and other competitors -- a jealousy that was liberally seasoned with apprehension. The new nation across the Atlantic was commercially aggressive, and few businessmen or statesmen of the time could conceive of commercial aggressiveness without linking it to monopoly and territorial acquisition. The mercantilistic tradition of monopoly was still so strong that many men could see no other end than the complete elimination of all competitors, an objective that required territorial possession or at least a territorial base. If American ships in large numbers continued to enter the Indian Ocean and undercut British trade with the Orient, it was only a question of time until the Yankees would occupy territory from which they could eliminate all competition.

There were some Americans who favored the idea of an American settlement on the East African coast. In 1796 a ship from Boston, the *Hercules*, was wrecked at a point some five hundred miles northeast of Cape Town, near where the Indiaman *Grosvenor* has been wrecked fourteen years earlier. The ship's captain, Benjamin

Stout, upon returning to the United States, addressed a memorial to the "President of the Continental Congress of the United States of America":

> I would draw the attention of the President to those commercial benefits which may be obtained by establishing a colony from America on that part of the coast where the ship was unfortunately wrecked . . . A single settlement on the coast of Caffraria would amply repay its expenses and the number of people necessary to the completion of such an undertaking might be limited to 1,000.[45]

Very early in the history of American traffic to and through South Africa, British officials began to worry about ultimate American intentions. In 1800 Sir George Yonge, the governor at Cape Town, informed London that U.S. trade with China and the East Indies was increasing rapidly and was entirely dependent upon supplies and services available in the Cape Colony. Implicit in his report was the belief that the Americans would not want to remain dependent indefinitely upon a foreign power for the continuation of their new commerce; sooner or later they would have to have their own base or bases. Yonge added, to give point to his statement: "Here have been many fine American ships since my arrival and here is now a fine American frigate of 32 guns [the *Essex*] and another expected, sent to protect the American commerce in India, which has been much harassed by French privateers fitted out at the Mauritius." Moreover, he said, the newly arrived American consul had informed him that the United States was fitting out fifteen frigates and five seventy-fours (ships of war carrying seventy-four guns) to operate against the French.[46]

After the War of 1812, when large numbers of American ships again appeared in the Indian Ocean, British officials, settlers, and traders in southern Africa became increasingly uneasy about U.S. intentions. Reflecting an important segment of British opinion, the London *Times* urged measures such as emigration from Britain to solve pressing problems at home and at the same time to forestall American ambitions in Africa: "Make the Cape a free port . . . and we banish North America from the India seas." And Captain Owen of the Royal Navy reported to his superiors in London that "should the Bay [Delagoa Bay] fall into the possession of either the French, *American*, or the Russian, it would be most ruinous not only to our colony, but to our East India possessions and commerce."[47]

Today such fears are patently absurd, but to the British colonials of the 1830s the American peril seemed very real. Dr. John Philip,[48] the superintendent in South Africa for the London Missionary Society, visualized Americans from Delagoa Bay arming the natives and reenacting on the South African frontier the horrors that had occurred on the frontiers in America. Nathaniel Isaacs, because of his open friendship with Americans, was accused of being secretly a U.S. consul with the mission of training the Africans in the use of firearms. And in spite of this accusation (of which he was probably ignorant), Isaacs vehemently urged the governor of Cape Colony to annex Natal before the Americans could do so. That responsible British colonial officials took the American peril seriously is attested by a letter from the governor at Cape Town to the Colonial Office in 1831: "With reference to . . . the possibility of the United States forming a settlement [in Natal], it is hardly necessary to remark how embarrassing such neighbours might actually prove to this Colony."[49]

In 1834 a large group of British merchants and settlers in the Cape Colony sent a petition to London urging the immediate annexation of Natal. Dr. Andrew Smith, a well-known medical officer who had visited Natal in 1832, wrote in proof of the urgency of the situation that the

> belief [in American designs on Natal] has lately gained ground from the circumstance of an American vessel of war, with a political commissioner on board, having run along the coast and observed the situation ... Let the intention of the Government be what it may, we know from undoubted authority that the nation [the United States] is about to send out missionaries to labour in that vicinity.[50]

English merchants had pressured to annex Natal, but the Colonial Office had refused. In 1835 Governor D'Urban repeated the request for annexation,

> putting forward the additional argument that the arrival of American missionaries presaged imminent annexation by the United States, which might be averted by a company of infantry and a few guns. The response of Lord Palmerton, the foreign secretary, was that the United States was welcome to this territory which had no significance for any British interests.[51]

Even though the United States took no action in the still unclaimed territory of Natal and the Portuguese officials continued to doze undisturbed at Delagoa Bay, British suspicion of American intentions lingered for years. The fears that American traders and ships on the coast and in East African waters were forerunners of American annexation quite probably helped stimulate the government in London in 1843 to add Natal formally to the British Empire.

During the period of excitement over the possibility of an American colony in South Africa, the fears of British officialdom and British colonists could not have been allayed by the action of two Salem Yankees, Jonathan Lambert and Richard Cleveland, who took possession of the then unoccupied island of Tristan da Cunha in the South Atlantic not far from St. Helena and only a few hundred miles from the Cape. Though Lambert and Cleveland attempted to establish a colony there, their intentions were not at all imperialistic: They hoped to turn a profit by selling fresh provisions to Indiamen, whose usual course took them close to the island. The two adventurers even offered to place their bit of preempted real estate under British authority in return for aid from the Cape. A few months after they had established themselves, a British visitor reported flourishing fields and gardens and urged the governor of Cape Colony to annex the island along with its settlers. Although the Americans planted corn, potatoes, pumpkins, onions, and other garden truck and slaughtered sea elephants to render a large quantity of oil, they were unable to attract enough customers or colonists to make the scheme a success. Eventually they had to admit defeat.[52]

There can be little question that an American base in southeastern Africa would have facilitated U.S. commerce in the Indian Ocean, but without doubt the last thing the U.S. government wanted was to become territorially involved in Africa. The American people as a whole would not have supported an annexation of territory outside North America, no matter how much the merchants of the Atlantic seaboard might desire it. Nor did the suddenly flourishing trade with Zanzibar and other African dominions of the sultan of Muscat change the government's mind.

Zanzibar and Muscat

The American sloop of war *Peacock*, sailing up the African coast in 1832 on a commercial mission to Muscat and other Eastern principalities, constituted recognition by Washington of what had rather quickly become an accomplished fact – a growing and highly lucrative trade with Zanzibar and the east coast of Africa. It is quite probable that American whalers and occasional traders touched at Zanzibar early in the century, but one of the first U.S. vessels of which there is any record was the brig *Laurel* of Salem, which presumably anchored there in 1825. The following year the *Virginia*, also of Salem, spent eighteen days at Zanzibar and, carrying a cargo that included "117 elephant's teeth," became the first vessel to sail from there directly to Salem.[53] The commerce thus opened grew rapidly. Three more Salem vessels arrived at Zanzibar in 1826, and in the following year seven American ships, most of them from Salem, anchored there.

Most significant for the future of American trade and American relations with East Africa was the *Mary Ann* of New Bedford, with a cargo consigned to Edmund Roberts. Roberts, although still a young man, already had a wide mercantile and quasi-diplomatic experience. Having recently suffered financial losses, he decided that the virgin trading field of Zanzibar and East Africa would be a good place to recoup. He chartered the *Mary Ann* with borrowed capital and sailed on June 10, 1827. On arriving at Zanzibar, he was extremely annoyed by the delays put in his way by the local Arab officials and by what he regarded as their discrimination in favor of the British: Only British merchants were permitted to trade freely at Zanzibar; all others had to deal through local agents who frequently overcharged, substituted unwanted goods, and seized upon all sorts of opportunities to line their own pockets. Such practices threatened any prospect of a promising American trade. Consequently, when the sultan of Muscat, sovereign of Zanzibar, visited that African island in January 1828, Roberts obtained an audience and complained vigorously about the agents and the special privileges accorded the British. The sultan listened sympathetically. He was interested in obtaining American munitions to use against his old enemies, the Portuguese, as well as against his rebellious African subjects on the mainland, and he saw in American trade an opportunity to free himself from complete dependence upon Europeans. The sultan thus not only welcomed Roberts and gave orders for immediate relief from the difficulties he had encountered, but went even further and suggested a commercial treaty between the United States and his own government.[54]

Roberts returned to the United States and lost no time in imparting the information to his old friend Levi Woodbury, secretary of the navy and former senator from New Hampshire. As a result, Roberts was appointed a special commissioner empowered by President Jackson to negotiate commercial treaties with the sultan of Muscat, the king of Siam, and "such Asiatic potentates, as he might find favourably disposed." He was ordered to keep his mission secret from the European powers, and in dealing with oriental rulers he was enjoined to distinguish the United States from the European countries by stressing its "non-imperial character."[55] Roberts sailed from the United States on his commercial/diplomatic mission early in 1832 on board the USS *Peacock*. To maintain secrecy his nominal status was merely that of ship's clerk, but the secret was evidently not well kept: As mentioned earlier, in South Africa a "political commissioner" was known to be on board.

The *Peacock* arrived at Muscat in September 1833 after some misadventures upon an uncharted reef on the Arabian coast. Roberts was warmly welcomed by Sultan Seyyid Said, who was flattered to be treated as an equal by the president of a great country. He saw the opportunity for expanded trade with his dominions, increased wealth for himself, and a new political friendship that might be of value someday against the dominant power of Great Britain. Furthermore, he was having difficulty in subduing a rebellion at Mombasa and was glad to get aid from any source. The negotiations took only three days, and on September 21, 1833, a treaty was signed by the sultan and by Roberts as the authorized representative of the president.

The sultan was more than generous in the terms that he conceded. His kingdom depended on the trade in ivory and slaves, imported from the African mainland, and on the production of cloves on island plantations. The sultan's government was anxious to enlarge its commercial contacts; hence Americans received the same status as the "nation most favored," a provision that placed them on a position of equality with the British. The Americans obtained full authority to travel and trade without restriction in all parts of the sultan's dominions and to arrive and depart without hindrance; they were to be charged not more than a 5 percent impost on cargoes actually landed. The United States was authorized to establish consulates at the principal commercial centers (i.e., at Zanzibar itself), with full diplomatic immunity and protection for the consuls; the consuls, moreover, were to have full and exclusive jurisdiction over disputes between Americans. The sultan agreed further to return shipwrecked American seamen without compensation, and outside the treaty, he voluntarily undertook at once to recover the guns and anchors that had been jettisoned from the *Peacock* when it struck the reef just before arriving at Muscat. The sole restriction in the treaty was a curious provision that at Zanzibar munitions were to be sold only to the sultan's government; elsewhere in his domains "the said munitions of war" could be "freely sold without any restrictions whatever to the highest bidder."[56]

In return for all this, the United States granted the sultan's subjects and ships the rights of the most-favored nation if they should ever land in America – not a particularly important concession, as the sultan knew. But in spite of the apparent inequality, the sultan was very happy with the agreement and sent President Jackson a glowing letter full of oriental rhetoric and promises of enduring goodwill. Upon Roberts's return to the United States, the U.S. Senate promptly approved the treaty; he was again dispatched on the *Peacock* to exchange ratifications, a mission completed on September 30, 1835.[57]

During the negotiations the sultan offered to allow American settlements to be made on the African mainland if the United States would assist him in suppressing the rebellion at Mombasa. The offer was declined, of course, but it seems to have come to the ears of the suspicious and watchful British. Combined with the presence of an American war vessel – the *Peacock* had touched at Zanzibar on the way to Muscat–and the recent arrival of American missionaries in Natal, the offer seemed to justify the fears of the British regarding U.S. intentions in Africa. Lord Palmerston is supposed tò have dismissed the idea; nevertheless, in 1834 a British warship was dispatched to Zanzibar. As has already been brought out, Englishmen remained nervous about the "American peril" for years to come.

The real threat to British interest came not from the U.S. government but from American traders and whalers–particularly from the Salem merchants and traders, almost the only Americans who were at all interested in East Africa. While Roberts was negotiating the commercial treaty with the sultan, the Salem men were making every effort to secure the East African trade for themselves. Their near monopoly was such that, of the thirty-two American vessels touching at Zanzibar between September 1832 and May 1834, twenty were from Salem. During the same period, only nine vessels from European nations entered the ports.[58]

The Salem men tried at first to keep the Zanzibar trade a secret within their own group. Failing in this aim, they acted swiftly, as soon as the news of Roberts's treaty became generally known, to make sure that the consul at Zanzibar would be from Salem. Largely through the efforts and lobbying of the merchants John Bertram and Michael Shepard, the man appointed was Richard P. Waters of Salem.[59]

Waters arrived at Zanzibar and assumed his duties on March 17, 1837. He was accorded a cordial welcome by the sultan, who also gave him his choice of any house in the city, rent free, for his consulate. Waters had been warned by the State Department not to take advantage of the unusual privileges he enjoyed under the treaty, but in those days a U.S. consul was never a career man. A consul's official salary and fees were hardly enough to pay for his groceries, and it was taken for granted that he was also in business, either for himself or as a representative of some business concern.

Waters crossed swords almost at once with the master of the customhouse, one Jairam Sewji (or Jeram Sewejee), who was paying large sums for his office and fully intended to make a profit. In addition to other practices, Jairam had devised a simple and effective system of extortion from local merchants who sold goods to Americans; thus he compensated himself for the loss of the export duty that he had collected before the treaty. He required Americans who purchased goods to bring them to the customhouse; even though he could not collect any duty, he controlled the hiring of coolies to transport the goods. And for reasons that are not clear, Waters quarreled also with African merchants. The result was that initially he was quite unpopular.

But after this unpropitious beginning the atmosphere cleared for the American consul, and his relationships became cordial. He and Jairam apparently decided that they could realize greater profits by cooperation than by competition, and they formed a quiet alliance that enabled them to dominate the commerce of Zanzibar. The rival British trading firm of Newman, Hunt and Christopher, finding itself operating at an annual loss, gave up the fight and left Zanzibar. Jairam, as master of the customhouse, could block, or at least make very difficult, any transaction that Waters did not approve. In return for this cooperation, Jairam became the unofficial middleman for the Salem merchants, determining what was to be sold, to whom, at what price. Both Waters and Jairam received a commission on each transaction, and it appears that Waters was actively engaged in business for himself as well as for the Salem merchants whom he represented.

Naturally, such a system did not appeal to those who were on the outside. Not only was the Zanzibar trade dominated by Salem merchants; it was also a monopoly in the hands of a small group determined to keep out all competitors. The British government in 1841 designated a consul for the first time in an effort to protect British commercial and political interests. By February 1842 Her Majesty's representative was able to report that British subjects had equal rights with Americans in the Zanzibar trade – a reversal of the situation of a few years earlier.[60]

In spite of his devotion to his own interests, Waters was a most capable and efficient consular representative of his country. Although Salem was unable to maintain a monopoly of the Zanzibar trade, Americans continued to dominate it until the Civil War, and the foundations of this preeminence were firmly laid by Waters. His commercial ethics were those of his times and he did nothing that his competitors would not have done, given the opportunity. He left Zanzibar a very wealthy man; his erstwhile enemy and later ally, Jairam Sewji, is said to have realized $100,000 annually from his position at the customhouse.

The treaty between the sultan and the United States provided for most-favored-nation treatment of Zanzibar vessels in the ports of the United States. American officials and the public were astonished when, on April 30, 1840, a bark flying the scarlet Zanzibar ensign dropped anchor in New York harbor. Owned by the sultan himself, it was the *al-Sultanah,* commanded by Ahmad bin Na'aman, one of the sultan's high officials, and laden with valuable cargo upon which His Highness hoped to reap a profit. The ship carried also a special representative on a mission of commerce and goodwill, who brought two Arabian horses and other princely gifts for President Van Buren. After several weeks in New York during which Ahmad bin Na'aman and his crew were lionized and feted and the ship was repaired and put into sailing condition at the New York navy yard, the *al-Sultanah* put to sea on its return voyage. Commercially, the voyage was a moderate success; diplomatically, it was a great one. In the somewhat confused relationships of the next few years, Ahmad bin Na'aman was the leader of what the British consul at Zanzibar bitterly called the "American party."[61]

During the prosperous years before the Civil War the American firms, led by Bertram-Shepard of Salem – known as the "Big Firm" – built a large trading complex embracing the whole East African coast, the offshore islands, and Arabia. Determined to expand their trade in the face of increasing competition from Europeans, the leading American trading companies soon had agents in Madagascar, Mozambique, Muscat, and Aden. By the middle of the nineteenth century they held a commanding lead in the commerce of the East African littoral. After Waters's departure, Jairam worked with various American merchants and even helped them when they were in need. During the Mexican War (1846–8), when American merchants had difficulty in obtaining specie, Jairam lent them what they required to stay in business.

But the American insiders, in spite of their influence, were not without competition. In 1849 the famous Hamburg firm of William O'Swald and Company opened a branch in Zanzibar with the avowed intention of making itself the leading trader on the island. Nor was the competition limited to Europeans. Ahmad bin Na'aman's voyage to New York had been undertaken despite the quiet but determined opposition of Waters and the Salem merchants and as a direct result of representations made by New York merchants who wanted to break into the dominance of Salem.[62] In 1852 Rufus Green and Company of Providence began trading in Zanzibar and quickly became a leading competitor of the Salem men. Although none of the newcomers succeeded in displacing the old, well-established Salem firms, their competition drove prices to new heights, thereby reducing profits and forcing merchants to extend their activities to other East African and Arabian ports to assure full cargoes for their ships.

Unfortunately, while American trade flourished at mid-century, diplomatic relations between the United States and the sultan deteriorated, with numerous petty disputes between Charles Ward, the American consul, and the sultan. First, there was an altercation over the status of the Indians of Zanzibar, who alternately claimed to be subjects of the sultan and of the British queen, whichever was more convenient at the moment. As subjects of the sultan, they could trade on the coast; as British subjects, they could claim the protection of Great Britain when they were threatened by foreign commercial firms. After a protracted dispute, the sultan, much to Ward's disgust, accepted the interpretation of the British consul that Indians were British subjects.

Other questions exacerbated Zanzibari–U.S. relations for a time. The sultan threatened to trade directly with the United States as he had done on a limited scale with the voyage of the *al-Sultanah*. Since his doing so would undercut American firms and traders, the threat caused considerable alarm. Then, too, in spite of the clear provisions of Roberts's treaty, the sultan refused to grant formal permission for Americans to trade in his dominions on the mainland. Ill feeling was intensified when Ward helped an American sailor to flee the island after conviction by a Zanzibari court. The series of disputes reached a climax on July 4, 1850, when the sultan refused to permit a public salute to the American flag. Ward demanded a written apology and, when it was not forthcoming, indignantly closed the consulate and left Zanzibar. Upon arriving in Washington, he advised the State Department to use force in recovering American honor. The department had received similar advice from other quarters, and on December 2, 1851, the USS *Susquehanna* anchored at Zanzibar. Its commander, John Aulick, served an ultimatum: He would bombard the town unless the required apology was made immediately. The sultan's governor acquiesced, American honor was satisfied, and the whole unfortunate affair was soon forgotten. A new consul, John F. Webb, quickly reestablished the former friendly relations, and no new causes of discord arose to mar them.

American domination of the Zanzibar and East African trade ended with the Civil War. American cotton goods were unobtainable for several years, and the United States ceased to export firearms and gunpowder. Americans were forced to seek new goods to sell. They shipped cargoes of soap and codfish, but neither of these products was in great demand at Zanzibar. They managed to get American gold accepted at par and worked up something of a market for that commodity, but gold could not possibly fill the holds of ships or take the place of other items. Some among the American merchants even imported cotton goods from England simply to fulfill their contracts and hold their customers. Often their purchases had to be transported to the United States in British vessels. American credit was maintained at a high level, and the American merchants hoped to regain their lost ground when the war ended; but the gains made by British, German, and Indian traders at American expense could not be overcome entirely. In 1859, in both tonnage and the number of ships entering the port, Americans had exceeded the British, Germans, and French combined; in 1866 they were surpassed by each of these, and in 1871 they were still lagging behind.

Salem and the African trade

During the years of American preeminence in nineteenth-century African trade, the dominance of Salem on both coasts was striking. Enterprising merchants of the Massachusetts town took the lead in opening trade with Africa, and throughout the era of direct commerce between the United States and Africa they provided by far the greater part of the cargoes; further, the cargoes were carried in vessels owned, manned, and usually built at Salem. The Yankee trader living and conducting business on the African coast was, more often than not, a man from Salem. As early as 1798 a Salem vessel sailed for Mocha in the Red Sea, a voyage that brought it to the shores of Africa; by 1805 no less than forty-eight Salem ships had "gone round the Cape."[63] A few years later, of a total of seventy-five American vessels known to have been in the waters of Madagascar and eastern Africa between 1824 and 1837, sixty-three were from Salem; several of the remainder were Salem vessels chartered by merchants of other cities.[64] On the west coast, Commander Joel Abbott of the USS *Decatur* reported in 1844 that there was a large trading factory at Ambriz (Angola) maintained by a group of Salem merchants and that eight or ten ships, mostly from Salem, visited that part of the African coast regularly.[65] A Salem trading house also had a permanent representative at Luanda.[66] In the fiscal year ending June 30, 1860, twenty-six vessels from West Africa and eight from East Africa docked at Salem. In 1857, when there were fifteen ships from Africa at Boston, there were thirty-two at Salem. The ships arriving at this single port in 1860 paid duties amounting to $36,739 – a large sum for those days.[67]

Salem's position in African commerce was partly the result of a natural accident: Its small and shallow harbor could not accommodate large vessels.[68] Hence Salem ships were in general small, with light draft, and much better suited to the dangerous waters of Africa than the bigger, less maneuverable craft typically built and owned by the merchants of Boston, New York, or Philadelphia. There were few harbors worthy of the name along the African coast. The innumerable sandbars, high surf, occasional tornadoes, and dry, sandy harmattan from the Sahara constituted perils that the light and handy schooner or brig from Salem could escape, whereas a bigger ship might come to disaster. The merchants of the larger cities consequently chose to trade in regions where natural dangers were less forbidding, leaving African commerce to the "poor relations" at Salem. Conversely, although the merchants of Salem sent vessels to India, China, and the Spice Islands, there they were handicapped in their competition with Boston and New York. Africa they had to themselves, and a very good thing they made of it.

From the United States the Salem ships carried a wide variety of goods wanted and needed in Africa: tobacco, rum, lumber, brown sugar, hams, cheese, crockery, sperm candles, tin buckets, brass kettles, bonnet ribbons, gloves, ladies' shoes, and cotton umbrellas. Besides these articles, traders found a ready market for brass wire, beads, gunpowder, muskets, and scores of other articles.

Probably foremost among the goods wanted from America, especially in East Africa, was coarse, strong, cotton cloth. Cloth manufactured in Massachusetts for the African trade proved to be superior to the products of Manchester and Madras for the Africans' needs and purposes. Over wide regions in East Africa, American-made cloth became the standard of trade – even the circulating medium, used instead of money. The word *merikani* passed into the languages of the region, and it is used to this day (although present-day *merikani* is made in Manchester or Osaka).[69] For the ivory hunter, a stout, heavy, sharp hatchet was as necessary a part of his equipment as his gun, and the best hatchets came from America: "Even sixty or seventy years ago, the old-time hunters tell us, they used 'superior American hatchets.' "[70]

To pay for ivory and other purchases, U.S. ships brought to Zanzibar wooden boxes packed with "Zanzibar dollars" minted in America. The near extermination of the elephant in western Africa made East Africa the primary source of ivory. With the growing population and wealth of the United States, ivory for piano and organ keys, billiard balls, knife handles, and various other uses came into wide demand.[71] One is likely to visualize ships returning from exotic, far-away countries as laden with exotic products – "ivory, and apes, and peacocks"; incense, jewels, and spices – but the small bulk of ivory and specie could not nearly fill the holds of the ships sailing back to America. To render a voyage profitable it was necessary to return with other and more readily obtainable articles. Commander Thomas Miller of the Royal Navy, urging his compatriots to extend their West African commerce, mentioned palm oil, beeswax, dyewood, orchilla weed (archil), white and yellow gum, and copper ore, in addition to ivory.[72] Hides, required in enormous quantities by the expanding shoe and leather industries of New England, became leading articles of U.S. import from Africa and anywhere else they might be obtained. A government report of 1855 shows that hides from Africa were of major importance, exceeded in value only by the more commonly known ivory and palm oil.[73]

Throughout most of the nineteenth century and before the rise of the mineral oil industry, the machinery of the new industrialism was kept operating smoothly by an African product: palm oil. In addition, the increasing trend toward personal cleanliness and sanitation called for vast quantities of groundnuts and palm oil for the manufacture of soap. The wastes from farm and slaughterhouse no longer provided enough material; it was necessary to call on Africa to fill the need. From 1865 to 1869, until peanut production increased in the United States, the South Senegal provided over $200,000 worth of peanuts.[74]

Before the rise of the chemical industry and the introduction of synthetic dyes, dyewoods were an important article of commerce, and Africa was especially rich in woods from which dyes could be extracted. Cabinet woods, too, were needed by American craftsmen who were building fine houses for wealthy merchants and constructing elegant furniture to fill those houses. Once again, Africa was a prolific source. The Yankee schooner or brig, laboring homeward with its hold crammed, was likely to have rough logs lashed as deckload wherever room could be found for them.

One major American product, and possibly the most profitable to the merchants of Salem, remains to be mentioned. Gum copal, the base for fine varnishes and lacquers, is found in many parts of Africa, but the arid highlands of East Africa proved to be the world's most important source. At first its use involved considerable difficulty, but in 1835 Jonathan Whipple of Salem invented a new and cheap process for cleaning the gum and preparing it for use, thus adding to the firmness of Salem's hold on East African trade and contributing to its continuing prosperity. Varnishes and lacquers used throughout the United States were made from gum copal received from Africa through Salem.[75]

For several decades, therefore, there was a procession of small ships across the Atlantic and down the length of that ocean, past the Cape of Good Hope and into the Indian Ocean, bearing lumber, tobacco, cloth, rum, hatchets, muskets, gunpowder, chinaware, brass wire, beads, and scores of other articles. On the return voyage to the United States they were heavy-laden with gum copal, ivory, hides, guano, cloves, peanuts, senna, ebony, or whatever else the shrewd Yankee skippers recognized as a possible source of profit. Yankee traders and skippers contributed notably to making the rest of the world aware of Africa and to bringing it into the orbit of world affairs.

The decrease in direct American trade with Africa after the Civil War can be ascribed to a number of causes. Probably the foremost was a general decline in the American merchant marine owing to the depredations of Confederate cruisers, a lessening of interest in foreign commerce, and the concentration of the American people (including many New England merchants) on the development and exploitation of their own Far West. Next, or equally important, was the transition from sail to steam as motive power for ships—steamships could transport bigger cargoes farther and faster. When the steamship took over the task of carrying the world's goods on the oceans, Salem was doomed as a major port. Its harbor could not accommodate steam vessels large enough to compete with those visiting Africa from Germany and Great Britain, and the small Yankee trading vessel, which could be operated in competition with other sailing craft, was unable to hold its own against the faster service and lower relative operating cost of the steam-powered ship. Furthermore, in the 1870s and 1880s cheap Hamburg gin began to replace American rum in the trade of West Africa.[76] The Stars and Stripes practically vanished from the coasts of Africa; the Salem trader was replaced by a trader from Hamburg or Liverpool.[77] And finally, the partition of Africa, under which European powers established sovereignty over the continent, also hurt the American traders: The colonial powers and their shipping conferences tended to discriminate against foreign shippers and traders.

CHAPTER 7

Missionaries and colonization societies

The eighteenth century was an age of religious ferment. The era saw a great religious revival, closely linked to the industrial revolution. Dissenting groups in England, in various parts of northwestern Europe, and in the United States prepared to preach the gospel both in the countryside and in the new factory towns that were often neglected by the older churches. Unlike French Jacobins, the new preachers did not look to revolution. Nevertheless, their message had far-reaching social consequences. Poverty, far from being a holy state sanctioned by immemorial tradition, was a disability to be remedied by the virtues of thrift, sobriety, and hard work; by cultivating a spirit of personal independence; and by constructive charity to all those who could not help themselves: the aged and the very young, the sick and the insane, slaves and, in the missionaries' interpretation, the ignorant savages in the bush.

English Methodists organized a regular system of foreign missions in 1787; the London Missionary Society was founded in 1797 and immediately started work in the Far East. The new movement quickly took root in northern Europe and in the United States, where the religious revival provided the principal inspiration for the abolitionist movement. It also led to missionary work overseas. The nineteenth century became the greatest era of missionary effort since the early days of Christianity as evangelists from Europe and America extended their activities into Asia, Africa, and even the tiny islands of the South Seas. Widespread interest found expression in the formation in 1788 of the Association for Promoting the Discovery of the Interior Parts of Africa. Religious and philanthropic interests in turn were linked to the rise of the antislavery movement in the Western, especially the English-speaking, world. The hostility to slavery was part of a wider revolution that steadily disrupted hereditary privileges throughout a large part of Europe, wiping out all manner of hereditary bondage, as well as seignorial and caste prerogatives. The critics of slavery, like the censors of serfdom, held strong convictions with regard to the personal dignity of each man and woman, irrespective of color or social origin. They had faith in the inalienable right of all individuals to sell their labor as they thought fit, without restraint from the shackles of caste. They tended to believe that people should be able to invest their earnings free from constraints imposed by accustomed notions concerning usury laws, or to spend their wages in the free market without restraint from sumptuary laws or similar restrictions.

Antislavery and colonization societies

Closely linked to the antislavery campaign were the movements to abolish the slave trade and to provide for the welfare of free blacks and slaves rescued from the slavers. On March 25, 1807, a law was passed in which the slave trade was forbidden to British subjects.[1] A few days later the U.S. Congress also enacted a law forbidding the slave trade as of January 1, 1808. The end of the legal slave trade for British and American citizens marked a revolution in the relations of Africa with the rest of the world.[2]

As we have seen, efforts to end the slave trade involved the United States in a long series of disputes with Great Britain over American rights at sea, and the United States was also charged with indifference to the horrors of the slave trade. On the other hand, the humanitarian interest of many Americans in ending slavery and the slave trade was closely linked with the establishment of Liberia as a homeland for free black Americans and as a refuge for blacks liberated from captured slave ships.

American slaves emancipated in the Revolution were among the first blacks to return to Africa. Some fifteen hundred ex-slaves who had joined the British army during the Revolution left the United States for London, the West Indies, or, chiefly, Nova Scotia in Canada in 1783. Their settlements in this latter bleak area failed, and a dream of going back to Africa led the majority of black Loyalists to sail for England, where they joined other black Loyalists.[3]

The Sierra Leone Company had been founded by British philanthropists and capitalists to encourage legitimate trade in West Africa; in early 1792 fifteen ships entered the mouth of the Sierra Leone River, and eleven hundred black Americans disembarked at what came to be called Freetown in the colony of Sierra Leone. The black Americans were not well received by the white officials, who thought them perverse and ungovernable.[4] The British officials especially hated the American habits of the black Loyalists, primarily their independence and opposition to arbitrary authority. The Americans were free black men and women, and they acted accordingly. They resisted paternalistic rule by company officials. Resentment over paying heavy taxes led to a short-lived rebellion in 1800. Because of company hostility no more American blacks were welcomed in Sierra Leone through official channels.[5] But after Fourah Bay College was established in 1827, one of its first presidents (in the 1840s) was an Afro-American, Edward A. Jones, a graduate of Amherst College.

The Sierra Leone Company failed, but the settlers succeeded. Life was harsh and commercial success rare; but the Loyalists, by their courage and skills, gradually won respect and acceptance. To them it seemed worthwhile to stay because of the greater opportunities and liberties they had in Sierra Leone. The black Americans helped create a new country in West Africa. Later arrivals swamped them and even surpassed them economically, but it was largely the black American component that created Creole society in Freetown and elsewhere in Sierra Leone. It was the Americans who put their stamp on the language, newspapers, and dress of the colony. They brought potatoes, wheat flour, and tea to the diet, as well as a good many American dishes and a preference for American trade goods that allowed American traders to dominate the colony's imports.[6]

Before the movement to set up an African colony for free blacks from the United States was given direction and form by the American Colonization Society, strong efforts to arouse sentiment in favor of colonization had been made by Samuel Hopkins and Paul Cuffee. The Reverend Samuel Hopkins, pastor of the First

Congregational Church of Newport, Rhode Island, had proposed a voluntary plan to send free slaves back to Africa. In 1773 he raised money to return a few freed slaves. They were to be given religious training; evangelization and colonization were to go hand in hand. Although nothing came of Hopkins's project, it found some support among New England black freedmen.

Cuffee, who was half black and half Indian, started life in Massachusetts under handicaps imposed both by poverty and by his ancestry. By the time he reached early middle age, he had educated himself and had accumulated a substantial fortune as a merchant and shipowner. Being deeply interested in the welfare of the black people, he made several voyages to Sierra Leone at his own expense to see for himself what the colony might offer for the future of the black American.[7] In 1816, in cooperation with the African Institution of England and the newly founded American Colonization Society, he transported seven families (thirty-eight persons) from the United States to Sierra Leone, using his own ship and largely his own funds. Cuffee was a devoted member of the Society of Friends, and his activities reflected the steadfast Quaker attitude toward slavery and the work of rehabilitating blacks. Thus he helped to lay the groundwork on the African coast for the later colonization efforts that would result in the formation of the Republic of Liberia.[8] Cuffee died in 1817.

On December 16, 1816, in Washington, the Reverend Robert Finley of New Jersey assembled a group of distinguished citizens to organize a society that would promote and assist the colonization in Africa of free blacks from the United States. Colonization interested not only humanitarians but also slaveholders who were eager to get rid of free blacks as undesirables. Finley's group, which included such men as Henry Clay, Bushrod Washington (nephew of George Washington), John Randolph of Roanoke, and Francis Scott Key, founded the American Colonization Society.[9] The movement thus initiated at Washington spread, slowly at first but with increasing tempo, until in 1826 there were forty-six auxiliary or local colonization societies. There were state affiliates in every state and territory except Rhode Island, South Carolina, Arkansas, and Michigan.[10]

Within two weeks after the society was formally organized in Washington, a memorial was submitted to both houses of Congress calling attention to the unfortunate condition of the free blacks in the United States and urging that they be colonized in Africa. Colonization, the society stressed, would help those blacks and would prevent the greater evils certain to follow if the problem were not solved. A few months later a committee from the society obtained a personal interview with President Monroe, who proved to be sympathetic toward the society and its aims. The society subsequently appointed two agents to visit Africa to reconnoiter possible sites for a colony.[11]

The two agents, Samuel J. Mills and Ebenezer Burgess, arrived at Sierra Leone in March 1818. They spent two weeks observing conditions and affairs at the British colony and then started a detailed, six-week examination of the African coast in search of likely sites.[12] In a small sloop manned by Africans, they explored southward from Sierra Leone. Acceptance of the substance of the report submitted by Burgess committed the American Colonization Society to action in the area investigated by the two agents, and at the same time involved the U.S. government in African affairs despite its traditional policies of isolation and noninvolvement.

On March 3, 1819, a few months after Burgess returned to the United States, Congress enacted a measure that put some force into the 1808 law forbidding the slave trade. Slavers were declared to be pirates, and the recognized penalty for piracy was death. Of immediate importance to the American Colonization Society was a provision that slaves on board ships captured by the U.S. Navy should be returned to Africa and liberated. To implement this provision, Congress authorized an appropriation of $100,000.[13]

President Monroe, disagreeing with an interpretation of the law by the attorney general, sent a special message to Congress on December 19, 1819, stating his personal views and announcing the line of action he intended to take. The president said that the authority he had been given to return captured Africans to Africa implied authority to establish a depot or refuge at some place on the African coast where the rescued slaves could be cared for until their final disposition was determined. The society, meanwhile, had been actively trying to recruit free blacks who were willing to pioneer in the back-to-Africa movement. Eighty-eight such volunteers were assembled, and the society chartered the 300-ton brig *Elizabeth* for the voyage to Africa. But there the matter rested, for the society lacked sufficient funds to proceed further.

The founding of Liberia. The American Colonization Society's project at first aroused a good deal of controversy. Governor Charles MacCarthy of Sierra Leone, for instance, as noted earlier, suspected that the society was a mere cloak for the real purpose behind the American colony: to injure British interests. MacCarthy actually requested permission from London to seize the island of Sherbro in order to forestall the suspected American peril. The British government did not back its proconsul over this matter, but even in the United States the American Colonization Society met with a good deal of hostility. Many abolitionists believed that the emigration of free Afro-Americans would simply strengthen slavery in the South. The great majority of black Americans had little interest in the scheme and no more wanted to leave for Africa than the Pennsylvania Dutch desired to return to their ancestral villages in western Germany.

At this point President Monroe's personal interest in the society's aims cleared the way. A month after his message to Congress, on January 8, 1820, he appointed Samuel Bacon as the U.S. Agent to supervise the repatriation of rescued slaves, with John B. Bankson as assistant. Bacon was directed by the secretary of the navy, acting on behalf of the president, to board and take possession of the *Elizabeth* and to assume its charter in the name of the U.S. government. He was then to load the vessel with stores and materials necessary to build "barracks" for three hundred persons, enrolling as many artisans as necessary to do the work directed, and then immediately sailing for the coast of Africa. Upon arrival he was to arrange for permission to land and then "make preparations for buildings to shelter the captured Africans and to afford them comfort and protection until they be otherwise disposed of."[14] All this was accomplished by the end of 1820. But the first settlement, at Sherbro Island, was a failure; the survivors were transported to Sierra Leone, where the colonial governor granted them temporary asylum.

A second ship, the *Nautilus,* brought another company, but dissension broke out among the leaders. In 1821 Dr. Eli Ayres, appointed to be the society's new agent, was commissioned by the government as a naval surgeon and furnished with a naval vessel to convey him to Africa. He found the colonists ridden with fever, the agents dead, and the survivors in terror and almost mutinous from fear. Ayres promptly assumed the duties of both government and society agent and used a firm hand to establish necessary discipline. A short time later Lieutenant Robert Stockton of the navy arrived with the USS *Alligator.*

After almost two years the Americans still possessed no land upon which to erect a settlement. Having selected Cape Mesurado as a suitable site, Stockton and Ayres approached the local potentate, King Peter, to arrange for the purchase, but the king refused. After hours of haggling, during which Ayres and Stockton suspected that their lives might be in danger, Stockton dramatically held a loaded pistol to King Peter's head. Next day the king and five of his principal chiefs formally agreed to the sale. It thus took the draconian intervention of a U.S. naval officer and a naval surgeon before the American Colonization Society finally owned a site upon which free blacks from the United States and Africans rescued from the slavers could make a new start in life.[15]

The fate of the new colony remained in doubt because of the hostility of local tribes, who resented the loss of their land and feared that the new colonists would endanger the slave trade. For generations, tribes on this part of the African coast had been among the most notorious slave traders, and their fears were undoubtedly incited by European and American slavers who did not want an end to their lucrative traffic.

In 1826 a remarkable white man, Jehudi Ashmun, assumed command of the colony, already called Liberia. He felt that the colony was at this point strong enough to take direct and drastic action. Angered by slave raids that had stolen men, women, boys, and girls almost from the doorsteps of Monrovia, the main Afro-American settlement, Ashmun led a force of twenty-five or more men in a sudden attack on a slaving center called Digby. He destroyed a large Spanish-owned barracoon and liberated the slaves. Then, reinforced by officers and men from two American men-of-war that had put in on the coast, he descended upon a notorious slave center known as Trade Town, where the expedition met a third American warship. The Liberians and Americans landed, under fire from the slavers, and Trade Town was destroyed. Few slaves were liberated, but the town was burned, a powder magazine was blown up, and a considerable number of slavers and their African allies were killed. The slave trade on that part of the coast of Africa never recovered. When Ashmun demanded guarantees from the chiefs that they abstain from the trade in the future, they had no choice but to yield.

During the period between the initial establishment of the colony and the Liberian declaration of independence in 1847, the position of the U.S. government was anomalous. Officially, the only interest of the United States in the colony was in its use as a depot to hold slaves rescued by vessels of the U.S. Navy until their final disposition should be determined. The instructions given to Bacon in 1820 were to the effect that the government had no concern with the affairs of the Colonization Society. Nevertheless, it was the threat of force by a U.S. naval officer that had enabled the colonists to obtain the land they required, and naval officers and men had erected buildings and fortifications after Ashmun's forces defeated the local tribes. The navy lent aid in Ashmun's expeditions against slavers, and there is little doubt that the American flag flew over the Liberian forces in these affairs.

Although the major efforts at colonization were made by the American Colonization Society,[16] it was not the only one to establish settlements of free blacks on the African coast. Several of the proliferating state and local colonization societies formulated policies and developed programs independent of – and sometimes in direct competition with – those of the parent society. From 1830 to 1840 a number of settlements thus were established between Sierra Leone and the Ivory Coast that were not connected with the older settlements of the American Colonization Society.

Spurred by a disagreement within that society and fortified by a substantial appropriation from the state legislature, the Maryland State Colonization Society was the first to embark upon an independent program. Maryland organized its society in 1831 after the Nat Turner rebellion and sent settlers to Cape Palmas in 1834.[17] (One family of former slaves that settled near Harper on Cape Palmas came from Georgia with the name Tubman – a name of great significance in the twentieth century, for William Tubman became president of Liberia in 1944.) The Maryland society reflected more of the fear and hatred of the free black than did the American Colonization Society; laws passed but not enforced in Maryland tried to deport blacks forcibly. About twelve hundred people from Maryland went to Cape Palmas. They signed treaties for land with the local Kru people, built stockades, and tried to farm on the poor land they had annexed rather than to depend on trade, as the Monrovian settlement had done.

Like the Americo-Liberians around Cape Mesurado, the Cape Palmas group did poorly, with few immigrants and little aid from the parent organization. It had good leadership, however. The feeling that the society was dominated by people who wanted to get rid of freed blacks did not endear it to the blacks themselves, and few signed up to go to Cape Palmas. Still, the colony survived, despite all the sufferings and failures experienced by the American Colonization Society; its most famous governor, John Russwurm (1836–51), was a black Jamaican and an early Negro College graduate who despaired of enjoying citizenship in the United States and emigrated to Liberia in 1829. In 1853 the Cape Palmas settlement became the Republic of Maryland; it joined Liberia as a county in 1857.[18]

The Mississippi Colonization Society decided to establish its own African colony in 1836, and sent an agent to Africa to obtain land for the purpose. With colonists from Mississippi and Louisiana, a settlement was founded on the Sinoe River. Although started with enthusiasm, the Mississippi/Louisiana settlement in Africa failed to prosper, and in 1842 the sponsors were easily persuaded to merge their colony with that of the American Colonization Society.

A third independent effort was made at Bassa Cove in 1834 and 1835 under the joint sponsorship of the American Colonization Society of Pennsylvania and its New York City organization. The pacifistic Quakers were strong in the former group; the appointed agent in charge of the settlement sternly refused to permit ownership of arms and even rejected offers of protection from Monrovia. The tragic result of such strict adherence to pacifism was well illustrated only six months after the colony was established, when the helpless settlers were massacred and the settlement was all but destroyed by hostile tribesmen. Under a new and more realistic governor, the Bassa Cove settlement was reestablished, and although relations between it and the older colony were excellent, it was maintained for several years as a separate settlement.[19]

Liberia, from its establishment until the 1840s, was a political anomaly. The de facto governing bodies were the colonization societies, with the American Colonization Society responsible for the greater part of the settlements; but neither by act of Congress nor by any international agreement was any society authorized to exercise governmental powers. Nevertheless, a government was necessary and, whether willing or not, the American Colonization Society found itself involved. In 1839, in order to give a semblance of legality to its actions, the society designated its settlements collectively as the Commonwealth of Liberia and conferred the title of governor upon its agent. Difficulties arose when British traders refused to recognize the society's government as a legal authority and British officials in Sierra Leone threatened reprisals against efforts to enforce commercial regulations and collect customs duties. In accordance with tradition, the U.S. government refused to annex Liberia or assume any official connection. The society took the only feasible course under the circumstances: In 1846 the colony was directed to proclaim its own independence, and in 1847 the Republic of Liberia came into formal being.

The new republic faced a variety of ills. The dominant Americo-Liberians remained a small minority. Their country was in financial straits; the colony's international position was in doubt; there were disputes centering on the question whether the colony should break all links with the Colonization Society. Liberia, moreover, was rent by various social divisions. The more conservative element consisted mainly of mulattoes, many of them adherents of the society, some of them prominent traders and shipowners. The mulattoes were better educated than their darker-skinned neighbors; some had inherited property from their white fathers; and they regarded themselves as a social elite and considered themselves entitled to the better jobs in commerce and government. They looked to new immigrants from the United States to replenish their numbers. Fearing the danger of "mobocracy," they subsequently tried to defend their political interests by founding the True Liberian Party (later known as the Republican Party).

The mulattoes were opposed by darker-skinned settlers who, in the main, made up the less affluent element of the population. This group, assigned land outside Monrovia, the main settlement, often accused the Colonization Society's white agent of discriminating on the mulattoes' behalf in the allocation of town lots. The darker-skinned later formed the True Whig Party; they called for the unification of all tribes and classes in the country and professed a more democratic outlook than the rival party.

The Americo-Liberians of all hues in turn formed a small ruling minority. They were surrounded by a vast indigenous majority who may have outnumbered them by a hundred to one. The colonists, like early white frontier settlers in other parts of Africa, faced all manner of difficulties: lack of capital, markets, and military resources; a difficult climate and difficult soils; tropical diseases against which no remedies were known. Above all, the settlers came into bitter conflict with the indigenous communities with whom they competed for land, trade, and labor. From the 1840s onward, the settlers began to destroy the indigenous domination of the coastal trade; by regulating labor recruitment and taxing returning labor migrants, the Liberian oligarchy managed to turn existing patterns of labor migration to its own profit. The indigenous communities resisted; there were numerous wars, especially against so-called Kru people; but the variegated tribes of the coast and the hinterland never managed to create a united front against the newcomers, who gradually established an uneasy predominance over the littoral.[20]

Despite these political and economic difficulties, most of the settlers were converted to the cause of independence. They felt that they had received inadequate support from the United States in Liberian disputes with the British. Liberia's governor under the Colonization Society, Joseph Jenkins Roberts, a Virginian of mixed white and black ancestry, argued that only independence would relieve the Liberians of future embarrassment and settle the objections raised by Great Britain concerning Liberia's sovereignty. In the end, the matter was put to a so-called popular vote. Only two-thirds of the electorate, including a few hundred African aborigines, cast votes. But a majority of them backed Roberts on the independence issue, and in 1847 a constitutional convention worked out a new instrument of government, largely on the American model. Roberts, who had been governor since 1841, was elected Liberia's first president.

This action changed the mission and purpose of the American Colonization Society; it became an emigration society, encouraging and helping freed blacks to migrate to Africa, but it had no responsibility for the operation and management of the colony. No longer burdened with the expenses of governing Liberia, the society was able to free itself from debt and to devote increasingly large sums to assisting the migration of blacks to Africa. Thus, between 1848 and 1854, the society was able to charter forty-one ships carrying nearly four thousand persons to Africa; by 1860 it had sent a total of around eleven thousand blacks. The Civil War, with resulting emancipation and adoption of the Fourteenth Amendment, lessened the attractiveness of Africa to most blacks, but the society's activities continued on a decreasing scale until near the end of the century.[21] In addition, slave ships captured in African waters were turned over to the Colonization Society. In 1860–1, for example, three captured slavers brought 2,310 recaptured blacks to Monrovia, the transfer subsidized by the U.S. government. Many recaptives died from the poor conditions on land, but a total of 5,457 were brought to Liberia, most of them between 1846 and 1862.

Despite the lack of formal recognition, the U.S. government maintained relations of a sort with the Liberian government, as evidenced by a report of the secretary of the interior in 1861, which noted that about forty-five hundred Africans rescued from slave ships had been landed in Liberia in a little more than a year, "under contract with the Government of Liberia."[22] But the bombardment of Fort Sumter and the exodus of slaveholding Southerners from Washington changed the situation radically. President Lincoln said in his message to Congress on December 3, 1861: "If any good reason exists why we should persevere longer in withholding our recognition of the independence and sovereignty of Hayti and Liberia, I am unable to discern it."[23] In the press of wartime business, Congress did not act upon the president's recommendation immediately, but in June 1862 it finally gave its approval to recognition of the two black republics. Shortly after, an American consul, John Seys, took his post at Monrovia, and the president was able to report in his annual message for 1862 that an advantageous treaty had been concluded with Liberia and was awaiting Senate confirmation.[24]

Seys, the first representative of the United States to be accredited formally to

Liberia, was one of those men whose quiet influence is deeply important but is too often overlooked by historians. A native of the British West Indies and a convert early in life to Methodism, he spent several years in the ministry and in missionary activities in Trinidad and other West Indian islands. Shortly after coming to the United States he was appointed to a missionary station among the Oneida Indians, where his energy, sincerity, and tact gained so many converts that in a few months he had an interracial church composed of 100 Indians, 7 whites, and 1 black. The newly established Methodist mission in Liberia meanwhile was engaging the attention of the church's authorities, and on April 7, 1834, upon the recommendation of Bishop Elijah Hedding, the board of managers appointed Seys to that station. He arrived in Liberia on October 18, 1834. Except for a few short visits to the United States, he remained in Liberia until 1841, when his wife's failing health and difficulties with Governor Thomas Buchanan compelled him to resign. In 1842, however, on learning that the country was without a Methodist minister, Seys volunteered his services; he continued until his wife's ill health again forced him to resign in 1845, but he was far from through.

In 1858 he was appointed U.S. government agent for freedmen in Liberia, and as just noted, he was the first U.S. consul.[25] Early in 1863 the president appointed John J. Henry commissioner and consul general to Liberia, but Henry resigned before taking the post. In his stead, Abraham Hanson formally presented credentials to the president of Liberia on February 25, 1864, but succumbed to an African fever two years later. The office was then tendered to John Seys, who became minister resident and consul general in the fall of 1866.[26]

Formal recognition and the designation of diplomatic representatives placed relationships between Liberia and the United States on a regular basis. Before recognition, however, the Liberian government drew moral strength – and sometimes a degree of physical aid – from the friendly interest of the parent country. The presence of the U.S. naval squadron in African waters enabled the struggling Liberian government to act decisively against slavers, and the occasional visit of an American warship was a definite object lesson to African tribes; in 1852, for example, the sudden appearance of the USS *John Adams* had a noticeably quieting effect upon the chiefs at Grand Bassa. The withdrawal of American ships during the Civil War deprived the Liberian government of this moral and physical aid, and for several years Liberian officials found themselves handicapped in their efforts to extend their authority, and sometimes even to maintain themselves in places they already held.

One of Seys's main interests was the securing of a suitable armed vessel from the United States to enable the Liberian government to suppress slaving and to maintain order among the coastal peoples. As early as 1864, in his last annual message, President Lincoln had urged that he be given authority to sell to Liberia a gunboat no longer needed by the U.S. Navy, and in 1866 Congress approved such a sale on terms that would have made the craft practically a gift. Unfortunately, none of the surplus war vessels was suitable; they were either too small for African service or too large for the scanty resources of the Liberian government.

Delany and the back-to-Africa movement. The basis for the American Colonization Society's activities in Liberia was the widely held idea that the black of the Western hemisphere should better his lot by migrating to the ancestral homeland.

Back-to-Africa schemes enjoyed a degree of popularity, especially among a number of educated blacks who were discouraged by the handicaps imposed upon their people in a predominantly Caucasian society.[27] Such a person was Martin Robison Delany, born in 1812 of free black parents in the region that is now West Virginia, and supposedly a descendent of Mandinka royalty of the Niger Valley. After a boyhood troubled by racial discrimination, he took up journalism, studied medicine, received a medical degree from Harvard College in 1852, and established a practice at Chatham, Ontario. But even in Canada he felt racial prejudice and discrimination.

While in medical school, Delany aspired to be a medical missionary to Africa. He seems to have dropped the idea for several years, although he never lost sight of the unhappy condition of his race in the United States. In 1854 he was a member and leading spirit of a convention called to consider a scheme of emigration from the United States to some other parts of the Western Hemisphere; Africa was specifically excluded from consideration. The convention adopted appropriate resolutions and established a national board of commissioners to endeavor to implement the resolutions.

Delany, however, had been maturing a scheme to organize and finance an exploration of the Niger Valley with a view to settlement there. He planned to obtain a cargo of trade goods in Philadelphia and exchange these for beeswax and ivory at Loango; with the profits he would go to Lagos, and thence to the Yoruba country of Nigeria. The board approved this proposal and on August 30, 1858, published an announcement:

> The object of this Expedition is to make a Topographical, Geological and Geographical Examination of the Valley of the River Niger, in Africa, and an inquiry into the state and condition of the people of that valley, and other parts of Africa, together with such other scientific inquiries as may by them be deemed expedient, for the purposes of science and for general information; and without any reference to, and with the Board being entirely opposed to any Emigration there as such. Provided, however, that nothing in this Instrument be so construed as to interfere with the right of the Commissioners to negotiate on their own behalf, or that of any other parties, or organization for territory.[28]

The dichotomy in the announced objectives was reflected in selecting personnel for the expedition. From the start, Delany's activities lacked coordination with those of some of his subordinates. When his sailing was delayed until May 1859, his assistant – Robert Campbell, a Jamaican-born chemist – departed for England and on his own initiative persuaded several wealthy Englishmen to support the project financially. Campbell stressed the need to find a supply of cotton for the Manchester mills, and prevailed upon Lord Malmesbury, secretary of state for foreign affairs, to give him a letter of introduction to various officials in Africa. Arriving at Lagos on July 21, 1859, Campbell, without waiting for Delany, moved upcountry to Abeokuta in August in the company of the sons of Samuel Crowther, a famous and highly esteemed black Nigerian missionary.

Delany arrived later without introduction, but managed to get to the court of the king of the Egba tribe. On December 27, 1859, he obtained a treaty. In return for pledges that none but people of good character would come to Africa, immigrants of the black race were granted the privilege of settling in Egba territory, where they would be subject to Egba law and custom. They would bring with them "Intelligence, Education, a Knowledge of the Arts and Sciences, Agriculture, and other Mechanical and Industrial Occupations."[29] Though the treaty was later repudiated by the alake (king), allegedly because of pressure from British missionaries, it is interesting to note that Delany and Campbell found one black American already settled in the region they proposed to colonize.[30]

Delany and Campbell returned first to England and then to the United States to raise the necessary funds and to assemble emigrants. They were supported by numerous influential persons and by organizations such as the African Aid Society of London. There was nothing inherently impracticable in Delany's plan for the colonization of black Americans in the Niger Valley; certainly the difficulties would have been no more formidable than those encountered in Liberia and Sierra Leone. But soon, in the turmoil of the Civil War in the United States, the status of the American black was to be redefined and all schemes for African colonization were to be suspended. Delany went into the war effort intensely and was finally commissioned in the Army Medical Corps. After the war he served as a federal official in South Carolina – one of the few carpetbag officials who earned the praise of the Carolinians for his honesty and efficiency.

Although the plan for resettlement of black Americans in Nigeria was never put into effect, the explorations made by Delany and Campbell were not without value. Both made definite contributions to the world's knowledge of African life.[31]

On the eve of the Civil War there were many schemes to move black Americans to other parts of the world: the Caribbean, Kansas, Australia, and Haiti, as well as Africa. Most black national leaders paid some deference to emigration schemes and to black nationalism; Central America interested some; Canada, a few; and Haiti, still others. Frederick Douglass at first opposed emigration projects as a distraction from solving problems in the United States. But so much pressure was put on him after the 1860 election that he began to shift his ground. While he ruled out Africa, he looked favorably on Haiti. The outbreak of the Civil War ended the scheme, and emigration movements remained largely dormant until the 1890s.[32]

The missionary movement

Closely related to the colonization movement was the missionary venture designed to bring Christianity to the peoples of the so-called Dark Continent. In the history of religion, the nineteenth century indeed stands out as an age of paradox. On the one hand the era saw a widespread assault on all religious creeds, more thorough and better founded intellectually than any launched in the past. The followers of Marx, Nietzsche, and Thomas Henry Huxley might disagree on many things, but they all had one conviction in common: God was dead and man must step into God's place. Skepticism or outright unbelief became an accepted part of the ideological scene, and the impact of the Christian faith weakened in many segments of Western society.

Yet at a time when many prophets believed that religion was on its way out, Christianity gained a new access of strength as theologians of many schools tried to reformulate their respective creeds in the light of the new intellectual challenges. Simultaneously, the churches embarked on a worldwide crusade that promised to make up for losses at home by new conquests overseas. European and American evangelists were fired by a profound enthusiasm; the age that sent white explorers, prospectors, traders, and soldiers of fortune to the remotest corners of the world witnessed a similar outburst of ecclesiastical pioneering, financed, for the most part, by small contributions from a great mass of the faithful rather than by donations from a few wealthy magnates. The missionary profession to some extent acted as a ladder of social promotion: People of humble background might make ecclesiastical careers for themselves in the wilds of Africa. Missionary work moreover attracted all kinds of men and women who, in a later age, might have sought livelihoods in a score of secular welfare services that developed during the course of the twentieth century.

Religious interest in Africa was not of course new to Americans. A short time after the Revolution, a former slave known as Olaudah Equiano, an African who had been owned in Virginia and probably converted to Christianity there, had pleaded for the extension of Christianity to Africa. Equiano was a gifted writer and an able theoretician. Like many supporters of the missionary movement both before and after him, he believed that there was a close link among the spreading of the Gospel; the destruction of the slave trade; the development of a new economic system founded on free labor and free trade, with resultant prosperity for the new manufacturing industries; and material progress for all. Equiano himself, an admirer of the British Empire at its best, petitioned the bishop of London for ordination, with the intention of going to Africa as a missionary. The bishop refused: The world was not yet ready to attempt to evangelize Africa; but the seed had been planted and was ready to germinate.[33]

Even earlier, five years before the outbreak of the Revolutionary War, Samuel Hopkins of Newport, Rhode Island, proposed to train a number of carefully chosen free blacks for the ministry and to send them to Guinea, where they were to settle quietly and watch for favorable opportunities to teach Africans the doctrines and precepts of Christianity. Each was to constitute himself a focus for Christian effort and teaching. The war prevented Hopkins from putting his plan into effect immediately, but after the war he selected a number of candidates and began to train them. He died in 1803 before the education of any of his missionaries had been completed, but at least two of his men – identified as S. Nubia and N. Gardner – went to Africa later under the auspices of the American Colonization Society.[34]

West Africa. The first American religious impression upon Africa seems to have been made at Sierra Leone, the earliest of the colonies established for repatriating freed Africans in their ancestral continent. As noted previously, an important element among the colonists, possibly a majority, was formed by the black Nova Scotians, slaves who had fought with the British forces during the Revolution. Most of the Nova Scotian blacks were deeply religious, giving their loyalties to the Baptist, Wesleyan, or Huntingdonian churches. The first arrivals from the United States included entire congregations led by their pastors; among the ministers, some of whom were also ex-Revolutionary captains, were Cato Perkins and William Ash, natives of Charleston, South Carolina. Churches were among the first structures erected in the new colony.[35]

It was not long before the Church Missionary Society of London and other religious bodies sent missionaries to Sierra Leone to keep the colonists within paths of denominational orthodoxy and to begin work among the pagan natives.[36] Probably the first black American to serve as a missionary in Africa was a man (his name is not recorded) who was added to the staff of the Sierra Leone mission of the Church Missionary Society in 1814 because of his knowledge of several African languages.[37]

The first missionaries to go directly from the United States to Africa were blacks, and their efforts were directed toward Liberia. It was assumed by most churches that a black could work among the heathen peoples of Africa more readily than could a white. Many churchmen believed that devout, Christian, free blacks were anxious to return to their ancestral homeland. Furthermore, the African coast was "the white man's grave," so that the odds were against any white missionary's surviving long enough to accomplish any good; black Americans were sent in the hope and belief that they were immune to the deadly fevers of Africa.

None of these assumptions were accurate. Immunity to disease proved to be an individual matter rather than a racial characteristic, and the death toll among the black American missionaries was as frightful as among the whites. To the native African, the black American was not a compatriot but another foreigner – and a foreigner who had much more in common with whites than with any African. Cultural ties between American and African blacks were practically nonexistent. Nevertheless, the black American in Africa played an important role.

It is true that at certain times and among some denominations there was opposition to the black as a missionary, but during the nineteenth century blacks were nevertheless sent to Africa as missionaries by white missionary groups. Such a statement as this one, made by Harold Isaacs, hence seems extreme and open to question: "With but rare exceptions, the large white Christian denominations seldom wished to send Negro workers into the African vineyards. Even when they did wish it, they seldom did so, and when they did, they did it sparingly and not for long."[38] The evidence indicates that at least some of the Christian bodies supporting African missions were anxious to send black missionaries and were limited partly by the availability of suitably qualified candidates. But a very high proportion of the missionaries sent to Liberia were blacks.

The Presbyterian mission group sent seventy-three people to Liberia between 1832 and 1899; of these, forty-nine were blacks. Only one black, a light-skinned woman named Miss Harding, was sent by the Presbyterians to serve in the Gabon and Corisco mission, but many white missionary pioneers to this area were accompanied by black assistants. Thomas J. Bowen of the Southern Baptist Church, for example, in establishing missions for his church in Nigeria, in 1849, was accompanied by black missionaries. William H. Sheppard, a black missionary, set up the earliest Presbyterian missions in the Congo and remained in that field for many years, assisted by both whites and blacks. The Reverend Charles W. Thomas, cruising the African coast as a navy chaplain in the 1850s, found black missionaries wherever Christian missions existed.[39]

In 1821 the first shipload of colonists from the United States to the region that was to become Liberia included among its passengers the Reverend Daniel Coker from Baltimore. A former slave who had managed to purchase his own freedom and obtain a liberal education, he was a member and minister of the African Methodist Episcopal Church from its origin as a national organization in 1816. During the voyage to Africa he organized a congregation, and after landing, when the three Colonization Society agents died, he assumed leadership of the colony. It was he who led the decimated remains of the first Sherbro Island colony to Sierra Leone for refuge. He remained in Sierra Leone after the Americans returned to the reestablished colony, and for many years he was the highly respected pastor of the African Methodists of the British colony.[40]

In addition to Daniel Coker, early colonists in Liberia included two black ministers from the Baptist Board of Foreign Missions, Lott Carey (or Cary) and Colin Teague. Little has been recorded about Teague, but Lott Carey is better known. He was born a slave in Virginia about 1780, and with help from a minister he taught himself to read and write. He was rented to the owners of a warehouse and soon made himself so valuable that they paid him a regular wage in addition to the rent paid to his master, and thus enabled him to purchase freedom for himself and his children. In 1819, accepted by the American Colonization Society as a missionary and ordained by the Baptist General Convention, Carey sailed for Liberia, where he remained for the rest of his life.[41]

Within a few years the other principal Protestant denominations in the United States sent missionaries to Liberia to work among the repatriated settlers. They met with varying degrees of success, but without exception all suffered from the climate and from deadly fevers. One after another, often within a few days or weeks after their arrival in Africa, the earnest, hopeful young Americans succumbed. The first Methodist missionary, Melville B. Cox, died four months after reaching Liberia.[42] On New Year's Day 1834 a second group of Methodists arrived, five men and women; two of them died within three months, and two of those remaining lost heart and returned to America. A lone, courageous woman, Sophronia Farrington, stuck to her post, and through her efforts and example the Methodist mission survived.[43] The Reverend John Pinney, who arrived in Liberia in 1833 as the first missionary ever dispatched to a foreign field by the Presbyterian Church in the United States, similarly survived. One assistant after another succumbed to African fevers, but Pinney retained his health and determination. In addition to preaching the gospel, for some time he acted as agent of the American Colonization Society and was in charge of the colony, so he is justly numbered among the founders of Liberia. Not until 1839 did he retire from the mission and finally return to America.[44]

The missionaries mentioned thus far were concerned primarily with the spiritual welfare of the black colonists from the United States. Although they all considered their work among the Liberians as a preparation for the later conversion of seemingly countless hordes of heathen who surrounded the colony, none of them came equipped or prepared for that further labor. A few years earlier, however, the American Board of Commissioners for Foreign Missions (ABCFM) had been formed on an interdenominational basis for just such work. The board in 1825 adopted a resolution looking to the establishment of a mission in West Africa as soon as practicable and shortly thereafter appointed a black Presbyterian minister to work among the Liberian people. For some unspecified reason the minister was not sent, and the project remained in abeyance until 1833, when "the Committee were constrained, by their views of the imperative claims of Africa, to resume the subject."[45] Later in the same year the Reverend John Leighton Wilson volunteered his services, and on November 28 he departed for Africa with Stephen R. Wyncoop as his assistant.

Wilson was instructed to determine the suitability of Cape Palmas as a location for a mission; if he found no serious objections or obstacles, he was to "take measures for the speedy commencement of a mission there." He would then devote himself to acquiring all possible information about Liberia and the native tribes, with a new departure in missionary work as his final objective – the training of Africans for the evangelization of their fellows:

> The information you will . . . seek concerning the native tribes, will relate
> to the character of their superstitions; the hold these have on the minds of
> the people; the nature of their vices; their social condition; their various
> languages; how far the gospel may be preached to them; their disposition
> in respect to schools; . . . the probability of procuring helpers from among
> the sons of Africa, or of the colonists; and the expediency of sending them
> from among the colored people of this country.[46]

The important feature of Wilson's instructions was the directive to train Africans to carry on the work of evangelization rather than to rely solely on his own efforts or on the efforts of other Americans: "The main dependence of our mission in western Africa . . . must be upon the labors of pious natives and colonists, trained for the work in seminaries provided for the purpose, and acting under the superintendence of missionaries sent from this country." Wilson's major personal objective was to form an educational and training program that would enable Africans to evangelize and convert their own people.[47]

With his assistant, Wyncoop, Wilson arrived at the Liberian coast in the latter part of January 1834. They spent the next several weeks between Cape Mount and Cape Palmas, exploring, observing, and asking questions; they decided that Cape Palmas, where the Maryland colony had recently been established, was the most suitable location. On hearing their findings when they returned to New York on April 13, 1834, the board quickly approved their recommendations; and on November 7, a little less than a year after his first embarkation, Wilson, with his wife and a black woman teacher as assistant, sailed again for Africa. By August 1835 Wilson reported from Cape Palmas that a small school had been opened, with both Africans and the children of colonists as pupils. Mrs. Wilson was conducting two Sabbath schools, one for Africans and the other for Americans. Wilson himself was exploring the surrounding country, studying the people, learning their customs and beliefs, and trying to gain their confidence.[48]

During the next few years several other missionaries from the United States, as well as a number of teachers and craftsmen, followed Wilson to Cape Palmas. The Grebo language was reduced to writing, and textbooks, tracts, parts of the Bible, and a life of Christ were translated for use in the schools and in teaching Africans the principles of the Christian faith. A black printer, B. V. R. James, arrived from the United States with a press that was soon printing books, pamphlets, and tracts for the board's mission and for other missions as well.[49] The mission at Cape Palmas, under Wilson's leadership, appeared at this point to be fairly on the way to becoming a center of Christian activities in West Africa.

But the missionaries of the American board, as well as those of other churches and nationalities, often found themselves struggling, somewhat unsuccessfully, against all sorts of difficulties. There was always the danger of the dreaded and deadly "African fever"; the country was unsettled and frequently turbulent; and there were annoying administrative troubles with the colonization societies. The Americo-Liberians, like many white settlers in Africa, were lukewarm in their attitude toward Christianizing or civilizing the aborigines, and there was marked indifference and sometimes downright hostility among the Africans – this in spite of the happy optimism of nearly all missionary reports. Even those who welcomed, or accepted, the missionaries often saw no reason to extend their benefits to neighboring communities and tribes. In 1836, for example, Wilson reported that the natives at Cape Palmas were decidedly antagonistic to his proposed establishment of a mission among their traditional enemies at Rocktown, only a short distance away.[50]

The worst enemy, however, was disease. The medical and sanitary knowledge of the time was insufficient to solve the problem. West Africa continued to live up to its ancient reputation as "the white man's grave," and there was soon abundant evidence that it was as fatal to the black American as to the Caucasian. In 1834 the American Colonization Society learned that of 649 colonists dispatched to Liberia in the few months preceding, 134 had died already. The Church Missionary Society of London recorded that 89 missionaries had been sent to West Africa between 1804 and 1825 and that 54 had died there.[51]

Wilson and his wife enjoyed several months of apparent immunity, but eventually the fever struck them too, and for months they were near death. That they recovered and did not succumb either to the initial attacks of the fever or to any of the subsequent periods of relapse was remarkable in the missionary annals of West Africa. Others who arrived to assist in "promoting the Kingdom of God" were not so fortunate. The Reverend David White and his wife arrived at Cape Palmas on Christmas Day 1836; less than a month later he was dead, and his wife lived only a few days longer. At almost the same time a black American teacher named Polk, whom Wilson had praised highly in several reports, was fatally stricken. In 1841 the first medical missionary, Dr. Alexander Wilson, died suddenly, and in 1842 the wife of the Reverend William Walker died after seeming to be on the way to recovery.[52]

Many people will take a chance on possible martyrdom, but there are very few who would willingly face almost certain death. That it became increasingly difficult to obtain missionaries for West Africa is not surprising, especially when the evangelical fervor of the 1820s and 1830s began to decline. Hence, in the early 1840s, the American Board of Commissioners decided to transfer its activities to some other region of West Africa.

The board's mission and activities at Cape Palmas were turned over to missionaries of the Protestant Episcopal Church who had been working in the Maryland Colonization Society's settlements since 1836. With this exception, Protestant missions in Liberia were virtually abandoned during the period between the proclamation of Liberia's independence and the Civil War in the United States. The toll of missionary lives was too heavy to be sustained. Nevertheless, the Episcopalians hung on doggedly, although in three years' time ten missionaries died (out of twenty-two), and eight were invalided home. There were times when the missionaries were endangered by uprisings; on two or three occasions they had to close the mission temporarily. They also faced the shortsighted opposition of the Americo-Liberian citizens to missionary work among the indigenous people. But in spite of such discouragements, the Christianizing and educational work initiated by Wilson was continued without significant interruption for many years.[53]

The survival of the Episcopal mission was largely due to the determination of Bishop John Payne, who was born in Westmoreland County, Virginia, and educated at the College of William and Mary and the Alexandria Theological Seminary. He went to Liberia as a young man and spent the greater part of his life there; in 1853 he was consecrated as bishop. It was he who was instrumental in bringing the Reverend Alexander Crummel to Liberia and starting him on his lifework.[54]

Because of disease and the friction with the officials of the Maryland colony, the ABCFM was eager to relocate. Captain Richard Lawlin, a veteran American trader and a good friend of the missionaries, suggested Cape Lahou (Ivory Coast) and Gabon as possible sites. He offered to take the missionaries John Leighton Wilson and Benjamin Griswold on a trading voyage down the coast to check on possible new locations. The evangelists landed with Lawlin at Glass near the mouth of the Gabon River – a center of English, French, and American trade in Gabon – on June 23, 1842. In a few days they had decided to stay. The site seemed healthy, the presence of a trade center meant better communications, and the Africans received them cordially. The people, too, Wilson reported, were "a good deal more advanced in civilization than any natives I have before seen or expected to see on the western coast of Africa."[55]

Contrary to Lawlin's assurances, however, Gabon did not prove to be very healthy. "Everyday," reported the Reverend William Walker, "we are reminded that this is not a New England clime."[56] And the local Mpongwe were interested in the schools only so they could become literate traders.

As at Cape Palmas, the missionaries started work almost as soon as they landed. Just when they felt that they were beginning to make progress, the very existence of the mission was threatened by a new factor in African affairs: the imperial ambitions of Europe. In a letter written on May 8, 1843, Benjamin Griswold informed the ABCFM that a French naval officer, with a small squadron, had attempted to purchase land for a fort on the south bank of the river and that officers from two French men-of-war had later made a similar attempt on the north shore; he believed that they had been successful in their purchase. Griswold, as a devoted evangelical, feared that this purchase might give an entry to the "Romanists," but apparently he saw no other danger.[57]

A year later, in April 1844, Walker informed the ABCFM that efforts made almost weekly by the French to bring the Africans under French protection had finally, by pure chicanery, succeeded. King Glass – the local chief – had while very drunk signed a paper that was supposed to be a letter of friendship to King Louis Philippe but was actually a treaty in which King Glass submitted to French overlordship. The next day the commander of a French warship exhibited the paper to the chief and received his acknowledgment that he had signed it. Thus was the treaty signed and "ratified."[58] In the ensuing difficulties, the American missionaries found themselves in a dangerous position. After several futile attempts to persuade the Africans to accept the treaty and admit French sovereignty, the French realized that they would have to use force. They sought an excuse to consider themselves insulted. A French officer brusquely informed the missionaries that he could not guarantee their safety if he had to bombard the town – and added curtly that the mission had no official status whatever. Since the Africans still refused to hoist the French flag, the bombardment began. The missionaries had displayed an American flag, but a thirty-two pound shot smashed into the mission church.[59] A French landing party fired indiscriminately at all natives, further endangering the Americans and their property.[60]

Wilson reported a few weeks later that the local French commander had hinted broadly that he would be glad to have the Americans leave Gabon, a hint to which Wilson had replied that he would not leave until he had received a formal, written command to do so. In another three months the French still held the mission's boats and other property seized at the beginning of the trouble, and Wilson fully expected to be expelled as soon as the anticipated French Jesuits arrived. By January 1846, however, the situation appeared more hopeful. A representative of the French admiral came to the mission, apologized in the admiral's name for the dangers to which the mission had been exposed, and assured Wilson of the admiral's friendship. The mission quietly continued its educational and religious programs with what Wilson considered a promising degree of success. Nevertheless, he recommended that locations be selected outside the French sphere to which the mission could be transferred quickly if necessary.[61]

During the height of the trouble the missionaries were unable to appeal to their own government because of the distance involved and because no U.S. warship was on that part of the coast. A newly arrived missionary and his wife found the local French authorities reluctant to permit them to land; a temporary permit was grudgingly granted after a delay and some argument. But the situation changed completely when Commodore George C. Read, commander of the American naval squadron, reached Gabon in mid-1846. He wrote a letter – apparently a strong letter – to the French admiral in command of all French forces on the coast, and the admiral soon made a personal visit to the mission. Wilson's report read: "Since the visit of the French admiral and Commodore Read, both of whom showed us much kindness, we have experienced nothing but the most civil treatment, from both the local authorities, and such of the officers of the French navy as have occasionally visited the river."[62]

The worst of the difficulties of the ABCFM's mission in West Africa thus were over; it was not long before French authorities recognized that the American missionaries were a positive force. From then until the mission was turned over to the Presbyterians, some thirty years later, the Americans enjoyed good relations with both the French overlords and their African subjects.[63]

In 1848, when it became apparent that the French were not going to expel the mission, eight new evangelists were sent to Gabon. Six Mpongwe were baptized, others were "inquiring," and the field "never was more encouraging." However, several outstations that had been created reported "fanatical movements," especially among the women; and the influx of American rum, which did the Mpongwe "ten thousand times more injury than the French guns," soon clouded the evangelical outlook.[64] Disease had thinned the clerical ranks by 1852, and religious interest had declined. The frustrated and disease-wracked missionaries quarreled among themselves; "personal vanities and feuds became as important as policy decisions." Younger missionaries criticized the conservative "preach and hope" tactics of their elders, tactics that failed to attract or to hold converts and that had not produced an indigenous clergy. Most of the dissidents eventually either quit or joined the Presbyterian mission on Corisco. William Walker and Albert Bushnell, despite their strained personal relations, doggedly stayed on at Baraka for another decade, but in 1860 it was evident that the ABCFM venture in Gabon had failed.[65] The Gabon station was taken over by the Presbyterians in 1870; the American Board of Commissioners was glad to get rid of it.

American Presbyterian missionaries began work on the island of Corisco in modern Equatorial Guinea in 1850. There was a high death rate among the pioneers, but the evangelists succeeded in spreading stations along the Rio Muni coast and in training local African catechists and pastors. In 1874, four years after the Presbyterians took over the ABCFM station in Gabon, the Reverend Robert H. Nassau became the first missionary to work on the newly opened Ogowe River station.[66] During the 1880s the Americans were under considerable pressure from the French colonial regime, and they finally handed over the Gabon and Ogowe stations to French Protestant missionaries. The Presbyterians then shifted their attention to southern Cameroon, where they did well.

As in all other regions, the first efforts of the missionaries at Gabon were spent in studying the local languages and in translating religious material into idioms that could be understood. Because of the uncertainty and vicissitudes of the first years at Gabon, the printing press brought from Cape Palmas was not set up and put into operation until 1849, although books were printed in the Mpongwe tongue in Gabon as early as 1844. Wilson himself had to act as printer. Walker meanwhile had translated the Gospel of St. Matthew into the Mpongwe language; this was probably the first book published in Gabon.[67] By the time the mission was turned over to the Presbyterians, both the Mpongwe and the Bakele languages had been reduced to writing and their grammatical principles worked out; vocabularies had been compiled and extensive passages from the gospels translated and printed.[68]

For years after the first establishment of missions on the west coast of Africa, the vast region that is now called Nigeria remained untouched. The Niger River valley itself was still largely unknown.[69] Nevertheless, disturbed by the probability that recovered slaves repatriated from Sierra Leone would revert to paganism, the British Wesleyans and the Church Missionary Society of the Church of England made a beginning in Nigeria in the early 1840s. In 1846, after spending almost two years on the coast while vainly trying to get to the interior, Henry Townsend and Samuel A. Crowther established the first Christian mission at Abeokuta, the capital of the Yoruba.[70]

In the United States, meanwhile, the Southern Baptists were giving anxious consideration to an African mission. In 1849 the Reverend Thomas Jefferson Bowen arrived in Nigeria to explore for a suitable location. In background and early life, Bowen was almost unique among missionaries. A native of Georgia, he had raised and commanded a company of Georgia volunteers in the war against the Creek Indians in 1836. Later in the same year, his taste for adventure and excitement still unsatisfied, he went to the Southwest, enlisted in the army of the infant Republic of Texas, was immediately commissioned a captain of cavalry in that redoubtable force, and spent the next two years on the frontier in the Far West fighting Indians and bandits. After leaving the Texas service and returning to Georgia in 1840, he underwent a deep emotional experience and devoted the remainder of his life to preaching.[71]

Once in Nigeria, Bowen established friendly relations with the Church of England missionaries; they gave him every assistance and encouragement, and he was deeply impressed by them and their efforts.[72] Anxious not to duplicate their work or to interfere with missions already established, he set off to explore Nigeria and spent the next two years searching for a site. He usually traveled alone except for a few bearers, and he ran into a number of difficulties. Some Nigerian chiefs were friendly; more were suspicious or even hostile. The traditional religious authorities by this time suspected that missionary influence meant the end of their own, and the numerous Muslims used every means to prevent this penetration into their areas. Nevertheless, by a combination of sincerity, earnestness, and humor, as well as an impressive skill with firearms, he won his way and visited parts of the Niger Valley that no white man had ever seen before. In every sense of the term, Bowen was an explorer, although he did not regard himself as such.[73]

Bowen found himself in Nigeria at a most critical time. There was civil war within Yorubaland, and the slave-raiding Dahomeans chose the early 1850s to attack. They were finally repulsed and defeated, but not until they had attacked the Egba capital of Abeokuta, where Bowen had taken refuge with his Church of England friends. It was largely through the leadership and example of the missionaries that the Egba people were able to defeat the Dahomeans in battle at Aro in 1851.[74]

Bowen returned to the United States in 1852, married, and was again in Nigeria the following year, this time as the head of a small group of Southern Baptist missionaries. They established themselves at Ogbonoshaw (Ogbomosho), north of Abeokuta, in the heart of the Egba country. In spite of the usual deaths and difficulties, the mission survived. Bowen and his wife returned to the United States in 1856; his health was shattered, although he lived many years longer.

Bowen's work is significant in several ways to the story of U.S. relations with Africa and American interest in the continent. He was one of the foremost explorers and linguists. His researches into the Yoruba language were among the first scholarly studies of that idiom, and for a long time his Yoruba grammar and dictionary were standard works. His accounts of the interior of Nigeria gave the Western world a far more accurate description of the region and its people than had existed before.[75] As a sincere friend of the people of Nigeria, he was a bitter enemy of the slave trade, and his name appears along with those of the Church of England missionaries as witnesses to the Treaty of Abeokuta (1852) by which the local king pledged himself to abolish the traffic.[76] He tried in 1857 to get Congress to negotiate a trade treaty with the Yoruba and to support an exploration of the Niger River, and he was interested in promoting back-to-Africa schemes.[77]

Although the majority of free blacks remained opposed to colonization movements, Edward Wilmot Blyden, born in the Caribbean in 1832, became a great advocate of the return of Afro-Americans as missionaries to Africa. Blyden went to the United States in 1850 to study theology, but left for Liberia in 1851 when he could not gain admission to any American school. In Liberia he developed his theory of "providential return," arguing that slavery had been part of God's plan to prepare blacks by putting them into a higher civilization in the United States and then returning them to Africa better educated than those who had remained. According to Blyden, Afro-Americans therefore had a duty to return to Africa to teach, civilize, and Christianize their fellows.

Blyden had indeed a special part to play in history. To him the African was God's "Suffering Servant." Blyden, a "Pan-Negro Patriot" and an outstanding scholar deeply concerned with the "racial vindication" of his people and with the defense of their traditional culture, thereby bequeathed an important legacy to Africanist thought of a later period. The doctrine of the Suffering Servant later became secularized by men such as W. E. B. Du Bois, the black American scholar, a radical freethinker and finally a Marxist who believed that those who had suffered most had most to teach to their Marxist comrades.[78]

No mention has yet been made of the missionary efforts of the American Roman Catholics in West Africa. The American missionary movement of the early nineteenth century was largely Protestant; the Catholic Church was still establishing itself in the United States at the time. Nevertheless, American Catholicism was represented early in West Africa, and Catholics from the United States were among the pioneers of their faith in that area.

In 1833 the bishop of Charleston, South Carolina, suggested sending Catholic missionaries to Liberia, especially since the settlements of the Maryland Colonization Society at Cape Palmas presumably included a number of Catholic residents. Some time later Pope Gregory XVI asked the bishops of New York and Philadelphia each to designate a priest, and late in 1841 Monsignor Edward W. Barron, the vicar-general of Philadelphia, and the Reverend John Kelly of Albany, New York, accompanied by a young lay catechist, sailed for Africa. They established themselves in the Maryland colony at Cape Palmas in late January 1842. Monsignor Barron, having meanwhile been designated prefect apostolic of upper Guinea with responsibilities extending from Liberia to the Gold Coast, soon left to raise funds in the United States. He then sought additional missionaries in France, and while there was promoted to bishop and had his mission raised to the status of a vicariate apostolic.

When he returned to Africa he found disaster. Two of the seven French priests whom he had sent ahead were dead, as was the young lay catechist. Father Kelly, his health broken, had given up and returned to America. One by one the remaining priests were succumbing to the fever, and in 1844 Barron petitioned to be discharged from his impossible responsibilities and allowed to return to the United States. The sole survivor among the priests from France, Father J. R. Bessieux, transferred himself to Gabon, hoping—like the Protestants of the ABCFM—to escape the high death rate. There he grimly remained, and his work is considered the beginning of Roman Catholic missions in that part of Africa.[79]

It is impossible in a brief discussion to relate all of the nineteenth-century efforts for the conversion of West Africa made by Americans or sponsored in the United States. The experiences of the missionaries of the American Board of Commissioners in Liberia and of the Baptists of Nigeria, however, are illustrative of the difficulties encountered and the results achieved by the devout, hopeful, enthusiastic men and women who took it upon themselves to carry the message of Christianity to pagan Africa and who were in many parts of Africa the missionary pioneers. Since the United States did not share in the later partition of Africa and the flag of the United States was never planted over an African empire, American missionaries have not received the historical credit that is their due.

South Africa. West Africa was not the only part of the Continent in which ABCFM missionaries labored. While John Leighton Wilson was working in West Africa, another group of American missionaries was devoting itself to converting the indigenous people of South Africa. In 1832 Dr. John Philip, superintendent of the London Missionary Society's missions in South Africa, received a letter from a young American Christian enthusiast named Purney asking for information on missionary needs and conditions in the country. Purney, a student at Princeton Theological Seminary, wrote on behalf of a student organization in which he was active, the Society of Inquiry on the Subject of Missions to the Heathen.

Philip found Purney's letter awaiting him when he returned to Cape Town from a several months' tour of the London society's missions and stations on the frontiers of the colony, during which he noted vast regions and whole tribes without missionaries. It was beyond the resources of the London Missionary Society to provide people to work in such places, and Philip replied to Purney at once with a long, detailed, and informative letter. He strongly emphasized that there was a "noble field for missionary labour" among the "Zoolahs" and added that the two principal chiefs (or kings), Dingaan and Mzilikazi, were friendly and highly favorable toward having missionaries among their people.[80]

All information that the student society received was forwarded to the ABCFM, which published Philip's letter in full in the November 1833 issue of the *Missionary Herald*. In the next issue the board published a notice that "a mission [is] . . . contemplated to the Zoolahs, a populous tribe on the southeastern coast of Africa." A number of volunteers offered themselves, and on December 3, 1834, the first group of six missionaries and their wives sailed from Boston for South Africa. Included were Henry Isaac Venable, Daniel Lindley, Alexander Erwin Wilson, Aldin Grout, George Champion, and Newton Adams. Wilson and Adams, in addition to being ordained ministers, were also physicians and thus were among the first medical missionaries.

The voyage to South Africa consumed several months. After reaching Cape Town, the missionaries had to procure necessary equipment and supplies, begin the study of native languages, and complete their final preparations. More than a year thus elapsed between their departure from Boston and their arrival at their destination. In the summer of 1836 Lindley, Wilson, and Venable finally reached Mosega, far beyond the Vaal River, the outer limit of civilization at the time. Adams, Grout, and Champion established themselves in Natal, near the coast and somewhat closer to urban settlements, but still on the far frontier.

The climate of South Africa is healthful and well suited to Europeans, but the three who went beyond the Vaal were taken ill and Mrs. Wilson died shortly after they reached Mosega. The remainder of the party recovered and for weeks labored with their own hands to erect necessary buildings and to make their surroundings habitable. They were completely isolated from white civilization; everything depended entirely upon their own efforts.

They had barely completed their mission buildings when they found themselves in the midst of perils as likely to prove fatal, both to themselves and to their hopes, as the dreaded West African diseases. Their mission was directly in the path of the pastoral Boers from the Cape who were beginning to migrate northward in the "Great Trek." In September 1836, very shortly after the missionaries' arrival at Mosega, the local Ndebele warriors attacked a party of emigrants, murdering some fifteen and stealing their sheep and cattle. A few weeks later Mzilikazi attacked a second party but was repulsed with the loss of a large number of his warriors. In January 1837 a Boer commando (a fighting band of mounted burghers) retaliated, and the Americans found themselves literally in the thick of bitter fighting. At this time the Boers often regarded the Ndebele somewhat the way their contemporaries on the American frontier regarded Indians – as dangerous foes to be exterminated as quickly and ruthlessly as possible. Although the Americans almost miraculously escaped harm in the battle that took place around their mission, the mission building was riddled by bullets and *assagais* (short spears), and they decided to return to the coast under protection of the Boers: The danger was very great that the Africans might fail to distinguish between friends and foes and might regard any white as an enemy.

Wilson wrote on April 17, 1837:

> Early in the morning [January 17] I was awakened by the firing of guns; I arose and . . . saw the farmers on horseback, pursuing and shooting the natives, who were flying in every direction. As soon as they had finished the work of destruction at the village near us, the commander [probably Andries Hendrik Potgieter] rode to the house and assured us that they intended no harm against us or our property, and invited us to leave the country with them, as they thought it would not be safe for us to stay behind . . . It now became a question with us, what was the path of duty . . . There was some reason that Moselekatsi and his people would no longer regard us as their friends. Even if there has been no reason to think thus, yet it was plain that our field of labor was destroyed . . .
>
> This emigration of the farmers from the colony, is going to form a new era in the history of the native tribes beyond the colony . . . We are now on our way to join our brethren in the country of Dingaan. We have our fears, that the farmers and Dingaan will come into conflict in a few years.[81]

At the coast, Wilson, Venable, and Lindley joined the Americans who had remained in Natal working among the coastal Zulus. Champion, Grout, and Adams appeared to be making progress. They had readily obtained the consent of Dingaan to the establishment of a mission, and they had opened a school, made a considerable number of converts, and commenced the publication of textbooks and religious works in the Zulu language. But the fears Wilson had expressed about Dingaan's future actions were well founded. Land-hungry Boer farmers from the

Cape were moving into Natal in large numbers. Dingaan became fearful for the freedom of his domain and his people and decided to end the danger once and for all by the complete extermination of the unwelcome immigrants. Early in June 1837 Champion noted in his journal that the Zulus were preparing for war. An immigrant party headed by Piet Retief, a noted Boer leader, entered Dingaan's domain in January 1838 and endeavored to negotiate for lands and permission to settle. The negotiations seemed to be proceeding smoothly, but Dingaan was merely biding his time. On February 6 he invited Retief to a conference at the royal *kraal*. Retief and his group entered unarmed, according to custom, and at a signal from Dingaan the entire Boer party, about sixty in number, was set upon and murdered. In the next few days hundreds of Boer settlers all over Natal died under the war clubs and *assagais* of the Zulu warriors.

Dingaan sent messengers to the missionaries, English and American, to assure them of his friendship and protection, but in the existing horrors they could not feel safe. His benevolence did not extend to their African converts, many of them from other tribes for whom the Zulus felt contempt. They were slaughtered like cattle, and there was always the grim possibility that the king might not be able to control his warriors. The missionaries thus decided to leave the country, and after a difficult journey they finally reached Port Natal and took refuge on board a British ship. Lindley remained behind for a time to keep in touch with the situation, but even he at last decided to leave.[82]

Dingaan's power was crushed and the massacre of Retief's party avenged, but the battle put an effective stop to all missionary effort in Natal. The ABCFM decided to discontinue its missions, and the American missionaries were authorized to return to the United States. Lindley and Adams, however, elected to remain. Even before the outbreak of the war with Dingaan, Lindley had grown friendly with the simple, hardworking Boer farmers who were migrating to Natal from the Cape in large numbers. They were without a minister, and Lindley, finding that the theology of the Dutch Reformed Church was essentially the same as that of his own church, agreed to be their pastor. For several years he traveled among them summer and winter, wherever his services were needed. When the British authorities and the migrating Boers came to blows in the early 1840s he stuck to his post, serving the British prisoners of war as well as his Boers. He also stood up for the rights of the conquered Zulus against his Boer parishioners. He was so trusted that in 1847, after Great Britain annexed Natal, he was placed on the official payroll as a government missionary, an appointment that continued after the ABCFM resumed its South African efforts and Lindley reentered its service.

Religion was not the only field in which the American missionaries were active. The Dutch farmers migrating into Natal found a need for some form of government, and with their tradition of democracy and independence, a republican government was inevitable. Little disorder was associated with the establishment of a republic with an elected assembly, the *Volksraad*. Its administration was weak at first and had to struggle to establish its authority.

> By the end of 1840 [the *Volksraad*] was finding its feet. Helped doubtless by the gift of a copy of the United States Constitution from one of the American missionaries, it had developed its procedure by trial and error,

fixed a reasonable franchise, regularized candidature and election, done something to instill a sense of duty into its officials, and even checked the vagaries of public meetings and petitions.[83]

Dr. Newton Adams, like Lindley, gained the trust of the people with whom he came into contact, though he was unsympathetic toward the Zulus. In 1847 he was named mediator on a commission to supervise the apportionment of land in Natal. Because there was a conflict among others on the commission, the governor, to redress the balance, named Lindley a member as well, "no doubt because of his known fairmindedness and also, possibly because he was *persona grata* with the Boers and familiar with their views."[84]

A major problem faced by both the short-lived Republic of Natal and the succeeding British colonial regime was that of coexisting with the Zulus while simultaneously rendering them incapable of future warfare. The solution reached, largely as a result of the land commission's labors, was the establishment of a series of "locations" similar to the Indian reservations then being established in various parts of the United States. This seemed to be a fair and humane solution to people of that period, and it appealed especially to missionaries (including the Americans) because the Zulus—whose numbers were increased daily by immigrants from across the Tugela River—could in this way be protected from the real or supposed rapacity of settlers and traders and more of them would be available to be taught.[85] It is not unreasonable to suppose, although this is conjectural, that Adams and Lindley, who were members of the land commission and had some knowledge of Indian affairs in the United States, may have influenced the decision. It is possible, too, that Aldin Grout, who had a considerable influence among the Boers, may have suggested locations to the people of Natal as a humane means of solving the problem. Lindley returned to the Zulu mission field in 1846 and worked as an American missionary until he retired in 1873.

Since the missionaries' major work lay among peoples with whom they could communicate only by learning the local idioms, language study was an important part of their program. James C. Bryant and Lewis Grout, both of whom arrived in 1846, distinguished themselves as linguists and contributed considerably to the study of South African linguistics. Bryant picked up the local idiom so quickly that he was able to deliver a sermon in Zulu only ten weeks after his arrival; eighteen months later he wrote an article on the Zulu language that is still considered accurate.[86]

Unfortunately, Bryant contracted tuberculosis; it was aggravated by exposure to the weather, and he died only two years after reaching the mission. During the last few months of his life, unable to preach or to perform the usual duties of a minister, he devoted himself to linguistic studies and to translating and writing. Lewis Grout collaborated with him. "James [Bryant] taught him all that he knew and had the comforting realization that . . . Lewis Grout would continue with the translation of the Bible into Zulu and with the provision of lesson-helps and textbooks."[87]

To the early missionaries the world owes most of its knowledge of the cultures of the places and the regions in which they worked. They were not conscious or intentional anthropologists; they observed tribal customs, practices, and mores not so much for the sake of information as for evidence of the presence of what they felt to be evil – what they proposed to attack and destroy. Their observations were often biased, but in many instances their reports afford the only knowledge available today of tribal life in Africa before the indigenous cultures were sharply modified by the onset of European civilization.

CHAPTER 8

Explorers and frontiersmen

The American frontier has exercised unending fascination on the world at large. Eighteenth-century philosophers idealized the trappers and woodsmen as noble savages in the wilderness. Nineteenth-century theoreticians considered the frontier a foundation of American democracy, a faraway land where even the poorest might achieve both prosperity and social esteem. Twentieth-century moviegoers and television viewers have accepted the frontier as a dreamland of heroic virtue. The real frontier, of course, in no wise resembled the poet's creations; it did, however, develop a multiplicity of skills that could be put to use in many backward regions of the world. At the same time the frontier provided a large number of opportunities for men and women anxious to seek their luck in regions far from the land of their birth. The frontier, of course, was not a rigidly fixed geographical entity. Soldiers of fortune might take part in an Indian war and later enlist in some irregular formation raised to fight an African war somewhere in the Cape. There was likewise an informal international of gold prospectors, hard-bitten men who would attempt to make their fortune in areas as far afield as California, Australia, and Rhodesia.

Among American military men who put on foreign uniforms must be included the score or more of young men numbered in the garrisons of Mozambique and in the Portuguese captaincies in East Africa in the 1790s. They may have been fugitives from justice or they may have been sailors or farm boys from New England impelled by romantic dreams, but there they were – Americans in the Portuguese army in Africa, and explorers as well.[1]

One of the first was John Ledyard of Groton, Connecticut. Born in 1751, he received the usual New England grammar school education and for a time studied law, but found it uninteresting. He next entered Dartmouth College with a view to becoming a missionary among the Indians, but this dream soon palled, and he shipped before the mast on a voyage to Europe. At Gibralter he jumped ship and enlisted in the British army. The military authorities returned him to his ship; he made a brief visit home; and he then went to London in 1776 and offered himself to Captain James Cook, who was assembling a crew for his third voyage of exploration. Cook was evidently impressed favorably: The young Yankee was enlisted for the voyage as a corporal in the Royal Marines. He was captivated by the unknown wilderness that Cook's ship touched, especially by the possibilities of what is now called the Pacific Northwest. A few years later he took a walking trip across Europe and through Siberia to the Pacific, traveling without permission of the Russian government. He got as far as Irkutsk in Siberia (and was undoubtedly the first American to penetrate that part of Asia), where he was caught and summarily expelled from Russia with a warning not to come back.

Ledyard had attracted the attention of Sir Joseph Banks, the president of the Royal Society and one of the moving spirits in a new Association for Promoting the Discovery of the Interior Parts of Africa, founded in 1788. Arriving in London from his Siberian misadventure, Ledyard went immediately to Banks, who felt him to be the man needed on an expedition to discover the source, course, and mouth of the Niger. Asked when he could start, Ledyard replied, "Tomorrow morning." He did not get further than Cairo, where he contracted a fatal disease and died before his trip was fairly under way. The information he transmitted before his death nevertheless was considered invaluable, and his reports on Egypt were models of what the association wanted. Behind the facade of impulsiveness he had planned coolly and carefully, leaving nothing foreseeable to chance. His death in January 1789 was a great loss to African exploration.[2]

Another American who threw some light on Africa was Archibald Robbins, even though he never entered the regions south of the Sahara. A native of Connecticut, Robbins passed a considerable part of the War of 1812 as a prisoner of war. In 1815 he sailed on the brig *Commerce* for a voyage to Gibraltar. The vessel was wrecked in September of that year near Cape Barbas, in what is now Rio de Oro, and the survivors were captured and enslaved by the desert Arabs. Robbins spent three years in slavery, accompanying his nomadic master over a wide area of northwestern Africa. He was a careful observer, and his narrative of these travels is one of the earliest firsthand accounts of a region that is still little known.[3]

The mystery of the vast interior of Africa fascinated many people. Even the scholarly Jared Sparks—clergyman, educator, chaplain of the U.S. Senate, and idolatrous biographer of George Washington—in his youth caught the fever. He visualized himself as an African explorer crossing the great desert, going from "Tombucto" to the mouth of the Niger, "wherever it may be," and to other unknown parts of the continent.[4]

Nothing ever came of Sparks's plan—it was a romantic dream—but it revealed both the ignorance of Africa among educated people and the extent to which Africa had excited the curiosity of Europe and America. As the nineteenth century unfolded, the fog of ignorance and myth that blanketed the continent was gradually dispelled by explorers and adventurers of many nations. Their accomplishment was not an easy one. A major obstacle to investigation of the African interior was the determination of many of the coastal peoples that no European should pass through their territories. The Africans of the seacoast were middlemen between the white traders and the people of the interior; they effectively controlled the highly lucrative traffic in slaves, ivory, gold dust, and other products that came from deep in the continent. The coastal tribes feared that if Europeans succeeded in getting to the interior, their own position would be lost and their monopoly destroyed.

John Leighton Wilson and his fellow missionaries repeatedly informed the American board that Africans had refused to let them pass, using every expedient possible to block the way from the coast. Paul du Chaillu (discussed shortly) at the start of his explorations found that his boyhood friends at the mouth of the Gabon were determined to dissuade him from going inland.[5] It was not until Africans learned to fear the white man's weapons and power that the rivers and trails into the heart of the continent were opened to the explorer.[6] This is not to say that the European and American punitive forces that landed from time to time at different places on the African coast came for the explicit purpose of making the country safe for explorers; such expeditions had other and more immediate missions. But opening the gates to the interior was an accidental by-product of military punishment and conquest. And even though the United States never held any ambitions toward an African empire, the protection of American interests led to punitive measures on several occasions.

When Commodore Matthew C. Perry arrived on the West African coast in 1842 with the first U.S. squadron to be stationed permanently in African waters under the recent Webster–Ashburton Treaty with Great Britain, one of his first concerns was to look into cases of outrage and violence against American traders. The crew of an American vessel, the *Mary Carver,* had been massacred at Berribe on the Ivory Coast. At a village called Fishtown, two men from the schooner *Edward Burley* had been killed and Captain J. R. Brown of the bark *Atlanta* had been viciously attacked. The people of Fishtown were also boycotting all American traders and threatening to attack the nearby settlements of the Maryland Colonization Society at Cape Palmas.

Perry acted promptly. A landing force from his ships destroyed Berribe, killing the local king and several of his warriors during the fighting. At Fishtown, with his ships' guns trained threateningly on the settlement, Perry went ashore with such a display of pomp and power that there was no resistance. A brief investigation exonerated the tribesmen for killing two sailors from the *Edward Burley;* it was found that the Americans had started the trouble. But for boycotting Americans and threatening the American settlements, Perry exacted a penalty: He compelled the tribesmen to evacuate the town and move inland from the coast, and he then burned the town.

Perry's measures were ruthless, but they ended the boycott, secured the Maryland settlements, and left whites safe on that part of the African coast for a long time to come.[7] Other nations and other navies also took sharp action on the African coast from time to time until whites were no longer stopped just beyond the high-tide mark by Africans guarding their monopolies.

American adventurers, explorers, and missionaries were among those who took advantage of the new possibilities, and among the most notable was Paul Belloni du Chaillu. As his name indicates, he was of French blood and birth, the descendant of a long line of Huguenots. Because his father was connected with a French commercial house having extensive African interests, du Chaillu spent several of his early years in Africa at his father's trading post on the Gabon River. He migrated to Philadelphia in the early 1850s, became a naturalized citizen, and throughout his adult life and career continued to regard himself as an American. Sponsored by the Philadelphia Academy of Science, he returned to Africa in 1855 for the express purpose of scientific exploration in an area that was still terra incognita to the world at large.

Du Chaillu based himself in Gabon, where he had lived as a youth. "My arrival," he reported, "was hailed with joy by my former acquaintances, who thought I had come back to trade." On being assured that he did not intend to trade, his Mpongwe friends were puzzled and became alarmed lest he should "secretly try to wrest the trade of the interior out of their hands."[8] Welcomed by the American missionaries in Gabon, he acclimatized himself and assembled the stores and equipment he would need.

The American missionaries who began work in the Gabon estuary in 1842 made numerous short exploring trips into the hinterland. Their most dramatic exploit was the first reconnaissance of the Ogowe River by literate observers. Deciding to investigate African reports on the then mysterious Ogowe, the evangelists were seeking possible station sites and a river route to the interior. The Reverend William Walker and his colleague, Ira Preston, secured permission from a local ruler to ascend the mouth of the river in September 1854, and they went by canoe to Orovy, about eighty miles inland, in three days. Here they were prevented from going further, probably because the riverine people feared a breach in their middleman system of controlling trade with the interior. The Americans then returned to Gabon and made a report that remains an important source for the history of the area. Walker and Preston were never recognized for their pioneering venture: The French officers who steamed up the Ogowe in 1862 successfully claimed credit for discovering new regions (it is possible that they were unaware of their American predecessors), and later writers ignored the missionary journey.[9]

With his boyhood knowledge of Africa reinforced by information obtained from the missionaries, du Chaillu spent several years systematically exploring and collecting specimens of the flora and fauna found on both sides of the Gabon and deep in the unknown interior. When his reports were published, the detail that made him both famous and controversial was his assertion that somewhere in the tropical forest was a species of giant ape—gorillas. He had collected an impressive amount of evidence but had been unable to obtain a specimen.

Du Chaillu was greeted with disbelief, almost by hoots and jeers, by savants who had never been in Africa. Many naturalists and biologists asserted vehemently that no such creature existed outside du Chaillu's imagination, even though John Leighton Wilson had forwarded convincing evidence in previous reports and several skeletons and pelts had been sent to Europe by others. As for du Chaillu's geographical observations, the German explorer Heinrich Barth, who had not been in the part of Africa du Chaillu traversed, gravely asserted that du Chaillu's map was the product of a mind deranged by fever; mountains could not possibly exist nor rivers flow where they were shown.[10]

Du Chaillu led a second expedition into Africa in 1863, and this time he brought back evidence of the gorilla that could not be controverted. This was fortunate, for on the second trip he made a discovery even more startling and unbelievable than that of the giant ape: Deep in the tropical forest dwelt a race of pygmies, tiny human beings whose very existence was previously unsuspected by the literate world.[11] Although there were references to pygmies in a number of ancient Egyptian documents and in Herodotus, such people were thought to be purely mythical. By the time du Chaillu announced his discovery, however, the world had become accustomed to the idea that Africa hid unbelievable marvels. His veracity was no longer questioned.

The discoveries of the gorilla and the pygmies were enough in themselves to place du Chaillu in the forefront of scientists and explorers. Unfortunately for his later fame, his accomplishments were soon to be overshadowed by the more spectacular and more widely publicized achievements of another explorer, Henry M. Stanley. But it was du Chaillu who had pioneered in the opening of equatorial Africa.

Du Chaillu was a good friend of the American missionaries, especially of William Walker. He spent much time with them, both in his youth and later when he returned for his two periods of exploration in Gabon. Yet he failed to credit Walker with his exploration of the Ogowe River in 1854, claiming that he himself had solved the Ogowe question. Du Chaillu's contributions were real, but his failure to admit that his theory was far from unique and his omission of the details of Walker's trip seem to have been deliberate and malicious. Du Chaillu did explore much unknown territory, and he often made accurate observations of peoples and places, but he was prone to sensationalism over such matters as cannibalism among the Fang or the number and ferocity of the gorillas he shot. Later observers, while noting the value of du Chaillu's work, delighted in pointing out his exaggerations. Yet despite his limitations, du Chaillu deserves great recognition for his pioneering explorations of some very difficult terrain.

The Civil War in the United States marks a dividing line in many phases of American life, and nowhere is the division more conspicuous and significant than in American relations with Africa. By the destruction of the major slavery stronghold in the Western world, the war virtually ended American participation in the slave trade. With emancipation, and with the opening of a greater degree of opportunity for blacks than they had ever had before in the United States, schemes for migration and colonization temporarily declined. For a variety of reasons, direct U.S. trade with Africa – except for South Africa – also diminished almost to the vanishing point. The American merchant marine to all intents and purposes disappeared from the sea. The nation turned its attention increasingly to the vast and undeveloped regions of its own continent, leaving Africa to the Europeans. Africa was carved up and divided among the powers of Europe; the American flag was never officially hoisted over a single port or stretch of beach.

Nevertheless, during the first half of the nineteenth century the impact of the United States upon Africa was significant. Vast regions of Africa became aware of the products from the West because of the commercial activities of American traders. American missionaries were among the pioneers in the effort to bring Christianity to Africans in Liberia, Gabon, and South Africa. Adventurous American explorers and scientists were among the first to investigate the mysteries of the African interior. Further, the fear of possible American encroachment in Africa and jealousy of the success of the American traders in Africa may have contributed momentum to the annexation of African territories by imperialistic European powers.

U.S. interest in Africa did not end after the Civil War, however. Missionaries continued with their work, and there were Americans who were fascinated by the lure of the unknown or by the promise of opportunities denied them in North America. American interest in Africa in the latter part of the nineteenth century was quiescent rather than dead. It was merely waiting to be aroused by the exploits of Stanley and by the discovery of gold, copper, diamonds, and products unknown to the shipmasters and traders of an earlier age.

III

The United States and Africa, 1865–1900

The Senate, Monrovia, Liberia. Courtesy Library of Congress.

Bishop Hartzell and ministers, Monrovia, Liberia. Courtesy Library of Congress.

CHAPTER 9

The vanishing flag

In West Africa, as in other parts of the continent, the era following the U.S. Civil War saw American trade decline almost to the vanishing point. At the outbreak of the war, however, American traders were conspicuous in the area from Senegal to Angola; the U.S. flag floated over scores of small craft anchored off many African villages and in rivers, inlets, and tidal estuaries along thousands of miles of coastline. A network of consuls, vice-consuls, and consular and commercial agents along the coast fostered U.S. interests and watched over U.S. trade.

In the early 1890s, in contrast, a report by the British consul general at Tangier showed not a single American ship among more than a thousand vessels entering that port during a specific period.[1] The organization used by the State Department to safeguard and extend U.S. commerce in Africa nevertheless remained virtually intact. It included seven paid consuls and a score or more of honorary consular agents. But the pay of the honorary agents, derived from their fees, was admittedly no pay at all, and the total value of U.S. trade with tropical Africa was less than that of trade with the kingdom of Hawaii. For commercial information on Africa, the United States was almost entirely dependent upon the reports of British officials.[2]

Direct commerce between the United States and West Africa declined for the same reasons as those which caused the decay of commerce with other parts of the continent. The Civil War struck the first heavy blow against American foreign commerce. On March 1, 1862, the acting consul at Bathurst reported: "The unfortunate differences in the United States have, during the last twelve months, severely affected the importation of American goods, which has fallen off nearly one-third."[3] For four years American shops and factories devoted their major effort to war production, with very little surplus left for export. Erstwhile farmers, mechanics, and factory workers were in the trenches before Petersburg or were shouldering muskets in Tennessee or Georgia. The sailors and shipmasters who had carried the U.S. flag and American products to all parts of the world were manning the blockading fleet that strangled the South. Many of the schooners and brigs that had borne American products to the coasts of Africa sailed up and down the American coast bearing coal, hay, lumber, blankets, and barrels of beef to the blockading ships and the Union garrisons from Matamoros to the mouth of the James River.

American merchants who maintained African connections found it difficult to procure the goods their African customers wanted, and there was no immediate market in the United States for most of the products from Africa. To keep their businesses alive, U.S. merchants frequently purchased goods in Europe and transported them to Africa in British, French, or Hanseatic ships. Moreover, the Confederate cruisers that captured and destroyed large numbers of Union ships all over the world placed a direct premium upon trading under a European flag. The *Alabama* burned Yankee vessels in African waters; the *Shenandoah*, in the North Pacific, destroyed the American whaling fleet that hunted along the African coasts.

There were some exceptions. The demands of the Union armies for boots and shoes stimulated the importation of hides into the United States. Trade between the United States and South Africa, instead of declining, thus increased as a direct result of the war, and the trade in hides picked up sporadically in other African areas as well. Surprising increases occurred for short periods in the trade with Senegal and Gambia.

American foreign commerce nevertheless started on the downgrade during the Civil War, and the downward movement accelerated owing to the worldwide transition from sail to steam. Steam transportation proved to be cheaper than sail, and it had the additional advantage of regular schedules made possible by its relative independence of winds and weather. Although American trade with Africa held up fairly well during the 1870s, the appearance of European steamships on the African coast doomed the American merchant or trader who depended upon a small sailing vessel. His merchandise could not compete in price with goods brought from Europe by transportation that cost a fraction of what he had to pay. As early as 1872 there were complaints from dissatisfied customers on the Gold Coast that American goods were procurable from Europe as cheaply as from the United States.[4]

Steam navigation first affected West African trade and commerce on the Gold Coast, where steamship service was introduced in 1852. Merchants there began to deal directly with Great Britain, thus breaking the near monopoly that had been maintained for years by a handful of London firms. In 1869 a second steamship line lowered transportation costs still further, and the cutthroat competition that followed eventually froze out the Americans.[5]

The decline in U.S. trade with Africa was continued by the westward expansion of the American people in the decades following the war. Foreign commerce became a minor activity as farmers, entrepreneurs, investors, and adventurers swarmed into the economic and social vacuum of the Great Plains, the Rocky Mountains, and the Pacific Coast to develop farms, mines, industries, and transportation. For the entire period from the Civil War to the end of the century, American capital found such abundant opportunities within the boundaries of the United States that there was relatively little incentive to seek opportunities and profits overseas. It was a period of isolationism, economic as well as political and diplomatic, during which almost no serious attempt was made to regain the position that American merchants had once held in the world's commerce.

British historians have commonly linked the expansion of the Victorian empire to the triumph of free trade. Compared to French and Portuguese colonizers, the British indeed took a relatively liberal attitude toward the commerce of their foreign rivals. Yet as the British Empire extended its sway in Africa, the British often made deliberate attempts to eliminate or at least reduce American competition. On the Gold Coast, for example, the handful of American traders on the spot faced all manner of discriminatory ad valorem duties. Revision of the colony's tariff schedules in 1876 and 1877 sharply raised the duties on the two American products that were still imported into Africa in large quantities, rum and tobacco.[6]

In other parts of West Africa the picture was similar. In Sierra Leone in 1872 the duty on tobacco was raised from 1.5 pence per pound to 4.0 pence; on spirits it was increased to 2 shillings per gallon. Smuggling (to which the Americans were not averse) increased sharply but could not offset the decline in trade. Beginning in 1873, for example, U.S. purchases of raw hides, which had been the major American import from Sierra Leone, began to drop off. Within a few years American trade was no longer of great importance in the colony's economic life.[7]

In French West Africa the United States established a consulate at Gorée in 1883. Like many of the others, the consul was unsalaried and was expected to reimburse himself from the fees of his office. Any hope that this appointment might stimulate American trade with the French colonies soon disappeared, for by the early 1890s the new French tariffs (Méline tariff) and other conditions finally squeezed out the Americans. The U.S. consul at Gorée did not bother to submit an annual report, and in 1895 the State Department noted that the French and British trade with Senegal was, "for all practical purposes," the sum total of the commerce of the country. In short, U.S. trade with French West Africa had virtually ceased to exist.[8]

The story of vanishing American commerce in Angola is similar. American interests once were so extensive that U.S. merchants maintained permanent establishments at Ambriz and Luanda; however, the last U.S. consul posted at Luanda reported in 1892: "Since the closing of the United States naval store at Loanda . . . no American traders have settled in Angola; but since 1881 several American missionaries [have become] an important factor in the population."[9]

The decline of direct trade did not mean that no American goods were sold or traded to West African customers or that no African products found their way to American factories and consumers. But these items were no longer carried across the Atlantic in American vessels; in most instances they were contained in the inventories of British, French, or German traders who had supplanted the Yankees. The United States was still the world's greatest tobacco producer, and Africans consumed enormous quantities of tobacco; the production of kerosene (coal oil) was almost an American monopoly, and kerosene quickly replaced native animal and vegetable oils in the lamps and under the cooking pots of Africa. In spite of the cheapness of German gin, many Africans continued to prefer the American rum that had formed their tastes in alcohol.

But U.S. trade with Africa (South Africa excepted) remained an unimportant item in U.S. commerce during the latter years of the nineteenth century. Few American merchants or firms were sufficiently interested to try to regain the position that Americans once held in the African economy. American businessmen forgot how to conduct business in Africa and with Africans, and casual attempts to maintain customary American mercantile practices were foredoomed to failure. Not until the 1920s did America again attain a position of importance in West African commerce.

CHAPTER 10

Liberia

The lamb and the wolves

As already noted the Civil War marks a dividing point in nearly all aspects of U.S. history and development. Afro-American relationships were no exception, and nowhere was the change more distinct than in the relations between the United States and its African protégé, Liberia. Although the United States had actually fathered the African republic and maintained an informal protectorate over it, no formal diplomatic recognition had ever been extended to the new state. Recognition would have entailed the presence of Liberian diplomats in Washington and Liberian consuls in the nation's major ports. That black diplomats, some of whom might have been former slaves, should rub shoulders with slave-owning aristocrats seemed unthinkable to the American establishment of that period. But, as noted in Chapter 7, Congress in June 1862 finally approved recognition of Liberia and Haiti, and John Seys, the former Methodist missionary, went to Monrovia as U.S. consul.

Intergovernmental matters that marked the first years of formal diplomatic relations between Liberia and the United States included the arrangement of a postal convention and supervision of the immigrants who continued to reach Liberia from the United States in small numbers. The U.S. government still furnished their transportation and supplies for the voyage to Africa, and the U.S. minister's major activities seem to have been caring for them after their arrival and watching out for the interests of the government he represented.[1] Seys resigned in 1870 at the age of seventy-one, after a lifetime spent in the service of his church and his adopted country; he died in 1872.

Numerous Americans showed a personal interest in the black republic during the time when Seys represented the United States in Liberia. One of these was Benjamin J. K. Anderson, a young Americo-Liberian surveyor who volunteered his services when Liberia's president, D. B. Warner, expressed a desire to learn more about the regions that abutted on the country. With the financing of two New York philanthropists, Henry M. Schieffelin and Caleb Swan, Anderson left Monrovia on February 14, 1868, accompanied only by a few carriers and canoemen, his mission to penetrate the interior and, if feasible, to visit Musardu, the so-called capital of the western Mandingoes.

Anderson was alone because Liberians other than his canoemen and carriers, terrified by tales of the dangers and of the cruelties of the Mandingoes, refused to join him. He reached Musardu ten months later on December 7, after repeated delays caused by desertions among his carriers and by continuous attempts to make him turn back. His life was threatened more than once. By a combination of tact, determination, and an occasional threat to use firearms if necessary, he won his way through and could claim to be the first outsider to see the forbidden city of the western Mandingoes. He returned to Monrovia in March 1869, thirteen months after starting on his journey.

Anderson's exploration of the Mandingo country was nearly contemporaneous with Henry M. Stanley's more spectacular achievements in the Congo; it was not widely publicized at the time and has since been almost forgotten. Nevertheless, Anderson gave the Western world its first knowledge of a part of Africa never before penetrated by Western man. The tribesmen of the territory he traversed always called him an American and he frequently referred to himself as such, although he was a Liberian citizen. His account of the journey – modest, clear, and concise – was sufficiently important to warrant distribution by the Smithsonian Institution, with a preface written by its secretary, Joseph Henry.[2]

Seys was succeeded as minister and consul by general J. Milton Turner, who represented the United States in Liberia until 1878. In his reports to Washington, Turner continually urged closer commercial relations, in the interests of the United States and its businesspeople and in those of Liberia itself. He transmitted detailed information, gained at first hand, on the soil, climate, resources, geography, and ethnology of Liberia. Late in his tour of duty he sent Washington a careful study of the coffee-growing potential of the area, urging that the crop's cultivation in Liberia would benefit his own coffee-drinking nation and would also solve Liberia's economic difficulties.[3]

During Turner's time in Liberia numerous Americans still visualized Africa as a refuge for blacks from the United States. On February 15, 1878, Turner reported that the American bark *Liberia* had just reached Monrovia with fifty-three immigrants, most of them from North Carolina and Mississippi, along with two "commissioners of emigration" prospecting for homes for blacks from Arkansas.[4] Neither Turner nor any of his successors, however, seem to have found it necessary to give much time to problems arising from this migration of black Americans. Blacks in general had shown little interest in returning to the land of their ancestors, and emancipation had effectively killed whatever may have existed.

Other matters claiming Turner's attention were of direct interest to the U.S. government in its capacity of informal sponsor and protector of Liberia. In a dispatch of October 25, 1871, shortly after he had presented his credentials, Turner reported that the administration had been overthrown by a revolution.[5] The revolution was bloodless, but it indicated a problem that would beset Liberia off and on for many years: the instability of the government because of the country's economic weakness. Of more immediate and pressing interest was the relationship of the Liberians to the indigenous people, who regarded them with dislike and suspicion, as though they were white.

The Africans were bitterly resentful of all attempts at control by Liberian authorities, and Americo-Liberians looked on the indigenous people with contempt. Trouble broke out in September 1875 when the Grebos, who numbered nearly thirty thousand, revolted and formally declared war on the Liberian government. On September 13 Turner notified Washington that the Grebos – well supplied with Snyder rifles and ammunition (of French manufacture) and in some cases thought to have received military training at the Episcopal mission schools in their country – had attacked the settlement at Cape Palmas. The attack was repulsed only because the Liberians were able to muster the needed artillery.[6]

Turner's messages took more than a month to reach Washington from Monrovia, but Secretary of State Hamilton Fish reacted promptly to their urgency. A U.S. warship was ordered to Cape Palmas because it was "understood that some American citizens were located there." The ship's arrival enhanced the prestige of the Liberian government; the Grebos fully understood the threat in its marines and guns; and the rebellion died out, leaving the Liberians firmly in possession of Cape Palmas and the Grebos reluctantly acknowledging their authority.[7] Liberian political instability continued, however. In January 1878, for example, Turner reported that the president and several members of the cabinet had been impeached and that a former president's son had been arraigned for conspiring to assassinate certain members of the Congress. But in spite of intense feelings and animosities, Liberian political disorders seldom became extreme: A new administration took office quietly, and the would-be assassin, on being convicted, was fined $100.[8]

Liberia lay well outside the mainstream of world politics during the 1870s, but the little country was hurled violently into the current when the Great Powers began their scramble for African territory in the 1880s. France, endeavoring to regain the world position it seemed to have lost in 1871, was vigorously expanding its African empire – and French territory was adjacent to Liberia.

The first indications of a movement that would cause trouble for Liberia and diplomatic complications for the United States appeared in an incident that did not immediately concern either country. In 1880, almost two years after the fact, Minister John H. Smyth, Turner's successor, reported that French troops had landed in March 1878 on the island of Matacong, about twelve miles off the mouth of the Mellacourie River. The governor of Sierra Leone protested at once, as Great Britain claimed the island and had recently begun to collect customs duties there. But the French were actively extending their African empire in the region in which Liberia lay and were even willing to take the chance of offending Great Britain in realizing their colonial ambitions.[9]

A short time later Smyth was informed by the Liberian secretary of state that France desired to assume a protectorate over Liberia. "As evidence of this," the U.S. official wrote, "a dispatch was shown to me from the Liberian consul-general [Leopold Carrance, at Bordeaux], addressed to the secretary, in which a protectorate was proposed and urged by that officer, who indicates the advantages to accrue to Liberia from such a relation with France."[10] The acting secretary of State, William Hunter, on receipt of Smyth's dispatch, directed the U.S. minister in Paris to make "judicious and confidential inquiries." Minister Edward F. Noyes replied six weeks later that the French government had no desire to assume a protectorate over Liberia. The proposal had originated with Carrance himself and was probably seconded by M. Huart, the Liberian consul in Paris, both of whom had special interests. Huart, in fact, had spent most of his time and effort in trying to persuade the Liberian government to institute a decoration for which he would be eligible.[11]

Smyth later reported the arrival at Monrovia of the French man-of-war *Talisman*, with orders to salute the Liberian flag and carry out any mission that the president of Liberia might indicate, a gesture obviously intended to set Liberian fears and suspicions at rest. At Monrovia, Smyth remained deeply suspicious of

French motives. He reported the details of a proposed mining concession that was being promoted by Huart in Paris, a concession that would have granted complete control over all mines and mineral resources in Liberia for a period of fifty years. Smyth openly expressed the belief that Liberia was a most desirable annexation for any nation hunting for African possessions.[12]

Liberian affairs – and American involvement with them – were further complicated in the fall of 1879 when the Grebos, still chafing under the authority of the Americo-Liberians, again revolted, this time proclaiming themselves British subjects. Any hopes of British intervention they may have had were not fulfilled. Firm measures taken by the Liberian government, supported by two U.S. warships, soon squashed the movement. The Grebo chiefs complained that they were "menaced" aboard the *Essex* and were threatened by the arrival of the *Ticonderoga,* but they yielded.

In their relations with Liberia, the European powers tacitly recognized the special position of the United States. The commanding officer of the French warship *Talisman,* for example, upon arriving at Monrovia after the flurry over a French protectorate, first called on the U.S. minister and requested him to arrange an audience with the president. Similarly, in December 1879 Captain Doerman of the Royal Netherlands Navy sought Smyth's good offices when he brought his ship, the *Alkmaar,* to Monrovia. Smyth accompanied Doerman to his interview with the president and seconded the Dutchman's suggestion that it would be desirable to open additional Liberian ports to trade.[13]

The U.S. minister at Monrovia seemed to acquire an international position, frequently representing the United States, Liberia, and some third power simultaneously. Early in 1881, when a German merchant ship, the *Carlos,* struck an uncharted rock on the Kru coast and sank, the officers and crew escaped in the ship's boats but were attacked, beaten, and robbed by the Krumen. The German minister in Washington informed Secretary of State William N. Evarts that the German imperial government was sending the corvette *Victoria* to Liberia to help the authorities punish the looters in "the general interest of all commercial nations." The German government requested that the U.S. minister at Monrovia be informed of the German ship's mission and be instructed to render any possible assistance. Evarts directed Smyth to do what he could. It was understood, Evarts wrote, that the Krumen were not pirates but "wreckers," outlaws over whom the Liberian government had no effective control, and the United States presumed that Liberia would be glad to avail itself of German assistance.[14] Had the case involved an American ship and crew, the United States would have considered it proper for Liberia to request such aid as Germany was offering.

Smyth had already acted on his own initiative. The German consul at Monrovia had formally protested to the Liberian government, but the latter was unable to take effective punitive measures against the tribesmen. The *Victoria* reached Monrovia on February 26, 1881; Commander von Valois called immediately at the American legation to pay his respects and, on orders from Berlin, to request the U.S. minister's aid. No available records indicate Smyth's advice to Liberian officials, but Liberia's president, A. W. Gardiner, and Secretary of State Edward W. Blyden agreed at once to pay a moderate indemnity of $3,500 and to accompany von Valois to the scene of the crime. After a brief investigation the president ordered the guilty village evacuated, and the *Victoria* then shelled it. The destruction was completed by a landing party from the corvette, accompanied by a Liberian officer.[15] Late in 1881 the *Victoria* again came to Monrovia, because Liberia had failed to pay the indemnity; on November 10 Smyth informed Washington that von Valois, having received $5,375, which the Liberian government had somehow managed to scrape together to pay the fine and the penalty for the delay, had finally sailed for the Cape Verde Islands.[16]

When the Great Powers of Europe were building their empires in Africa (see Map 2), Great Britain and France seemed to pose the main threats to Liberian territory. The boundaries between Liberia and Sierra Leone were vague, both countries claiming certain areas, and by 1866 the expansionists of Sierra Leone demanded regions to which Liberia had acquired rights as far back as 1852. In addition, some of the tribes in the areas bordering on Sierra Leone unfortunately were beyond the control of the Liberian government, and British traders resented any attempts by the government to enforce its laws. The two African countries agreed upon an international boundary commission with an American, Commodore R. W. Shufeldt, as arbitrator. It was first scheduled to meet in the early fall of 1878, but Liberia failed to appoint its members in time; when the commissioners finally got together in the spring of 1879, they found themselves unable to agree. The British commissioners denied being bound by the decisions of the American arbitrator, and the commission broke up without accomplishing anything.[17]

The disputed boundary had been unsettled for several years when suddenly, on March 20, 1882, a flotilla of British gunboats appeared without warning at Monrovia. Sir Arthur Havelock, governor of Sierra Leone, was aboard the flagship and served what amounted to an ultimatum upon the Liberian government: British claims to territory up to the River Maffa must be acknowledged immediately and an indemnity of £8,500 be paid to certain British traders for injuries inflicted upon them in 1871 by tribes in the territory being claimed by Great Britain.[18]

The United States took such diplomatic action as was possible to aid Liberia. The difficulty lay in the fact that British expansionists were ready to use force; the United States was not. President Chester A. Arthur informed the U.S. Congress that the government had "endeavored to aid Liberia in its differences with Great Britain touching the northwestern boundary of that country," using the services of its ministers at London and Monrovia, and added that the prospect was good for a compromise by which Liberia would not lose any territory.[19] Nevertheless, Sir Arthur Havelock returned to Monrovia with his gunboats in September, demanding immediate ratification of the treaty that he had dictated earlier in the year. The Liberian Senate refused, and a few months later British troops from Sierra Leone marched into the disputed territory. Recognizing the futility of further resistance to the British colossus, Liberia finally acknowledged British claims by a treaty signed in London on November 11, 1885.[20] The area has been part of Sierra Leone ever since.

For a few years Liberia ceased to be the focus of American diplomatic interest in Africa, but in the mid-1880s the calm was shattered. French empire builders could no longer be restrained. Early in December 1886 Smyth sent a dispatch to Washington saying that Lieutenant P. Aroux of the French gunboat *Gabes* had paid a courtesy call on the president a few days earlier. During the conversation it was

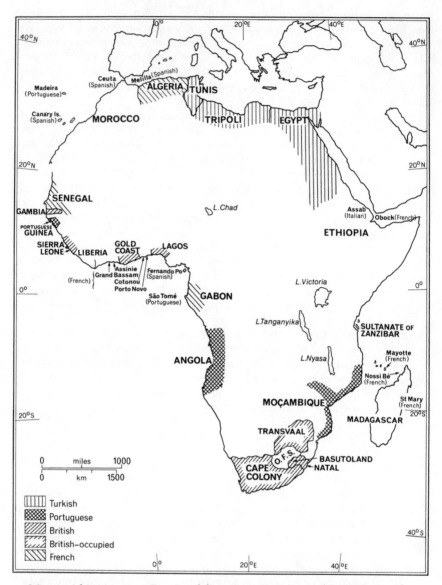

Map 2. Africa in 1879. Reprinted from Peter Duignan and L. H. Gann, eds., *The Economics of Colonialism*, vol. 4 of *Colonialism in Africa, 1870–1960* (Cambridge: Cambridge University Press, 1975).

learned that the *Gabes* had anchored for several days at Berribe before coming to Monrovia. But Smyth heard from the agent of the German trading firm of A. Woermann that Aroux failed to mention a treaty he had negotiated with the Africans at Berribe, which lay some distance east of Cape Palmas and in territory that was clearly and unmistakably Liberian. Smyth reminded the State Department of Carrance's attempt to bring about a French protectorate over Liberia; he also mentioned that in 1884 a French firm had leased Kent Island in the River Mana without any reference to the Liberian government, dealing with the islanders as though they were an independent people. When the United States brought the Kent Island matter to the attention of the French government, the latter disallowed the lease, but such precedents left Smyth suspicious of all French activities. He urged an investigation of Aroux and any treaties with which he was involved.[21]

The secretary of state at once directed the minister at Paris to ask the French foreign office whether there was "any foundation for the report that France [had] assumed to treat with Liberian tribes as independent."[22] It became apparent not only that France was treating with the tribes as independent, but that French policy and ambition in the region included encroaching upon territory supposed to be a part of Liberia. Information reached Washington in July 1886 that another French naval officer, Captain E. Dumont of the *Voltigeur*, had been ordered to Berribe by his government with directions to "protect" the people there. In response to inquiries, the French foreign office was polite but unyielding, maintaining that France was undertaking no aggression against Liberia, entertained no designs upon Liberian territory, and was merely claiming what belonged to it by "the ties, already old, which unite to France the populations of Grand and Petit Beriby."[23]

The U.S. minister at Paris, Robert M. McLane, was shown a treaty negotiated in 1868 by a Lieutenant Crespin of the French navy, a treaty that, it was asserted, gave France a paramount and incontestable right to the territories it was claiming. In the treaty three of the local potentates – Mané, "King of Little Beriby," Damba-Gué, "King of Grand Beriby," and Rika, "King of Basha and Bassa-Wappoo" – had agreed to full French sovereignty over their territories and had conceded to France the right to erect fortifications and build naval bases. They had further agreed never to make treaties with other countries without French permission.[24]

The diplomatic interchange between Washington and Paris continued for months. Secretary of State Thomas F. Bayard pointed out that Liberian title to the lands in question was based on purchases made by the American Colonization Society in 1846. When Liberia became an independent state, he added, the society had reserved ownership of every other square mile of the country for future immigrants from the United States; in other words, half the disputed territory was legally owned by U.S. citizens.

President Grover Cleveland, in his annual message to Congress on December 6, 1886, remarked upon the affair:

> The weakness of Liberia and the difficulty of maintaining effective sovereignty over its outlying districts, have exposed that republic to encroachment. It cannot be forgotten that this distant community is an offshoot of our own system, owing its origin to the associated benevolence of American citizens ... Although a formal protectorate over Liberia is contrary to our

traditional policy, the moral right and duty of the United States to assist in all proper ways the maintenance of its integrity is obvious, and has been consistently announced during nearly half a century.[25]

Unhappily for Liberia, the significant word in President Cleveland's remarks was "distant." The American people could not become passionately interested in the fate of a small country on the other wide of the world. The United States, moreover, for all its impressive size and population, was militarily a second-rate state, whereas France was one of the foremost military and naval powers of the world and was energetically extending its dominions in every direction.

In these circumstances the only recourse for Liberia and the United States was continued diplomatic correspondence and interchange. Many Americans, possibly even those in high office, believed optimistically that reason, right, and argument would prevail over selfish national interests. Late in 1887 the Liberian secretary of state wrote to Bayard, saying that Carrance – still representing Liberia in his own country – believed that he must be granted special powers to handle the negotiations since the French foreign ministry had refused to treat with the U.S. minister on the matter. Bayard's reply was that the U.S. minister was acting as a disinterested conciliator, not as a Liberian representative.[26]

A rebellion among the tribes of part of the disputed territory, during which a party of American missionaries was plundered and abused, complicated the situation. The president of Liberia begged for active U.S. assistance or intervention, maintaining that such action was called for under existing treaties. Bayard, somewhat legalistically, denied the right of Liberia to demand American military help; such a demand, he said, must come from the injured American citizens – and none of the missionaries involved in the incident had presented any such request.[27]

Meanwhile, French appetite for African territory was unsatisfied. The dispute was still going on when French emissaries made a treaty with a Muslim ruler known as Almamy Samadu (now better known as Samori ibn Lafiya Ture) with whom Liberia had concluded treaties several years earlier. He asserted that his treaties with the French were commercial ones only, but the French maintained that he had agreed to their protection, and French troops, to enforce the claim, immediately occupied his country in the eastern part of Liberia.[28]

The U.S. minister in London, Robert Todd Lincoln, discussed this development with the Liberian minister, Edward Blyden, and on August 14, 1892, met with the prime minister, Lord Salisbury. Salisbury was noncommittal, referring Lincoln to a parliamentary paper (Africa No. 7, 1892) in which he had given directions to the British ambassador at Paris: The ambassador was told to notify the French government that British acknowledgment of French treaties on the Ivory Coast was not to prejudice Liberian claims. Further than that Salisbury declined to go.[29]

Since France would yield to no argument but the sword, and since the United States would not, and could not, resort to force, Liberia was defeated. An earlier treaty placed the boundary between Liberian and French territory at the Cavalla River, and the Liberian government signed an agreement in December 1892 that formally ceded to France an area occupied by Liberia almost from its inception as a state.

These disputes by no means put an end to Liberia's difficulties. In 1903 Great

Britain forced Liberia to sign a treaty adjusting its boundaries with Sierra Leone. The French put additional pressure on Monrovia to make territorial concessions along the frontiers of Guinea and the Ivory Coast. Blyden himself, one of the foremost scholars and diplomatists in Liberia's service, became so despondent regarding the future of Liberia that he actually considered a scheme whereby Liberia would be placed under British protection. He warned the Liberians that they had little time left to develop their hinterland and improve their relations with the indigenous African communities. Likening the Americo-Liberians to the Afrikaners in Africa, he insisted that the dominant Liberians must integrate the subject African peoples into the Liberian body politic: Unless Liberia reformed its ways, it was doomed.[30]

Events almost bore out Blyden's pessimism. Monrovia had to deal with a variety of ills: financial stringency and corruption; repeated indigenous rebellions, especially among the Kru people; dissensions within the Liberian oligarchy itself; and, above all, renewed French ambitions. (A boundary delimitation treaty in 1911 cost the Liberians a large strip of land along the borders of the Ivory Coast and Guinea.) Between them, the French and British won control of more than one-third of the hinterland claimed by Liberia. In the end, Liberia somehow pulled through. Without U.S. diplomatic support, however, it would probably have vanished from the map during the European powers' "Scramble for Africa."

CHAPTER II

Bula Matari and the Congo

In Africa, Liberian affairs constituted the main diplomatic concern of the U.S. government during the period between the Civil War and the end of the century. Americans collectively had little interest in matters outside their own country, and the United States took no part in the seizing of African territory in the 1870s and 1880s. That is not to say that individual Americans were indifferent to developments on the African continent. American merchants continued to trade with Africa; American prospectors, engineers, and technicians played major roles in developing its mineral resources; American missionaries worked to bring the gospel to Africans; and American explorers and adventurers were among the foremost in solving the geographical and ethnological puzzles of the interior.

The name that stands out in the annals of African exploration is that of Henry Morton Stanley. Late in life Stanley resumed British citizenship and accepted a knighthood, but at the time of his explorations in Africa he regarded himself as an American, and his efforts were largely financed by Americans.

Born John Rowlands at Denbigh, Wales, on June 10, 1841, Stanley was abandoned by his family and placed in the St. Asaph Union Workhouse, where he remained until 1856. He then thrashed the headmaster for his brutal tyranny and ran away. He shipped for New Orleans as a cabin boy, was befriended in 1859 by a local merchant, and assumed his benefactor's name, Stanley. When the Civil War broke out, he enlisted in the Confederate army, was taken prisoner at Shiloh, and was released after a brief captivity to enlist in the Union army. Ill health caused his early discharge from the army, and he wandered for a time until he enlisted in the Union navy.

Stanley supplemented his naval pay by acting as an unofficial correspondent for the New York papers, and after the war he joined the staff of the *New York Herald*. He soon became a star reporter, covering a wide field from Indian campaigns in the Far West to the British expedition to Abyssinia in 1867. Two years later he was writing on a civil war in Spain when he received a telegram directing him to report in Paris to James Gordon Bennett, the owner of the *Herald*. Bennett's instructions were broad. Stanley was to find Dr. Livingstone, the famous missionary-explorer, who had vanished into central Africa in 1866 and had not been heard from since. Stanley was given a free hand and a blank check for expenses.

Arriving at Zanzibar on an American whaler in January 1871, Stanley noted that most of the vessels in port were American, principally from New York and Salem: "They arrive loaded with American sheeting, brandy, gunpowder, muskets, beans, English cottons, brass-wire, china-ware, and other notions, and depart with ivory, gum-copal, cloves, hides, cowries, sesamum, pepper, and cocoa-nut oil."[1]

It took weeks of preparation at Zanzibar before Stanley could load his supplies and equipment, his soldiers and porters, onto four Arab dhows and sail for Baga-moyo on the mainland. The American consul helped in his preparations, and his equipment included two boats purchased from Americans and a horse presented by a Salem merchant who had lived in Zanzibar for many years. As the dhows moved out from port, Stanley hoisted an American flag, a present from the consul's wife.[2] He had the flag carried at the head of the column as he led his large expedition across Tanganyika to Ujiji, several times fighting hostile Africans. At Ujiji he found Livingstone and supplied him with food and medicines. Together they explored Lake Tanganyika, but when Stanley was ready to turn back, Livingstone refused to leave Africa. He was still fired with his mission to find the source of the Nile.

Stanley returned to England to find himself famous. Certain professional explor-ers and so-called experts on Africa at first refused to believe that he had found Livingstone, declared that the geographical information he published was unbeliev-able, and accused him of being a fraud; these charges, however, were soon refuted by evidence that he was telling the truth. Some of this opposition and a degree of prejudice against him personally may have come from the fact that he was re-garded as an American and not a Britisher. The unfavorable reception in England led to his emphasizing American mannerisms and an American accent.[3]

Stanley's brief contact with Africa and with David Livingstone convinced him that his mission was to open the continent. In 1873 he accompanied Lord Wolse-ley's expedition to Ashanti as a war correspondent, attracting the attention of the commander-in-chief by his coolness under fire. The short, smoothly conducted Ashanti campaign provided him with insight into African psychology and customs and let him observe and study Wolseley's meticulous plans and arrangements. When it ended, Stanley left for England and learned that Livingstone had died months earlier. The body of the great explorer, medical man, and humanitarian arrived in England on April 15, 1874, and three days later was buried in West-minster Abbey with Stanley as one of the pallbearers.

A few days after the funeral Stanley suggested to Edward Levy-Lawson, the owner and manager of the London *Daily Telegraph*, that a new expedition to Africa be organized to complete the explorations that Livingstone had not lived to finish and to unravel the African mysteries that Livingstone's death left unsolved. Levy-Lawson agreed tentatively, and a cablegram inviting James Gordon Bennett's participation was sent off. The reply was simple and to the point: "Yes. Bennett";[4] and thus was conceived in 1874 the Anglo-American Expedition for the Discovery of the Nile and Congo Sources. Following approximately his old route from Zanzi-bar, Stanley plunged again into Africa and vanished from the world for almost three years. He emerged from the forest 999 days later near the mouth of the Congo. Despite much personal brutality, his had been an astonishing military achievement and an incredible feat of endurance; he was the only white survivor, and more than half of the Zanzibaris who formed the party had died or been killed in fights with people along the river.

Stanley had crossed the continent. Geographically, he had resolved many of the unanswered problems of Africa. He had measured the length and shoreline of Lake Tanganyika and had determined the size of Lake Victoria and proved that it was a single lake. He had discovered a previously unknown body of water, Lake Mweru, and had traversed the hitherto unknown course of the mighty Congo. Politically, his letters from Uganda urging that missionaries be sent to the court of M'Tesa (Mutesa) extended British interests into the interior of East Africa and led ultimately to the establishment of the Uganda protectorate. Commercially, Stanley's expedition opened vast regions of Central and East Africa to European and American merchants. In Belgium, Leopold II hoped to gain wealth from the Congo; in Great Britain, Sir William Mackinnon and his associates of the Imperial East Africa Company looked for profits in Kenya and Uganda.

Stanley's reappearance after he had been given up as lost electrified Europe and the United States. In the months following his return to Europe, statesmen and scholars vied in honoring him: the king of Italy sent a portrait of himself with a complementary inscription; the principal geographical societies awarded him their gold medals; Queen Victoria received him in audience and gave him a diamond-studded gold snuffbox. The explorer was especially proud of a vote of thanks passed unanimously by both houses of the Congress of his adopted country.[5]

Another monarch interested in the man who had braved the Congo was Leopold II, king of the Belgians, a wily and capable diplomat and the most astute businessman among the crowned heads of his time. For some time Leopold had considered various projects in the tropics, including Africa, but in the competition for African territory he was handicapped by the fact that his country was not a great power. Nor did Belgium have any time-honored claims or status in Africa that could be used to bargain or to extend its influence. On September 12, 1876, while Stanley was still in the Congo, Leopold convened at the royal palace in Brussels a distinguished gathering of geographers and travelers, including delegates from Great Britain, Germany, France, Austria-Hungary, Russia, and Italy, as well as Belgium. There were no American delegates, but near the king's right hand stood Henry Shelton Sanford, who in the 1860s had spent eight years as U.S. minister to Belgium.

Leopold, in his opening speech of welcome, expressed his hope that the meeting would result in an international organization that would finally suppress the slave trade and would open Africa to civilization. Three days later the conference adjourned, having laid the foundation for the International Association for the Exploration and Civilization of Central Africa. Leopold was president, and there was an executive committee consisting of three members, one for each of the three principal language groups of the Western world, English, Germanic, and Latin. The British government, however, was reluctant to become involved, even though the International Association was supposedly an unofficial organization. The British member, Sir Bartle Frere, who was to represent English-speaking peoples, soon was appointed governor of the Cape of Good Hope, and Great Britain withdrew. Frere was replaced at once by Henry Shelton Sanford.[6]

The Anglo-American expedition had established Stanley as one of the world's greatest explorers and as the leading authority on Africa. A few still regarded him as primarily a notoriety-seeking poseur, but his reputation was firmly founded in popular estimate and in scientific circles even before he returned to Europe from the Congo. Leopold and the executive committee of the newly formed association decided that Stanley was the man to undertake and execute their African projects. On Stanley's arrival in Marseilles early in 1878, Sanford and another member of the committee were on hand to meet him and sound him out. Stanley listened to what they had to say. He was interested, but at the time he had had his fill of exploring; he was willing to give the International Association the benefit of his experience, but he told Sanford that he would not then consider returning to Africa.[7]

An aspect of Stanley's character that is usually overlooked by historians made him an obvious choice to execute Leopold's plans. Stanley combined steel-like resolution and hardness with a military loyalty toward those for whom he was then working, along with an ability to drive both subordinates and himself beyond accepted limitations. Some of Stanley's contemporaries recognized this facet of his character. His African name was Bula Matari, "the breaker of stones." An elderly African who had known him said to Emory Ross, "Mr. Stanley, he was a har-rd man," and no less a person than Queen Victoria, after her audience with him, characterized him as "determined."[8] Stanley resembled the hard-driving American frontiersman and businessman, and many of the Americans who went to Africa seemed cast in the same mold.

Leopold and his committee persevered. By August 1879 Stanley had recovered his health and spirits, and a life of relative idleness was beginning to pall. He was rebuffed in Great Britain; in spite of the honors he had received, he was unable to persuade anyone in the kingdom to take more than an academic interest in the Congo. A letter from one of the committeemen suggested a meeting in Paris, and he was much more receptive than he had been at Marseilles. Accepting Leopold's invitation to the palace at Brussels, Stanley expressed willingness to consider the proposals of a group of financiers, explorers, geographers, and philanthropists from several countries who had gathered there. They evinced a deep interest in Africa and plied him with questions throughout the day.

Some of their questions Stanley could answer offhand; others were unanswerable. Before the meeting broke up, a new organization had been formed – the Comité d'Etudes de Haut Congo – with an initial fund of £20,000 subscribed for immediate use and with every subscriber bound to donate more if necessary. An expedition would be sent to Africa as soon as possible to obtain accurate information on doubtful points and to establish bases for later activities. By unanimous vote, Stanley was invited to take command of the expedition and to act as the committee's representative.

Henry M. Stanley thus became the mainstay of Leopold's plans in Africa, the driving force that made their fulfillment possible. Without his services, the vast Congo basin could have been taken over by one or another of the Great Powers, and the course of Central African history would have been far different. Stanley, believing thoroughly in the benevolence and disinterestedness of Leopold's purposes and the value to Africa and Western civilization of the committee's projects, supported and fostered both.[9]

Stanley's activities during the next few years covered the beginnings of the Congo Free State, with Leopold as its sovereign, and the inception of European penetration into the still unknown regions of the Congo. Stanley set to work with his usual energy; he purchased equipment, interviewed applicants, and engaged suitable men. His task – the organizing of settlements intended to be permanent bases – required that he foresee and provide for all contingencies. Enormous amounts of equipment and supplies were needed; the numbers of men whose employment was anticipated and the extent and complexity of the expected operations required an elaborate organization and a grasp of details not to be expected of persons without practical experience in the tropical forest. Stanley arrived at the mouth of the Congo within a few months, ready to start on his mission.

Unlike his two previous expeditions into the wilds of Africa, this venture was international, but the United States was still a factor. In addition to Sanford in Belgium, the International Association included an American committee in New York City presided over by John H. B. Latrobe, president of the still-active American Colonization Society and one of the founders of Liberia.[10] Stanley's immediate staff of assistants included an American named Sparhawk, an old "Africa hand" upon whom he could rely.

Stanley lived in Africa for most of the next five years, extending his explorations, establishing and supervising stations, surveying and building roads, and negotiating treaties with numerous African dignitaries and potentates who would place themselves under the protection of the International Association. This part of Stanley's mission was not publicized, a circumstance that tended to cast an air of mystery about the expedition and led to the groundless suspicion in some quarters that Stanley, a U.S. citizen, was laying the foundations for an American empire in Africa.[11]

Stanley's contemporaries did not suspect that the association's primary motives were other than philanthropic, humanitarian, and scientific. Its commercial motives were open and apparent, but the public assumed that the commercial development of the Congo would tend automatically toward civilizing and improving the condition of the indigenous people.

While Stanley was establishing stations and obtaining concessions and treaties from local kings and tribal chiefs, other claims to Congolese territories suddenly threatened to disrupt everything the association was trying to do. Portugal, by reason of the discoveries of the early Portuguese explorers, had always maintained a shadowy claim to the Congo, but none of the European powers paid much attention to its claims. In the mid-nineteenth century a rather feeble Portuguese effort to establish authority had been firmly vetoed by Great Britain because traders of several nations were already installed in the Congo and because the slave trade flourished under the Portuguese flag wherever it was seen. Moreover, Great Britain itself had somewhat nebulous claims to Congolese soil, owing to treaties negotiated with several chiefs during British operations against the slave trade. Even so, the vast territory which Stanley had explored and in which he was working on behalf of the association was still not held under international law by any "civilized" power.

Two sets of circumstances suddenly rendered the Congo important. First, Stanley's explorations suggested that the Congo basin was a region of great potential wealth and could be made accessible; second, the announcement of Pierre de Brazza's explorations and annexations adjacent to the Congo, in the name of France, caused immediate alarm in London and Lisbon. French colonial policy was exclusive. If the French established themselves firmly, then the merchants, missionaries, and traders of all other nations would be shut out.

British fears of French designs resulted in a long, complicated series of confidential negotiations with the Portuguese that ended in the treaty of February 26, 1884.

In its broad provisions, the treaty recognized Portuguese territorial claims and provided for a joint Anglo-Portuguese commission to control navigation and traffic on the Congo River. Although the treaty assured freedom of navigation on the Congo and its tributaries to shipping of all nations, the two powers had disposed of the matter as though only they were concerned. Other nations whose traders were already in the region were completely ignored, and the establishments formed by Stanley for the International Association went unmentioned.[12]

The treaty caused a wave of protest. In March 1884 the French government announced that France would neither recognize the treaty nor consider itself bound by it, and on April 18 a similar announcement was made by the German government. Nor did the treaty meet with unanimous approval in Great Britain. British businessmen with existing interests in the Congo were distinctly displeased at the prospect of subjecting themselves to the inefficiency, maladministration, and corruption that they regarded as almost synonymous with Portuguese colonial government. Humanitarians were aghast at the idea of putting additional Africans under the power of a nation that still winked at the slave trade; Protestant missionary bodies were indignant at the possibility that Protestant missions might be handicapped or thwarted by a staunchly Roman Catholic government. Even the strongest proponents of the treaty had to admit the neither governments nor private parties with interests in the Congo had been consulted.[13]

The association's legal status in Africa at this time was extremely vague. Its position was somewhat analogous to that of the American Colonization Society in early Liberia: It was exercising sovereignty without any legal or technical right to do so. It was a corporation – a private individual – in competition with recognized sovereign powers. As Stanley said in a letter to an unidentified friend, "De Brazza with his walking stick, a French flag and a few words in the presence of the whites at Leopoldville, is really stronger than Stanley with his Krupps and all material of war, faithful adherents, aid of natives, etc."[14]

Looking to potential American commercial interests, President Chester A. Arthur in his annual message to Congress on December 4, 1883, gave the first hint of official U.S. interest in the Congo:

> The rich and populous valley of the Congo is being opened to commerce by a society called the International African Association, of which the King of the Belgians is the president, and a citizen of the United States [Stanley] is the chief executive officer. Large tracts of territory have been ceded to the association by native chiefs, roads have been opened, steamboats placed on the river, and the nuclei of states established at twenty-two stations under one flag which offers freedom to commerce and prohibits the slave trade. The objects of the society are philanthropic. It does not aim at permanent political control but seeks the neutrality of the valley. The United States cannot be indifferent to this work nor to the interests of their citizens involved in it. It may become advisable for us to cooperate with other commercial powers in promoting the right of trade and residence in the Congo Valley free from the interference or political control of any one nation.[15]

Not surprisingly, the United States promptly recognized the sovereign rights of the International Association. There was not only a genuine American interest in the possibilities of the Congo, stimulated by national pride in the fact that an American, Henry M. Stanley, was a key figure in efforts to open the region, but also a suspicion that Great Britain—widely believed by Americans to be a notoriously predatory power—was seeking, unjustly, to preempt the Congo.

The association's position was clarified and strengthened on April 22, 1884, while the controversy over the Anglo-Portuguese treaty was in full sway, by a formal American pronouncement:

> Frederick T. Frelinghuysen, Secretary of State, duly empowered therefore by the President of the United States of America, and pursuant to the advice and consent of the Senate heretofore given . . . declares that . . . the Government of the United States will order the officers of the United States, both on land and sea, to recognize the flag of the International Association as the flag of a friendly Government.[16]

U.S. recognition of the association's sovereign status was followed within a few days by French recognition and on November 8 by that of Germany. In due course the other powers followed suit; the association took its place among the recognized governments of the world, and Leopold II of the Belgians reigned over a vast African region as well.

CHAPTER 12

Neutrality and philanthropy

With the International Association established in the Congo and recognized there as sovereign by several powers, Great Britain and Portugal were faced with the almost unanimous opposition of all Europe. They had no choice but to abandon the attempt to treat the Congo as a private matter between themselves. Consequently, when Chancellor Bismarck, of Germany, after consultation with France, invited the United States and other interested powers in early October 1884 to send representatives to Berlin to consider (among other items) the question of "freedom of commerce in the basin and the mouths of the Congo," the area was positively placed within the scope of international interest.[1]

The United States traditionally remained aloof from Old World politics, so the government had some hesitancy in accepting Bismarck's invitation. However, with the understanding that the conference was purely for discussion and for the establishment of general principles, and that the United States could reserve the right to decline to accept conclusions reached, the government at Washington decided to participate.

The designated representative was John A. Kasson, the American minister at Berlin. Kasson was no novice in international diplomacy and politics. He had served several terms as a member of Congress and as a state legislator. Under President Lincoln's administration he was an assistant postmaster general, and he represented the United States at the International Postal Congress in Paris in 1863. In 1867 he was on the commission to negotiate postal conventions with Great Britain, France, Belgium, Germany, Switzerland, and Italy. He was U.S. minister to the court of Vienna from 1877 to 1881, and at the time of Bismarck's invitation he had recently been promoted to the more critical diplomatic post of minister to the German Empire.[2]

After he was informed that he would be the U.S. representative, Kasson heard from the German Foreign Office, on October 20, 1884, that the conference probably would hear experts on Africa. He wrote to Henry M. Stanley to ask, "Can you hold yourself at liberty to be present at Berlin a week before the meeting of the Conference on West African affairs, and during its deliberations?" He was well aware that Stanley was concerned with the International Association and, in view of his government's attitude toward the association, he welcomed the opportunity to have Stanley present the association's case before the conference. His letter continued, "This action will be in harmony with the interests which you represent." Three days later, having learned from the German Foreign Office that each delegate would be allowed an associate, Kasson at once thought of Sanford, an experienced diplomat familiar with the matters to be discussed and officer of the association. He cabled Washington on October 23, 1884, to ask "that the usefulness of Mr. Sanford, as such an associate, be taken into consideration." Secretary of State Frelinghuysen authorized Kasson to use Sanford at his own discretion, provided that no additional expense to the U.S. government was incurred.[3]

A further American official – W. P. Tisdale, the government's commercial agent in the Congo state – hurried to Berlin to observe the conference proceedings. Tisdale was not formally accredited as an associate delegate, but "at the same time his position as the first and only representative sent by any Government to the State of the Congo" was to be borne in mind.[4]

The delegates assembled for the first session on November 15, 1884. Bismarck, as host, accepted the chairmanship and suggested the agenda for consideration. On the second day Kasson made a brief speech, citing the reasons for U.S. participation and the bases of American policy and attitudes. He stressed that vast regions in Central Africa had been first explored by an American citizen and that the International Association, which had established a de facto government in the region, included Americans in its membership, adding that "the blacks will learn from it [the Association] that the civilization and the dominion of the white man means for them peace and freedom and the development of useful commerce, free to all the world."[5]

Kasson, because of his position of neutrality and international impartiality and because he was aided and advised by Stanley and Sanford, had a strong influence on the conference, and his words carried weight. When it became clear that many of the delegates had only vague ideas on African geography, Kasson suggested that Stanley enlighten them.

> He went to a chart suspended in the room, and immediately engrossed the interest of every delegate, by a vivid description of the features of the Congo basin; and finally of the [adjacent] country necessary to go with it under the same *régime* to secure the utmost freedom of communication with the two oceans.[6]

Kasson thus persuaded the conference to adopt his suggested definition of the Congo basin, and he steadily used his influence toward the adoption of free trade with and within the areas defined. In other particulars, too, Kasson was active, and the final general act, or convention, of the Berlin conference bears the imprint not only of Sanford, Stanley and Leopold II, but of Kasson as representative of the United States.

The U.S. government never ratified, and hence was never formally bound by, the results of the Berlin conference. Nevertheless, the U.S. representative signed the convention, and the U.S. government acted in accordance with the principles finally agreed upon.

Stanley's exploratory and colonizing work in the Congo had ended before the Berlin conference, but he was not yet through with Africa. He went to the Congo a fourth time in 1887 to lead a difficult expedition that rescued Emin Pasha (Eduard Schnitzer), a German in Egyptian service who was isolated in equatorial Africa by the Mahdist uprising in the Egyptian Sudan. On the outward journey, after the rescue, Stanley discovered the great Ruwenzori Range (the legendary Mountains of the Moon), the Albert Edward Nyanza (lake), and the great southwestern gulf of Lake Victoria. He returned to England and resumed British citizenship in 1892, was knighted, and was elected to Parliament in 1895.[7]

At the Berlin conference, for the first time, U.S. representatives sat in a multilateral international conference considering issues and territories outside the Western Hemisphere. Despite the government's reservations, many people "viewed with alarm" what they regarded as a radical deviation from the traditions of a century and from the almost sacred precepts established by the Founding Fathers. The isolationist die-hards, led by Congressman Perry Belmont, attacked at once. On January 5, 1885, Belmont introduced a resolution demanding that President Arthur inform Congress just why the United States was participating, and shortly before the inauguration of the new president, Grover Cleveland, he sponsored a resolution that went further:

> The House of Representatives, heedful of the admonitions of Washington, and faithful to that neutral policy of separation and peace which our situation and the wisdom of a free people have hitherto enabled us to maintain, hereby explicitly declares its dissent from the act of the President of the United States in accepting the invitation of Germany and France to participate in the International Conference at Berlin.[8]

These opponents refused to regard the Congo as a matter of concern for the whole civilized world; Belmont, for example, to the end of his life maintained that this was a purely European problem with which the United States had no concern. In addition, there was an absurd fear that international agreements concerning navigation on the Congo might somehow be twisted into a precedent for international control over the Mississippi.[9]

Belmont, as a Democrat, easily gained the ear of President-elect Cleveland, who was inclined to suspect anything suggesting international entanglement. In his annual message to Congress in 1886, Cleveland stated that, since acceptance of the Berlin convention would have made the United States a party to an alliance, he had withdrawn the treaty and expressly refrained from asking the Senate to ratify it. Somewhat ambiguously, he added that the American delegates, despite the reservations under which the United States participated, had signed the convention just as had the plenipotentiaries of the other powers.[10]

Nevertheless, the concern of the United States with what was happening in Africa and the government's policy of maintaining the rights of its citizens in that part of the world were matters that transcended temporary mutations of party politics. The outward thrust from the United States was becoming too powerful to be restrained by a tradition of isolationism that even then was beginning to lose its vitality.

The tradition that the government should aid and foster foreign commerce was as ancient as the tradition and policy of political isolation. American industries were growing with tremendous speed. Though numerous merchants and other businesspeople undoubtedly regarded the domestic market as capable of indefinite expansion, there were many others who foresaw a time when the United States would no longer be able to absorb all the products of its own mills, factories, and farms. In addition, the railway network was approaching completion, and heavy industry no longer needed capital from London or Amsterdam. American capitalists and entrepreneurs began to think of overseas investment opportunities that promised greater returns than domestic loans.

Political isolation and the concentration of the American people upon domestic affairs did not lessen the considerable latent interest in Africa, and particularly in the possibilities offered by the still-unknown country of the Congo. This interest had shown itself, even before the Berlin conference, in the assignment given to Commodore Robert W. Shufeldt in 1878 as commander of the USS *Ticonderoga*. He was directed by the secretary of the navy to proceed first to Liberia, where he would, if necessary, act as umpire in the boundary dispute between Liberia and Great Britain. He would then "visit both the western and eastern coasts of Africa and hold such intercourse with the natives to whom he could obtain access as would enable them to appreciate the advantages of trade with the United States." He was also instructed to visit Madagascar and other places around the world, all with a view to promoting foreign commerce.[11]

In its cruise down the west coast of Africa, the *Ticonderoga* touched at the mouth of the Gabon, where Shufeldt observed with approval the activities of the American missionaries and spent several days at Fernando Poo. In May 1879 the ship anchored in the Congo River as "the first American ship of war which can be said to have really entered the Congo – the others having anchored at its mouth off Shark's point" – while Lieutenant Francis J. Drake and Paymaster William J. Thomson investigated the commercial possibilities of the region. They found that millions of dollars' worth of such raw materials as ivory, palm oil, rubber, sesamum oil, gum copal, groundnuts, and orcin were being exported annually from the river's mouth, while vast amounts of cotton goods, liquors, gunpowder, brass rods and rings, and all sorts of metal utensils were being imported. The only article of American production coming into the Congo was tobacco, and it was imported by Dutch and British, not American, traders. Drake's brief survey, moreover, led him to believe that the country was well adapted to the cultivation of almost anything that could be raised in Southern Europe.

In spite of the generally optimistic tone of his officers' reports, Shufeldt was skeptical about U.S. commercial possibilites in the Congo. Dutch traders established at Banana near the mouth of the river, scenting a threat to themselves and their trade in the *Ticonderoga*'s arrival, had but poorly concealed their animosity toward Shufeldt and his officers and crew. Shufeldt reported, in substance, that these traders were so firmly entrenched that any effort to break their monopoly would be virtually hopeless.[12]

One American commercial venture was launched. The Sanford Exploring Expedition established in 1886 was given the first trade concession in the Congo. Starting with $60,000 in capital, the company hoped for quick profits from the ivory trade. Henry S. Sanford hired Lieutenant Emory H. Taunt (on leave from the U.S. Navy) to lead the expedition, and planned four stations along the Congo River, to be connected by a steamer. Some ivory was brought out in 1886, but a boat that had to be taken up country in sections was not ready until 1887, and Stanley then borrowed it for forty-five days to aid the Emin Pasha relief force. By late 1887 the steamer *Florida* was busy in commercial trade; it was soon joined by the *New York*. In one year Sanford's group brought thirty-five thousand pounds of ivory and sixty-one thousand pounds of rubber. Taunt meanwhile had returned to Europe to be fired as an alcoholic by the U.S. Navy and court-martialed as AWOL; Sanford got him a job in 1888 at $4,000 a year as U.S. commercial agent for the

Congo Free State. By 1888 the company needed new capital, but Sanford's appeal was ignored by American businessmen. A merger was concluded in 1889 with a Belgian firm, and the first U.S. commercial company in the upper Congo River ended its operation.[13]

To the average American in the last few decades of the nineteenth century, however, the commercial possibilities of tribal Africa were secondary to a resurrection of the earlier missionary fervor. Missionaries had focused primarily on Africa, and the publication of Stanley's sensational accounts of cannibalism and other "depravities" stimulated evangelical Christians in both Europe and America to carry the gospel to what they saw as a benighted region.

None of the American or European missionaries who had been prominent in Africa since the start of the missionary movement had penetrated the wilderness of the Congo basin before the 1870s. Once it became known that the Congo Valley could be entered via the river's mouth, evangelical associations quickly responded. The first to make the attempt came from England in 1878, sent by a group of dissenter philanthropists. Calling themselves the Livingstone Inland Mission, they pioneered at the time when the hard-bitten adventurers under Stanley's direction were cutting roads and establishing stations for the International Association. By 1884 the Livingstone Inland Mission had set up a thin chain of missionary stations along the south bank of the river as far up as Stanley Pool. They suffered heavy casualties from disease, and they were handicapped by friction with Stanley, who had seized their steamboat, along with the association's, for use in his expedition to rescue Emin Pasha.[14]

By 1884 the philanthropic group that sponsored and supported the project was in financial difficulties. The missions themselves were not prospering as had been hoped, and the missionaries gladly accepted the American Baptist Missionary Union's offer to take over their work. This was an old, well-established organization that had developed a policy very different from that of the Livingstone Inland Mission. The Livingstone missionaries conducted their work in several languages and regions; the American Baptists preferred to concentrate in a central mission using one language, and from this base to extend their efforts gradually, one step at a time. From the central mission the Baptists branched out to a circle of satellite stations and eventually advanced to new regions.[15]

For some years the Baptists and the Disciples of Christ, who maintained a single mission, were the sum total of American missionary efforts in the Congo. During the 1880s Bishop William Taylor and Bishop Joseph C. Hartzell of the Methodist Episcopal Church investigated the Congo at different times with the idea of establishing a chain of Methodist missions, but the plans were not carried out during the nineteenth century.

After the Baptists, the next major American missionary effort in the Congo was undertaken by the Southern Presbyterian Church, prodded originally by a young black minister, William H. Sheppard. A native of Virginia and a graduate of Hampton Institute and Tuscaloosa Theological Institute, Sheppard had aspired from childhood to be a missionary to Africa. Shortly after his ordination in 1887 he approached the mission office of his church, which was reluctant to send him to Africa alone. In 1890 a second volunteer presented himself, the Reverend Samuel N. Lapsley of Anniston, Alabama, and that same year the two young ministers, one white, the other black, set out for the Congo to explore for a site where they might commence their work.[16]

The two young men traveled together until Lapsley died of an African fever, like so many Europeans and Americans before him. Undiscouraged, Sheppard continued alone. Suspicous tribesmen once spared his life because they believed him to be the reincarnation of a legendary chief (he did not disillusion them). Eventually he established himself at Luebo in a region deep in the interior. Before his final return to the United States many years later, he had the satisfaction of seeing the mission he had founded attracting converts by the hundreds and expanding into one of the most important centers of Christianity and modernization in Central Africa.[17]

The Baptists and the Presbyterians virtually complete the nineteenth-century story of American missionary efforts in the Congo. The Disciples of Christ, at the station at Balenge that they took over from the Baptists, had many misfortunes, including the inevitable deaths from fever, and did not become firmly established until the end of the century; their work in the Congo did not really begin until the twentieth century.

During the 1880s and early 1890s the attitude of the American people was changing, and the traditions of isolation and noninvolvement were gradually ceasing to be regarded as immutable laws. When a second conference to discuss the Congo and African affairs assembled at Brussels in 1890, the United States took part without the opposition that had attended its participation in Berlin. The American delegate was Henry S. Sanford, who had left Leopold's service and was selected because of his familiarity with the diplomatic and legal problems of the Congo. The original Berlin convention was amended slightly to enable Leopold's government in Africa to raise needed revenue by charging nondiscriminatory tonnage and duties, and a further agreement was adopted that, it was hoped, would restrict the traffic in liquor and firearms.

After the Brussels conference, U.S. official diplomatic interest in Africa subsided for the rest of the century. But no account of the United States and the Congo is complete without mention of Richard Dorsey Mohun. Ever since the recognition of the Congo Free State, U.S. policy had maintained a commercial agent there to represent American interests, and in 1892 Mohun was appointed to the position. He went to Africa by way of Brussels, where he paid his respects to Leopold II, the sovereign of the Free State, and became convinced of the king's determination to bring peace and civilization to the region.

Since trade between the United States and the new state was still almost nonexistent, Mohun began to investigate its commercial potential, traveling into areas not seen by Westerners previously. Among his earlier reports to the State Department is one that is extraordinary as an official dispatch but typical of Mohun:

> I desired to see the natives making cloth, and asked permission of the chief to visit the town, which was readily granted. I took only six men with me armed with revolvers under their shirts. When I had gotten about ten minutes distance from the town I was most foully attacked from the bush with spears and poisoned arrows. Fortunately none of my men were struck, and before they could throw their arrows again we opened fire. We captured the village and I burned it to the ground to teach them a lesson. This is

only one of five or six times I have been compelled to fight during the past six months.

The whole eastern boundary of the State is now shut by the Arabs, and all the white men who were in the different posts have been killed. Their bodies were afterwards eaten by the large number of cannibal slaves attached to the caravans.[18]

The latter part of Mohun's statement refers to the fact that the Congo Free State authorities suddenly found themselves at war with the Arab slave traders from the east coast who were established well within the boundaries of the state and who were bitterly resentful of the efforts to suppress their commerce. Such a war was regarded in Europe and America as a struggle between barbarism and civilization – between slavers and the heralds of peace and freedom. The Congo forces were heavily outnumbered by the Arabs and their native allies, and when Mohun was asked to replace a Belgian officer who was seriously ill, he did not hesitate to join the conflict. In a short time he was acting as chief of Free State artillery, and in this capacity he took a leading part in most of the battles.[19]

Before the war ended with the complete defeat of the Arabs, Free State authorities sent an expedition to determine the practicability of a water route from Lake Tanganyika to the Lualaba River (the upper Congo), with Mohun as second in command. The Belgian commander to the expedition fell ill, and Mohun took charge and continued until the expedition completed its task.

The oddest feature of Mohun's career is the fact that the U.S. government, of which he was the accredited official representative, never took the slightest exception to his highly undiplomatic activities. The State Department evidently was satisfied by his explanation that he refused to accept pay from the Congo Free State for his services as an officer. Far from disavowing Mohun and his actions, the government seemed to approve; after the completion of his term of office, he was appointed to the still important post of consul at Zanzibar – a promotion that he would not have received had he been persona non grata. He remained at Zanzibar for three years before resigning from U.S. service to devote the remainder of his life to Africa and the Congo Free State. He led exploring parties into Katanga to verify rumors of the extensive mineral wealth in that region, and later travelers found him constructing telegraph lines through the wilderness.[20]

With Mohun, the more spectacular part played by Americans in opening the Congo area comes to an end. Americans have continued to take part in the affairs of the Congo, but their roles have been prosaic in comparison with those of Stanley, Mohun, and Sheppard. Before Stanley's incredible voyage down the river, inner Africa was the land of Rider Haggard's romances, a lost world where any day the impossible might become reality; after Stanley and his successors, inner Africa became almost as familiar as the prairies of Kansas. The Americans who assisted in opening the Congo were filling roles in the tradition of the many other pioneers who subdued the wilds of North America.

CHAPTER 13

Traders, explorers, and soldiers of misfortune

Zanzibar

American interest in eastern Africa centered throughout the nineteenth century on Zanzibar, the commercial focal point for the entire east coast region. In the years just preceding the Civil War, American merchants and traders largely dominated the commerce of Zanzibar, and their goods filled the shops and bazaars. The Africans of adjacent continental areas dressed themselves in *merikani* (cotton cloth), refusing to accept substitutes from Manchester or Madras. Ivory hunters preferred American hatchets. Ships flying the Stars and Stripes crowded the ports and anchorages.[1] The commercially minded ruler Sultan Seyyid Said, finding that trade within his dominions was handicapped by the lack of small coins, ordered a supply from the United States, and when he decided to engage in a trading venture of his own, his ship was dispatched to the United States.[2]

The Civil War, as discussed earlier, struck a body blow to this commerce. American merchants at Zanzibar, struggling to survive commercially, had to substitute goods manufactured in Great Britain or Germany of those usually sent from the United States, and their cargoes were transported to Africa under the British, French, or Hanseatic flags. They maintained their credit, but their businesses inevitably declined before the end of the war, while competitors took full advantage of the opportunity thus offered them to promote their own interests.[3]

For several years after the war the Americans, against the fierce competition of British, Indian, German, and French traders, seemed to recover their position. In 1869 Robert S. Rantoul, the collector of customs at Salem (the port most deeply concerned with African trade), announced somewhat oratorically that "a large fraction of the dates, gums, spices, ivory, ebony, sheep skins and goat skins brought into this country" and "the delicious Arabian coffee, the aromatic berry of Mocha," were again passing through Salem.[4]

In spite of the revival, conditions were taking an unfavorable turn for American merchants in East Africa. The typical American sailing vessel could not compete with the larger, faster ships from England and Germany. The opening of the Suez Canal in 1869 and the replacement of sail by steam-powered craft reduced shipping costs and time so that European goods could be sold more cheaply than American. One by one, most of the merchants and merchant firms that had supplied East Africa with American cotton cloth, tools, and trinkets closed their Zanzibar offices and went out of business.

American commercial interest did not, however, entirely lapse. The Africans still preferred American cotton goods to all others; the bulk of the gum copal gathered annually found its way to the factories of New England; and until well into the twentieth century the greater part of the East African ivory was carried to the

United States. The ivory trade illustrates the fact that commerce is a two-edged weapon. In 1882, when the supply of ivory was cut off by tribal warfare in Tanganyika, people in Connecticut suffered severely as factories closed down and employees were thrown out of work – much as had happened in England when the Civil War cut off the supply of American cotton.[5]

Even though commerce with the region declined to a fraction of its earlier volume, there was still enough to justify maintaining a U.S. consul at Zanzibar. Maintaining a consulate cost the government very little in the days before the consular service became a government career. The salary was extremely small; a consul was expected to support himself from the fees and other perquisites that went with the office. The U.S. consul at Zanzibar was almost invariably one of the merchants residing and doing business there, and the office came to be regarded as the just prerogative of certain Salem traders and merchant families. There was considerable resentment when an outsider was appointed. In 1865 Edward D. Ropes of Salem became consul; he was succeeded in 1869 by Francis Ropes Webb of Salem, who in turn was succeeded in 1872 by John F. Webb, also of Salem.[6]

The consul's duties were diplomatic as well as commercial, since he was the only official American representative in the sultan's dominions; but in actual fact, his diplomatic duties were negligible. On only one occasion in the period after the Civil War did the consulate attain, for a brief time, some political importance. Great Britain, determined to suppress the slave trade on the East African coast, in 1845 obtained a treaty from the sultan that banned slave export from his African territories but authorized the shipment of slaves from the mainland to Zanzibar and Pemba and between the islands. Since it was almost impossible to prove that a dhow loaded with slaves was really going to Muscat or Persia if the master asserted that his destination was Zanzibar or Pemba, the enforcement of the treaty was extremely difficult. Beginning about 1868, the Royal Navy intensified its campaign against the illegal slave trade, at times in a manner unquestionably high-handed and arbitrary. Francis R. Webb, who had been in business in Zanzibar for years and who was later, as noted, to be appointed U.S. consul, estimated that the British sank or burned at least seventy Arab craft, many of which, he believed, were innocent of any part in the slave trade. Webb feared that the British meant eventually to abolish slavery itself, not merely the overseas trade in slaves, and that this outcome would injure business.[7] In 1868 he urged the State Department to send an American warship to Zanzibar as a preventive measure. Washington, however, took a broader view, and replied with a sharp reprimand for even suggesting opposition to the British policy: "So far from protesting against it, the influence of this government would be exerted in its favor."[8]

The abusive British activities were corrected shortly by the establishment of a vice-admiralty court at Zanzibar with John Kirk as both British consul and justice of the court. Kirk was a noted African explorer in his own right who had been on the continent since the 1850s, when he was a member of Livingstone's expedition to explore the Zambesi River. He was grimly determined to stop the traffic in human beings. But Kirk felt some of the contempt for traders and merchants characteristic of numerous British colonial officials; he also had an innate dislike and suspicion of Americans. Moreover, he was deeply imbued with the idea of promoting and advancing the British Empire and enhancing British prestige. This was an attitude that could not make for smooth personal relations in the tiny foreign community in Zanzibar, where most of the Europeans and Americans were traders or merchants who were at all times deeply suspicious of British motives. Kirk clashed with some of the Americans in Zanzibar, including Webb, who was by then consul.

Her Majesty's government in 1872 decided to clarify the situation at Zanzibar by dispatching Sir Bartle Frere to persuade the sultan to modify the treaty of 1845 and stop the intradominion shipment of slaves, the subterfuge under which thousands of blacks were illegally transported out of Africa every year. On March 6, 1872, Sir Edward Thornton, the British minister at Washington, wrote at length to the U.S. secretary of state, Hamilton Fish, calling attention to the numerous reports and explorers' accounts of the horrors and ravages of the slave trade in the East African interior and emphasizing the need for cooperation among the Great Powers to end the slave traffic.[9] In addition to abrogating the objectionable provisions of the treaty, Great Britain suggested governmental support of steamship and mail service to East Africa as a means of fostering "legitimate" trade, a term at that time almost synonymous with "civilization."

The secretary of state cautiously refused to commit the United States to common or joint action with another power, but in view of the praiseworthy objective of British policy, the U.S. consul at Zanzibar would be instructed to "intimate to the sovereign of that country that we would be glad to see that provision of the treaty between him and Great Britain terminated." The commander of the first U.S. warship to visit the East African coast would be ordered to carry the same message.[10]

This exchange occurred in March 1872, but the matter was in abeyance for some time. All that summer the USS *Yantic* lay in the dockyard undergoing repairs and refitting in preparation for sailing to the Asiatic station via the Suez Canal. Not until after it had sailed did anyone realize that it would pass not too far from Zanzibar on its voyage. On September 3, five days after the *Yantic*'s departure, the Navy Department cabled the necessary instructions to the U.S. consul at Gibraltar, to be transmitted to Commander Byron Wilson when the ship arrived there. The *Yantic* was not a fast vessel, and it was the end of October before Fish was able to inform Sir Edward Thornton that Wilson had received orders to proceed to Zanzibar and cooperate with Frere's mission to the sultan.[11] The *Yantic* anchored at Zanzibar in January 1873, several days ahead of the arrival of Sir Bartle Frere and his staff, and Wilson, hoping to emulate "Stanley and Livingstone over again," composed a "long and strong dispatch" for the sultan. Himself a Union veteran of the American Civil War, Wilson urged the sultan to follow the lead of "the last among the great civilized nations to abolish slavery as an institution in their midst."[12]

Wilson hoped to present an accomplished fact to the British mission when it arrived, but he did not reckon on the opposition – even the active hostility – of his own country's consul. Acting Consul John F. Webb believed that Frere's mission was simply a British scheme to drive out business competitors, and the consulate's interpreter, whether with Webb's knowledge or not, so altered Wilson's communication in translation that the commander seemed to be urging the sultan to stand firm in resisting changes. Webb would have nothing to do with the matter beyond advising the sultan to uphold the treaty of 1845, as his instructions from Washington – by his interpretation – required him to do. He then considered that he had complied with his orders, refused to back up Wilson in any way, and declined all cooperation with Frere's mission, even failing to return the courtesy calls made by the mission's members.

Fortunately for the reputation of the United States, the acting consul became ill and Francis Ropes Webb resumed the consulate. Although he had been lukewarm in supporting previous antislavery measures, his point of view was more realistic than that of his colleagues, and he recognized that slavery and the slave trade were doomed. As a result, when Sir Bartle Frere gave the sultan an ultimatum – either consent to the revised treaty or see Zanzibar blockaded – the American consul advised the sultan to comply.[13]

Apart from this episode, the U.S. consulate at Zanzibar during the late nineteenth century dealt almost entirely with commercial matters. Consul Francis R. Webb assisted Stanley in preparing for his expedition in search of Livingstone. He and his successors did little else except further their own businesses and sign consular papers.

American merchants continued their struggle through the 1870s, and managed to secure most of the gum copal and ivory. But there were difficulties. In 1872 a disastrous storm, the worst in local recorded history, caused such damage as to disrupt the economy of Zanzibar and of all East Africa. Many African middlemen were unable to meet their obligations, and one American firm was forced out of business, unable either to pay its creditors or to collect from its debtors. Other American firms, somewhat more resilient because of working arrangements with leading Indian merchants, managed to survive but were badly hurt. American business at Zanzibar was helped at this time by the introduction there of kerosene for lighting – a cheaper fuel than the locally produced animal and vegetable oils, which was made attractive when the U.S. promoters of the new industry furnished a serviceable lamp at a price even the poorest could afford.[14]

Nevertheless, American predominance in Zanzibar's commerce was being undermined. The Suez Canal provided advantages in cost and speed to European shipping and brought increasing numbers of British and, especially, German merchants to the east coast of Africa. American merchants, in addition to fighting cutthroat competition, had to combat the prejudice and dislike of empire builder John Kirk, who had become the power behind the sultan's throne and who missed no opportunity to discredit the Americans. When a group of merchants of several nationalities presented to the sultan a petition urging new regulations to improve the efficiency and operation of caravans, Kirk portrayed it as an underhanded attempt by the Americans to revive the slave trade; in consequence, the U.S. consul received an unwarranted reprimand from Washington. Charging that "American officials and others in these parts are in the habit of buying slaves," Kirk strongly supported the Royal Navy's illegal search of an American ship and the arbitrary removal of two black crew members on the grounds that they were slaves, in spite of the captain's firm denial. In other ways, too, Kirk went out of his way to be disagreeable to Americans and to exhibit his contempt; his successor, Charles Euan-Smith, referred to the American consul as a "vulgar pushing fellow anxious to make his position felt in Zanzibar politics."[15]

American trade with Zanzibar and East Africa has never ended, but one by one the old American firms found it expedient to close their Zanzibari offices and discontinue their efforts to survive in the African trade. As Great Britain and Germany absorbed the dominions of the sultan of Zanzibar into their colonial empires, merchants and traders of other nations were quietly and decisively pushed aside. Yet the results of U.S. dominance in commerce and shipping at Zanzibar and other East African ports cannot be measured by commercial statistics. Concentrated as it was in a few New England ports that would otherwise have been of minor importance, the East African trade created capital that contributed directly to the development of areas and resources within the United States itself. The financing of railroad construction in the Far West was, in large part, furnished by New England capital seeking investment opportunities after the African trade declined.

The Blue and the Gray on the Nile

The Civil War, while it began the decline of U.S. commercial supremacy in East Africa, led indirectly to American activity in the upper valley of the Nile and in the Sudan. The war's end left a large number of Americans with their taste for adventure and military life unsated and with little opportunity to gratify it in the minuscule U.S. Army of the time. Many experienced professional soldiers of the defeated Confederacy also had no means of livelihood in the United States, and for several years after the war the nation was a reservoir of highly trained, seasoned staff officers and combat commanders.

The availability of such men coincided neatly with a demand for them in Egypt, where the khedive Ismail aspired to transform the ancient land of the pharoahs into a great modern empire. He inaugurated railway projects; built roads, schools, and hospitals; and laid plans to extend the borders of his country into the region of the Central African lakes and the still unexplored reaches of the Sudan. Further, Ismail wished to be free from interference from his nominal overlord at Constantinople; he thus needed to strengthen and modernize his fighting forces. He brought in foreign experts, and in the early 1870s he took more than thirty Americans into his employment. Not only did they have good professional military qualifications, but to Ismail they were untainted by any connection with ambitions or interests in Egypt likely to clash with his own: They could give him their unqualified allegiance and loyalty. These men were more than specialists in combat, for their experience included mapping, surveying, and exploring. In numbers, the Americans were about equally divided between former Confederates and former members of the Union army; about half were graduates of West Point or Annapolis. Five were second lieutenants of the U.S. Army permitted by William T. Sherman, commanding general, to take indefinite leave of absence for the sake of the practical experience they would gain in Egypt.[16]

Heading the American group was Brigadier General Charles P. Stone, a capable, energetic engineering officer to whom the Civil War had brought nothing but professional misfortune. A staunch and loyal Unionist, he had lost a minor battle early in the war and, without trial, was practically convicted of treason by the press and the secretary of war. His consuming ambition was to vindicate his honor, and in the judgment of history, he did so by his service with the khedive. Next to

Stone was Brigadier General William W. Loring, a battle-scarred veteran of the Mexican war and numerous Indian campaigns and a noted explorer of the American Far West. When the Civil War broke out, he resigned from the U.S. Army and cast his lot with his native South, but early in the conflict he disagreed on a matter of professional judgment with General Thomas Jonathan Jackson – the redoubtable Stonewall Jackson – and this stand blocked his advancement in the Confederate army. Loring was far from embittered, but he too was anxious to restore his reputation.[17]

In the khedive's army the Americans were primarily involved in organization and training, yet several found themselves in the thick of fighting. At Gondet, according to the English general and hero "Chinese" Gordon, an unidentified American commanding a detachment of black troops in 1875 "made a gallant fight" against an overwhelming body of Abyssinian invaders, until he and his entire force perished under the Abyssinian spears.[18] Loring, probably to his disgust, found himself chief of staff and adviser to an Egyptian prince who commanded a field force against the Abyssinians on another occasion – a prince who was ignorant of the very elements of war, felt no martial enthusiasm, and ignored all advice. When the demoralized prince fled the battlefield, it was Loring who saved the remnants of the command and prevented what was admittedly a defeat from becoming a disaster.

In the same battle, Surgeon Major Thomas D. Johnson of Tennessee, also a Confederate veteran, was wounded and captured. He was rescued by an Abyssinian *ras* (prince) when he was about to be murdered along with other prisoners, and was treated as a guest during the forty-odd days of his captivity. He was finally released after a long interrogation by King John of Abyssinia and upon his solemn promise to try to deliver a letter from the king to Queen Victoria unbeknownst to the "Turks" (i.e., the Egyptians). Many Europeans had earlier been in close contact with the Abyssinians, but Johnson was the first American to observe them intimately and to have a long audience with their ruler; his account of his experiences as a prisoner gives a balanced and objective view of his captors.[19]

In their efforts to modernize and discipline the Egyptian army, the Americans faced heavy odds. Nevertheless, they accomplished much that was positive:

> When the American officers accepted the invitation of Ismail Pasha the writ of the Khedive did not run throughout the Sudan. The Equatorial Provinces were closed to civilization. Under American leadership the Sudan was won back to Egypt, and during the period of their primacy the Egyptian flag was respected as far south as the Equator.[20]

The significance of these American "soldiers of misfortune" lies not in their ultimate failure to transform the Egyptian army into a first-class combat force, but rather in the trails they blazed into Central Africa. Incidental to their military duties, they reconnoitered and mapped thousands of miles of territory that Western men had never before seen. Their names are forgotten or little known, and others have received credit for discoveries and explorations actually made by them, yet these men put their stamp upon the Sudan and the vast regions south of the Sahara. General Loring has recorded some instances:

Lieutenant Colonel Mason and Colonel Prout navigated and surveyed Lake Albert Nyanza, discovered by Baker in 1864. General Raleigh Colston, formerly an officer of the South Confederacy, was more recently one of our American explorers in the interior of Africa. His geological and botanical collections, maps, and reconnaissance add much to the interest of a visit to the Citadel at Cairo. Devoted to duty, he penetrated into the comparatively unknown region between the Debbé, Mantoul, and Obeyail, and far into the provinces of Kordofan and Darfour in Central Africa.[21]

Colston's exploration of Kordofan under orders from the khedive took place in 1873 and 1874. It was Colston's second exploration, and came perilously close to being his last. Deep into Africa he became dangerously ill, so weak as to need assistance to mount his horse or even to walk, but he stubbornly refused to turn back until he reached El Obeid. Too ill to continue, he turned the expedition over to his second in command, Colonel Henry G. Prout, an engineer from the University of Michigan who had had experience in mapping the American West. Prout continued on into Darfur, where he joined an expedition under Major Erastus Purdy that had penetrated the region from another direction. Meanwhile – contrary to all expectations, including his own – Colston was recovering; his labors resulted in a substantial body of accurate and scientific knowledge concerning a part of Africa previously known only in legend.[22]

Americans responsible for other noted explorations and surveys included Major Oscar Eugene Fechet of Michigan – one of the five lieutenants granted indefinite leave of absence by General Sherman – who conducted surveys in Nubia and the Sudan and who designated Aswan as the most suitable site for a great dam to control the waters of the Nile. Major William P. A. Campbell, a former Confederate naval officer, took part in exploring the desert between Berenice on the Red Sea and Berber on the Nile. He became fluent in Arabic and in 1874 accompanied General Gordon to Khartoum, where he died of cholera. Lieutenant Colonel Alexander McComb Mason, a graduate of Annapolis who had served in the Confederate navy, was initially in charge of the khedive's steamers on the Nile, since there was no Egyptian navy; he found the assignment too restrictive, however, and soon joined the explorers. Mason discovered the Semliki River flowing into Lake Albert and proved that the waters that fed the Albert Nile came from the deep heartland of Africa; he also established and mapped the exact configuration of Lake Albert and determined its true extent.[23]

Colonel Charles Chaillé-Long, a native of the Eastern Shore of Maryland, was a college student when the Civil War broke out; most of his relatives and friends "went south," but Chaillé-Long entered the Union army and finished the war as a captain. Restless and looking for further military life, in 1870 he was commissioned a colonel in the khedive's army, and when Gordon arrived in Egypt in 1874 Chaillé-Long was designated his chief of staff by the Egyptian war ministry.[24]

Shortly after arriving in Equatoria with Gordon, Chaillé-Long was sent to Uganda, where, according to his own account, he concluded a treaty with M'Tesa by which the king acknowledged Egyptian overlordship. The political mission, however, was probably the least significant part of Chaillé-Long's journey. On his return, fighting his way through several attacks by tribesmen, he traversed a portion of the Nile never before explored by a white man and discovered Lake Kioga. Gordon wrote to his sister from Gondokoro on September 11, 1874, remarking that for more than six months he had not heard from Long, who had gone to Uganda. Six weeks later he wrote:

> Long came in the day before yesterday. He has had a hard time of it. He left this place for Fatiko on April 24; got there in ten days, and from thence went on to Karuma Falls . . . He went to Mtesa and got a very good reception. He went down to Urundongani, and thence, with two canoes, descended the Nile to Foweira. He found no cataracts at all on the route . . . Long says he passed through a large lake between Urundongani and Foweira. He was attacked by Kaba Rega's men and had to fight his way through near Mrooli.[25]

In 1875 Chaillé-Long commanded the Egyptian land forces in the McKillop expedition to undertake an amphibious operation in the Indian Ocean. To obviate some of the difficulties of communication between Cairo and Equatoria via the Nile, the khedive – probably encouraged by Gordon's advice – decided to establish an Egyptian base in what is now southern Somalia. The expedition sailed from Suez on September 18, 1875, and on October 16 and 17 landed at the mouth of the Juba River without any opposition. As a precaution, the McKillop expedition seized the antiquated fort, held by a nominal Zanzibari garrison, and occupied the slave-trading port of Kismayu (Chisimaio), liberating more than five hundred slaves.[26]

The port and the territory occupied were within the domains claimed by the sultan of Zanzibar, and it was not long before he took action. Even though he provided one of the expedition's ships with coal and sent a present of fresh fruits and other supplies to Chaillé-Long, he also cabled Great Britain: "Egyptian pirates have seized my army and country and massacred my people. Come to my aid." It was no part of Great Britain's policy to permit Egyptian expansion into areas in which British commercial interests were expanding, so the khedive was pressured to change his plans, and the Juba River expedition was withdrawn.[27]

Chaillé-Long resigned his Egyptian commission in 1877. Except for a brief period of conspicuous and distinguished service as U.S. consular agent at Alexandria at the time of the British bombardment in 1882, he had no further concern with Africa.[28]

The British occupied Egypt in 1882, and the Americans gradually departed from the Nile and from Egyptian affairs. The great colonial powers of Europe carved up most of Africa among themselves. The United States, except for participating in the Berlin conference of 1884–5 and the Brussels conference of 1890, remained aloof from Africa during the last quarter of the nineteenth century. The few Americans who went there did so quite unofficially and on their own. There were no massive subscription drives to outfit exploring expeditions, nor was there an official organization to represent the government's interest or to advance money and add prestige.

Journalist-explorers

Popular interest in Africa did, however, produce the journalist-explorer, a characteristically American phenomenon. The greatest was Stanley, who in 1887 disappeared into the African interior to "rescue" Emin Pasha, the governor of Egyptian Equatoria. Emin Pasha was not in fact very anxious to be relieved, but finally departed in Stanley's company. The *New York World*, a bitter rival of Bennett's *Herald*, decided to emulate its enemy by sending out Thomas Stevens. Stevens had already achieved a degree of fame by riding a bicycle around the world and by riding a mustang across the Russian Empire. He was directed to investigate the troubles between the Germans and Arabs in East Africa, to look into the slave trade, and to find out everything possible regarding the fate of Stanley and Emin. The newspaper authorized Stevens to organize a relief expedition at Zanzibar, as Stanley had done in his search for Livingstone.

Stevens led his expedition to the borders of the Masai country (hundreds of miles from where Stanley actually was), but when word reached him that Stanley had reappeared and was en route to Bagamoyo through territory that had been acquired by Germany, Stevens resolved to be the first person from the outside world to greet him. Outwitting German authorities who forbade him to cross the territory and operating on a combination of courage, brazen audacity, and pure luck, Stevens finally caught up with the great explorer. He did not quite achieve his goal of being the first to meet Stanley, for Baron von Gravenreuth of the German army arrived at Stanley's camp ahead of him, but he got there in advance of Frank Vizetelly, correspondent for the *New York Herald*. Stanley was unfeignedly glad to see the two Americans as well as the German officer, and he broke out a bottle of champagne carefully saved for just such an occasion.[29]

An explorer of a different sort was A. Donaldson Smith of Philadelphia, who led his own expedition from Somaliland into Central Africa in 1894 and 1895. Smith was a wealthy man educated and trained as a physician (he studied medicine at Harvard, Johns Hopkins, and Heidelberg) who was by choice a sportsman and biologist. He wrote:

> The keen love of sport and adventure that is innate in most of the Anglo-Saxon race had always prompted me to go into the remotest corners of the earth, and I suppose it was my seven years medical training in America and Europe which taught me never to lose a chance of doing scientific work when it presented itself.[30]

A hunting trip to Somaliland with a friend led Smith to attempt a more extensive expedition to combine exploration of unknown country with the collection of zoological, botanical, and geological specimens for scientific study. He was wealthy enough to finance the project himself, and in 1894, when he was thirty years old, he set out from Berbera with a single American companion and a large and carefully equipped expedition. For several months they hunted, researched, and occasionally fought across Somaliland and southern Abyssinia. Smith and his party made a detailed examination of Lake Stefanie, discovering an unknown smaller lake nearby (which he named Lake Donaldson), and continued westward to Lake Rudolf – a feat that had been considered impossible – returning to the coast along the Tana River through parts of Africa until then unexplored.

Smith's journey through East Africa, while not as epoch-making as Stanley's earlier voyage down the Congo, was important scientifically and geographically. His zoological collection included twenty-four previously unknown species of birds, eleven new reptiles, and scores of insects that naturalists had not seen before. He reported vast reaches of East Africa to be suitable for white colonization and capable of cultivation.[31]

Off the southeast coast of Africa in 1884 an American naval officer, Lieutenant Mason A. Shufeldt, explored the interior of Madagascar and made what may have been the first crossing of the entire breadth of the island for purely exploratory purposes. Shufeldt was a son of Commodore Robert W. Shufeldt, who had commanded the *Ticonderoga* on its round-the-world voyage of commercial investigation. He was graduated from the U.S. Naval Academy in 1873 and spent most of his sea service in the Far East. As an officer of the *Ticonderoga* under his father's command, he became interested in Madagascar and its problems when the ship stopped there for some time. He conceived the idea of exploring the unknown interior and wrote to Washington requesting permission to do so. Authorization from the secretary of the navy reached him months later, when he had all but forgotten his request. At that time, in November 1883, he was on board the USS *Enterprise* in Korean waters, and it was not until late in May 1884 that he was able to reach Tananarive (then known as Antananarivo), the inland capital of the huge island. The queen's government had received advance notice of his coming, and upon his arrival at the east coast Shufeldt was received by a high official with a letter of welcome.

The eastern part of Madagascar was fairly well known to the world; the western part was little known to Europeans. The tribes of the west were in revolt against the somewhat fumbling efforts of the queen and her ministers (who were resisting French aggression at the same time) to extend their authority into that region.[32] The country was disease-ridden, and a powerful slave trader named Rakatava was bitterly opposed to anything that might interfere with his business. The few European inhabitants of the capital assured Shufeldt that any attempt to cross to the west coast would be suicidal. Nevertheless, he started on May 28, 1884, with one European companion and a considerable army of local people: In addition to 180 bearers whom he hired himself, some 350 soldiers with their families were to escort him to the west coast and to remain there as settlers and as a garrison.

The march across the island took almost a full month, and both Shufeldt and his lone white companion nearly died of fever. On at least one occasion Shufeldt, with his revolver, suppressed a mutiny among his followers. There were several fights with hostile tribes, presumably Rakatava's followers. The expedition suffered from hunger and found the country destitute of anything edible. Nevertheless, on June 24, 1884, Shufeldt reached the Mozambique Channel after traversing regions not described previously by any European. Dismissing the army, he and his companion hired a native canoe and two weeks later reached the mainland in Mozambique; there they saw the American flag flying over the *Sarah Hobart* of Boston, on which they would return home.

Scientifically, Shufeldt's expedition accomplished little. However, he formed the conclusion that the "Zizibongy" (Mania) River could be a commercial channel into the heart of the island and that Madagascar's potential as a producer of agricultural and mineral products was enormous. This nearly forgotten expedition occurred during a period when the United States was committed to isolation and when foreign commerce was receiving relatively little attention from American businessmen. But the fact that a naval officer was detached for months from his normal duties – and, presumably, provided with the money to pay his passage from Korea to Madagascar, to hire 180 bearers, and to buy food for them to consume over a period of weeks – argues that some persons in the U.S. government were interested in future possibilities.[33]

A. Donaldson Smith and Mason A. Shufeldt were typical in many respects of the Americans who took part in the exploration and opening of East Africa in the latter part of the nineteenth century. They did not brave the very real dangers of disease, martial tribes, and wild beasts because of a duty imposed by their own government and people. They were not building an American empire. The only empire builders among them were those who, owing temporary allegiance to the khedive of Egypt, conscientiously furthered his expansionist policies during their years in his service. By far the greater number of Americans who took part in African affairs were inspired by altruism (the missionaries, for example), by the traditional ambition of Americans to better themselves through pioneering, or by the motives that prompted Smith and Shufeldt to leave civilization and venture into the wilds: love of adventure, science, and sport and the new desire for publicity fostered by the popular press serving a mass public.

CHAPTER 14

Miners and adventurers

Gold and diamonds

Gradually the American Far West was reduced to law and order. The farmer replaced the mountain man and the trapper, the Indian ceased to be an enemy and became an anachronism secluded in a reservation, and the men who had pushed westward began to look elsewhere for riches and adventure. Africa beckoned to such men. They were rapidly working out the California gold fields, but they heard of the new strikes of gold in Africa; and the hostility of the Matabele warrior or Arab slaver appealed to some of the men who had fought the Apache or Sioux.

The Americans who flocked to the southern regions of Africa in the latter part of the nineteenth century went there in search of wealth and, except for the missionaries, often were not particular about the means by which they might achieve success – a characteristic they shared with men of other nationalities. Their ranks included educated men and illiterates, devout men and atheists, farmers and sharp city types, bookkeepers and soldiers of fortune. Whatever their backgrounds, they were tough, mentally and physically. To survive under frontier conditions, to endure hardship and overcome an environment that was often bitterly hostile, required a temperament hard as steel. The idealist had to be as tough as the grossest materialist. The men who left the United States to search for quick riches in southern Africa, like all other white pioneers on that continent, possessed such hardness to a conspicuous degree.

A gold rush is an international affair. The California gold rush attracted men from every continent. Similarly, the discoveries of gold and diamonds in South Africa drew prospectors from everywhere, including an appreciable number of veteran American prospectors who were still young and vigorous enough to try again. Since the Americans, almost alone among the gold seekers, had practical experience and know-how, their prestige and influence was disproportionate to their actual numbers.

During the early 1850s the white Boer settlers of the newly formed Transvaal Republic, possibly influenced by the discovery of gold in California and in Australia, became mildly interested in the mineral possibilities of their new country. Consequently, when Pieter Jacob Marais returned to Africa from several years' prospecting for gold in California and suggested to the legislative assembly, in the autumn of 1853, that he be authorized to search for gold, his suggestion was eagerly accepted; a contract between the government and Marais was signed, and he began to prospect. He did not have to look long; he was in the midst of what would prove to be one of the richest gold fields in the world. On January 7, 1854, Marais exhibited a quantity of gold dust from the Witwatersrand, causing a local sensation. But the discovery was not publicized, and the excitement quickly died down. Most of the Boers wished to live as farmers; they were not at all anxious to start a movement that would bring large numbers of Englishmen into their rural Utopia and return them to British rule. The *Graaf Reinet Herald* commented on March 4, 1854: "Gold was discovered here a few months ago by Mr. Marais . . . The Vaal River Government have closed the diggings, until it is decided whether they shall coin their own gold, and whether the Sovereignty will be retained or abandoned by the British Government."[1]

The gold fields did not become important for thirty more years, but in 1867 another mineral transformed the South African economy and dragged the subcontinent into the mainstream of world affairs. The major source of the world's diamond supply until then was India, with a small part of the supply coming from Brazil. This status changed shortly after a Boer's child accidentally discovered a single diamond on his father's farm in 1867. The first stone caused no particular excitement. The leading geological and mining savants of Great Britain shook their heads glumly; South Africa was positively not a diamond country. Sir Roderick Murchison, the most eminent geologist of the day, went so far as to say that he would stake his professional reputation on there being no diamond matrix in the country.[2]

The discovery of a second diamond several months later, however, brought an influx of hopeful fortune seekers. As in the California and Australian gold rushes, few actually struck it rich, but some realized their dreams and thus encouraged others. Among the lucky ones was an Irishman turned American whose total assets were thirty shillings in small coins. When this amount was exhausted, he joined the horde of vagrants who drifted from claim to claim, living by their wits. Finally staking a claim at Bulfontein, he formed a partnership with two brothers who owned a claim nearby – and a few years later the three sold their rights to the newly formed De Beers corporation for a sum in excess of £5 million.[3]

An American, Jerome L. Babe, whose name still survives in the diamond fields, was among the earliest arrivals in 1870. Babe was in South Africa as a salesman for the Winchester Repeating Arms Company and as part-time correspondent for the *New York World*. After completing his business at the frontier settlement of Colesberg, he found that he had a few months to spare and decided to try his luck in the diamond fields, some forty miles distant. Babe had been a prospector in California and was unpleasantly impressed with the amount of sheer physical labor in "dry" digging, a process that involved carrying huge amounts of excavated material to the nearest water, or vice versa. To eliminate this step, he devised a simple, easily constructed apparatus for the dry screening of the earth and gravel. By the time he left the diamond fields a few months later, there were hundreds of his "Yankee Baby" devices in use, and the "baby" is still used by African prospectors. Babe was moderately successful in his search for diamonds, but he prospered more by selling diamonds that he bought from miners who needed immediate cash. He also grubstaked a number of American and English prospectors and arranged for the purchase of a large tract of land for an American company.[4]

The presence of gold became widely known in the late 1870s, and the gold fields began to attract hordes of prospectors, among them many Americans.[5] In the 1880s, in addition, prospectors who failed to realize fortunes in gems began to wash the gravels, looking for gold dust and nuggets; in due course, perhaps partly as an accidental by-product of the diamond rush, the surface deposits of South African minerals that attracted independent prospectors were exhausted. To explore, determine, and exploit the deep ore veins and ledges required capital and knowledge far beyond the resources of the "shovel and blanket-roll" prospector. Highly trained and experienced geologists, mining engineers, mine managers, and smelter operators were needed for operations that involved the sinking of shafts hundreds of feet deep, the installation and use of heavy and complex machinery, and the construction of huge industrial plants.

In the 1870s and 1880s the United States, the foremost mining country in the world, probably had more of these expert mining engineers and skilled mine operators than any other nation. Thus, even though most of the capital invested in South African mines was British or was locally raised, Americans supplied the expert knowledge when and where it was needed. In contrast to the rough-and-ready miners of the frontier and the prospectors of the gold-rush days, most of these men were educated and trained in technical colleges in the United States, and several had studied at the Royal Saxon School of Mines at Freiberg, Saxony, which was then one of the most advanced mining schools in the world. Typically, they came to South Africa with years of experience behind them and with established reputations in their professional field. Upon the reports of these Americans, capital was raised and shares of stock fell or rose to several times their nominal worth.[6] The significance of the American contribution to the South African mining industries therefore lies not in the presence of prospectors but in the fact that so many of the experts who developed the mines and smelters were from the United States.

The first noteworthy arrival was Ethelbert Woodford in 1876. Woodford was exceptional in that he was an engineer and an authority on mining without benefit of a college degree. He became a railway construction engineer by practical experience, and he seems gradually to have directed his interests into mining. Within a short time after his arrival in South Africa he was appointed town engineer for Kimberley; later he was chief engineer for the mining board. In 1887, after an interval in South America, he returned to become the consultant mining engineer for the Transvaal Republic, and in this capacity he drew up the mining code that is still the basis for much of the mining law of South Africa. Woodford made himself considerably unpopular among the mining population by bitterly opposing the efforts of mining adventurers (including many Americans) who sought to escape the control of the Transvaal government and to undermine the republic in order to bring about British annexation.[7]

Important though Woodford's work was, his greatest significance was in being the forerunner: He pointed the way for other American mining engineers and technicians who came a few years later to play an even greater part in developing what would become South Africa's major industry. Among the scores, possibly even hundreds, are four whose contributions were outstanding: Hamilton Smith, James Hennen Jennings, Gardner Williams, and John Hays Hammond.[8]

Hamilton Smith, whose influence was far-reaching, was a Kentuckian of New England ancestry. Like Woodford, he achieved a high place in his profession without academic preparation. His early education was supervised by his grandfather in New England; at the age of fourteen he went to work in his father's Indiana coal mines to learn about mining engineering and accounting; and when barely out of his teens he was a recognized expert in both subjects. He went to the Pacific Coast in 1869, and within a few years he was probably the world's foremost authority on hydraulics. In California he attracted the attention of Baron Rothschild, then in the United States to inspect Rothschild properties, and was engaged by him as a consulting engineer and sent to El Callao, Venezuela, where he gathered about him a small group of young mining engineers destined to leave their mark upon South Africa.

Smith did not actually spend much time in Africa. He visited South Africa twice, in 1892 and 1895, but his influence upon subsequent developments in gold production has been immeasurable. It was his report on the potential of the South African gold fields after his first visit that persuaded the Rothschilds to expand their interests in the country and invest heavily there. The men who developed the industry were men whose training and thought he had influenced deeply.[9]

James Hennen Jennings was one of Smith's protégés and, like him, was a native of Kentucky and born to a family with coal-mining interests in Indiana, but he approached the profession of mining engineer by the academic route. Jennings attended school in England and graduated from the Lawrence Scientific School of Harvard University. He was associated with Smith in both California and Venezuela, and in 1889 was a consulting engineer in London. Within a few months the firm for which he was consultant sent him to South Africa, where he quickly attained a position of influence in the mining industry. When the Transvaal government appointed a commission to inquire into various aspects of mining, Jennings's testimony was said by the chairman to have given the commission a clearer insight into the working of the mines than that of any other witness.[10]

Although most of the American mining experts who applied their training and abilities to the South African mines were concerned with the production of gold, Gardner Fred Williams was a diamond expert. He was a native of Michigan who decided on a mining career while still quite young, and he became one of the first graduates of the newly established University of California. He then went on to the Royal Saxon School of Mines at Freiberg, and returned to California for his master's degree. Only after his academic foundation was firmly laid did he commence practical professional work in the mining districts of the Far West and in Mexico. In 1884, upon the recommendation of Hamilton Smith, he was engaged to take charge of some gold-mining properties in the Transvaal, a project that led directly to an acquaintance and association with Cecil Rhodes. This connection brought him to the attention of the Rothschilds and – with a shift of his interest from gold to diamonds – to the management of the De Beers properties. Williams's seventeen-year management of the De Beers mines helped make them the monolithic center of the world's diamond production.[11]

Perhaps the most noteworthy – certainly the best known and most spectacular – of the Americans in South Africa was John Hays Hammond. He was a protégé of Gardner Williams, who had persuaded him to turn down an attractive offer from the mining magnate George Hearst and accept a less lucrative position with the U.S. Geological Survey for the sake of the experience and knowledge he would thus gain.[12] Hammond did not arrive in South Africa until 1893; he was engaged by Barney Barnato, an Anglo-Jewish speculator who had amassed a fortune in the mines, to inspect and oversee various properties at the then enormous salary of

$50,000 a year. But since Barnato ignored his advice on several occasions, Hammond resigned within a few months and was immediately hired by Cecil Rhodes at an even greater salary (rumored to have been $75,000). As one of Rhodes's principal agents and as consulting engineer for Consolidated Gold Fields of South Africa, Hammond had influence second only to that of Rhodes himself in the economic development of South Africa. He hired and fired; he opened and closed mines and plants; and when Rhodes's interests and ambitions caused him to intervene in South African politics, Hammond became deeply involved in the bitter feud between the Boers and the *Uitlanders* (the foreign residents, chiefly British) in the Transvaal.

Large numbers of foreigners were attracted to South Africa as the richness of its mineral resources became apparent. The agrarian Boers of the two independent republics, the Transvaal and the Orange Free State, regarded this influx with deep distrust. They feared Great Britain; the parents of most of them had migrated on the Great Trek for the express purposes of escaping British rule. The Boers had no desire to kill the mining industry, but they were determined to keep political control of the republics in their own hands. At the same time, somewhat shortsightedly, they imposed upon the *Uitlanders* a highly discriminatory revenue system under which the foreigners paid most of the taxes. The mining industry still earned large profits, but some of the British mine and plant operators feared, or professed to fear, that unless drastic steps were taken the Boer farmers would fail to supply the supporting services needed by the industry, while taxing it out of existence.

The measures taken by the Boers, intended primarily to maintain their control of the country, conflicted directly with the Rhodes dream of a great British empire in Africa extending from the Cape to Cairo. A head-on collision between the two opposed ideals was almost inevitable. During the several years of agitation that preceded the actual break, most of the Americans in South Africa saw only one side of the case and failed to understand that a monopoly by Cecil Rhodes and his group would be as oppressive as the Boer oligarchy. They saw only that the *Uitlanders,* of whom they were a part, were virtually without civic rights, even though in some areas they claimed to be in a majority. Finally, aided and abetted by Rhodes, the foreigners began to plot a revolution.

One of the principal conspirators was John Hays Hammond, who maintained that he was doing only what the Americans of 1774 and 1775 had done. Over a stretch of months he and Gardner Williams smuggled arms and ammunition into the country. Hammond was also instrumental in swinging the support of the Americans in the Transvaal to the revolutionary side. In describing his activities, he wrote:

> I may begin . . . with a meeting held by five hundred Americans in Johannesburg . . . in December, 1895. What we had met to decide was whether or not we should give our support to a Revolution which was then brewing against the Boer oligarchy. Our grievances were so well known that there was no need for me to enlarge upon them; all I had to do was to take the sense of those present – and every class of American was represented – on the question of whether the point had not been reached to which the signers of the Declaration [of Independence] referred.[13]

The plot did not proceed as planned. An armed force consisting mostly of police of the British South Africa Company (the "Chartered Company") and led by Rhodes's close friend Dr. Leander Starr Jameson – a physician turned miner, soldier, explorer, and administrator – entered the Transvaal from Bechuanaland. These so-called raiders were captured January 2, 1896, at Doornkop, and the movement was nipped in the bud. Hammond's part in the conspiracy became known; he was arrested, tried by a Boer court-martial, and sentenced to be shot, but the sentence was commuted to payment of a huge fine and a pledge to abstain from meddling in Transvaal politics.[14]

Other Americans helped in various ways to bring South Africa to the important position it has attained in the world's economy.[15] Louis Seymour revolutionized the operation of the diamond mines with his self-winding engines. Leslie Simpson, a graduate of the University of California who had no previous practical experience, established world records for speed and depth in digging mine shafts. George Labram, who attained fame during the Boer war, erected a crushing plan for De Beers and designed an efficient grease table for catching diamonds in the sorter. And Anthony Robeson designed a pulsator for the last stages of diamond sorting.

The United States thus provided a reservoir of men, devices, and ideas – second only to Great Britain in importance for South Africa. Frontier conditions in the United States widely resembled those in southern Africa. The United States therefore could supply technological and scientific expertise of a particularly useful kind. Americans, used to moving from state to state within their own country, were widely willing to try their luck in other countries where English was universally understood in business. A great many inventions pioneered or perfected by Americans helped to transform the South African economy, including the typewriter, vulcanized rubber, the telephone, the paraffin and the incandescent lamp, the steam-driven and the gasoline-driven tractor, the sewing machine, barbed wire, the wind pump, and especially the automobile and the motor truck. American argicultural scientists, veterinarians, physicians, astronomists, biologists, and a host of other experts worked in South Africa to good effect. Americans established a variety of new industries; for instance, William Russell Quinan and Kenneth Bingham Quinan introduced the manufacture of dynamite into South Africa. These men were so numerous that a full listing of their names would turn this chapter into a tedious catalogue.

The adventurers

The hundreds of Americans in southern Africa in the late nineteenth century were by no means all professional men or highly trained technical specialists. The redoubtable breed of frontiersmen produced by the American West – men versed in the arts of the wilderness, of hunting game and finding their way through unknown country – were masters in the specialized craft of subduing untamed nature and resisting the attack of Indian warriors. These skills were equally in demand on the frontiers of South Africa's "Far North," and Americans soon made their appearance in the heart of Africa. Adam Renders, a German-American hunter and prospector, was one of these. He apparently quarreled with his family, abandoned them, and then "went native" while he hunted elephants in the unknown regions of what became Rhodesia (now Zimbabwe). There he discovered the ruins of the ancient Zimbabwe—as far as is known, he was the first white man ever to see them—and the prehistoric gold mines in the vicinity.[16]

Another American was the picturesque Guillermo Antonio Farini, who seems to have been a showman. He had walked across Niagara Falls on a tightrope; in the 1870s he operated the famous London Aquarium; and he first went to South Africa in 1882 to obtain some real Bushmen to take to London; at least one of those Bushmen later went with Farini to the United States. In 1885, accompanied by his son, Farini made an exploring and sporting trip into the Kalahari Desert, where, if he is to be believed, he discovered the extensive ruins of a prehistoric city. His book about the Kalahari was one of the first reports of that remote area by an eyewitness, and his descriptions of the flora and fauna were acclaimed at the time as important contributions to the knowledge of a previously unknown region.[17]

In 1890 Rhodes organized a picked body of young men, the Pioneer Corps, to occupy Mashonaland and take advantage of a concession he and his associates had obtained from the Matabele king, Lobengula. Rhodes instructed Frank Johnson, a young British adventurer to whom he entrusted the details and command of the corps, to select only first-class marksmen and horsemen and also to use men representing varied trades and professions. The Pioneer Corps erected a fort in Salisbury, disbanded, and established Rhodes's claim to the vast country that became known as Rhodesia (Zimbabwe). Soon farmers and ranchers, men, women, and children, flocked into Mashonaland. As one of his company commanders and as a key assistant Johnson chose an American who had been in Africa since 1879, Maurice B. Heany (or Heaney—the name was spelled both ways).[18]

Little is known of Heany's background and career before he went to Africa. It was widely believed that he was a Virginian by birth and a cousin of Edgar Allan Poe, that he was an officer of the U.S. Army, and that he had seen considerable service in the Indian wars in the United States.[19] What took him to Africa is unknown, but he first became prominent as an officer in the Pioneer Corps and he continued for years thereafter to play a conspicuous part in the affairs of Southern Rhodesia. He and Johnson had become acquainted when they were members of the Bechuanaland Border Police and later, with a man named Borrow, they formed a business triumvirate that had a marked influence on the economic development of the newly opened territories. In 1885, in one of their first joint enterprises, Heany and Johnson tried to find the source of the quills of gold dust that the Africans often used to pay for imported luxuries. Heany thus was one of the few white men who had already been in the country to which the corps was sent and which Rhodes proposed to settle.

Heany later served with distinction in the Matabele war of 1893 and in the Shona and Ndebele rebellions of 1896. In the abortive Johannesburg revolution of late 1895, the Jameson Raid, he was the trusted confidential messenger sent by Rhodes with an important message for Jameson. He is said to have been the only raider not captured; he was ungentlemanly enough to violate the tacitly understood rules by shooting his way out through the encircling Boer commandos.[20] Heany spent the remainder of his life in Rhodesia (he died in 1928), living to see the country in which he had pioneered become a modern state.

The Pioneer Corps included other Americans, among whom was William

Harvey Brown, a young biologist employed in the U.S. National Museum. On an afternoon in the early autumn of 1889 he was astonished when the museum's director, without warning, asked him if he was prepared to sail shortly for Africa: The government was sending an expedition to Cape Town to observe a solar eclipse, and the museum was authorized to send along a naturalist to obtain specimens for its collections. The American scientific party was in South Africa while the Pioneer Corps was being formed. Brown and a friend in the museum group liked the idea of exploring new country, and Brown saw in the corps an opportunity to obtain for the museum rare zoological, botanical, and anthropological material. With the permission of the chief of the party and the approval of both the navy captain in charge of the expedition and the U.S. consul at Cape Town, he and his friend enlisted as Pioneers and Brown continued to collect and forward scientific material to Washington.[21] Upon the breakup of the corps he stayed on in Africa. He fought in the Matabele and Mashona rebellions – in the latter he was badly wounded – and did not return to America for almost eight years. His half brother from California, joining him, helped to establish the Salisbury Botanical Gardens.

Frederick Russell Burnham may have been the best known among the Americans who pioneered in Southern Rhodesia. He had been a prospector, a rancher, and a well-known scout with the U.S. Army in the Apache wars in Arizona before coming to Africa and joining the British in the Matabele war, where his skills and experience soon made him almost a legend. At the time when the Boer republics and the British Empire came to open blows in 1899, the British commander in chief, Lord Roberts, invited Burnham to return to Africa to serve as chief scout for the British forces; by special decree he was permitted to accept a commission in the British army without renouncing his U.S. citizenship.[22] Among the hard-bitten frontiersmen of southern Africa there were not many who could glance at a trail and say approximately how many men and horses had passed and at what time, or who could sniff a passing breeze and say confidently that an enemy force was so many miles distant. But Burnham was reputedly able to do all these things, and the Burnham legends grew.

More important was the part Burnham played in discovering some of the copper deposits situated near the Kafue River in Northern Rhodesia. The areas of Arizona and northern Mexico where he had prospected were rich in copper, and he spotted a bracelet of native copper worn by the slave wife of a Matabele who was digging a well for him. Questioning disclosed that the Matabele had acquired his wife on a raid into a country far to the north. Painfully slow interrogation – the woman could not speak a language that could be readily understood, even by her husband – revealed how her people obtained the red metal: "Messages repeated back and forth from interpreter to interpreter through four languages brought out these facts: her country was the same number of days march beyond the Great River as it was from Bulawayo to the Zambesi [and] this metal came from ingudines, holes in the ground."[23] As a result, Burnham obtained financing by a group of British and South African capitalists; in 1895 he undertook a systematic exploration for the "holes in the ground" and found where they were.

Pioneers of a different kind followed the Pioneer Corps; they were civil servants and technicians who laid the foundations of good government without which the country could not have prospered. Once more Americans were among those in the forefront. John Hays Hammond and Gardner Williams drafted Southern Rhodesia's first mining laws, which have remained substantially unchanged, and an American was responsible for laying out the streets and avenues of the capital, Salisbury.

Once a European administration had been set up, settlers with their families began to establish permanent homes in the country. American enterprise took an important share in this colonization process by contributing to early transport. Before the railroad was constructed from the Cape into Southern Rhodesia, the familiar American stagecoach – shipped across the seas from the Far West, where it had outlived its usefulness – was the de luxe transportation on the African frontier. Cobb and Company, a California firm, is credited with responsibility for this particular stroke of acumen.

The Boer war

The press and people of the United States were largely sympathetic toward the Boers in their disputes with the British Empire, but Americans in South Africa were almost without exception on the British side: In the Boer war (1899–1902, discussed in greater detail in Chapter 16) many Americans fought on the British side, and very few joined the Boer commandos.[24] The Americans who were cut off from the outside world in the besieged cities or mining camps of Mafeking and Kimberley took an active part in their defense. As the Boers closed in on Kimberley – its defenders equipped only with small arms and a few pieces of light artillery – Rhodes called into conference one of his American engineers, George Labram. As a result, Labram commenced work in the De Beers shops on December 27, 1899, and three weeks later a heavy gun of 4.1 caliber began throwing shells to a range of 8,000 yards. Even before he started to build "Long Cecil," as the gun was nicknamed, Labram had turned the shops into an improvised munitions factory producing ammunition for the light artillery. Without the inventive and mechanical genius of this American, Kimberley might have been forced to surrender.[25]

A few Americans in South Africa joined Boer fighting forces. A famous commando unit, the Irish Brigade, was composed largely of Americans and commanded by Colonel John Y. Fillmore Blake,[26] a graduate of the U.S. Military Academy. It seems that a sizable proportion of the Americans on the Boer side were Irish of birth and descent, men whose emnity for Great Britain was traditional and almost hereditary. Certainly, forty volunteers from Chicago who pretended to be Red Cross volunteers to the British army and then joined the Boer forces, being assimilated into Blake's command, were motivated largely by such a sentiment.[27] Blake's brigade took part in all the principal battles of the war (during which Blake himself was wounded), and was not disbanded until the Boer forces finally disintegrated at the end of the war.

Both the Boers and the British availed themselves of American scouting talent and experience. Captain John A. Hassell, a native of New Jersey, organized and commanded a group of Americans as a reconnaissance force, the American Scouting Corps.[28] Because the Boer side of the war was not well publicized in spite of efforts to gain American sympathy, nothing can be said of the actual exploits of Hassell's men, but their services were greatly valued by the Boer high command.

This was a time when the American people were becoming increasingly aware of the world outside their own country, and the war attracted a good deal of attention in the United States. One of its immediate effects was to stimulate interest in furnishing a hospital ship, along with other humanitarian measures. A group of socially prominent American women led by Lady Randolph Churchill (the mother of Winston Churchill) raised nearly $200,000 and chartered the SS *Maine*, which was equipped to care for the sick and wounded of both sides. The surgeons and nursing staff were Americans, and the ship was fitted with the most modern hospital equipment available, including the X ray. Goods and stores offered by British firms were accepted by the *Maine* committee, but subscriptions for the ship came from the American public.[29]

Agricultural impact

Although mining and the related industries are of major importance in the economy of southern Africa, the region has always been basically agrarian. American agronomists and horticulturists in southern Africa have been less spectacular in their achievements than prospectors and mining engineers, but from the United States came many of the fruits, vegetables, and other farm products basic to today's agriculture. Maize, tobacco, and the potato, items that have revolutionized agriculture all over the world, are of American origin. California, having provided initial training and experience for most of the American mining experts who took part in developing South Africa's mines, also sent its agricultural skill; it was recognized as the world's foremost fruit-producing region in the latter part of the nineteenth century.

The first impact of Americans upon the agriculture of southern Africa occurred in the 1890s when South Africa, long famous for its wines, saw phylloxera devastate its viticulture. The insect threatened the industry with extinction. As in France a few years earlier, the infected stock was dug up and replaced with resistant vines from California, but the vineyardists faced several barren years before the imported vines could mature and produce. At this juncture a young American, W. E. Pickstone, entered the scene; he seems to have been related to W. Fox Pickstone, a member of a firm that shipped fruit from South Africa to Great Britain. The American Pickstone was an adventurer who went to Africa seeking action in the tribal wars, but his education and training in California had made him a skilled horticulturist. He became acquainted with Cecil Rhodes and convinced the magnate that this was an opportune time to buy vast areas of vineyard land cheaply; the owners were glad to sell at any price.

Rhodes purchased twenty-five vineyard estates and, under Pickstone's management, had them planted to citrus and other fruits. As in his other enterprises, Rhodes set about raising fruit on a mammoth scale, and he shortly augmented the staff by bringing Rees Alfred Davis, an authority on citrus culture, from California. Other orchard crops, too – the loquat and pecan nut and new varieties of such old fruits as the Satsuma plum and Calimyrna fig – were introduced into South Africa from the United States.[30] South Africa ultimately became one of the leading fruit-producing countries of the world, with annual exports (mostly to Great Britain and the United States) to the value of millions of pounds sterling carried in fleets of fast refrigerator ships.[31]

Tobacco was an early crop in Southern Rhodesia, and it became one of the most successful. A few of the first settlers experimented with tobacco without much success; they produced a satisfactory leaf, but lacked the knowledge of how to cure and season it. Urged by Earl Grey, a director of the British South Africa Company, G. M. Odlum went to the United States to study all phases of the tobacco industry in American plantations and warehouses; he returned to Southern Rhodesia in 1904 with several American specialists to apply what he had learned. From that time tobacco cultivation and manufacture increased, and with some ups and downs, tobacco became one of the country's major economic resources.[32]

Americans also exerted a degree of influence in other fields of agriculture, particularly among the Africans. American missionaries are believed to have introduced into South Africa the cultivation of cotton, sugarcane, and rice, although the evidence is not conclusive. Certainly the trade and agricultural schools, which grew out of the missionaries' need to establish farms for their own food, have had a marked effect upon African life.

CHAPTER 15

Capitalists and missionaries

During the period between the Civil War and the end of the nineteenth century, American relationships with southern Africa, as with the rest of the continent, depended largely on the individual interests of private persons. Political isolationism was so deeply ingrained that the U.S. government, while endeavoring to keep itself fully informed, remained strictly aloof from intervention in African affairs. Thus it was an exceptional event when President Grover Cleveland, the arch-isolationist who had withdrawn the Congo treaty from the Senate, stated in his annual message to Congress on December 1, 1889:

> In the summer of 1889 an incident occurred which for a time threatened to interrupt the cordiality of our relations with the Government of Portugal. That Government seized the Delagoa Bay Railway, which was constructed under a concession granted to an American citizen, and at the same time annulled the charter. The concessionary, who had embarked his fortune in the enterprise, having exhausted other means of redress, was compelled to invoke the protection of his Government. Our representations, made coincidentally with those of the British Government, whose subjects were also largely interested, happily resulted in the recognition by Portugal of the propriety of submitting the claim for indemnity, growing out of its action, to arbitration.[1]

The foundation for this statement had been laid several years before. On December 22, 1884, the U.S. minister at Lisbon wrote in a dispatch to the State Department that the Portuguese government had just granted permission to Colonel Edward McMurdo, an American, to build a railroad from Lourenço Marques on the Mozambique coast to the Transvaal frontier. The country the railroad would traverse presented few natural difficulties or serious engineering problems, and construction proceeded rapidly. But the project soon became inextricably involved with the Anglo-Boer disputes. Portugal may have begun to fear that it had acted hastily in granting the concession: McMurdo's railroad might provide an excuse for the seizure of Mozambique by the British. Portuguese fears, though not in fact justified, were not allayed by such pronouncements as this, made by a British commentator on current events:

> In South Africa . . . our first consideration is the consolidation to their natural limits of the territories to the south of the Zambesi. We must stretch out to the banks of the river; on the North-West we are limited by the German claims; on the North-East every legitimate effort must be made to obtain command of Delagoa Bay and its railway, which, commercially and politically, would render us supreme over all South Africa.[2]

Fear of British seizure of Mozambique was reinforced by the knowledge that London was where McMurdo had sold most of the bonds to finance the railroad and that the chief engineer in charge of the construction was an Englishman, Sir Thomas Tancred. Combined with vociferous opposition from the Transvaal authorities, who were outraged at the prospect of losing revenues accruing from the transportation of goods to the interior, these factors caused Portugal to renege on its concession. On the morning of June 29, 1889, without warning, Portuguese soldiers forcibly seized the property and equipment of the railroad and Portugal declared the concession canceled. The breach of contract was so flagrant that the U.S. government soon felt constrained to take diplomatic action to protect the interests and lawful rights of an American citizen, and Great Britain took similar action. As President Cleveland remarked in his message, Portugal consented to arbitration.

The Delagoa Bay arbitration case dragged along for ten years. The Portuguese government, nearly bankrupt at the time, must have regretted many times the impulse that led to the seizure of the railroad. It was soon apparent that the Portuguese legal case was weak and that Portugal would have to pay a large indemnity. In 1900 the Swiss arbitration tribunal finally handed down its decision – against Portugal on all points.[3]

The Delagoa Bay case marks a shift in American relationships with Africa. The latter half of the nineteenth century had seen hundreds of individual Americans contributing to the future of Africa. Missionaries, soldiers of fortune and misfortune, farmers, prospectors, explorers, sportsmen, technologists – all had gone to Africa on their own initiative. Edward McMurdo, even though his enterprise was ultimately a failure, marked a new approach: He represented the American capitalist who went to Africa vicariously through his purchasing and hiring power.

The year 1900 was a turning point for Africa in other ways. At the opening of the nineteenth century, Africa seemed to white men a continent of mystery; at its close, much of Africa had been explored by Europeans and, in many cases, by Americans. By 1900 the modern political borders of Africa had largely been established, boundaries that for the most part have survived to the present day. The colonizers thereby laid the foundations of the newly independent countries that became the legatees of empire in the wake of World War II. Having laid out their claims, the imperial powers gradually subdued the surviving kingdoms, statelets, and autonomous neighborhood societies that had once covered Africa. The newcomers established their own *pax:* They built cities, ports, and railroads; they sunk mine shafts and laid out plantations; they built schools and hospitals; they introduced a host of new agricultural and veterinary techniques; they transmitted a great variety of new skills, those of the Western-trained physician, educator, plant breeder, geologist, surveyor, and administrator. They helped to transmit literacy; they created new systems of wage employment that linked Africa to the world markets overseas and that, despite all its inequities, immeasurably increased the physical wealth of Africa. Africa underwent the greatest revolution in its history, and in this revolution Americans played a conspicuous part.

Americans, of course, did not directly participate in the political conquest of Africa; apart from Liberia, Washington made no direct attempts to assert its will anywhere on the continent. American reluctance to join the "Scramble for Africa" requires some explanation: After all, America's links with Africa were more extensive than those of Kaiser Wilhelm's Germany or King Leopold's Belgium when the partition of Africa began in the 1880s. The Americans, however, were preoccupied at first with settling their own continental frontier. When the Western frontier had finally closed (about 1890), Americans turned their attention to Cuba, Central America, and the Philippines, rather than to Africa. Americans, moreover, retained a strong tradition of antiimperialism, widespread especially among literary people, journalists, professors, pastors, schoolteachers – the very people who in France and Germany were often inclined to call for imperial glory. Civil servants anxious for proconsular appointments and admirals and generals eager for military glory were not as influential in the United States as they were in Germany or France. On the contrary, there was widespread suspicion among politicians and businessmen of imperial ventures that would risk the taxpayers' money overseas, while courting war abroad. American merchants with a stake in overseas commerce looked to the Open Door; but provided foreigners did not maliciously exclude Americans from foreign markets, they were quite satisfied to carry on trade under foreign flags.

Black Americans were equally reluctant to participate in imperial ventures. During the 1890s, a black-led emigration movement swept many parts of the South, supported mainly by the illiterate and the poverty-stricken, who saw emigration as a means of escaping from oppression at home. But the black poor had neither the knowledge nor the means to take up a life of pioneering in an unknown continent. The bulk of articulate, middle-class blacks, on the other hand, bitterly opposed emigration as a solution to America's racial problem. They accepted the American system, but they wished to garner its full benefits. They accepted current notions concerning the need to civilize Africa, but they warned of white domination over the continent. Africa should be uplifted, in their view, not through colonization or emigration, but through missionary activities and business ventures – an assumption widely shared among white as well as black progressives.

Americans accordingly took a most active part in what became known to Victorians as the "opening up" of Africa. In this process, missionaries played a particularly important role. For example, the American Board of Commissioners for Foreign Missions (ABCFM), which sponsored the first American religious representatives in South Africa in 1835, quietly maintained and extended its evangelical effort. By the close of the century, the ABCFM had become one of the foremost missionary groups in Africa.[4] The board's activities included schools, a theological seminary for educating and training African pastors, and several dispensaries and hospitals. Medical work among Africans received an impetus in 1893 with the arrival of Dr. Burt Nichols Bridgeman, a man who combined medical skill with Christian humanitarianism.[5] Numerous biographical and autobiographical works testify to the vigor of the board's handful of missionaries. The foremost authority on missions in South Africa pays this tribute to them: "The translation of the Bible into Zulu ... was made wholly by various members of the Mission [and] has proved of inestimable benefit to all Christian missions in Natal."[6]

To stress the work of the ABCFM missionaries as pioneers with the most prominent American religious body in South Africa is not to detract from the accomplishments of others. Particularly important was the African Methodist Episcopal (AME) Church, one of the leading black churches of the United States, which expanded into South Africa during the 1890s in response to a new interest in the "redemption" of Africa and a desire to affiliate with the separatist church movement that was gaining strength among black South Africans during the period. In 1892 Bishop Henry McNeal Turner traveled to South Africa on behalf of his church. He proclaimed a militant doctrine of "Africa for the Africans," denounced white imperial oppression, and alarmed white South Africans with aggressive speeches that extolled African separate development. Turner felt convinced that the black race would never receive a chance for self-development in the United States. But he saw a "providential design" for bringing black Americans back to their African homeland to convert, civilize and develop the continent.

Turner's church received further support during 1896 and 1897 when the African Wesleyans (Methodists) broke away from the parent British church and affiliated with the AME Church. The union was cemented in 1898 by another visit from Turner, who ordained a number of African ministers and took other steps to make South African churches integral parts of the American body. In 1900 another outstanding black minister, the Reverend Levi Jenkins Coppin, was designated bishop for South Africa; the position of the AME Church was further strengthened when the government of the Union of South Africa recognized his episcopal status.[7,] From this beginning black separatist churches in the United States increasingly influenced the twentieth-century movement for independent African churches.

In a wider sense, the AME Church helped to apprise black South Africans of the black struggle in America; black South African leaders increasingly became familiar with the work of black American thinkers such as Dr. W. E. B. Du Bois and Booker T. Washington; in addition, a number of African political and ecclesiastical leaders acquired university training in the United States before comparable facilities became available to them in their country at Fort Hare. The most prominent of these was the Reverend John L. Dube, a founding member of the African National Congress (set up in 1912) and one of the foremost spokesmen of its new policy of welding the African tribal communities into a united South African people.

In 1879 the ABCFM decided to establish a mission in Portuguese East Africa (as Mozambique was then called). The mission would use Inhambane as a base and then move into the interior to contact the tribes of Gazaland in what would become Southern Rhodesia. The Reverend Myron W. Pinkerton, a missionary with almost ten years' experience among the Zulus, arrived at Inhambane in October 1880 but almost immediately died from a fever. His successor, the Reverend Erwin H. Richards, succeeded the following year in reaching the region chosen by the board for its major effort and was received with cordiality by Umzila, the local king, who was anxious to have missionaries among his people. Portuguese authorities, however, were openly hostile, and the region was as unhealthy as the deadly west coast. After much trouble, the mission finally obtained a tract of land, but the missionaries were forbidden to preach or to carry on the usual missionary activities outside its limits. To overcome such handicaps took many months of protracted diplomatic correspondence between Washington and Lisbon.[8]

ABCFM missionaries were (as far as available records show) the first Protestants to work among the East Africans, and in 1885, acting on a suggestion from the Reverend Erwin H. Richards, a small group from the Free Methodist Church commenced work at Inhambane.[9] The first Methodist Episcopal missionaries reached Mozambique in 1890 and found that Richards, unwilling to abandon the country and migrate to the board's new mission to Rhodesia, had remained. He changed his denominational allegiance to the Methodists and clung grimly to his post until his death in 1928. Under his leadership the Methodist mission in Mozambique grew from inauspicious beginnings until it became the most influential Protestant mission in the region. In addition to the usual preaching and attempts to convert, the Methodists found time to translate the Bible into the Shitswa language and the New Testament into the Gitonga language.[10]

In 1888, when the board decided to close its mission in Portuguese territory and transfer its work to the interior, its representatives again encountered difficulties. Two missionaries who visited Gungunyana, the son and successor of King Umzila, found that he did not share his father's favorable attitude toward them. His mind had been turned against missionaries, and the permission that his father had granted was no longer valid. "Your feet have been too slow in coming," he said curtly, indicating that he wanted nothing more to do with them.[11] The setback, however, was only temporary. Cecil Rhodes's Pioneer Corps entered Mashonaland in 1890 and cast the power, authority, and prestige of the British Empire – albeit indirectly through the British South Africa Company – over Gungunyana's domain. Rhodes wanted the missionaries to work among the African peoples of his newly acquired dominions, and he offered the American board a tract of land upon which to establish a mission.

A party headed by the Reverend George Wilder explored Gazaland in 1892 and selected a site near Mount Selinda, where "the hills and mountains lend grandeur to the scenery and healthfulness of the climate." The site was well within the area preempted by Rhodes's company and was almost exactly on the spot that Rhodes had previously indicated as a suitable location for a mission. For a nominal quit-rent of twenty-four pounds per annum, the board was granted a princely domain of more than thirty thousand acres in two separate tracts.[12]

In June 1893 the missionaries bound for the new mission station arrived at Beira in Portuguese East Africa and began the journey inland to their new home, bringing huge quantities of supplies and a prefabricated boat made of corrugated iron. The party – including a physician, three American and four Zulu missionaries with their wives and families, and a lone American woman missionary – ascended the Busi River by boat and canoe as far as the falls and cataracts, which impeded further movement by water; using bearers, they traveled the rest of the distance on foot. The Reverend Fred R. Bunker reported to ABCFM:

> The ladies were introduced to their pioneer experiences by having to sleep on the deck of our sailboat without any mattress. Overhead was stretched the sail of the boat to keep off the dew, which is like rain here, while we were entertained (?) and kept awake all night by the beating of drums and dancing in a kraal nearby.[13]

Everybody, including the Zulu assistants, suffered from fever during the journey, but increased knowledge of the nature of the disease prevented casualties. The Reverend Francis Bates remarked, "Everyone full of malaria and quinine – a bitter feeling to the world."[14]

Once at their new station, the group constructed a station that would be at least livable until something more permanent could be erected. Huts with grass roofs and dirt floors were uncomfortable but sufficed to keep off the rain and the dew. The transportation of supplies kept Bunker running pack trains from a point a hundred miles distant, and he found that "donkey-driving did not leave much time for evangelistic work."[15] The country was already filling with land-hungry settlers who supplied the mission with butter and milk and with horses, donkeys, and pigs. But the missionaries feared the effects upon the Africans of close contact with the newcomers. It was necessary to take immediate possession of the westerly tract allotted to the mission before completing work on the site where the station was to be established and before the squatters who were moving in became so firmly planted that the mission would forfeit its title. The danger was forestalled, however; the mission retained ownership of both its allotted tracts, and there was no marked friction with the incoming settlers.

In addition to the purely material activities of building, transporting supplies, and organizing, missionaries toured villages, preaching and exhorting. They started schools, although the initial response was discouraging. In their curriculum they stressed agriculture and practical training, although they did not ignore literary skills. Settlers accused them of teaching the doctrines of equality and self-government to Africans, but there seems in fact to have been little difference between the Europeans and Americans in what they taught. Dr. W. L. Thompson, the medical member of the group, found his services in demand over a vast area, and he responded whenever he was needed, regardless of the weather or how he felt.[16] The goodwill the Americans built up among the Africans was such that the mission and its people stood undisturbed during the uprising of 1896, when the Mashona joined the Matabele in a desperate effort to expel the white settlers.[17]

The newly opened lands in southern Africa soon attracted the attention of Protestant religious bodies all over Europe and the United States. In 1894 American Seventh-Day Adventists received land granted by the British South Africa Company and established a mission in Southern Rhodesia not far from the town of Bulawayo. They were followed in 1898 by Bishop Hartzell and the American Methodists, who were granted the company's abandoned post at Old Umtali.[18] The Brethren in Christ settled near Bulawayo in 1898.[19]

Land grants to British and American missions were part of Rhodes's scheme for Anglo-Saxons to rule the world; further, they reduced the humanitarian criticism of his company in Great Britain. But he may also have had a tactical reason for supporting the American missionaries: He gave them land along the border of Portuguese East Africa, where, it has been suggested, he would be able to use them as a diplomatic *cause célèbre* in case of trouble with the Portuguese.[20]

In 1892 a strange, idealistic, visionary, and almost fanatical enthusiast named Joseph Booth, an Englishman who had spent several years in Australia, arrived in Nyasaland to found the Zambesi Industrial Mission. Deeply religious from childhood, he questioned the ideas and practices of the established churches, so his doctrines were held suspect by more orthodox missionaries. His success in making converts may have aroused their envy and apprehension; certainly his ideas of racial equality were disliked by both authorities and settlers, and eventually he was forced from the country. But one of his earlier converts was an earnest, intelligent young African named Chilembwe, who was educated and ordained in the United

States. Chilembwe, on his return to Nyasaland, established a mission upon the same lines as that founded by Booth, an industrial mission in which Africans were trained in arts and crafts as well as in the principles of Christianity. During World War I Chilembwe and his mission, with black Americans among his missionaries, attempted a violent coup that was suppressed by force.[21]

In another part of southern Africa religious bodies were attracted to the vast Portuguese domain of Angola, which was practically a blank on the mission map. In 1880 three missionaries of the American board, one of them a black, arrived in Angola to establish a mission among the Ovimbundu people of the Benguela highlands at Bailunda, deep in the interior.[22] The mission expanded and the future seemed to be promising until 1884, when the local king suddenly ordered the missionaries out of his realm. Since the government of Portugal had approved the establishment of the mission, the matter called for diplomatic intervention by the U.S. government. Correspondence between Washington and Lisbon dragged along for more than two years.

The expulsion apparently was prompted by an unscrupulous local Portuguese trader, Eduardo Braga, who saw a threat to his trade and profits if the missionaries became too influential, and by the Portuguese governor of Benguela, who for private reasons appears also to have been interested in getting rid of the strangers. The king (or sobo) of Bailunda had a considerable degree of autonomy under Portuguese rule, and when Braga persuaded him that the Americans were fugitives from justice in their own country and meant no good to him and his subjects, the king acted promptly. The culmination of the affair, late in 1885, was an apologetic letter from the king to the Reverend W. H. Sanders in which he explained why he had felt compelled to act as he did, and then added, "But I have orders from the governor at Loanda to take you back." The king was willing to return the missionaries' confiscated property and effects for a consideration, and he naïvely included in his letter a demand for a monthly payment from them. Beyond this there are no published records, but it is assumed that the missionaries recovered their personal effects without the payment of a ransom or a monthly bribe.[23] The ABCFM mission in Angola expanded and within a few years was one of the most influential in that part of the world.

Angola was a promising field. In 1885 the American board missionaries were followed by a group of Americans representing the Methodist Episcopal Church and led by Bishop William Taylor, who had been designated the year preceding the Methodist Missionary Bishop of All Africa.[24] Taylor, who was somewhat of a visionary, was convinced that missions should and could be self-supporting. He succeeded in convincing the laymen and clergy of his church that his ideas were sound, and was directed by the General Conference of 1884 to found new missions in Africa on the self-supporting plan wherever possible. He arrived at Luanda in 1885 with thirty men and women who were spurred on by Taylor's exuberant personality and by their own enthusiasm.

The Methodists established five stations in Angola, but they soon found that the good bishop's ideas were completely unrealistic; simultaneously to support themselves, build and maintain missions, and conduct evangelical work was impossible. "They all endeavored to make ends meet by engaging in commerce, cattle-raising, working at a trade, or farming generally," said an optimistic account by Héli

Chatelaine, a member of the group, in the London *Christian* of March 9, 1888. At Luanda they established a school that seems to have been successful, although it "would not have kept the teachers without the addition of income from private lessons in languages." The missionaries set up a farm at a village station that the bishop established about three hundred miles from the coast. "A large tract of land was cleared, well laid out, ploughed and planted, and houses built on it." But, Chatelaine added later, "As farming in a new country is rich in disappointments, it has not yet paid sufficiently to support the station." One member of the party was "earning his support by collecting medicinal plants for the Congo State."[25]

Héli Chatelaine was a naturalized American citizen, Swiss by birth, gifted with remarkable ability as a linguist. His function in the mission group was to acquire sufficient knowledge of the native languages to instruct the missionaries so that they might preach to the Africans and converse with them in their own idiom. Chatelaine's activities were handicapped by the needs of the self-supporting scheme, but he managed to prepare a dictionary and grammar of the Kimbundu language, translate a gospel into that tongue, and make a scientific study of some of the Angolan folklore. In 1897 he resigned from the Methodist mission and established an independent and nondenominational project, the Mission philafricaine, to teach the Africans useful arts as well as Christian principles.[26]

In spite of their optimism, the Methodists' experiment was doomed to failure. At about the time Chatelaine was writing his account, the *Northwestern Christian Advocate* quoted one of the missionaries as saying that their destitution was pitiable. This missionary noted that when they could obtain remunerative work, it was often of a kind they could not conscientiously perform, such as repairing stills or keeping accounts for unscrupulous traders.[27]

Bishop Taylor continued to maintain his enthusiasm, but when he was succeeded in 1896 by Bishop Joseph C. Hartzell, the Methodist missions in Angola were on the edge of extinction. The church's Missionary Society took over the financial responsibilities, placing their missionaries on salary (as those of other churches were). The Methodist missionaries in Angola and other parts of Africa were then free to devote themselves to evangelism, without having to expend their time and energy in a struggle for survival. Their missions began at last to gather strength and grow.[28]

Christian missionaries took an equally important part in the history of Nigeria. American missionary endeavor there began in 1851 when the Reverend Thomas Jefferson Bowen, a Baptist, visited Ketu in Yorubaland. The Yoruba were a highly developed people with a flourishing agricultural economy and a complex state system. Bowen's initial mission was a failure, owing to stiff opposition from the local Muslim community to Christian penetration. Bowen, however, persisted in his endeavor and subsequently established a mission for the Southern Baptist Church at Ogbomosho. During the American Civil War, American missionary enterprise in Africa languished as funds from the United States dried up and as missionary recruits largely ceased to work in Africa. During the Civil War period, the Ogbomosho mission was entirely in the hands of the church's Yoruba members, who kept the spark alive and even made additional converts. "The period produced a confidence and pride in African achievement and a belief in African ability which was a cause of conflict when white missionaries returned and expected the old deference and dependence."[29]

Christian evangelization, among the Yoruba as in the rest of Africa, produced a variety of new social problems. The Christians transmitted a new creed, new skills (including literacy in English), and new attitudes, including a new sense of time – time measured mechanically by the pocket watch and the church bell, rather than by the position of the sun during the day and the seasons. The missionaries spread knowledge of the Bible and Bible stories; they taught their hymns, and with the hymns, Western forms of music. The missionary churches, like the church in medieval Europe, created the first modern social services: schools, clinics, hospitals. The missions created a new demand for cash, which their parishioners required to pay school fees and church membership fees; the missions thereby assisted in the spread of a cash economy. The missionaries preached a new creed of individualism, founded in part on an individual sense of sin. The churches became communities of a new kind that transcended the traditional boundaries of the extended family and local community.

Christianity, at the same time, shook the people's faith in traditional religions, and drastically reduced the impact of traditional religious cults and the influence of the traditional priesthood. In western Yorubaland, as in other parts of Africa, there were numerous conflicts between Christians and the traditionalists who regarded Christianity as a menace to their accustomed beliefs and way of life. The Christians moreover insisted on revolutionizing vital customs, such as the Yoruba marriage and burial institutions; they tried to replace polygamy by monogamy; they attempted to do away with the custom (familiar to the ancient Hebrews) whereby a surviving brother could inherit the wife and children of a deceased person. Traditional Yoruba believers buried their dead inside their own lineage houses, whereas the Christians insisted that the deceased must be buried in cemeteries, usually situated at some distance from a town. The cemeteries served the Christian congregation as a whole, irrespective of kinship links; the Christians thereby tried to substitute the community of the church for the community of the lineage.

The churches also developed new tensions within their own ranks, often – though not invariably – hinging on differences between white and black. When financial support from the United States was cut off, the Baptist mission was at first maintained by the Reverend J. M. Harden, the black minister who had accompanied Bowen from the United States when the mission was first established. (He supported himself and his family, and obtained funds for the mission, by making and selling building bricks, the first ever used in Lagos.) But Harden died in 1864, and his wife had to take over the responsibility and burden. At the same time, a number of African converts assumed positions of leadership. The most outstanding among these was M. L. Stone, who became a lay preacher, conducted prayer meetings, and kept the primary school in operation. He also maintained friendly relations with other missions, especially the Methodists.

In 1875 two new American missionaries (one white, the other black) arrived to resume the work of the mission. The African Baptists, while welcoming them, were by now entirely indisposed to submit to their authority. The new white missionary, W. J. David, at once sent Stone from Lagos to Ogbomosho, where he functioned as de facto pastor for nearly seven years, gaining the affection and confidence of his congregation to such an extent that, in 1878, they formally licensed him as their preacher. David remained unconvinced of the ability of Africans to manage the church without a white missionary's supervision; hence there was conflict of a kind paralleled in other Protestant churches of Nigeria. As a result, all but a handful of African Baptists seceded from the American Baptist Mission in 1888 and formed the Native Baptist Church – a name they chose themselves.

The break of 1888 marked the beginning of African control of the churches of Nigeria. Without being aware of it, the Native Baptists in 1888 ushered in a new era of Christianity among the Yoruba. A spell had been broken; a door opened for Christians of every mission affiliation to find a dignified means of escape from the rule of the missionary societies. Over a period of years similar difficulties arose in every other mission, with the same ultimate result: the establishment of an African church, following the theology and with the same general organization as the parent European or American church, but still distinctively African. The missionary societies of America and Europe did not yield without a struggle. Most of them attempted to maintain control over the religious organizations and institutions of Africa, but in the long run their efforts to this end proved unavailing.

Other U.S. missionaries established themselves on the island of Madagascar. They were never as prominent in religious work on the island as were missionaries of other nationalities, yet they reinforced activities already established. In 1888 the American Lutheran Missionary Society, founded and maintained largely by Norwegian immigrants to the United States, sent representatives to Madagascar to establish a mission with headquarters at Fort-Dauphin. Two years later a second body, the Lutheran Board of Missions, founded a station at Manasoa in the province of Tullear. According to available information, no other American missionary bodies were represented in Madagascar, though the missions of the Society of Friends (Quakers) in the country included a number of Americans among their personnel.[30]

The part played in Africa during the latter half of the nineteenth century by Americans – or by people so closely associated with the United States that they may reasonably be considered Americans – was not negligible. Nevertheless, it has been largely ignored or overlooked by both European and American historians.

White missionary societies kept preaching about the obligations of blacks to evangelize Africa, but so did some blacks. Bishop Turner was the leading black churchman who stressed the duty of American blacks to help their African fellows. In 1893, during the Chicago World's Fair, a World Congress on Africa was held under the sponsorship of the American Missionary Association. The purpose of the congress was to stimulate black missionary work in Africa. The theme was that, as a better approach than emigration, talented blacks should be encouraged to go to Africa to Christianize and civilize the people there.

The World Congress on Africa achieved at least two things: It introduced many black Americans to people who had lived in Africa and who spoke with respect about the peoples and their culture, and it focused attention on what many believed was the obligation of blacks to redeem their fellows.[31]

White church groups took the lead in encouraging black missions to Africa. The Methodist minister W. J. Stewart provided funds and a library to found the Stewart Missionary Foundation for Africa within the theological seminary in Atlanta of the Methodist Episcopal Church. Stewart wanted "to awaken in the more intelligent and better educated young Negroes of the United States a deep and warm interest in their African kindred and country."[32]

The Stewart Missionary Foundation hosted a major conference in Atlanta, "Africa and the American Negro," in December 1895. White and black missionaries spoke–for example, Alexander Crummell, a black who spent twenty years as a missionary in Liberia, and Bishop Turner. Once again the theme was one of black responsibility to return to Africa.[33]

Despite the expressed need for blacks to go to Africa as missionaries, few appeared to want to go. The AME Church established itself in Liberia, Sierra Leone, and South Africa; the African Methodist Episcopal Zion (AMEZ) Church sent people to Liberia and the Gold Coast between 1890 and 1900. Like emigrationism, however, the black missionary movement suffered from an ambivalent view about Africa: Was it the land of promise or the land of savages? Afro-Americans responded proportionately in far smaller numbers than did their white colleagues to the call to preach the gospel. There were, after all, too many problems at home.

Nevertheless, as a result of missionary and emigration movements and the daring deeds of Livingstone and Stanley as reported in the *New York Herald,* there was a growing interest in African affairs among black intellectuals and churchmen in the 1880s and 1890s. The focus was twofold: to discover Africa's past and to protest against the abuses of colonialism. One such intellectual was the able black historian George Washington Williams, who was sent on a fact-finding mission to the Congo Free State by President Benjamin Harrison and the railroad baron Collis P. Huntington. His reports on Congo conditions helped start the campaign to end Leopold's rule.

James E. Bruce, a New York black journalist, corresponded with African intellectuals such as Casely Hayford and subscribed to West African newspapers. He thus knew about conditions in Africa, and his columns attacked abuses in the African colonies. Still, Williams's and Bruce's writings were unusual. Not until W. E. B. Du Bois became editor of the *Crisis,* the journal of the National Association for the Advancement of Colored People, did black Americans get regular critiques of European rule in Africa.

After 1890 black American interest in Africa revived and revolved around four issues: emigration, Christianity, black identity and education. Emigration was supported by both whites and blacks as the only way to save black Americans and to give them a chance to improve themselves. Henry McNeal Turner, bishop of the AME Church, was the leader of the back-to-Africa movement after 1890. Turner had worked with the American Colonization Society in its efforts to get settlers to Liberia. His activities and the visit to the United States of Dr. Edward W. Blyden had coincided with economic depression and violence in the South and had stimulated interest once again in going to Liberia. In 1892 over three hundred farmers from Arkansas and Oklahoma came to New York to swamp the society's facilities: Only fifty people could be accommodated in a ship going to Liberia. Poor, untrained farmers had little chance of success in Africa, so the society became less a sponsor of colonization and more an agency to spur economic and educational developments in Liberia.

But this approach left unanswered the needs of black farmers and others who wished to flee the United States. With these people in mind, Turner organized in 1893 his back-to-Africa movement for ordinary poor blacks. His lectures and his newspaper, the *Voice of Missions,* spread the gospel of emigrationism to large numbers of blacks. After visiting West Africa, Turner toured the States and called for a conference in November of 1893 to launch his movement.[34]

The conference, however, failed to support Turner's idea of emigration as the solution to the black's problems. Middle-class blacks opposed sending uneducated blacks to Africa and were not interested in going there themselves. Frederick Douglass said in opposing Turner, "I do not believe in any wholesale plan of colonization to Africa. Emigration? Yes. Exodus? No."[35] Turner was defeated, but he continued to believe that thousands of blacks would go to Africa if money and shipping were available. Throughout the South schemes for shipping and migration were launched, and though none succeeded in sending very many people to Africa, the International Migration Society of Birmingham, active from 1894 to 1900, actually got five hundred people to Liberia.

Turner became discouraged, although he remained active in plans to repatriate blacks; he died in 1915. Perhaps a thousand blacks went to Liberia between 1890 and 1914, and many of those who went either died or sickened there and returned home disappointed at the harsh realities and poverty of life in Liberia. A song popular among immigrants went like this:

> Love of Liberty Brought us Here
> But lack of money keeps us here. [36]

Emigration, missions, education, black identity, and Pan-Africanism were to be the major forces involving Afro-Americans with Africa in the twentieth century. But these themes attracted only small numbers of people. Black Americans had too many problems in the United States to care much about events in Africa. Though the sense of links with Africa remained, only a few intellectuals, such as Du Bois, began to see the fates of blacks in Africa, in Europe, and in the United States were closely linked. In Du Bois's view, they had suffered together at the hands of whites, and together they could redeem themselves and perhaps the whites as well.[37]

IV

The United States and Africa, 1900–1939

Theodore Roosevelt with his party in Kenya, 1909. Courtesy Hoover Institution Archives.

Martin and Osa Johnson and others. Neg. no. 118532, courtesy Department Library Services, American Museum of Natural History.

Mrs. Carl Akeley and party, East Africa, 1926. Neg. no. 335107, courtesy Department Library Services, American Museum of Natural History.

Members of the Akeley expedition to East Africa. Neg. no. 412196 (photo Carl Akeley), courtesy Department Library Services, American Museum of Natural History.

178

The skin of a giraffe for African Hall, American Museum of Natural History. Neg. no. 412195 (photo Carl Akeley), courtesy Department Library Services, American Museum of Natural History.

St. Paula River Industrial School, Liberia. Courtesy Library of Congress.

Edward Blyden. Courtesy Library of Congress.

Marcus Garvey on parade in New York City. United Press International photo.

W. E. B. Du Bois. Courtesy Library of Congress.

The staff of Tuskegee Institute. Courtesy Library of Congress.

William A. Taft and Booker T. Washington. Courtesy Library of Congress.

183

Tuskegee Institute. Courtesy Library of Congress.

CHAPTER 16

Official America

Official America, until the outbreak of World War I, had but little concern in African affairs. The United States had taken no part in the partition of Africa. The State Department largely considered the African continent an extension of Europe in both the political and the diplomatic sense (see Map 3). American empire builders looked to Cuba and the Philippines, not to the so-called Dark Continent. Similarly, the American economic stake in Africa amounted to little. Most American capital was invested at home, and what there was of U.S. foreign trade centered on Europe and the Americas. U.S. commerce with Switzerland by 1913 was worth more than the American traffic with the entire African continent. If Egypt and South Africa are excluded, American mercantile dealings with Africa hardly equaled the value of American traffic with Ecuador (see Table 1).

Naval strategists turned toward the Panama Canal and the Pacific for their country's security, not toward the Cape route or the Suez Canal. Washington viewed with approbation all colonial powers prepared to keep their respective possessions open to the commerce of all nations; the British and, to a lesser extent, the Germans met these criteria and garnered little criticism from U.S. policy makers. The Portuguese and the French, protectionist in attitude, offended against American principles regarding the Open Door, but the American stake in the French and Portuguese dependencies was too small to engender much friction. American penetration was left to the private enterprise of merchants, missionaries, and mining magnates — an ill-assorted group with disparate interests that never combined into a single lobby.

Table 1. *U.S. foreign commerce, 1913 (in dollars)*

		Imports	Exports
Total Europe		864,666,103	1,499,573,363
Total North America		389,814,744	601,176,159
Total South America		198,259,005	146,514,635
Total Asia		281,407,363	126,122,651
Oceania		34,791,505	81,702,676
Africa		23,729,760	28,928,808
Egypt	17,249,585		
South Africa	3,066,349		
Total		1,792,668,480	2,484,018,292

Source: The New International Year Book (New York: Dodd, Mead, 1913), pp. 717–18.

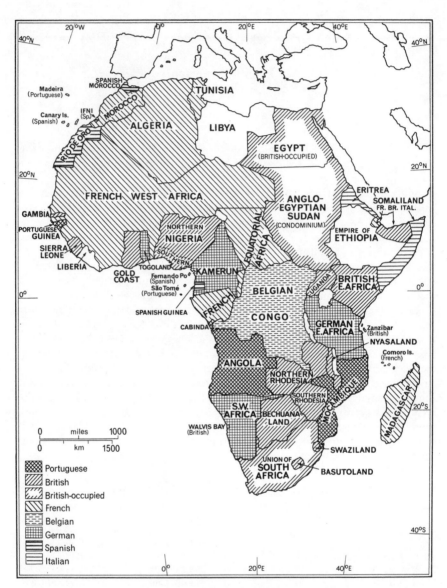

Map 3. Africa in 1914. Reprinted from Peter Duignan and L. H. Gann, eds.,
The Economics of Colonialism, vol. 4 of *Colonialism in Africa, 1870–1960*
(Cambridge: Cambridge University Press, 1975).

The end of isolationism

American humanitarians sympathized with the great mass of black Africans, supposedly sunk in heathen darkness and in need of material uplift and moral salvation; with white Afrikaners (then known as Boers), who struggled against the might of the British empire; and with Americo-Liberian settlers, who had created a small but insecure black commonwealth in West Africa. But the United States in general had been committed to a policy of isolation during the nineteenth century. This attitude was exemplified in the attitude of the Honorable Perry Belmont when he opposed bitterly the participation by the United States in the 1884–5 Berlin conference on the Congo. To people who held such views – and such people and such views were quite general in the later nineteenth century – the United States was completely self-contained, and the advice of George Washington and the Founding Fathers to avoid entangling alliances was almost a divine injunction.

The Spanish-American War, the subsequent war in the Philippine Islands, and American participation in the Boxer Relief Expedition to Peking would have been unthinkable in 1884; in 1900 such action was taken for granted. The strong stand taken by the United States in Liberian matters and the growing prominence of the role played by the United States illustrated a veritable revolution that took place in the American attitude toward the rest of the world following 1898, the year of the Spanish-American War. A body blow had been given to traditional isolationism, and the United States was growing increasingly aware of its own strength and position as one of the world's great powers.

The shift in American policy did not bring demands for a U.S. empire in Africa. But Americans became increasingly insistent that their nation's voice should be heeded – not only in Liberia, a traditional sphere of indirect influence, but also in other parts of the continent. American interests in Africa quickened after Theodore Roosevelt acceded to the presidency, determined that the United States should play a role in world affairs. Roosevelt took a well-publicized hunting trip to East Africa. In 1908 he also called on Sir Harry Johnston – a British explorer, writer, and ex-administrator – to provide him with advice during an extended stay at the White House.[1] Roosevelt's personal concern with Africa, linked with his determination that the United States should be heeded in world affairs, led to an involvement that would have horrified the isolationists of 1884–5 who objected so strongly to American participation in the Berlin conference.

Early in 1906 the tension between Germany and France became even more acute than usual. Conflicting interests and aspirations in Morocco threatened a crisis and possibly a major war, especially when Kaiser Wilhelm, with his usual bombast and lack of tact, attempted to humiliate France over the issue of French colonization in Morocco. President Roosevelt conceived it his duty to do everything possible to avert an open rupture, and the resulting Algeciras conference to discuss Moroccan affairs was largely his handiwork. American representatives, not confining themselves to the role of observers, took an active part in the conference; in a sequel unlike that following the Berlin conference, the U.S. Senate promptly approved the resulting treaties. Further, when at one time during the conference the kaiser's objections and intransigence threatened to wreck the proceedings, it was Roosevelt who persuaded him to relent.[2]

South Africa, 1899–1913

The South African War of 1899–1902 (commonly known as the Boer war) was a milestone in the history of Africa. The conflict began, as far as the British were concerned, as a colonial venture of the limited-liability variety, financed on a shoestring and fought against an enemy thought by most British fighting men to be hardly superior to warlike Indian mountaineers. But the struggle turned into a major conflict with many facets. White English-speaking South Africans took up arms against their Afrikaner neighbors. In addition, the British Empire as a whole made the greatest military effort in its history. The dispatch of four hundred thousand British soldiers to fight on the other side of the world was an unprecedented feat. The struggle, so confidently begun, ended as a halfway house to total war in which farms were burned, civilians rounded up, and the Boers driven to the border of despair. British public opinion became divided, and for many Englishmen the imperial image was forever tarnished.

The United States stood aloof. But Secretary of State John Hay stressed his country's attachment to Great Britain. Impartial enforcement of America's neutrality legislation in fact worked in London's favor, owing to British naval and financial supremacy. American capital had a stake, however small, in the gold-mining industry of South Africa. American mining engineers and mine managers had played a part in developing the gold mines of the Transvaal and the diamond mines in Kimberley. There was also a small "reverse" flow of capital from South Africa to the United States, directed by mining magnates such as Cecil John Rhodes.

The American establishment tended to sympathize with the British. The Boer cause, on the other hand, found much support among Irish, German, and Dutch Americans, as well as among humanitarians who considered the Boers a small, downtrodden people rightly struggling to be free. To many Americans of all classes, moreover, Great Britain was still the traditional enemy: Every schoolchild was taught about Paul Revere and his ride to warn the Minutemen of the approaching Redcoats; and to several million Americans of Irish descent, England was still the merciless oppressor. In addition to the people of Irish descent, the American population included millions of Germans and a smaller number of people of Dutch ancestry, a segment of the population with an influence far beyond what was indicated by its numbers. To many of these people the war in South Africa was an inexcusable and ruthless act of aggression by Great Britain against their kinsmen, even though the degree of kinship was extremely remote. Hence Dutch-Americans supported the Boers in their war of independence. The Boer republics sent representatives to speak in the American Midwest; they received money and enrolled some volunteers to go to fight against Great Britain.

During the Boer war, strong efforts were made by various elements of the population to swing the power and influence of the United States to the Boer side. In New York City, one George W. Van Siclen, who described himself as a "Son of the American Revolution," financed and directed through various churches a poll to determine the proportion of American citizens who were "in favor of the United States offering to mediate between Great Britain and the two South African Republics, for the purpose of putting a stop to the war now going on."[3] Charles D. Pierce, also a "Son of the Revolution," who had held the honorary position of representative of the Orange Free State in the United States (he was never accorded diplomatic or consular recognition by the U.S. government), was indefatigable in his efforts to enlist American sympathies for the Boers. Among other activities, he seems to have been instrumental in starting a Boer Relief Fund, ostensibly for the relief of Boer widows and war orphans and for Boer families detained by the British in concentration camps. Branches and auxiliaries were organized in various parts of the United States, and numerous prominent people were persuaded to lend their names as members of committees.

The prevalence of a strong humanitarian sentiment among the American people is well known. It was this sentiment that gave strength and impetus to the missionary movement of the nineteenth century, and it even strengthened the imperialism of the early twentieth century: The conquest of the Philippines was believed necessary in order to provide for the enlightenment of the Filipinos and to prepare them for independence and democracy. Intervention in Cuba was largely justified on humanitarian grounds; stories of the horrors of the Spanish concentration camps and of brutalities inflicted upon helpless women and children confined in them aroused the American people to a veritable fury.

When the British in South Africa found it necessary to establish a system of concentration camps for the civilian population of the war zone, a perfect weapon was placed in the hands of Boer sympathizers and propagandists in the United States. Montagu White, who had been a consul general for the Transvaal Republic in Europe and who was named Boer representative in the United States (his exact position is vague), stated firmly and categorically that all reports of atrocities perpetrated by Boers were false, but that Boer women and children in the concentration camps were being fed on half rations of weevilly corn and damaged sugar. Moreover, the British policy of destroying farms and crops in the battle areas was causing unbelievable hardship amounting to famine and starvation.[4]

Somewhat earlier, Professor Cesare Lombroso had made a confident prediction for the benefit of American readers that the Boers would easily "conquer the English," and such journals as the *Outlook* reported every skirmish as a great Boer victory. Usually no mention was made of any incidents that could be interpreted as Boer reverses. Anti-British elements among the American population gloated over the series of British defeats that marked the opening phases of the war.[5]

Secretary of State John Hay's son Adelbert was appointed consul for the Transvaal Republic on December 2, 1899. He arrived in Pretoria during the war and soon impressed the British and the Boers by his impartiality. Young Hay (twenty-four years old) acted as neutral representative of the five thousand or so British prisoners of war in the Transvaal, doling out half crown pieces to them. After leaving South Africa, at a point when he was due to become private secretary to President William McKinley, he died tragically after a fall from a balcony on June 23, 1901.

A number of Americans, mostly of Irish ancestry or birth, enrolled in an Irish-American Hospital Corps and promptly, upon arrival in South Africa, discarded their red crosses and joined Colonel Blake's Irish Brigade. The fortunes of war made some of these men prisoners of the British, and they became the subject of a long and complicated series of diplomatic problems for the U.S. government. Although their status was clear under well-recognized principles of international law, they (or their friends and relatives) nevertheless began to demand that the United States obtain their release. Quite naturally, their captors were made to appear in as unfavorable a light as possible. It was learned that some of the Americans were confined at a prisoner of war camp in Ceylon, a fact which gave their petitioners a weapon to wield: Confinement in a tropical country, it was charged, would inevitably result in the death of most of them from tropical diseases. A few were held at St. Helena, where Napoleon had been a prisoner; St. Helena thus must be a terrible place where prisoners would suffer untold hardships. A few were in prison camp in balmy Bermuda; one American sympathizer went so far as to describe in detail the miserable condition of the Bermuda prisoners – in rags, without adequate fresh water, and suffering terribly from the cold![6]

On November 28, 1900, a G. J. Diekema of Holland, Michigan, a community that to this day is peopled largely by descendants of Dutch immigrants, wrote to Congressman William Alden Smith on behalf of a young man named Frederick Versluis: "Whatever is done must be done quickly if the life of this young American captured by the British in South Africa is to be saved. It is feared that he is in great danger of death by a process of drumhead court-martial. He fought under Colonel Roosevelt at Santiago."[7] A certain H. Wood, who claimed to be a native-born American captured while fighting the Boers, was reported to be critically ill in Ceylon. On the contrary, the governor of that dominion replied, Wood was in excellent health; he consequently refused to order the man's release. Patrick Lennon asserted that he was an American citizen and a resident of Butte, Montana, and that he had been arrested by the British arbitrarily, although he had never borne arms and had scrupulously observed all regulations governing civilians in the war zone. Investigation, however, indicated that Lennon had been released from jail by the Boer authorities (he had been confined for beating his wife) on the condition that he enlist as a commando, and that he had formally become a Boer citizen before his capture.[8] James L. Molloy, one of the prisoners in Bermuda, inadvertently gave the Boer sympathizers a shock when he asserted that he had been given his choice, upon dissolution of the Irish-American Hospital Corps, between enrollment as a commando or being shot. His complaint, however, was about being held as a prisoner of war: The United States should demand his immediate release.[9]

These incidents are of no importance in themselves, nor are they of any considerable historical significance. They indicate, however, the considerable amount of pro-Boer or anti-British feeling in the United States, particularly among elements of the population that were of Dutch or Irish extraction. They also indicate the relationships and complications between the United States and Great Britain that grew out of the situation in South Africa. The correspondence concerning Americans taken prisoner by the British grew voluminous before the war ended and the proclamation of peace brought about their release.[10]

Despite the partisan interest of numerous Americans in the South African War, the general feeling of the great mass of the American people was humanitarian in origin; they hoped to end the war, and their deepest sympathies were for the helpless – the wounded, and the women and children of the war zone. That humanitarian interest continued after the guns fell silent. America's strongest impact, for the time being, was in the medical field.

Africa at the turn of the century was still widely regarded as "the white man's grave," as it had been in centuries past. The beginning of the twentieth century, however, saw a medical revolution of far-reaching importance. Scientists proved that malaria – the deadly "African fever" – and the equally perilous yellow fever were not contagious diseases but were borne by mosquitoes. Americans took a prominent part in changing conditions that made life in Africa almost as deadly as a game of Russian roulette, a part in which the U.S. government became indirectly involved.

In the autumn of 1913 an outbreak of a virulent form of pneumonia among the African laborers in the Rand mines of South Africa, linked to poor living conditions in general, drove the death rate among them to the horrifying figure of 35 percent. Since the laborers were recruited in such tribal areas as Nyasaland and Basutoland, under the direct control of a British government that regarded itself as responsible for the Africans' welfare and safety, notice was served upon the mines' management that, unless the disease was checked at once, all further recruitment of labor would cease. This step would close the mines. At this juncture, the secretary of the Transvaal Chamber of Mines, Samuel Evans, learned of the success of William Crawford Gorgas, then a colonel in the U.S. Army Medical Corps, in reducing the incidence of disease in Panama, where the United States was constructing the interocean canal. Panama for centuries had had a reputation for deadliness comparable to that of the African coast, and the first efforts to construct a canal there, by the French, had foundered largely upon the high death rate among the workers. Within a short time Gorgas made the construction of the canal possible by reducing the disease toll until it was not appreciably higher than that in more temperate places.

Evans went to Panama to consult with Gorgas and to observe his methods at first hand. Gorgas shortly after was invited to South Africa to study the sanitary and health problems of the mining industry, a visit requiring government approval, since he was an officer on active duty. The president approved. Gorgas was granted a lengthy leave of absence, and he spent several months in South Africa studying and observing the conditions. His recommendations were adopted at once and in toto. As a result, the death rate from pneumonia among the African mine laborers dropped quickly from 35 percent to three per thousand – less than 1 percent. At the same time, deaths from other diseases dropped to sixty per thousand per year, a death rate that compared favorably with the mortality figures of Europe and the United States.[11]

While he was still in South Africa, Gorgas was appointed surgeon general of the army with the rank of major general, the highest rank then possible in the U.S. Army. The Senate confirmed the appointment unanimously, and the British governor formally notified Gorgas of his new position at a reception given in his honor – probably one of the few instances in which a U.S. official received formal notice of his promotion from a foreign official in a foreign land.

The Congo and Liberia

Major medical obstacles to white penetration in Africa were removed in the early years of the twentieth century. Dr. Donald Ross of the Indian Medical Service finally showed that the deadly African fever that had made the continent's coasts so dangerous for the white man was a virulent form of malaria transmitted, not by the climate or by miasmas in the air, but by the anopheles mosquito. At the same time, Dr. Walter Reed of the U.S. Army Medical Corps proved that yellow fever, a tropical scourge almost as devastating as malaria, was also mosquito borne. Within a few years these facts became so widely known among missionaries, traders, explorers, and officials that the dreadful diseases abated, and regions previously denied to whites or to unacclimatized black Americans were open for exploration, trade, and evangelism.

It was in the early years of the twentieth century, also, that large numbers of Americans directed their attention toward the Congo and attempted to persuade the U.S. government to intervene diplomatically in the affairs of that presumably independent country. Americans and Europeans had generally welcomed the establishment of the Congo Free State, seeing in it an instrument for the final abolition of the slave trade and of such abominations in Victorian eyes as cannibalism, wife purchase, and other tribal practices. The Congo Free State, it was believed, would be an agency to facilitate the spread of Christianity and would bring law, order, and civilization to peoples who were universally believed to be deep in savagery. But shortly before the close of the nineteenth century, disturbing rumors reached Europe and the United States that all was not well in the Congo. The Congo Free State, far from being an instrument of enlightenment, seemed as brutal, ruthless, and savage in its treatment of the Africans as Tipoo Tib's slave raiders. According to some reports, Leopold II's officials were as predatory a pack of human wolves as ever disgraced the race, their only interest was in enriching their royal master and themselves, and many of their activities in pursuit of this goal were so fiendish as to defy description.

The Congo was Leopold's private fief. The Belgian Parliament unfortunately had permitted Leopold's assumption of sovereignty over the Congo Free State on condition that the national treasury of the Kingdom of the Belgians should incur no responsibility whatever. The funds to defray the Congo's necessary expenses must come from its own resources and from the king's private fortune. Since Leopold hoped to reap a profit from the Congo, about half of its vast area was designated as royal domain. The sudden rise in the world's consumption of rubber seemed to solve the Congo's financial problems, for wild rubber was one of the region's major products. But to obtain sufficient quantities of rubber to cover the state's expenses and give Leopold a satisfactory income, it was necessary to assign quotas to each district. No questions were asked about the means by which the Africans were persuaded to turn in the required amounts of rubber – and they were people who were accustomed to working for subsistence only; they had no desire to do anything else. There can be no doubt that some of the officials, as well as concessionaires, were brutal and callous in their methods of persuasion.[12]

Among the first to call attention to the abuses caused by the quota system was an American Baptist missionary, J. B. Murphy, who sharply criticized the "rubber system" in 1895. The following year a Swedish missionary named Sjöblom confirmed Murphy's statements and added his own. Two years later an article in the *Century Magazine* entitled "Cruelty in the Congo Free State," by Edward James Glave, a young English adventurer-explorer, served further to bring attention to conditions and practices in the Congo.

Glave had been with Stanley in 1883, establishing the first stations in the Congo basin. He was familiar with Africa and was by no means predisposed to criticize Leopold's government or officials, nor did he have any inhibitions toward using force in compelling Africans to obey. In 1889 Glave resigned from service in the Congo Free State, went to the United States on a lecture tour, and shortly left with a single companion to journey into the then unexplored interior of Alaska. He was engaged in 1893 by *Century Magazine* to return to Africa (it may be more accurate to say that he persuaded the magazine's management to finance his return). He proposed to go afoot across the continent studying conditions, observing, photographing, and doing whatever possible to combat the dying but still lively slave trade. He reached the mouth of the Congo in April 1895, having walked across the continent – a feat comparable to Stanley's original achievement. Before he could embark for Europe, however, he died unexpectedly from the African fever that had taken such a toll of white men's lives.[13] Writing shortly before his death, Glave noted that even in a district administered by a Belgian official noted for justice, enlightenment, and humanity,

> the natives have complained that they are compelled to bring rubber, which is bought by the officers of the Congo Free State; half of the price paid goes to the mgwana, or chief, of the district, and half goes to the natives. Many villagers refuse to bring rubber; they are attacked, and killed, or taken prisoners.[14]

As just mentioned, Glave was not squeamish about using force to compel Africans to work. Like most people of his time, he believed that inculcating in Africans "habits of industry and thrift" to replace their supposed idleness was highly desirable. Likewise, in accordance with accepted Western beliefs and values of that time, he accepted without question the dictum that civilization and commerce were practically synonymous terms, and that opening the Congo to trade would automatically civilize the indigenous peoples. Nevertheless, he indicted the administration of the Congo Free State in bitter words:

> The state conducts its pacification of the country after the fashion of the Arabs, so the natives are not gainers after all. The Arabs in the employ of the state are compelled to bring in ivory and rubber, and are permitted to employ any measures considered necessary to obtain this result. They employ the same means as in days gone by, when Tippu Tib was one of the masters of the situation. They raid villages, take slaves, and give them back for ivory. The state has not suppressed slavery, but established a monopoly by driving out the Arab and Wangwana.[15]

In the last part of his journey, Glave noted deserted villages and found that the Africans were in open revolt against their new masters. For example, his journal entry for February 27, 1895, reads:

> Reached Mdmumba at nine o'clock this morning. Found that the chief of the station, a Norwegian officer, Sundt, was away on a war expedition ... The persistent badgering of the natives for rubber and ivory has led to the revolt. All are agreed on this point.[16]

Equally devastating were the reports derived from the pen of George Washington Williams, America's first major black historian. Williams, a Pennsylvanian by birth, had begun his career by serving with distinction in the United States Colored Troops; he subsequently became an attorney, a member of the Ohio state legislature, a journalist, and an author. In 1883 Williams published his two-volume *History of the Negro Race in America,* a pioneer work, and made a name for himself as a distinguished figure in black intellectual life. Williams originally favored Leopold's enterprise in the Congo as a humanitarian venture. But having visited the Congo in 1890, Williams changed his mind and submitted Leopoldine rule in the Congo to a devastating analysis that presaged all later criticisms.

The conditions in the supposedly philanthropic Congo Free State quickly attracted the attention of humanitarians in Europe and the United States. In Great Britain a noted humanitarian, Edmund Morel, was instrumental in organizing the Congo Reform Association, and in several books he castigated in vitriolic terms Leopold's government and administration in the Congo.[17]

But defenders of the Congo Free State, despite the allegations and a certain amount of circumstantial evidence, categorically denied the truth of the statements made by Morel, Glave, and others. The correspondent of the *Chicago Tribune* found no evidence at all to support the stories of wholesale atrocities and cruelty.[18] Likewise, Edgar Wallace – whose fame as a writer of mystery stories has obscured the fact that he was an outstanding newspaper correspondent and, later in life, a hard-working member of Parliament – investigated the Congo stories on behalf of the London *Daily Mail* and found little to substantiate the charges.[19]

Henry Wellington Wack, a prominent New York attorney interested in African affairs, came to the defense of the Congo Free State and charged unequivocally that the allegations of wholesale abuse of Africans and atrocities against them were part of a program designed to discredit Leopold's government so that other powers and interests could take over.[20] Wack took particular exception to the reports of Sir Roger Casement, the British consul at Boma, in which all sorts of horrors were related. Wack asserted that Casement's reports, which were regarded by many as completely authoritative because of his official position, were almost entirely based upon hearsay, and that one instance which Casement claimed to have investigated would not stand analysis.

The gruesome stories coming out of the Congo were not all true. But the facts were grim enough, and reports concerning abuses found wide credence in the United States and Europe. Almost immediately an American branch of the Congo Reform Association was organized, and a lengthy memorial was submitted to the U.S. Senate.[21] In September 1904 Morel, who was in the United States to assist in organizing the association, obtained an interview with President Theodore Roosevelt and presented a petition urging the diplomatic intervention of the United States. Roosevelt was not moved; it might be said that he was unfavorably impressed with Morel. He saw no reason to involve the United States in a diplomatic controversy in which it would be unable to take action and in which neither treaty obligations nor national interests were involved. In a letter to Eugene A. Philbin on September 28, 1904, Roosevelt quoted Secretary of State John Hay: "It is a well-meant impertinence . . . for Englishmen to come to us to take up their Congo quarrel." Two years later, the Congo Reform Association having been very active in the meantime, Roosevelt wrote to Henry Cabot Lodge: "The only tomfoolery that anyone seems bent on is that about the Congo Free State outrages, and that is imbecile rather than noxious."²² Strictly speaking, the U.S. government did not enter into the Congo controversy, though American public opinion and inquiries made by the State Department exercised some influence in bringing about reforms.

American interest in Africa before World War I centered overwhelmingly on Liberia's difficulties. From its beginning, Liberia had been plagued with a lack of economic resources to be exploited or maintained by Liberians. The country's economic potential, in fact, was virtually unknown. Dependent entirely upon import duties and uncertain taxes from an impoverished people for its revenue, the Liberian government was almost constantly insolvent. The situation was further complicated by the fact that Liberia abutted on the African possessions of Britain and France, two Great Powers whose appetite for African territory appeared unsated and many of whose officials seemed to feel that the Americo-Liberians were unfit to rule and develop either themselves or the indigenous peoples. Only with considerable reluctance did London and Paris accept the fact of Liberian independence.

The persistent isolationism of the people and government of the United States forced Liberia in the nineteenth century to turn to Great Britain as a mentor, despite British imperialistic interest in Liberian territory. American bankers had no funds available to loan outside the United States. In return for loans from London, Liberia accepted British tutelage and, toward the end of the century, agreed to undertake certain reforms proposed by the British, including reorganization of the Frontier Force—the Liberian army—under a British commander. The officer selected for this duty conducted himself as though he were dealing with a disorderly and difficult segment of a British colonial population; he was arrogant and condescending to the point of actually refusing to obey orders from the country's president. When it was found that he was enlisting in the force large numbers of British subjects from Sierra Leone in direct violation of Liberian law, the Liberians wrongly began to suspect him of planning a coup that would lead to British annexation. The Liberian authorities consequently took their courage in hand and dismissed him.²³

By 1908 the danger to Liberian independence seemed to be so pressing that President Roosevelt felt impelled to invite Sir Harry Johnston, one of the world's foremost authorities on Africa, to the White House in order to obtain firsthand information from an impartial and disinterested observer:

> The affairs of Liberia at the opening of 1908 had got into such a condition
> of confusion, owing to French rapacity on the frontier and German in-
> trigues for permission to establish great wireless stations . . . that I felt a
> strong disposition to go over to the United States, and endeavor to put
> before the American Government the whole situation.²⁴

In the same year, 1908, the Liberian government, anxious for the future, sent a commission to the United States to plead for American financial and diplomatic assistance. In particular, the commission wanted the United States to gain British cooperation for Liberia; otherwise they feared that their country would soon be swallowed by the great French colonial empire or would fall prey to aggressive

German colonial expansion.[25] Roosevelt decided to send a commission to Liberia to investigate and report upon the situation, meanwhile strongly urging Great Britain to join with the United States in maintaining the status quo in Liberia until some solution for the country's difficulties could be found.[26] Roosevelt regarded Liberia with extreme concern. The commission was taken to Monrovia by no less than three warships, which were ordered to remain there until the group completed its labors.

The impressive squadron sailed from Hampton Roads on April 23, 1909, with the commission aboard: three well-known public men, Roland P. Falkner, George Sale, and Emmet J. Scott, the latter a distinguished black educator and an associate of Booker T. Washington. The three powerful cruisers, USS *Chester, Birmingham,* and *Salem,* together constituted a stronger force than any European power maintained in African waters: It was a force calculated to give pause to both European powers and recalcitrant coastal peoples. Accompanying the commission on board were George A. Finch as secretary; Major Percy M. Ashburn of the Army Medical Corps, a recognized authority on tropical diseases and health problems, as medical consultant; Captain Sydney A. Cloman as military consultant; and Frank Abial Flower, a specialist on African affairs. The ships arrived at Monrovia early in May, and the commission set to work immediately. Within a month it had completed the investigation and was ready to submit its report.

In broad terms, the commission concluded that Liberia was not so much bankrupt as the victim of mismanagement and of encroachment by both France and Great Britain. The commissioners reported:

> In pursuit of their policy of building up a great West African Empire, the French have been a thorn in the side of Liberia . . . The British foreign office has protested that Great Britain has no designs on Liberian territory. We find it hard to reconcile this protestation with the acts of her officials in Sierra Leone.

The commissioners found, too, that although the British commander of the Liberian Frontier Force had greatly improved its efficiency, he was unquestionably guilty of grave irregularities. He had mismanaged funds, he had filled the ranks with British subjects, and on at least one occasion he had even threatened the president of the country. In short, he had acted as though Liberia were a British dependency and he himself superior to all Liberian law and authorities. The commission's conclusions were damning to Great Britain:

> But for the prompt and judicious action of the Liberian Executive [in dismissing the British commander of the Frontier Force], aided by the American minister resident, the following would presently have been the situation: A British gunboat in the harbor, a British officer in command of the frontier force and a large number of British subjects among the enlisted men, a British official in charge of the Liberian gunboat *Lark*, a British regiment in the streets of Monrovia.[27]

According to the commissioners, Liberians widely believed that there was a deliberate plot among the British residents of the country and of Sierra Leone to make it appear that the republic was tottering to its fall, so as to bring about

British occupation and annexation. The actual existence of a plot of this sort is more than doubtful, but there is no question but that many British in West Africa would have welcomed such a contingency. Any immediate danger was quashed by the presence of the three American naval vessels at Monrovia, and the rumors of impending British intervention subsided.

The commission recommended against any U.S. guarantee of Liberian independence or territorial integrity. This stand was, of course, strictly in accord with the traditional U.S. policy of avoiding anything that might be considered an alliance. The report, however, included a strong recommendation that the United States help the black republic to reorganize its finances and to reform its armed forces. Negotiations for a loan, to be sponsored by American bankers, began shortly after the commission submitted its report. Roland Falkner, the commission's chairman, was appointed Liberia's financial representative, with full authority to negotiate with the European bankers who had made previous loans to the country. Both Great Britain and France, acting upon diplomatic suggestions from the United States, agreed to settle their respective boundary disputes with Liberia, each power finally accepting much less than it had originally demanded. And—possibly the most important measure—Liberia appointed an American, Reed Paige Clark, as receiver general, with full authority to administer the country's treasury.[28] The loan negotiations continued well into 1912, with the situation complicated by the undisciplined state of the Frontier Force. A border incident, apparently precipitated by Liberians on the still undelineated Sierra Leone frontier, resulted in bloodshed and a sharp protest from Great Britain. The Liberian officers involved coolly ignored President Daniel Edward Howard's orders to return to Monrovia to give an account of themselves.

Meanwhile, in 1911 Liberia requested that U.S. officers be detailed to organize and train the Frontier Force, asking especially for the services of First Lieutenant Benjamin O. Davis, military attaché at the American legation in Monrovia. Davis, who was one of the few black officers of the regular army, had served in the Spanish-American War and the Philippine insurrection. Although he was still a young man and comparatively junior in rank, he could point to a wide professional experience. (He would later achieve distinction as the first black general in the U.S. Army.) Because he had been in Liberia for some time and was thoroughly familiar with the country and its problems, the choice was sound, but the War Department refused to approve. Forgetting or ignoring the precedent established by General Sherman when he permitted several junior officers to serve as military advisers with the Egyptian army in the 1870s, the War Department could find no legal authority by which Lieutenant Davis could be detailed. The U.S. government, instead of sending an officer on the active list, arranged for three qualified black ex-officers to enter the Liberian service: Major Ballard and Captains Brown and Newton.[29] The three arrived in Liberia on May 1, 1912, to work under the supervision of Major Charles P. Young, who had replaced Davis as military attaché. Young, however, because of his position and diplomatic status, could not exercise direct authority.

One of the few black graduates of West Point, Young was an outstanding soldier. He had seen active combat service in the later Indian wars, in the Spanish-American War, and in the Philippine insurrection, and he had served as military attaché in Haiti before being assigned to Liberia. He was known as a man of unusual tact, steel determination, and tireless energy, who maintained discipline with a firm hand and was respected by his subordinates as well as his superiors. Later, after returning from his first duty in Liberia, he commanded with distinction and conspicuous gallantry a squadron in the Mexican punitive expedition of 1916. He was retired for physical disability, over his own vehement protests, shortly after the United States entered the war against Germany, but soon was recalled to active duty and promoted to the rank of full colonel. Ordered to Liberia a second time, he died there in 1922.

In 1912 Young was directed by the War Department to advise and assist the Liberians in every possible way, but he was specifically forbidden from exercising command or taking personal part in the affairs of the Liberian Frontier Force. He soon found that even the advisory task was discouraging. He reported "a dearth of men from whom to make . . . officers in the Republic. The old Liberian officers of the old force cannot be trusted . . . either on the frontiers or elsewhere."[30] The three black American officers thus found themselves unable to accomplish much in reforming the force. Because of the protracted loan negotiations, the Liberian government could not give them the pay they had been promised, and it failed to support them in their efforts to eliminate nepotism, favoritism, and other deeply entrenched forms of graft. To complicate matters further for them, in 1913 Young became so seriously ill that he had to return to the United States, leaving his colleagues without the support of his strong personality and official position.

Almost simultaneously, in 1913, many communities along the Sierra Leone frontier broke into open revolt. The Liberian government feared that the disorders might provoke – or provide a seemingly reasonable excuse for – British intervention, especially as some of the tribesmen were reportedly claiming to be British subjects with no allegiance to Liberia.[31] It was also reported that the coastal Kru, who had always chafed at Liberian rule, were becoming restless. Only their respect for and fear of Major Ballard, the senior of the three Americans, had kept them quiet, and when Ballard was transferred to Monrovia after Young's departure, it was feared that his restraining influence on the Kru would vanish.

Although the border peoples remained restless through the remainder of 1913 and the first part of 1914, the situation did not change materially. The rebellious communities on the Sierra Leone frontier were defeated in several engagements by Frontier Force detachments commanded by Americans. The British made no overt move threatening Liberia's independence, but in other ways the little country's troubles continued to mount. The bankers who were considering credit for Liberia insisted that before the loan became final, arrangements must be made for its prompt repayment and for the protection of their interests. Liberia, the United States, and the European countries whose bankers had previously made loans together negotiated an agreement that would establish an international receivership to take over collection of the Liberian customs. The head receiver would be named by the president of the United States, and the others would be named by Great Britain, France, and Germany.[32]

But all harmony was at an end once the basic agreement had been reached. The jealousies and tensions that were leading Europe rapidly toward war made any real agreement in Liberia impossible. All negotiators agreed that the American chief receiver, Reed Paige Clark, would be stationed at Monrovia, but where would each of the other three receivers be located? In the absence or disability of the American chief, who would act in his place? Matters of international prestige were involved, and discussions became somewhat stormy. Germany insisted that the German member also should be stationed at the capital because the greater part of Liberia's commerce was with Germany. The French objected strenuously to such a suggestion, but hinted broadly that a liberal slice of Liberian territory would overcome their objections. Huntington Wilson, the acting secretary of state, wrote sharply to the French chargé d'affaires in Washington: "The [State] Department would . . . be surprised to find the view seriously entertained that territorial compensation [at the expense of Liberia] would be a proportionate counterpoise to a matter of no graver import than the present location of the respective Receivers."[33]

Despite its absurdity, the quarrel lasted for some time. New causes of friction appeared when the receivership was formally inaugurated after completion of the loan negotiations. The three European receivers unanimously denied the authority of the American receiver general, and especially his right to assign them to stations. Their action violated an understanding that Washington had reached with their respective governments and seems to have sprung from personal pique of the British and German receivers, both of whom had previously held consular rank and who felt it beneath their dignity to take orders from an American without diplomatic status. The French receiver merely went along with his colleagues in putting into his place this interloper from across the Atlantic. The squabble was finally smoothed over when Clark was directed to assign each receiver to a post of his own choice adjacent to his own national territory.[34]

But Liberia was not yet out of the woods. On a night in September 1912 someone, presumably a Liberian, threw stones at some foreigners in Monrovia. When the news reached Europe, the incident had been blown into a serious antiforeign riot endangering the lives of all foreigners in Monrovia. Two months later, in November, New York bankers heard from Hamburg that Monrovia was torn by riots that the Liberian authorities were unable to suppress; a German cruiser had been ordered to Monrovia. The bankers were naturally hesitant about proceeding with the loan. In response to inquiries from Washington, the American chargé d'affaires at Monrovia said flatly that the stories of riot and disorder were exaggerated. It was his opinion that such rumors had been started deliberately by German merchants, and he added that a small uprising at the River Cess, suppressed without difficulty, had been instigated by some Germans in that region.[35]

In the midst of the so-called crisis, the German gunboat *Panther*—the ship that had precipitated the Agadir incident and almost started a world war in 1911—arrived at Monrovia and then proceeded immediately to Bassa. The *Bremen* reached Liberian waters a few days later, and the diplomatic situation became grave when the Germans loudly complained that a German naval officer had been deliberately insulted by a Liberian officer. The kaiser's government demanded a full apology from Liberia, the immediate dismissal of the Liberian officer, and a guarantee that he would never again be employed.

Although it is not possible to document the statement, there can be little doubt that the aggressively imperialistic German Empire of that time would have welcomed an excuse to intervene in Liberia. To forestall possible German landing forces, the United States had to move. The American ambassador in Berlin received somewhat pointed instructions from Secretary of State Philander Knox: "Make it clear . . . that in view of the marked consideration of German wishes from the very beginning of the Liberian negotiations, this Government feels justified in expecting on the part of Germany a patient and liberal attitude."[36] The outbreak of war in 1914 ended any immediate danger to Liberian independence and sovereignty. German war vessels temporarily vanished from the seas in that vicinity. Every available French citizen or subject was needed on the Western front; Great Britain had neither resources nor desire for further commitments.

Although immediate threats to Liberian independence vanished as the Great Powers of Europe began to fight, Liberia, like all countries dependent upon the factories and shipping of Europe, began to suffer. For years past, most of the country's necessities and virtually all of its few luxuries had been imported from Europe, and the greater part from Germany. This source of supply was cut off overnight. The Liberian government's scanty revenue was derived almost entirely from import duties; with no imports entering the country, the treasury quickly emptied. Liberia had to reduce the Frontier Force because there was no payroll money. Payment of interest on the promised loan was suddenly impossible. Some schools were closed for lack of funds, and since the emergency was worldwide, even some missionary activities were sharply curtailed. Under the circumstances, Wall Street bankers found it impossible to relieve the situation by an emergency loan.[37]

As noted, the Kru people of the coastal areas had always resented Liberian authority; in the past they had revolted numerous times.[38] With the world in arms and the Monrovia government barely able to maintain itself, the Kru – not surprisingly – again rebelled, proclaiming themselves British subjects and demanding that Great Britain annex them. Unable to handle the situation with its own resources, the Liberian government urgently asked for help from the United States, and the USS *Chester*, en route to the United States from Turkey, received radio orders to alter its course and sail for Monrovia. A somewhat surprising incident occurred at this juncture. Though Liberia had long suffered at the hands of Great Britain, and though the Kru rebels were calling themselves British subjects and demanding help from Britain, on October 18, 1915, HMS *Highflyer* anchored at Monrovia and its captain at once tendered his services to the Liberian government, pending the *Chester*'s arrival, to assist in suppressing the revolt. Liberia declined the offer with thanks, however, suspecting British intentions and fearing that its own neutrality would be compromised in accepting such help from a belligerent power.

The *Chester* reached Monrovia on November 8 and sailed at once for the scene of the rebellion, carrying the Liberian government's commission of inquiry and a strong detachment of the Frontier Force. On November 23 the American chargé d'affaires, who was also on the *Chester*, reported to Washington that all efforts toward a peaceable settlement had failed and that fighting had begun. A week later he wrote that government forces had opened the port of Sinoe and were again in possession; two soldiers and some twenty tribesmen had been killed. Faced by a superior force, the Krumen subsided. The rebellion was over.[39]

No marked change in Liberia's condition or in American involvement in Liberian affairs occurred during the next two years. In April 1917, when the United

States entered the war against Germany, Liberia was persuaded without much difficulty to follow. Liberia's declaration of war against Germany was, of course, a pure formality, but it was a matter of some importance for the Allies. German submarines ranged the whole northern Atlantic Ocean, and a neutral Liberia would have been a potential source of supply for them and a possible center for German espionage activities. A year later, in April 1918, a German submarine unexpectedly appeared before Monrovia; its commander submitted a series of impossible demands upon the Liberian government before proceeding systematically to shell the town. Since Monrovia was unfortified and without military importance other than that conferred by its status as the nation's capital, this was an act of pure frightfulness and a clear violation of international law. The sole effect, apart from a few casualties among the civilian population and damage to nonmilitary targets, was to confirm the world's belief that Hohenzollern Germany would be restrained by no consideration of law and humanity.

Liberia after World War I

During the late 1920s and the early 1930s Liberia went through a crisis that threatened its existence as an independent country. In all essentials, Liberia was a settler state dominated by a number of interlocking families: the Barclays, the Coopers, the Colemans, the Gibsons, the Tubmans, and a few others. The Liberian constitution continued to be modeled on that of the United States, but Liberia administered its indigenous people in a manner reminiscent of the way in which the worst of European colonial powers governed their African possessions.

There were at least sixteen major indigenous groups in Liberia. Administration of the coastal region constituted a species of dyarchy, with one set of rules for the Americo-Liberians and another for the indigenous people, who were governed by traditional authorities under the control of the Liberian government. Most of the indigenous people lived in the hinterland, where the Liberians had installed a system of indirect rule that attempted to utilize traditional chiefs and traditional codes of tribal law, subject to the control of Liberian district commissioners. "Uncivilized" Africans were subjected to hut, poll, and educational taxes; they were compelled to render *corvées* on road building and other projects. Military control over the hinterland was maintained by the Liberian Frontier Force, which took an active part in recruiting Liberian labor for shipment abroad.[40] For all the Liberians' pride in their African past, a black tribesman was doubtless better off under British governance in neighboring Sierra Leone or on the Gold Coast than he was under the sway of Monrovia.

Liberia's troubles, however, were not all of its own making. European colonies could draw on their respective governing powers in the metropoles for capital, administrative, and technological skills. The ruling Americo-Liberian stratum in Liberia, on the other hand, numbered scarcely more than twelve thousand persons; their resources were small, their administrative and governmental responsibilities enormous. Liberian exports – coffee, rubber, palm nuts, and palm oil – were scanty, and suffered from sharp price fluctuations on the international market. The country's transportation system was inadequate, the banking system was weak, and markets were few, so that much of the trade in the hinterland continued to rest on barter.

Liberia also suffered from unsound financial management. The prewar loan, administered by American officials, was a heavy drain on the country; it also caused increasing resentment in many Liberians as an affront to their national integrity and a threat to their sovereignty. A proposal for a loan of $5 million from the U.S. government was rejected by the U.S. Senate as that body became more and more hostile to any form of foreign commitment.[41]

This was the broad situation when, in 1926, Harvey Firestone, the American rubber manufacturer and financier, entered the Liberian scene. The Firestone enterprises in Liberia are discussed more fully in Chapter 17. Briefly, however, in the eyes of its critics, the company's entry into Liberia marked the start of Liberia's neocolonial phase. But without Firestone production of rubber, Liberia could hardly have survived financially.

Within a few months after the conclusion of the first agreement between Liberia and the Firestone Company, Liberia was the subject of a widespread attack that for a time threatened its very existence. The Americo-Liberians were charged with engaging in practices that seemed disagreeably close to those of the former slave trade.

The charges were first aired when a defeated candidate for the presidency, Thomas J. R. Faulkner, wrote a lengthy letter to the secretariat of the League of Nations (of which Liberia was a member) claiming that Liberia's indigenous people were forced to labor without pay upon roads and other government projects for as much as nine months a year. They were required to furnish their own food and tools and to supply food for the soldiers who forced them to work, as well as for the public officials who supervised them. Further allegations stated that government officials rather than the public benefited or profited from many of the projects upon which people were compelled to labor. A chief or headman who failed to furnish his quota of laborers was heavily fined and often publicly humiliated; laborers paid heavy fines for trivial offenses and often were punished so severely that they died. As a result, Faulkner charged, tribesmen were fleeing to other places to escape oppression and abuse, leaving whole districts depopulated. Even more pernicious, he stated, was the practice of shipping laborers under contract to the Spanish colony of Fernando Po. Certain high government officials, according to Faulkner, and particularly the Honorable Allen C. Yancey, vice-president of the republic, profited to the extent of ten dollars per head in this traffic. Faulkner charged further that the Liberians who conducted this twentieth-century slave trade did not hesitate to use force or any other kind of skulduggery to obtain recruits, and that the Frontier Force was used freely for this purpose.[42]

The migration of Liberian workers to Fernando Po, São Tomé, Libreville, and other places in West Africa where labor was at a premium was an old problem. For many years, under agreement with the Spanish government, Liberian laborers had been taken in large numbers to the cocoa plantations of Fernando Po. In 1921, because of the ill treatment of Liberians there, the Liberian government denounced the agreements with Spain and forbade further shipments of Liberians to the Spanish colony, as well as recruiting of labor by Spaniards within the country. The Spanish Sindicato Agrícola in 1928 approached the Liberian government with a new proposal, which guaranteed good care, humane treatment, proper housing, adequate wages, and return to Liberia at the expiration of the contract period. To ensure compliance with this agreement, a Liberian consulate would be established at Fernando Po, the consul having full right to investigate conditions affecting Liberians and free access to all necessary places and records.[43]

Grim rumors still continued to circulate. In 1929 an unnamed American clergyman was said to have noted a large group of unhappy young men being herded, under guard, aboard a Spanish ship at Monrovia. On inquiry, he was informed that they were contract laborers bound for Fernando Po, and he reported his observations and impressions to the State Department in Washington.[44] Adding to the unpleasant impression caused by Faulkner's statements and those of the anonymous clergyman were the comments of Raymond Leslie Buell in a massive two-volume study entitled *The Native Problem in Africa*, written in 1928 after twelve months of personal study and observation in all parts of Africa. Buell's remarks concerning forced labor in Liberia were moderate in tone and all the more damning for their restraint:

> While the 1924 convention [concerning shipment of laborers to Fernando Po] attempts to erect certain safeguards protecting Liberian labor, two main criticisms against the system have been made: first in regard to recruiting such labor, and second, in regard to its treatment at Fernando Po. At present each recruiter in Liberia is paid five dollars for each boy, a system which several years ago at least encouraged compulsion. In some counties native commissioners engaged in recruiting, sharing the profit with the chiefs; and in one county at least the County Commissioner carried on these activities. Recently a government official was reported to have arrested wholesale a batch of natives and brought them to the coast ostensibly for placing them in jail; but instead he shipped them to Fernando Po.[45]

Such charges, combined with difficulties the Firestone Company was having in clarifying its relations with the Liberian government, aroused a certain amount of interest in the United States about its African protégé. There was occasional mention of Liberia in the press; the U.S. government took official cognizance of the allegations when, on June 8, 1929, Secretary of State Henry L. Stimson sent to the chargé d'affaires at Monrovia a sharp message, with instructions to bring it to the attention of the Liberian officials at once. Stimson's dispatch, described as "scathing," stated that evidence which had to be regarded as reliable and authentic "definitely indicate[s] that existing conditions incident to the so-called 'export' of labor from Liberia to Fernando Po have resulted in the development of a system which seems hardly distinguishable from organized slave trade." Stimson added that the Frontier Force was employed in enforcing the system, and that high officials of the Liberian government furnished their authority and influence. The dispatch also included a thinly veiled threat of foreign intervention if Liberia did not quickly and thoroughly "clean house."[46]

Liberian officials at first issued an unqualified denial of the charges. The Liberian secretary of state, on receiving the American note, remarked that it was "an old story. The Department does not say if the charges are true but assumes that they are. They are serious and we will investigate, but there being no specific instance charged, investigation may be difficult."[47] Otherwise, the Liberian reaction was all that the most critical could desire. The Liberian government itself suggested an investigation by a "competent, impartial and unprejudiced commission."[48] After some diplomatic correspondence, President Charles Dunbar Burgess King formally appointed a commission of inquiry whose members included representatives of the League of Nations, the United States, and his own country. The league member was an Englishman, Dr. Cuthbert Christy; the American was Dr. Charles S. Johnson, a noted black educator and sociologist; and the Liberian was the Honorable Arthur Barclay, a former president of the republic.[49]

The commission spent several months in its investigation, and its final report, in spite of earlier Liberian denials, was damning. It found that chattel slavery, as understood in Europe and the United States, did not exist. Traditional African domestic slavery was still practiced by indigenous groups, and the local custom of "pawning" a dependent had developed into something indistinguishable from real slavery. These considerations, however, were not particularly important. What really shocked the world were the commission's findings on the export of labor to Fernando Po, São Tomé, and French Gabon, and on forced labor in so-called public works: "The Commission finds that a large proportion of the contract laborers shipped to Fernando Poo [*sic*] and French Gabon from the southern counties of Liberia have been recruited under conditions of criminal compulsion scarcely distinguishable from slave raiding and slave trading, and frequently by misrepresenting the destination."[50]

The commission found, too, that high officials of the Liberian government were deeply involved, making full use of their authority and influence to line their own pockets at the expense of the hapless tribesmen.

> The Commission finds that Vice-President [Allen N.] Yancey and other high officials of the Liberian Government, as well as county superintendents and district commissioners, have given their sanction for the compulsory recruitment of labor for road construction, for shipment abroad and other work, by the aid and assistance of the Liberian Frontier Force; and have condoned the utilization of this force for purposes of physical compulsion on road construction, for the intimidation of villagers, for the humiliation and degradation of chiefs, for the imprisonment of inhabitants, and for the convoying of gangs of captured natives to the coast, there guarding them till the time of shipment.[51]

It appeared to the rest of the world that Liberia was unable to solve its own problems without outside help. The council of the League of Nations set up a special Liberian Committee in which the United States agreed to participate, in spite of its previous policy of having nothing to do with the League. King and Yancey both resigned and Edwin J. Barclay was elected to the presidency, pledged to abolish the conditions discovered by the commission and to reform the country.

In December 1932 the League's committee announced a plan to assist Liberia. It provided for a chief adviser, a man who could be neither American nor French nor British and whose advice the Liberian government would be obliged to follow. Under him would be a series of provincial commissioners and medical officers who would actually administer the country for five years. In case of disagreement between the chief adviser and the Liberian government, the League's council would have final decision. In addition to these officials, the country's finances would be administered by a financial adviser; the United States, backed by the obvious needs of the Firestone interests, insisted that this official be an American.

The proposal raised strong opposition and vociferous criticism. Many U.S. liberals feared that it would lead to a dictatorship such as, some asserted, the United States had imposed upon Haiti. Liberians saw in it the death of their independence and sovereignty. Some liberals pointed to a disturbing symptom of this threat: the fact that the United States recommended greater authority for the chief adviser than had been indicated by the League's committee. Buell, whose word carried considerable weight, believed that the plan would benefit nobody but Firestone. Other liberals, in a period when liberal opinion in the United States was deeply suspicious of all activities of large-scale capitalism, detected a Machiavellian scheme to fasten the tentacles of Wall Street upon another guileless and helpless people.[52] An editorial in the *New Republic* urged that the only solution to Liberia's problems was a League of Nations mandate "or its equivalent," a solution that would effectively prevent "such a dubious liaison as now exists between the Liberian government and the Firestone Rubber Company."[53] The editorial expressed the contradictions that plagued liberal thought over the Liberian issue during this period: The writers did not see the inconsistency of urging a forced colonial condition upon a previously independent state; neither did they realize that such a solution might simply benefit those other capitalist interests that were hostile to Firestone's Liberian projects.

Despite all sorts of diplomatic pressure, including withdrawal of U.S. recognition for a period, the Liberian oligarchy refused to submit to what passed for international opinion as expressed by the League of Nations. The situation was further complicated by the Great Depression and by the rise of openly aggressive, imperialistic, and racialistic dictatorships in Italy and Germany. In 1935 Mussolini's government presented an unprecedented and brazen demand that Italian nationals in Liberia be granted all the privileges of Liberian citizenship – a demand that caused considerable apprehension, as it coincided with Italy's conquest of Ethiopia and was obviously another step in its attempt to build a great African empire. In 1936 the prime minister of South Africa, James Hertzog, blandly suggested that the League give Nazi Germany a mandate over Liberia, simultaneously satisfying Germany's colonial aspirations and solving the Liberian problem.[54] The threat to Liberia's national existence, however, abated somewhat when the United States again recognized the Liberian government. When the USS *Boise*, on its maiden cruise, anchored at Monrovia in 1938 for a courtesy visit, it signaled to the world that the United States was still interested in the little African country.[55]

To sum up, America's major official interest in Africa before World War I centered largely on Liberia. Diplomatic concern in the United States was complicated by the fact that the very existence of an independent black republic lacked, for many European colonialists, the kind of legitimacy that the colonial powers accorded each other. The real and alleged abuses found in Liberia and in Haiti widely served as arguments for withholding self-government to black Africans. Even black Americans were divided. Some felt disgust at the iniquities committed by Monrovia; others sided with Liberia on the grounds that white Americans or white Englishmen had no business to set themselves up as judges over the black republic.

The United States, on the whole, came out of the affair with credit. The Americans avoided taking direct responsibility for Liberia. Yet they supported the country in such a manner as to preserve Liberia's independence while, at the same time, salving the exaggerated pride that then was widely characteristic of the Great Powers in their attitude toward small and weak states. In the end, it was in all probability only American influence that prevented Liberia from being absorbed by one or another of the major colonial empires.

Americans in Africa, 1919–1939

Africa played only a small part in the calculations of U.S. policy makers during the years preceding World War II. Except for a handful of missionaries, commercial employees, and mine managers, few Americans chose to live in tropical Africa. The only colonial city with a self-consciously American community was Nairobi, of all African cities the best publicized in the United States at the time. In addition, a handful of U.S. consuls served in various parts of Africa, but a spell in a consulate in tropical Africa did not count much for promotion. Occasionally, a commercial agent came to Africa on behalf of the U.S. Bureau of Foreign and Domestic Commerce, but overall, such efforts counted for little.

U.S. commerce with Africa did increase significantly after World War I, however. In 1914, the value of America's trade with the entire African continent had amounted to just over half that of U.S. commerce with the small island of Puerto Rico; by 1920, this traffic had increased by more than six times (from $47 million to $325 million). The U.S. government attempted to stimulate commercial exchange with Africa, but failed to make this trade significant except with South Africa. Until the 1920s, American ships did not carry much American-made merchandise to Africa. Nevertheless, exports expanded. Heavy machinery, cars, and trucks stood at the top of the list, followed by petroleum, lumber, cement, motion pictures, musical instruments, sporting goods, and arms. Africa sent essentially the same goods as during the nineteenth century: palm oil, cocoa, spices, peanuts, cashews, woods and dies, manganese, iron, and copper ore.

The major obstacle to expanded U.S. trade with Africa, besides imperial preference tariffs and distance from the market, was the lack of American flag shipping rights to Africa: European shipping conference lines monopolized the passenger and goods trade with Africa.

The U.S. government, through the Shipping Act of 1916, expanded American ship-building facilities and encouraged the growth of new shipping lines, some of which went to Africa. The first was A. H. Bull's West Africa Line, which started in 1921. The Barber Lines of New York bought out Bull in 1928 and established a more efficient service, the American West African Line, which was still operating in the 1970s. By 1936 four American lines had service to sub-Saharan Africa and operated a fleet of twenty-three medium-sized ships.[56] The most successful company was the Farrell Lines (discussed in more detail in Chapter 17).

In dollar value, automobiles and trucks were the major U.S. export to Africa between 1919 and 1939. Edward H. McKinley reports one estimate that 93 percent of cars in British East Africa in 1923 were American made.[57] Ford dominated the car market, but Buick, Willy-Knight, Chevrolet, and Overland also did well; in

Table 2. *U.S. foreign trade, 1939 (in dollars)*

U.S. imports/exports	Amount
Exports to Africa	69,118,000
Imports from Africa	28,721,000
Exports to the Netherlands	96,809,000
Imports from the Netherlands	28,930,000
Total trade with foreign countries	
Exports	12,900,000,000
Imports	13,910,000,000

Source: World Almanac and Book of Facts (New York: New York
World Telegram, 1942), pp. 494–5.

southern Africa the Chevrolet reigned supreme up to 1960. The reasons for the
success of the American cars were their low gas mileage, power, speed, durability
and ease of repair. Other good sellers for the United States, as noted, were movies,
which had a near monopoly of the African market. American musical instruments,
phonographs, and records also dominated the market. Yet, although American
commerce with Africa had indeed considerably increased since the early 1900s, by
1939 the total value of American trade with Africa was still of less value than that
of U.S. traffic with the Netherlands (see Table 2).

In the cultural field, African influences on America were more profound. Developing almost parallel with the Garvey movement, there was a black American movement known as the Harlem Literary Renaissance. Claude McKay, Langston Hughes,
Countee Cullen, Jean Toomer, Georgia Douglas Johnson, and many others made
their names in the realm of letters. They tried to rebuild a bridge to the lost African
homeland of their imagination, but their mood was apt to be wistful, rather than
confident. As McKay mused over his motherland in a mood of nostalgia:

> For the dim regions whence my fathers came
> My spirit, bondaged by the body, longs
> Words felt, but never heard, my lips would frame;
> Thy soul would sing forgotten jungle songs.[58]

Americans were also becoming conscious of their debt to Africa in music and the
arts. Aided by the new technology of the gramophone and the radio, ragtime, jazz,
and rhythm and blues became America's true folk music, its most distinctive contribution to music in the world at large. Alain Leroy Locke, a black Harvard
professor, published in 1936 a major study entitled *The Negro and His Music*
(1936), in which he traced the African impact on American music. African sculp-
tures came to be widely admired and exercised a profound influence on modernis-
tic art forms. But most Americans continued to regard Africa as a continent of
mystery and darkness, of no conceivable concern to their personal lives.

There was little scholarly concern with Africa at the time, but few pioneers (such as
Raymond Leslie Buell and Melville J. Herskovits) made distinctive contributions to
American knowledge of Africa. At Harvard University, the Peabody Museum started

Harvard African Studies after World War I, though there were no departments of African studies in the major American universities for years to come. Harvard and the Rockefeller Foundation sponsored Buell's work in Africa in 1925–6. W. D. Hambly of the Field Museum of Chicago, an earlier student of African ethnology, worked in West Africa and edited the *Source Book for African Anthropology* in 1937.[59] Professor Edward A. Ross's *Report on Employment of Native Labor in Portuguese Africa* (1923) led to a League of Nations investigation of Portugal.

Among black American intellectuals, W. E. B. Du Bois made a name for himself as a radical critic of racism and colonialism. Du Bois wrote extensively on a broad range of subjects. One of his many interests was promotion of a Negro History Week campaign designed to foster black pride, although it was ultimately Carter G. Woodson who got Negro History Week established. Du Bois bitterly fought against the views of those who, like Anson Phelps Stokes and Booker T. Washington, believed that black Americans and Africans alike would specially benefit from vocational instruction of an industrial or agricultural kind, an education that would cater to peculiarly black needs. Du Bois, instead, was convinced that industrial education alone could not cure the ills of society, and that teachers would do best by developing their students' intelligence through "hard" academic subjects. According to Du Bois, black academic institutions such as Fisk and Howard in the United States had accomplished infinitely more than industrial institutes like Hampton and Tuskegee. In his view, the vocational programs begun by Hampton and Tuskegee had not been successful in training a skilled working class; hence these institutions could not provide a pattern for education in Africa – current missionary orthodoxies notwithstanding. Du Bois's views on education and culture went with an intensely held faith in black unity and Pan-African solidarity, and he helped to organize a series of Pan-African conferences (discussed in Chapter 19). But even Du Bois's influence was limited; few white Americans during the 1920s or the 1930s could even have identified his name.

The Americans' lack of interest in African affairs went with a more general mood of isolationism. Senator Gerald P. Nye and others conducted a veritable crusade during the 1920s and 1930s to convince their countrymen that U.S. involvement in World War I had been occasioned by the greed of American munitions makers looking for markets and by the machinations of American investors, who had put their money into allied government loans. American isolationists further argued that the nation's neutrality would be assured if U.S. citizens, in the event of war, were required to stay at home and mind their own business: Any Americans who entered the war zone would do so at their own risk; any Americans who transacted business with a belligerent country would do so at their own risk. At the same time, the United States sponsored and ardently promoted the Kellog-Briand Pact, with which the majority of the world's sovereign states pledged themselves to renounce war as an instrument of policy. This pious but meaningless document met with almost universal approval in the United States – without, however, making an impact on the realities of power politics.

In the pacific intellectual atmosphere of the mid-1930s, the Italo-Ethiopian crisis and the war of 1935 burst like a bomb. A small minority of Americans supported Mussolini, while the bulk of American public opinion swung in favor of the Ethiopians. Pacifists, believers in the League of Nations, anti-Fascists of all persuasions united with Jews, black Americans, and believers in the Popular Front (an attempted alliance of anti-Nazis, ranging from moderates to the extreme left, led by Communists) to condemn Mussolini's adventure. At the same time, American public opinion insisted that the country should remain neutral at all costs, that the job of thwarting Mussolini's ambition should be left to the League of Nations and—above all—to the British and the French. In August 1935 Congress adopted a Neutrality Resolution that imposed a mandatory embargo on arms and ammunitions exports to the belligerents in the event of war. The League's hesitant policy on sanctions gave little encouragement to official appeals asking Americans to limit to normal amounts their sale of oil and other merchandise useful for war. (American exports to Italy, in fact, rose considerably during the early months of the war.) Neutrality, as in the Boer war, worked in the aggressor's favor.

The neutrality issue led to a tug-of-war between the president and the isolationist leaders in the U.S. Senate over the precise terms of neutrality legislation. The president preferred discretionary powers; the isolationists insisted upon rigid legal requirements. In a mood of bitter apprehension, they feared that discretionary powers would allow the president to follow whatever action the League of Nations might take, thus involving the United States with that body. In August 1935, as the Italian concentration of troops in Eritrea and Somaliland was building up, the Ethiopian Emperor, Haile Selassie, appealed to the U.S. government under the Kellogg-Briand Pact, but because he had already appealed to the League of Nations, he received a rapid dismissal. Meanwhile, if the United States moved to join in any sort of collective action, the isolationists would be outraged; if the United States refused or failed to support any sort of collective action, efforts of the League of Nations to ensure peace would be largely nullified.

When the president and Congress resolved the terms of neutrality legalities by a compromise, the ensuing proclamation of an embargo upon war materials was narrowly limited to actual munitions and weapons, which Italy was not procuring in America and which Ethiopia, for obvious geographical reasons, could not obtain in America. Oil, vital to modern armies, was not embargoed; should the League of Nations endeavor to bring Italy to terms by withholding essential fuel for Italian vehicles and vessels, Italy could, presumably, obtain all that was needed from the United States.

The U.S. government thus found itself on the horns of an African dilemma: how to remain apart from the League of Nations and avoid even the appearance of cooperation while supporting and assisting the League's efforts to thwart an aggressor and stop a war; how to maintain peace in a tense world and at the same time avoid any involvement in international effort. The dilemma remained unsolved until the rapidity of the Italian conquest of the ancient empire appeared to make the issues obsolete.[60] The Ethiopian war, however, left a deep imprint on black consciousness in the United States. Once again, a white nation apparently had treacherously attacked a black people; Emperor Haile Selassie, the "Lion of Judah," had heroically tried to defend his country. In exile, he continued to plead the fate not merely of his own country, but of the world at large. Educated black opinion became even more firmly riveted to the progressive alliance among New Dealers, anti-Fascists of all persuasions, labor, and certain ethnic minority groups such as the Jews in what appeared to all participants as the cause of humanity at large.[61]

CHAPTER 17

Private interest groups

During the nineteenth century, Africa appeared to whites as a continent of mystery. Missionary reports and travelers' tales made popular reading; tales of Africa to some extent supplied the place that science fiction would fill half a century later. Many parts of Africa, moreover, remained almost blank spots on the map, and explorers like J. H. S. Speke, Karl M. Mauch, Richard Burton, and scores of others continued the work of Livingstone and his contemporaries in filling in the blank areas.

Explorers, hunters, and scientists

The regions of northern British East Africa, abutting upon Ethiopia, were at the turn of the century almost as unknown to Europeans as in the days of Stanley and Livingstone. Some of the mystery of this part of Africa was dispelled in the early 1890s by Dr. Arthur Donaldson Smith's expedition. In 1892 another American amateur explorer entered the country with a large safari. William Astor Chanler, accompanied by Lieutenant Ludwig von Höhnel, an officer of the Austrian navy who had made a previous trip into that part of Africa, undertook to investigate "that portion of East Africa hitherto unexplored, lying between the Tana and Juba rivers . . . My journey was undertaken purely in the interest of science."[1] Chanler's safari added materially to the available information about that part of Africa, even though he failed in one of his main objectives, the penetration and exploration of the great Lorian swamps.[2] Americans continued to supply a substantial share of travelers, and another explorer-writer, William Edward Geil, shortly after 1900 followed Stanley's route across Africa from Mombasa to the mouth of the Congo. His principal purpose was to gather material for a book; he did not claim to be an explorer. He did, however, make an original contribution to ethnographic knowledge with his picture of the pygmies in the tropical forest region before their ways were modified by contact with European culture. (He also gave what now appears an unduly favorable account of the Congo Free State administration.)[3]

President Theodore Roosevelt's interest in Africa and African affairs created and fostered a degree of interest in Africa among the American people. His hunting trip to Africa after he left office certainly aroused an interest in Africa among people who otherwise would never have given the subject a thought. He had planned his safari for a long time, and in March 1909 he sailed from New York accompanied by one of his sons and a small party. A month later he landed in what was then called British East Africa. Roosevelt was an amateur naturalist, with a deep knowledge of wildlife. His African safari was not for sport alone, but had as a major objective the collection of specimens for the U.S. National Museum and the

American Museum of Natural History. He and his party got to the business of collecting within a few days after arriving in Africa, and almost a year later they emerged in the valley of the Nile, having traveled and hunted in British East Africa, Uganda, a corner of the Congo, and the Sudan. Unlike Stanley, Livingstone, and other early explorers, Roosevelt was never "lost"; his daily adventures were followed eagerly in the newspapers by millions of people in the United States.[4]

While in Kenya (as the country is now called), the Roosevelt safari, by pure chance, encountered another American safari. This one was led by Carl Akeley, who was, like Roosevelt himself, hunting for scientific specimens. The two men had known each other for years; each knew that the other was in Africa; but their encounter on the Uasin Gishu plateau was unplanned.[5] Akeley's lifelong interest in Africa and in the natural sciences was aroused during his formative years largely by a man whose name is now all but forgotten, but who probably had more to do than any other individual with awakening scientific interest in the world's wildlife.

Henry Augustus Ward provided the original impetus for Akeley, William T. Hornaday, and other men who became famous as naturalists and artists. Ward was born in 1834 near Rochester, New York, to a family of New England origin. A disrupted family life during his childhood, rather than having a traumatic effect, seems to have strengthened his character and increased his self-reliance. He became fascinated with the natural sciences while still a child. After various ups and downs, he finally achieved an education far in advance of what was usual in his day, largely owing to the friendly interest and generosity of General Wadsworth, a wealthy landholder of the Genesee Valley who engaged Ward as a companion for his own son, financed collecting trips for the two, and finally sent them to Paris to study at the famous French School of Mines. Together they made a trip to Egypt and Palestine during which Ward investigated and wrote a paper on the "singing sands" of the Sinai desert. The paper resulted in his election to the French Geological Society as perhaps the youngest person ever to receive the honor.

General Wadsworth meanwhile had suffered business losses and was unable to maintain the two young men in Europe longer. Ward decided to remain until he had completed his courses; to support himself, he became a purveyor of geological specimens to the museums of Europe, an occupation that took him to all parts of Europe, from Spain to Russia and from the British Isles to the Balkans, without seriously impairing his training. His studies ended, Ward yielded to the pleas of his family and decided to return to the United States via Cuba, but at Lisbon he missed that ship and sailed instead for the west coast of Africa as a deck passenger.

Probably to the scandal of conventional Europeans on the African coast, he lived for brief periods among the Africans in their villages, collecting specimens, taking notes, and observing. There are indications that he may have ascended the Niger alone to a point farther than any previous white man had ever reached. He contracted African fever and was dumped on the beach at Fernando Po and left there to die. He recovered instead, and finally, none the worse for his experiences, returned home to be appointed to a newly established professorship at the University of Rochester. Within a few years, however, he began to devote himself entirely to Ward's Museum of Natural Science. In a way, he became a showman, for he was unable to obtain grants or donations and was forced to try to make his museum self-supporting. He was never entirely successful in this attempt, but fortunately he had a wealthy uncle who, grumbling, always made up the annual deficit.

Ward's significance, beyond his own studies, lay in his idea of the purpose and function of a museum. He conceived a museum to be an educational institution, not a collection of curios. Through the students and his employees – whom he trained – his ideas spread, and Henry Augustus Ward has justifiably been called "the father of American museums."[6] He was a great scientist in his own right, and though his name is little known, he had a profound influence upon scores of others, not the least of whom are those in whose minds he stimulated an interest in the animal life of Africa.

Carl Akeley, as a teenaged youth, became interested in the art of taxidermy. After serving for four years under Ward, he decided that true representation of specimens in museums and other displays required an accurate knowledge of the habits, habitat, movements, and anatomy of the animals. His studies in these and related fields made him one of the foremost naturalists of the age and a sculptor of international fame. He first went to Africa in 1896 as an assistant to Professor Daniel G. Eliot, the curator of the Field Museum in Chicago. Once he acquired the African habit, Akeley returned time after time, eventually attaining recognition as a leading authority on Africa, on many of its varied peoples, and on the animals of the continent.

While Akeley was gaining scientific knowledge and obtaining numerous specimens for major American museums, he became deeply concerned over the continued lessening of the numbers of animals he observed on his successive trips, especially over the possible extermination of the gorilla if measures were not taken promptly for its protection. In his first published book, *In Brightest Africa,* he said, "The gorilla is on his way to extinction. He is not particularly numerous. He is neither wary nor dangerous. He is an easy and highly prized prey to the 'sporting instinct' . . . These considerations materially led my mind to the idea of a gorilla sanctuary."[7] Upon his return to the United States, Akeley immediately embarked upon a campaign of lecturing and of correspondence with influential people throughout the world in an effort to arouse sentiment for the protection of the threatened species in Africa, and especially of the humanlike gorilla. Ultimately he was successful, and the creation of the Albert National Park in the Congo can be attributed largely to his efforts.[8]

Among the members of Akeley's party in his first quest for gorillas were Mr. and Mrs. Herbert E. Bradley of Chicago, accompanied by their five-year-old daughter. It was purely a sporting and sightseeing expedition for the Bradleys, although they reinforced Akeley at all turns. They became so enamored of Africa that in 1924, with a party organized among their friends, they returned this time planning to penetrate regions of the Congo that were virtually unexplored and were reputed to be inhabited by cannibals. They were successful and do not seem to have encountered any serious dangers. The Bradleys were neither scientist nor intentional explorers. Nevertheless, the fact that they made two trips into the still mysterious interior of the Congo, both times with a child who suffered no ill effects, helped to dispel the horror that many people felt for the deep tropics and proved that, with reasonable precautions, Africa could be traversed as safely as any other out-of-the-way part of the world.[9]

Coincidence and chance often combine to produce results that a fiction writer would hesitate to employ in a novel. In 1908 a young man named James L. Clark joined with a photographer friend named Dugmore in a trip to East Africa. Clark was primarily an artist trained in the plant of the Gorham Silver Company and the Rhode Island School of Design; he had been employed for several years as a taxidermist at the American Museum of Natural History. The museum's director, Dr. Herman C. Bumpus, knowing of Akeley's work in Chicago, wanted to develop a staff at the American Museum that could produce the same realistic, natural displays. Akeley was persuaded to give Clark a course of instruction—a personal contact that resulted in a lifelong friendship and an amazingly close parallel between the careers of the two men. To quote Clark, "Akeley became my mentor and idol."[10]

Clark was intrigued by what Akeley had told him of Africa, and when he learned of Dugmore's plans for a free-lance trip to Africa to obtain animal pictures, he jumped at the chance to go along. The two reached Africa shortly before the Roosevelt party, but they met the former president's safari on several occasions and were permitted to photograph Roosevelt and many of the safari's activities. Dugmore returned to the United States after six months, but Clark remained in Africa for more than a year to observe and study the animals in their natural habitat, and to study the country and collect specimens. When Akeley arrived, Clark joined him, although not as a permanent member of his party, and through Akeley he became well acquainted with Roosevelt.

Like Akeley, Clark had many sides to his interests and activities. The two were closely associated in developing and producing Akeley's motion-picture camera, and both wanted to be out of doors and to take active part in procuring specimens. They collaborated closely in preparing the African Hall in the American Museum, and upon Akeley's untimely death in the Congo in 1926, while on an expedition into gorilla country, Clark was appointed to take full charge of the work. During the course of a long career as a scientist, artist, and explorer—although he never regarded himself as such—he made five trips to Africa.

At the time of Theodore Roosevelt's safari, Africa fairly teemed with American hunting expeditions. In addition to Roosevelt, Akeley, and Clark, there were expeditions organized and headed by Paul J. Rainey and a colorful character known as "Buffalo" Jones. Rainey, who was also collecting specimens for the U.S. National Museum, was a young man of great wealth who found a life of adventure and hunting very much to his taste. Previous to his African trip, he had conducted an expedition to the Arctic at his own expense, during which he captured a polar bear alive. He owned a huge private hunting preserve in Louisiana, as well as other properties where wildlife was carefully protected. He took to Africa with him a pack of his own bear hounds in order to try hunting lions by the methods used for hunting bears in the canebrakes of Mississippi. Rainey found that hounds were able to bring a lion to bay as easily as and with no more risk to themselves than in a bear hunt.[11]

"Buffalo" Jones's expedition to Africa was probably the most extraordinary African safari of all time. C. J. Jones was a Western plainsman who had developed, over a period of years, a specialty of capturing wild animals by roping them in the way cattle are roped. His captures with the lariat included mountain lions, buffalo (hence his nickname), deer, elk, moose, and – on a trip to the Arctic – a musk-ox. He determined to try his methods in capturing such large and dangerous African animals as the lion, the African buffalo, and the rhinoceros. He interested a financial backer, and in 1909 the Buffalo Jones African Expedition sailed for British East Africa; besides Jones himself, the party included two experienced American cowboys, a motion-picture cameraman, and various technicians. Jones carefully selected top-string cow ponies, and like Rainey a short time before, he took his own pack of hounds.

In spite of doubters, Jones's efforts were spectacularly successful. A rhinoceros, a giraffe, and many smaller animals were deftly roped and secured by Jones and his two cowboys. Since Jones was in Africa to prove a point rather than to collect, all of the captured animals were released. He never killed except for food or in self-defense. The climax of the safari was the roping and capture of a full-grown lion without injuring horses, hounds, or men. This was the single animal that was not released; Jones presented it to the Bronx Zoo. More significant, however, than pursuit and capture were the motion pictures taken of the action with the animals. These may have been the first motion pictures ever taken of African animals in their natural habitat, and certainly they were the first pictures ever taken of the capture of such animals.[12]

Still another American hunting party to enter East Africa was that of Stewart Edward White, a popular author who specialized in outdoor articles and stories. White made a hunting trip to British East Africa in 1910 and 1911 to explore hunting possibilities and obtain material for his writing. From the purely sporting point of view, the trip was a great success, but White decided that "most of British East Africa is a beaten track"; he wanted to get into regions that were still unspoiled. In 1913 he made a second safari with a single white companion, this time penetrating into a part of German East Africa (now Tanzania) that was previously unknown to Europeans other than, possibly, a few professional hunters.[13]

White was primarily a hunter and sportsman rather than an explorer and naturalist, but he was a close observer. His previous hunting excursions had taken him into the almost unknown interior of Alaska and into the Arctic. His observations on the country he traversed – its geography, topography, inhabitants, and flora and fauna – hence were definite contributions to the world's knowledge of Africa. World War I exploded simultaneously with the publication of his story, however, and the hunters' paradise that White and his companion found was destined in the next few months to become the scene of savage fighting between British and German patrols.

Shortly after the opening of the twentieth century, another American entered the African scene. William Northrup McMillan (or Macmillan), a native of St. Louis, Missouri, was educated in the United States and, like Arthur Donaldson Smith and William Astor Chanler, was wealthy enough to be able to indulge a taste for exploring unknown places. His first trip to Africa was made in 1902; its most dramatic event was the murder of one of the European members of his party by a Danaki tribesman during an expedition into Abyssinia (as Ethiopia was then called).[14] Nonetheless, McMillan's expeditions were carefully planned and organized. His wife usually accompanied him, and his staff included a physician, a taxidermist, an engineer, and other specialists and technicians whose presence assured that the expedition's results would be positive. He made several trips into Ethiopia. In 1903 he attempted unsuccessfully to navigate the Blue Nile to its source; the boats, which he had had specially built for the purpose, proved to be unsuitable. The next year, with more appropriate craft, he renewed his effort to determine whether there was a waterway feasible for commerce between the Sudan and Ethiopia. This time he proved that small craft could proceed as far as the Gambela cataract, and he found that a scarp previously believed to be impassable could be traversed easily by loaded pack animals.

After several years of exploration, McMillan decided to live permanently in Kenya, becoming a pioneer in the cultivation of sisal, flax, maize, coffee, and other agricultural products. Theodore Roosevelt spent considerable time with the McMillans, both at their town house in Nairobi and at their great farm. Few scientists or sportsmen passed through East Africa, in fact, without availing themselves of the McMillans' hospitality and intimate knowledge of the country.[15]

McMillan was in the United States when the war erupted in the summer of 1914. He returned immediately to Africa and was shortly commissioned as a major in the colony's forces; he was also named as a member of the War Council. He took part in the campaigns against the Germans in East Africa, and contributed both his town house and his farm for use as hospitals. In 1919, having become a British subject in the meantime, he was knighted in recognition of his services in peace and war. Sir William Northrup McMillan died in 1925 at the relatively early age of fifty-three, a man who might easily have spent his life as a gentleman of leisure but who preferred, instead, the life of an adventurer, explorer, and pioneer. In 1931 Lady McMillan established the McMillan Memorial Library in Nairobi housing the best Africana collection in East Africa. The McMillans also helped establish a system of public libraries throughout Kenya.[16]

Theodore Roosevelt's hunting trip to Africa thus had served a distinct purpose in the history of the relationships and interactions between the United States and the peoples of black Africa through World War I. Roosevelt enjoyed a popularity that few presidents have had. He was the idol of millions of Americans, so his trip focused on Africa, however temporarily, the attention and interest of multitudes of people to whom that continent had been previously an obscure and distant part of the world populated by ferocious animals and wild cannibals.

No mention of the various Americans who taught their countrymen something of Africa and helped to dispel the atmosphere of mystery that still covered the continent in popular imagination would be complete without a brief account of Martin and Osa Johnson, who spent months in Africa in the 1920s. It is difficult to place the Johnsons in a category. They were neither scientists nor explorers, but they achieved distinction in both fields. A husband-and-wife team, they might best be described as professional adventurers who profited from a popular interest in strange and out-of-the-way places. Martin Johnson was a photographer, an artist with the camera in both still and motion pictures. Osa Johnson became a writer, transforming the dry facts of their experiences into vicarious adventure for her readers without loss of accuracy. Before going to Africa, they had been to the remote islands of the South Seas and to the unexplored interior of Borneo; it was Carl Akeley who suggested to them, on seeing the pictures of their Borneo adventures, that they film and describe the wildlife of East Africa. "I've made it my mission," he said, "to perpetuate vanishing wildlife in bronze and by securing specimens for the Museum. You are doing the same thing in film which is available to millions of people all over the world."[17]

The quality, accuracy, and artistry of Johnson's photography made his work of high scientific value, so much so that his second and third trips to Africa were sponsored by the American Museum of Natural History. Between the last two trips he took flying lessons and qualified as a pilot, so that he was able on the last trip to achieve results impossible to anyone restricted to the ground. He thus pioneered in using the airplane as an adjunct for scientific and artistic purposes.[18]

The Johnsons' first trip to Africa was financed by George Eastman, the world's foremost manufacturer of photographic materials and a philanthropist who was keenly interested in the continent and who had financed some of Akeley's expeditions. In 1926, upon retiring from the active management of his business, Eastman utilized the information given him by his protégés and undertook a safari in East Africa. With two companions, one of them his personal physician, he landed at Mombasa in April 1926. He was met by the Akeleys, and the Johnsons accompanied him throughout most of his time in Africa. Incidentally, he noted in his account of the trip that on the ship from England to East Africa there were no fewer than four hunting parties (including his own), all of them American and one of them – the Chrysler party – going to Tanganyika to obtain specimens for the National Museum.[19]

These numerous hunting and scientific expeditions to Africa in the 1920s and 1930s largely shaped the American vision of Africa. Motion pictures, magazine articles, and books about the expeditions provided the only information most Americans had about the continent. The captured specimens from these expeditions assembled in the African halls of museums made it appear as if all of Africa was a land of jungles and animals – an image reinforced by Tarzan movies – whereas in fact, much of Africa is desert or dry lands, and only 7 percent is tropical rain forest.[20]

From the end of World War I on, American museums and zoos were fearful that Africa's wildlife was doomed to extinction. For this reason they sent numerous expeditions to Africa to capture or to shoot specimens. African halls developed in New York, Chicago, San Francisco, and Oakland, as well as other cities, as a result of this concern. In 1926 two of the biggest and most costly scientific expeditions ever sent to Africa departed from the United States: the Akeley-Eastman-Pomeroy African Hall Expeditions for the American Museum of Natural History in New York and the Smithsonian-Chrysler East African Expedition for the National Zoological Park in Washington, D.C.

Two men acquired the entire African collections of two museums. Henry A. Snow built up the African Hall for the Natural History Museum in Oakland, and Leslie Simpson shot the specimens for the California Academy of Sciences Museum in San Francisco. Snow also made a successful movie of his adventure in 1922 under the title *Hunting Big Game in Africa*. Simpson, a graduate of the California School of Mines, in 1901 moved to South Africa and became superintending engineer of the great Consolidated Gold Fields Company. He retired a wealthy man and became a formidable hunter. For years he shot specimens for the California Academy of Science; the twenty-four groups he contributed to the academy's

African Hall are among the nation's best, and the unmounted Simpson material is outstanding.

It is impossible to mention all of the Americans who made scientific studies in Africa or who went there in search of sport. Ernest Hemingway, for example, spent a great deal of time in Africa and made it the locale for a number of his stories. Many American universities, museums, and other learned organizations also devoted significant parts of their effort to Africa. The National Geographic Society sponsored some fourteen African projects before 1965. These included, to mention only a few, a photographic expedition in 1937 to obtain pictures of South African wildlife, the investigations by Dr. and Mrs. Louis S. B. Leakey in the Olduvai Gorge of Tanzania, and geological explorations in Ghana and the Ivory Coast. The Field Museum of Chicago sponsored sixteen scientific expeditions to Africa between 1895 and 1962, including three led by Carl Akeley. Numerous titles on Africa were published by the Peabody Museum of Harvard University, and an entire series – the *Harvard African Studies* – is devoted exclusively to African subjects.

Whereas these people and institutions, and scores of others, played honorable and often distinguished roles in opening and developing Africa, there were other Americans of whom their countrymen have no reason to be proud – except, possibly, for the unquestionable courage that many of them displayed. The African frontier, like its counterpart in the American West, attracted characters who were social misfits or who found it expedient to avoid officers of the law. Men like Carl Akeley were deeply concerned over the threatened extinction of African wildlife; yet there were scores of others who, like the buffalo hunters of the American plains, saw in the vast African game herds nothing more than quick and easy wealth. The numerous poachers who played havoc with the elephant herds in defiance of the law – and sometimes in armed defiance, at that – included a number of Americans. Such men were unscrupulous, tough, and usually fearless. Theodore Roosevelt, while not condoning in the least their lawless activities, openly admired the qualities that made them thorns in the sides of constituted authorities.[21] Unfortunately for the historian, men of this stamp do not normally leave any record of their activities. Information regarding them thus is likely to be vague and inaccurate.

The Americans in the unsavory crew that preyed upon elephant herds included one known only as Forbes, a skillful, cautious, and uncannily successful rogue. Dextrously avoiding the officials of German East Africa who were determined to capture him, he shot his way across that country and cut across a corner of the Congo into the Lado Enclave. During his safari he killed more than ninety elephants and garnered ivory worth thousands of dollars (many dealers willingly paid high prices for ivory and asked no questions). From the Lado Enclave, Forbes shot his way again across German East Africa to add several thousands more to his illicit profits, with the conscientious German officials straining after but never sighting him.

Even more striking than Forbes was another American, James Wood Rogers. Rogers was a human anachronism. He was out of place, even in the rough and questionable society of professional poachers. He would have been more nearly in his proper niche on the quarterdeck of a buccaneer ship or with Jesse James. A husky, barrel-chested six-footer with a bulging stomach that could hold any quantity of whiskey, purchased, donated, or stolen, he gained a fortune in the Klondike and promptly lost it all at Monte Carlo. He transferred himself to South Africa, where, in a short time, the authorities suggested pointedly that he betake himself to other parts. So he went to Rhodesia, where he quickly outwore his welcome. From Rhodesia he somehow made his way to the Lado Enclave, and from there he appeared in Uganda in April 1911 with over four thousand pounds of ivory. In July of the same year he was again in the enclave at the head of a large safari. Practically everything he did was in violation of the law, but Rogers was not a man to let such a detail worry him. Sudanese officials, however, learning of his reappearance within their jurisdiction, determined to stop his activities and make an example of him. For several weeks he was trailed through the wilderness by a small party consisting of one young British officer, a few porters, a noncommissioned officer, and six privates from the Fourteenth Sudanese Battalion. On the afternoon of October 14, 1911, Rogers was surprised in an African village by two or three of the soldiers who were scouting ahead of the main party. Contemptuously, he tried to disarm them, there was a burst of gunfire, and he fell with a bullet near his heart. Rogers died three days later, unmourned by anyone.[22]

Businesspeople, entrepreneurs, and experts

In the period following World War I, the traditional isolationism of the United States revived sharply and in even greater strength than before. The revival was destined to last for only a few years, but during that time the official attitude and policy of the U.S. government toward Africa and other parts of the world was strictly "hands off." At the same time, the continuing development of transportation systems and the invention of new methods of communication were making the world smaller and increasing the dependence upon each other of the various countries. In spite of isolationist sentiment and official policy, the United States and its citizens became more deeply involved in Africa.

World War I changed the United States from a debtor nation that needed European capital for its own internal development into a creditor country, with billions of dollars owed to the government and to private bankers and industrialists. How to pay these debts, which reached such astronomical heights as to be virtually unpayable, was one of the most baffling problems ever faced by the world's statesmen and economists. The problem bore particularly heavily upon the political and financial leaders of Great Britain, and therein lay the seed of an American involvement in Africa that would have seemed unlikely not many years earlier.

Between 1900 and 1920 the American people, without realizing it, became dependent upon a newly invented, self-propelled vehicle, the automobile. By 1918, over a large part of the United States and particularly in the cities, the motor vehicle had already replaced the horse as a means of motive power; rural areas were rapidly becoming motorized. Manufacturers of harness, carriages, wagons, saddles, and buggy whips found their businesses declining. Railroads and express companies were feeling the pinch because motortrucks carried an increasing portion of the freight formerly moved only by rail. The American people continued their westward migration at an accelerated pace, but not by prairie schooner or oxteam: Hordes of migrants rode westward in cheap automobiles. Increasing industrialization and the relative decline in the importance of agriculture caused the expansion of such cities as Detroit and Los Angeles to geographical limits that made their inhabitants completely dependent upon motor transportation.

Within a very brief time the motor industry became one of the nation's basic. To maintain it, certain products not produced in North America were vital, and foremost among these was rubber. Rubber – which an American, Charles Goodyear, first made practicable for daily use – was (and is) produced on a large scale only in the tropics. The first rubber introduced into American and European industry came from wild trees in the forests of the Amazon, the Congo valleys, and West Africa. In the Amazon and the Congo, around the turn of the century, fantastic profits from rubber caused international scandals, with charges of horrors perpetrated against helpless Indians and Africans by greedy and unscrupulous European exploiters. But as the number of motor vehicles continued to grow, especially in the United States, supplies of wild rubber from the Amazon and Congo rapidly became inadequate to keep automobiles and motortrucks rolling and also to provide electrical insulation, raincoats and overshoes, hot-water bottles, and scores of other necessities. The American people had grown dependent for their daily welfare – almost for their very existence – upon a tropical product.

Early in the twentieth century experts found that the Malay Peninsula and the island of Ceylon, both of them parts of the British Empire, were ideal for the cultivation of the rubber tree. Plantations, scientifically planned and operated along business lines, soon became primary sources of the world's rubber, which thus was virtually a British monopoly. American farmers hauling their produce to market or storage, western ranchers mending fences or carrying feed for cattle, merchants and their customers, workers riding in buses or driving Model-T Fords to and from work – all were dependent upon a product the price of which was controlled in London.

Shortly after the end of World War I, an economic depression hit the world. Rubber planters, who had expanded their plantations and activities during the war, suddenly faced a world temporarily glutted with raw rubber. Prices dropped; planters were unable to meet their obligations; shareholders in London failed to receive their accustomed dividend checks; bankers in the City of London had to be very cautious in advancing loans secured by rubber-producing properties; and the British government found it difficult to obtain funds with which to pay the interest on debts owed to the United States.

A plan was formulated that seemed to promise relief for the rubber planters and British investors while bringing a flow of American dollars into the British money market that would help pay the long-overdue war debts. Urged by the planters of Malaya and Ceylon, the British Colonial Office on November 1, 1922, approved the Stevenson Rubber Restriction Scheme, which sharply restricted and controlled the production of raw rubber. The colonial governments of Malaya and Ceylon enacted the necessary legislation, and within three years the price of raw rubber rose from $0.14 a pound to a record high of $1.23 per pound in the world market.[23]

Large stocks of crude rubber were on hand, purchased when the price was low, so the United States did not immediately feel the effects of the Stevenson plan. Some rubber manufacturers, moreover, were directly interested in Malayan plantations; they benefited from the plan. Others would pass increased costs on to their customers. But the secretary of commerce, Herbert Hoover, was indignant at what he regarded as a brazen attempt to mulct the American consumer. The United States absorbed by far the greatest part of the raw rubber produced; estimates vary from 70 percent to 93 percent, the latter figure amounting to 900 million pounds annually. According to Hoover, the rubber planters could realize a very satisfactory profit at $0.20 per pound. American consumers thus were contributing nearly $180 million annually to the British rubber monopoly, thereby paying dividends to British shareholders, underwriting the return of prosperity to Malaya, and contributing toward the payment of debts owed to their own government.[24]

Hoover's statements and his efforts to protect American interests, as he conceived them, provoked an acrimonious diplomatic correspondence and a storm of domestic controversy that go beyond the scope of this book. His suggestions were received with cold indifference or open antagonism by some American rubber manufacturers, especially those who owned Malayan properties. It was a period when liberals in the United States were deeply suspicious of big business and looked askance at any efforts to facilitate business. It was a period, too, when pacifism enjoyed great popularity, and the argument that it was dangerous for the United States to be dependent upon a foreign monopoly for a vital product was greeted with scoffs and sneers in many quarters. Finally, Hoover's suggestion that efforts be made to develop sources of rubber under American control were decried as "imperialistic" – by then a pejorative expression.

Harvey S. Firestone, however, was a major rubber manufacturer who agreed with the secretary of commerce and opposed the other rubber magnates. Despite their opposition, he sponsored investigations of potential rubber-producing areas in the Western Hemisphere and in the Philippines. For various reasons, mostly political, both areas were rejected, and the investigations were extended to Africa in December 1923 by Donald A. Ross, a Firestone expert.[25] Ross found the climate and soil of Liberia to be almost perfect for cultivation of the rubber tree. A two-thousand-acre plantation started near Mount Barclay in 1910 by some British capitalists had long been abandoned but was found still flourishing, in spite of years of complete neglect. After further investigation and somewhat extended negotiation, in 1926 the Firestone Company was granted the right to lease up to a million acres of land at an annual rental of six cents per acre. Firestone, in return, agreed to pay an export tax upon all rubber shipped out of Liberia and undertook to act as an intermediary in renegotiating the country's financial arrangements.

Preliminary work commenced at once. Firestone's engineers surveyed and started clearing land, building roads and bridges, and making preparations for planting the trees. One of the first structures was a modern hospital staffed with American physicians and nurses. Firestone collaborated with the Harvard University Medical School in 1926 and 1927 to make an extensive health survey of Liberia and other parts of Africa; this survey provided information necessary to combat diseases that had made the region fatal to Europeans. The Yale University School of Forestry, also with Firestone's sponsorship, surveyed Liberia's forest resources. The Firestone program expanded to provide additional roads, sanitary villages for Liberian employees, an electrical power plant, and a telephone system; stores supplied Firestone employees with necessities and little luxuries at prices within their wage scale, and a Coca-Cola bottling plant appeared.[26]

Firestone's entry into Liberia began a revolution in the country's economy and in the ways of life of many of its people. Though its major objective was to increase the company's business and profits, the company's policies and methods were on the whole enlightened.

There was opposition. Certainly, Firestone's competitors in the world rubber market would gladly have sabotaged the enterprise had they been able to do so, and the segment of American liberal opinion that regarded all activity by American capitalists with suspicion was outspoken in its hostility, asserting that Firestone would soon reduce the people of Liberia to a condition of peonage, as (it was asserted) had happened when American capitalists began to operate in various Caribbean countries. Even before the Firestone plantations were fairly functioning, such charges were aired.[27] It was openly predicted that Liberia would be unwilling or unable to fulfill its agreement with the company and the United States would intervene, as it had done in Haiti and Nicaragua.

Liberia was but one area of U.S. business activity in Africa. In other parts of the continent American capitalists made their appearance, with the dollar as their proxy, and frequently with American specialists to manage their enterprises and safeguard their interests. In the early 1920s, when travel in the Congo was still attended with considerable difficulty, Isaac Marcosson, a noted freelance journalist, found the valley of the Kasai River in the Congo a beehive of activity carried on by the Société Internationale Forestière et Minière du Congo (known as Forminière), a Belgian corporation of which at least half the capitalization was American. Forminière was planned by Leopold II as one of his last measures as supreme sovereign of the Congo Free State before he formally ceded his right to Belgium. In 1906 Thomas Fortune Ryan, a multimillionaire traction magnate of New York City on holiday in Switzerland, received an urgent invitation from Leopold to attend a conference in Brussels. Ryan was somewhat cool at first, but Leopold was insistent. The king was in need of capital to fund his Congo plans, and he preferred American capital because the United States had no colonial or imperial designs in Africa: American capital was "nonpolitical." From this meeting grew Forminière, in which Ryan and his associates were accorded a 50 percent interest.[28]

Ryan was interested in the Congo primarily as a source of rubber (plantation rubber had not yet been developed), so he willingly turned over to the Guggenheims the right to explore for minerals and to develop them in the regions allocated to Forminière. The Guggenheims at once sent to the Congo their chief mining engineer, Alfred Chester Beatty, and under his direction American geologists and engineers systematically surveyed the Kasai Valley. Searching initially for gold and copper, they first found diamonds in fabulous quantities. Hence the opening and developing of the Kasai diamond fields resulted from the combination of American capital, mining knowledge, and management.

American influence continued to remain extensive, especially in finance, higher management, and technology. In 1921, for instance, Marcosson voyaged up the Kasai to view Forminière's operations. He was met at the company's main landing place by Forminière's chief engineer and its transportation head, both of them

Americans. They rode in a Model-T Ford car, possibly the most efficient form of backwoods transportation in the world at that time. At Tshikapa, the center and focus of Forminière's diamond mines, Marcosson found a community that he promptly dubbed "Little America," so obvious were the presence and influence of American engineers, technicians, executives, and others, with their families and with American tools, machinery, and equipment. Everywhere in the Kasai, a region of which few in the United States had ever heard, Marcosson found Americans, American ideas, and American ways of doing things.[29] Within a few years Forminière became second only to De Beers of South Africa as a producer of diamonds.

American expertise and capital likewise played a part in the development of Katanga (now known as Shaba) in the southern part of the Congo. During the last few years preceding World War I, Katanga began to develop as a producer of copper, and Elisabethville (now Lubumbashi) turned into the main center of the region. From its beginnings as a tough frontier town, the city was characterized by a rigid system of segregation – not only between whites and blacks, but also within the white community itself. Belgian officials disdained "Anglo-Saxons," that is, the British, American, and South African mine managers, miners, and traders. Well-to-do whites of any origin, in turn, were contemptuous of "low whites," small traders of Portuguese, Greek, Eastern European, or Sephardic Jewish origin. The Belgians feared a British political take-over. Speakers of English quarreled with speakers of French on the boards of the great mining companies. American and British Protestants competed with Catholics, especially Belgian Catholics, for souls. From the Belgians' standpoint, the few thousand resident Britons and Americans made more trouble for the Belgian administration than all the Africans in Katanga.

There was, in effect, a private war between the Belgians and the Anglo-Saxons in Katanga. This was settled only after World War I, when, between 1917 and 1922, the proportion of Belgians rose from 22.5 percent to 58 percent of the Union Minière's skilled white working force. Preston K. Horner, the African director of the Union Minière and one of the great American mining experts in the country, lost out to the Belgian faction led by Edgar Sengier and Jules Cousin; and Bishop John McKendree Springer, an American Methodist missionary, an educational pioneer among Katanga's incipient urban labor force, and a *bête noire* in the Belgian administrators' eyes, failed to gain the influence that the Belgians had anticipated.[30]

Of equal importance to the world's economy and to the future development of Africa were the enormous deposits of the copper belt of Northern Rhodesia (now Zambia). As was the case with iron ore, the copper mines of the United States, Mexico, and Chile seemed near exhaustion by the middle of the twentieth century. Although the existence of copper in Rhodesia and the southern part of the Congo had been known for a long time, it was not until after World War I that steps were taken to determine scientifically the extent of the deposits and to make them available for world industry. In developing the copper belt, American capital and American technical knowledge – gained from experience with the extensive copper deposits in Michigan, Montana, Arizona, northern Mexico, and Chile – were significant from the beginning, in spite of determined efforts in later years to limit American participation and restrict control to British hands.[31]

In the early part of 1917 Ernest Oppenheimer, later known as the financial giant of South Africa, was in London having difficulty, because of the war, in raising the necessary British or South African capital for a new corporation. He became acquainted there with Herbert Hoover, widely known as an able mining engineer and as the administrator of Belgian war relief. On April 17, 1917, Oppenheimer wrote to Hoover: "If American capital wishes to obtain a footing in South African mining business, the easiest course will be to acquire an interest in our company." The Anglo American Corporation of South Africa was incorporated on September 25, 1917, and it became one of the greatest mining companies in the world. The London *Times* of September 28, 1917, noted that the formation of the Anglo American Corporation "meant the beginning of a new epoch . . . for the employment of American capital on the Rand." From 1917 on, American capital flowing into South Africa sparked the South African industrial revolution and led to the development of the Northern Rhodesian copper fields.

An outstanding American engaged in the building of the Northern Rhodesian mining industry was Alfred Chester Beatty, a New Yorker by birth and a highly trained mining engineer. Possessing administrative as well as technical knowledge, he made a name for himself in the United States as an expert in the exploration and exploitation of low-grade copper deposits, and subsequently worked his way into the directorates of several important copper companies. He served for a time as chief mining engineer for the Guggenheims in their great mining developments. In 1913 he settled in London, and later he became a British citizen by naturalization. In 1923 Beatty joined Ernest Oppenheimer, by then the greatest of South African mining capitalists, to float the Rhodesian-Congo Border Concession, which carried out exploration on a huge scale. Beatty formed the Rhodesian Selection Trust in 1928 with American backing. His company, which controlled the great Roan Antelope and Mufulira mines, among others, became one of the two major mining corporations that developed the Northern Rhodesian copper belt and turned the area into one of the world's greatest producers of copper. (The other major mining group was the Anglo American Corporation. This centered on South Africa and, despite its name, depended mainly on South African and British capital.) Beatty ended his career as a full-fledged member of the British establishment, chairman or director of numerous companies with interests as far afield as South-West Africa (now Namibia), Sierra Leone, and Rhodesia (now Zimbabwe). He was a governor of the London School of Hygiene and Tropical Medicine and a trustee of the Imperial Institute, and he enjoyed a worldwide reputation as a collector of precious manuscripts.

In addition to financing the development of the copper belt, Americans made major contributions to its technology. P. K. Horner, an American mining engineer who, as already noted, had been associated with the Guggenheims and was a former director general of the Union Minière in the Congo, was instrumental in the adoption of a process devised by an American named Perkins for treating oxidized copper ores (most of the copper belt ores are sulphides, which are easier to treat than oxides). The first flotation tests of ores from the Roan Antelope mine were made by the American Metal Company and a specialist by the name of Weinig of the Colorado School of Mines.[32]

Early shipments of ore from the new mines coincided with the early phases of the Great Depression, and the finances of the mining companies were shaky. The price of raw copper on the world market fell to little more than four cents per pound. The American Metal Company, however, bought the entire output at prices that enabled the mining companies to meet their payrolls and continue in operation. The ores thus purchased were shipped to the United States for treatment by smelters in New Jersey.[33] Without American capital and American specialized knowledge of copper mining and production, the development of the copper belt would have followed courses far different from those actually taken. Opening the fabulous mineral deposits could have been delayed for years. Instead, American experts and American capital helped lay the foundations for the gigantic industrial complex that burgeoned within a few years in the barren, desolate, African plateau that constitutes the copper belt of Central Africa. Most of the development has taken place since the end of World War II. Today there are enormous mines with shafts descending thousands of feet into the earth; there are power plants, railroads, schools, hospitals, libraries, swimming pools, gardens, golf courses, tennis courts, theaters, stores, modern housing tracts – all the appurtenances of Western civilization, and all are still expanding.[34]

American business expansion and activities in Africa could not have occurred without ocean transportation. Before the Civil War, as noted elsewhere, the schooners and brigs of Salem and other small New England ports carried the American flag and American products to the lagoons, rivers, and tidal estuaries on both coasts of the African continent. After the Civil War, the American flag virtually disappeared from the seas around Africa thanks largely to British-built Confederate raiders. Though American products still found their way to Africa, and African raw materials were consumed in quantities in the United States, they were carried in ships flying the British, German, or French flags. There were almost no direct sailings between Africa and America, and so all commerce moved via London, Marseilles, or Hamburg, traversing thousands of added miles and thus arriving with increased product costs. Disappearance of the American merchant marine was, in fact, a major cause of the decline of American trade with Africa and of American contacts with Africa. Missionaries journeying to their African stations had, perforce, to go by way of Great Britain or Germany; there was no other way to reach their destinations.

Few Americans realized how dependent upon foreign shipping they had become until after the outbreak of World War I, when German vessels vanished from the seas and large numbers of British freighters were diverted from commerce to war services. There was a sudden shortage of shipping, with few American vessels and an inadequate number of other neutral ships to fill the gap. Some British ships were eventually made available for service between the United States and Africa, but at rates that discriminated against American shippers and products.[35]

The president of the U.S. Steel Corporation, James A. Farrell, found it necessary before the war to engage directly and indirectly in the shipping business because of the volume of the corporation's overseas business. This fact, together with the efforts of the U.S. government to revive the American merchant marine during the war, led to the 1925 acquisition by Farrell and his associates of the American South African Line. Operating initially with a small number of ships obtained from the U.S. Shipping Board, and fighting cutthroat competition from both American rivals and British shipping firms, the company managed to maintain itself. There was, for the first time, a regular steamship service under the American flag between the United States and Africa. The company survived the vicissitudes of war, in which a number of ships were lost, and in 1948 it became the Farrell Lines, the name under which it now operates.[36]

In terms of overall U.S. trade, these enterprises did not amount to a great deal. The percentage of American exports to Africa in comparison to those to the world at large rose but slowly – from 1.2 in 1913, to 3.8 in 1938, to 5.1 in 1949. The corresponding figures for American imports amounted to 1.5, 2.8, and 5.1.[37] African products nevertheless gradually increased and began to attain some importance in specialized sectors of the economy.

Americans in Africa, probably numbering no more than a few thousand before 1939, were mostly missionaries, commercial agents, salesmen, engineers, and consular officers. Hunters and photographers came by the scores in the 1920s and 1930s, but did not stay. Official U.S. representation was limited to four consulates and two legations. For Americans, Africa as yet remained a backwater.

CHAPTER 18

Preachers and teachers in Africa

Missionaries and educators

Historians of the future may well consider that the major contribution made by Europe and the United States to modern Africa lay in learning and medicine. Dispensaries and missionary doctors, schools and the education that they provided, helped to stir African villagers from their relative isolation. Education and evangelization, of course, were not the same. But missionaries used education as a means of imparting Christianity; the two became closely interwined, and chroniclers cannot consider them apart from each other.

All modern missionaries, Catholics as well as Protestants, were determined that proselytes should understand the new faith. No longer would a purely formal or ritualistic conversion suffice. To comprehend, the convert must be able to read and understand the hymnbook and catechism, the Bible and scriptural lessons. Missionaries were thus forced to become linguists and translators, to act as printers and distributors of books in the vernacular. Missionary commitments, however, did not stop at this point; the missionaries thought in terms of a cash economy. They believed that their charges should acquire new industrial skills. To save their souls, the Africans had to be taught a means of maintaining themselves in the world: They had to acquire the tools that would permit them to earn money.

American missionaries in Africa from the first were concerned with the health and physical needs of the people. The small group from the United States who served in South Africa in the 1830s included a physician, Dr. Adams, and the first American missionary-doctor in West Africa arrived there in 1841. It is true that the primary function of both of these men was the health of their fellow missionaries, but both of them gave time and attention as well to the Africans. The groups of American Board missionaries who walked from Mozambique to Rhodesia in 1893 included a physician, Dr. W. L. Thompson, who, as noted previously, reported a year later that he had responded to 590 professional calls during the year.[1]

The opening of the new century found no less than nineteen hospitals and dispensaries scattered from Natal to Kamerun (Cameroun), administered and maintained by various American missionary bodies, treating the illnesses and injuries of thousands of Africans.[2] The Free Methodists, upon taking over the mission and fieldwork in Mozambique from the American Board, took care to include a physician, and to found a hospital and dispensary as soon as their limited finances permitted. The first medical missionary joined their staff in 1904, followed a few years later by an American nurse. Probably the greatest contribution by the Free Methodist mission to the improvement of social conditions in Portuguese East Africa has lain in the training of a considerable number of African nurses who, in addition to assisting at the hospital, have been able to carry their training, their medical experience, and information to their native villagers.[3] In the vast country of Angola, thousands of patients, both black and white, for years have looked for help to the mission hospital administered by Dr. Aaron Manasses McMillan, a black American physician who gave up a lucrative practice and a promising political career to become a medical missionary in Africa.[4]

Other examples are so numerous that to mention them would be redundant, but note should be made of the leprosariums established by the American Mission for Lepers (ca. 1914) and by the American Baptist Mission in the Congo in 1938.[5] Americans in many cases pioneered medical treatment of Africans. The American Presbyterian Congo Mission at Luebo and the American Baptist Board at Tondo were among the first to establish hospitals in the Congo, and for years the Presbyterians at Bibango operated "the only active hospital in the Momami and as far east as Lake Tanganyika."[6]

Mission hospitals and medical missionaries filled a genuine need in the African countries in which they were established by supplementing the medical and sanitary provisions inaugurated by various colonial administrations. Governments, government physicians, and officials were primarily interested in what may be termed "mass medicine": the control of epidemics, innoculation of the populations in entire provinces, urban sanitation. The missionary doctor, while supporting such measures and often assisting in many ways, was basically interested in the health and ills of the individual African patient, whose problems required an individual approach and often the overcoming of opposition from African medicine men and from the European community as well.

Dr. James B. McCord, a medical missionary of the American Board working among the Zulus of South Africa, found such opposition. In the early part of the century, when he finally accumulated sufficient funds to establish a hospital for the Zulus in Durban, many influential members of the white community were bitterly hostile: They feared that the Zulus would impinge on the whites and depress property values in the vicinity of the hospital. He persisted, however, founded his hospital on a small scale, and finally overcame the opposition to such a degree that the McCord Zulu Hospital became a recognized medical institution; in addition to caring for patients, it was a training school for African nurses and medical assistants and a center that worked to improve the Zulus' health and physical condition.[7]

Nearly all missionaries in Africa opened schools as a first step toward bringing the gospel to the Africans. Few missionaries, American or foreign, held the narrow view expressed by one of the Christian pioneers: "We didn't come to Africa to educate the Natives, but to convert them—to put Jesus Christ into their hearts and save their souls from eternal damnation."[8] During the first half of the nineteenth century almost all the schools for Africans on the continent were those set up and maintained by missionaries, and wherever the missionaries endeavored to establish themselves, their first act, almost invariably, was to found schools.

The Reverend Charles W. Thomas, the navy chaplain visiting Liberia in the late 1850s, noted that the staff of the Episcopal mission in that country included thirty teachers, of whom twelve were Africans, and that the Southern Baptist Board was supporting a high school in Monrovia.[9] In 1878 the U.S. minister to Liberia, J. Milton Turner, reported to the State Department that Bishop Pinnick of the

Episcopal Church, a native of Virginia, had just arrived in the company of two young men whose purpose was to establish missions and schools among the previously unevangelized Vei people in the vicinity of Cape Mount.[10] The American minister to Portugal informed the State Department in 1885 that Bishop William Taylor of the Methodist Episcopal Church had spent several months establishing mission schools in Angola.[11]

The close of the nineteenth century saw an impressive number of educational institutions on the African continent founded and supported by American missionary and religious bodies: colleges, theological schools, high schools, elementary schools, and both boarding and day schools located everywhere from Liberia in the north through the Cameroons and Congo into Angola and to the southernmost part of South Africa.[12]

Between the opening of the century and the outbreak of World War I, American missionaries quietly expanded their activities and entered fields that had been previously closed. In the 1880s the Presbyterian Board of Missions had arranged with the newly established German colonial authorities to establish missions in Cameroon, and between 1890 and 1900 their activities slowly and gradually increased. In spite of irritating friction with the German authorities on occasion, the American missionaries acted as peacemakers between the Africans and their German overlords. On one occasion the U.S. government representatives supported the missionaries, thus causing the kaiser's government to overrule local officials.

The Reverend Adolphus C. Good, a pioneer American missionary, commenced his work in Cameroon shortly after it had become a German possession and continued after the country became a French mandate. Good made lengthy trips to the unknown interior in search of suitable sites and actually became an explorer, although he did not consider himself one. He wrote:

> The Church in South Cameroun is the leading educational agency in the uplifting of the race. Here church and school go hand in hand. Every Mission Station has a large school. Every outpost church building is a schoolhouse. When a native evangelist worker is sent out to take charge of the religious work of a district, a school-teacher is sent with him, or else he combines in himself the functions of both preacher and teacher . . .
>
> There are schools at every Station (which teach courses prescribed by the mandatory French government, as well as other courses).[13]

The first mission school in Cameroon (apparently the first school of any kind in the country) was started by the American Presbyterian missionaries at Efulan in the summer of 1894, with seventeen Bulu boys as the first students. One of the missionaries sawed the letters of the alphabet out of thin boards; with some sheets of paper upon which hymns were inscribed in the Bulu language as additional visual aids, the lessons started. The Americans expanded their educational program at the turn of the century, obtained full recognition from the German colonial government, and in 1913, just before the outbreak of the war and the end of German dominion, were maintaining 97 schools with a total of more than 6,500 pupils.[14] Sixteen years later the number of "bush" (village) schools totaled some 630, maintained by the missionaries. In addition to schools established by the French mandatory government after World War I, there were also a number of girls' schools (including a high school), a normal school, a school for evangelists, an industrial school, and a theological seminary.[15]

Early mission schools, and some more recent ones, had dual and concurrent purposes: to give the Africans the ability to read the Scriptures for themselves, and at the same time to develop a body of African clergy and teachers who would be qualified to carry the message of Christianity to other Africans. Consequently, the curricula of early mission schools and mission-supported institutions stressed religious and theological subjects, with emphasis upon literary, as distinguished from vocational, studies. A modern criticism of the missionaries' educational efforts, in fact, has been that they taught little that related to the needs of life in Africa. Such a criticism reflects a twentieth-century point of view and takes no account of the intellectual climate of the time or of the preoccupation of the earnest, serious-minded men and women with the ultimate salvation of souls, rather than with the affairs of this world. Nevertheless, there was early recognition by many missionaries and mission bodies that an essential part in winning Africa for Christianity was to give the Africans skills that would enable them to maintain themselves decently and to adapt themselves to a changing world.

Hence many mission schools, especially those that were established late in the nineteenth century and early in the twentieth, from the start included vocational and agricultural subjects in their curricula. Agricultural training was introduced into Rhodesia by the Seventh-Day Adventists. The schools started by Bishop Taylor in Angola, in his optimistic plan for self-supporting missions, included industrial and vocational schools. The school founded by John Chilembwe (an African educated in the United States), which became the focus of the uprising of 1915, was an industrial school that taught trades and vocations.

In Cameroon early in the twentieth century, the American Presbyterian Mission established the Frank James Industrial School, named in memory of a young American hunter who had been killed by a wounded elephant and whose sister contributed to its foundation. Africans in the school were taught carpentry, tailoring, masonry, blacksmithing, tanning, garage and machine work, and two very lucrative crafts, the manufacture of rattan furniture and ivory carving. The demand for products from the school's shops soon made it virtually self-supporting.[16]

In spite of their natural preoccupation with things of the spirit, then, the missionaries – especially American missionaries – did not neglect needs of the flesh.

Most of the people of Africa have always been – and still are – directly dependent upon the soil for their existence, and American missionaries were in the forefront of efforts to improve African agriculture. Contrary to widespread popular belief, only about 7 percent of Africa is covered by tropical rain forest, and even this area is declining as cultivators continue to make inroads into the jungle. The greater part of the continent actually consists of desert, semidesert, or savannah, often with poor soil and little or irregular rainfall. Moreover, the traditional practices of the indigenous peoples sometimes destroyed what little natural fertility the soil had once possessed. Customary methods of shifting agriculture, dependent on slash-and-burn techniques, worked well as long as the population was scanty, as long as farmers owned only a limited number of livestock, and as long as cultivators were able to permit fallow acres to recover their natural fertility. But once the population began to increase and land became scarcer, the balance of nature was often upset. The white men's plows enabled peasants to cultivate more land, and erosion caused by torrential rains completed the ruin. Africans had long been accustomed to moving from one farmed area to a new one, remaining there until it in turn became useless, then moving to another and still another, with the result that multitudes of Africans were only one step ahead of hunger, often laboring for bare subsistence under unfavorable conditions that they could not easily change.[17]

Missionary efforts to improve the Africans' material condition as a step in bettering their spiritual state began late in the nineteenth century. In Southern Rhodesia, Jesuit missionaries initiated a program to teach agricultural and industrial skills in 1892, when the country was barely penetrated by whites. Other Roman Catholic missions followed suit, but because of lack of funds and inadequate personnel, their programs remained more or less static. The Seventh-Day Adventists, an American group, were among the first Protestant missionaries to train Africans in modern agriculture. In the early 1900s they began farming on a twelve-thousand-acre tract at Solusi in Southern Rhodesia; in 1912 they exchanged four thousand acres of this tract for a similar area near Salisbury, where they established an agricultural and industrial school. The Adventists in 1907 began a program of cotton culture and dairy farming in Nyasaland on a two-thousand-acre tract near Malamulo.[18]

At the Methodist mission at Old Umtali the young George Arthur Roberts arrived in 1907 for his first assignment. Roberts was born on a farm in Iowa; he attended Iowa State College (as it was then called) to train as a scientific farmer, his boyhood ambition. His interests turned toward religion during his student days, and upon meeting the famous Bishop Hartzell at a religious convention in Nashville, Tennessee, Roberts volunteered for service as a missionary in Africa. Shortly after arriving at the mission, he noticed the waste of uneaten food from students at the mission school; though other staff members objected, he finally was permitted to invest a small amount of the mission's funds in some pigs to be raised on that wasted food.

From this beginning came years of work to improve the African's knowledge of animal husbandry and agricultural practices, all in addition to teaching and preaching. The most revolutionary innovation may have been in persuading the local African farmers to use the plow. For a variety of reasons in which custom, convenience, and sheer inertia were intermixed, the Africans regarded the plow with suspicion, but in 1908 one farmer was persuaded to try it. The results were so astounding that others followed suit, and agriculture in that part of Africa received a major stimulus. Using their cattle as draft animals to help till the soil had never occurred to the Africans; on the mission farm, Roberts taught a number of them how to use oxen to lighten their own tasks, and in 1914 he added dairy cows to his teaching efforts. Nor did his work stop there. The Africans kept great numbers of chickens but had no idea how to control or prevent disastrous poultry epidemics. Simple sanitary precautions, emphasized by unfortunate episodes that he could use as demonstrations, enabled Roberts to teach them proper care of their poultry.

Roberts introduced a number of other practices that affected the Africans in the immediate mission area. He used contour plowing to stop the damaging erosion that accompanied tropical rains; he organized agricultural shows to stimulate competition and provide for an exchange of ideas; he taught irrigation methods when rainfall did not furnish enough water; he tried new crops, vegetables, trees, and pest controls; and he improved stockbreeding, ditching, and draining. At the end of his long career as a missionary, he was able to say with modest pride, "Where starvation was rife sixty years ago, there is now plenty of food." He did not claim the credit, but much of the credit is his.[19]

As significant as was Roberts's contribution to the improvement of African life, his influence was largely local, confined to the vicinity of his mission. An American who may reasonably be regarded as a successor to Roberts and whose activities and influence eventually covered a much wider field with far-reaching effects was Emory Delmont Alvord, who arrived in Rhodesia in 1919 and spent the rest of his life serving the Rhodesian people. Alvord was born in Utah and was originally a member of the Latter-Day Saints. His family moved to Nebraska when he was a small child, and he attended primary and secondary schools there; but for his college he chose Washington State, where, as an undergraduate, he was a star athlete in football and wrestling. After graduation he taught manual training for a while before reentering Washington State to train as a teacher of agriculture. With a master of science degree in agriculture, he served for a short time as a county agent and then volunteered as a missionary of the Congregational Church, of which he had become a member. Alvord arrived at Mount Selinda in 1919 and spent the next seven years there, introducing a course in agriculture in the mission school and devising a comprehensive scheme to work and demonstrate among the African villagers who could not be reached directly by the school.

Alvord's work at the mission school soon attracted the attention of H. S. Keigwin, a commissioner for native affairs who was trying to develop schools in which the Africans would be taught useful vocations and agricultural skills. In 1920, when Alvord had been in Rhodesia only a year, Keigwin asked his help in planning a new government school recently authorized at Domboshawa. Alvord spent some time there instructing the staff and the African students in such things as crop rotation, proper plowing, manuring, the use of legumes, and row planting. In the following year, 1921, Keigwin and Alvord arranged an exhibit at the Salisbury Agricultural Show that amazed the Europeans. It may have aroused some jealousy, for Keigwin's efforts to train African artisans[20] met with bitter opposition from some Rhodesian Europeans who wanted to keep Africans in a permanent state of dependence. In 1926, unable to succeed, Alvord resigned in disgust, and at about the same time the government decided to establish the office of Agriculturist for the Instruction of Natives. In spite of the hostility of one female member of parliament, Alvord was offered the position and he accepted.[21]

Alvord spent the remainder of his active life in the service of the Southern Rhodesian administration, trying to improve the agricultural practices, and hence the standard of living, of Africans in the country. He remained a missionary at heart, but left direct mission work when it became apparent that he could influence more Africans as a government official than he could as a missionary. As an American citizen, he found his work somewhat handicapped and his personal status diminished, so he became a British subject; in 1937, after only ten years in his position, he was awarded the King's Coronation Medal in recognition of his achievements. In 1948 his name appeared upon the King's Birthday Honours List as an Officer of the Order of the British Empire.[22]

Alvord's success in improving the methods of the African farmers was based upon his early observation that Africans were so wedded to the ways of their ancestors that only visual demonstration would persuade them to change. Such demonstration, moreover, must be made by an African; otherwise the farmers would attribute any success to the white man's "magic" and be unconvinced. Successful demonstrations also required that the demonstrator spend weeks and even months living in African villages; again, only an African, not a white man, could succeed. Beginning with six men, Alvord trained a large number of intelligent Africans, who were sent – with seeds, fertilizers, and tools that were easily available to the African farmers – to places where some headman or farmer had indicated his willingness to be taught. There the demonstrator prepared, seeded, and tended a small plot until the crop was ready for harvest.

Teaching the Africans how to conserve and maintain their soil and how to plant and tend their crops was only part of Alvord's self-imposed mission. To produce adequate foodstuffs, he also had to persuade and teach the Africans to care properly for their cattle and to maintain proper pasturage; in order to increase the amount of arable land available, he introduced irrigation in areas where rainfall was inadequate. For several years he kept up somewhat of a feud with ill-advised conservationists who insisted upon preserving trees that Alvord knew should be cut to develop grasslands. He taught Africans to live in planned and well-constructed villages rather than to scatter at will, planting their crops haphazardly wherever there seemed to be space; by congregating they could increase their water supplies, improve sanitary conditions, keep pastures and cultivated fields separate, and provide for communal effort.

Alvord's activities brought opposition from both blacks and whites. After Keigwin's departure, the principal of the school at Domboshawa relegated agricultural training to a minor level and employed as simple laborers on the school farm those who were supposedly being trained to work among other Africans. This step led to a confrontation between Alvord and the principal, a battle that Alvord won. The Africans, too, were suspicious of his motives. One paramount chief argued to his people that Alvord was merely testing their land: If it was found to be good, the government would take it away from them (an opposition that may have been based upon bitter experience). This chief eventually became an enthusiastic convert, but it took time.

Alvord's work was complicated by several drought and famine years as well as by opposition and by the inherent difficulty of overcoming the inertia of ancient tradition. His duties required constant travel under difficult conditions and frequent exposure to danger. He was affected by sunstroke while working on an irrigation project in 1933, but recovered quickly, and in January 1936 he was attacked by a banded cobra while inspecting a demonstration spot. While helping his son construct a new house in 1947, Alvord fell and injured his back, an injury that left him paralyzed from the waist down; the physician was sure that he would never walk again, but he continued to direct the affairs of his department from his hospital bed and to try to use his legs. Twenty days after the accident he was walking again, convinced that his recovery was miraculous and resulted from the power of prayer. In summary, no missionary-educator had a greater impact on African agriculture than did Alvord.

American influence on African education also came from experts sent to Africa and from Africans trained in colleges in the United States. One of the best known of the expatriate students was James Emman Kwegyir Aggrey, an outstanding educator. A native of what is now Ghana, he was descended from African royalty, and he evinced early an unusual aptitude for learning and teaching. He was educated by the AME Church and then worked in mission schools in his native country and served as an interpreter with British forces in the Ashanti Expedition of 1896 before leaving for the United States to study at Livingstone College, also an AME institution, in North Carolina. On graduation he was appointed to the faculty. He meanwhile served as pastor in two small country churches and continued his own studies of the classics and of several languages. He also found the time and energy to form farmers' clubs and to organize a Negro Community League to work for the improvement of black life in the locality.

Aggrey acquired several degrees in the United States, including an honorary doctor of divinity degree, but he was ambitious to earn the doctor of philosophy degree; accordingly, in 1904 he matriculated at Columbia University. For financial reasons he could not take consecutive courses at Columbia; several years would elapse before he resumed his formal education and even then his studies were interrupted because of his need to save money. Aggrey nevertheless continued, taking summer courses as opportunity offered. He was becoming well known in educational circles, and in 1920 the state of North Carolina conferred upon him its Teacher's Life Professional Certificate, the state's highest certification and an honor that had been previously awarded to only thirteen persons. Aggrey was the first black man to receive it.

An additional honor came to him at this time, when he was invited by Thomas Jesse Jones, a former adviser to the president of Hampton Institute and an old friend of Aggrey's, to join the Phelps-Stokes Commission to survey African education, the work of which will be discussed shortly. In 1920 and 1921 the commission, with Aggrey as a prominent member, toured West and South Africa, examining schools and educational facilities. On this occasion, while voyaging from Liberia to his native Ghana, Aggrey met Francis Gordon Guggisberg, the Canadian-born governor of the Gold Coast Colony – a meeting destined to have important consequences. The commission returned to Africa in 1924, revisiting South Africa and touring East and Central Africa, and about this time Guggisberg persuaded the brilliant and still young African to accept a key position on the staff of a new college planned at Achimota. For three years Aggrey worked hard on its establishment, becoming involved in local politics, yet retaining the respect of all parties and factions. In 1927 he was granted a lengthy leave of absence to return to the United States and complete the requirements for his doctoral degree in New York. He was preparing the final work on his dissertation when he was stricken with meningitis and died within a few hours on July 30, 1927.[23] Aggrey was an outstanding example of the African student educated in the United States, but there have been scores of others, their numbers increasing steadily since the African countries gained their independence.

The African-born Aggrey did important work for African education, but American-born blacks also gave outstanding missionary service. For instance, Sam Coles, Alabama-born of former slave parents, went to Angola in 1923 as an agricultural missionary and stayed for thirty years. He brought to his work the philosophy of self-help in the Tuskegee tradition and the practical skills of a farmer, blacksmith, and ox driver. With these he transformed the lives of people in a three-hundred-mile area around his mission station at Galangue. He was, as he said in his autobiography, the preacher with a plow.[24] Coles was a man of practical genius; he seemingly could do or make almost anything, and he could teach others both to do what he could do and, most important, to want to improve. His work experience was the key to his success. He had laid steel rails; he had been in logging camps handling oxen and making bows and yokes; he had been a dairy farmer, a blacksmith, a farrier, and a wheelwright; he knew how to haul timber, turn wood, can fruit and vegetables; he had been a farm carpenter and a brickmason.[25] But it was his ability as a driver of oxen that gave him his first success with Africans.

Although the Ovimbundu people had cattle, they did not use them for work or for milling. They did not exploit the rich land along the river because they could not break up the heavy soil. Coles taught them to use all their land and to train their oxen to pull plows, to help carry water, to stump trees, and to transport logs or crops. He insisted on hard work ("be early in the field"). He introduced new crops. In the words of his first sermon, "Upon these hoes, spades, shovels, seeds and plows, I shall build my church and all the pains of hunger, fear from the lack of tax money, superstition, poverty and nakedness shall not prevail against it."[26] Africans welcomed him as one of their own who had returned to help them. He learned that preaching was not much use if people were hungry, so he set out to improve their lives first; the preaching could come later. With patience, tact, imagination, and a sharp tongue, he got Africans to change their work habits, adopt new tools and crops, and learn new skills. He worked and lived among them and was always teaching and demonstrating, encouraging and remonstrating.

For seven years Coles also served as the mission doctor. He operated, set bones, and prescribed for every imaginable illness; he never lost a patient. And he never lost his determination to improve the lives of the Africans he served for thirty years. No matter how tired he was or how discouraged, when he looked at African men and women toiling without plows or wagons he simply roused himself for another effort and asked, "How can I sleep?"[27] Even after he retired, he was preparing himself to return to Africa to run a school for crippled and homeless children when he died in 1957.

As economic growth produced changes in African societies, missionaries had to learn to play a new role among temporarily urban Africans involved in a wage economy as miners or factory workers. Outstanding among this new breed of missionary were men like John Merle Davis, an American churchman who had first made a name for himself by a survey of multiracial problems on the Pacific Coast and by his work as secretary of the Pacific Institute of Pacific Relations. Davis's work made a considerable impression on the International Missionary Council, which placed him in charge of its newly created Department of Social and Industrial Change, and which supported a major study concerning the problems of industrialization in the copper belt in what is now Zambia.[28] Davis cooperated with a number of distinguished academics and with others, the new approach resulting in an attitude of mind very different from the old-fashioned, unquestioning fire-and-brimstone faith. Davis and his collaborators recommended, among other things, a better anthropological training for missionaries, and the churches were urged to pay more attention to social welfare problems at the mines and to acquire a better understanding of the implications of indirect rule. More important still, Davis suggested the formation of an interdenominational Protestant church in the copper belt that would tackle the evangelical problems raised by the new mining economy, problems the churches had hitherto neglected.

Ray E. Phillips followed a similar tradition. Like Davis, the Reverend Dr. Phillips worked among urban Africans engaged in the mining industry. He was born in Hawthorne, Wisconsin, and held bachelor's degrees from Carleton College and from Yale; in 1937 he received a doctorate from Yale. Phillips and his wife went to Johannesburg for the American Board of Commissioners for Foreign Missions in 1918 and served there until 1958. He pioneered welfare work among the Bantu brought to work on the mines, Africans who were temporarily dwelling in cities. The government considered them to be temporary workers and provided no services or social institutions to help them adjust to the new conditions of the city. White authorities and missionaries had won improvements in wages and hours for the black workers, but they had ignored the workers' situation outside the job. Phillips sought to alleviate their conditions. Slums, crime, prostitution, drunkenness – things unknown in tribal society – were now daily problems to the new men of the mines. Soon after his arrival he persuaded mine owners to be more concerned with the transplanted Africans' leisure hours and to provide them with canteens, recreation areas, and free movies. In the 1920s he and his wife helped organize the Helping Hand for Native Girls and the South African Bantu Men's Social Center, the only groups in the entire city concerned with the well-being of Africans.

In 1940 Phillips founded in Johannesburg the interracial Jan H. Hofmeyr School of Social Work, which sought to train social workers to operate among the temporarily urbanized Africans and to help them adapt to the new conditions of urban society. He was also one of the founders of the South African Institute of Race Relations, dedicated to study and improve relations between the peoples of multiracial South Africa.[29] The institute also acted as protector of African rights, and sought to reform conditions for Africans. In a foresighted book, *The Bantu Are Coming*, Phillips described the plight of urban Africans and predicted the continued flight from the back country to urban centers of South Africa.[30] His work eased the transition to urban living of African migrant workers.

The philanthropists

Between World Wars I and II private American philanthropic foundations joined the missions in support of African education. In 1909 Caroline Phelps, a wealthy American philanthropist, donated a substantial sum to the cause of black and Indian education, and in 1913–14 the resulting Phelps-Stokes Fund sponsored an extensive survey of black education and black schools in the United States. In 1919, with the cooperation of various missionary bodies and the approval of several colonial governments in Africa, the fund's trustees allocated money for a similar survey of education in Africa. The report of the commission conducting the survey did more to stimulate the interest of American educators and foundations in Africa than any other single document.

The Phelps-Stokes survey was the first – and to date, the only – broad investigation of schools and educational activities to cover the greater part of the African continent. The commission tried to be objective, and its report was intended to reveal the educational needs of the peoples of Africa and to evaluate the available facilities. Both the commission and its report were bitterly criticized, however: W. E. B. Du Bois, for example, charged that the commissioners wished only to force Africans into the peculiar mold desired by their Caucasian oppressors. The report also met with wide disapproval from a number of white colonial administrators and settlers who claimed that the commission's educational recommendations were far beyond African capabilities.

According to the report, virtually all of the educational activities in Africa were conducted by missionaries. The colonial governments had, at that time, done little for education in their respective countries except to give grants-in-aid to mission schools. "In none of the colonies visited did the governments include a Director of Education within the Executive Councils." The commission found, too, that in many of the African schools the prescribed curricula bore little relation to the actual needs of the people and the country. Many among the missionaries thought of education as no more than imparting information; others thought of it as a means of enabling Africans to read the Bible. "This group has been content with an education in books. For the masses they have provided the three R's. For the catechists and the advanced pupils they have endeavored to give a knowledge of literature, including, of course, an interpretation of religion."[31]

To correct this condition and to provide education adequate for the actual needs of Africans, the commission urged that "the adaptation of education to the needs of the people is . . . the first requisite of school activities. Much of the indifference and even opposition to education in Africa is due to the failure to adapt school work to African conditions."[32] The commission found, too, that many of the mission schools suffered from faulty organization and inadequate supervision, in spite of the enthusiasm of the earnest men and women who conducted them. And in all of Africa, at the time of the commission's first tour, there were only two institutions of higher learning for Africans. An even more serious fault was the fact that among educational institutions offering vocational curricula, the subject most essential for Africa – agriculture – was conspicuously ignored.

In addition to such general estimates and criticisms, the Phelps-Stokes Commission detailed its findings in each of the countries visited. For example, the courses offered at Fourah Bay College in Sierra Leone, one of the two college-level institutions, were entirely theological and classical; entrance requirements for African students included Latin, Greek, mathematics, English, religious knowledge or ancient history, and geography. In the Gold Coast Colony (now Ghana), although education was far ahead of that found in most African countries, the commission was entertained at one school by "a reproduction of English songs and recitations, with no reference to Africa."[33]

On its second visit to Africa the commission – this time including Homer Leroy Schantz, an agricultural and botanical expert of the U.S. Department of Agriculture who had previously made a study of soil conditions, agricultural practices, and animal life from the Cape of Good Hope to Cairo – found nothing that changed, in any way, its earlier conclusions. "The facts assembled in 1921 by the Education

Commission to West, South and Equatorial Africa are emphatically confirmed by the facts ascertained by the Education Commission to East, Central and South Africa in 1924."[34] In spite of the generalized criticism that education in Africa was not adapted to the actual needs of the countries and their people, the commission acknowledged many contrary instances. It also reported that American missionaries were prominent in education in every country visited, and that practically all education in Angola was conducted by Americans.

It is a moot question just how much influence the Phelps-Stokes Commission may have had in determining the future course of education in Africa, but there is no doubt that its report gave the world its first general view of the requirements of African education. Contrary to Du Bois's opinion, the commission did not recommend educational plans designed to make Africans more useful to their European overlords; on the other hand, neither did it recommend schemes calculated to increase the African's independence and to foment their nationalism – a fear expressed by some ultracolonialists. The commission was interested solely in recommending measures for the "hygienic, economic, mental, and spiritual development" of the individual African, and its report recommended a heavy missionary input for African schools as a necessary ingredient in "character building."[35]

There were other foundation undertakings in Africa during this period. Since the early 1920s the Phelps-Stokes Fund has made grants to African educational institutions, for instance, the Booker Washington Institute in Liberia. Both the Rockefeller Foundation and the Carnegie Corporation of New York took an interest in African education at this time, and as early as 1925 Carnegie Corporation grants helped establish a Jeanes School at Kabete in Kenya. The Jeanes Schools had their origin in a bequest by an American, Miss Anna T. Jeanes, for the training of teachers for Negro schools in the United States; with help from Carnegie and encouragement from the Phelps-Stokes Fund, the Jeanes program was applied in eastern and southern Africa, with great success in some areas though only moderate results in others. Since the 1920s the Carnegie Corporation has spent over $5 million on activities in Africa, much of which has been devoted directly or indirectly to education. Numerous foundations have followed the lead of Carnegie, Rockefeller, and Phelps-Stokes, and after World War II the Social Science Research Council, the Wenner-Gren Foundation for Anthropological Research, the Guggenheim Foundation, and particularly the Ford Foundation would make Africa a major interest of America's largest foundations (see Chapter 23).

Separatist churches

Alien rule, the coming of a cash economy, and a new religion helped to disrupt traditional African mores. European ways, often introduced by force, replaced customs and habits that extended deep into the past and were part of the Africans' legacy. Many tribal chiefs and their councils lost their authority, and old gods lost their vitality. African migrants came into the cities, mines, and industrial plants, especially in southern Africa; there they were suddenly sundered from the obligations of village life and left without adequate standards to replace those which were lost. The Africans' efforts to adapt themselves to new conditions confirmed the beliefs of whites in their own superiority and further convinced them that

Africans were mentally children incapable of ruling their own destinies, who must be kept in subjection for their own welfare and their neighbors' safety.

Most Christian missions, from their entry into Africa, held as an ultimate objective the training of African clergy who would be able to administer African religious affairs and to carry the Christian message to other Africans. But throughout the colonial era, few Africans managed to reach the higher ranks of the ecclesiastical establishment. Discontented Africans therefore attempted to strike out on their own, to free themselves from alien tutelage, and to establish independent African churches. The dissidents were encouraged by the Protestant respect for individual interpretation of Holy Writ. African Protestant Christianity has shown a remarkable tendency to form new denominations and new cults with one feature in common: They are African without any supervision by whites. Evidence indicates that in some part this tendency springs from inspiration furnished by Americans, and particularly by the evangelical, millenarian, and black churches of the United States. The movement is significant as a feature of the impact of America and Africa upon each other.

The missionary impact was greatest in South Africa, the most Westernized country in Africa south of the Sahara. Initially, the control of religious institutions was as firmly in the hands of whites as was the control of government and industry. As long as the great mass of Africans was illiterate, this monopoly caused little resentment. But as soon as a body of literate African Christians developed, the condition changed. African ministers and lay preachers began to feel that they were as capable of managing the affairs of African congregations – of interpreting the Word of God to Africans – as any white, and many began to resent deeply what seemed to them to be treatment as children.

Although resentment at the white's domination and their attitude of condescending superiority affected the Africans' attitude toward the institutions of the new religion decisively, of coordinate importance was the Protestant doctrine of the freedom of the individual to read and interpret the Scriptures. This doctrine, like the whites' superior position, had no significant effect as long as most converts remained illiterate. When Africans acquired education, however, the freedom of the individual to interpret the Scriptures became an explosive issue.

Mention was made earlier of the secession of South African native Wesleyans from their parent church and their subsequent fusion with the AME Church of the United States. This event may prove to have been one of the most decisive events in the religious history of Africa.

The gold fields of South Africa were focal in religious significance because they were centers where large numbers of partially detribalized Africans assembled as laborers in the mines. In 1892 a considerable number of African ministers and missionaries worked among the tribesmen, gaining a fair number of converts. In that year one of them, the Reverend Mangena M. Mokone, deeply hurt because of racial discrimination within the Wesleyan Church, resigned from the Wesleyans and formed at Pretoria a new organization that he called the Ethiopian Church. Mokone at first envisioned a completely African church under purely African leaders.[36] He corresponded with Bishop H. M. Turner of the AME Church in the United States, however, and finally proposed that his Ethiopian Church be merged with the American body. At a Pretoria conference in 1896, the Ethiopian Church's membership voted in favor of affiliation, and James M. Dwane was sent to the United States to arrange the merger.

Dwane was an extraordinary person. By heritage, he was chief of one of the major clans. He was well educated, a forceful and convincing speaker, and, like Mokone, an ordained Wesleyan minister; in addition, he had almost an excess of personal ambition. He arrived in the United States in June 1896 and found the AME Church favorable toward amalgamation. The House of Bishops and the Missionary Board agreed, and Dwane was appointed general superintendent for South Africa. Two years later, when Turner visited South Africa, Dwane was appointed vicar bishop in recognition of the ability he had displayed in persuading the greater part of the Wesleyans of South Africa to join the American church. This step, however, was not enough for Dwane. After a second visit to the United States in 1899, he decided that control by black Americans was as objectionable as control by Europeans. As a result, he abandoned a black Methodist Episcopal church and then formed the Order of Ethiopia within the framework of a white episcopate, the Church of England. He was unable, however, to persuade more than a small fraction of the Methodists to follow him; to the present day, the AME Church of the United States is the parent body of the black Methodists of South Africa.[37]

The secession of the Wesleyans from the parent British church and Dwane's later secession from the AME Church were the beginning of a trend: the African's increasing impatience with white domination and consequent resentment of it. To the people who followed Dwane into his Order of Ethiopia, the black Americans who headed the AME Church were not Africans; they were merely whites with dark skins. What increasing numbers of Africans wanted, above all else, was complete freedom to decide their own activities and objectives. At the same time, while the black American bishops and church officials were not Africans, they were living proof that blacks did not need whites to manage their religion: Africans could approach God directly without white intermediaries.

The white people of South Africa and the missionaries under authority from Europe were more than a little alarmed by the movement for religious independence and were inclined to ascribe it to the subversive influence of blacks from the United States. "American Negroes Making Mischief in South Africa" was the alarmed title of an article published in the English *Missionary Review of the World* in 1902.[38] Many colonial officials and settlers, confusing symptoms with causes, were convinced that the AME Church was a dangerously subversive force and that its ministers and missionaries were agitators and agents of African nationalism — and African nationalism was something they saw no reason to encourage.

The use of the word "Ethiopia" in these first two secessionist movements is significant. Ethiopianism, although the term is loose and cannot be defined exactly, is practically synonymous with African nationalism. In many instances there has been little distinction between African nationalism and simple hostility to all foreigners, and to this extent, the unhappy colonial officials had a certain basis for their fears. Distinctly African churches with African ministers and church officials, and eventually with African rituals and theological variations, were definitely part of the yearning for an "Africa for the Africans." The name "Ethiopia" seems to have been selected deliberately by the African Wesleyans who first broke away from the British church; it is based upon Psalm 68:31, "Ethiopia shall soon stretch out her hands unto God."³⁹

The entering wedge once driven in, not many years passed before further secessions and new African churches emphasized the Africans' hopes for churches that would fully express African religious ideals. Two distinct trends soon became evident, trends to which Bengt Sundkler has applied the terms "Ethiopianism" and "Zionism." The terms are admittedly inexact, and often the two movements overlap or are so closely interlaced that sharp distinction is impossible; nevertheless, the expressions are useful in attempting to understand the separatist tendencies of African Christianity.⁴⁰ In general terms, the Ethiopian churches follow closely the ideologies and rituals of the mission churches from which they are derived. They are characterized by conservative theology, coupled with enthusiastic African nationalism and a degree of anti-Europeanism.⁴¹ The AME Church provided the example; it is the ancestral body for some of the Ethiopian churches. The Zionistic churches, with their strangely assorted rituals, represent an entirely different trend, although, as just mentioned, it is often difficult to distinguish between the two in actual practice. Whereas the Ethiopian churches express the longing of Africans for a Christian African (Ethiopian) nation, under the symbolism of the "Lion of Judah, King of Kings," Zionism is an emotional effort to connect the African directly with the Land of Zion, the Promised Land, and the "Heavenly Jerusalem."⁴²

Just as the Ethiopian movement among South African black Christians had its origin in the United States, the Zionist movement also received its stimulus from across the Atlantic, in the Watch Tower movement and the denomination now called Jehovah's Witnesses. The movement was started in 1896 by John Alexander Dowie, a religious enthusiast of Scottish birth who had spent most of his adult life in Australia. The initial doctrines of the Christian Catholic Apostolic Church in Zion (to use the original name), as Dowie propounded them, were simple and of a nature to appeal to a largely illiterate people suffering under a deep sense of oppression and injustice. He taught, first, that the Bible was literally – word for word – true: "Any statement the Bible makes is . . . the infallible Word of God, and the ultimate explanation of any matter, whether scientific, ethical, or religious."⁴³ To this rigidly fundamentalist view of the Bible, Dowie added faith healing, strict Sabbatarianism, unquestioning obedience to God's decrees as expressed through his ministers, and the imminence of the end of the world as foretold in the Apocalypse. Dowie's visionary church was transformed, under the leadership of Charles Taze Russell, into the worldwide Watch Tower movement and the new denomination, Jehovah's Witnesses. Stimulated by a missionary fervor that still carries its votaries to the ends of the world, the Watch Tower movement soon reached Africa, where the first converts were baptized at Johannesburg as early as 1904. Not until several years later did the Watch Tower "reach its stride," with significant results.⁴⁴

The importance of the movement in Africa was in part the work of a remarkable individual, a sincere and devoted religious fanatic as idealistic, visionary, and selfless as any of the saints of a more conservative tradition. Joseph Booth, like Dowie, was born in Scotland and spent the formative years of his life in Australia. As a deeply religious young man, he went through a long period of emotional storm, unhappiness, and doubt, but finally resolved his difficulties when he felt that he had received a call from God to go to Africa. He eventually established himself as an independent missionary in the highlands of Nyasaland, where he founded several missions in which he not only propounded the precepts of Christianity, as he conceived them, but also taught various trades, arts, and crafts. Booth was impressed with the injustices and oppression suffered by the Africans under European rule, and he soon became an outspoken advocate of "Africa for the Africans," a forthright enemy of racial discrimination, and a supporter of African self-determination and independence. Before long Booth had become thoroughly unpopular with settlers and orthodox missionaries and was regarded with deep suspicion by colonial officials.[45] Booth was deported from Africa several times because of his activities, but he always managed to return. During at least two of his periods of exile he went to the United States, and in 1906 he met Russell. Booth had long been dissatisfied with both the doctrines and the practices of orthodox churches (he had changed his denomination several times), but meeting Russell seems to have provided an answer to his personal religious problems, and when he returned to Africa it was as the official agent of the Watch Tower movement. In this way a connection was established between the Watch Tower and the "Africa for the Africans" ideal.[46]

One of Booth's earliest converts in Nyasaland was an intelligent and earnest young mission-trained African known as John Chilembwe. Chilembwe accompanied Booth to the United States in 1897 and, after some initial difficulties, was matriculated at the Virginia Theological Seminary, a black Baptist institution. When he was graduated, he was ordained as a minister of the Baptist Church. Returning to Nyasaland in 1900, Chilembwe established a mission similar to those which Booth had set up earlier: He preached Christianity and he tried to teach useful trades and crafts. He was aided by contributions from the National Baptist Convention Foreign Mission Board, and as the mission grew under his dynamic leadership, two black American missionaries were sent from the United States to assist him – an event regarded by settlers and colonial officials with great misgiving. Such persons were, prima facie, dangerous; even if they did not preach subversion, their very presence was likely to give the "natives" undesirable ideas.

Chilembwe had disengaged himself from Booth's influence during his theological training ("broken" is too strong a word, for they remained friends). Booth was apparently still changing churches, whereas Chilembwe never forsook his allegiance to the Baptists. But Booth's influence in Nyasaland had resulted in the establishment of a number of African independent churches resembling Russell's churches in varying degrees. There is no indication that Chilembwe himself was ever influenced by Watch Tower doctrines, but as he became more impressed with the injustices the black people suffered under European domination, his mission became a focal point for African resentment. To be concise, early in 1915 (a year foretold by some self-appointed prophets as the time indicated in the Apocalypse for the end of the world) a rebellion broke out in Nyasaland, centering about Chilembwe and his mission. The rising, however, lacked mass support and was easily suppressed with only a small number of casualties, including Chilembwe himself, who was killed on February 3, 1915.[47]

As a result of this abortive uprising, the Watch Tower movement and all of the African independent churches came under suspicion, which also extended to millennial and apocalyptic denominations and even further. The Seventh-Day Adventists and the handful of Seventh-Day Baptists found themselves under a cloud and were suspected of sympathizing with, if not actively fomenting, rebellion against the European overlords. An idealistic young American missionary of the latter church was abruptly ordered to leave the country; even the missions of churches that were strictly orthodox needed to prove their innocence. The highly conservative Calvinists of the Church of Scotland were tarred with the same black brush that smeared the Watch Tower and the numerous independent African churches that had sprung up. A. G. B. Glossop, an archbishop and High Church missionary of the Church of England who was a member of the commission appointed to investigate the uprising, believed firmly that the trouble arose from permitting "undisciplined," "childlike" African minds to formulate their own interpretations of the Scriptures. The result was somewhat odd: The missionaries of the Church of Scotland found themselves standing shoulder to shoulder with Adventists, Baptists, Watch Tower ministers, and others in vehement defense of the principle of religious freedom.[48]

Once started, the separatist tendencies exemplified by James M. Dwane and by the churches in Nyasaland expanded. In South Africa, especially, new churches sprang up and proliferated until there were literally hundreds of native African denominations – a movement that has profoundly affected organized Christianity in all of southern Africa and has affected, for the worse, the relations between the black and white races in that part of the world. Millennial doctrines such as those of the Watch Tower movement often have been transformed in the minds of illiterate or barely literate Africans to mean that social roles will be reversed in the rapidly approaching millennium; when that day arrives, blacks will reign supreme and Europeans will be subject to them. An incident demonstrating the lack of reality in this situation occurred when James Aggrey, the African educator, visited South Africa in 1921 as part of the Phelps-Stokes Commission. To his amazement, Aggrey was heralded as the forerunner of an army of black Americans who would arrive shortly to drive the white people into the sea and return Africa to the ownership of the blacks. At a meeting in Transkei, he found that many people arrived with empty sacks and baskets to carry away the merchandise that he was expected to compel the merchants to give them, or at least to sell them at bargain prices.[49]

In at least one other incident in southern Africa, the results of millennial separatism were tragic. A forceful but utterly ignorant "prophet," one Enoch Mgjima, who had been excommunicated by the Church of God and Saints in Christ (a small black American denomination), assembled in 1921 a new following of Israelites. Mgjima and his followers established themselves on crown land near Queenstown, without permission, and ignored all orders to leave; in fact, they ignored all orders. The government's patience was interpreted as weakness, and Mgjima assured his disciples that they had nothing to fear – the white man's bullets would be miraculously turned to water. When the police appeared, Mgjima and his people attacked, and in the ensuing melee more than 150 were killed and scores were wounded.[50]

Such tragedies as Chilembwe's rising and Mgjima's mistaken prophecy fortunately are exceptions. It is only fair to note that the Watch Tower and its successor denomination, Jehovah's Witnesses, are inclined to be pacifistic and categorically deny being subversive. Yet their doctrine of the approach of the millennium – when the poor, weak, and oppressed will come into their own – has made a profound impression upon many semiliterate people in ways that Dowie and Russell did not foresee. Certainly the Watch Tower's emphasis upon individual reading and study of the Bible leads directly to individualistic interpretation. Jehovah's Witnesses claim, perhaps with some justification, to be the most rapidly growing church in Africa. It can hardly be coincidental that the growth of the denomination in Africa has been followed in every country by a wave of secessions, not only from the older churches but from newly established African churches – secessions leading to other secessions.[51]

Among the non-European Christians of South Africa, the combination of causes that has been touched upon resulted in a condition close to religious and denominational anarchy. The need to create new socioreligious communities, the desire for religious independence, resentment at continued European control, individual interpretations of the Bible, rising Bantu and African national feeling, conflicts of personalities and personal ambitions – by 1950 these forces together operated to produce within the geographical limits of South Africa more than two thousand separate and distinct African churches.[52] The total is reportedly increasing daily.

Separatism prevalent among the South African Bantu speakers has been stressed for two reasons: First, it is further advanced and more conspicuous than that in other parts of Africa; and second, the information available is more complete than that for other regions. But in all other parts of Africa the same tendency toward separation of African churches from the parent body and the subsequent fissure between African churches is apparent and is rooted in the same causes. The actual number of distinctively African churches, however, is not as large in other regions as in South Africa, nor does it now seem likely that it will ever reach the total indicated for South Africa.

In the copper belt, for example, shortly before independence was granted to the republic of Zambia in 1964, the authorities listed only nineteen denominations, including such settled churches as the Roman Catholic, Methodist, and Anglican. The Jehovah's Witnesses continued to be strong on the copper belt, where the British colonial authorities, after initial hesitation, concluded that the sect was not subversive in its intentions or in its effects. The African nationalists, however, came to a different assessment. Jehovah's Witnesses would not take part in the organization of the United National Independence Party (UNIP), or any other nationalist body. After Zambia had attained independence, the Witnesses refused to vote, sing the national anthem, or salute the new flag. They thereby provoked the wrath of local UNIP branches; there were widespread clashes between UNIP and the Witnesses; and the government then greatly restricted the freedom to hold meetings and preach from door to door that the Witnesses had enjoyed in colonial times.[53]

In Ghana, the development of the missions into full-fledged churches and the Africanization of those churches proceeded somewhat faster than in most other African countries. Initial steps toward African control were taken during World War I; the process proceeded smoothly and with a minimum of friction and was virtually complete by the end of World War II. A considerable number of missionaries, many of them from the United States, remained in the country, understanding fully that they were there for the sole purpose of assisting with their advice in the African administration and operation of the churches.[54] It is a possible indication of a happier relation in Ghana between Africans and Europeans than holds in some African countries that in 1954 the Methodist Synod for the country, composed of 137 African and 22 European members, unanimously elected a white man, G. Thackray Eddy, as chairman. Objections in the nationalistic local press were answered by a Ghanaian minister.

Even in Ghana, however, the same fissiparous tendencies have shown themselves as have been seen in other parts of Africa, though the number of separate sects is small in comparison with South Africa.[55] One observer ascribes the divisiveness to the tendency to stress only a part of the Scriptures, or to "one-sided" interpretations – also common among white Protestants in Europe and America.[56] Another commentator remarks:

> An important feature of the Christian situation has been the emergence of African sects, the so-called "African" or "Ethiopian" or separatist churches. When these first arose in the early years of this century they were partly aimed at independence from foreign control, and sometimes influenced by the Negro churches of America. But their main doctrines have generally been orthodox and they have been the expression of African religious experience, often in conscious opposition to the formality of the older churches.[57]

In East Africa the same basic causes of discontent among African Christians existed, but for a number of reasons the separatist movements took a different course from that which they followed in southern Africa. Roland Oliver summarized the difference: "The problems which beset the Church in East Africa today arise less from rival beliefs of local origin than from the unbelief and half-belief of the secular west."[58] As in all other parts of the continent, in East Africa the whites' assumption of innate superiority aroused deep resentment. Even missionaries, who should have been more attuned to the people whom they wanted to convert, were sometimes guilty of extraordinary lack of tact. The intense desire of the African for spiritual as well as political freedom resulted, in East Africa, in a separatism that differed from that of southern and West Africa in that there was no great proliferation of small sects. The East African separatist churches tend to be orthodox in their theology, and are well exemplified by the most prominent, the African Orthodox Church.

The African Orthodox Church was originally an offshoot of the schemes and dreams that Marcus Garvey devised in the 1920s. Garvey, a Jamaican who migrated to the United States in 1916, was obsessed with the ambition to uplift his race. He organized the Universal Negro Improvement Association and developed a visionary program to establish a great black empire based in Africa and embracing blacks of all the world.[59] His program favored distinctively black churches, and in eastern Africa it inspired a remarkable preacher named Reuben Spartas, a man born in a Christian family who had received an education far beyond that of most Africans at the time. Deeply religious by nature, he became convinced of the need to maintain strict apostolic succession. Hence he eventually broke away from the Anglican communion in which he had been raised and became a member of the African Orthodox Church, where his intelligence and personality led him to leadership. Under his guidance, the African Orthodox Church was recognized by the Greek Orthodox and eventually became a part of that church, an African branch with full apostolic powers.[60]

In Tanganyika (now Tanzania), the same strong desire for complete religious independence without supervision or interference by Europeans manifested itself, but without the strong tendency toward orthodoxy that appeared in Kenya and Uganda. Studies among the Nyakyusa, a rural people around Lake Nyasa, reveal that most of the African Christians who grew dissatisfied with missionary leadership became members of two principal separatist churches, the Last Church of God and His Christ and the African National Church. It is significant that the foremost leader of the Last Church of God and His Christ was, at one time, a follower of the Watch Tower movement, from which he broke in 1925, and that the new church follows Watch Tower practices in several particulars. It is also significant that the organizer and first leader of the African National Church, Gordon Nsumba, was a Nyasa who had spent considerable time in South Africa, where he may have had contact with Watch Tower enthusiasts.[61]

There are many other separatist churches in eastern Africa, but nothing like the staggering numbers found in South Africa. The Watch Tower movement and its successor, Jehovah's Witnesses, seem to have made relatively little headway compared with other parts of Africa, in spite of the enthusiasm of its missionaries. A few were noted among the Nyakyusa, maintaining only a tenuous connection with the headquarters of the movement in Cape Town. In Kenya, as recently as 1953, Jehovah's Witnesses claimed only a single congregation and minister; in Tanganyika they had achieved a mere thirteen congregations.[62]

No discussion of African religious separatism and of possible American influence in African religion would be adequate without mention of the Kitawala movement in the Congo (the former Belgian colony, now Zaire), which is a direct offshoot of the Watch Tower – an African variation of Charles Russell's doctrines. The Kitawala movement was started, or at least stimulated, in the first decade of the century by a Nyasa named Elliott Kimwana, who studied the Watch Tower doctrines under Joseph Booth himself. Under Kimwana's preaching, the movement became definitely anti-European, and aimed for the day when the Africans would "make our own powder, and make or import our own guns."[63] Since the Kitawala movement unquestionably influenced many of the people in Chilembwe's revolt, it was logical that the authorities should make every effort to suppress it; and since they did not distinguish between Kitawala and the legitimate Watch Tower movement, the latter was under suspicion for a long time.

The combination of the Watch Tower movement (and its variations) with the opening of the mineral resources of Central Africa made relatively easy the spread of new ideas – often out of sight and beyond the knowledge of colonial government officials. Workers from Rhodesia and Nyasaland swarmed into Katanga, frequently bearing more than their meager material possessions, so it is not surprising that local adaptations of Watch Tower doctrines began early to reverberate through the Congo. In that enormous land, it appears that some of the ideas of the Watch Tower movement, especially in their Kitawala form, merged with the ideas of an indigenous movement known as Ngunzism, although some of the latter's early pronouncements show a remarkable similarity to some of Russell's doctrines.

At some time before 1920 a devout Christian convert of the lower Congo Valley, Simon Kimbangu, began to preach a new faith that stressed miraculous healing. Kimbangu gradually became a prophet in the eyes of his followers – and possibly in his own as well. At some as yet undetermined point, the Kitawala movement came in contact with laborers from Rhodesia, and the ideas, doctrines, and followers of the two movements were merged. At the same time there may have been injected some traces of Marcus Garvey's dreams of the redemption of the African race and the expulsion of the whites from the continent. Without the intention of Kimbangu himself, at least initially, Ngunzism became rabidly nationalistic, antiwhite, and revolutionary.[64]

The degree to which ideas and doctrines originating in the United States may have influenced radical prophetic dreams and schemes in the Congo is conjectural. But certain coincidences should be noted. As previously mentioned, when Aggrey was in South Africa in 1921 on behalf of the Phelps-Stokes Commission, he found that some of the Zulus were living in anticipation of the arrival of an army of black Americans that would drive the whites into the sea. During the same period in the Congo, the Ngunzists' "hopes for the future were sustained . . . by the good news that the Congo was to be conquered by Negroes from America, hastening to the aid of their afflicted brethren."[65] It will also be recalled that when Mgjima's deluded followers charged the police, their courage was multiplied by the faith that "the white man's bullets would be turned to water." In the Congo, according to a legend that circulated in the 1920s, when the Prophet Kimbangu stood before a firing squad for execution only water came from the soldiers' rifles.[66] Bullets that turn into water have been legendary in nearly all parts of the world from time to time, when Europeans and less-advanced peoples have been in contact. The appearance of this legend in widely separated parts of Africa should not be surprising; but its nearly simultaneous emergence in South Africa and in the Congo, at a time when ideas were infiltrating from one region to the other, suggests that in this instance there was a common origin. Admittedly, this view is conjectural, but the possibility should not be dismissed that Joseph Booth, through the perversion of his ideas during years of word-of-mouth transmittal, was the ultimate ancestor of Ngunzism and of Mgjima's Israelites in South Africa.

As elsewhere, in the Congo there are numerous other separatist churches. It would seem, however, that the diversity and confusion that characterizes separatism in South Africa does not exist in the Congo solely because the number of professed Christians is small. A writer on the subject of Christianity and Christian missions in Africa says:

> In Congo the land is large enough to have a fantastic tapestry of churches, sects and missions which conform loosely to the word "Protestant" and have a community of about a million with the Baptists, Presbyterians and Disciples counting a membership of about 80,000 each, the Adventists (20,000) and many other groups ranging from Assemblies of God, Free Methodists, Mennonites, and Independent Baptists to the labels Interdenominational and just Independent.[67]

In Nigeria the secessionist tendency, once started in 1888, continued, though not as vigorously as in South Africa. New denominations were established after 1888 at the average rate of one every second year, and by 1922 there were seventeen African churches. Twelve originated and maintained their headquarters at Lagos. Four came from schisms within mission churches, six originated as schisms within existing African churches, and the others arose elsewhere in the country and from different sources.

Official reactions

The records of colonial policy toward black missionaries tell a contradictory story. Colonial officials did not want to be accused of overt discrimination, but the results in fact limited the number of black missionaries – for example, there were none in East Africa between the two world wars.[68] Missionary societies changed their policies: Groups that had sent blacks in the nineteenth century did not do so, or did so reluctantly, in the early twentieth century. The blacks themselves resented this form of exclusion from the African field; the black American scholars W. E. B. Du Bois and Carter G. Woodson both were outspoken for many years on this point.

The 1912 conference on Africa assembled by Booker T. Washington had charged white governments, and especially South Africa, with discriminating against blacks. Not until 1916 did black Americans come to East Africa, when Max Yergan arrived to serve ably as YMCA secretary among African troops. But even though his group had done outstanding work, the British Colonial Office refused to let him return in 1920 as head of the International YMCA in East Africa: The administration did not want well-educated black Americans working in the colony.[69] Blacks then suspected that white mission bodies and white governments did not want black missionaries in Africa. Thomas Jesse Jones, chairman of the Phelps-Stokes Education Commission touring Africa in 1921, delayed Yergan's appointment until he could check to see if Yergan was a moderate, cooperative black or a "Pan-African Negro with a violent antipathy to cooperation with white people."[70] Similar caution about black missionaries must have motivated other missionary groups, philanthropic bodies, and colonial governments. Like Jones, these groups wanted to be sure that they were sending cooperative blacks, those who had the accommodative attitudes in race relations of Tuskegee and Washington, as opposed to the "troublesome" followers of Marcus Garvey or Du Bois.[71]

Missionary leaders such as J. H. Oldham cooperated with colonial authorities in discouraging black American missionaries – even of the Tuskegee kind – from going into East Africa.[72] Oldham felt in 1921 that Tuskegee-trained blacks should be kept out of white-settled Africa; they could find productive work in East Africa when conditions were better. Secretary Turner of the Foreign Missions Conference of North America agreed to discourage the societies from sending black missionaries to Kenya; so in effect the Colonial Office did not have to make a discriminatory ruling.[73] This policy was apparently applied throughout Africa in some form or other. Although black Americans were encouraged to become missionaries to Africa and white groups kept talking about the need for them, few blacks were actually sent. J. E. Kwegyir Aggrey's visit with the Phelps-Stokes Commission surveying African education led to an increased demand for black Americans, and the fund itself brought missionaries from Kenya and Uganda to tour Southern American black colleges and to see how their students were trained; visitors saw the obvious applications of the Tuskegee and Hampton models to training in Africa. Yet obstacles to bringing black American missionaries increased; East Africa was, in fact, shut off as a field of work. The Le Zoute conference on Christian Missions in Africa, held in 1926, tried to find ways of sending more black missionaries. Blame was placed on colonial governments and on the poor performance of black Americans in Africa, but no blame was assessed against the missionary boards themselves, although their failure in responsibility is evident. White churches failed to train black Americans for work in Africa. They had done better in the nineteenth century. The pressures of colonial governments and settler interest groups overrode the clear call of conscience and practical need. In some cases, individual mission groups were simply prejudiced, for they sent no blacks anywhere in Africa; other church bodies were timid and acquiesced to government pressure.

Even when they represented orthodox and conservative bodies such as the Methodist Church, black Americans were often suspected of being agitators, and in some instances, years after their departure from Africa, the legend of their subversive activities would not die. For example, as Efraim Andersson notes: "According to Karstedt, Thwaite and Schlosser . . . it was the bishop of the black branch of the American Methodist Episcopal Church, H. M. Turner, one of the leaders connected with the introducing of American Negro christianity and the motto 'Africa for the Africans,' who was active [in introducing the Watch Tower into Africa]."[74]

In what was formerly British Central Africa the first black American missionary to arrive encountered such suspicion that he was finally forced to leave the country, his efforts a failure. Thomas Branch was a Seventh-Day Adventist, and it is possible that he was sent to Africa as a result of Joseph Booth's recommendations. At any rate, he and his family arrived in time to have the alarmed colonists and the almost hysterical colonial press link his name with the growing spirit of resentment among the Africans. From the small amount of information available, Branch seems to have been a quiet, devout man who was intent only upon preaching the gospel as he understood it, with no interest in African nationalism. But the color of his skin damned him, and his mere presence was terrifying to the settlers.[75]

A little later, when L. N. Cheek arrived to work as an assistant to Chilembwe, the very heavens seemed about to fall. This was years before Chilembwe's rebellion and long before his mission became a center of subversion, but Cheek "was a Negro minister, and that was enough!"[76] There was a widespread fear that the black Americans might provoke a general uprising – indeed, it was believed that they came to Africa for that purpose – and if they did not accomplish such an aim, their mere presence would give the blacks ideas that the ruling whites could not stomach: that Africans could be educated and civilized, could hold positions of responsibility, and need not always be subordinate to whites.

As late as 1912 the suspicious attitude of the colonial authorities was exemplified by the disagreeable experience of two black American missionaries who were denied permission to land in South Africa. After a lengthy detention, the authorities grudgingly gave permission for them to remain six months. A twelve-month extension was reluctantly granted, with the express stipulation that they would not be permitted to remain longer. At about the same time (1912), another black American missionary, J. E. East, was charged with a minor offense by South African officials, and strong efforts were made to expel him from the country. He was finally exonerated and permitted to remain, but apparently was branded in the minds of officialdom as a dangerous agitator. In 1925 the annual report of the National Baptist Convention (Negro) mentioned that black missionaries were regarded with uneasiness by European officials. "What will happen if all Africa awakens as the black man in America has awakened?" was a question that disturbed the governing powers.[77] Emory Ross succinctly summarized the problem that worried colonial officials and settlers, a problem not yet entirely solved:

> Many an administrator in Africa, particularly but not exclusively those whose mother tongue is other than English, believes that all American Negroes are Garveyites, that Pan-Africanism is one of their major concerns, that communism claims them by the million, that dangerously emotional religious vagaries are their usual style, that their attitude is predominately anti-white and that, as a consequence of all this, they are not exactly desirable fellow residents in Africa.[78]

The attitude toward black American missionaries was not, however, universally hostile. In recent years, in fact, the part that they actually played in raising the intellectual level of the Africans has been widely recognized, and they received full cooperation from colonial and dominion governments after World War II. Even in the late 1930s, when Amos Jerome White, a well-known black educator and clergyman, went to South Africa with his wife to accept the presidency of Wilberforce Institute in the Transvaal, he received every courtesy. On at least one occasion a friendly official classified the two as "Europeans" so that they would be exempt from the operation of pass laws and could travel first class.[79]

This outline is necessarily incomplete. From vast areas of the continent there is no information available at all; even in South Africa, where information is full, there are many gaps and needed explanations. Enough, however, has been brought out to demonstrate that Americans played a leading role – possibly a decisive part – in developing the Africans' sense of their own religious individuality. The colonial authorities who, not long ago, doubted the wisdom of permitting black American missionaries to enter their domain had, from their own point of view, considerable justification. Few if any black missionaries from the United States were subversive, but their mere presence proved the untruth of certain widely held colonial assumptions. They were living evidence that blacks were not in the least children by nature – brave, imaginative, and loyal perhaps, but nevertheless children who, for their own good, should be kept under guardianship for many years to come. The favorite colonial myth was just a myth.

In recent years another facet of African religious separatism has become clearer than before. African converts widely interpreted the new creed in their own fashion; they developed their own theology; they become reluctant to accept the infallibility of the white missionary's interpretation of the Bible and attendant doctrines. Without realizing it, Africans who established their own churches according to their own ideas and interpretations may exemplify the individual "priesthood of the believer." Resentment, conscious or unconscious, of the assumption of superior knowledge and superior character by the non-African has expressed itself in the proliferation of unnumbered African sects. One result has been that missionaries, American as well as European, now stand in a new relationship with Africans.

They no longer speak with final authority, and this is especially true since the attainment of independence by the Africans in the greater part of the continent. African Christians are now resolved "to practice what the foreign missionaries had been preaching to them all along—to stand on their own feet."[80] One of the unintended consequences of missionary endeavors was the training in their schools of most of the important first generation of modern nationalist leaders.

CHAPTER 19

Black nationalism and the search for an African past

The first British Empire owed much to the triangular trade between Africa, the West Indies and North America. The last British Empire has not been uninfluenced by another triangular trade, a trade not of pocatille, slaves and molasses, but a commerce of ideas and politics between the descendants of the slave in the West Indies and North America and their ancestral continent.[1]

Black Americans, like European immigrants, have traditionally been ambivalent in their attitudes toward their respective homelands. Blacks were among the earliest Americans. They helped to build the United States and to defend it. The vast majority of them had no other home, and they naturally resented nineteenth-century projects of a racist kind to repatriate them to Africa as if they were undesirable aliens. But Africa has also had a special appeal for black Americans, prized as the place of their origin, as the home of a unique culture, or as a lost homeland on which they might fix their sights.

The homeland concept was harder to accept for black Americans than, say, for Italian- or Polish-Americans linked to the Old Country by ties of a common language and by their connection with a specific country rather than a continent. But as black Americans gained increasing confidence in their status as American citizens, they increasingly looked to Africa as a fountainhead of the dignity, identity, and racial achievement denied so often to them in the United States by their slave heritage. The focus of black nationalism has shifted at various times. But three major themes have persisted through the last two centuries: black missionary activity in Africa, emigrationism, and Pan-Africanism. In their efforts to create a black nationalism in the United States, black Americans have at the same time deeply influenced African nationalism.

Intellectual springs of African nationalism

The West Indies occupied a place of particular importance in the formation of black consciousness in the New World. People, merchandise, and ideas traveled freely from the mainland to the islands and back again, creating in the process a reverberating effect. Haiti's war of independence against the French, which occasioned untold hopes and fears on the American mainland, provided the one outstanding example of a successful black insurrection against white rule. Later on, Haitian men of letters discovered their African heritage, which they blended with French culture. So did intellectuals in the French West Indies and Guiana, men such as Félix Eboué, an outstanding colonial administrator, and Aimé Césaire, apostle of the African cultural heritage.

The British West Indies had an even more important role in the cultural history of the New World, for blacks in North America, in the British West Indies, and in many parts of West Africa shared a common language. And the British West Indies were a generation ahead of the United States in emancipating slaves. The social structure of the British West Indies, moreover, at first allowed "people of colour" a greater degree of social mobility than they enjoyed in most of the Southern states of the United States. Because West Indian whites formed a small percentage of the population, there was room for a mulatto middle class.

From about the turn of the present century onward, West Indians began to migrate to the United States in sizable numbers. The newcomers settled mainly in the urban centers along the Atlantic seaboard, particularly in New York and Boston. The majority of immigrants were probably unskilled; but some of them (for instance, the Jamaican cigar makers) were highly trained. In addition, the immigrants contained men with professional qualifications that, allied to a knowledge of English, opened the door to prosperity. By the 1930s, therefore, a high proportion of New York's black physicians, dentists, and lawyers had been born in the West Indies. Many of the newcomers did well economically (by the late 1970s, the West Indians' average family incomes had come to approach more or less the national average). But the West Indians found social adjustment more difficult. They were, on the whole, better educated than black Americans; their religious affiliation was Episcopal rather than Baptist or Methodist; because they were used to a society where status derived only partly from color, they were particularly upset at America's biracial pattern. Not surprisingly, they began to take an active part in black politics and intellectual life, where their importance far exceeded their numerical strength.[2]

One of the most outstanding of these black intellectuals was Edward Blyden, who was born on the island of St. Thomas in 1832, just a year before the British abolished slavery throughout their empire. He visited New York in 1847 seeking admission to a university. Upon being refused, he went to Liberia, where he established himself as a scholar-politician-minister. Blyden became the leading participant of the triangular trade in ideas. He made eleven trips to the United States between 1872 and 1888, and he came to know and influence many black Americans through his writings, his letters, and his visits.[3]

Two other West Indians who exerted a profound influence on the attitude of American blacks toward Africa were Marcus Garvey and George Padmore. Garvey, a Jamaican, spent eleven years in the United States. He moved the black masses, especially in the early 1920s, as no leader had previously done. His Universal Negro Improvement Association helped to ignite racial consciousness around the world.[4] Padmore, born in Trinidad, emigrated during the 1930s to the United States, where he attended Fisk and Howard universities and became active in the Communist movement. Some years later he left the United States for Europe. He left the Communist Party in 1935 and subsequently formed the Pan-African Federation. By his life and writing, especially in *Pan-Africanism or Communism?* he showed "the existence of this triangle [of intellectual exchange] and tried to estimate its significance for Africa."[5]

A few other West Indian figures worthy of mention are Albert Thorne, an emigration activist between 1897 and 1920, who tried to launch a back-to-Africa movement for Central Africa; Henry Sylvester-Williams, the driving spirit behind the first Pan-African movement; and Alexander McGuire, who was named bishop of the African Orthodox Church in 1921 as part of the Garvey movement. (The African Orthodox Church, as we have seen, was important in the development of African independent churches in East and South Africa.)[6]

West Indian and American blacks were drawn together by the mutual need to find an answer to the question whether Africans had a past and a history of significant achievements. In addition, they shared a feeling that only in Africa could blacks be treated with respect and dignity. If Africa had no past, then people of color had to create a sense of African nationalism and to find collective achievements. If Africans had made cultural contributions, then black scholars should uncover them. In the answers to these questions and the solutions to these problems lie most of the sources for black American influence on Africa and for the rise of black nationalism and Pan-Africanism.

Black American interests in Africa had many roots. Already in the eighteenth century, some blacks had shown an interest in emigrating to Africa. Freedmen especially longed to return to their homeland. Some black Loyalists after the American Revolutionary War chose to depart for Sierra Leone. Even before Paul Cuffee, a black shipowner from New England, took some freedmen to West Africa in 1811, some American blacks had dreamed of emigrating to Africa. As we have seen, Liberia, founded in 1821, became the realized dream for black colonization societies. Before the Civil War, back-to-Africa movements attracted some blacks; they comprised ventures such as Martin R. Delany's efforts to establish a settlement for American blacks in Nigeria in 1859. Like many black intellectuals, Delany was concerned as much with the search for identity as with dignity. Along with Blyden, he preached "Africa for the Africans" and the need to preserve African customs and traditions.[7] Delany felt convinced that blacks in the United States formed a nation within a nation and that black Americans should prize separation rather than assimilation. Yet his own career belied his thesis. A Harvard-trained physician, a pioneer black novelist, a leader in the antislavery cause, the ranking black officer in the Union army, an influential official in the Freedmen's Bureau, and finally a respected Charleston judge well regarded even by many white conservatives, he achieved the kind of success that proved to ambitious black youngsters that some Afro-Americans at least might indeed pursue successful careers within the framework of white-ruled society.

Emigrationism. The victory of the North in the Civil War legally turned the blacks into citizens. However hard and unjust conditions might be in the New World, there was at least hope for a better future. Accordingly, emigrationism to Africa declined after 1865, although it was somewhat revived, owing to falling cotton prices, in the 1890s.[8] The blacks who did return to Africa derived mainly, though not wholly, from the lower class. It was an untidy, disorganized movement, mostly of Southern black farmers who had long been victimized by sharecropping, debt peonage, and cotton cultivation. Between 1890 and 1910 perhaps a thousand blacks emigrated to Africa, a negligible number in relation to America's total black population.

Africa was of concern, not to people who wanted to better their social condition, but to humanitarians, missionaries, scientists, and reformers of all persuasions who wanted to explore or "improve" the African continent. As noted previously, the leading figure after 1890 in the back-to-Africa movement was Henry M. Turner (1834–1915), bishop of the AME Church, who returned to the dream of emigration during his many periods of despair with white America. He wanted a migration of about five hundred thousand black people who would raise pride and respect among blacks everywhere. Through his extensive travels on church business in the United States and Africa, he had many opportunities to air his views. Even the U.S. Congress in the 1890s sponsored several bills to promote black emigration, bills that were never passed but that caused much discussion among blacks and whites.

All efforts to promote emigration by Turner's American Colonization Society eventually failed because of lack of interest and because of the constant flow of disillusioned returnees, who told horror stories of death and suffering. There were blacks who went to Oklahoma in the 1890s, became disillusioned, and then sought to go to Liberia. They and some Arkansas blacks were stranded in New York City when their leaders defrauded them. New York blacks tried to dissuade people from emigrating, and only a few managed to get to Liberia. The United States and Congo National Emigration Company and the Reverend Benjamin Garton also attempted to promote emigration, but both failed because of fraud, dishonesty, and ineptness. Yet the fervor was there. In Atlanta, Georgia, 2,500 people assembled in 1896 to be transported to Africa; 42 wound up going. Transport was usually the major problem. Turner also supported a white, profit-oriented organization, the International Migration Society, which did get 200 Southern blacks to Liberia in 1895 and 321 in 1896. But conditions were so bad for the emigrants that more than half died or left.

After 1900 the general prospects in the United States and the rival message of self-improvement within the country hurt the emigration movement. Rural blacks lost interest in going back to Africa. Turner gave up his efforts in 1906, although he still believed in emigration for some blacks. The emigrationists desired free land, economic security, freedom, and security from lynching. They lost hope for progress in the United States, and felt that in Africa they could reestablish black pride. But the band of people Turner needed – educated blacks – did not emigrate. (Garvey, whose work will be discussed shortly, had more success among urban blacks than did Turner.) Nevertheless, Turner's lectures were listened to and his book was widely read. For example, Chief Alfred Sam of the Gold Coast, taking action on Turner's words, got sixty Oklahoma blacks to the Gold Coast in 1917.

But all emigration movements were bound to fail for essentially the same reasons. Conditions for blacks might be bad in the United States, but they were never bad enough to drive out black Americans in large numbers. The vast majority of blacks felt themselves to be Americans, and they had no wish to be anything but Americans. They had come "up from slavery"; they had experienced a slow but steady rise in their social condition; rural serfs were advancing into the ranks of the unskilled and skilled working class; a small middle class had come into existence, anxious to expand its economic opportunities. Like their white countrymen, black Americans assumed that, however bad their present condition, the future would surely be better rather than worse.

Africa, moreover, could never attract black Americans in large numbers. Black Americans had no wish to live under the tutelage of a European colonial power or even of an Ethiopian monarchy. Liberia lacked both the economic potential and the will to become a black Zion. Black Americans who did desire to build a new future for themselves in Africa lacked the social resources available to Swedes, Irishmen, Germans, or Jews determined to migrate from Europe to North America: cheap transportation; a network of friends, relatives, churches, and secular societies already established in the new country; and – above all – the economic opportunities provided by an expanding economy and a political system geared to the absorption of newcomers.

Black missionaries. Meanwhile, another more important movement had developed: Christian missions led by black Americans anxious to "save" and to develop Africa.[9] From the founding of Liberia in 1821 until the 1920s, the major influence of black Americans on Africa came from black missionaries. The colonization movement gave birth to the black missionary tradition and to the theory of "providential design," which taught that black slaves were brought to the United States and Christianized and educated so that they might be able to send their children back to redeem Africa.[10] Missionary societies seemed to believe that blacks could withstand the African climate and resist the diseases of Africa better than whites. Furthermore, evangelical clergymen felt that Africans could be converted more easily by black than by white missionaries.

In spite of their words, most white missionary societies, as we saw in Chapter 18, were reluctant to send black preachers to Africa. This reluctance, with the resistance of settler and colonial governments to receive them, meant that few black missionaries actually went to Africa. Still, there were a few. They worked successfully in West and Central Africa, but before 1945 they were practically excluded from East Africa. Although some black ministers served with white mission groups, the impact on Africa of black Americans was probably greatest among the missionaries sent out by black church groups, the most important of which were the AME Church, the African Methodist Episcopal Zion (AMEZ) Church, and the three Negro Baptist conventions.

Contrary to some colonial opinion, black missionaries seldom organized political resistance among Africans, but they did stand as symbols of what Africans could aspire to. Black-led churches were eager to accept African breakaway groups from white mission churches. Black missionaries brought a small but steady stream of African students to the United States to study at black colleges and universities, usually in the South or at Wilberforce in Ohio or Lincoln in Pennsylvania.[11] The resources allotted and the schools and stations erected in Africa were significant both in number and in influence. Bishop Alexander Walters of the AMEZ Church noted in 1912 that his group was running five mission stations in Liberia and eleven in the Gold Coast, and that it had three schools serving these areas.

Besides Liberia, the Congo Free State was at first seen by many black Americans as offering special missionary opportunities. Their dream was shattered in the 1890s by the atrocities committed in the Congo and by the criticism of Leopold's regime brought by black missionaries such as William H. Sheppard of the Southern

Presbyterian Church.[12] Because of attacks on the Congo government, black missionaries were restricted from serving in the Congo after 1909. Still, men like Sheppard, C. C. Boone, and others who went out to the Congo from 1901 to 1906 under the auspices of the Lott Carey Baptist Convention and the American Baptist society thought the Congo would be a place where they might seek new dignity and useful service.[13]

The black missionary movement was always intermixed with a spirit of Pan-Africanism. Africa seemed to offer black Americans a chance to emigrate, to prosper, and to Christianize their African kin, but also to help Africans to rise economically. Furthermore, black Americans believed it was God's design that educated blacks should return to Africa and develop it. Turner and his newspaper, the *Voice of the People* (1901–7), continually preached this message of "providential design" and emigrationism:

> The Negro race has as much chance in the United States . . . of being a man . . . as a frog has in a snake den . . . Emigrate and gradually return to the land of our ancestors . . . The Negro was brought here in the providence of God to learn obedience, to work, to sing, to pray, to preach, to acquire education . . . and imbibe the principles of civilization as a whole, and then to return to Africa, the land of his fathers, and bring her his millions.[14]

The British colonial authorities were never happy about admitting black Americans, be they Garveyites or missionaries, into their African colonies. If, as noted earlier, black missionaries were none too welcome even when they worked within white-led churches, they were even more unpopular when they came as leaders of black separatist churches. South Africa opposed the Ethiopian movement beginning in 1896–8, when Africans tried to become members of the AME Church or to associate with it. Turner's visits to South Africa in the 1890s established a relationship, and the AME Church spread north to the Rhodesias after 1900. Africans from South Africa went to the United States for education in black American colleges, and some, such as John L. Dube, Solomon Plaatje, and D. D. T. Jabavu, became important figures in the African National Congress.[15] These contacts, inspirations, and associations made the South African and Rhodesian governments fearful of the black American's influence on the Bantu. The Zulu rebellion of 1906, Garveyism, and the "Bulhoek Massacre" of 1921 seemed to confirm official fears that contact with black American separatist churches was a source of unrest and violence among local blacks.[16]

But other colonies were almost as inhospitable to black missionaries. The Congo reversed itself from welcoming blacks to opposing and restricting their entry. The role of such black American intellectuals as Booker T. Washington in speaking out against Belgian misrule in the Congo may in part have accounted for Belgian hostility. Basically, however, it was probably the fear that black Americans might implant in the local black population certain dangerous ideas about self-rule, liberty, equality, and rights. In Kenya, colonial officials won the cooperation of missionary groups in restricting admittance of blacks to Kenya until 1945, and similar attempts were made in other European colonies to restrict the activities of black Americans in Africa.[17]

Black leaders. Despite the long history of setbacks and obstacles, the image of Africa as the place where freedom, dignity, and success could be won has persisted with some American blacks to this very day. Stokely Carmichael, who migrated to Guinea in 1971, is but a recent example of a goal that has beckoned blacks for over 150 years. Almost since the beginning of American history, leaders have arisen periodically who tried to turn this dream into reality. Although the majority of the leaders of black American communities have always rejected the emigration-ist urge in black nationalism, the persistence of the sentiment throughout the nineteenth and twentieth centuries and the mass appeal of Marcus Garvey imply that among many lower- or working-class blacks there has been some desire to return to Africa.[18]

During World War I large numbers of blacks migrated to the northern United States, where unemployment and race riots produced frustration and disillusion-ment among them. Appearing as a secular savior, Marcus Garvey exploited this discontent and built the greatest emigrationist movement the United States has ever known. After the war he was to play on the disillusionment felt by many blacks when their hopes for liberation were not met. Garvey had set up his Universal Negro Improvement Association (UNIA) in Jamaica on August 1, 1914. He preached racial pride and power through commercial success and the eventual establishment of independent African states throughout Africa. His short-term goal, however, was to establish an educational institution in Jamaica, and for that reason he arranged to visit Booker T. Washington in Tuskegee (although Washing-ton died in 1915, before he arrived).

When Garvey came to Harlem in March 1916, he quickly captured the attention of the black population. He had a gift for self-dramatization, coupled with great energy and remarkable powers of persuasion. Though he had little understanding of the indigenous societies of Africa, of Africa's cultural and ethnic peculiarities, or of the part played in African history by Arabs, Berbers, and other lighter-skinned races, he was fired by a strong missionary impulse. Garvey was an accomplished propagandist, moreover, a man who claimed that Mussolini had only copied fas-cism from him. His weekly newspaper, the *Negro World*, started in 1918, brought militant ideas to thousands who might not see his parades or hear his talks.[19] With his plumed hats, street parades, marching bands, medals, and titles (knight or duke), Garvey appealed primarily to less-educated blacks.[20] In 1920 the UNIA held a convention in New York City and drafted a Declaration of Rights of the Negro Peoples of the World, which called for "Africa for the Africans at home and abroad."[21] Historian Benjamin Quarles estimates that at the height of his influence in the early 1920s Garvey may have had over a million adherents.[22] Throughout the years when Garvey was captivating the blacks of Harlem and elsewhere, his message of black nationalism also reached Africans of the diaspora but especially on their continent and spread as far as Kenya, Malawi, Rhodesia, and South Africa, especially through the work of the African Orthodox Church.

Garvey's appeal, however, rested on more than showmanship, appeals to vanity, or the desire for power. His calls for "pride of race . . . served to give meaning to [blacks'] lives and worth to their personalities."[23] A sense of self-respect and pride in blackness emanated from the UNIA. Garvey, in fact, became a black suprema-cist: The blacker the skin, the better the person; light-skinned blacks were scorned and ridiculed. He called for racial success and political achievement. He taught that the United States was a white country where blacks could never be happy or prosperous; his solution was to find an independent nation for blacks in Africa. His slogan was "Back to Africa!" and he proclaimed himself "Provisional President of Africa."

Although he was called the Black Moses, Garvey rejected most of black folk culture and music, calling for blacks to master European civilization instead. Success was to be measured solely by the criterion of white achievement, even though Garvey was a vociferous opponent of European colonialism. He even adopted the titles, degrees, and symbols of rewards and grandeur associated with Europe's royalty and achievements. Garvey essentially accepted the capitalist system. Though widely denounced as a radical, in fact he created a movement of the extreme right. His Negro Factories Corporation and his Black Star Line (an attempt to organize his own steamship company) were attempts to set up black-owned corporations so that blacks would not have to beg white men for jobs. He would have nothing to do with trade unionism; on the contrary, he believed that black workers should effectively compete on the labor market by keeping their wage demands a little below the white level. Neither would he have any truck with socialism or communism. He was equally critical of the educated black elite. According to Garvey, the National Association for the Advancement of Colored People (NAACP) was dominated by white socialists and their mulatto lackeys and failed to speak for the black masses. He also entertained strong prejudices against the Jews.

Garvey's role in history is ambivalent. Though the African Orthodox Church spread his influence to East and southern Africa, he failed to do for the blacks what Theodor Herzl had achieved for the Jews; he was unable to create a viable movement. Garveyism depended on the personal qualities of a single leader whose autocratic method, slipshod financial practices, and lack of administrative experience alienated many potential supporters. His Black Star Line did not succeed; neither did he get far in his attempt to form a small army corps, the African Legion. He had a striking sense for the showy and the dramatic; but he lacked the abilities of an apparatchik. At the height of his power, he was tried and convicted for fraud (1923), and he was finally deported to Jamaica from the United States in 1927. He died in London in 1940, almost unknown and forgotten.

Garvey and his UNIA never succeeded in sending a single black settler to Africa. Nevertheless, Garvey was an influential figure in Afro-American history in the twentieth century, and he deeply influenced nationalism in Africa. He had a profound commitment to black dignity. He believed that blacks had a splendid history and would yet create an equally splendid future. Garvey at his best was far removed from the brutal chauvinism of European Fascists. His notions, artlessly summarized in these moralizing verses, corresponded rather to those of early German romantics like Herder:

> Each race should be proud and stick to its own
> And the best of what they are should be shown;
> This is no shallow song of hate to sing,
> But over Blacks there should be no white king.

Every man on his own foothold should stand,
Claiming a nation and a fatherland!
White, Yellow, and Black should make their own laws,
And force no one-sided justice with flaws.[24]

The Philosophy and Opinions of Marcus Garvey was read by Africans across the continent. The prominent Gold Coast intellectual Casely Hayford considered that "the U.N.I.A. had done more than any other agency to bring to the notice of world opinion the disabilities of the African race."[25] Kwame Nkrumah has written how Garvey moved him: "I think that of all the literature I studied, the book that did more than any other to fire my enthusiasm was *The Philosophy and Opinions of Marcus Garvey*."[26] From the Gold Coast to Kenya to South Africa, people read Garvey's writings and his newspaper and discussed the activities of his movement. Nationalists and separatist church groups heard his message: "Be proud you are black." Not only were political leaders such as Nkrumah inspired by Garvey; his inspiration reached trade unionists such as Clements Kadalie of South Africa and religio-nationalist movements such as Kimbanguism in the Congo. As Garvey put it in a speech in London in 1928: "I am only the forerunner of an awakened Africa that shall never go back to sleep."[27] His influence was, however, strongest in West Africa, where nationalism derived support from conservatively minded African middle- and lower-middle-class groups who first of all aimed at advancement under British imperial tutelage and subsequently fought for independence. Having shaken off colonial rule, they preferred state capitalism to socialism, economic nationalism, and centrally planned development of the Communist variety.

Garvey, then, was essentially a propagandist and organizer. In five years, with few resources and opposed by racists in the United States and elsewhere, he made the world conscious of blacks and of Africa. Garvey was important in the struggle of black Americans for equality and justice. Contemporary Black Muslims in the United States and Rastafarians in Jamaica represent current forms of Garveyism, and African nationalism owes him a tremendous debt, as we have seen. His UNIA was both a fraternal body and an imperial federation of the world's blacks. It was the greatest Negro movement ever; it had more members enrolled throughout the world than all previous black organizations put together, according to Robert Hill, the editor of the Garvey papers.

Garvey prophetically foresaw an independent Africa; his movement, the UNIA, and his writings played a major job in instilling black nationalism among blacks not just in Africa but everywhere the diaspora took them.

Garvey's influence was later rivaled by that of William Edward Burghardt Du Bois. A mulatto of French, Dutch, and African ancestry, Du Bois derived from a distinguished and cultured colored family from Haiti, although his mother's people were poor New Englanders. He was born in 1868 in the small community of Great Barrington in western Massachusetts. Though later professing to speak for the black masses, Du Bois had few contacts with the ordinary working person, either black or white. He made himself a member of a small but self-conscious black elite, by gaining an excellent education, graduating first from Fisk University and later receiving a doctorate from Harvard. As we shall see shortly, Du Bois was one of the pioneers of Pan-Africanism. He also made an academic reputation for himself by empirical enquiries into the black condition; his work *The Philadelphia Negro: A Social Study* (1899) stands out as the first case study of a black community in the United States. Originally convinced that the social sciences could provide the knowledge required to solve the American "race problem," he subsequently placed his hope in militant agitation, and ultimately ended as a supporter of communism. He died in Ghana in 1963 at the age of ninety-five.

In 1905, Du Bois took the lead in forming the Niagara Movement, which made a special point of attacking the moderate position taken by Booker T. Washington. Du Bois also played a prominent part in the creation of the NAACP in 1909. Whereas Booker T. Washington had sought piecemeal reform, backed by blacks, Northern businessmen, and white leaders in the New South, the NAACP operated from a Northern power base; it heavily relied on the new black elite, and sought, not to mend racial injustice, but to end it. Du Bois's book *The Souls of Black Folk* (1903) showed some of the concern for the conditions of black people that Garvey was to display many years later. Du Bois's work in Paris in 1919 on African questions had deep significance for black nationalism in the United States, as well as for African nationalism within Africa.

The growth of black American self-consciousness and concern about black history affected African nationalism during this period. Earlier work by Blyden and his relations with American blacks had already helped to stimulate in the United States the black history movement and its search for the black past, its roots, and its achievements.[28] In 1915 Du Bois published *The Negro*, only one of many efforts being made in the United States at that time to make blacks aware of their African past.

Du Bois followed Blyden's lead, seeking through his writings to pursue in a different way the same goal as Garvey – "to bolster both Negro American and emergent African nationalist self-esteem."[29] Du Bois and Garvey had much in common: Both aimed at political and economic freedom for blacks; both believed that blacks should see "Beauty in Black"; both emphasized the role of economics. Du Bois for long looked to the development of a separate black "group economy" in the United States, centering on producer and consumer cooperatives, which would provide a weapon for fighting discrimination and poverty. Du Bois regarded Garvey as an unschooled demagogue, and Garvey reciprocated the dislike. Garvey saw himself as more closely allied to the philosophy of Washington – the success ethic, racial improvement, practical education – than to Du Bois's program of educating the "Talented Tenth." Garvey also attacked Du Bois over his Pan-African Congresses. But neither Du Bois nor Garvey grasped either the integrative power of American patriotism or the enormous potential of the American economy, its ability to expand and to provide vast new opportunities both to the expanding black middle class and the skilled black workers. Booker T. Washington did and organized the National Negro Business League accordingly.

Other prominent black American intellectuals between 1900 and 1920 were James Edward Bruce, James Weldon Johnson, and Carter G. Woodson. Bruce was a black journalist in New York who, with Arthur Schomburg, a Puerto Rican black, established in 1911 the Negro Society for Historical Research to study the African past. Many African intellectuals and professionals knew of Bruce's work. African members and officers in the society included Paramount Chief Lewanika of

Barotseland, Blyden of Liberia and Nigeria, and Casely Hayford of the Gold Coast. Schomburg built up a library of books written by blacks to show that the "Negro had a long and honorable past." (The library survives in the Schomburg Collection of the New York Public Library.) Interest in the black's past and pride of race were spread by the work of the society, and both black Americans and African nationalists began to take pride in their blackness. Bruce, Blyden, and others foreshadowed the concept of an "African personality" and of African culture,[30] as embodied later in what some called negritude.

During the same period, James Weldon Johnson's editorials in *New York Age*, which linked the black American's fight for civil rights with the 1914 war and African rights, exerted a strong influence. Johnson wrote a piece entitled "Africa at the Peace Table" in *Africa in the World Democracy,* a pamphlet that called for black self-determination in Africa and, by implication, for black self-determination in the United States as well. Johnson later became executive secretary of the NAACP.

Carter Woodson was a major force in the founding of the Association for the Study of Negro Life and History (ASNL) in 1915 and of its *Journal of Negro History* in 1916. His work was of great importance to African nationalists in their search for identity and dignity. All nationalist movements, of course, live by the myth of a glorious past, and Woodson helped to nurture for Negroes this sense of black historicity. A professional historian trained at the University of Chicago and Harvard University, Woodson devoted his life to studying the role of blacks in human history and to popularizing his own and other scholars' research. From 1915 to 1950 the *Journal of Negro History* was the only American scholarly periodical seriously devoted to African history and culture.[31] Long before most American scholars were concerned with Africa, the journal promoted objective writing about a broad range of African subjects.

Woodson's reviews, essays, and notes aimed to show that blacks had a history, that they were not an inferior people, and that Africa had its heroes and kingdoms and cultural achievements. The major African themes covered by the *Journal of Negro History* were African culture and history, African relations with the New World and Europe through the slave trade and commerce, American migrations to Africa, Liberian history and affairs, colonial policies, and the impact of colonialism on African societies.[32] The NAACP journal, the *Crisis,* also traced African history and colonial rule. Thanks to the two journals, important articles on Africa and its peoples and their cultures served to inform and to influence generations of Afro-Americans about their African heritage. Woodson also helped to popularize the study of black history – perhaps more than anyone else – through his annual Negro History Week programs, started in 1926.

The birth of Pan-Africanism

During the later part of the 1920s, black American interest in Africa declined. The Garvey movement had failed; problems of unemployment, made infinitely worse by the worldwide Great Depression, affected American blacks to an infinitely greater extent than did questions concerned with Africa, as remote and unknown a continent for black Americans as for white. But institutionalized contacts between

Africa and America did not diminish. European missionaries and colonial officials continued to visit Southern black schools such as Hampton and Tuskegee to learn how to teach Africans industrial and agricultural skills. African students, including future leaders, came in greater numbers to study in the United States, most of them attending black schools. Kwame Nkrumah, for instance, went to Lincoln University; Hastings Banda to Meharry College; and A. B. Xuma to Tuskegee Institute, the University of Minnesota, and the University of Chicago. Nnamdi Azikiwe studied at Storer College, Lincoln University, and Howard University; Leo Hansberry of Howard, he once said, first introduced him to the history of Africa. During the late 1920s Azikiwe also became acquainted with Alain Locke, the first black Rhodes Scholar, later professor of philosophy at Howard, and editor of a then most influential anthology entitled *The New Negro* (1925). Locke was one of the early leaders of the black protest movement in the United States; Azikiwe learned a great deal from him, and became convinced that the problems of America were also those of the world at large. Azikiwe, like many other African expatriates resident in the United States at the time, concluded that the position of the black American in many ways resembled that of Africans under colonial rule.

But nevertheless America, to many Africans, also seemed a land of promise. In Zambia, during the aftermath of World War I, some militant African preachers were fond of telling their flocks that the British were only in what was then Northern Rhodesia by American sufferance, that all British aircraft were manufactured in the United States, or that an army of black Americans would come to redeem the people from British governance. As we have seen, during his visits to Africa in the 1920s for the Phelps Stokes Commission, the American-trained J. E. Kwegyir Aggrey was regarded by some Africans as the member of a black American advance guard preparing a black American invasion to crush imperialism.

Black missionaries from orthodox and separatist churches continued to play their part in awakening African self-consciousness. And America, as the jazz and sports center of the world where black men played, fought, and won prominence, served to make Africans aware of the achievements of men of color and enabled them to dream of better days. By knowing of such men as Du Bois, Washington, Bruce, Woodson, Padmore, and Garvey, blacks in the United States and Africa could feel more pride in being black. Afro-Americans became more conscious of Africa's past as they learned of the Sudanic kingdoms and of the quality of the continent's arts and crafts. As George Shepperson pointed out: "Negro Americans, in a complicated Atlantic triangle of influences, have played a considerable part ideologically in the emergence of African nationalism: in conceptualization, evocation of attitudes, and through the provision of the raw material of history."[33] Black expatriates from Africa and the New World went on to meet freely in the metropolitan capitals of London, Paris, and Brussels, as well as in North America. The intellectual diaspora became a fountainhead of ideas and of political agitation — with far-reaching effects for the future of the African continent and of blacks in the United States.

Pan-Africanism: the beginnings. The prefix "pan" is defined as "the entirety of a diversified group," and the "pan concept" as the idea that all of the different and diverse peoples of a particular ethnic or cultural group have qualities in common that set them apart from other peoples of the world, and that the common heritage of a particular group is so important that it transcends all other considerations, religious, economic, political, or indeed cultural. The concept includes, along with the essential unity of an ethnic group, the usually unspoken corollary that a self-conscious group is in some way superior to other groups.

With the growth of nationalistic feeling throughout the European world in the nineteenth century, the pan concept became the psychological or spiritual foundation for an imperialism which demanded that all of the peoples of a common ethnic stock must, both of right and of necessity, be united under a common rule. Thus the concept, in the forms of Pan-Germanism and Pan-Slavism, became the foundation for aggression and international skulduggery on a large scale: All Germans must be united in one Reich; all Slavs, regardless of other factors, must be joined together under the reign of the Romanoff czars. With the emergence of Africa from a nearly universal state of colonial dependence to independence in the mid-twentieth century, the ideals of Pan-Africanism or of a United States of Africa suddenly made their impact upon the world.

The ideology of Pan-Africanism, which is not of recent origin, has changed several times during the twentieth century. It is therefore difficult to define the term precisely. The American social anthropologist St. Clair Drake defines the Pan-Africanism that arose in North America under Du Bois and Garvey as

> independent activity on the part of Negro Americans designed to establish relations with Africans and people of African descent everywhere for the development of trade between dispersed groups of Negroes, for cooperation in the fight against color discrimination, for protesting against the derogation of the Negro race and for participation by Negroes returning to Africa in the nation-building process on that continent.[34]

Pan-Africanism, then, was a response of blacks to their subordinate position in society and to the charge that they were an inferior race biologically, with no history or culture.[35]

The responses to this assumption of inferiority were varied. Men such as Booker T. Washington said that the difference between the races was not biological but cultural. This view led to a stress on education and self-improvement so that blacks might acquire higher skills. Leaders such as Marcus Garvey – and before him, the American Colonization Society – called for the segregation of the races and the establishment by blacks of separate communities, preferably in Africa. Other blacks responded to the charge of inferiority by pointing to the cultural contributions made by blacks to humankind and by fighting for black rights. The formation of black history societies, the writings of Bruce, Du Bois, and Woodson, all sought to disprove the racist notion of black inferiority. Du Bois, moreover, took on the additional role of organizing blacks politically to protest and pressure for equal rights in a Pan-African movement aimed at improving the conditions of black men everywhere.

Political organization. Pan-Africanism as an organized movement really began around 1900. Black intellectuals in the United States, Africa, and the West Indies became more militant in their demands for equal rights. They defended the independence of the black states of Liberia, Ethiopia, and Haiti, and they called for more political rights for Africans in the colonies. They spoke out on black history, its achievements and its glories. They demanded equality as a natural right. "The fight for the rights of Negroes in North America, the fight for the rights of Africans in Africa, the revival of Negro interest in African history all began to blend. One of the first fruits of this blending was "pan-Africanism.' "[36]

The first Pan-African conference, called together by Henry Sylvester-Williams, a West Indian lawyer, was held in London in 1900. The chairman and the secretary of the conference were Americans: Alexander Walters, bishop of the AMEZ Church, and Du Bois. The delegates were mostly blacks from the New World, with a sprinkling of Africans and whites living in London. According to Walters, the conference had three objectives:

> First, to bring into closer touch . . . peoples of African descent . . . ; second, to inaugurate plans to bring about a more friendly relation between the Caucasian and African races; third, to start a movement looking forward to the securing to all African races living in civilized countries their full rights and to promote their business interests.[37]

The theme of the conference and the emphasis of Pan-Africanism for the next four decades was racial equality. It was in London that Du Bois made his prophetic statement "The problem of the twentieth century is the problem of the color line." Almost as an afterthought, the London group expressed its concern to Joseph Chamberlain, British minister of colonies, for the interests and welfare of the peoples in South and West Africa. Pan-Africanism thus was to remain until 1945 primarily a protest movement against racial inequality and essentially a black American reaction to racism. This London conference of 1900 is significant for two reasons: It was the first attempt by blacks to establish racial unity, and it marked the debut of the man who would be the main leader of Pan-Africanism for the next forty-five years, W. E. B. Du Bois, who at this time made his first published suggestion of "a great central Negro State of the world."[38]

During his early years Du Bois had "almost no experience of segregation or color discrimination."[39] But travel and education at Fisk University in Tennessee and Harvard College made him acutely aware of color bars and discrimination against blacks. His feelings of personal injury led to a militantly hostile attitude toward certain aspects of white society, and out of this awareness of white racism, black inequality, and intellectual dependence developed his mission to teach and to reconcile the two groups. This was to be his lifework, first as a teacher and scholar, later as a journalist and activist.

For a number of years after the conference of 1900, all thoughts about Pan-Africanism lay dormant in Du Bois's mind, although Sylvester-Williams kept the movement alive. Du Bois's ideas were crystallizing during this period, and his polemics on the subject of racial discrimination were bringing him into national prominence as spokesman for the more radical blacks. He joined with a group of white liberals and black intellectuals interested in improving conditions for blacks, and in 1909 they formed the National Association for the Advancement of Colored People (NAACP). The purpose of the NAACP and its magazine, the

Crisis, started in 1910, was to fight for black equality in the United States and elsewhere.[40]

The *Crisis* dealt in a more popular and more polemical way than did the *Journal of Negro History* with events in Africa and with the lives of ordinary Africans under colonial domination. Du Bois was the semi-independent editor of the magazine from 1910 to 1932, and he brought to it his interest in black rights and African history. He brought also his critical mind, along with a style that made the journal a leading publication promoting black rights around the world and protesting against injustice and discrimination. To make blacks proud of their race, Du Bois felt that he had to change their misconceptions of Africa as a land of savages and darkness. The NAACP supported his work in African history as well as his interest in the various Pan-African conferences that he would organize in 1919, 1921, 1923, and 1927. He was sent by the NAACP to Paris in 1919 to take part in the Versailles Peace Conference, and to the First Pan-African Congress in order to fight for black rights, especially in Africa.

The pages of the *Crisis* were filled with the news of the various Pan-African conferences, ranging from summaries of speeches to full texts of resolutions and manifestos. The journal also covered African history and aspects of tribal life, and attacked colonialism's methods and abuses – both real and alleged. There were editorials, pictures, and profiles of African leaders and reports on forced labor, on pass laws, and on hut taxes. The readers of the *Crisis* were probably the best-informed people in the United States on the subject of Africa.

> Between 1911 and 1945 *The Crisis* probably printed more about Africa and Africans than all the other general magazines put together. It was *The Crisis* that pioneered in the publishing of pictures of noted Africans and Africans in the daily round of their lives. . . . It was, however, the department of the magazine called "The Horizon" which was actually a news section that printed more information about Africa than all the other American magazines put together.[41]

In 1911 Du Bois made his second trip to London in order to attend the First Universal Races Congress, a convocation of representatives of all the races of humankind. He found the atmosphere particularly stimulating. To him, it was inspiring to hear the world's foremost anthropologists state categorically that the traditional superiority of one race over another was pure myth, that in the last analysis there was no such thing as race – all mankind was one. He met, on terms of social and intellectual equality, people of different nations and colors, all of whom were opposed to the customary assumptions upon which white supremacy was ideologically based. And he shared the optimism of other members of the congress that their resolutions were epoch-making and were the beginning of a new era.[42] The 1911 congress was not especially concerned with Pan-Africanism; in fact, the basic idea that lay behind the congress was opposed to such an ideal. Nevertheless, the congress definitely stimulated the latent movement by insisting on the equality of all races.

The events of August 1914 dispelled any possibility of black or African unity in the near future. During the war, as Du Bois became increasingly bitter toward whites – who, he thought, oppressed and exploited blacks – his eyes turned more toward Africa, the homeland of his race. In May 1915 he published a major piece in the *Atlantic Monthly* entitled "The African Roots of the War," which predated Lenin's famous explanation that colonial rivalry led to political tensions and caused the war.

At the same time, he began to think of Africa as the place where a great black state could readjust humanity's balance and enable blacks to assume their rightful place in the world:

> Africa is today held by Negro troops trained under European white officers. These Negro troops have saved France. They have conquered German Africa. They and their American Negro brothers are helping to save Belgium. It would be the least that Europe could do in return and some faint reparation for the terrible world history between 1441 and 1861 to see that a great free Central African state is erected out of German East Africa and the Belgian Congo. Surely after Belgium has suffered almost as much from Germany as Africa has suffered from her, she ought to be willing to give up the Congo to this end; and it would be right that England should refrain from taking German East Africa as well as refrain from handing it back. Out of this state we could make a great modern effort to restore the ancient efficiency of the land that gave the iron age to all the world, and that for ages led in agriculture, weaving, metal working, and the traffic of the market place.[43]

The powers, however, took no more note of black American than of Armenian or Kurdish aspirations. In the Versailles Peace Conference, Africa figured only in a marginal capacity. The former German territories were divided among Great Britain, France, Belgium, South Africa, Australia, and New Zealand – all under the guise of the new mandate system. President Woodrow Wilson believed in self-determination for the former subjects of the Hohenzollern and Habsburg monarchies in Europe; he had no wish, however, to engage in an anticolonial crusade or to alienate his allies. The United States declined to accept responsibility for any of the mandated territories. By its failure to ratify the Versailles treaty and to join the League of Nations, the United States deprived itself of any influence over governance of the mandates. According to American policy makers, the American national interest in Africa was confined to maintaining the Open Door, to making sure that American traders, investors, and missionaries would have free access to the continent on a nondiscriminatory basis.

Du Bois hastened to Paris in 1919 as correspondent for the *Crisis,* with the intention of participating in the peace talks and organizing and directing a Pan-African congress. With the help of an African member of the French Chamber of Deputies, Blaise Diagne (from Senegal), he obtained Clemenceau's consent, and in February 1919 the First Pan-African Congress convened in Paris. It was to carry more influence than the 1900 gathering in London. Dominated by Du Bois and composed almost entirely of well-educated blacks from the Americas, it claimed to speak for blacks of the whole world. Du Bois wanted rule by an international body for the development of the African peoples, rather than administration of the former German colonies by other colonial powers. Drawing their inspiration from the liberal and reformist thought of the time, the delegates advocated trusteeship principles in terms not very different from those of enlightened colonial administrators. The congress insisted that the colonial powers in Africa should safeguard African rights against loss of land, forced labor, exploitation, and sundry other abuses. The colonial powers should be more concerned, it argued, with the welfare of the colonized peoples and should promote more education and give the indigenous population a share in local and tribal government.

With the optimism and belief in the importance of his cause that often characterizes the idealist, Du Bois felt at the time that the congress had accomplished world-shaking results. (Later, he made a more realistic appraisal in his autobiography.) Actually, the statesmen and politicians assembled in Paris to make a peace treaty (and to divide the spoils of war) were not unaware of the congress, but they had no intention of establishing a new and independent African state, as Du Bois requested. The influence of Du Bois and of Diagne, however, may have carried some weight with the Paris Peace Conference in establishing the mandates system. At any rate, Du Bois believed this to be the case: "The Congress specifically asked that the German colonies be turned over to an international organization instead of being handled by the various colonial powers. Out of this idea came the Mandates Commission."[44]

The congress of 1919 was the first of a series, in all of which Du Bois was the driving force. Another was held in 1921, with its first sessions in London and subsequent meetings in Brussels and in Paris.[45] At Brussels, according to his own statement, Du Bois caused consternation by introducing resolutions that had already been adopted by the sessions held in London:

> Diagne, the Senegalese Frenchman who presided, was beside himself with excitement after the resolutions were read . . . His French was almost too swift for my ears, but his meaning was clear: he felt that the cause of the black man in Belgium and France had been compromised by black American radicals; he especially denounced our demand for "the restoration of the ancient common ownership of the land in Africa" as rank communism.[46]

The portion of the resolutions that stirred up the hornet's nest in Belgium and France was a paragraph that illustrates how Du Bois intermixed race issues with Marxist ideology in a manner similar to Lenin's analysis:

> If we are coming to recognize that the great modern problem is to correct maladjustment in the distribution of wealth, it must be remembered that the basic maladjustment is in the outrageously unjust distribution of world income between the dominant and suppressed peoples; in the rape of land and raw material; the monopoly of technique and culture. And in this crime white labor is *particeps criminis* with white capital. Unconsciously and consciously, carelessly and deliberately, the vast power of the white labor vote in modern democracies has been cajoled and flattered into imperialistic schemes to enslave and debauch black, brown and yellow labor, until with fatal retribution, they are themselves today bound and gagged and rendered impotent by the resulting monopoly of the world's raw material in the hands of a dominant, cruel and irresponsible few.[47]

The third congress was held in London and Lisbon in 1923, and the fourth in New York in 1927; no more were convened until after World War II. At all of these conferences, American and West Indian delegates were in the majority. Though few Africans were present, it is certain that they were influenced by the proceedings. Yet Du Bois's Pan-African dream appealed mainly to the small black intellectual group and to the middle class rather than to the average black. The movement remained basically a reform movement and limited itself to appeals for black rights; but even this aspect made it appear dangerous to whites and to colonial authorities.

During the 1920s, as we have seen, Du Bois encountered a rival in Marcus Garvey's back-to-Africa movement and found that its parades, its uniforms, and its appeal to race moved the masses in a way he never could. Recognizing the danger to Pan-Africanism from Garvey and his black racism, Du Bois fought the Garvey-ites bitterly. The danger passed not when Garvey was discredited and imprisoned in 1923, but when he was deported in 1927; then his organization fell apart. But Pan-Africanism still failed to attract black Americans in any numbers. There were too many problems at home to worry about African rights in the colonies, and the linkage between African rights and black American rights was too nebulous for most to see. The increased flight of blacks north to the cities, followed by the depression and unemployment, further weakened black interest in Africa. Communist propagandists who became vocal and influential during the 1930s spoke in terms of race, class, and capitalist exploitation, not of a back-to-Africa movement or Pan-Africanism.[48] After 1927 Du Bois had hoped to organize yet another Pan-African congress, to be held this time on African soil, but the depression killed his chances for financial support and put a damper on the movement until the end of World War II. The NAACP concentrated on black rights within the United States, giving but scanty support to the Pan-African congresses. The Communists dismissed the Pan-Africanists as petty bourgeois nationalists, and Pan-Africanism drifted into the doldrums.

Booker T. Washington, Tuskegee, and Africa

Scholars such as Blyden and Du Bois made major contributions to the newfound sense of black pride. But the most influential black in the United States during the last two decades of the nineteenth and the first ten years of the twentieth century was Booker T. Washington (ca. 1859–1915). Washington was an unusual man. Whereas the bulk of the nineteenth- and early twentieth-century black leaders in the United States had descended from the middle class, the ranks of antebellum "free persons of color" and their descendants, Washington had been born a slave. Washington made his name as an outstanding black American educator during the two decades preceding and the decade following World War I. He turned Tuskegee Normal and Industrial Institute from a small, ill-funded school in the backwoods of Alabama into a major center of vocational education and teacher training. The institute came to provide instruction for blacks in a variety of crafts, nursing, agriculture, and commercial subjects. Washington also wished to promote black entrepreneurship and in 1900 organized the National Negro Business League for the purpose. He was convinced that there could be no black advancement without white goodwill; he believed that education, especially vocational instruction, had to take precedence over the struggle for civil rights, that moderation would work better than militance. He regarded himself first and foremost as an American; hence he would have nothing to do with projects designed to return blacks to Africa.

Time has not dealt kindly with Washington's reputation; to radicals of a later era he became the very prototype of an "Uncle Tom." Even the titles of most of his many books—*Sowing and Reaping* (1900), *Character Building* (1902), *Working with the Hands* (1904), and others—now have an archaic air reminiscent of the Victorian era. But Washington in no wise betrayed his principles. Unlike his latter-day censors, he had actually risen from the ranks of the unskilled black workers, and he understood them much better than the middle-class intellectuals who so often came to snigger at his name. He tried to make the best of conditions as he found them, not as they might exist in the future.

The emancipation of the American slaves, including the young Washington himself, and the emancipation of the Russian serfs had occurred at about the same time; the two acts of general manumission had many features in common, a fact obvious to contemporaries. But whereas the czarist autocracy had made some provision to furnish the liberated slaves with land, American democracy had made no similar concession. Emancipation had left the greater part of black Americans landless laborers without specialized industrial or agricultural skills and without much formal education. Washington felt convinced that no amount of political agitation would succeed unless American blacks could improve their occupational and educational status. He emphasized practical work, not to keep the blacks in their place, but to further their advancement. He ran Tuskegee in a spirit similar to that of many other white training institutions of the time, characteristically American in their stress on useful arts, self-reliance, and hostility to aristocracy, slavery, and rum.

Washington had but limited success. He encountered bitter opposition from highly placed politicians like William Howard Taft; even President Wilson, for all his liberal rhetoric, endorsed racial segregation in government offices. Institutionalized racism proved too powerful to overcome, except in a partial fashion. Nevertheless, Washington's work had considerable influence, not only in the United States, but also in colonial Africa (for example, he influenced James Aggrey of Achimota College in the Gold Coast, now Ghana, and John L. Dube of the Ohlange Institute in Natal in important ways). Many English-speaking reformers became certain that his work in America could be adapted to what they regarded as the needs of Africa: the task of turning subsistence cultivators into skilled wage workers, entrepreneurs, and farmers producing crops for the market. Washington's concepts of self-help and practical educational training also had a marked impact on moderate African nationalists of his era and on educators of all political persuasions. His interests in Africa were far-reaching; he was determined to encourage black American missionaries, teachers, and businesspeople to seek opportunities in Africa, rather than to confine their interests to American soil. Insofar as their aspirations for black advancement were concerned, Washington and Du Bois had indeed more in common than Washington's critics realized.

After his death in 1915, Tuskegee and other black schools in the South carried forward his ideas and his practices. His autobiography, *Up from Slavery*, which became a best seller, was translated not only into European languages but also into Zulu. His accomplishments as an educator at Tuskegee Institute earned him the admiration of Americans, Europeans, and Africans, and his opinions were highly respected. Under his direction, Tuskegee Institute became world renowned as a practical training school in which young blacks were prepared to compete in a world dominated by whites. The institute became famous for successfully promoting the most practical techniques of scientific agriculture.

As was to be expected, because of his hopes for the advancement of the black race, Washington held a deep personal interest in Africa and the Africans. His attitude toward the various movements that were current during his lifetime is of particular significance. Strangely enough, he looked upon such movements and on the men who organized and sponsored them with the eye of a detached outsider. It seems clear that he viewed Africa exactly as did most white men at the time – as an uncivilized wilderness continent peopled by men who were culturally retarded. Although he was black, Washington never regarded himself or other black Americans as Africans. He corresponded with some of the leaders of African nationalism, yet he probably never understood – and certainly never encouraged – the attitude of the more militant nationalists and Pan-Africanists.[49]

Washington nonetheless had a considerable degree of influence upon African thought and upon events in Africa because of his prominence and because of the respect accorded him. His success in developing black artisans and technicians at Tuskegee may have influenced the officials and labor leaders of South Africa in a negative way when they adopted measures to exclude Africans from the skilled trades: Washington had strongly recommended industrial training for the Africans of the Union of South Africa, but the whites of that country wanted no competition from a future skilled, educated, black working force that greatly outnumbered them. The Tuskegee approach (or the Hampton–Tuskegee approach) emphasized practical education, training in Christian ethics, and accommodative race relations – that is, an acceptance by blacks of an inferior social position in order that they might be permitted to seek opportunities in technical and agricultural education. Because Washington's work had been so successful in the American South, its supporters, and even colonial authorities, felt that it could be useful in Africa as well.

With the formation of the Congo Free State in 1885, Washington and other black intellectuals had become greatly interested in Africa. In 1895 African affairs were discussed at a congress on Africa that was held at Gammon Theological Seminary in Atlanta concurrently with the exposition where Washington made his famous "Atlanta Compromise" speech. Support for missionaries was stressed, and the possibilities of emigration were considered (this meeting might even be called the "First Pan-African Congress").[50] Washington was not involved in the Gammon conference, but following the wide publicity given to cruelties and maladministration in the Congo Free State under Leopold II, he became prominent in agitating for reforms in the Congo. Washington, in fact, through his sponsorship of the Congo Reform Association and his acceptance of its vice-presidency, and also through his many lectures and articles, probably exerted as much influence as any other single person in swinging a large segment of American opinion to the reform side. How seriously the opposition regarded his contributions may be seen in the correspondence that passed from Leopold's chief propagandist in the United States to his royal employer.[51]

Washington was also naturally interested in the tribulations that beset Afro-Americans in Liberia. In the summer of 1908, when the Liberian commission to seek American help arrived in the United States, he served as its host. His friendship with President Theodore Roosevelt enabled him to guide the members through the labyrinths of the capital. Washington was intended to be a member of the American Commission sent to Liberia to study the country's problems, but President Taft, the new incumbent in the White House, was unwilling to name him, intending instead to keep him close enough to serve as the principal advisor on problems of the blacks. Emmet J. Scott, Washington's private secretary, ultimately became the black member of the commission.[52]

In 1910 Washington visited England and discussed African problems with local experts. And in 1912 he held at Tuskegee a large international conference on the Negro. Addressing this conference, Washington outlined his views on the role of black Americans in Africa: They should be teachers and technical assistance experts; black colleges should train able African students. On this occasion as on many previous ones, few Africans attended the meeting; but delegates from eighteen foreign countries and thirty-seven religious groups were there. Pan-Africanism, the missionary movements, and black education were among the topics discussed. High hopes were held out for interracial cooperation and the educational development of Africa by black Americans. World War I and the death of Washington in 1915 temporarily reduced Tuskegee's influence, and the opposition to black American educators and missionaries in Africa limited their opportunities between World Wars I and II, especially in East Africa. But an important direct impact had already been made.

Although it is difficult to evaluate Washington's influence in Africa, there can be no question that Tuskegee made a significant contribution. Washington's social philosophy and his ideas on education for blacks unquestionably influenced African intellectual leaders and colonial officials. The colonial administrator preferred the Tuskegee type of educated black to the supposedly more radical followers of Du Bois or Garvey. The example provided by Tuskegee Institute was followed more or less closely by numerous educational institutions established in Africa, including the Zulu Christian Industrial School of Natal, the South African Native College at Fort Hare, Cape of Good Hope, the Lumbwa Industrial Mission of Kenya, the Mittel und Gehilfen Schule of German East Africa (Tanganyika), Achimota College in the Gold Coast, and several others.

Washington and Tuskegee had a more direct impact upon Africa, however. Although the statesmen and politicians of Europe scrambled for African territories for the sake of national prestige and the glory of being known as empire builders, once they occupied the territories they wanted to make them productive. And in accordance with the universally accepted beliefs of the age, it was taken for granted that if the Africans could be persuaded or trained in the ways of industry and agriculture, they would soon become "civilized." If they could be educated to produce for export, they would soon commence wearing European or Western clothes voluntarily and, wanting European manufactured goods, would have to buy these goods from Europe.

This belief led directly to Tuskegee's first recorded overseas venture. In the late 1890s the German Kolonial-Wirtschaftliches Komitee (KWK), an organization of colonial-minded German businessmen, officials, and other persons dissatisfied with the small returns Germany had so far realized from its new colonial empire, conceived the idea that some of the colonies were probably suitable for the production of cotton. The small colony of Togoland (now called Togo) on the Gulf of Guinea seemed the most promising. If the culture of cotton could be introduced there as well as in other colonies, the manufacturers of Germany would be freed of their dependence upon the United States and Egypt for an essential raw material. The colony then would become self-supporting and would be an asset to Germany instead of an economic liability. However, Germany had no experience in cotton cultivation. It was logical, then, that the KWK should seek information, advice, and assistance from the foremost cotton-producing country of the world and from the black institution that was well known as a place where practical cotton farmers were trained in large numbers – Tuskegee.

After some correspondence between Washington and the German ambassador to the United States (correspondence in which the State Department and the Department of Agriculture were interested), a committee from the KWK was invited to Tuskegee to observe the institute's methods and to engage a small team of expert black cotton farmers. Four young men, recent graduates of Tuskegee, were hired. Apparently at Washington's insistence, James Nathan Calloway, a member of the faculty and a graduate of Fisk University who was familiar with the German language, was also engaged to head the group. They sailed from New York in November 1900, arriving at Togoland on New Year's Eve after what Calloway described as a very pleasant voyage down the West African coast.[53] They were fascinated with their first glimpses of Africa, but there is no indication of any sense of relationship to the Africans whom they saw at the various ports where their ship touched. The Africans were "natives," exotic peoples of an exotic country, peoples of an unrelated culture and outlook; the men from Tuskegee were Americans.

Put ashore with their effects and their equipment on New Year's Eve, they found that there were no roads, nothing but trails and footpaths. To reach the place where their experiment was to be conducted, they had to walk. The equipment – plows, a cotton gin and press, and a wagon that they had constructed themselves in the shops at Tuskegee – had to be carried by manpower to the interior. Not only were there no roads in the country, but no draft or pack animals were available. They took only what could be carried in the customary headloads of African porters and set out for Missahöhe, their interior destination, a hundred miles distant. Once arrived, however, they found that preparations had been made for them with proverbial German thoroughness, and they suffered few hardships and faced no dangers; they looked upon their march almost as a pleasant outing, in fact, and they set to work with a will. Grass huts were built for temporary shelter. Aided by numbers of Togolese provided by the German authorities, the Americans attacked the trees and elephant grass and planted their first crop. In May 1901, five months after their arrival, S. L. Harris, one of the group, wrote to Washington that they had cleared over a hundred acres of elephant grass and thicket and had planted "cotton, corn, peanuts and other things as well."[54]

But in spite of the support of the German colonial authorities, the sailing was not all clear. Locusts, ants, and chiggers added to the normal difficulties and discomforts. The farmers found, too, that the local Africans were not at all interested in improving their cotton. Cotton, to them, was distinctly a secondary crop, they wanted only the small amount necessary for their immediate needs. Their main farming interest was in food crops, and cotton was judged a waste of time and field space. In the beginning, moreover, they regarded these strange black Americans with deep suspicion. The Togolese felt no more sense of kinship with the Americans than the Americans reciprocated: They were foreigners, strangers, or "white men with dark skins," and as such they were not to be trusted too far. The Africans at first refused to accept the cotton seeds that the Americans offered them, fearing that "if they should accept our seeds we would come again and claim our own with usury."[55]

The Americans found the Togolese so confirmed in the ways of their ancestors (as had other agricultural missionaries) that it took time to accustom them to the implements of Western agriculture.[56] Never having seen a wagon, the Africans were so amazed when the Americans finally assembled the one they had brought from Tuskegee that, as soon as the Americans' attention was diverted, they carefully took the vehicle apart. They were prepared to carry the parts on their heads instead of hauling the wagon along the ground. Such naïveté, however, was purely temporary, for Robinson informed Washington later that the Togolese had come to take it "as a hardship if they are asked to carry anything."[57] And in addition to the difficulties arising from human relationships, it was found impossible to maintain draft animals: The tsetse fly killed them before they could be broken to harness.

Nevertheless, in spite of handicaps and in spite of several deaths from the old African fever, Tuskegee's first overseas agricultural mission struggled on. It soon turned out that American cotton was not adapted to the soil and climate of Togoland; American seed produced a luxuriant tropical plant with almost no usable fiber. So the Tuskegee men, being practical farmers and teachers of agriculture, became botanists and agronomists as well; their cross-pollination finally resulted in a hybrid that did produce usable fiber.

Once the young black Americans were established, they erected comfortable living quarters for themselves and furnished them in the American manner. The local Africans, seeing the American-style houses, liked what they saw, and it was not long until the Togolese, at least in the immediate vicinity of "Tuskegee in Africa," were building American houses for themselves.[58] But personal example was only one result of their influence upon the conditions in Togoland. From their initial crop of only twenty-five bales, they managed within a very few years to convince the German colonial authorities that cotton would become an important feature of Togoland's economy.

Members of the group returned to America (others of them had died), until John W. Robinson was the only Tuskegean remaining. To make a success of his mission became almost an obsession with him. In 1904 he wrote to Washington, "It has become the main object of my life to do most successfully that so-called simple thing 'Grow Cotton.' "[59] He returned to the United States briefly, married, and took his bride – also a Tuskegee graduate – to Africa. In 1905 the experimental farm, with a hundred students drawn from all parts of the colony, became an agricultural school devoted to teaching the culture of cotton. The following year the student body was increased to two hundred, with Robinson himself virtually the entire faculty. In 1907 he wrote to Washington that he began work at 5:30

a.m. daily, showing the boys how to harness the oxen, how to fire the engine, "how to build a straight wall on a house, how to hold a plow to run a straight furrow"; then he went to his office for a full day's work. He planned all the buildings and supervised their construction. He was hired as agent for the German government in purchasing cotton from Togolese farmers who had overcome some of their early inhibitions. He bought and trained animals for the farm and school. He experimented with various fertilizers and wrote reports of all his activities. On top of such duties, he had to keep the school's books in order and to account to the German authorities for his receipts and expenditures.[60] By 1908, worn out by ceaseless work, his health undermined by the climate and, no doubt, by bouts with malaria (although he never alluded to this), Robinson decided to resign in two years and return to the United States. Before he could do so, however, he was drowned when his canoe collapsed in a swift river.[61]

It is impossible to evaluate precisely the effect of Tuskegee in Africa upon subsequent developments in Togoland. The quick seizure of the colony by the French and British in 1914 disrupted all German establishments, and division of the country into two separate mandates produced a state of historical confusion. Records either have been lost or have not been made accessible in Lomé or Potsdam. Some facts, however, are certain. Cotton production at seven stations in Togoland increased from 129,797 kilograms in 1904–5 to 530,763 kilograms in 1910–11 – a sizable crop. German manufacturers began to make gins and presses for the colonial market and to supply power for gins and presses in Togoland. No fewer than ten power stations were constructed.[62]

Although the agricultural school founded by Robinson did not survive World War I, it did have a permanent effect. The successful introduction of cotton culture was important in improving Togoland's economic position, and cotton has since become a major crop in the country.[63]

The Tuskegee cotton mission to Togoland was the first – and probably the most significant – instance in which Tuskegee Institute and Booker T. Washington exercised a direct influence upon Africa, but Tuskegee graduates and students were instrumental in introducing cotton culture into other parts of Africa. In 1903 Leigh S. J. Hunt, a former president of the State Agricultural College of Idaho who had abandoned teaching and become wealthy in business, visited the Sudan. Impressed with the agricultural potential of the region, he discussed with the British governor-general, Sir Reginald Wingate, the possibilities of establishing plantations on which skilled blacks from the United States would act as technical demonstrators and instructors for the Sudanese. By 1906–7 the project was well under way, and Hunt brought three Tuskegeans – a carpenter, a blacksmith, and an agriculturist – to assist. Beyond this bare fact, information is lacking, but it is sufficient to note that the three men from Tuskegee were in at the birth of one of the world's foremost cotton-growing enterprises.[64] Tuskegeans were employed also to introduce cotton culture in Nigeria and the Belgian Congo.

Tuskegee was not an old institution in the early twentieth century but its substantial contributions to raising the economic, moral, and intellectual status of people depressed by generations of slavery were already world famous. And since Tuskegee was an educational institution exclusively for people of African descent, it was natural that it attracted – as it still does – numbers of students from African countries. In 1907 Washington noted that a young Zulu former student of Tuskegee Institute had won oratorical honors at Columbia University.[65] In the same year a young African from Cape Colony graduated from the Phelps Hall Bible Training School (a part of the institute), and in 1916 A. B. Xuma from the Transvaal received his high school diploma at Tuskegee. Until 1917 the number of African students entered at Tuskegee grew slowly. During the interwar years, from 1919 to 1939, the number remained almost constant, but a few students began to come from the countries of East Africa, a region previously unrepresented in the student body. As could be expected, the number of African students attending Tuskegee, as well as all other American colleges and universities, declined drastically during World War II. Immediately after the war, however, the numbers began to climb sharply until, for example, the enrollment for 1964–5 included eighty-six Africans from ten countries.[66]

The ideals of practical education, Christian ethics, and racial accommodation represented by the Hampton–Tuskegee approach were carried forward by the Phelps-Stokes Fund, founded in 1911 with the aim of educating Negroes, both in Africa and the United States.[67] In the 1920s, as we have seen, it sent the American specialist on black education Thomas Jesse Jones and J. Kwegyir Aggrey to Africa to study means of providing education for Africans. The Jeanes Schools experiment in mass literacy was one of its programs, and as a tribute the fund established the Booker T. Washington Institute in Liberia. African students in increasing numbers were brought to the United States before and after World War II by the fund, as were colonial officials and missionaries, to learn about the Hampton–Tuskegee approach to practical education for blacks.[68]

Missionary and philanthropic groups believed "that the experience of Negro educational institutions in the Southern States was directly relevant and transferable to educational and political development in Africa."[69] While Du Bois preached one variety of Pan-Africanism, an English missionary, J. H. Oldham, and Thomas Jesse Jones stressed a missionary brand. All were united on the goal of developing links between blacks in Africa and the United States, but they differed on the means to be employed. Jones and Oldham feared that Du Bois's politics would impede their efforts to improve Africa by transferring techniques developed to educate blacks in the American South.[70] Colonial officials, in reaction, might let no blacks in.

Those who controlled missions and education in Africa, then, favored the Hampton–Tuskegee approach to education – that is, an agricultural and industrial training program that produced in the American South artisans and teachers who did not challenge white supremacy. Visitors to the South from British Africa spread the schools' fame and methods.[71] The World Missionary Conference meeting in Edinburgh in 1910, reflecting a growing dissatisfaction with European-type literary training and looking to the United States for a different model, began a formal period of imitation of the two schools' model of education through practical training.[72]

Visits to Hampton in 1912 convinced British missionary officials that the key to training Africans was the Hampton–Tuskegee method. Oldham, as editor of the *International Review of Missions,* publicized the merits of Hampton. His campaign to get industrial arts and agricultural training introduced into missionary schools was helped by two major studies that appeared in 1917: C. T. Loram's *Education of the South African Native* and Thomas Jesse Jones's *Negro Education: A Study of the Private and Higher Schools for Colored People in the United States*. Loram, a South African, had visited American Southern schools, and he called for African education to be more practical – and hence less literary – in its goals. Jones, a Welsh-born naturalized American, was educational director of the Phelps-Stokes Fund and a champion of the Hampton–Tuskegee model. In 1918 Oldham wrote a major review article on these books for the *International Review of Missions* that would serve as the design for mission educational changes after World War I. The theme was to be practical education adapted to train Africans to live better in their villages; literary education would no longer be stressed.

In 1919 Jones persuaded the fund to make a major survey of education in West, South, and equatorial Africa. Oldham ensured cooperation by mission bodies and colonial governments.[73] Loram and Aggrey were to travel with the commission, which was "to study and report upon the industrial education adapted to the needs of the African."[74] The commission not only gathered data on African schools, but also suggested features of the Hampton–Tuskegee method that might be adopted. The Phelps-Stokes reports (1922 and 1925), though they were monumental surveys of education in Africa, still would not have had much impact if Oldham had not espoused them through his various positions on mission boards and royal commissions.[75]

Not only was the training in industrial arts and agriculture more useful to Africans than academic training, according to Oldham, but it had been demonstrated that the Tuskegee method turned out more moderate and cooperative blacks.[76] The suitability of Tuskegee-trained blacks for missionary posts in Africa was thus clearly recognized by most white leaders, although, paradoxically, Oldham never succeeded in having people of this type assigned to work in East Africa. Oldham later spent two weeks at Tuskegee, and he continued to push the school's approach. His visit confirmed his belief that there were two types of blacks, the Du Bois type and the Tuskegee type.[77] Oldham's *Educational Policy in Africa* (1923) incorporated the first Phelps-Stokes Report into British colonial thinking in education and showed that the work of the Hampton and Tuskegee scholars was an effective method of training Africans.

Additional visits to the American South were arranged, some of them financed by the Rockefeller Fund in 1926. By 1931 more than 250 educators had been brought to Tuskegee.[78] The influence of Hampton and Tuskegee was both direct and indirect. Achimota College (Gold Coast), under Aggrey and Fraser, both of whom had visited the schools in the American South, reflected the Tuskegee model and philosophy very closely. The Jeanes School in Kenya, started in 1925, embodied the American philosophy of differential education for blacks and concern for African welfare; the school was supposed to quiet settler fears about educating Africans. Although the Carnegie Corporation granted $37,500 to run the Jeanes School for five years, the school did not achieve its goals. Not only did it fail to enroll the best students, but it was unsuccessful in deflecting African ambitions for a Western as opposed to a "Negro-type" education.[79]

At the 1926 Le Zoute conference on Christian missions and education in Africa, Oldham and Jones succeeded in communicating "the insights of the Southern states to African educators."[80] But Oldham lost hope that he and the missionaries could

win concessions from colonial and settler interests in Kenya through the accommodationist philosophy of Tuskegee. Yet even though his belief faded that the Tuskegee way would reduce racial and political injustice, he did not lose faith in the
practical education for rural development, self-help, and service that the school
represented.

Thanks to Oldham's efforts, to visits to Southern schools in the United States by
missionaries and colonial officials, and to the Phelps-Stokes reports on education,
the Hampton–Tuskegee approach of practical education was adopted in English-
speaking Africa. Although rural development was the objective, Africans seemed to
resist agricultural and industrial education; according to Du Bois and according
also to educated African nationalists during the 1920s and the 1930s, the run-of-
the-mill African student preferred the European model of education, and looked on
"practical" education as a way of being kept subordinate.[81] This is too easy an
explanation: Wherever Africans had a chance to learn skills that immediately
improved their lives, they were eager students. The few missionaries trained in
farming and practical skills who managed to be sent to Africa had great success
with the Africans. Much depended on the missionaries themselves, on their apti-
tudes and outlooks, and on their ability to demonstrate the advantages of their
newer techniques. Just as white missionaries such as G. A. Roberts or E. D. Alvord
in Rhodesia were able to transform African agriculture, so was the black missionary Samuel B. Coles (a product of Talladega College, a Tuskegee-like school) able
to revolutionize agricultural practices around his mission station in Angola. Hundreds of Africans came to Coles to learn how to plow, to yoke and train oxen, to
plant new crops, to make bricks, or to ply the carpenter's trade.

Africans did not simply prefer a solid literary education to practical instruction.
What good did a Jeanes School do for most adult African farmers? The African
farmers willingly came to learn from Coles, for they saw by example how they
could profit from the new ways. Whenever they were shown how to improve their
land and its yield, most farmers were willing to learn. Too few missionaries or
colonial officials, however, could teach them. Africans did not reject the Tuskegee–
Hampton approach solely because it seemed to shut them out from the white
man's world; all too rarely were they taught by example, in the way that Coles
taught in Angola or Alvord in Rhodesia.

Few schools taught the practical skills with immediate benefits that Africans
needed and wanted. Few missionaries were farmers who could plow, let alone
make a plow or teach Africans to break in their cattle as beasts of burden. The
schools all too often were removed from the daily needs of village and farmer, and
teachers often were unable to adapt themselves to the working conditions of the
African tiller. When a school or teacher could overcome the difficulties, then the
Tuskegee approach met with success. Coles and Robinson accomplished this; so
did Alvord and Roberts. Their incredible successes proved that the Tuskegee techniques of practical agricultural education could have worked. Because those techniques were seldom tried, the lessons of Hampton and Tuskegee failed to improve
conditions in Africa significantly. Of course, the failure of agricultural missionaries
may have lain in a much wider causal network, including lack of markets, of roads,
of communications, or of incentives. All of these factors may have militated against
the success of some schools that stressed practical agricultural education.

But if the Jeanes School failed in Kenya, Tuskegee-like institutions did not fail elsewhere. Two government-sponsored institutes offering industrial and agricultural training were opened in Southern Rhodesia in the 1920s: Tjolotjo and Domboshawa. As mentioned elsewhere, the head of Domboshowa, H. S. Keigwin, visited the United States and Tuskegee and adapted many of the techniques he observed for use in the Rhodesian schools.

But Africans were also influenced by liberal arts colleges in the United States. Lincoln University (first called Ashmun Institute) was founded in 1854 by a Presbyterian minister, John Miller Dickey, who had been associated with the American Colonization Society and the settlement of Liberia. Its goal was to elevate Africans in America and Africa and to train them in the liberal arts so that they could be leaders of their people.[82] The first building, dedicated in 1856, was called Ashmun Hall in honor of the great white Liberian leader Jehudi Ashmun. By 1900 Liberian students were about the only African students to have attended Lincoln (thirty-three out of thirty-five). When the Presbyterian Church in the United States broke its ties with its mission church in Liberia, Liberian students stopped coming to Lincoln.[83]

South Africans made up for the loss of Liberian students—twenty-two attended between 1896 and 1924. Lincoln's most famous graduates attended the school in the early 1930s: Azikiwe came in 1929, Nkrumah in 1935.[84] No African entered during World War II, but sixteen enrolled in 1946 and the numbers have increased ever since.

Lincoln University's goal, a blend of rationalism and Calvinism, was to redeem Africans in the United States and Africa. The school was dedicated to the belief in human equality, and it pursued, against strong criticism, a program of liberal education in the arts, humanities, and sciences.[85] Yet Lincoln was not a radical school: No Negro served on the governing board until 1928 or on the faculty until 1931.

The African students at Lincoln got a good liberal education; lived in a beautiful, isolated, small campus; and conversed and studied with American Negro students. They read the Negro press of the day, and from the 1920s on this press was strident and sensational. Azikiwe especially seemed to have been influenced: He worked for the *Baltimore Afro-American* and when he returned home founded the *West African Pilot,* which had more of the flavor of an American Negro newspaper than of a staid English-African paper.[86]

Many thousands more Africans were to come to the United States after World War II than came before 1940. And many thousands of Americans and Afro-Americans were to go to Africa as teachers and missionaries to continue the work not only of Booker T. Washington but also of W. E. B. Du Bois and Marcus Garvey.

V

The United States in Africa, 1939–1983

Clean water program, Sudan. Courtesy USIA.

Ethiopia–U.S. clean water program. Courtesy USIA.

Road building in Upper Volta. Courtesy USIA.

Senegalese foreman displays crops made possible with well provided by Peace Corps volunteers. Courtesy AID.

USIA library, Monrovia, Liberia. Courtesy USIA.

Caterpillar tractor in Zambia (AID). Courtesy Hoover Institution Archives.

Feeding station in Mauritania. Courtesy USIA.

The Reverend James Robinson of Cross Roads Africa, receiving books for Africa. Courtesy National Archives.

CHAPTER 20

Africa between East and West

On October 15, 1945, shortly after the end of World War II, a Pan-African congress met at Chorlton Town Hall in Manchester, England. Delegates included a whole brain trust of future prime ministers, including Kwame Nkrumah and Hastings Kamuzu Banda, both of them graduates of American academic institutions. The congress, in retrospect, stood out as a landmark in modern African history. Delegates adopted a policy of reformist socialism; they vigorously denounced imperial rule and called for independence as a cure for the ills of Africa. By the standards of subsequent generations, the demands of the congress were moderate; at the time, however, its program seemed almost utopian.

Except for the defeated Italians, the Western empires in Africa appeared to have emerged from the war almost unscratched. Great Britain's might stood unchallenged in the colonies. South Africa basked in the glory of having helped to defeat the Axis powers and to found the United Nations. The Free French had drawn heavily in their war effort on those territories in Africa loyal to the cause of de Gaulle; Belgium was firmly entrenched in the Congo; the Portuguese Empire seemed somnolent. White rule appeared to be safe for a long time to come, but the Pan-African Congress in Manchester and similar meetings in francophone Africa signaled that changes would have to be made if the colonies were not to be lost. Changes were made, but they were not made fast enough.

The cold war in Africa

During the North African campaign, American soldiers had fought and died on the northern littoral of the African continent. U.S. troops had been stationed in various parts of sub-Saharan Africa for the purpose of keeping communication lines open and transporting war materials to the Middle East and Africa. President Roosevelt, in line with his New Deal coalition, was actually more hostile to British imperialism than to Soviet communism; he regarded the British system of imperial preferences as an obstacle to world prosperity, and the British Empire as a potential threat to peace. The State Department looked to a policy of accelerated reform whereby the colonial regimes would become accountable to an international authority in which the United States would have a predominant voice. American pressure was far from negligible in its effects. The colonizers, especially the British, became more defensive in their attitude; colonial reformers in the Western European capitals had as an additional reason to defend their projects the desire to cement the American alliance and improve conditions in the colonies. (The Colonial Development and Welfare acts, passed by the British Parliament, were in part designed as a reply to American criticism of British colonial practice.)

After World War II, however, American official interest in Africa began to wane. The present chapter cannot attempt to provide a history of U.S. and Soviet policy toward emergent Africa. Such a task will be accomplished only when the newly available archives in the former metropolitan countries and the United States have been fully exploited, and when scholars can draw on more detailed studies concerning specific aspects of American foreign policy, such as the books written by William Roger Louis and Richard D. Mahoney.[1] At this point, we can do no more than to point to certain major determinants. One of these was the Soviet threat, as perceived in Washington. As the Soviet menace waxed, Washington grew more concerned with Moscow's real and suspected designs than with the future of the Western colonial empires in Africa. Preoccupied with the restoration of Europe and the rise of Russian power, the U.S. government was content to regard the bulk of the African continent as a colonial appendage of Western Europe, although some Marshall Plan aid was to be used in the colonies. The ways to Dakar, Lagos, and Leopoldville still lay respectively through Paris, London, and Brussels. Even during the 1950s the global policy of containing Soviet expansion took absolute priority over African matters. Within the State Department, the Bureau of European Affairs insisted on a policy that would balance the theoretical advantages of self-government against the practical needs of strengthening the North Atlantic Treaty Organization (NATO) alliance. Washington had no wish to quarrel with its European supporters over the affairs of a continent known to so few of America's citizens. Even the organizations of black Americans, preoccupied with the civil rights struggle, took but a minimal interest in the great landmass from inhabitants of which some tenth of all Americans had descended.

During the immediate postwar period, Moscow's relative indifference to sub-Saharan Africa mirrored Washington's lack of concern. Soviet trade in the subcontinent was negligible. Soviet strategists looked for strength to land power in Europe rather than to naval power overseas. The orthodox Communist parties counted for little in Africa, and they initially received but scanty support from the Soviet Union. During World War II Stalin had made no attempt to embarrass his Western allies in Africa. After hostilities ended, his interest in black Africa remained small. A hard-liner at home, he believed that "bourgeois" nationalists like Kwame Nkrumah of Ghana were imperialist lackeys who represented only the *comprador* class, the African agents of white colonialism in Africa. Leadership of the future revolution, Stalin believed, must fall to the nascent proletariat. In any event, Stalin's line for black Africa did not provide for future revolutions in Africa unless foreign policy gains for the USSR were involved. Stalinism provided for a period of co-operation between proletariat and national bourgeoisie as a stage leading toward socialism in colonial areas.

Stalin's death in 1953 brought about major changes in Soviet African policies, and from the mid-1950s the Communists revalued their African stance in the light of policy changes at home. In 1956 the congress of the Communist Party of the Soviet Union (CPSU) admitted that national independence in Africa might be won under African "bourgeois" leadership. The small Communist parties in Nigeria, Senegal, and South Africa all stressed the need for a broad-based alliance that would include the "national bourgeoisie" as well as the peasants, the "petty bourgeoisie," and the working class in the struggle for "national democratic revolutions" as stepping-stones to socialism.[2] The new policy was much more realistic than Stalin's narrow orthodoxy. The Soviet Union took a leading part in the UN debates that called for the end of Western empire in Africa. Moscow established friendly relations with the newly sovereign states, no matter whether they were bourgeois in orientation or professed to take the "noncapitalist road," as did Guinea and Ghana. Communists in sub-Saharan Africa concentrated on infiltrating trade unions; on African nationalist movements; on building up networks of agents and supporters through local "peace movements," cultural fronts, youth leagues, women's associations, and scholarship programs for study in the Soviet Union; and on similar measures. Communists of the pro-Soviet (as opposed to the Maoist) persuasion played down the need for armed struggles except in the Portuguese colonies, Rhodesia, and South Africa. But in practical terms, such efforts at that point did not amount to a great deal. American policy makers shouldered little risk by attacking Portuguese colonialism or South African racialism at a time when the Soviet Union and its allies seemed ill prepared to intervene.

The Americans responded to the African challenge in a slow and ambivalent fashion. They stood committed to decolonization; yet they had no wish to alienate their NATO allies by hurrying the pace.[3] Washington tried to escape from this dilemma by backing the reformers within the metropolitan countries. The most significant change in U.S. African postwar policy involved the transformation of the Gold Coast from a British colony to the independent state of Ghana as a member of the Commonwealth – a development warmly welcomed by Washington. The British Labour Government installed after the end of World War II had initially framed its African policy in terms of gradual and piecemeal reforms. In 1946 the British introduced a new constitution that embodied much of the Gold Coast's nationalist program of the 1920s. The new constitution, however, did not prove acceptable to the new African nationalists, and in 1948 there were serious disturbances in the colony. These troubles made a profound impression at the Colonial Office, where the Gold Coast had always been regarded as a model colony with a contented population. The pace of constitutional change rapidly accelerated, and in 1957 Ghana became independent. This transformation opened the floodgate to rapid decolonization, not only in British, but also in French-speaking Africa (see Map 4). In 1958 Guinea opted for independence from France; two years later nearly all French dependencies in sub-Saharan Africa had become sovereign states, eligible for Washington's largesse.

In the former British states of Central Africa, colonialism staged a holding action, designed to combine economic progress with limited concessions to Africans and far-reaching demands on the part of the local European colonists. In 1953 white Southern Rhodesians and the British imperial power agreed to the formation of the Federation of Rhodesia and Nyasaland. The architects of the Federation had divergent and contradictory motives. They wished to create a British bastion against both Afrikaner nationalism in South Africa and African nationalism in the north. They meant to create an economic unit larger and more credit-worthy than any of the three constituent territories (Southern Rhodesia, later Zimbabwe; Northern Rhodesia, later Zambia; and Nyasaland, later Malawi). They also hoped to resolve the clash between an emergent white Rhodesian and an even more potent African nationalism by an ill-defined policy of "partnership" that, for a long time to come, would leave the whites as senior partners. The only effective

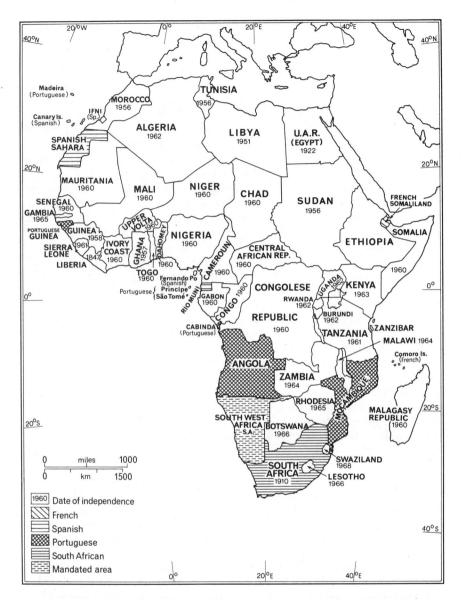

Map 4. Africa in 1968. Reprinted from Peter Duignan and L. H. Gann, eds., *The Economics of Colonialism*, vol. 4 of *Colonialism in Africa, 1870–1960* (Cambridge: Cambridge University Press, 1975).

partnership, however, was a short-lived understanding between the imperial authorities and London and a settler-dominated government in Salisbury. This partnership broke down as African nationalist sentiment grew apace in the northern territories, and London decided that the Federation could not survive. In 1963 the ill-starred state broke up amid bitter mutual recrimination. Southern Rhodesia (now known as Rhodesia) reverted to its previous ambiguous position as a "self-governing colony" run by a mainly white electorate. Malawi and Zambia became independent members of the British Commonwealth – a transformation that was by now both welcomed and enthusiastically endorsed by Washington.

The African challenge also led to far-reaching changes within the American bureaucracy. African affairs assumed a more important role than before. In 1958, for instance, an independent Bureau of African Affairs came into being within the State Department, and eventually a number of consulates were replaced by full-fledged embassies. In addition, the Americans began to promote the academic study of African cultures and languages in the 1950s; they channeled loans and grants to Africa; and above all, they changed their political line. Anticolonialism came to be interpreted as a policy that was moral in itself, as a device for expanding American trade, and as a means for strengthening the American position where the newly independent states were endowed with a voting strength in the United Nations quite out of keeping with their military or economic power.

The accession of John F. Kennedy to the U.S. presidency gave promise of an even more drastic overhaul of American policy. Kennedy regarded anticolonialism as a weapon in the cold war, even as an influence that would ultimately "undermine the great Communist Colonial empire."[4] "In unfriendly hands, the African coasts would threaten the lines of communication of the Free World." African products, moreover, had come to play an important part both for military and for peaceful purposes. The uranium required for nuclear power came mainly from the Congo, and African copper continued to be "a vital element in our peacetime economy."[5]

Above all, anticolonialism and foreign aid became means of spreading the American liberals' concepts of civil rights and of advancing the New Frontier to the most distant corners of the globe. The United States, in the view of these liberals, had a moral duty to help Africa in developing stable and independent nations able to make their own unique contributions to the world community. The United States had an obligation to help the governments of Africa in meeting the legitimate aspirations of their respective peoples, and to assist the African peoples to develop free societies and free institutions in harmony with the Africans' own beliefs and cultures.[6] The Americans, in other words, set themselves a task whose magnitude and complexity they hardly understood. But no matter which party held power in Washington, there was an element of continuity in American policy; this aimed throughout at supporting moderate and constitutional demands from African nationalists while, at the same time, countering Soviet moves to gain influence on the continent.

The change in American policy went with a transformation of the American bureaucracy. The civil service grew enormously in size and complexity, and in expense (between 1930 and 1950 the State Department's budget increased more than twenty-two times, from $15 million to $331 million). This growth was, however, nothing compared with the bureaucratic expansion that occurred during the subsequent three decades. By 1978 the State Department spent much more on its operating expense in Africa alone (more than $51 million) than had been disbursed for the department's work throughout the world a quarter century before. But the State Department by this time had become only one of many agencies dealing with Africa. As foreign aid to that continent expanded (reaching $475.7 million for civil aid and $67.9 million for military assistance in 1978), bureaucratic power became increasingly fragmented. By 1980 a total of twenty-nine U.S. government departments, agencies, and permanent commissions were concerned with African affairs in some form, ranging from major bodies like the departments of the Interior, Defense, Agriculture, Housing and Urban Development, and Health, Education, and Welfare to the National Aeronautics and Space Administration, the Export–Import Bank of the United States, the Agency for Volunteer Services (Peace Corps), and the National Endowment for the Humanities.

These new technical departments deprived the Department of State of an ever-increasing number of functions. To give just a few examples, the State Department lost operational responsibility for intelligence to the Central Intelligence Agency (CIA), for foreign assistance to the Agency for International Development (AID), and for information to the International Communication Agency. Other departments developed their own "mini-State Departments"; the Defense Department built up its own Office of International Security Affairs. The State Department further declined in influence as heads of state were able to communicate by telephone with Washington or to travel by jet aircraft without paying much heed to the advice of locally accredited ambassadors.

There were also changes within the social structure of the American bureaucracy. Before World War II the State Department, like the Foreign Office in Great Britain, had drawn most of its personnel from the establishment – more so than any other government agency. There was some truth to the stereotype of the State Department official drawn from "old" Anglo-Saxon stock, educated in eastern Ivy League schools, anglophile in orientation, and English in manners. The Foreign Service Act of 1947, however, broadened the social and geographical basis of recruitment, and by the late 1970s the people recruited in the 1950s and the early 1960s were beginning to move into senior positions. (The new personnel included black Americans like Donald McHenry, who joined the State Department in 1963 as a Foreign Service officer and later was U.S. ambassador to the United Nations. Others were liberal intellectuals like Anthony Lake, a Harvard graduate and a Princeton Ph.D., appointed Foreign Service officer in 1962. He later became a Democratic Party campaigner, a Carter supporter, and subsequently director of the policy planning staff under the Carter administration.)

The State Department did not, as some conservatives have maintained, simply mirror the politics of the liberal media and of academia. Power within the department was widely dispersed. Moreover, within the bureaucracy as a whole, the State Department's policies with regard to issues like South Africa and Rhodesia went by no means unchallenged. Departments like Defense thought, above all, in military terms; the National Aeronautics and Space Administration (NASA) liked to cooperate with South Africa on problems of space tracking; the Treasury did not want to complicate relations with the world's principal gold producer. By and large, however, the "political" branches – the State Department, AID, the U.S. mission to the United Nations–tended to hold the balance of power. These agencies were concerned particularly with the real or supposed power of the newly emergent Third World nations. Their bureaucrats were apt to take an anticolonial–and even more, an anti-South African–line, both from political conviction and from the standpoint of what they conceived to be America's long-term interests.[7]

Within the State Department, the Bureau of African Affairs was concerned primarily with the new African countries; the Bureau of International Organization Affairs and the U.S. mission to the United Nations were preoccupied with America's international position within the United Nations itself; the Bureau of Intelligence and Research shared the preconceptions of liberal academia. The State Department became increasingly responsive to liberal lobbies, lobbies drawn from the ranks of academia, the missionary societies, the labor union movement and, to a minor extent, black Americans. The process accelerated from 1960 onward, when President Kennedy asked for policy recommendations from his newly appointed Task Force on Africa, made up of specialists recruited from universities, philanthropic foundations, and business firms.[8]

Contrary to widespread misconceptions within conservative ranks, the New Frontier administrators at first played their cards quite skillfully when it came to countering the Soviets in Africa. Americans, with support from their Western allies, effectively resisted a Soviet challenge in the newly independent Congo (later Zaire), as well as an attempt by the mineral-rich Katanga province to secede from the Congo, which would have stripped the central government of essential revenue and left it crippled. The United States also supplied military assistance to a number of countries, including Liberia, the Congo, and Ethiopia. The Americans set up space-tracking stations in countries as far afield as Nigeria, Madagascar, and South Africa. They watched the Soviets make mistake after mistake, allowing countries like Ghana, Guinea, and Egypt to weaken or break former ties with Moscow.

The Kennedy administration marked the high point of the traditional liberal alliance among the disparate groups within the Democratic Party–liberals, ethnic groups, Catholics, Jews, blacks, other minorities, trade unionists, academicians–committed to domestic reforms. The liberal alliance was committed, above all, to civil rights. Washington looked with approval on Western decolonization in Africa, a process equated in some measure with the civil rights struggle at home. The whites' unwillingness to hand over power to the blacks in South Africa and Rhodesia, on the other hand, appeared to Washington as an aberration inspired by the bigoted folly attributed to white diehards in Alabama and Mississippi.

Other factors also entered the equation: the breakdown of British, French, and Belgian imperial rule in Africa; the emergence of a new and vocal African voting bloc in the UN at a time when this body still commanded widespread admiration within the United States; the faith placed by many American academicians and journalists in "nationbuilding," "mass mobilization," "guided democracy," foreign aid, and rapid economic development in postcolonial Africa; the ideological slur cast upon anticommunism in the wake of the McCarthy era; the political and economic gains made by black Americans within the United States; and the growing liberal lobbies in Washington committed to the policy of backing the nations of black Africa. The South African government seemed discredited by implementing apartheid, especially after the Sharpeville riot (1960). The U.S. government therefore judged that it would best serve the national interest by cutting adrift from the losing side of white racism.

This proved a difficult policy to pursue. The Kennedy administration in 1961 briefly went further in supporting African nationalists than any administration before or thereafter. In 1961 Washington provided some covert financial support to Holden Roberto, leader of the Frente de Libertação Nacional de Angola (FLNA), one of several independence movements engaged in guerrilla warfare against the Portuguese overlords of Angola. Kennedy's policy, designed to strip a NATO ally of its possessions, had no precedent. The Portuguese, however, held a trump card through their hold on the Azores, a group of strategic islands in the Atlantic that had been used by the United States in a succession of crises as a refueling, communications, and antisubmarine base. (In 1961, for instance, the Americans relied on the Azores to send troops and equipment to Berlin and to transport UN troops to the Congo.) The Joint Chiefs of Staff insisted that the Azores were indispensable to any emergency buildup of Western forces in Europe and the Middle East. After a long and bitter debate, intensified by the sudden chill in U.S.–Soviet relations over Cuba in the summer of 1962, Kennedy yielded to the Portuguese, and U.S. contacts with Roberto and other African nationalists came to an end.

The Kennedy administration also went further than any previous in its attacks on South Africa; Kennedy did not confine his opposition to verbal condemnation, but announced that the United States would cease selling arms to South Africa after 1963. Senior officials like Chester Bowles, Adlai Stevenson, W. Averell Harriman, and G. Mennen Williams were all strongly pro-African, and the ambassadors appointed by Kennedy to African diplomatic posts were liberal American intellectuals. The Johnson administration followed the precedents established by Kennedy, and in some ways went even beyond them; in 1964, for instance, the United States voted for a UN Security Council resolution to study the feasibility of sanctions against South Africa.

In practical terms, however, hostility to Pretoria did not exact much of a price from Washington. No matter what the politicians might say, trade between the United States and South Africa grew in a striking fashion, leaving the United States with an increasingly favorable trade balance. The Western powers denied themselves the use of South African naval and air bases in the South Atlantic and the Indian oceans, facilities that might have been theirs for the asking. But such military advantages seemed to be outweighed by the political disadvantages, especially at a time when, on the sea and in the air, the Americans evidently maintained a decisive superiority over the Soviet Union throughout the world, and especially in Africa.

The 1970s, however, saw a striking decline in the Western position. Communist victories in Vietnam, Laos, and Cambodia; worldwide inflation; increasing dissatisfaction with both real and imagined shortcomings of the Western welfare states; a shift in the global military balance in favor of the Soviet Union; a loss of Western political confidence; an international energy crisis following striking increases in the price of Arab oil; President Nixon's resignation after the Watergate scandals; and the overthrow of the Portuguese dictatorship in Lisbon by the Portuguese army (1974) all brought about far-reaching changes on the international scene and in

Africa. Portugal decided to grant independence to its colonial possessions. At the tail end of the war in Mozambique, Portuguese troops actually helped to install a Marxist regime, headed by Frente de Libertação de Moçambique (FRELIMO), against opposition from local white settlers and from various African ethnic groups, such as the Makonde. In Angola pro-Communist officials, backed by the then influential Portuguese Communist Party, supported the Popular Movement for the Liberation of Angola (MPLA) in its struggle against its rivals, and in July 1975 MPLA expelled the other liberation movements from the capital.

Above all, there was a dramatic difference in the form taken by Soviet intervention in Africa, as in other parts of the Third World. Determined not to suffer another humiliation like the Cuban missile crisis, the Soviets began to take steps to change the worldwide military balance of power in their favor. From the mid-1960s onward, Soviet military spending and military investment began to exceed American; Soviet expenditure in absolute terms increased as American expenditure declined. The Soviets were therefore enabled to make their power felt in areas such as the Middle East, Africa, and Southeast Asia, once undisputed Western preserves. Until 1975 the Soviet Union and its allies had confined themselves to training guerrillas and subsidizing pro-Soviet organizations in Africa, thereby encouraging partisan warfare through leftist liberation fronts.

By intervening in southern Africa, the Soviets hoped to weaken the West strategically, politically, and economically. In addition to the goal of encouraging communism, Moscow may have thought of safeguarding its future access to scarce raw materials; but such speculations must necessarily be based on guesswork. The Soviet Union certainly looked also to weakening China's influence in the world and to reinforcing its own claims as a global superpower. In all likelihood Moscow meant to strengthen relations with its allies by entrusting them with new responsibilities. Moscow's main coadjutors in these new tasks were Cuba and, to a lesser extent, East Germany. Their respective regimes embarked on these new commitments in order to strengthen their shaken domestic prestige and to enhance their international position in relation to the capitalist world, their Communist allies, and the Soviet Union itself.[9]

From 1975 onward, the Soviet Union, able to rely on its newly built naval strength and airlift capability, began to intervene directly through the use of Cuban ground troops and East German and Soviet supporting staff. In September 1975 strong Cuban forces disembarked in Luanda, thereby initiating a new phase in Soviet foreign policy designed to spread communism and perhaps to compensate for weaknesses at home by military victories abroad.

The United States did not respond directly to the new challenge, but confined itself to supplying small amounts of arms and cash to the anti-MPLA forces. Along with such African states as Zambia, it also gave covert encouragement to South Africa, which in October 1975 sent a small fighting force across the Angolan border to assist União Nacional para a Independência Total de Angola (UNITA). The South Africans and their Angolan allies nearly succeeded, but in December 1975 the U.S. Senate, by an overwhelming majority, imposed a ban on all further assistance, overt or covert, to the anti-Communist forces in Angola. At a crucial point in their advance, the South Africans were suddenly bereft of further American support; afraid to face the Communist bloc, the South Africans pulled back.

Guerrilla warfare continued in Angola, but the way was open for the MPLA and the Cuban forces to seize power throughout the greater part of the country.

The new strategy of direct intervention, carried out under the banner of "proletarian internationalism," had far-reaching consequences. The Soviet Union and its allies worked out a military division of labor in which the USSR provided the higher strategic direction, logistic support, and arms; East Germany supplied experts, technicians, and instructors (especially those to train intelligence agents and secret police officers); and Cuba became responsible for the bulk of the combat forces. This formula was also applied with much success to Ethiopia, where the Soviet Union and Cuba airlifted large numbers of troops and heavy supplies over great distances in an impressive display of military strength, enabling the Ethiopians to defeat a Somali invasion (1977–8) and largely suppress a widespread rebellion in Eritrea. Impressed by real or imagined analogies between the fall of the "feudal" monarchies in Ethiopia and czarist Russia, the Soviets became convinced that Ethiopia was one of the keys to Africa. Ethiopia became to them a testing ground for the ability of a Marxist–Leninist revolution to survive in a hostile world; a touchstone for the efficacy of proletarian internationalism as a revolutionary instrument in a backward society; a strategic bastion in the Horn of Africa; and a potential manpower reservoir for military operations in other parts of Africa, the Persian Gulf, and Saudi Arabia.

By the end of the 1970s, Marxism–Leninism had made considerable gains. More than forty thousand troops – East German, Soviet, but mainly Cuban – were deployed in Africa to support Marxist–Leninist governments. The new regimes of Angola, Mozambique, Ethiopia, the People's Republic of the Congo, and Benin all claimed to be based on Marxist–Leninist principles. Libya was allied to the Soviet Union by a treaty of friendship and by providing air and naval facilities. In practice, of course, these regimes varied widely. Marxism–Leninism in the People's Republic of the Congo was largely rhetorical. Power in Ethiopia remained with the army. Even Mozambique and Angola, for the time being, sharply diverged in many respects from the Soviet pattern. Nevertheless, the balance of power had begun to change in Africa. Marxism–Leninism, far from being an exiles' creed, had become a continental challenge to the West.

U.S. policies in South Africa

The theoreticians of the New Frontier and the Great Society believed in linking liberal policies at home with liberal policies abroad. They were apt to identify the blacks and the poor within the borders of the United States with those of the Third World nations overseas; conversely, they were inclined to associate white regimes in Africa with the worst features of Middle America, with all its real or supposed privileges and prejudices. The Kennedy and Johnson administrations both attempted, therefore, in a halfhearted manner, to side with the Third World nations in criticizing South Africa. On reaching office in 1969, President Nixon somewhat diverged from this policy, assuming that the white regimes in Rhodesia, in the Portuguese colonies, and in South Africa were interconnected and that they would last for a considerable time. After Nixon's resignation in 1974, however, his successor, President Ford, largely reverted to earlier policies.

In Rhodesia, the regnant white government had in 1965 cut all existing constitutional links to Great Britain through a "Unilateral Declaration of Independence" (UDI). Most experts assumed at the time that UDI would not long prevail against the combined forces of world opinion, an international boycott, and African guerrilla war. In fact, the white Rhodesians initially held their own. The country's economy at first rapidly expanded. (Between 1964 and 1974 the gross national product nearly doubled, and gross fixed capital formation increased almost fourfold.) The collapse of Portuguese rule in Mozambique enormously enlarged the white Rhodesians' military frontier; the Rhodesians could no longer effectively impede guerrilla penetration, and they became increasingly dependent on South African financial support. The South Africans, anxious to end their diplomatic isolation, and determined to shed a never-ending financial burden, put pressure on Salisbury in a manner that Smith could not resist.

The change in the South African line coincided with a shift in American policy. After Nixon's resignation in 1974, his successor, President Ford, partly reverted to earlier policies. Henry Kissinger did his best to persuade the South Africans to oppose Smith; Kissinger put pressure of his own on the UDI government, and, by collaborating with Pretoria, achieved what Washington could not have achieved on its own – public Rhodesian acceptance in 1976 of early African rule. (This was accomplished by a transitional government installed in 1979 and an African nationalist government, headed by Robert Mugabe, who obtained a stunning electoral victory in 1980.)

The Ford administration's policy toward South Africa was, however, marked by ambivalence. The new administration, for instance, wanted to bring the Namibian conflict to a swift conclusion, no matter what Pretoria's preference. The existing U.S. embargo on South Africa was extended to include goods such as U.S. airplane engines made in France. The United States would not allow South Africa to sell gold to the International Monetary Fund. The United States also declared in the Security Council that South Africa was a threat to peace, and that South African control over South-West Africa (Namibia) was illegal.

From the U.S. standpoint, these policies were in fact counterproductive. Pretoria became, if anything, more intransigent; U.S. influence on South Africa lessened; criticism of the United States within the United Nations failed to diminish. The arms embargo on South Africa deprived the United States of sales and contributed to South Africa's decision to build up its own arms industries while turning to France, Israel, and West Germany for imported weapons. The order forbidding U.S. naval ships from using South African ports increased the cost of naval operations and deprived U.S. ships of much-needed logistic support in the area.

When President Carter assumed office in 1977, he was determined to put increasing pressure on South Africa. His assumptions concerning South Africa reflected the views of the liberal "New Politics" wing within his party: South Africa was Georgia writ large, and South Africa must be freed. Carter's platform had called for U.S. support to those forces pledged to majority rule in South Africa. The United States was to refuse recognition to the Transkei (nominally an independent "Bantustan" within the South African framework) and to intensify the arms embargo; tax credits were to be refused to American corporations doing business in Namibia. Even more striking was a statement made in Vienna by Vice-President Mondale (backed by Carter and by his UN ambassador, Andrew Young), calling for the introduction of the one-man–one-vote principle to South Africa.

Table 1. *U.S. arms transfers to Africa, 1966–75 and 1976–80*

	1966–75		1976–80	
Country	Value ($ million)	% of total	Value ($ million)	% of total
Algeria	3	1	—	—
Cameroun	3	33	20	80
Ethiopia	120	79	80	5
Gabon	—	—	5	5
Ivory Coast	1	5	—	—
Kenya	7	14	50	30
Liberia	2	100	5	50
Libya	66	6	—	—
Morocco	52	33	380	20
Nigeria	8	4	40	10
South Africa	24	6	20	5
Sudan	2	2	140	25
Tanzania	2	2	—	—
Tunisia	36	67	60	25
Zaire	29	24	30	15
Zambia	6	10	—	—
Totals	361	11.5	830	3.8

Notes: Data for all African countries except Egypt in current dollar figures. Values for 1976–80 rounded independently by the Arms Control and Disarmament Agency and thus imprecise; approximate percentages calculated from them rounded to the nearest 5. Figures for South Africa include commercial sales of such U.S. Munitions List items as inertial navigation systems for civilian airliners, data encryption devices for U.S. corporate subsidiary use in electronic funds transfer and ADP applications, and other nonmilitary equipment for use by nongovernment entities. Dashes indicate no data.

Source: Joseph P. Smaldone, *World Military Expenditures and Arms Transfers, 1966–1975,* U.S. *Arms Control and Disarmament Agency Publication 90* (Washington, D.C.: ACDA, 1976), table 5, p. 77; *World Military Expenditures and Arms Transfers, 1971–1980,* ACDA Publication 115 (Washington, D.C.: ACDA, 1983), table 3, p. 117.

The United States, however, soon realized that South African support was essential in order to reach settlements of the Rhodesian and Namibian issues. The Carter administration was compelled to cooperate, at least diplomatically, with South Africa. From 1978 on, Donald McHenry led the five Western powers' negotiating team to find a solution to the stalemate in Namibia. The South Africans agreed to hold elections, dismantle apartheid, and concede independence to Namibia. Negotiations kept breaking down over questions of Marxism in the South-West African People's Organization (SWAPO) and the UN's lack of impartiality: Even before elections, the UN had recognized SWAPO as the legitimate ruler of Namibia.

Deeply rooted in the political and moral assumptions of the New Politics school, the Carter administration at the same time attempted to do business through what became known later as disarmed diplomacy. In 1977 Congress and the president cooperated in curtailing arms transfers to the Third World (see Table 1). Carter's arms control restraints went along with his human rights and moral principles approach to foreign policy matters. Disarmed diplomacy became his guiding principle. The rationale was that if the United States did not sell arms to Third World nations, the Soviets would not either. On May 19, 1977, Carter issued his Presidential Termination 13, by which arms transfers were to be unilaterally restricted. The result was that Soviet exports of almost all forms of military equipment surpassed in quantity the export of similar equipment from Western nations during Carter's four years in office. Under Carter, the United States naïvely refused to help some African governments to build up their security forces; even though trouble increased in Africa, the administration was giving less than it had done before. U.S. restraint did not stop Soviet intervention or arms transfer. By the early 1980s the Soviet Union had become the leading supplier of arms to Africa, providing eleven times more than the United States.

President Reagan's accession to office in 1981 marked a swing to the right both in domestic and in foreign policy. Reagan appointed Chester Crocker as assistant secretary of state for African affairs. Crocker toured Africa, trying to convert African states to the U.S. view that the Soviet Union and its proxies were the real menace to peace in the region. The Reagan administration rejected Carter's approach of disarmed diplomacy and set out to bolster the security requirements of America's friends around the world. There were five components to the Reagan security program: foreign military sales, economic support funds, grants of military assistance, international military education and training, and peacekeeping operations. By increased spending on all of these programs, President Reagan sought to reestablish the conventional arms equilibrium with the Third World, in order to diminish Soviet domination and consequent danger to the United States and its friends.

At the same time, Reagan took a more pro–South African line than his four immediate predecessors had done. Jean Kirkpatrick, the U.S. ambassador to the United Nations, vetoed in the Security Council (along with Great Britain and France) an African-sponsored set of sanctions against South Africa designed to punish Pretoria for not holding UN-approved elections in Namibia. The Reagan administration believed that South Africa would not accept a settlement unless further concessions were made. Crocker accordingly agreed that a constitutional conference should be held before the elections to draw up clauses that would protect white interests. This policy gave South Africa a way out of holding elections, perhaps for years, and put the United States in the invidious position of having to sell this new plan to SWAPO and to the African states.

The Reagan administration further shifted toward South Africa by linking Soviet and Cuban withdrawal from Angola, and the bringing of rebel leader Jonas Savimbi into the government, with U.S. recognition of Angola and a settlement in Namibia. There was talk even of reviving limited military relations with South Africa.[10] But in actual fact, the continuity between Reagan's and Carter's policies, in Africa as in the rest of the world, remained greater than both proponents and critics of the Reagan administration had assumed. There was no American–South African alliance. Foreign aid continued, albeit with less enthusiasm than before in Washington. Assistance on a substantial scale continued to be provided also for such revolutionary regimes as Zimbabwe's, which, under Robert Mugabe's guidance, embarked on a neutral foreign policy inspired by Marshal Tito's example in Yugoslavia.

At the time of writing in 1983, "constructive engagement," as formulated by the Reagan administration, was under severe attack. According to an administration spokesman (Princeton Lyman) appearing before the Sub-Committee on Africa of the House of Representatives on December 2, 1982, the policy had the following objectives: Constructive engagement should foster a movement toward a system of government by consent of the governed and away from apartheid and the political disfranchisement of blacks. The new policy should, at the same time, make for continued access to strategic minerals for which the United States and the countries of the Organization for Economic Cooperation and Development depend on South Africa. There was special emphasis on strategic security for Cape sea routes vital for U.S. and Western European oil and mineral supplies from the Middle East and South Africa. At the same time, regional security should be maintained in southern Africa against the Soviet-Cuban threat.

This approach was designed to secure five distinct aims: first, internationally recognized independence for Namibia under a non-Communist regime; second, internationally supported programs of economic development in all the developing countries of the region; third, negotiations for the withdrawal of Cuban troops from Angola; fourth, a détente between South Africa and its neighbors; and fifth, peaceful evolution in South Africa away from apartheid, toward a system of government (with a makeup never clearly defined) that would be based on consent of the governed and would provide security for all South Africa's ethnic groups.

The United States attempted to combine this program with bilateral negotiations with South Africa on Namibian independence. The major new element in these talks lay in the two partners' insistence that Cuban forces must evacuate Namibia in order to counter what the Reagan administration regarded as an integral part of a Soviet drive for world domination. While stigmatizing apartheid as incompatible with basic American values, President Reagan insisted that the United States should take up a friendly and encouraging attitude toward South Africa, as long as Pretoria was prepared to modify its racist system of government. Constructive engagement therefore depended on the achievement of effective reform within South Africa and the attainment of internationally recognized independence for Namibia.

These objectives all proved equally hard to attain, and after three years of the Reagan presidency constructive engagement was in serious trouble. The administration faced bitter hostility over these issues in the Third World (especially the African) nations. Namibia, at the time of writing, was no nearer to independence than it had been when Reagan took office. On the contrary, the South African army stood more firmly entrenched in Namibia than before and by 1984 had forced both Angola and Mozambique to end support for partisans.

In South Africa a new constitutional arrangement had gone into effect providing representation through separate parliaments for Indians and Coloureds. But the new settlement had done nothing for Africans. The government, in fact, continued its policy of eliminating so-called black spots from white areas by uprooting African communities such as the Bakwena and Ba Mogopa people and shifting them into separate ethnic Bantustans.

Many white liberals in South Africa had hoped that Zimbabwe might turn out to be an acceptable countermodel to white ethnocracy in southern Africa, a multiracial state built on democratic foundations. But Zimbabwe by 1984 seemed to be drifting into a one-party dictatorship; the struggle between whites and blacks had been supplanted by a new interblack conflict between Ndebele and Shona, a conflict that belied revolutionary expectations of an earlier era. In the face of real and imagined foreign threats, South Africa had increasingly militarized its relations with its neighbors; South African troops could strike at guerrilla bases in Angola and neighboring Mozambique with near impunity; and southern Africa seemed likely to drift into a new form of "Israelization."

In the face of this unpalatable situation, liberals argued that constructive engagement was bound to be ineffective or run into covert collaboration. Yet their alternative plans promised no solution either. The truth is that external pressure had failed to produce reform, and it will continue to do so until the internal conditions for change develop in South Africa. Only Pretoria can help the United States to continue its policy of constructive engagement by making bold domestic reforms, by cooperating on Namibian independence, and by cooperating with its neighbors. If it does not take these steps, the United States will probably distance itself, perhaps even disengage itself, from South Africa, assuming that Reagan is re-elected. If the Democrats should win in 1984, the United States will probably return to diplomatic harangues and new sanctions.

The international campaign against South Africa has not brought about any direct changes in South Africa. But the campaign has helped to strengthen and legitimize black consciousness. There is no evidence that the antiapartheid movement will lessen its pressure in the future to isolate South Africa and to reduce the amount of assistance South Africa receives. Although the abolitionists cannot defeat South Africa – only internal subversion and massive external assaults can do that – they can isolate South Africa, deny it goods and services, and thus raise the cost of continuing the apartheid system.

An unreformed South Africa will never again command the friendly respect that it enjoyed in the United States when Smuts was at the helm in Pretoria. U.S. commitment to racial equality and to human rights is now too strong to embrace apartheid. South Africa will have to make more significant reforms and share power with blacks before the American people will accept an alliance, no matter how important the Cape route is, how much the West needs South Africa's strategic minerals, or how strong the Soviet-Cuban presence becomes. South Africa's anticommunism, or its value as a military base during wartime, will not prove sufficient to overcome hatred of apartheid during a time of peace.

The United States and Africa today and tomorrow

Given these apparently insoluble difficulties in Africa, what policy should the United States pursue? There are many conflicting answers, but our own is unequivocal. As we see it, the West cannot eliminate Soviet aggressiveness, but an attempt to contain it should be made. The West's best option is to shore up key states, assisting them to develop economically and to govern themselves. For the 1980s, however, the picture looks gloomy and full of violence – ethnic, regional, and ideological – that will further draw in rival foreign powers. Indeed, World War III might conceivably begin in Africa. The Afro-Marxist and the military dictatorships will probably be economically worse off by 1990 than they were in 1980.

The condition of the masses in many states in all likelihood will deteriorate steadily.

What of the future? The United States has been overly inclined to shape its foreign policy in Africa to meet the approval of the Third World – the "uncommitted" nations of Asia and Africa that are supposed to hold the future world balance of power in their hands. This point of view neglects the military realities of power and looks on the present struggle for world supremacy as an ideological beauty competition between East and West, a competition in which the panel of judges is made up of Asians and Africans. Nations are indeed influenced by ideas, but economic and strategic factors play an even larger part in world affairs. In our view, the West would hardly be justified in subordinating its interests to the real or imagined demands of neutralists. It is in fact only the strength of the West, and nothing but its strength, that has made it possible up to the present time for Afro-Asian countries to afford the luxury of neutralism. Once the West weakens, the fate of new countries is itself imperiled.

There cannot be a simple rule of thumb for U.S. foreign policy in Africa as a whole. There are many African countries, and the United States accordingly needs many different African policies. The United States should aim at flexibility, realism, and avoidance of the view that American policy must somehow always be ideologically acceptable to others. Political and economic warfare against South Africa would not liberalize the republic nor improve the lot of its black people. The United States should seek to cooperate with a reform-minded Pretoria insofar as collaboration is in its strategic interest. The West should try to support moderate forms of government in Namibia rather than aid its declared enemies. Similarly, it should consider recognition of Angola only after all foreign troops – Cuban and East German – and Soviet military experts have left. This step would force the MPLA to form a coalition government with the two guerrilla organizations that now oppose it from the bush. Such a withdrawal should be a necessary condition for U.S. recognition.

In a more general sense, the United States must become more realistic in the conduct of its African affairs, and be sufficiently firm to make it clear to African governments that certain policies they advocate are not in the best interests of the West. The United States will have to take sides on issues, and not simply always back blacks against whites, or radicals against conservatives.

The West has yet to develop a coherent policy toward African development and security problems. The United States needs to focus its aid to shape events in countries that receive it; the United States should also aid countries directly rather than channel funds through international bodies. Arms and security programs should be instruments of diplomacy in Africa. The Reagan administration has wisely revived its military assistance program.

The United States therefore must reinvigorate its African policy, by devoting more aid and military assistance to Africa. The United States would be well advised to denounce Soviet-Cuban involvement in Africa for the instability it has caused, to respond positively to requests for security assistance when the states requesting do act in their mutual interests, and to praise the French for maintaining regional security and do likewise. The United States must point out to African nations that it is in their mutual interest to discourage Soviet domination and to develop policies that will promote both prosperity and peace.

CHAPTER 21

Economic activities

The private sector

Before the European powers partitioned Africa, American merchants played a considerable part in many regions of the African continent. But once the European powers planted their respective flags on African soil, American economic influence declined; the colonizers generally favored their own nationals. In the colonial era, three-quarters of American financial interests in sub-Saharan Africa were concentrated in Liberia and South Africa. American entrepreneurs sought profits mainly in countries free from European control; American trade and investments in Africa thus remained small throughout the first half of the twentieth century.

America's main interest in sub-Saharan Africa centered on a few but critically important strategic minerals. By the beginning of the 1980s, the United States imported about 99 percent of its cobalt from the African continent (Zaire producing about half the world's total output, and Zambia about one-tenth). Zaire also accounted for something like half the world's production of industrial diamonds. The United States had to import virtually all of its manganese, a mineral essential for the production of high-grade steel; and it relied on Gabon for about one-third of its needs. Africa also had turned into a large supplier of oil. Nigeria, the world's seventh largest oil producer, provided about one-fifth of U.S. crude oil imports, ranking second only to Saudi Arabia. Equally important was South Africa, which provided approximately 65 percent of the United States vanadium imports, 44 percent of its antimony, 33 percent of its platinum group requirements, over 30 percent of its chromite, and its ferro-chrome, 27 percent of its gold, and 10 percent of its manganese. In addition, the African continent continued to supply American markets with a variety of tropical crops, such as cocoa, peanuts, palm oil, sisal, wattle bark, and tanning extracts.

The expansion of this trade owed a major debt to the American merchant fleet; for instance, the Farrell Lines, which pioneered in a variety of fields, helped to introduce the export of American diesel-electric locomotives for use on South African railways and to import fruit and lobsters into the United States.[1] The Farrell Lines were not the only steamship operators making regular sailings between the United States and Africa. The Lykes Africa Lines, the Moore-McCormack Lines (which absorbed Farrell's old rival, the Robin Line), and the Delta Steamship Lines all provided scheduled service to Africa. America and Africa thus came to be more closely tied than ever before, linked by ships sailing under the American flag. After the end of World War II, in fact, British and French vessels and lines that once monopolized the traffic between the United States and Africa declined in the business. As in the sailing-ship days, Americans and Africans once again began to exchange products without European intermediaries. The Farrell Lines were foremost in bringing about this condition; perhaps Farrell's greatest achievement has been the effort to make Americans conscious of Africa in general, and of its trade and investment possibilities in particular.

In America's foreign commerce as a whole, sub-Saharan Africa nevertheless still occupied but a modest place – a point to which we shall return. Trade figures fluctuated, but on the average sub-Saharan Africa, between 1950 and 1980, purchased no more than between 3.5 percent and 4 percent of American exports as a whole. South Africa initially was by far the best African customer of the United States, exporting minerals and purchasing trucks, cars, machinery, and other investment goods. In addition, Zaire occupied a major role as a supplier of uranium, diamonds, copper, and other primary commodities. At a time of rising oil prices, Angola came into its own as an oil producer; so did Nigeria, whose trade with the United States had come to exceed the value of American–South African commerce by the mid-1970s. (In 1975, the United States imported from South Africa merchandise to the value of $587 million and from Nigeria goods, mainly petroleum products, worth $3,525 million. Exports from the United States to South Africa amounted to $1,341 million, and those to Nigeria $536 million.)[2]

Investment and multinational enterprise

Commerce and capital exports commonly go hand in hand. Experience in trade familiarizes banks and manufacturing corporations with new opportunities; investments, in turn, get new forms of commerce. During the late 1940s and the early 1950s, as shown, American trade with Africa remained relatively small. American firms mostly lacked a sound knowledge of African conditions; their contacts with Africa remained scanty, save for a few firms – especially those with links to Liberia and South Africa. At the end of 1956 *private* American investments overseas stood at $33.0 billion (American billion, here and throughout), whereas total U.S. investments abroad amounted to $49.5 billion. Exclusive of Egypt and the Sudan, however, Africa accounted for no more than $836.0 million, a negligible share – only 1.68 percent of America's total foreign investment. The largest single recipient of American investment was Liberia, with a total of $338.0 million; but even this figure was deceptive, as it included the value of oil tankers (estimated at $263.0 million) registered under the Liberian flag but owned by U.S. companies. Excluding this unique form of investment, U.S. direct investment in Africa at the end of 1956 had a book value of only $573.0 million. Of this sum, about 30 percent had gone into mining, 30 percent into the production and distribution of petroleum products, 20 percent into manufacturing, and 20 percent into such other activities as trade.[3]

During the next two decades American investment in Africa, particularly in South Africa, began to expand. Between 1968 and 1973 the book value of American investments in Africa went from $2.67 billion to $4.07 billion; earnings increased from $671.00 to $852.00 million; the balance-of-payment income to the United States fluctuated between $663.00 million and $526.00 million. Thereafter, American investments in sub-Saharan Africa remained almost stationary. Only 3 percent of overall American investments abroad had been placed in sub-Saharan Africa and these investments were concentrated in a few major countries, especially South Africa, Nigeria, and Zaire; South Africa accounted for about 1 percent of

U.S. investments abroad. Most U.S. involvements were concentrated in a limited number of industries. By 1973, $555.00 million was invested in mining and smelting, $2.28 million in petroleum, $701.00 million in manufacturing, and $798.00 million in other activities.[4]

At first sight the figures seem impressive, but these funds counted for little within the wider framework of American capitalism. By 1970, to be exact, America's investments in the United Kingdom amounted to more than twice its investments in the whole of Africa, and American investments in the European Economic Community were three times as large as those on the African continent. When compared with America's total foreign investments, the U.S. African stake seemed even more insignificant: $4.07 billion out of $78.00 billion in 1973.[5] For all that the critics of American neocolonialism and the advocates of the "dependency" school might say, the bulk of America's foreign holdings went to the developed countries of the world.

But even these funds played only a minor part in generating American wealth. By 1970 all American investments overseas accounted for less than one-twelfth of America's gross national product (GNP) – just over $78.0 billion out of a total of $974.0 billion. By way of comparison, American expenditure on clothing, accessories, and personal care alone was nearly as much as all American funds invested outside the borders of the United States ($72.4 billion as against just over $78.0 billion). American earnings from the Third World thus formed but an insignificant part of America's total wealth. (U.S. revenue from investments made on the entire African continent amounted to $845.0 million in 1970; of this, $141.0 million derived from South Africa.)[6]

American financiers mostly operated in Africa through international consortia. Taken as a whole, few modern institutions have enjoyed a worse press. In Europe, conservatives of the old school often identified such international bodies with the American challenge, the much-publicized *défi américain*. To Marxists, the international consortium was an engine of international capitalism and a tool of worldwide exploitation. To adherents of the dependency school – often, but not necessarily, Marxists – the international consortia were global bloodsuckers likely to empty the pockets of Third World peoples and to corrupt their souls.

The worldwide hostility against multinational corporations is not hard to explain. Old-time captains of industry – Rhodes, Alfred Beit, Ford, Rockefeller, and Carnegie – might have been disliked for their riches and power, but at least they were recognizable as individuals. The multinational corporations, on the other hand, appeared to their critics as vast, anonymous aggregates with subsidiaries all over the world, a complex network difficult to comprehend. Multinational corporations, their critics said with much justice, were hard to control and even harder to break. Such corporations were in a strong position when dealing with national governments because of their size, complexity, and technical expertise.

Multinational bodies, however, also had much said in their favor. They served as effective agencies for diffusing scarce skills and scarce capital throughout the world. They were usually run more efficiently than state or UN agencies. They contributed to the economies of backward countries by creating new forms of enterprise and new social services and by making major contributions to public revenue. Ironically, the bitter accusations made by Communists and their allies all over the world against the multinationals did not prevent Communist or Marxist–Leninist governments from welcoming them to countries under Communist control: By 1973, of the 500 major multinational corporations in the West, at least 140 had significant dealings with the Communist world; this tradition was maintained in independent Africa, where Gulf Oil continued to operate within the newly independent People's Republic of Angola. And dependency theories notwithstanding, the multinationals remained cautious about operating in the more backward parts of the globe. According to UN estimates published in 1973, the aggregate value of all multinational corporation activities amounted to about $500 million; but three-quarters of the multinationals' business was concentrated in the industrialized parts of the world.

Within the local African context, however, multinationals were important. From the American investors' standpoint, there were peculiar advantages, both financial and political, in operating through the medium of great consortia. Huge multinational corporations could negotiate more safely with national governments than a host of small private firms, vulnerable to expropriation in the event of a revolutionary take over. By combining with European companies, moreover, American firms spread their risk, while sharing the task of deploying the vast capital sums required for huge development projects. According to the theories put forward at the time – and put forward with almost equal relish both by socialist planners and by capitalist entrepreneurs – huge projects such as dams, power plants, and irrigation schemes were essential means of priming the economic pump. The importance of small enterprises and the small investor, on the other hand, was played down: They lacked chic in the eyes of society hostesses and prestige in the estimation of development economists. In addition, huge undertakings such as the Volta River dam and the Cabora Bassa dam provided psychological rewards to both bankers and politicians, rewards not afforded by smaller, less ambitious enterprises of the kind that pioneered the industrial revolution in countries like Rhodesia in the 1930s and the 1940s.

The investors who put their money in these projects were a varied group of people with multifarious interests. But they had one feature in common: a remarkable ability for working under governments of whatever description – capitalist, colonial, nationalist, or socialist.

What of the social and political effects produced by the multinationals' operations in Africa? According to their critics, the huge internationals formed interlocking monopolies that used vast financial resources for the purposes of keeping down African wages and subverting local political movements, or at least steering them along lines profitable to their paymasters. Historians will not be able to reach definitive conclusions until the records of both the newly independent governments and the multinational corporations become open for inspection. The evidence that we ourselves have been able to unearth does not, however, support the dramatic charges made against the multinational corporations.

Multinationals, as we have seen, were responsible for developing the copper belt of Northern Rhodesia (now Zambia). Their local power was immense. Like the Fria of Guinea (which became known as Friguia in 1973), the Rhodesian Selection Trust and the Anglo-American Corporation between them created the basic infrastructure required for a great mining enterprise; by the early 1960s, the two conglomerates had provided most of the facilities required to house, feed, care for, and entertain something like a quarter of a million Africans and some thirty-five thousand Europeans in the heart of Africa. But the two combines were far from united. Their labor policies, for instance, sharply diverged, reflecting their national backgrounds. Rhodesian Selection Trust, an American-controlled firm, consistently worked for the advancement of Africans into skilled positions at a time when black Americans were moving into more responsible jobs in the United States itself. The Anglo-American Corporation (controlled, despite its name, by South African interests) took a much more cautious position regarding the promotion of Africans, a position in line with the practices inherited from South Africa.

The two companies joined in supporting the formation of the Federation of Rhodesia and Nyasaland in 1953. But the companies' support was halfhearted. When Roy (later Sir Roy) Welensky, one of the leading European politicians, went cap in hand to the Northern Rhodesian copper trust, he obtained but a few thousand pounds to support the federation movement.

The copper lords neither paid the piper well nor called the tune. The two companies did not even manage to formulate a common policy with regard to the federation. Whereas Anglo-American proved reasonably steadfast in its policy of supporting the federation as a political and social counterweight against South Africa, Rhodesia Selection Trust soon lost interest in the experiment and by the late 1950s had come round to backing African nationalism, by then the winning horse in Northern Rhodesia.

Multinationals on balance have clearly played a progressive role. They have brought capital, technical skills, and entrepreneurship to African states lacking all three. They have developed local resources, generated subsidiary economic development, and provided wages for workers and taxes for governments. Resources that previously could not be exploited or were inefficiently exploited have been made useful and profitable through their actions. As Marx foresaw, capitalism has operated as a revolutionary force in backward economies – partly via multinationals.

West Africa

World War I was economically disastrous for Liberia, but World War II proved to be an economic blessing. For the Western allies, northern Africa was one of the principal theaters of operation. Hence sub-Saharan Africa was extremely important in the transportation of men, supplies, and equipment from the United States. Transatlantic flying was in its infancy; the shortest way across the Atlantic with reasonable safety was between the continental "bulges" of South America and Africa, a route that put Liberia temporarily on one of the most important airways of the world.

Shortly before the United States became involved in the war, Pan American Airways negotiated with the Liberian government for the construction of a modern airport in the country. In February 1942 Liberia granted to the United States the right to build and maintain civil and military airdromes and, if necessary, to provide for their defense. This step resulted in the quick construction of Roberts Field (named in honor of Liberia's first president) and the presence of a garrison and maintenance force of several thousand American soldiers. The pay that burned holes in the pockets of the soldiers, the high wages – by local standards – paid to thousands of Liberian workers who labored at the American installations, and other funds expended by the United States in various ways all had a stimulating effect upon the Liberian economy.[7]

Another wartime development was important to Liberia's economic future. From the start, the country had been handicapped by the lack of an adequate seaport. Shipping was impeded by shifting sandbars and by heavy surf – as dangerous in the twentieth century as it had been in slave-ship days – that required the lightening of cargoes. The Firestone Company, in its original agreement with Liberia, agreed to construct a modern port, but after sinking several hundred thousand dollars into the venture at Marshal, adjacent to the company's other installations, the company was forced to give it up as being beyond the financial resources of a private corporation. After a brief meeting at Roberts Field between the U.S. and Liberian presidents, Franklin D. Roosevelt and Edwin Barclay, following the Casablanca conference, lend-lease funds were made available and work started at once. A modern seaport was formally opened at Monrovia in 1948 with two breakwaters and a port area of some 750 acres, 150 of them dredged to a depth that enabled vessels of twenty-eight foot draft to lie safely; warehouses and docks accommodated six vessels simultaneously. Monrovia had become one of the best ports on the West Coast of Africa.[8]

The development of Monrovia's harbor brought new and unexpected revenue to the Liberian government. Shipowners discovered that registering vessels under the Liberian flag entailed definite advantages, such as freedom from some of the regulations and restrictions imposed by other maritime countries, lower labor costs, and the availability of large numbers of capable seamen from the Kru folk. Registration fees brought considerable sums into the country's treasury, and every major port of the world began to see ships flying the Liberian tricolor, with "Monrovia" inscribed on their sterns as their home port.

American investors took part in developing Liberia in close cooperation with the government and with local moneyed men. As the middle of the twentieth century approached, the iron ore deposits of the Western Hemisphere became increasingly scarce and the world's steel mill operators and manufacturers began an intensive search for new sources. The interior of Liberia was supposedly rich in minerals, but because of the impenetrable terrain this belief could not be verified. The prospect of an adequate seaport, however, quickened interest in exploration. A known deposit of iron lay in the Boma Hills, some forty miles from Monrovia, previously unworked because of its inaccessibility. The new port changed this condition, even before it was complete, and in 1945 the Liberia Mining Company was formed under Canadian incorporation to open and work the field. In 1946 the Republic Steel Corporation, an American firm, and L. K. Christie of New York purchased a controlling interest. To carry the ore from the Boma Hills to the port required construction of a railroad, bridges, and roads, along with the usual facilities for officials and employees of the firm. Work proceeded rapidly, and in 1951 the *New York Times* noted the arrival at Baltimore of the first cargo of 1,000 tons of ore.[9] By 1960 some $40 million had been invested in Boma Hills, and production after that time increased steadily; in 1963 the Boma Hills mines exported more than 2.5 million tons of high-grade iron ore.[10]

Once the market for Boma Hills ore was assured, the Liberia Mining Company agreed to renegotiate the concession, for the express purpose of including Liberian members on its board of directors. This cooperation with Liberians foreshadowed the pattern for financing a second ore deposit on the Mano River. This concession has likewise been developed by a private corporation, the National Iron Company, but in this case, 50 percent of the voting stock in the company is held by the Liberian government. An additional 35 percent of the stock is in the hands of more than sixteen hundred Liberians living throughout the country, and only the remaining 15 percent is held by American interests.

Meanwhile, under President W. V. S. Tubman's policy of attracting foreign capital to Liberia, geologists had been carefully exploring the country and had discovered that the Nimba range, some 170 miles from the coast, was one of the greatest undeveloped iron deposits in the world. In the 1950s a complex international consortium was organized to open and develop the Nimba field. The Bethlehem Steel Corporation acquired a quarter interest in the project, thus adding to the American share of the capitalization. If the Nimba ores were to be available to the world, a deepwater port would be needed, and an American engineering firm, Raymond International, undertook construction of both port and railroad. Making the port entailed constructing a breakwater almost two miles long into the open waters of the Atlantic, building both iron-loading and commercial quays, and dredging to a depth that would take heavily laden vessels. The railroad was built to standard American gage (4 feet 8.5 inches), the only one of that width in Africa south of the Sahara. With heavily metaled roadbed and steel bridges, it can carry at high speed ninety-car trains loaded with nine thousand tons of ore.

Preparing to produce ore, of course, included other details as well: roads, living facilities for employees, hospitals, schools, shops, and all the multitudinous things necessary to modern life. The Nimba project cost over $220 million before a single ton of ore was shipped out; it has been characterized as one of the largest industrial projects undertaken in Africa to the present time. Production began in August 1963, and before the end of the year 1,797,445 tons of ore were shipped. In 1964 production rose to 7.23 million tons.[11]

African financial participation was even greater in the large-scale Volta River project in Ghana to develop the country's aluminum resources. The idea of damming the Volta River had been conceived forty years earlier, but it was not until 1952 that British concerns took an active interest in the plan and prepared preliminary surveys. The high cost of the project discouraged the British companies, and the scheme was dropped until President Nkrumah's visit to the United States in 1958 prompted a reassessment of the scheme. Kaiser Aluminum and Chemical Corporation engineers were selected to perform the reappraisal, and in February 1959 they submitted their report. The key to the scheme was the aluminum smelter, for only the production of aluminum required the enormous amounts of electricity needed to turn the hydroelectric project into a paying proposition. Through reduced construction costs, the price of power became sufficiently cheap to make its purchase for smelting aluminum economically feasible. The Volta River was developed as a complex of hydroelectric dam and power plant, estimated at a cost of some $168 million, to provide electricity for an aluminum smelter costing $128 million. The Akosombo dam and power plant were financed half by Ghana and half by the World Bank, the Development Loan Fund, the Export–Import Bank of Washington, and the government of Great Britain. To construct the smelter, a consortium of American aluminum companies – Kaiser Corporation, Reynolds Aluminum, and Olin Mathieson – formed the Volta Aluminum Company (Valco) to work in conjunction with the construction of the dam and power plant.

Thus the Volta River project entailed all the financial arrangements that had been employed on other large development schemes in Africa: a consortium of firms to spread the risk and raise the capital, the cooperation and financial investment of the African government itself, and finally the involvement of the U.S. government. Participation by Africans not only helped to provide the massive sums required, but spread and protected the risks taken by the private investors. African cooperation eliminated fears of foreign exploitation, engendered pride in cooperative effort, and provided a check on the activities of the developing company.

Major consortia often became privileged bodies, achieving a specially protected position denied to independent small firms. In Guinea in 1957, for instance, a group of international investors formed the Fria Compagnie Internationale pour la Production de l'Alumine for the purpose of mining and manufacturing aluminum. Nearly half the company was financed by Olin Mathieson, an American undertaking; the remaining half was provided by French, German, Swiss, and British firms.[12] Initial arrangements were made while Guinea was still under French sway. When Guinea became independent, in 1958, relations between Guinea and France were ruptured; Guinea decided to embark on what its defenders called the "noncapitalist way to development." But the construction of the plant, one of the largest and most modern in the world, proceeded nonetheless. When it was finished, it had an installed capacity of 480,000 metric tons, with facilities planned to more than double its output in the future. Two-thirds of the development costs derived from the construction of an adequate infrastructure – railroads, highways, harbor works, and a city to house seven thousand people with all the necessary hospitals, schools, utilities, and recreation areas. The lack of such facilities in Africa, elsewhere usually provided by the government, had clearly discouraged smaller American investment and thereby contributed to the use of the international consortium as a means to acquire the necessary capital. By the mid-1960s investment exceeded $150 million and was comparable to the entire gross national product of Guinea.

Relations between Fria and the government of Guinea remained reasonably friendly. The management of Fria adopted the policy of training Africans as rapidly as possible for advancement into positions of trust and responsibility. Hence, although Guinea was one of the more radical of the newly independent African countries, there was – and has so far been – little hostility toward the consortium and no lessening in its planned expansion and activities.[13] The shareholders benefited from the prospect of a steady supply of aluminum; Guinea benefited from an industrial city with all the technical and administrative training necessary for the Africans to cooperate in Fria operations. The taxes from Fria provided revenue for the state, and the sale of aluminum provided the major source of Guinea's foreign exchange. The common interests of the government and the multinational corporation guaranteed the investors against expropriation and promised even greater profits to come.

The Olin Mathieson Chemical Corporation did not pretend to be a philanthropic organization, and was frankly operating in Africa for profits. Nevertheless, the company realized from the start that whatever was done for the good of the country was good business and in the long run would result in increased earnings for the firm. Following this policy, the company established a one-year fellowship at the Harvard Graduate School of Business Administration for a Guinean student to be named by the government of Guinea, a scholarship for a Guinean student preparing for the foreign service at Rutgers University, and sponsorship of another Guinean student at the Eli Whitney Technical School. One of the company's senior research scientists was loaned for several months to the Guinean Ministry of Production to survey methods to improve the country's agriculture, and the firm assisted directly in carrying out his recommendations. In addition, through E. R. Squibb and Sons, an Olin Mathieson subsidiary manufacturing pharmaceuticals, came the donation of a large supply of antibiotics and vitamins to the Guinean Ministry of Public Health. The Fria project was not Olin Mathieson's only interest in Africa, but at the time it was undertaken it was one of the largest investments of private capital in West Africa. Through the Squibb International Division, the firm maintained scientific offices in Egypt and Kenya. In South Africa it had a manufacturing plant and a foundation that provided grants for medical research and allied activities.

The consortium that included Olin Mathieson had a happier experience than one in which American, French, and Canadian investors were deeply involved financially. Bauxites du Midi, a French-owned subsidiary of Aluminum Limited, received the first rights to the Boké bauxite deposits in northwestern Guinea in the 1920s and to deposits in Los Islands near Conakry in the 1930s. Aluminum Limited, a Canadian corporation mainly owned by Americans, did preliminary work in the 1950s at a cost of $12 million. When Guinea received its independence, the new government honored existing commitments. Unable to raise on its own the huge funds required to develop the Boké deposits (nearly $200 million), Aluminum Limited decided to form an international consortium on the lines of Fria in order to meet the target date, 1964. The greater part of the money invested went to build an extensive infrastructure: a deepwater port at Kakande, a railway from Kakande to Boké, townsites, schools, hospitals, entertainment facilities, corporate enterprises. Aluminum Limited, in other words, took up the burden that government agencies would have shouldered in more-developed parts of the world. The project promised to be even more extensive and ambitious than the Mathieson one. In 1961, however, the company found itself unable to meet the promised completion date, so the government expropriated its properties and ordered its withdrawal from Guinea.[14]

In addition, the United States acquired an increasing stake in the commerce of Nigeria, which had traditionally supplied the world market with such tropical crops as palm oil, palm kernels, cocoa, and groundnuts. In 1956 Shell-British Petroleum, a United Kingdom company, made the first important discoveries of oil. American companies, especially Mobil Oil, joined in the work of exploration, and by the late 1960s Nigeria was on the threshold of modernization. The transition from the peasant economy to a semi-industrialized economy was reflected in the composition of Nigeria's imports. By the mid-1960s, Nigeria had become an important purchaser of industrial materials, machinery, and transport equipment, rather than consumer goods, as in the past. The Nigerian civil war seriously set back development. War occasioned heavy casualties and widespread destruction; and the government spent nearly all of its income for military purposes; prices rose; and there was a serious balance of payments crisis. The Nigerian peasant economy suffered seriously from the government's policy of transferring financial resources from the villages to the towns: Government marketing boards insisted on underpaying the peasants for their produce and applying the surplus to urban development, industrial enterprises, and the growing bureaucracy.

Nigeria's growing petroleum industry, however, helped to tide the country over these difficulties, and American entrepreneurs took an important share in developing its oil resources. In addition to Mobil Oil, American entrepreneurs active in Nigeria by the late 1970s included Gulf Oil, Phillips Petroleum, Tennessee Nigeria (Tenneco), Union Oil, Texas Overseas Petroleum, and California Asiatic Oil. Oil overshadowed Nigeria's export economy, and the United States had become one of its most important customers: In 1977, for example, United States imports from Nigeria represented about 47 percent of all Nigerian exports. Dazzled by its apparent oil wealth, Nigeria, like so many other Third World countries, took up huge foreign loans; debts owed to foreigners rose from 350.1 million nairas in 1975 to 1,186.7 million in 1978. When oil prices dropped, Nigeria therefore faced a difficult financial position whose gravity contributed to what had become, by the early 1980s, a worldwide banking crisis.[15]

Southern Africa

Americans also enlarged their foothold in the Portuguese colonies. The outbreak of guerrilla warfare in Angola in 1961 coincided with a remarkable upswing in Portugal's domestic economy. Having realized that it must develop its empire or lose it, Lisbon began to invest more funds in its overseas dependencies. At the same time, the Portuguese began to open their doors to foreign lenders, whom they had previously viewed with mistrust. Foreign – including American – capitalists received a number of advantages denied to smaller domestic entrepreneurs in matters such as repatriating profits. Gulf Oil's operations in Cabinda, for instance, became a major enterprise, left inviolable by the Portuguese as well as by the Angolan guerrillas. By 1973 the United States had become Angola's largest customer and its third most-important importer.[16] Up to 1977, when the Marxist government insisted on joint enterprises, the oil companies had purchased concessionary rights to explore for and exploit oil. The government oil company Sonangol now has 51 percent or more of all oil ventures in Angola.

Gulf Oil is the biggest of the American investors, with $532 million currently invested. Other American oil companies operating around Cabinda are Mobil, Texaco, Cities Service, and Marathon. Yet the United States does not recognize the Angolan government. And the oil companies, in effect, have become lobbyists for a Marxist–Leninist state that oppresses its people, has threatened its neighbors Zaire and Namibia, and wages a civil war against one-third of its people.

The most controversial American investments have been those in South Africa. Seen within the wider context of American capitalism as a whole, these investments have accounted for little (1 percent of all American direct investment overseas and, for most firms involved, less than 1 percent of total corporate assets). Within South Africa itself, however, the American impact has been far from negligible. In 1979 just under 5 percent of all capital stock in the South African manufacturing industry was in American hands; the American share was considerably larger in petroleum, computer, and automotive industries. Total American investments in 1979 stood at about $2.01 billion and were derived from a relatively small number of companies.[17] Major corporations comprised Union Carbide (a great chrome producer), Newmont Mining, Kennecott Copper Corporation, Phelps Dodge, United States Steel, American Metal Climax, and others.

In addition to capital, these Americans have been particularly important in the transfer and development of advanced technology, and the manufacturing component of American investment has been especially valuable. In 1970 over 50 percent of these funds were placed in manufacturing industries, 10 percent in mining, and 25 percent in petroleum. Ford and General Motors held about one-third of the automobile market. American firms dominated the market for computers, which at the present time are still being imported from abroad. Caltex, Mobil, and Exxon had a 40 percent share in South Africa's market for petroleum products; U.S. firms helped to build up South Africa's refining capacity and thus contributed to supplying the country with energy, about one-quarter of which derives from petroleum. U.S. capital was invested in the mining of gold, diamonds, and various base metals. In addition, Americans have participated in heavy engineering; in the manufacturers of agricultural, mining, and construction equipment; in the rubber industry; and in electronics. American interests have been involved in a wide variety of services, including banking, shipping, and insurance.[18]

In South-West Africa (now Namibia) Americans also played a major part in developing the mining industries. Before World War I began, the Germans had opened a small copper mine in a remote township then named Tsumeb. The original operators were allowed to continue during the interwar period, but on the outbreak of World War II the South African government confiscated all German properties, and shortly after the war had ended the Tsumeb mine was put up for sale to the highest bidder. The mine shafts meanwhile had filled with water, and the installations had deteriorated to the point where it was impossible to determine accurately whether the property could be rehabilitated and made to pay. The outlook was so unpromising that many major mining firms refused to bid, but a syndicate formed by American Metal Climax and the Newmont Mining Corporation decided to gamble, and bought the mine.

The actual operation and management of the enterprise was undertaken by the Newmont Mining Corporation. When the first American officials and engineers reached the mine, they found the African employees living in huts made of tin cans, burlap, and other scavenged materials, without sanitary or recreational facilities of any sort, and existing on such foodstuffs as the desert provided. Many local Europeans informed the Americans that the Africans preferred to live that way and that any attempt to better living conditions would be a waste of time, money, and effort. Disregarding this advice, the Americans tore down the ramshackle huts and replaced them with neat, sanitary cottages for married workers and modern dormitories (or barracks) for men without families. A sewer system and a modern water system were installed. Laundries, sports fields, a motion-picture theater, a hospital and dispensaries, a truck farm to provide vegetables, a dairy farm, herds of beef cattle, schools for the workers' children – all were provided before an ounce of ore was taken from the mine. And before the mine could operate, it was necessary to build a railroad from Tsumeb to the sea, a distance of some 235 miles. A smelter was completed in 1962, the mine was pumped dry and completely rehabilitated, and the American syndicate soon found that its gamble would pay rich dividends.

Before rehabilitation of Tsumeb was complete, a second rich mineral deposit was discovered at Kombat, about sixty miles distant, where similar facilities were needed before operation could be undertaken. Curiously, the actual operation of the mines and smelters disclosed that copper, the original attraction, was but one of the metals found in the complex deposits. Today, though copper is an important product of Tsumeb and Kombat, it is minor to lead, zinc, and other minerals that constitute the major output.

Measures to benefit the African employees (including a 30 percent wage increase made voluntarily by the management), though regarded by old "Africa hands" as useless waste, have paid off in the form of a dependable, efficient, contented labor force. Workers were recruited in "tribal reserves," but increasing numbers of them returned to Tsumeb year after year; under the company's program of education and training, many of them began to advance steadily to more responsible and higher-paid positions.[19]

By the end of the 1970s, southern Africa had assumed an important role as a supplier of urgently needed metals for the American economy. The so-called Santini report issued for the congressional subcommittee on mining and minerals revealed in 1980 that "American dependency on South African mineral resources is without question." By 1980 South Africa was a major supplier to the United States of the following amounts of imported strategic minerals: chrome ore, 38.3 percent; ferrochrome, 76.3 percent; manganese ore, 49.7 percent; manganese metal, 98.0 percent; ferromanganese, 39.2 percent; palladium, 51.4 percent; and platinum, 73.8 percent.[20]

In the 1980s a reverse flow of capital and technology is linking the United States with South Africa. South Africa, starting in 1950, pioneered the making of oil from coal. The South African Coal, Oil and Gas Corporation (SASOL) produces liquid fuel from coal and provides South Africa with 70 percent of its energy requirements. A SASOL II plant was begun in 1979. South Africa has become the world's leading oil-from-coal processer, and in 1981 an agreement was reached between SASOL and Fluor Engineers and Constructors, a subsidiary of Fluor Corporation of California, for the future marketing and use of SASOL's coal-conversion technology in the United States. With SASOL's technology and Fluor's qualified personnel, the United States will also be able to reduce its dependence on imported oil by processing its own extensive coal deposits. The flow of businesspeople, technicians, engineers, and scientists, who for over a century have trekked to South Africa, may be about to be partially reversed.

American investments in South Africa met widespread criticism within the United States in the 1970s and 1980s. The opponents of the apartheid system (most notably, the NAACP, militant student groups, and some church groups and universities) called for "disinvestment," the withdrawal of American funds from South Africa. Advocates of moderate reform – such as the Reverend Leon Sullivan, a black minister from Philadelphia and a director of General Motors – recommended that South Africa be changed from within: Apartheid was to be overcome through a strict code of business conduct for American firms, which outlawed racial discrimination, assisted the technical training and promotion of blacks, and encouraged the formation of trade unions. In 1977 more than a hundred American firms signed the resulting Sullivan Code. It required desegregation of eating facilities and toilets; equal employment opportunities; equal pay for equal work; apprenticeship and management trainee programs for blacks and browns, as well as whites; improvements in living conditions for nonwhites; support for unionization; and promotion of nonwhites to higher posts.

In 1972 a group of investing bodies founded Investor Responsibility Research Center (IRCC) as a non–profit-making body to conduct research in South Africa and to publish impartial reports on social policy issues and their impact on major corporations and international investors. IRRC was financed primarily by annual subscription fees paid by more than a hundred investing bodies; it was governed by a twenty-one member board of directors, most of whom represented subscribing institutions. Its reports included such detailed documents as *Labor Practices of U.S. Corporations in South Africa* (1976), *U.S. Business and South Africa: The Withdrawal Issue* (1977), and *Bank Loans to South Africa* (1979).

The makers of the Sullivan Code and other critics have assumed that American capitalists have the power to change Third World countries, especially South Africa, by manipulating their power structures through economic pressure. This assumption is a dubious one. South Africa, by the 1960s, had developed a relatively mature economy, engendering the bulk of its capital from domestic resources; foreign investments accounted for a relatively small share of the capital produced by its economy. Of the foreign funds placed in South Africa, American investments amounted to only about 18 percent. Even this share was on the decline, for the pace of new capital investments made by European and Japanese firms greatly exceeded the pace of American investments. U.S. investments, moreover, became increasingly "South Africanized" as the bulk of American profits made in South Africa came to be locally reinvested.[21] Advocates and critics alike of American investment in South Africa were inclined to overestimate grossly the importance of American investments within the wider framework of the South African economy.

The same judgment applies to the advancement of Africans and Coloureds in South African industry. The promotion of both groups in industry did not start with the Sullivan Code; it was linked to wider structural changes in South Africa's economy and the shortage of skilled and semiskilled white workers. The impact of the Sullivan Code can at best be marginal, as can American industrial investments in general. The industrial revolution in South Africa was not brought about by American enterprise; American firms merely strengthened existing trends. The new industries developed new skills, and these skills, in the long run, benefited the entire labor force. Manufacturing industries, on the whole, paid higher wages than did extractive industries, and the benefits of these wages percolated downward, albeit slowly. Lastly, the development of manufacturing has encouraged the development of an internal market. Blacks and Coloureds began to be valued not merely as hands, but also as customers – perhaps the most far-reaching departure in the social history of South Africa.

American corporations with holdings in South Africa have not, however, constituted a very effective pressure group in the United States. According to a considerable number of intellectuals on and off college campuses, American multinational corporations, allied to the Central Intelligence Agency and the military, have wielded far-reaching and malignant power throughout the land; they have controlled the media; they have provided money and hence have controlled policies. In practice, this has not been the case. Business lobbies can be extremely effective where specific, narrowly defined issues, bearing on the direct financial affairs of a particular firm, are concerned. But American entrepreneurs, for the most part, have not been interested in the collective – as opposed to the sectional – interests of capitalism. Gulf Oil, for example, continued to do business in the Marxist–Leninist Republic of Angola, where it supplied a major part of the country's revenue. Gulf Oil managers favored U.S. recognition of Angola; Cuban and MPLA troops guarded Gulf Oil installations in Cabinda from guerrilla attacks. Strikes were made illegal because Communists and capitalists had discovered a most profitable form of coexistence.

Overall, U.S. businessmen have tended to be defensive rather than aggressive, especially on questions of "social responsibility," including apartheid – issues of particular concern to South Africa. The stakes held by American firms in South Africa have not been of sufficient importance to their worldwide interests to justify serious public relations risks. U.S. firms with financial stakes in South Africa are unlikely to take part in a political confrontation unless they are forced to disinvest in a manner that will cost them a great deal of money. Otherwise, they are likely to go along with piecemeal reforms under the Sullivan Code, which American managers tend to approve on economic as well as moral grounds.

The closest thing to a pro–South African lobby has been found in some conservative elements within the United States. These groups have sympathized with South Africa for a variety of reasons. Some perceive South Africa as either a Christian country or an anti-Communist bastion; others see it as a strategic asset, a bulwark of white supremacy, or a defender of capitalism. White South Africa receives a good deal of sympathy among members of the American gun lobby and among former Green Berets, who regard it as a stronghold of the West. South Africa often enjoys high regard among evangelical Christians, respectful of a country that bans pornographic literature. But the defenders of South Africa, like its opponents, think primarily in American domestic terms: They are apt to project American concerns on the African screen; African issues on their own cut no ice in American politics. Senator Dick Clark, a liberal and head of the influential subcommittee on African affairs of the Senate Committee on Foreign Affairs, failed to be reelected in 1978. His defeat owed only a little to his African policies – his opponent called him "the Senator from Africa" – but derived more from internal American issues such as the taxpayers' revolt, discontent with the performance of public services, and above all, the right-to-life question.

CHAPTER 22

Economic Activities

The public sector

The history of American philanthropy overseas is a long and honorable one. Americans, as individuals, are easily the most generous in the world. The nationals of no other country can equal Americans when it comes to writing checks for charitable organizations designed to help the poor and unfortunate in foreign lands. During the nineteenth and the first decades of the twentieth century, foreign aid hinged on the private enterprise of mission societies, charitable bodies, and privately organized relief operations such as Herbert Hoover's Commission for Relief in Belgium, set up during World War I. Private philanthropy rivaled private investment in extent and effectiveness.

During the course of World War II and afterward, however, the American state became increasingly powerful as an agent for channeling public investments overseas and as an instrument of charitable work; indeed, the two functions widely came to be seen as interlocked. Lend-lease given to Great Britain and the Soviet Union in World War II, followed by the Marshall Plan during the war's aftermath, created a new climate of opinion and new expectations. There was a sense of optimism in the air. The Nazi and the Japanese warmongers had been crushed. Fascism had been extirpated. A new world was in the making, free from poverty, fear, and war. Where President Wilson had failed after World War I, the democratic leaders of the emergent Third World nations would succeed. The new nations, freed from the shackles of colonialism, would help to inaugurate an era of prosperity, and for this purpose they needed Western technology and finances. Guided by the precepts of John Maynard Keynes, John Kenneth Galbraith, and Walt Rostow, the leaders of the world would eliminate sickness, want, and poverty throughout the globe. The road to economic salvation was straight; all that was wanted was the will to embark on the great journey to worldwide brotherhood.

Foreign aid programs

Within a short period of time, foreign aid became an accepted means of national policy, challenged only by a handful of outsiders on the extreme right and the extreme left. Foreign aid was all things to all people, for it appealed to a great body of disparate constituents who otherwise had little in common. Foreign aid seemed a sovereign means of defending the free world against communism, a way to achieve international stability, an instrument for strengthening democratic government, a bribe to buy over unfriendly governments, a Keynesian device for stimulating international demand and thereby avoiding worldwide slumps, a pork barrel for American farmers and manufacturers, a blueprint for international planning, a means of saving life, a control on runaway population growth, a plan for assuring international literacy, and a form of international income tax that would even out disparities of wealth between the rich and the poor countries in the world. Aid became a form of Western reparation for both real and alleged iniquities committed against the Third World.[2]

Foreign aid supposedly would provide a New Deal on a global scale, a reborn sense of purpose to the nation at large; it would help in stabilizing the world's population, would spread popular education and enlightenment, would curb disease, and would make Americans beloved throughout the world. Foreign aid became part of America's secular religion, one that almost equated economic, civic, and spiritual progress. In addition, foreign aid generated a new and powerful lobby of its own: administrators, planners, academicians, bankers, and businessmen, all with a vested interest in expanding foreign aid at the taxpayers' expense. In this as in other spheres, public and private enterprise began to fuse, creating a power structure of a kind new to the American body politic.

In Africa, the foreign aid program did not seriously get under way until the end of European colonial rule, despite some trickling down under Point Four of the Marshall Plan. Even after the Union Jack and the French tricolor disappeared from most parts of the continent, an American committee appointed by President Kennedy and headed by General Lucius Clay of Berlin fame, reported in 1963 that the Western European countries should continue to bear the main burden of assisting the former colonies.[1] Yet between 1946 and 1961 the United States made available a worldwide total of $90.5 billion in foreign aid (including $29.0 billion for foreign military assistance). Foreign aid took many forms: loans, both "hard" and "soft" direct grants; technical assistance; and so forth. The U.S. government, moreover, negotiated investment-guarantee agreements with most of the new countries, under the terms of which the American taxpayer provided American entrepreneurs with coverage against such risks as war, revolution, insurrection, and expropriation.[2] The terms of these agreements differed from country to country, but they all had one feature in common: Special groups of investors received specific benefits at public expense not available to investors in other sectors of the economy. In the eyes of their critics, such programs became boondoggles for special-interest groups.

Within this new bureaucratic financial empire, Africa counted for only a minor share of funds. The entire African continent received only $1.8 billion, or 2 percent of the total. Of this amount, 95 percent was disbursed for economic assistance; military assistance, such as it was, remained largely the responsibility of the colonial powers. Black Africa during this period received very little U.S. aid; the bulk of the funds spent on Africa (a total of $1.1 billion) went to the Muslim states of north Africa.

After 1961, U.S. assistance to Africa rapidly expanded; by 1980 the American taxpayer was spending, in a single year, as much on assistance to the African continent as that taxpayer's parents had spent during the entire first fifteen years following World War II.[3] However limited this amount appeared in terms of the total U.S. gross domestic product, within Africa American aid was enormous. Africa received the largest per capita share of aid in the world.

Foreign aid was different in kind from the assistance proffered by the traditional colonial powers to their dependencies. The Europeans dealt with a limited number of territories under their own suzerainty, and there was some continuity in policy. There was rigid accounting for money disbursed and elaborate supervision through the civil service and through parliamentary debates. Above all, the European colonizers exercised direct control on the spot, working through a permanent staff of administrators and technicians whose careers were tied to the colonies for the entire spell of their working lives. These safeguards did not prevent instances of gross mismanagement and incompetence – such as the British "Groundnut Scheme" undertaken in Tanganyika after World War II to provide food oil for Great Britain – but on the whole, wasteful expenditure was kept in bounds.

Foreign aid, on the other hand, proceeded on very different principles. American and foreign aid officials had to work through bureaucracies that they could neither control nor hold accountable. The direction of American aid was apt to veer from one country to the next, in accord with shifts in the international kaleidoscope. Economic policies likewise changed in emphasis, reflecting changes in the climate of academic and bureaucratic opinion.

The complexities of American policy and the multiplicity of lobbies – congressional, bureaucratic, and entrepreneurial – concerned with Africa militated against steadiness of purpose and public accountability for the vast sums expended on the American taxpayers' behalf. The sheer size and diversity of the American bureaucracy further militated against efficient administration. By the end of the 1970s some twenty-nine U.S. government departments, agencies, offices, administrations, and permanent commissions were engaged in activities concerning Africa,[4] often in virtual ignorance of one another's operations. The Department of Defense provided military assistance, with personnel stationed throughout much of Africa. The Department of State maintained diplomatic missions in most parts of the continent. The National Endowment for the Humanities and other agencies (especially the Department of Education) awarded grants for research and similar projects. Fulbright scholars were sent to African universities. A variety of official bodies carried on international training programs, or supported private voluntary agencies in Africa, or contributed to the UN organizations with interests in Africa. The Export–Import Bank and the Overseas Private Investment Corporation offered financial aid to American businesspeople investing in Africa. A considerable number of agencies administered economic and development assistance of various kinds, including the Department of Agriculture and, above all, the Agency for International Development (AID), first set up in 1961 to expand the foreign aid programs. AID was itself the latest in a long line of postwar aid agencies whose complex structure would require an entire administrative manual for its proper elucidation.[5]

Given the extent of bureaucratic proliferation and its scope, the total extent of U.S. aid to sub-Saharan Africa is hard to evaluate. In 1977 alone, U.S. assistance to Africa south of the Sahara totaled $543,618,000, including $475,718,000 devoted to economic, and $67,900,000 to military, aid. The Americans, in other words, were spending in one year more in aid than the entire gross national product of the Somali Democratic Republic ($425 million), a sovereign member of the UN and a substantial military power in the Horn of Africa. AID alone disbursed $230 million in 1977. Few human activities were excluded from AID's scope, from growing maize or learning the alphabet to birth control.[6]

The advocates of aid were usually committed to long-term international planning, but American aid, like international assistance in general, was subject to rapid and unpredictable fluctuations that made long-term planning impossible. The development campaign was vast, its expenditure impressive but ill coordinated and subject to great administrative overheads. The traditional colonial powers, in trying to develop their overseas possessions, had worked within a strictly defined territorial framework. International aid of the postcolonial kind had no such limitations. American aid administrators, like their colleagues abroad, bestowed public largesse for the most varied and contradictory purposes.

Following its independence in 1960, Nigeria was singled out as America's most-favored recipient of aid. Much the most populous state in Africa, Nigeria impressed the Americans by its supposed stability and its dedication to democratic principles and a free-enterprise economy – this at a time when danger signals were already heralding a military take-over (1966) and a bloody civil war (ended only in 1970). Immediately upon gaining independence, the Nigerian government set in motion a six-year plan for developing the country's resources. Favorably impressed with the plan, and persuaded of the ability of the Nigerians to carry it through, the United States made outright grants and advanced loans totaling, together, some $225 million. At the same time a guarantee agreement was concluded under which Nigeria hoped to attract significant amounts of private American capital for investment inside its borders. One U.S. program for the technical training of Nigerians was inaugurated in 1977, and AID had by 1982 brought twenty-four hundred Nigerians to the United States for two-year training programs.

Liberia received a substantial amount of aid because of the long-established relationship between the two countries. The postwar American assistance program was aimed at helping Liberia to achieve basic reforms in budgetary policies and public administration, as well as promoting Liberia's general economic development, especially its infrastructure. Loans totaling several million dollars were granted to improve sanitation in the capital, to establish a hospital, and to construct schools. Governance by Liberia's Afro-American ruling stratum hardly represented American democracy in the form preached by AID officials, but this matter was overlooked because the government was a staunch defender of American interests and President Tubman was considered a moderating influence in Pan-African politics.[7]

Ethiopia was another important client with dubious democratic credentials. Between 1965 and 1973, it was the largest recipient of American aid in sub-Saharan Africa. Ethiopia occupied an important strategic position in the Horn of Africa. Emperor Haile Selassie, moreover, had acquired an international reputation for himself as a liberal statesman during the dark days of the Italo-Ethiopian War and World War II; his image as a philanthropist-king for long stood unchallenged. Further, Ethiopia provided to the United States a variety of military facilities. The Ethiopian king received his reward in the form of substantial grants-in-aid at a time when few anticipated the monarchy's disastrous collapse and none foresaw its transformation into a Marxist–Leninist People's Republic.

The Congo (later Zaire), on the other hand, was a newcomer and moved to the top of the United States' most-favored list in Africa during the 1960s – not because of its strength, not because of the supposed stability of its democratic institutions, but because of its weakness: American policy makers feared that the Congo might disintegrate and fall into Communist hands, with disastrous consequences both to itself and to its neighbors. Between 1960 and 1962 the Congo, previously ignored because it was a Belgian colony, suddenly received more American aid than any other state in Africa. Private investors had been discouraged by independence, a sudden Belgian exodus, mutinies within the Congolese army, warfare between differing black ethnic communities, and reports – sometimes true, sometimes exaggerated – of atrocities. Concern over the influence in the Congo of Ghana, Guinea, and other radical states stimulated counteraction. The U.S. government therefore provided aid in many different forms, amounting to a total of over $100 million for the years 1960–2. Aid included, among other items, $4 million in development grants, $17 million for food, $5 million for technical assistance, and $38 million through UN agencies. According to the State Department, this vast transfer of cash materially assisted the strife-torn country in its recovery.[8] Such assertions, however, cannot be verified, given the absence of a proper system of inspection and audit.

A substantial amount of assistance went to Guinea, not as a reward for good democratic conduct, but as a bribe designed to wean it away from its initial pro-Soviet policy. The U.S. government did not at first take much interest in Guinea's major strategic asset, its bauxite deposits. In 1959 official contributions stressed humanitarian considerations: Famine threatened the country, so the United States shipped five tons of rice and three thousand tons of wheat flour. Despite Guinea's apparent orientation toward the Soviets and its acceptance of aid from Communist China, the United States in 1960 also extended a credit for $1 million to purchase rice, flour, and milk. In the same year a technical and economic aid agreement provided for a large number of scholarships in the United States for students from Guinea. In 1965 two loans were provided to Guinea for the procurement of aircraft, the construction of a hangar, and the addition of increased electrical power facilities in the Conakry.

Tanganyika (known as Tanzania after its 1964 union with Zanzibar) became a beneficiary of America largesse shortly after attaining independence in 1961, when the United States added $10 million to funds provided by Great Britain to expand communications and improve the school system. In addition, the United States advanced substantial long-term loans and supplied humanitarian aid. In the winter of 1961–2, for instance, when a prolonged drought, followed by disastrous floods, threatened much of Tanzania with famine, the United States provided large quantities of food, in some instances air-dropping supplies directly into isolated villages where food was desperately short. During the late 1970s Tanzania became the most substantial recipient of American assistance in sub-Saharan Africa.

And so it went on. The Malagasy Republic (Madagascar) obtained a loan to rehabilitate its railroad system – specifically to replace a major bridge and realign the tracks. Cameroun received a loan to construct roads. Kenya was helped to procure services and goods for the expansion of the Kenya Polytechnic. The list seems endless.[9] Yet, despite the enormous amount of literature produced to justify foreign aid, there is in retrospect no conceivable correlation between the dollar amounts contributed by the American taxpayer to the various African countries and the ostensible objects of such largesse, if we judge by the recipients' political stability, economic development, democratic proclivity, or willingness to provide long-range support to the United States in foreign affairs.

African governments also asked for and received military and police training after they became independent. The United States has had a strong military assistance program since 1946. By 1966 some 2,721 officers and noncommissioned officers had come to the United States to study, at a cost of $13,861 million. There was also a five-year cost-sharing program, offered to a limited number of students from Ethiopia, Ghana, Liberia, Mali, and Sierra Leone, to provide four years of undergraduate study at a school with a Reserve Officer Training Corps program and then one year of officer training at a service school such as the Army Infantry School. Ethiopia sent the largest numbers of men to be trained in military science.

The United States operated several of these programs for African governments as well. The International Police Academy in Washington, D.C., had trained 175 African officers by 1966. Much less military and police training took place in the 1970s, because African governments no longer felt the need to send people overseas for such courses and because, under President Carter, far less military assistance was available (see Table 1).

Dissent on aid

The objects for which foreign aid was given were subject to changes of intellectual fashion. Initially, policy makers emphasized large-scale projects like the Niger Dam, designed to expand Nigeria's electricity supply and thus stimulate the economy. By the late 1970s AID operations had greatly diversified; far more stress was laid on food and nutrition, health, and population planning, the latter a subject that by this time had become dear to academicians, with overpopulation coming to be regarded as a global danger. Even on their own terms, aid policies failed to follow a consistent line, responding as they did to a variety of bureaucratic, academic, and economic pressure groups within the United States and the recipient countries.[10] There was no consistent plan, no consistent object, and – worst of all – no efficient system of accounting or design for follow-up studies.

American motives for *not* giving aid, or for withholding assistance once given, were as mixed as the motives for supplying it. A prospective recipient might disqualify itself either by success or by failure. South Africa was left out because of its economic prosperity and because of the evil reputation of apartheid. Ideological considerations apart, bodies like the Department of Health, Education, and Welfare (HEW) or AID, concerned with giving aid and advice to backward countries, naturally sympathized with the newly independent black countries rather than with South Africa or Rhodesia, which received no development funds and did not rank as financial clients. Libya was dropped from the list of beneficiaries because of the ample revenue produced by its newly found oil deposits. Congo-Brazzaville was eliminated following its leftward swing after the ouster of President Fulbert Youlou in 1963. Ghana received sizable loans from 1961 to 1963, at a time when President Kwame Nkrumah was in good standing because of his anticolonial reputation; subsequently, however, Ghana fell into disfavor, partly because of Nkrumah's economic mismanagement and partly because of his increasingly hostile stand toward the United States. Ghana redeemed its reputation in 1966 through a military coup that ousted the dictator, only to plunge the country into new and unforeseen difficulties.[11]

The U.S. foreign aid program undertaken after the end of World War II has been

Table 1. U.S. Training of sub-Saharan African Military Personnel, 1970–9

Country	Number of people trained											% receiving operational training[a]
	1970	1971	1972	1973	1974	1975	1976	1977	1978	1979	1970–9	
Cameroun	2	—	—	—	—	—	—	—	—	—	2	—
Ethiopia	154	140	160	158	148	129	354	137	—	1	1,381	27
Ghana	22	11	9	14	8	41	118	43	78	66	410	16
Ivory Coast	8	12	8	2	—	—	—	—	—	—	30	—
Kenya	—	2	2	1	—	3	39	97	70	54	268	34
Liberia	44	38	36	34	36	20	26	16	30	9	289	46
Mali	9	—	—	—	—	5	—	—	—	3	17	18
Nigeria	5	108	35	—	—	4	428	825	406	482	2,293	32
Senegal	5	—	—	2	—	—	—	2	7	11	27	48
Sudan	—	—	—	2	5	—	—	17	184	53	261	36
Togo	—	—	—	—	—	—	—	4	—	—	4	—
Upper Volta	—	—	—	—	—	—	—	—	—	9	9	44
Zaire	114	160	50	35	57	37	110	120	94	88	865	36
Totals	363	471	300	248	254	239	1,075	1,261	869	776	5,856	

Notes: Data are by fiscal year and include training under the International Military Education and Training (IMET) and Foreign Military Sales (FMS) programs. However, figures for 1970–5 represent IMET only and are greatly understated owing to unavailable or noncomparable FMS data. Dashes indicate no data.

[a] This column shows percentage of students who received weapons, equipment, and operational training, as opposed to managerial/administrative, supply/maintenance, and indoctrination/orientation training.

Source: Joseph P. Smaldone, Statistical Data on Department of Defense Training of Foreign Military Personnel, FGMSD-80-48 (Washington, D.C.: GAO, 1980).

adjudged in many different ways. Aid has constituted but a negligible proportion of the gross national product; hence the assistance given has seemed parsimonious to critics. On the other hand, aid has involved a public gift unequaled in history. Keeping in mind the complexities of American administrative organization, the varieties of financial transfers involved, and the slackness that has so often characterized accounting for official funds, no one can be quite certain how much wealth has ultimately been transferred abroad from the United States. No one knows exactly what has happened to all the transfers made. We can only be sure of one thing: The funds involved have been enormous. Between 1945 and 1970 alone, at a time when the value of the dollar as yet remained relatively stable, total U.S. aid was estimated at about $125 billion. This amount alone greatly exceeded the value of reparations actually paid by Germany to the victors of World War I – money transfers thought so onerous that they have been widely held to have contributed to the failure of the Versailles peace settlement and the breakdown of the Weimar Republic. Given the extent of America's foreign aid program and given the abuse often showered on the donor by beneficiaries of American largesse, the Americans' willingness to pay has been almost miraculous. The U.S. foreign aid program has become part of an accepted orthodoxy, and, as already noted, official aid has been paralleled by assistance given through private sources – missionary societies, humanitarian bodies, and the great foundations.

What good has come of this foreign aid? The question is hard to answer, for the full story remains to be written. By and large, the World Bank has secured an excellent reputation for itself in administering multilateral aid; its staff has acquired a well-earned reputation for the efficiency and competence with which it administers and invests the funds entrusted to the bank's care; the bank's performance has not often been matched by that of other aid-giving bodies, however. Foreign aid has certainly provided a large guaranteed market to U.S. farmers, to manufacturers, and to suppliers of services, including a substantial body of academicians who formulate plans, draw up blueprints, and provide counsel of varying quality. All these lobbies have benefited from the American taxpayers' largesse. Foreign aid has also transferred a substantial amount of wealth from the donor to the recipient countries. Great projects such as the Niger and the Volta dams were probably constructed at less cost to their respective owners than would have been the case had Nigeria or Ghana been forced to raise the requisite capital on the private money market. American aid likewise has transferred a substantial amount of food to needy countries at prices much below those that would have been required on the world market.

The exact impact of this aid is, however, hard to assess, as many consignments went into the wrong hands, and as the donors have found it very hard (and often have had not much incentive) to learn exactly what has been done with each shipment. There are the inevitable stories of waste and abuse, of scientific equipment rusting on tropical wharves for want of delivery, of unsheltered bags of cement turning into stone, of UNICEF milk being fed to cattle, of prize breeding bulls being consumed at banquets. Such instances of waste must be set against the many examples of able and honest administration of aid. The best results have come from aid dispensed through competent local bodies (such as the Catholic Relief Services in Senegal, an organization familiar with local conditions and known for its probity).

More serious have been the more general deficiencies of foreign aid, both in concept and in execution. In the early days of foreign aid, assistance to Third World countries was widely likened to the Marshall Plan, which had helped the recovery of Europe from World War II. There is, however, no analogy between *restoring* advanced economies, temporarily disrupted by war, and *developing* underdeveloped economies to a higher level of production. Even the experiences of the Marshall Plan should have taught foreign aid experts a lesson they were inclined to forget – that there is no necessary connection between the amount of aid received and the progress made. (Great Britain obtained more Marshall aid than West Germany, yet West Germany's economic recovery was much more impressive than Great Britain's. Belgium received no Marshall aid at all, and yet staged an economic miracle of its own, based essentially – as were Germany's and Austria's – on the operation of private enterprise.) In Africa these lessons had to be learned again.

The Portuguese, though NATO allies, obtained no American aid for their colonies. Nevertheless, Angola and, to a lesser extent, Mozambique benefited from a striking economic upsurge from the early 1960s, when, after a long period of relative stagnation, the Portuguese began to open the doors of their empire to foreign lenders whom they had previously viewed with mistrust. This economic expansion continued until the two territories attained their independence; thereafter, they experienced disastrous economic breakdowns, ones that foreign aid could neither prevent nor greatly alleviate. Rhodesia, far from obtaining Western aid, was subjected to sanctions imposed by the international community to punish the ruling whites for Ian Smith's decision to proclaim unilateral independence from Great Britain in 1965. Yet during the first ten years of Smith's premiership (1964–74), the Rhodesian GNP nearly doubled (from Rh.$668 million to $Rh.$1.252 billion, at constant 1965 prices), a development that went contrary to all the experts' forecasts.[12] Aid, the experts said, should not go to a repressive country such as white-run Rhodesia. Such arguments did not, however, prevent Western assistance from reaching President Idi Amin, whose bloodstained rule in Uganda benefited from Western aid as late as 1978. Neither did such considerations prevent the World Bank from granting in the same year a new loan to benefit Mengistu Haile Mariam's Ethiopia, at a time when large-scale slaughter of political opponents and of many ordinary people had become the order of the day in that trouble-stricken land.

Whatever the theoretical pros and cons of foreign aid, assistance to poor nations had not, by the late 1970s, achieved any of the objectives that the original advocates of aid had meant to achieve. It did not add to America's popularity abroad; in fact, the American aid record was hardly known. Foreign aid certainly did not produce prosperity. By the late 1970s, for instance, the economies of Zaire and Ghana, both of them substantial beneficiaries of American grants, had sunk to a dangerous level.

Tanzania was in a particularly parlous condition, even though it had been one of the principal recipients of foreign aid and of "soft" loans ultimately guaranteed by taxpayers of the United States or of other industrialized nations. Tanzania had for long aroused the admiration of what passed for progressive opinion in the United States. By the early 1980s, however, its economy was in shambles. The cultivators, widely underpaid for their crops and often forced into collectivized villages against their will, were discouraged; the principal beneficiaries of socialism in the country-side had turned out to be a new class of local party functionaries and bureaucrats. A considerable number of Tanzania's nationalized companies had gone bankrupt or were producing at a loss, despite their monopolistic position in the local market. Taxation had reached a level vastly higher than under the much-abused British colonial regime. Wages were fixed, strikes forbidden, human rights abused, incentives to work diminished.

But Tanzania's case was in no wise unique. Aid recipients all over Africa were struggling with horrendous problems that variously included inflation, high prices for imported oil, excessive fluctuations in the prices received for raw materials, large foreign debts, declining food production, a pervasive shortage of skills and capital, rising military expenditure, corruption, political instability, and a widespread reluctance among private investors to risk their savings in Africa.

Foreign aid alone could not cope with the real problems of Africa: political instability, ethnic rivalry, political and bureaucratic parasitism. Foreign aid did not curb, but perhaps even encouraged, the tendency of the new states to favor investment in the inefficient and graft-ridden public sectors, rather than in the private sector.[13] Foreign aid did not correct the widespread tendency in both socialist and nonsocialist states to exploit, or at least to neglect, the village cultivators in favor of urban people – industrial workers, school teachers, and civil servants. The aid givers, for instance, never insisted that cultivators be paid the world market prices for their produce by state marketing boards; on the contrary, the theoreticians of foreign aid were apt to welcome designs for "mobilizing" rural surpluses for the purpose of financing industrial enterprises. They saw nothing wrong in development plans that provided but a small fraction of a developing nation's national resources for the purposes of agriculture. Not surprisingly, sub-Saharan Africa's rural problems were becoming ever more severe as the 1980s began; because agriculture was declining, the advocates of foreign aid in turn gained new arguments for extending the scope of official Western philanthropy.

According to its critics, foreign aid may have created new difficulties of its own by contributing to inflation, by discouraging governmental thrift, by saddling the recipients with unanticipated costs of an indirect kind, by inefficient forms of national planning, and – above all – by promoting the interests of the party functionaries and bureaucrats rather than the common people. As P. T. Bauer, an outstanding British economist, puts it:

> Official aid goes to governments, not to poor people. Its expenditure is governed by personal and professional ambitions of politicians and civil servants. Much is spent on politically inspired projects: airlines, inefficient industries, Western-type universities, the graduates of which cannot find jobs, and the construction of new capitals at vast cost (Brasilia, Islamabad, Dodoma in Tanzania). These projects have to be subsidized by local taxes, including those of the poor.[14]

In a wider sense, foreign aid represents the ideals of the American welfare state applied to the world at large. Assistance-giving agencies, such as AID, have themselves been apt to turn into lobbies for actual or potential assistance, and to link with congressional and private pressure groups in pursuit of their departmental aims. After Reagan's elevation to the presidency some changes were made, and AID began to send out teams to advise governments on how to convert public agricultural and industrial companies to private enterprise. But there remains a legacy of faith in public spending, high taxation, the redistribution of incomes on a global scale, and a pervasive distrust of private enterprise unrestrained by regulatory agencies.[15] But for all its deficiencies, aid has also represented a transfer of resources for productive purposes. The aid givers have solid achievements to their credit; their total impact as yet remains to be evaluated.

CHAPTER 23

American interests in Africa, 1945–1983

The American academic and philanthropic response

Sir Charles Dilke, a well-known English radical, visited the United States just over a century ago. Dilke was fascinated by the new system of education set up in the new western universities, such as the State University of Michigan:

> It is cheap, large, practical . . . but all work with spirit, and with that earnestness which is seen in the Scotch universities at home. The war with crime, the war with sin, the war with death – Law, Theology, Medicine – these are the three foremost of man's employment; to these, accordingly, the university affords her chiefest care, and to one of these the student . . . often gives his entire time.[1]

American scholarship never lost this moral earnestness, practicality, and dedication to solving the real or assumed problems of society by the application of the scientific method. In 1939, for instance, Robert S. Lynd argued in a series of lectures entitled "Knowledge for What?" that learning ought to lighten the burdens of man. After World War II Harold Lasswell and his colleagues elaborated and popularized the pragmatic orientation in their idea of the "policy sciences." The stress placed on "social problems" facilitated the rise of research centers as an integral part of academia; the research centers, in turn, placed particular emphasis on the interdisciplinary approach to scholarship. The many learned private foundations – especially those named for Ford, Carnegie, and Rockefeller – were important in developing such research centers and in diffusing the optimistic secular philosophy, linked to Wilsonian idealism and the New Deal, that shaped the social sciences in mid-twentieth-century America.

World War II had a profound impact on the social sciences in the United States. American colleges and universities had been traditionally oriented toward Western Europe; with few exceptions, they either neglected non-Western areas or limited their research and teaching in these areas to classical languages, ancient history, and literature. As a result, universities, defense agencies, government, business, and many professions found themselves increasingly handicapped during and after the war by a shortage of specialists with competence or experience in Asia, Africa, the Middle East, and even Eastern Europe. War broke long-standing habits of intellectual isolation, as millions of Americans put on uniforms and for a time lived and fought in countries that previously they would hardly have been able to identify on a map. War also affected the social sciences in professional ways. The Army Research Branch, interested in the various aspects of a fighting man's life, helped to pioneer new survey techniques and caused the Department of Defense to sponsor more research in the behavioral sciences. The Research and Analysis Branch of Strategic Services provided jobs to numerous intellectuals, schooled them in teamwork, and acquainted them with new problems and new countries.

A few American scholars, of course, had been interested in Africa since the United States began. Some black colleges and universities had taken an honorable part in spreading academic interest in Africa. Missionary bodies had likewise helped in the task of pioneering. As early as 1911, Hartford Theological Seminary had given instruction in African languages to intending missionaries. A regular course on Africa was offered from 1927 on by Melville J. Herskovits, a professor at Northwestern University, and dissertations on African studies were being written, primarily at Northwestern and Indiana universities, in the 1930s. The first formal African studies program was founded at Northwestern with funds from the Carnegie Foundation. Then the Ford Foundation provided funds for a Foreign Areas Training Program and for centers at Boston University (1953) and the University of California at Los Angeles (1957). Another early development was the Program of African Studies at the School of Advanced International Studies of Johns Hopkins University, started by Dr. Vernon McKay in 1957; the program trains a variety of students for careers in African studies.[2]

Until the late 1950s these area studies were located only in departments of anthropology and geography. When independence reached the colonial world, however, the political sciences also became interested. History departments examined little African history until the mid-1960s. Beginning in 1967, programs in Afro-American studies, African and Afro-American studies, Africana studies, and Pan-African studies, subsumed under the generic rubric black studies, were established on many U.S. campuses; and courses on African history, politics, and culture became part of their curricula. A few Afro-Americans took degrees in African studies and gained positions on university and college faculties. A small number of African scholars migrated to the United States and began to teach African studies at American schools, and a few blacks went to African universities to teach. A triangular trade in ideas was reborn among the United States, Africa, and the West Indies: Blacks from these areas taught and wrote about Africa and black history in both the United States and in Africa. For example, Ali Mazrui of Kenya taught at the University of Michigan; Hollis Lynch, a West Indian, taught in Africa and in the United States; the recently deceased West Indian Walter Rodney, who wrote *How Europe Underdeveloped Africa,* taught in Tanzania. St. Clair Drake of Chicago and Palo Alto served for over two years as professor and head of his department at the University of Ghana. There are probably more than two hundred scholars in this diaspora teaching and writing about Africa.

Since the late 1970s, these black studies programs have flourished. There are now about two hundred programs, with outstanding ones at Harvard, Yale, UCLA, and Cornell universities. And there are journals, such as the *Journal of Black Studies,* the *Black Scholar,* and the *Western Journal of Black Studies.*

By the mid-1960s the Carnegie, Rockefeller, and Ford foundations also supported area studies in the United States and Africa. One of the most important of these bodies was the Carnegie Corporation.[3] From 1953 onward, the corporation began to direct its attention to the British Commonwealth and its colonial empire, especially Britain's African dependencies. The Carnegie Corporation had long been committed to supporting academic departments of education, with their commitment to psychology as an educational tool, their dedication to "social adjustment" and "institutionalized change," their distrust of academic elitism, and their penchant for a behaviorist philosophy.

Under the tutelage of Stephen S. Stackpole, Alan Pifer, and Frederick Mosher, three senior staff members especially concerned with the corporation's new Commonwealth Program, the Carnegie Corporation began to apply this philosophy toward what its directors considered to be "creative philanthropy" in Africa. Mosher, Pifer, and Stackpole firmly believed that the new British-created universities in sub-Saharan Africa should move away from the elitist traditions of British universities, with their sense of detachment and their emphasis on purely academic work, toward a commitment to education that would aim at social change of a broader kind. The corporation specially favored providing funds for new departments of education, and it helped to found or to expand institutes or departments of education at the new universities at Makerere, Nairobi, Dar-es-Salaam, Lesotho, Nsukka, Ife, Ibadan, and Zaria.

The program organizers were in no sense anti-British. On the contrary, as long as the empire lasted, the corporation did all it could to cooperate with the British colonial authorities, which by this time had themselves become converts to the new gospel of development, higher education, and ultimate African self-government. (White-ruled Rhodesia and South Africa, on the other hand, were excluded from the corporation's purview, on the grounds that these countries were too inhospitable for its own brand of liberalism.) According to the corporation's historian, the Carnegie programs in fact benefited from cooperation with competent colonial administrators. Most of the corporation's failed or disrupted programs dated from the postcolonial era, by which time Carnegie had begun to expand the size of its grants considerably. (Between 1953 and 1973, for example, the corporation spent a total of $10,062,804 in Africa – nearly five times the 1961 revenue of the British colony of Gambia.)[4]

The corporation likewise provided assistance to universities and educational institutes to promote research in the United States and to support African students. Grants totaling $421,000 also went to other American-based groups concerned with African affairs, for instance, the African-American Institute (treated in greater detail in the following section). By 1982 geographical emphasis was focused on southern Africa, with special attention to educational projects that promote peaceful change. Whereas in South Africa Carnegie's emphasis is now on developing black leadership and communication among the various racial groups, in Zimbabwe projects focus on the educational needs of the country during its transition to black rule.

Carnegie's project grants in southern Africa totaled $471,000 for 1982. The University of Cape Town received $200,000 to look at poverty and development in South Africa; the Legal Resources Center, as a public interest law firm working for reforms of the legal system, received $180,000. The Centre for Intergroup Studies (given $60,000) works to improve race relations in South Africa by carrying out applied research. The Black Lawyers Association ($15,000) works to improve the education of black lawyers and to promote human rights in South Africa. Other grants were given to Yale University to look at American corporate interests in

South Africa ($6,000), to the United States–South Africa Leader Exchange Program ($15,000), and to the Institute of International Education of New York (IIE) to run the South African Education Program to provide scholarship to blacks to attend American colleges and universities ($75,000). The Ford Foundation also provides tuition grants for this project, and the U.S. Congress voted $4 million in 1982 for black South Africa students in the United States, $2.67 million of which went to IIE.[5]

The Ford Foundation arrived somewhat later in African studies than Carnegie and Phelps-Stokes, but the sheer size of the foundation has enabled Ford to equal the historic work of smaller organizations. Between 1952 and 1960 Ford spent over $5 million on its sub-Saharan African programs, reflecting in its rate of giving the sudden growth of American interest in Africa. Until 1958 the interests of the Ford Foundation were limited, confined to area fellowship programs for training American scholars in African studies and outright grants to strengthen programs of African studies at American universities. In 1956–7 Ford sent a reconnaissance team to Africa with a view to extending its Overseas Development Program to the continent. A second team was sent in 1958, and from that time the foundation decided to concentrate on African education and in particular on the institutions of higher learning in Africa. Grants were made, for instance, to Lovanium University in the Belgian Congo and to the East African Institute of Social and Economic Research at Makerere College in Uganda to enable these institutions to respond more readily to requests for information by African governments. Other grants have been made to the University College of Rhodesia and Nyasaland to provide regular staff in African studies and the social sciences, and in 1960 the Ford Foundation joined with Rockefeller in giving aid to Lovanium so that the university could open in spite of the turbulence of transition in the Congo.

Scores of institutions, programs, and projects have been sponsored by Ford in the United States, Europe, and Africa; overseas grants have gone increasingly to activities in the less-developed countries. Funds have gone to development programs for local institutions and to national governments and public service institutions for research, for development, for agricultural and rural development, and for population programs.

The Rockefeller Foundation, founded in 1913, has had a profound effect on Africa, Asia, and Latin America because of its concerns with problems of disease, illiteracy, and poverty. The foundation supports work worldwide in control of malaria, yellow fever, hookworm, tuberculosis, yaws, typhus, and schistosomiasis. Thanks to Rockefeller Foundation support a vaccine to protect against yellow fever was developed by Dr. Max Theiler in the foundation's research laboratories in New York City.

After 1963, the foundation also financed studies to produce the Green Revolution, with agricultural crop improvement in corn, wheat, beans, rice, and so on. In 1967 an Institute of Tropical Agriculture was established in Ibadan, Nigeria, to help serve the food needs of the developing world. In addition to food and health, the Rockefeller Foundation has been concerned also about population control. Grants have been made to the Population Research Office of Princeton University to do fertility studies in Africa and Asia and to the Population Council for information services.

The foundation started a program of university development in 1963 to assist such potentially important countries as Kenya, Nigeria, Tanzania, Uganda and Zaire; the idea was to provide enough scholars and teachers to launch development in these countries. The program was reoriented with a smaller budget in 1974, however, after criticism that its efforts had failed to improve the quality of education.

Scientific research in Africa has long been supported by American foundations, research institutes, and academies. Aided by financial support from these groups, American scholars have taken the lead in the scientific study of Africa in such fields as modern geomorphology (the geological study of the configuration and evolution of landforms), seismology, ecology and conservation, evolution, and animal research.

The Leakey Foundation for the Study of Man's Origins in Pasadena, California, was founded in 1968 to honor the work of Louis Leakey. The founder and president of the foundation is the noted Africanist Ned Munger. The foundation supported the work of the Leakeys (Louis, Mary, and Richard), but it has made more grants for primate research than for fossil studies. One of the foundation's most famous protégées is Jane Goodall, who did her work on chimpanzees at the Gombe Stream Reserve in Tanzania starting in 1960. In 1975 a band of Marxist guerrillas from eastern Zaire tried to kidnap Goodall, but she fled the camp, abandoning four Stanford University students who were doing research at Gombe. After long and tortured negotiations (made more difficult by the lack of cooperation of Goodall's husband, Derek Bryceson, minister of tourism in the Tanzanian government), the head of the Stanford Gombe Project, David Hamburg (now head of the Carnegie Corporation), secured the release of the students.

Dian Fossey, another protégée of Leakey's, studied the African gorilla in East Africa (Mountains of the Moon of Ruwenzori, Rwanda), starting in 1967 with a grant from the Leakey Foundation. After many years of arduous and dangerous research, her book *Gorillas in the Mist* appeared in 1983 (New York: Houghton Mifflin). Fossey's work built on previous field research of other American scholars, such as Hal Cooledge from the Harvard expedition in the 1930s and George Schaller, who spent a year with gorillas. A third major research project of the foundation was the work of Elizabeth Meyerhoff on female circumcision among the Pokot of western Kenya.

The National Geographic Society also supported the work of the Leakeys in tracing the development of early man in the Olduvai Gorge in northern Tanzania, as well as Goodall's chimpanzee studies in Gombe. The society continues to fund African projects each year on a variety of subjects. Throughout its history articles in the society's journal, *National Geographic*, have dealt with Africa, covering hunting, exploration, wildlife, animals, birds, plants, archaeology, conservation, animal survival, places, and especially the peoples and cultures of Africa.

Many other learned societies in the United States support scientific work in Africa. The National Academy of Science, for example, in the 1950s did work on the albino gorilla and sponsored research in Zaire on primates and the breeding of primates to supply laboratories with animals for biomedical research. A major project for the past ten years has been a study of the causes of environmental degradation of the Sahel and ways to reinvigorate the ecosystem there.

World Wildlife Fund–U.S.A. (Washington, D.C.) was founded in 1961. The group has an international network of scientists and conservationists who focus on world wildlife problems. Its Global Strategy for Primates, begun in 1978, has supported sixty projects in twenty-five countries. It has been active in conservation projects in Africa—assisting Sierra Leone to develop its first national park, for instance. Much of its work revolves around tropical forests, parks, and protection of habitat, migratory birds, and animal reserves, such as those in Madagascar, Rwanda, and Nigeria.

Wenner-Gren (New York City) has provided grants to scholars for work in archaeology, anthropology, and related sciences, especially through its "Origin of Man Program" started in 1964–5. Grants have supported field research, subsidized publications, and established new study centers. Research backing for African studies also comes from the National Endowment for the Humanities and the National Science Foundation.

Africare was founded by black Americans C. Payne Lucas and Joseph Kennedy after their service in the Peace Corps in the mid-1960s, in effect to continue the humanitarian work they had begun in the Peace Corps. Africare represents a unique blend of black American and black government concern. At present its budget is about $5 million a year, with a staff of sixty-seven. The primary focuses of the group are on problem solving in Africa's poorest countries in the Sahel and on involving the black American community in this work. The Lilly Foundation was one of Africare's first major supporters, with a $2 million grant for well digging and irrigation projects in Chad, Niger, Mali, and Upper Volta. AID also provided several million dollars for this work, and AID is now the major source of funds for Africare. The black community (especially its notables) has continued to support Africare.

Other American groups involved in African relief, education or medical care include: the Institute of International Education (student exchange), the American Red Cross, Catholic Relief Services (for distribution of surplus U.S. foodstuffs), and World Vision (especially for emergency assistance).[6]

What did these efforts amount to by the early 1980s? Conservative critics of the great foundations censured them for their liberal and behaviorist bias. Radical scholars, by contrast, accused them of serving as instruments of "cultural imperialism," of bending the social sciences to serve the interests of corporate capitalism, and of co-opting academicians for this undesirable purpose. Whatever the truth or falsehood of these charges and countercharges, the foundations did contribute to linking the continent to Western academic endeavors.

Major support for African studies also came from the U.S. government through Title VI of the National Defense Act of 1957, voted to encourage study of uncommon languages and cultures. Language programs expanded rapidly thereafter. In brick and mortar and in funds provided, personnel appointed, and publications released, the results were impressive. By the early 1970s the United States had created a total of 191 foreign area study centers. Of these, 131 concerned themselves with specific themes, with special interest in subjects such as economic development, political change, the growth of communism—the very titles of the subjects chosen reflected a preoccupation with dynamic change. The other 60 centers dealt with specific geographic areas, including 9 specializing solely in Africa.

This was a time of optimism, an era when American universities were expanding, when qualified candidates for academic jobs were in short supply, when a preoccupation with exotic lands and cultures promised interesting and worthwhile careers in academia or in government agencies concerned with diplomacy and foreign aid. Not surprisingly, fellowship programs developed after World War II attracted a large number of highly qualified and ambitious men and women. Between 1952 and 1971, during the heyday of foreign area studies, the Foreign Area Fellowship Program administered jointly by the American Council of Learned Societies and the Social Science Research Council provided training for a total of 2,050 young academicians (315 of them specifically concerned with Africa).[7]

Foundation support dropped in the 1970s, and new Afro-American studies programs began to take some students away from research concerning the continent itself, with a consequent decrease in the number of courses and programs in the United States. In 1972 the Office of Education cut back its support to only 6 graduate centers (UCLA, Indiana, Northwestern, Wisconsin, Stanford, and Illinois) from a high of 100. There are 20 African studies programs still thriving in the country, including 5 government-funded centers.

Before World War II, scholarship concerned with Africa centered on the colonial powers in South Africa; a handful of American scholars (for instance, Melville J. Herskovits) had reached international prominence, but the giants – Lord Hailey, Hubert Jules Deschamps, E. E. Evans-Pritchard – worked abroad. By the early 1970s the United States had acquired a decisive quantitative lead over the ex-colonial powers and the Soviet Union, and qualitatively, the best of American erudition was equal to the foremost scholarship anywhere in the world.[8] Whether in history, political science, anthropology, or the study of art, Americans were to be found in the front rank of learning; they made an enormous contribution to the study of Africa in every major discipline.

The new African studies programs also widened American interest in Anglo-African literature; the names of such outstanding African writers as Chinua Achebe and Cyprian Ekwensi became widely known on American campuses, and the growing taste for African literature in turn widened the market for African writers. Conversely, African writers such as Oswald Mtshali, Wally Serote, and Sipho Sempla – products of the segregated townships around Johannesburg, men full of bitterness against the South African white regime – took a special interest in militant black American literature.

The new academic interest in Africa had many sources. During the nineteenth and the early part of the twentieth century, these studies owed a great deal to missionaries with scholarly interests who carried out anthropological research and played a major part in the study of African languages by compiling dictionaries and translating the Bible, hymnbooks, and prayerbooks into African tongues. American scholarship concerned with Africa also stood indebted to black institutions such as Howard University, which had taken an interest in African questions at a time when the man in the street widely associated Africa with Tarzan's antics in the jungle. Later, in the 1950s and 1960s, African academic programs further benefited from the enthusiasm inspired by the black civil rights struggle in the United States and by decolonization overseas. New courses in African history, culture, languages, and social institutions became increasingly popular on American campuses at large. University presses and prestigious commercial publishers vied with one another in publishing titles with an African interest.

American scholarship also had far-reaching political implications. In a secular-ized society like that of modern America, professors enjoy a great deal of esteem for their technical expertise, and their views carry greater weight in secular matters than those of pastors. Professors, moreover, often share the clergy's self-image as shepherds destined to lead their flocks. For many if not most college teachers in the humanities and the social sciences, the right way leads to the left. Scholars like Seymour Martin Lipset and Alan Ladd provide a wealth of statistics indicating that professors, especially those in prestigious institutions, are far more liberal than their fellow citizens. Professional Africanists, as a body, stand even further to the left than humanities professors as a whole. Many American Africanists (like the great majority of Latin Americanists) have an intellectual and moral commitment to the real or assumed virtues of a planned economy, of state intervention for the public good. By far the greater number of Africanists incline toward the liberal end of the political spectrum. They wish to promote what they call nation building in Africa; they advocate massive U.S. aid to the newly independent states. At the very least, liberal intellectuals and their allies in the great foundations, the labor move-ment, and some of the great corporations feel that the United States has a mission to reform South Africa.[9]

The African studies establishment in the United States shares the strengths and weaknesses of American liberalism, its enthusiam and generosity and, somtimes, its sanctimoniousness. Academic publications have almost uniformly sided with inde-pendent, as against colonial or settler-ruled, Africa. Not that African states have been exempt from criticism. But, generally speaking, academicians sometimes prac-tice a double standard against whites in Africa of which the scholars are hardly aware. For instance, *Issue*, one of the organs of the African Studies Association (ASA, founded in 1957), in its first five volumes (1971–5) featured two special numbers and forty additional articles dealing with white minority regimes in south-ern Africa and their civil rights violations. By contrast, only one issue was devoted to Burundi, where the Tutsi had subjected the Hutu to genocidal terror unequaled in the modern history of Africa; only one article dealt with the expulsion of Asians from Uganda, a measure much more radical than anything Malan, Verwoerd, or Vorster in South Africa had considered. Atrocities committed by the ruling elites in countries as diverse as Equatorial Guinea, Angola, Mozambique, Ethiopia, or Gui-nea do not receive anything like the same academic scrutiny as is devoted to South Africa. The shooting that occurred in South Africa made Sharpeville an international word of horror: Sixty-seven persons lost their lives. Four years later, in 1964, the police in newly independent Zambia killed over seven hundred members of the allegedly subversive Lumpa Church without interfering in the slightest with Presi-dent K. D. Kaunda's reputation as a worthy defender of "Zambian humanism."

The liberal media have reflected and magnified the assumptions of liberal acade-micians, who helped to train the journalists and television commentators in presti-gious institutions. Prestige journalism has increasingly dealt with highly complex issues – ecology, nuclear weaponry, sociology – requiring journalists with an aca-demic background. Not surprisingly, the major television networks and national newspapers like the *New York Times* gradually came to share the intellectual's widespread disillusionment with American businesspeople and Middle America. (Investigations of TV soap operas during the 1970s revealed that businessmen were usually shown in an unfavorable light; the typical businessman as represented on the screen was apt to make his money in a manner immoral, illegal, or at least aesthetically repulsive.) The whites in South Africa or Rhodesia were apt to be identified with Middle America – to the equal discredit of both.[10]

The reasons for this state of affairs are complex. For one thing, relevant data are much harder to secure in countries like Guinea or Burundi than in a relatively open society like South Africa. Scholars, journalists, and pastors can travel about South Africa more easily than they can through most African countries. Above all, Western social reformers can identify much more easily with white South Africans than with Tutsi or Bemba; they thus feel a vicarious sense of guilt regarding South Africa not experienced concerning atrocities committed in Zambia or Burundi. It is not surprising, therefore, that many Africanists have accepted a double standard where South Africa is concerned. The ASA as a body does not object to official control of research in independent black African countries; yet these same scholars would protest furiously if South Africa – or, for that matter, West Germany or the United States – were to impose similar restrictions on American academicians working there.

African studies in the United States has suffered from other weaknesses. The student revolution of the 1960s and the early 1970s radicalized some faculty members and discouraged others. African studies came to be grouped with black studies, Afro-American studies, ethnic studies, and women's studies, all widely identified with liberal left politics; they generally excluded conservatives from their teaching staffs.

The ASA has contained few conservatives. Avowed conservatives have been, in practice, excluded from teaching positions in subjects like African, black, or Afro-American (or women's) studies at the major American universities. No self-confessed supporter of Ian Smith or D. F. Malan (former white prime ministers of Rhodesia and South Africa, respectively) could ever have aspired to an instructor's position at institutions like Stanford, Northwestern, Columbia, Yale, or UCLA. Conservative Africanists, grouped in the American African Affairs Association, have formed a negligible group.

The era of postwar academic prosperity came to an end at the very time when relations between liberal academia and Middle America had reached their lowest point. The economic decline of American academia coincided with a widespread slump in many parts of postindependent Africa: The fruits of independence seemed poisoned, and the academicians' old optimism began to wane. By the latter part of the 1970s, universities all over the Western world found themselves in difficult straits. Teaching positions turned out to be in short supply.

In the United States, black studies came under attack on the grounds that these programs encouraged a romantic withdrawal from American society, a society founded on a belief in the merits of the private enterprise system and material success. Critics complained that minority students in particular were being seduced from "practical" subjects, such as engineering and computer science, to take up unrewarding pursuits of a merely literary kind. Enrollments (including those of black students) in black and African studies widely declined. In addition, black militance (expressed with considerable vehemence at the ASA's annual meeting in Montreal in 1969) introduced a further element of discord into the ranks of Africanists at a time when academicians of all political stripes would have been well advised to cooperate. Black studies came under further criticism when white job applicants claimed to be discriminated against in favor of blacks, or when black militants insisted that blacks were better suited to teach African or black studies than whites.

Worse still, the academicians' own emotional commitment to Africa declined. Their disenchantment had many causes. The newly independent African states failed to live up to their own original expectations; sub-Saharan Africa failed to develop the free and prosperous democracies that so many academicians had anticipated during the independence struggle. Field research in black Africa, moreover, became increasingly difficult by reason of bureaucratic interference, public distrust, and rising crime rates in many independent African countries – at a time when travel funds and scholarships for studies overseas became increasingly hard to obtain in the United States. African studies, with their emphasis on the social sciences tradition, produced few narrative historians with a gift for style, men or women comparable to Thomas Bailey in American or Gordon Craig in German history. Caught within their terminological constraints, Africanists thereby isolated themselves further from the public at large. Worst of all, a number of leading Africanists (including Joseph Greenberg, Paul Bohannan, David Apter, and L. Gray Cowan) switched from Africa to other fields. The ASA thus was left with diminished numbers of prestigious members at a time when American academia, at the end of the 1970s, began to face a series of crises concerned with declining student enrollments, decreasing financial support, and a diminished sense of purpose.

American academia, on the other hand, also drew new strength from Africa insofar as American universities extended their student recruitment there. In the 1920s and 1930s only a handful of Africans had managed to study in the United States. After the end of World War II, however, the federal government, universities, and private organizations created a variety of new programs to finance the education of African students in the United States. By 1965 the number of Africans studying in the United States was 6,855. Almost 6,000 of these were men; and almost 4,000 were undergraduates, with the remainder studying for advanced degrees or pursuing special courses. The largest single number were studying in the social sciences, though the number studying the physical and natural sciences followed closely. Over a thousand were engineering students, but only a few hundred were studying medicine or education.[11] The largest African national group represented in the United States came from Nigeria (especially the Ibo), with 1,382 students in various American schools and colleges.

Private bodies

The most important American organization concerned with stimulating American interest in Africa has been the African-American Institute (AAI). In 1954 the AAI opened its first office in Washington, D.C., as an agency to which African students might turn for advice and assistance. The institute subsequently opened branch offices in various other cities (including New York, Lagos, Accra, Dar-es-Salaam, Lusaka, and Addis Ababa). At the same time, the AAI greatly managed to expand its staff and revenue; by 1967 it employed 130 staff members, and its budget amounted to $8 million. The institute has shouldered a great variety of tasks. It placed 197 American secondary school teachers in African schools; it organized lectures, provided advice and information to the mass media, encouraged educational exchanges, offered technical and professional training, supported a short-term visitors' program, and financed a series of minor programs of limited duration (such as a Books for Africa project). During the 1960s, it turned to what was to become its most significant operation, educational assistance to African political refugees from the so-called white redoubts in southern Africa. The AAI offered scholarships to refugees and also set up training centers in Dar-es-Salaam and in north central Zambia; in addition, it operated a graduate fellowship program that brought students from Africa to the United States for graduate work. Between 1960 and 1965 alone, the AAI's African Scholarship Program in American universities brought to the United States a total of 1,776 African students from thirty-two countries.[12]

The institute also publishes a bimonthly journal, known as *Africa Report*. *Africa Report* began in 1956 as a modest newsheet but subsequently expanded into a major organ of opinion, edited by Helen Kitchen. Right from its start, the journal received backing from a directorate composed of liberal academics, public servants, and business magnates (including Horace Mann Bond, president of Lincoln University; Chester Bowles, former U.S. ambassador to India; Lansdell W. Christie, president of Liberia Mining Company; and Harold K. Hochschild, chairman of the board of the American Metal Company and of numerous other major corporations). *Africa Report* soon became the foremost American organ for reportage on and interpretation of the African political and cultural scene, written mainly – though not exclusively – from a liberal standpoint.

The affiliates of the AAI after 1959 consisted of the Women's Committee and the United States–South Africa Leader Exchange (USSALEP). The Women's Committee sponsored research into women-related topics from a feminist viewpoint.[13] The USSALEP, which later separated from AAI, attempts to reach present and prospective elites. It seeks out "teachers of teachers" and attempts to provide by quality what it lacks in quantity. In 1982 something like twenty-two South Africans of all colors visited the United States under the program's auspices; by 1983 the number had risen to about thirty (50 percent of them blacks, 30 percent whites, 20 percent Asians and Coloureds). The program has created a special career-training plan for blacks, who have found internships in professions as varied as banking, labor relations, publishing, and urban planning. Unlike visitors invited from the State Department, these are not given Cook's tours of the United States as a whole but spend most of their time on the East Coast. In addition the organization has promoted research into South African educational problems. Unfortunately, however, the scope of the program (with a total budget of about $500,000 in 1983) is not sufficiently great to make a major impact.[14]

The AAI has focused in recent years on economic development and political freedom. In 1980–1 it increased its services to corporations and sought to gain for Africa greater access to U.S. technology. Three international conferences (in Boston, Wichita, and Freetown) strengthened the linkage between the U.S. private sector and the developing African economies. Under the auspices of the U.S. government's International Visitor Program, the AAI arranged more than two hundred itineraries for African visitors. A grant from the Carnegie Corporation also provided travel awards to African leaders for short-term visits to the United States. In addition, the AAI arranged travel and consultations for Nigerian officials.

In an effort to increase the role of women in African growth, the AAI started in 1980 the Women and African Development Program. It has also continued to support African university students – by now, more than a thousand of them – in development-related studies in the United States. The AAI maintains an active program to make Americans more aware of Africa through its publications, especially *Africa Report;* lectures and radio broadcasts by AAI staff; visual and performing arts programs; and seminars and briefings for U.S. congressmen and aides.

Critics of the AAI charge that its activities are ill controlled; that its programs favor members of Marxist bodies, such as SWAPO and the African National Congress (ANC); that organizations whose political orientations do not accord with the AAI's leftist preferences (such as Inkatha in South Africa or UNITA in Angola) have found themselves excluded from American largesse; and that the AAI has unjustly belabored the Reagan administration's African policy. The AAI's International Visitor Program, the critique continues, has largely prevented contacts between visiting Africans and American conservatives or advocates of the free-market economy whose political preferences do not coincide with the institution's.[15]

Several programs not affiliated with the AAI concentrate on southern Africa refugees and training. The Southern African Student Program (SASP) and the Southern African Refugee Education Project (SAREP) go back to the early 1960s. The largest program, started in 1976, is entitled Development Training for Southern Africans and is funded by AID. To date 645 southern Africans have received development training in the United States and Africa under its auspices.[16]

The South African Education Program provides fellowships for graduate study in the United States for black South Africans. The program, which began in 1981, is sponsored by the Ford Foundation, the Carnegie Corporation, U.S. business corporations operating in South Africa, and participating American universities.

American educators also played their part in shaping university education in colonial and postcolonial Africa. In doing so, they faced considerable opposition, as francophone Africa built its new universities on the French, and anglophone Africa mainly on the British, model. The commitment to the British connection derived to a considerable extent from African demands for degrees that would have international currency and meet the standards of the best British universities, irrespective of financial costs. New universities, such as the University College of Rhodesia and Nyasaland and the University College of Ibadan in Nigeria, thus initially granted London degrees.

In Nigeria this policy ran into opposition from men such as Dr. N. Azikiwe, who felt that the British system was too expensive and that Nigeria should rather look to the American land-grant colleges for a model. "We cannot afford," he said, "to continue to produce . . . an upper class of parasites . . . We can no longer afford to flood only the white collar jobs at the expense of . . . productive vocations . . . particularly in the fields of agriculture, engineering, business administration, education, and domestic sciences."[17] Azikiwe therefore helped to found an institution that he called the University of Nigeria at Nsukka, inspired by the land-grant philosophy and fostered by Michigan State University. The new university, set up in the East Central State of Nigeria, opened its doors to students in 1960, after preliminary recommendations made jointly by the British Inter-University Council and AID. Nsukka differed from its sister institutions in that it admitted students with a lower level of achievement in secondary schools than that insisted upon by Ibadan. Nsukka provided an extensive prospectus – in the American style – of hundreds of credit-earning courses.

Above all, Americans took a leading role in higher education in Ethiopia. After a brief and hateful period of Italian occupation, Ethiopia regained its independence in World War II. Resolved to modernize their country, the Ethiopians looked for aid from a variety of Western countries, so as to balance foreign influence. Traditional Ethiopian society had rested on an African form of feudalism, on a threefold division into nobility, church, and peasantry, with rigid divisions of status and wealth. Older education, such as it was, had derived from the Ethiopian Orthodox Church, and had aimed primarily at diffusing religious knowledge. From the latter part of the nineteenth century on, Western missionaries had entered the country. Forbidden to convert Ethiopian Orthodox Christians, and unable to make real headway among the Muslims, the newcomers emphasized education, both academic and technical.

After World War II, the Ethiopian authorities increasingly emphasized secular schooling, and an increasing number of elementary and secondary institutions opened their doors. In 1961 the Ethiopians inaugurated Haile Selassie I University at Addis Ababa, patterned on both British and American styles. This university formed part of the new African "academic frontier" that opened to Western professors, and the United States became deeply involved in the university's expansion. Roughly a quarter of the university's budget derived from foreign, especially U.S., funds. AID provided the wherewithal to build the new Kennedy Memorial Library; AID also sent a number of teams to assist the staff. Mormons from the University of Utah played a major part in getting the university started and taught in its Institute of Education. The University of Oklahoma ran the Agricultural College set up at Harare, the Law School, and the Business College, the latter completely American in style. Oklahoma State University became responsible for instruction, research, and extension work at the College of Agricultural and Mechanical Arts (established in 1957 at Almanaya near Harare through an agreement between the U.S. and Ethiopian governments). Equally important was the role of American-educated Ethiopian intellectuals, men such as Abraham Demoz, head of the Arts Faculty at Haile Selassie University and recipient of a doctorate from the University of North Carolina. American Peace Corps volunteers flocked to Ethiopia; Ethiopian students (including many military officers) sought advanced training at specialized institutions in the United States. Ethiopia's educational effort relied on aid from many Western countries, including Britain, West Germany, and Canada, but by the end of the 1960s, the United States had become by far the largest contributor to Ethiopian education.

American and other expatriate pedagogues assisted through their endeavors in transferring new skills and knowledge to Ethiopian society. However, in Ethiopia, as elsewhere, their work also had unforeseen consequences. The burden of education rested heavily on the peasantry. The Ethiopian fiscal system as a whole worked in such a way as to favor the wealthier at the expense of the poorer regions, the cities at the expense of the countryside. It was mainly urban people who sent their children to schools and to the university, whereas rural taxpayers, landowners and poor peasants alike, bore much of the cost. Education created new expectations that a ramshackle feudalism could not meet. There was widespread dissatisfaction among teachers and lecturers at what they regarded as low salaries; there was much discontent among graduates at what they conceived as inadequate prospects for jobs. The system as a whole did little for the mass of villagers whose needs went almost unconsidered, a state of affairs not improved by widespread corruption and by the manner in which funds ostensibly raised for educational purposes went for different objects. The resultant crisis in education itself therefore became a contributing factor in the demise of the Ethiopian imperial government, and finally of the complete disappearance of American influence from Ethiopia.

Black responses to Africa

During the years preceding World War II, the great majority of black Americans had little interest in Africa. Far from taking pride in Africa's achievements, they tended to repudiate past connections with the "Dark Continent"; alternately, theirs was an attitude of embarrassment at the poverty and backwardness, the tribal customs, and the supposed superstitions of Africa. But there were exceptions. Howard University Medical School (founded in 1868) and Meharry (set up in 1876), both of them black institutions, made a significant contribution to both the teaching and the study of tropical medicine, to the training of African physicians, and, indirectly, to the diffusion of black American thought to Africa. By providing an opportunity for Africans to graduate in medicine, these schools added to the pool of British-trained physicians who had originally come from Sierra Leone, part of a new Afro-Victorian elite. Between 1868 and 1978 Howard and Meharry Medical Schools trained some sixty-five African graduates, mostly from West Africa (twenty-nine came from Nigeria, ten from Liberia, seven from Ghana). Some of these had distinguished careers on their return. For instance, David E. Boye-Johnson, trained at Howard, rose to be chief medical officer in Sierra Leone in 1944. Dr. Hastings Kamuzu Banda, another Howard graduate, later turned to politics; he played a significant part in breaking up the Federation of Rhodesia and Nyasaland, established in 1953 by another physician-turned politician, Sir Godfrey Huggins. Banda became Malawi's first life president.

Banda's links to the United States were not just fortuitous, for American blacks had previously labored in Malawi (formerly Nyasaland) as missionaries, and Malawians had come to the United States to study. One of the best known of these was John Chilembwe, the trained African educator and radical whose work is discussed in Chapter 18. Chilembwe worked out a curriculum modeled on Tuskegee, emphasizing practical skills, but he lacked the financial support that Washington received in the United States from wealthy philanthropists like Andrew Carnegie. Starved of funds, Chilembwe's educational work made little headway, and he turned to radical politics. The small rising against the British that he led in 1915, in which he lost his life, lacked mass support and posed no immediate threat to British rule; but as an inspiration to African nationalism, Chilembwe and his Afro-American connexions played a significant role in history.[18]

Far more influential, because of his books, columns in newspapers, and frequent magazine articles, was George Padmore, another black man writing on African affairs prior to World War II. A West Indian who attended Fisk and Howard universities briefly, Padmore joined the Communist movement during the late twenties because it promised liberation of Asia, Africa, and the West Indies from colonialism. His 1931 pamphlet written for the Red International of Labor Unions, entitled *Life and Struggles for Negro Toilers,* showed the unity of black problems and called for blacks everywhere to unite to solve them in revolutions inspired by, and as part of, the worldwide Communist movement. He attacked emigrationists in the New World for evading the task of organizing for revolt, and missionaries for misleading Africans. Padmore lived and worked in Europe and Africa during the early thirties and broke with the Third International in 1935, organizing with Jomo Kenyatta, C. L. R. James, and Peter Abrahams the International African Service Bureau, which had evolved into the Pan-African Federation by 1944.

Though Padmore's antiimperialist writings were widely read and approved of by Afro-Americans, these writings contained no prescription for black liberation. In 1937 a few friends of the international Communist movement founded the Council on African Affairs, which eventually was able to mobilize some pressure on behalf of the African National Congress in south Africa; it never gained a wide membership base, however.

Black American intellectuals did not easily agree on a common program. During the 1920s they were divided, for instance, on the question whether to defend or attack Liberia and Liberian misgovernment. Padmore criticized the government in Monrovia. Du Bois argued that Liberia's rulers were no worse than those of most governments. George Schuyler insisted that Liberians had to reach a higher standard because they were black Americans and because many enemies of blacks were watching to see if they would fail.[19]

There was more unity over the Italian–Ethiopian war in the 1930s. Ethiopia was one of only two independent black states in Africa; it had long been regarded with pride and religious zeal ("Ethiopia shall stretch forth her hands unto God"). Black Americans attributed Ethiopia's defeat to its betrayal by the League of Nations because it was an independent black state. The flight of Emperor Haile Selassie to London and the obliteration of the only independent, indigenous black kingdom aroused intense feelings of anxiety and a sense of helplessness reflected in black editorial columns. Padmore wrote to Du Bois that he feared an extermination of the earth's black people.

Black awareness of Africa was greatly increased by the numbers of black American soldiers who went to Liberia, the Gold Coast, and Nigeria during World War II, mainly as service troops to load and unload ships and trucks. Even more important to developing the link between Americans and Africans were the Africans who studied in the United States after 1930, among them, as noted elsewhere, Nnamdi Azikiwe and Kwame Nkrumah, who became important leaders of African nationalism after 1945. Nkrumah worked with the African student newspaper *African Interpreter* and spoke to black church groups as often as he could. He worked with Paul Robeson and Max Yergan in the Council of African Affairs, and he visited Africa House in Harlem. During the war, Nkrumah read and was influenced by Padmore's writing on Pan-Africanism and socialism; he joined Padmore at the Fifth Pan-African Congress in Manchester in 1945 (discussed next). Later

Padmore followed Nkrumah to the independent state of Ghana, which Nkrumah headed, became his advisor on African affairs, and helped to train African leaders and to plan ways in which other colonies could become independent.

During the long depression years and the war years that followed, African nationalist and labor leaders became aware of themselves. African labor organizations were finally included in the Trades Union Conference at London in 1945 – the first time that Africans had been accorded admission to a labor assembly. At the conference, according to George Padmore, there arose a spontaneous demand for another Pan-African congress, a fifth one. The black delegates at the conference, after consultation and some correspondence, constituted themselves the Pan-African Federation and proceeded to the business of calling the congress.[20]

The Fifth Pan-African Congress, which the federation had originally intended to hold in Paris, assembled in England at Manchester on October 15, 1945, and met daily for several days. Du Bois's part in convoking this congress is not clear, but it is certain that he was one of the moving spirits; significantly, he occupied the chair during most of the sessions. Kenyatta was chairman, and Nkrumah and Padmore shared the office of organizing secretary. This fifth congress was the first in which a majority of the delegates were Africans, and a large number (possibly a majority) were workers rather than intellectuals. Western Hemisphere blacks were still important in the leadership, but real control had passed to African political figures about to go home. Nkrumah and Kenyatta reflected the change in Pan-Africanism from a protest movement against racial inequality by American blacks to an African movement for the liberation of African colonies.[21]

The congress assembled a few months after the British Labour Party had gained power, and the gathering displayed a mood of striking optimism. The congress adopted a philosophy of quasi-Marxist socialism and vigorously denounced Western rule. In addition, it called for justice for blacks all over the globe; sections were devoted to East Africa, West Africa, the Congo, North Africa, the Union of South Africa, the protectorates (opposing the annexation of South-West Africa by South Africa), the West Indies, Ethiopia, Liberia, and Haiti. Thus, although the majority of the delegates were Africans, the congress endeavored to cement black unity throughout the world.

The Fifth Pan-African Congress was an early milestone on the road to African independence from colonial rule. In this campaign, black Americans could play but a small part. Insofar as exerting pressure on behalf of Africa was concerned, they were divided into a number of competing bodies, several of which – such as the African Students Association of the United States, the African Academy of Arts and Research, and the Ethiopian World Nationalist Movement – were short-lived and lacked both leadership and expertise. The most important organization before 1955 was the Council on African Affairs (CAA), founded originally by Max Yergan (who ultimately became a militant conservative). In 1937 Yergan persuaded Paul Robeson, some other prominent Afro-Americans, one African, and five white liberals to join him in organizing the International Committee on Africa, the forerunner of the CAA. This group subscribed to Marxism and was friendly with the American Communist Party and the Soviet Union. The CAA petitioned and protested for African causes and helped to educate the public about Africa through its journal, *Spotlight on Africa*. Yergan broke with the CAA in 1948 and became an active anti-communist, testifying against the council before congressional hearings on subversive organizations in the 1950s. Du Bois also joined the council, but before he became a Communist in 1961. The council went out of existence in 1955, about the time that the civil rights movement was starting in the South. Although it had a small membership, it had been one of the most important American organizations specifically concerned with Africa.[22]

But the historian of the CAA, Hollis Lynch, finds it difficult to assess the council's influence on U.S. policy toward Africa. He believes it contributed to the formation of American policy favoring rapid decolonization after World War II. Members of the council lobbied the new Office of African Affairs within the State Department, and criticized the department for not pushing for decolonization in Africa. The council was the first American-based Pan-African group to form close links with African nationalists and labor organizations. Support for South African nationalists came from the printed word (a 1953 pamphlet was entitled *Resistance against Fascist Enslavement in South Africa*) and from money ($2,500 to aid the Defiance Campaign). Kenyan nationalists received council backing during the Kikuyu rebellion of 1952–4. The council had its closest contact with West Africans, especially with Nigerians, and Nigerian nationalist leaders were regularly in correspondence with its members. The council, for example, aided Nnamdi Azikiwe in his support of the 1945 and 1949 strikes in Nigeria. But if African leaders were not sufficiently leftist or took actions against Communist groups, the council sharply criticized them in *Spotlight on Africa*.

After 1952 Afro-American intellectuals took increasing interest in Africa. The Mau Mau rebellion in Kenya helped awaken ordinary American black interest, for example, in growing Kenyatta beards, as did the activities of Azikiwe in Nigeria and Nkrumah in the Gold Coast. But the history of black American involvement in Africa mainly centered on West Africa and on South Africa, the latter a country widely, though mistakenly, identified by Americans of all colors with the unreconstructed South. Black American activities hinged on a number of minor lobbies. During the 1950s black Americans placed special emphasis on cultural ties with Africa. The American Society of African Culture (AMSAC), founded in 1957, played an active political part by holding conferences in its New York City headquarters and cooperating with black American colleges. AMSAC invited prominent African leaders like Agostinho Neto of the MPLA, Sam Nujoma of SWAPO, and intellectuals such as Bloke Modisane and Lewis Nkosi to discuss cultural and political topics. The society maintained a fine library in New York City and published an excellent journal, *African Forum*.

The American Negro Leadership Conference on Africa (ANLCA) was founded by representatives from organizations including the NAACP, CORE, the Urban League, the National Conference of Negro Women, and several fraternities, sororities, and church groups. It had a full-time paid lobbyist in Washington; and it achieved several successes through lobbying with the State Department – as, for instance, when it blocked the visit of a U.S. aircraft carrier to Capetown. ANLCA never attempted to mobilize mass support among black Americans. In the late 1960s, when it was found to have unknowingly used CIA funds, it came under fire from black militants like John Henrik Clarke, a founder of the African Heritage Society of America, and from the radical black caucus within the African Studies

Association; it lost its Jewish and Irish financial backers after the black power upsurge alienated them. At this point ANLCA ceased to be effective.

The African Liberation Support Committee (ALSC), a more radical body, succeeded ANLCA in about 1968. Basically a black nationalist group, it held rallies and organized protests against Portuguese colonialism and white South African racism. It tried to influence American policy toward Africa and pledged aid for liberation movements in southern Africa. The ALSC split into many bitter rival factions after 1972.

One of these was Transafrica, headed by Randall M. Robinson, a black attorney trained at Harvard and a former assistant to Congressman Charles C. Diggs. Robinson, able and eloquent, established excellent relations with the delegation of the Organization of African Unity in New York and with the State Department, but given the divisive nature of black American society, Transafrica's effective influence also remains limited.

Another black splinter group evolved from the African Studies Association in 1969 and survived the 1970s. The African Heritage Studies Association (AHSA) is, like ALSC, a black nationalist group, but it is more scholarly than political. It runs a yearly conference dealing with African studies, just as does the ASA. The AHSA believes that white scholars should not dominate the field in granting funds for study and research and interpreting controversial questions.[23]

The Student Nonviolent Coordinating Committee (SNCC, discussed later in this section), CORE, and the Southern Christian Leadership Conference (SCLC) led the civil rights movement of the 1960s. SNCC split in 1966 into integrationist and separatist factions; when the separatists won, the whites left the organization. Stokely Carmichael sent up the cry of "black power." For a decade before Carmichael made his "return" to Africa, taking up residence in Sekou Touré's Guinea, a few individual Afro-Americans had been going as teachers and technicians, particularly to Liberia, Ghana, Nigeria, Kenya, and Tanganyika. Other black nationalists, influenced by the rhetoric of Frantz Fanon (for example, the Black Panthers or RAM) or attempting to emulate Mau Mau, embarked on domestic violence, hopeless revolutionary ventures whose scope and importance were vastly exaggerated by the media. But black nationalism perhaps found its most widespread expression in the black student protests that swept the campuses between 1967 and 1972.

Black nationalism looked to black self-determination in the United States and in Africa. The independence gained by the African colonies in the 1960s reinforced black nationalism in the United States, and many black intellectuals began to look toward Africa not only for their roots, but also to celebrate Afro-American culture. Ghana under Nkrumah became a symbol of the political, economic, and social liberation of blacks and an example of black capacity and worth. Some Afro-Americans, like Carmichael, went to Africa to participate in building the new postcolonial states.

Black Americans, in theory, have a greater stake in Africa than any other group of Americans, however well intentioned. Constituting about 12 percent of the population, black Americans are more numerous than Jewish, Czech, or Polish Americans, all of whom exercised considerable influence in bringing about the independence of their respective homelands. For all their social disabilities, moreover, black Americans during the 1950s and the 1960s formed the world's wealthiest and best-educated black community. Properly organized, black Americans might have exercised greater influence on Africa than any other segment of American society. There was a constant interchange between black American and African intellectuals. Black American popular music and culture found an echo in Africa, in a continent where even remote communities began to hear of the outside world through cheap transistor radios. There was also an interchange of political ideas. Nkrumah, the first prime minister of Ghana, owed a good deal to his American experience. Chief Walter Lutuli, a leader of the African National Congress in South Africa and the most notable spokesman of its constitutional wing, drew on the experience of black American leaders like Martin Luther King.

But on the whole, black Americans took only a peripheral part in the struggle for African independence. The reasons for their inability to play a decisive role are complex. Liberia, once the hope for black Americans, could not serve as a black American Zion. As I. K. Sundiata, a historian of Liberia, puts it:

> By the early twentieth century – when large-scale emigration from the diaspora became technically feasible due to improved communication and effective tropical medicine – the Americo-Liberians were no longer an extension of Afro-America. They were a group native to Africa hoping to maintain their supremacy against all comers. Racial solidarity, although used as a propaganda instrument, played little part in the policy decisions of the Monrovia government.[24]

Black Americans, even black militants, were far from united in their approach, especially once independence from European rule had been won for the African colonies. Black as well as white radicals would often interpret African issues in terms of American issues – a failing that they shared with their countrymen at large. The black power advocates, for example, were apt to side with the secessionist state of Biafra during the Nigerian civil war in the late 1960s. The Biafrans appealed to the Americans' romanticism. Moreover, the Ibo, the main supporters of Biafra, were among the best-educated black ethnic groups in Africa; many of their leaders had studied in the United States and Great Britain; they were skilled in putting their case in excellent English, quoting American revolutionary parallels. Black power advocates in the United States thus found themselves in a bizarre alliance with Ibo separatists, Chinese Communists, Portuguese colonialists, politicians of the French establishment, and missionary lobbies, while siding against a legitimately established African government. Black power slogans seemed to make more sense in South Africa, where the black consciousness movement owed a debt to American as well as South African theoreticians. This movement, developed in the 1970s, aimed at welding Africans, Coloureds, and Indians into a common alliance against the whites. This objective appealed to black power advocates; black and white Americans alike were prone to underestimate the vast differences between their own country and South Africa.

The cultural experience of black Americans likewise differed strikingly from that of Africans like the Kikuyu in Kenya or the Bemba in Zambia. Black Americans (like South African Coloureds) traced their ancestry to a multiplicity of African peoples and often also to Europeans of varied descent; black americans, like Angolan mestiços or South African Coloureds, spoke a European-descended, not an African, tongue. The black Americans' education, customs, and prejudices were American. Even the most militant black Americans could not help being taken aback when Tanzania's ruling party, for example, declared "cultural war" in 1969 on such American imports as "soul music" or Afro clothes, food, and wigs, on the grounds that these products served as a means of cultural penetration to further the interests of American imperialism.[25] The miniskirts worn by African fashion fans offended the new puritans in East and Central Africa: Such outlandish garments of Western provenance supposedly sullied the dignity of black womanhood and symbolized an attack on the traditional African family values. But few black American intellectuals agreed.

The black Americans' link to Africa was more tenuous than the Irishmen's to Ireland or the Poles' to Poland. Few black Americans could trace the country from which their ancestors had arrived, much less the province, the city, or the kinship group. The vast majority had in the past not been much interested in Africa; they considered themselves Americans, entitled to the civic rights that should be available to them in their capacity as American citizens. They were no more interested in learning Swahili or Hausa than the descendants of Irish immigrants were in learning Erse poetry, or third-generation Americans of German origin were with studying the lay of the Niebelungs. In schools and colleges the ethnic revival was apt to end where the irregular verbs started – a fact well known to all those who have ever attempted to teach foreign tongues to American students in high schools or colleges.

The much-heralded ethnic revival in the United States, complete with Oktoberfests and zithers, tartans and pibrochs, Swahili surnames and bongo drums, had nothing to do with the cultural irredentism of oppressed nineteenth-century European minorities in the Ottoman, Russian, or Austro-Hungarian empires. Ethnic assertiveness in the United States did not try to promote a genuine interest in Goethe, Calderón, or any other foreign literary genius; on the contrary, the revival coincided with a striking decline in language and literature teaching in high schools and universities. The real function of the revival was quite different: It was a means of asserting pride and dignity among hitherto despised or supposedly despised Americans in their relations with other Americans; it was but another instrument of Americanization.

In the same way, the back-to-Africa movements had always been unable to prevail against the irresistible force of Americanization. They had attracted but a relatively small number of blacks, few of them drawn from the middle and upper classes. Even during the dramatic years of decolonization, black American interests in Africa remained confined to the educated. Black Americans, with their white allies, were strong enough to serve as a veto group able to render nugatory any attempt to form an American–South African or an American–Rhodesian alliance. But black Americans for long were unable to build up a truly effective ethnic lobby of their own. The reasons are not hard to explain.

The politics of ethnic influence in America require a lobbying apparatus, the ability to mobilize an electoral threat, and a successful appeal to the symbols of American nationhood. Black Americans have acquired considerable influence in American politics, especially those of the big cities. By the early 1980s, their influence had further grown. Blacks sat in the mayoral offices of great metropolitan centers such as Los Angeles and Chicago. Black leaders like the Reverend Jesse Jackson could run in 1984 as a black presidential candidate.

Equally noteworthy was the Black Caucus in Congress. Founded in 1971 to coordinate the work of blacks in the U.S. House of Representatives, the Black Caucus was one among several similar bodies that met to discuss legislative strategy, electoral questions, and the like. Associated with the caucus were white liberals, like Stephen J. Solarz, who relied on black as well as white voters for their seats. Initially, the Black Caucus regarded itself as a single unified group representing the entire black national community. But soon thereafter the members of the Black Caucus increasingly identified themselves as "just legislators," primarily representatives of individual constituencies that contained voters of every hue. The achievements of the caucus were not negligible. Led by Representative William H. Gray, the caucus supported, for example, legislation to prohibit new U.S. investments in South Africa. At the same time, there was a growing campaign requiring the major state employee funds to sell all investments in firms doing business with South Africa. Divestiture of at least some existing holdings gained approval from state legislatures in, for instance, Nebraska, Kansas, and Michigan.

Nevertheless, black Americans still had a long way to go in making their power felt over issues connected with Africa. The Black Caucus was strong enough to stop legislation (such as the so-called Byrd amendment on Rhodesian chrome). But it could not easily initiate legislation. The caucus managed to achieve some representation on other congressional committees. (For example, Congressman Howard E. Wolpe's Subcommittee on Africa in the House in 1983–4 pushed for legislation to disassociate the United States from South Africa in the economic field by prohibiting new investments, new bank loans, and the importation of Krugerrands; it also sought to establish a tougher business code for American firms in South Africa.) But the Black Caucus proved unable to obtain increased aid for Africa. (Israel, at the time of writing, obtained three times as much American assistance as the whole of black Africa.) The twenty-one members of the Black Caucus lacked the numbers, organization, and unity to become a major force in America's African relations, or to assume a consistent national leadership for the black community in the United States.

There were many reasons for the black Americans' relative political weakness. Blacks were the last group in America to attain full legal equality. Racial segregation in schools was not outlawed until 1954, six years after D. F. Malan had entered the prime minister's office in South Africa with a militant program for apartheid. The main victories of the civil rights movement in the United States (for instance, the Civil Rights Act of 1964 and the Voting Rights Act of 1965) roughly coincided with the end of decolonization in British Africa. Black leaders during the 1950s were preoccupied mainly with domestic problems concerned with civil rights, poverty, and unemployment. There were few blacks in the higher levels of bureaucracy, business, or politics in the United States, and those blacks who were influential concerned themselves more with the American South than with South Africa.

During the 1950s and early 1960s the American civil rights struggle was led by men like Martin Luther King, who looked to peaceful legal change and who drew his inspiration from Gandhi rather than Lenin. From 1966 onward, however, black American aspirations were increasingly redefined by the militant youth in terms of black power, black consciousness, and militance. Many black American intellectuals attempted to find their ethnic identity in relation to their African heritage. There were widespread ghetto riots; there was a national mood of self-questioning intensified by the Vietnam War.

SNCC exemplified the turn from the struggle for civil rights to revolutionary socialism and solidarity with the Third World. SNCC began in 1960 as a peaceful and constitutional movement. During the 1960s it became increasingly militant, this trend accelerated in part as a result of contacts with Africa. SNCC's first mission to Africa departed in 1964; the delegates were James Forman, John Lewis, Bob and Dona Moses, Prathia Hall, Julian Bond, Ruby Doris Robinson, and other black activists. The American visitors received a warm welcome from Sekou Touré, president of newly independent Guinea and a leading proponent of African socialism and nonalignment in the cold war. Touré encouraged black Americans to take a global view of their struggle and to understand, as he put it, the close relationship between what SNCC did in the United States on the one hand and events in Africa on the other. The delegates were impressed, not only by the warm reception accorded to them by leading officials, but also by their observations of a country run by blacks, a country where blacks drove buses, blacks flew airplanes, and blacks sat behind big desks in bankers' offices.

Lewis and a companion subsequently traveled to Liberia, Ghana, Zambia, Kenya, Ethiopia, and Egypt. Their meetings with African student leaders and Afro-American expatriates persuaded them that the struggles in Africa and the United States formed part of a universal campaign against a vicious system controlled worldwide by a few white men, and that black Americans must cooperate with Africans. Following subsequent visits to Africa by Forman and other staff members, SNCC finally set up an office of international affairs. By 1968 Hubert Rap Brown, one of SNCC's leaders, was demanding that blacks move from "resistance to aggression, from revolt to revolution."[26] Ultra-militants, known as the "Atlanta specialists," went even further; they called for the expulsion of white activists from SNCC and, in a wider sense, for the blacks' repudiation of Western civilization as a whole.

SNCC, however, failed to attract mass support. Like others among the radical intellectuals of the time, all too many SNCC leaders lived in a dreamland of posters where flag-waving maidens and gun-toting youths were forever marching up a hill into the radiant sun. SNCC staff members could not agree on a policy designed to gain wider popular backing; there were bitter internal conflicts, made worse by police infiltration and staff desertion. For all their Marxist rhetoric, militant SNCC organizers (and also organizations such as the Black Panther Party) were ill equipped to tackle such basic questions as organization, intelligence, supplies, pay, arms—those humdrum details that make or break an army. The black masses would not rally in support of a revolution. The lumpenproletariat, though willing at times to riot and loot, could not be converted into a revolutionary force. Black American, like white American, militance ultimately formed part of the great religio-political pilgrimage in which Western intellectuals—from George Bernard Shaw, Sidney and Beatrice Webb, Louise Armstrong, Pablo Neruda, Jean-Paul

Sartre, Bertolt Brecht, Lion Feuchtwanger, and the Reverend Hewlett Johnson, to Eldridge Cleaver, Susan Sontag, Norman Mailer, Tom Hayden, Mary McCarthy, Noam Chomsky, and countless others – abased themselves before bloodstained tyrants claiming to embody the inner meaning of history.

In a more prosaic sense, black Americans found themselves at a political disadvantage compared to other ethnic groups. When Irishmen, Poles, Czechs, or Jews had organized in support of specific ethnic causes – in favor of Irish, Polish, Czechoslovakian, or Israeli independence – they had appealed to sentiments with a wide popular appeal to all Americans. Polish and Czech nationalists during World War I had played the antimonarchist card, and after World War II they had made use of anticommunism in America. Irish nationalists had appealed to long-standing American hostility to British imperialism. Zionists had American sympathies for the persecuted and American respect for the people of the Old Covenant. None of these issues were in conflict with the sentiments of the American majority.

By contrast, black revolutionary socialism or self-identification with Third World peoples had little appeal beyond the world of the campuses. During the 1930s a substantial number of volunteers, derived from many Western countries, had signed up for the International Brigades that fought in Spain. Almost no Americans, black or white, were willing, however, to participate personally in the guerrilla struggle against the Portuguese, the white Rhodesians, and the South Africans. (Yet about fifteen hundred white Americans served in the Rhodesian forces to defend Ian Smith's unrecognized republic, as against twenty-eight hundred Americans who did battle in Spain in the 1930s.) Middle America as a whole was alienated by strident calls for revolutionary violence and by the would-be revolutionaries' obscure or scabrous terminology. American revolutionaries consistently supported African exile movements, but because these were often split among themselves, their U.S. supporters were apt to become involved in the domestic issues of foreign states without relevance to American issues. Black radicals identified with the newly independent countries of black Africa and gained a new feeling of dignity from the influence of the African bloc at the United Nations. But publicity concerning Africa was by no means an unmixed blessing for black Americans; black prestige also suffered sometimes, as black Americans were unfairly identified with the turbulence and bloodshed that has characterized so many of the postcolonial regimes in Africa.

The black ethnic cause suffers from other disabilities. Because blacks traditionally vote for the Democratic Party, Democratic politicians are not afraid of mass black desertions to the Republican Party when they offend black voters. Congress has its Black Caucus, but blacks at the moment do not have an effective lobbying apparatus within the Democratic Party; hence they cannot easily make electoral threats. The traditional liberal alliance between Jews and blacks has weakened, partly over the issue of Israel, partly over domestic problems like busing, quotas, and competition for public service posts. The American black community remains heterogeneous in character and hard to mobilize. Black Americans are not likely to rally over South Africa, a country with which they have no religious, linguistic, or cultural links comparable to those that may tie, say, an Italian American to the ancestral country. Moreover, to help the revolution abroad, black Americans have tended first to join the establishment at home, especially at a time when the radicalism of the 1960s was on the wane and a cautious conservativism was in the ascendant.

But above all, the black power theoreticians, like many American academicians and many other ethnic politicians in general, did not truly understand their own society. They underestimated alike the strength of American patriotism, the assimilative power of American society, the Americans' pride in their political inheritance, and their distrust of socialism. The critics of American society, including President Carter himself, had often asserted that Americans, by the end of the 1970s, were subject to a severe crisis in confidence and to nagging doubts that their political and civil liberties would endure. But American migration statistics and pollsters' reports both told a very different story: America remained what it had always been, a magnet to attract immigrants. Native-born Americans, on the other hand, stayed at home. No matter what complaints may have been levied against the United States, Americans preferred their own country to others. Jewish Americans, for instance, did not normally settle in Israel; the mass of Mexican Americans did not desire to live in Mexico, much less in Cuba; black Americans for the most part never even dreamed of going back to Africa.

Patriotism remained a powerful force in the United States, stronger perhaps than in any other Western country. If the pollsters are to be trusted, an enormous majority (98 percent) felt proud in 1981 of being American; 84 percent (including 80 percent of the blacks) thought that their country had a special role to play in the world; 94 percent (86 percent of the blacks) believed that the United States was the best country in the world in which to live. At a time when Americans supposedly were suffering from a profound national malaise, they prized their constitutional liberties, approved of the private enterprise system, and distrusted socialism: 91 percent of the whites and 85 percent of the blacks agreed that "the U.S. business system works better than any other for industrial countries."[27] Given these assumptions, the black masses remained as hard to mobilize for revolutionary change as the whites, and black separatism in a political sense seemed a lost cause.

Earlier predictions to the contrary notwithstanding, black Americans remained firmly wedded to constitutional politics of the conventional kind. Potentially, their influence was considerable, with many states where blacks might swing an election either way. But there remained the problem of effectively mobilizing and coordinating the vote of a community for long distinguished in the past by a low voter turnout. During the early 1980s the willingness of black citizens to go to the polling booths substantially increased, partly as a result of rising black educational standards and partly owing to the efforts of men like the Reverend Jesse Jackson. At the same time, there was a growing commitment to the Democratic Party's presidential candidate, with blacks the most loyal and consistent supporters among any ethnic community of the Democratic ticket.[28] But even within the Democratic Party, black opinion remained divided and little concerned with African issues. Black voting patterns remained as complex overall as those of their fellow citizens of different ethnic backgrounds. Black American politicians as yet had a long road to travel in building an effective and united black lobby, able to sway Washington's policy toward Africa.

Anti–South African lobbies

Of all issues in America's African politics, none has aroused more emotion and more commitment than the campaign against apartheid. The fervor caused by opposition to South Africa's system of apartheid far exceeds the involvement of Americans with other governmental abuses in Africa. Opposition to apartheid unites blacks and many whites in the United States and extends all over the Western world. All human rights groups object to apartheid. These groups perform many functions in education, in welfare relief, and in the work of political lobbies. Some of them are long established (such as the Anti-Slavery Society in the United Kingdom), but most American anti-apartheid groups have come into existence only since 1962. Most have small budgets and rely on volunteer staff. They have nevertheless succeeded in putting some pressure on South Africa by their programs of education and aid to South African opposition groups, and by lobbying the UN and governmental and corporate bodies.

The anti-apartheid movement has legitimized the attempted South African revolution and gained recognition for liberation movements. This change has caused great problems for Western countries in their dealings with South Africa. South Africa has been condemned, boycotted, subjected to sanctions, and isolated from world politics. Only occasional U.K. and U.S. votes have prevented the use of stronger measures against South Africa.

The UN has been the major area of pressure, especially since the establishment in 1962 of the Special UN Committee on Apartheid. The West supported the committee until 1970, when the group backed liberation movements and called for economic sanctions. The Organization of African Unity also gave support to liberation movements and thus caused friction with the United States and the United Kingdom, who opposed the use of violence. Up to the 1960s, anti-apartheid groups were largely moderate and reformist. After Sharpeville (1960), they began to call for direct action and to support liberation. They took to direct action with marches, demonstrations, and campaigns to attack apartheid. The anti-apartheid movement became the central coordinating body for direct-action programs of boycotts, demonstrations, strikes, and campaigns against business and banking activities in South Africa, as well as sports engagements.[29]

By the late 1960s, educated opinion in the West had become overwhelmingly anti–South African.[30] The anti–South African alliance is a loose coalition that depends for its cohesion upon certain common assumptions, and not a tight organizational network. This alliance derives its support primarily from intellectuals and professional people, rather than from workers or the lower middle class, and comprises a wide spectrum. The Popular Front may have died in Spain, but it has revived to operate against South Africa on the grounds that the Pretoria regime represents the world's last Fascist holdout, the last country on earth where Communists, liberals, and progressive conservatives may cooperate against the common foe.

Conservatively minded Africanists, by contrast, have carried relatively little political weight. They are few in number. Until the election of President Reagan in 1980, at least, they wielded no influence in Washington. Indeed, they were seldom called to testify, much less to advise. Study projects such as those of the Rockefeller or Carnegie foundations on South Africa have no conservatives on the staff and seldom ask conservatives to consult or testify. Liberal professors, on the other hand, have served as advisers and consultants for government departments, they have helped to shape opinion as teachers, and their expertise has been drawn upon by the media and the bureaucracy. Academicians have also played an important part in lobbies like the American Committee on Africa (ACOA), the Association of Concerned Africa Scholars, and the Washington Office on Africa, characterized by interlocking directorates that tie together university people, liberal politicians, church people, labor unions, and the civil rights movement.

Critics of apartheid are apt to oppose with equal fervor the real or imagined machinations of multinational corporations, firms involved in nuclear power, or enterprises that pollute the environment or kill whales. They identify white South Africa with all the real or supposed ills of "Middle America." These groups are loosely tied through personal contacts, through bonds of political sympathy, and sometimes through linked directorates; they can therefore mobilize around particular issues with surprising speed and effectiveness and can readily assemble hordes of student demonstrators. They have also managed to preempt certain words for their use: Terms such as "concerned," "peace," "liberation," "majority rule," and "popular" have become widely identified with liberal and left-wing issues.[31]

The most important anti-apartheid group in the United States is the ACOA, founded in 1953 by the civil rights activists for the purpose of supporting African independence movements and advocating an American boycott of South Africa. ACOA, headed by George Houser, a white liberal and a former minister, cooperated with other liberal groups and helped to form numerous anti-apartheid organizations in the 1960s and 1970s.

The American Committee on Africa and its associated body, the African Fund, founded in 1966, have modest budgets but active programs; the 1980 budget for ACOA was about $95,000, and the African Fund spent $250,000. ACOA spent most of its money ($45,000) on campaigns and projects calling for the withdrawal of accounts in banks making loans to South Africa, the halting of sports contacts with South Africa, and the divestment of stocks in companies aiding apartheid. It continues to lobby in Washington for a U.S. policy sympathetic to the so-called liberation struggle in southern Africa. The next largest share of money ($33,000) goes for information and education on southern Africa for campus groups, churches, trade unions, and the media. Through congressional and UN testimony, national speaking tours, action meeting reports, and news releases, ACOA brings vital information on important events in southern Africa to the American people. For 1981, ACOA budgeted $5,000 for emergency assistance for refugees fleeing from South Africa.

The African Fund spends a larger sum on refugees (about $169,000 in 1980). It has devoted much of its efforts to giving material assistance to Namibian refugees, and Mozambique has received medical supplies and equipment valued at $50,000. Fifty grants worth $26,000 were made to individual refugees in 1980.

The African Fund's research and education program ($68,000) is one of the most extensive in the United States, providing information on southern Africa, with special emphasis on U.S. corporate and government policies. In 1980 it distributed 35,000 copies of African Fund publications and 6,500 other titles. Hundreds of requests for information are answered, and over 150 reporters and researchers use the files of the fund each year. Free labor is provided by college students. The African Fund also sponsors extensive speaking tours for exiled black and white South Africans. Both ACOA and the African Fund carry out research and publish studies on southern Africa. Their publications, which are listed in a five-page catalogue, include *ACOA Action News* (published twice yearly), *ACOA Action Mailing,* and the *ACOA Annual Report.* The African Fund also publishes a *Southern Africa Perspectives* series.

Lobbies like ACOA publish newsletters, background papers, research memoranda; they call upon congressmen and senior officials in the administration; they secure a good deal of coverage for their activities in liberal newspapers like the *New York Times;* they send speakers to college campuses and to church-related gatherings and seminars. They enjoy valuable links to the labor movement. Walter Reuther's personal involvement with ACOA probably exerted some influence on the anti-apartheid policy pursued by the United Automobile Workers (UAW).

The UAW's aversion to apartheid is shared in turn by the AFL–CIO. The AFL–CIO has a strong commitment to promoting reformist policies abroad; for this purpose, it set up three institutes in Washington, D.C., concerned respectively with Africa, Asia, and Latin America, in order to assist fellow workers overseas in trade union training, worker education, and vocational instruction; to provide information on general themes concerned with workers' interests; and to aid in the development of cooperatives, credit unions, and similar institutions. The AFL–CIO has taken a particular interest in South Africa; it sent a fact-finding mission to the country and did everything in its power to promote free collective bargaining for black and brown, as well as white, workers.

The Washington Office on Africa (WOA), in operation since 1972, has been a leader of the U.S. movement working to gain majority rule in southern Africa and to form, according to its brochure, "a progressive United States policy towards that region."[32] Its sponsors are mostly church groups and the American Committee on Africa. They have lobbied effectively in Congress to retain the Clark amendment banning U.S. covert military operations in Angola and to cut U.S. Export–Import Bank financing in South Africa.

The WOA serves two major functions: It coordinates public campaigns around southern Africa issues and supplies up-to-date information on U.S. policy toward the region. The office publishes a quarterly newsletter, *Washington Notes on Africa;* issues legislative alerts on pending bills affecting southern Africa; and provides resource papers on topics of current interest.

The Lawyers Committee for Civil Rights under Law was founded in 1963 to fight for civil rights in the United States. In 1967 it formed the Southern Africa Project to link the domestic struggle to the worldwide struggle for human rights. The project seeks (1) to ensure that defendants in political trials in South Africa and Namibia receive the necessary resources for their defense, including lawyers of their choice; (2) to initiate or intervene in legal proceedings in the United States in order to deter official or private actions that support South Africa's policy of apartheid; (3) to serve as a legal resource for those concerned with promoting the human rights of South Africans; and (4) to heighten the awareness, especially among the American legal profession, of the erosion of the rule of law in South

Africa. Since 1967 the Lawyers Committee has been directly involved in, or informed about, virtually every major political trial in South Africa and Namibia. The committee has also been active in seeking to extend the arms boycott against South Africa.

The Southern Africa Media Center brings together media people, educators, religious leaders, and citizens to improve the effectiveness of film in church, community, and academic education and action programs centering on southern Africa. In the five years since its founding, the Media Center (based in San Francisco) has become one of the leading distributors of anti-apartheid films.

Radical youth groups sprang up in the 1960s to lend support to liberation movements. The African Research Group (ARG) worked out of Cambridge, Massachusetts, and published a series of studies on southern Africa. It disbanded in 1973 and gave its files and publications to the black African Information Services based in Harlem. Many ARG members then joined the Southern African Committee (SAC).

The SAC was also a radical student group that focused on research on imperialism and racism and the role of U.S. corporations in the Third World. The group produced a radical monthly, *Southern Africa,* a radio Africa News Service, and a press service. The research of this group and of ACOA stimulated the sanctions, boycotts, and disinvestment debates of the 1970s. The SAC and ACOA led the campaigns against Gulf Oil, Polaroid, and leading banks. Perhaps the most successful campaign was conducted (in 1966) by the Committee of Conscience against Apartheid, established by the ACOA, clergy, and union officials, which was opposed to U.S. banks making loans of $40 million to South Africa. Banks were threatened with the withdrawal of church funds and gave into the pressure and did not renew the loans.

A new group emerged in late 1981, the Association of Concerned Africa Scholars (ACAS), to oppose the Reagan administration's Africa policy, especially its policy toward South Africa. The group, based in East Lansing, Michigan, is made up of leftist and liberal activists in academia. One of their objectives is to issue background papers on critical issues affecting Africa. These will be sent to key legislators, to the national network of organizations concerned with Africa, and to the media and members of the association. Political Education Action (PEA) will disseminate information quickly and coordinate national campaigns on various issues. Actions would include telegrams and letters to the State Department and congressmen, teach-ins, demonstrations, and so on organized by the PEA committee. A conference committee will seek to organize panels to appear at various scholarly conventions. The ACAS has attempted to coordinate and to share responsibilities with other activist African groups, for example, the 1981 Conference on Solidarity with the Peoples of Southern Africa and the Dennis Brutus Defense Campaign.

In the United States, Communist fronts opposing apartheid include the Coalition of Black Trade Unionists (CBTU), the International Association of Democratic Lawyers (IADL), National Anti-Imperialist Movement on Solidarity with African Liberation (NAIMSAL), a CPUSA front founded in 1973 to support revolutionary terrorism in Africa, National Conference of Black Lawyers (NCBL, an affiliate of IADL), National Lawyers Guild (NLG, an affiliate of IADL and the legal support group for the CPUSA and its fronts and unions), and Women for Racial and Economic Equality (WREE, a CPUSA front and an affiliate of the WIDF).[33]

The influence on U.S. foreign policy of these and kindred bodies can easily be exaggerated. Lobbyists come and lobbyists go. They speak with conflicting voices. They cannot impose their views on the country's foreign policy unless they find powerful allies within the legislature and the bureaucracy, which exercise a considerable influence through their financial expenditure in Africa alone. Academia's bureaucratic allies, however, are numerous and well endowed financially. The bureaucratic stake in massive public expenditure dovetails with the academicians' desire to promote "development," "nation building," and "political mobilization" in black Africa. When these lobbies join, they are too strong to be ignored.

CHAPTER 24

Americans in Africa, and Africans in America

The Peace Corps and other programs

The late 1950s and early 1960s were, for the United States, times of optimism. America was prosperous; American military power stood supreme. Most Americans looked to the future with assurance; many dreamed of opening a New Frontier, of creating a splendid future that would see the end of oppression and poverty both at home and abroad. Perhaps the most distinctive contribution made by American progressives to foreign aid was the creation of the Peace Corps, initiated in 1961 under the auspices of President Kennedy. The Peace Corps appealed, above all, to the energy, restlessness, and idealism of young men and women drawn from the professional middle class, that group in American society that had taken the leading part in supporting social reform at home, welcoming African independence, and commiserating over real or alleged grievances experienced by the Third World.

The Peace Corps was inevitably a gamble. African socialists like Kwame Nkrumah at first asked for its aid and then for various reasons denounced it as a cover organization for American propagandists, spies, and subversive characters.[1] Conservative Americans grumbled about wasting the taxpayers' money for the purpose of financing a new breed of Boy Scout, or for sending "underdeveloped youngsters to underdeveloped countries." As Rupert Emerson, a warm supporter, put it:

> To turn so many Americans loose in Africa, normally with only three
> months of training and often living by themselves in remote parts of the
> country to which they were sent is to invite trouble of many different
> kinds. [But] the amazing thing is how relatively slight and infrequent it has
> been and how cordially the Americans have been welcomed.[2]

The number of volunteers rapidly increased. By 1965 there were 4,474 in training, with 1,136 in Africa; later, when 8,356 were working abroad, 3,010 of them were in Africa. By the end of the 1970s the number of the Peace Corps volunteers serving abroad had somewhat diminished; they then numbered about 8,000.[3] A number of foreign countries, moreover, had paid to the Peace Corps the most sincere compliment possible: They had copied the Peace Corps concept in a variety of ways.

The Peace Corps men and women invite comparison with the earlier generations of young Englishmen, Scotsmen, and Irishmen who heeded Kipling's call to take up the White Man's Burden, serve the cause of empire, and thereby "Fill the mouth of Famine, and bid the sickness cease."[4] If anything, the Peace Corps' self-evaluation is even more resplendent than that made by the colonialists:

Peace Corps volunteers . . . make things happen—useful, appropriate and enduring things. They use technology that is affordable and technologically sound—which benefits the community while preserving local customs. They help increase knowledge and skills, economic development, income, housing, available energy, conservation and community services . . . As a result, volunteers leave behind far more than the wells dug or the schools and clinics built—more even than the millions of lives changed through better diet and cleaner water. They leave behind creativity. They leave a better sense of how to make the best of finite resources. They leave techniques that will help the Third World shape itself long after the volunteers go back home.[5]

The reality has not been so spectacular. The Peace Corps has tried to recruit specialists—foresters, agronomists, architects, engineers, technicians, businesspeople, nurses—as well as generalists with degrees in liberal arts, all of whom served for a pittance.[6] But specialists in technical professions have always been hard to get; the great majority of Peace Corps volunteers (80 percent of them in the mid-1960s) have served as teachers; most African nations, in fact, at first asked only for teachers. In 1961 the first contingent of Peace Corps teachers arrived in Ghana, and five years later more than 2,500 of them were working in elementary and secondary schools, universities, and vocational schools in nineteen African countries. In Cameroun the Peace Corps, teaching such subjects as English, mathematics, and science, by the mid-1960s had helped to double the enrollment in the country's secondary schools and had been instrumental in opening fourteen new schools. In Ethiopia more than 500 Peace Corps teachers had nearly doubled the number of students in the schools, from elementary grades to university level. In Liberia 320 Peace Corps teachers taught 17,000 students in elementary and secondary schools.[7]

In the same period, the Peace Corps provided technical services. Instructors with agricultural training tried to teach soil conservation and improved methods of farming in countries as far afield as Cameroun, Guinea, Niger, Senegal, Tanzania, and Togo. In Gabon, Guinea, and Tanzania, American Peace Corps engineers, equipment operators, surveyors, and repairpeople helped to build roads, water supply systems, public buildings, and other structures, at the same time training Africans for those duties. Peace Corps medical teams included physicians, dentists, nurses, pharmacists, and technicians who staffed hospitals and clinics, instructing Africans and attacking diseases that Africans have long regarded as unconquerable and inevitable.[8]

How effective were these efforts? Compared with the traditional colonial services, the Peace Corps served under great disadvantages. Colonial administrations, like any others, suffered from discontinuity of policy; governors and district commissioners would change, and the new people attempted to carry out new policies that in turn might be changed by their successors. They history of local administration in the colonies is full of projects that were started and not completed—bridges not maintained, roads begun and not kept in repair. Nevertheless, there was a sense of permanence during the heyday of empire. Young men who signed on for the British Colonial Service, for instance, meant to devote the whole of their working lives to Great Britain's overseas dependencies. Meteorologists, archivists, agronomists, and medical officers were apt to spend the greater part of their careers in the same colony, where they would gradually accumulate a great deal of local knowledge. Well or poorly conceived, their projects were supervised by their own superiors and debated in the local legislatures by men familiar with their work.

The Peace Corps volunteers, for the most part, come on short-term contracts. They generally go home just as they are beginning to acquire sufficient knowledge to become truly useful. There have been human problems. Young men and women, brought up in the egalitarian atmosphere of American campuses during the 1960s and 1970s, often found that the realities of life in a remote part of Zambia or the Ivory Coast bore no relation to what they had learned in the United States about the real or supposed qualities of the Third World. Young American graduates, for example, required a great deal of imagination and flexibility to adjust to the mores, of say, a remote Lamba village in Zambia, where etiquette was even more strict than in a traditional European household, where formality of speech and manner was accepted as the mark of the well-bred, where the young were taught to respect their elders, and where whites in general were apt to be derided as boors unfamiliar with the most elementary rules of courtesy. Even in the technical sense, the Peace Corps would encounter many failures. What was the use of the best-intentioned scheme of sinking a new well or of starting a local cooperative when the scheme could be discontinued and the well abandoned upon the departure of its designer?

The effectiveness of the Peace Corps is hard to evaluate. At its best, the corps has provided an outlet for the idealism of young Americans and an agency for transmitting technical and educational skills. At its worst, it has served as a short-term employment agency for young Americans unsure as yet what to do with their lives. Overall, the Peace Corps has done excellent work in teaching (itself a difficult assignment for many Americans, who, unexpectedly, have had to learn how to conform to the systems of British or French education implanted by the erstwhile colonizers). During the late 1970s and the early 1980s, the composition of the Peace Corps volunteers began to change. The youthful arts graduates of the 1960s were increasingly replaced by older men and women trained in a variety of technical and managerial skills, willing to sign on for longer periods than their predecessors, and increasingly efficient therefore at their jobs.

Nevertheless, given the expenditure of money and manpower involved (more than 80,000 Americans had served in the Peace Corps by the beginning of the 1980s), its performance has been somewhat disappointing. It has acquired a well-deserved reputation for Spartan living, for dedication, and for personal integrity. Its members generally have acquired much greater popularity, as individuals, than their competitors from the Soviet bloc. Nevertheless, the United States may have benefited more in the long run from the Peace Corps than have the Third World countries where the volunteers do their service. A great number of Americans have broadened their horizons, acquired new skills, and seen new countries, as they would have done had they served in the armed forces. But in structural terms, the Peace Corps has not fully attained its end.

Private initiative organized Cross Roads Africa, a kind of unofficial Peace Corps. The project began in 1958 under the guidance of Dr. James H. Robinson, a black

Presbyterian minister and the founder of the Morningside Community Center in New York. Robinson determined to set up an interracial, interreligious group, composed mainly of students, to be chosen by competitive examination and interviews. These young men and women would work in Africa for limited periods, contribute to African development, and serve as "ambassadors of good will." Cross Roads Africa works on a tiny budget; individual churches contribute some scholarships, but participants raise the bulk of their funds through their own efforts. The students come from a variety of schools and from many different backgrounds; their work is equally multifarious. For example, volunteers worked on a chapel in the Cameroons, on a model village in Ghana, on experimental farms, and even on the construction of a sewage system. They spend their weekends taking trips, talking to officials and to villagers, and answering sometimes difficult questions regarding the United States. The founders of Cross Roads Africa, like those of the Peace Corps, had extraordinarily high hopes; they envisaged "a mighty chain reaction on both sides of the Atlantic" that would "lead to fusion rather than friction . . . confidence and hope rather than despair."[9] As in the case of the Peace Corps, the high ambitions of these secular missionaries have contrasted with their relatively moderate achievements, yet Cross Roads Africa provides a genuine outlet for student idealism that historians of culture would be foolish to ignore.

The U.S. government has extended technical advice and assistance through agencies other than the Peace Corps. In 1965, under the AID program, almost fourteen hundred government employees or technicians under contract with the government were in various parts of Africa working in food and agriculture, industry and mining, transportation, health and sanitation, education, public safety, public administration, and community development and housing. The United States has also funded semiprivate bodies such as the AAI, whose work, as noted in the previous chapter, has been criticized by conservatives.

Less controversial have been American efforts to assist the work of schools and missionary societies in Africa. The U.S. government – to give just a few examples – helped to establish a teacher-training institute in Mali, supported a ten-year program to build a city school system in Monrovia, assisted in the establishment of regional pilot-model secondary schools in Nigeria, and provided funds for the expansion of the University of Nigeria. Some two dozen American universities provided staff and technicians who, with U.S. government funds, worked to improve numerous African educational institutions. One of the most interesting programs was at Columbia University Teachers College, which provided the staff and administrators to recruit and train nearly two hundred Americans for primary and secondary school teaching in East Africa under contract with the U.S. government. Known as the Teachers for East Africa project (TEA), it reflected the growing recognition that education was an important element in national development. As the administrator of AID, David E. Bell put it: "This is why we place so much emphasis on helping underdeveloped countries acquire skill and competence . . . to help establish institutions in the countries which can provide skilled competent leadership for those countries, without outside help, as soon as possible."[10] This project reflected the undeniably documented fact that the greatest bottleneck preventing the development of leadership competence in the about-to-be independent

British territories of Kenya, Uganda, and Tanzania was the shortage of qualified secondary school teachers, made even more critical by the projected departure of British expatriate teachers upon the arrival of independence.

With unprecedented speed from AID and with extraordinary care in planning from Teachers College, in cooperation with British and African educators in London and in the governments and ministries of education in East Africa, the TEA project was launched in February 1961. In the course of four years, 463 American college graduates were recruited, screened, selected, trained, and assigned to the secondary schools of East Africa, where they served for two or more years as fully qualified education officers appointed, paid, and supervised by the professional officials of the newly independent African governments.

The program had several major characteristics. It was based upon demonstrable need in the receiving countries. It grew out of detailed cooperative planning and careful preparation among the British who were giving up authority, the Africans who were assuming authority, and the Americans who were being asked to assist the transition (in fact, many new British teachers also became involved in the project). Furthermore, the teachers were carefully interviewed and selected to assure high professional qualifications, as defined in the educational codes of the East African countries; and they were given specialized training to meet the particular conditions of teaching and pay required of the educational services in the countries where they would serve.

The TEA project differed substantially from the early Peace Corps policies, which put great stress upon the motives of volunteerism and on the values of understanding other peoples, and which provided needed skills on a noncareer, temporary, emergency basis. In this view, specialized professional training or competence was not as important for teaching in Africa or elsewhere as was the generalized liberal education of an American college graduate. When it was decided in Washington in 1964 that the Peace Corps would thereafter take over the task of providing American teachers to the countries of the world, the governments of East Africa raised serious objections, but accommodations were eventually made. Teachers College thereupon trained Peace Corps volunteers and launched a significant but smaller program under AID contract to provide tutors for the teacher-training colleges of East Africa (totaling 168 professionals between 1965 and 1972); these tutors assisted in the improvement of training for primary as well as for secondary school teachers. In both cases the immediate shortage of teachers was relieved, schools were kept open and even expanded, Africanization was speeded up in the staffing of schools and government positions, and in many instances the nature of the curriculum and teaching procedures were modified as well.[11]

Missionaries

The Peace Corps volunteers were missionaries of a secular kind. They initially received great publicity and enjoyed almost universal approval as emissaries of a secular faith in human brotherhood and enlightenment. But in numbers, expenditure, and length of contacts with Africa, religious missionaries have remained by far the largest category of American citizens resident in Africa. In fact, the total number of American missionaries considerably increased between the early 1920s and the 1960s. By 1965 over 7,000 American missionaries were working in Africa in 47 states; there were 224 organizations supporting the 71 Catholic, 71 Protestant, and 82 interdenominational groups.[12] Nigeria, with over 1,200 Americans in 1960, had the largest U.S. contingent in Africa; these missionary links in turn helped to tighten other educational ties between Nigeria and the United States. The greatest American Catholic missionary effort centered on Tanzania, which in 1963 accounted for nearly 40 percent of all American priests working on the African continent. The total number of American Catholic missionaries in Africa in 1963 was 901, including 339 priests, 212 brothers, 243 sisters, and 107 laymen. By the 1960s some 9,000 Protestant American missionaries were working in Africa, as against fewer than 3,000 in the early 1920s. Of the Protestants, one-quarter were ordained clergy; 1,000 were medical missionaries; and the remainder were "general" missionaries or instructors in industrial, agricultural, and other subjects.[13]

American missionary efforts were impressive in their scale, drawing as they did on the world's largest reservoir of missionary labor.[14] American missionary expenditure was, if anything, even more striking. By the mid-1960s the American Protestant missions in Africa spent nearly $35 million per annum – more than the total of American official aid given jointly in 1965 to Nigeria and Ethiopia, the two most populous countries in black Africa. Or, to give another example, American Protestants spent more on their mission work in Africa than the total revenue of the British Nyasaland Protectorate (later Malawi) at the time.[15] Missionary funds did not derive from large corporations; they mostly came from the pockets of middle, lower-middle, and working-class people to whom even a relatively modest contribution was a financial sacrifice. These contributors commonly imagined that their hard-earned dollars would help to spread the gospel and convert the heathen. But the contributors' image was often out-of-date.

Nineteenth-century missionaries went to Africa not only as the apostles of a new faith, but as the representatives of a new way of life. They believed in individual salvation instead of tribal collectivism hallowed by the ancestral spirits.[16] They stood for a creed of individual economic effort and advanced production techniques instead of existing systems of tribal cooperation based on rudimentary technology; they represented the values of the Christian and monogamous family instead of extended kinship groups practicing polygamy. To bring about the transformations in which they believed, the early missionaries were willing to risk incredible hardships as well as the ever-present danger of tropical diseases whose causes were still unknown. Only people of inflexible character and an unshakable faith were prepared to take these risks. Half a century later missionaries and their families, if they were attentive to their health, had life expectancies in Africa about equal to what they might expect at home.

At the same time, there was a striking shift in the missionaries' function. Old-style evangelists, stuck in backwood stations, had by force of circumstances tried their hands at almost every employment under the sun; they had worked as preachers, teachers, builders, gardeners, craftsmen, and at times even as traders or local lords. White missionaries, assisted perhaps by African interpreters, had themselves taught village children how to spell. As expenditure increased and the churches expanded, however, more and more ecclesiastical and pedagogical duties devolved upon Africans. Missionaries increasingly became administrators, supervisors, and technical experts, leaving congregations and schoolrooms in African hands. Devolution accelerated as the various African countries reached independence. In Marxist–Leninist countries like Mozambique and Angola, foreign stations were largely eliminated; elsewhere their influence declined, as African governments (and the white government of South Africa) either increased official control over missionary schools or wholly supplanted missionary-sponsored education with that run by the government.

During the 1920s and 1930s there was a striking shift in attitudes. A whole generation of learned Christians–people like Henri Junod, Dietrich Westermann, and E. W. Smith–helped to change the older missionary views that widely regarded African villagers as a people without history or culture, empty vessels at best, which should be filled with the white man's truth. Catholic clergy argued on similar lines. As an encyclical issued later by Pope John XXIII put it, the Catholic Church had never identified itself with one particular culture, not even that Western civilization with which it had been so closely associated in history. On the contrary, the church could always draw strength from other beliefs; even pagan thought should be neither scorned nor completely rejected, but should be purified in its vision and perfected by Christian wisdom.[17]

At the same time, missionary leaders began to appreciate the importance of bringing the gospel to the growing African cities, as well as to the villages. The new town-oriented approach owed much to the initiative of John Merle Davis, an American missionary scholar of distinction. Davis belonged to a new generation of American churchmen who had made their names during the interwar period and who were greatly influenced by the study of sociology; Davis first became well known through a study of multiracial problems on the Pacific Coast, and later, during the 1930s, he served as secretary of the Institute of Pacific Relations and head of the Department of Social and Industrial Research of the International Missionary Council. There was a world of difference between a sophisticated scholar like Davis and old-time evangelists like H. Masters or W. E. Masters, missionary pioneers who, a generation earlier, had preached the gospel among the Lamba in what is now Zambia; the Masterses had been men of simple faith who had challenged the local "witch doctors" in a rainmaking competition to vindicate the name of Jehovah.[18]

Decolonization placed the churches in a difficult position. As a group, they had welcomed the partition of Africa during the latter part of the nineteenth century, and they had benefited from the creation of empire. Churchmen such as François Coillard, a veteran missionary statesman in Barotseland (in what is now northwestern Zambia) had actually taken an important role during the 1890s in persuading the Lozi (Barotse) king to place himself under British protection. A generation later, even militant negrophiles like Arthur Shirley Cripps, a missionary pioneer in Southern Rhodesia, had actively campaigned in favor of territorial segregation as a means of safeguarding African interests. But by the 1950s the churches' own past had come to appear discreditable in the eyes of many believers, and once the European empires began to crumble, the missionaries found themselves under fire from opposing flanks. The remaining defenders of empire accused expatriate clergy of meddling in politics, of applying double standards in calling for privileges from

Western governments that they would never dare to request from Communist regimes, or of malignantly concealing the churches' own role in the creation of colonial rule. African nationalists, on the other hand, accused the churches of serving – wittingly or unwittingly – as agents of colonialism or of practicing a spiritual form of domination. The churches' position was all the more delicate because a high proportion of Africa's anticolonial leaders had been trained in mission schools and had often taken an active part in the lives of their respective churches.

Slowly and hesitantly, the churches changed their stand from a position of benevolent neutrality to one of open hostility to colonialism and racism. In 1952–3 and 1959–60, for instance, the National Council of the Churches of Christ in the United States (NCC), at that time a fairly conservative body, undertook African studies programs that produced three books; in 1956 the council issued a declaration that called for ending any kind of domination exerted by one political or social group over another. The NCC unites within its ranks the Protestant establishment (including bodies such as the United Methodist Church, the United Presbyterian Church, the Episcopalian Church, the Church of Christ), but excludes evangelical churches as well as so-called fringe groups like the Unification Church (Moonies).[19] It soon took a more militant line, becoming more leftist in its leanings than the ordinary American churchgoer. It stresses social responsibility rather than personal salvation and has funded organizations like the Interfaith Center on Corporate Responsibility. Some NCC leaders considered Marxism closer to Christianity than capitalism, a system that they equate with selfishness incarnate. The NCC actively sympathizes with what it considers to be the black freedom struggle in South Africa, and church funds have passed into the coffers of African guerrilla organizations, ostensibly for humanitarian purposes.

When the World Council of Churches (WCC) was founded in 1948, its members stood committed to the Western tradition of democracy and human rights. Thirty years later, many of its council members had become respectful of the new liberation theology. The WCC assembly at Nairobi in 1975 took a political line that in many ways hardly differed from the established orthodoxies of Havana and Moscow. The world's principal villains allegedly had their headquarters in Tel Aviv, Pretoria, and Washington, D.C. The religious oppression practiced in Communist countries was largely passed over in silence.[20]

"Progressive" organizations of a secular kind with church connections included Clergy and Laity Concerned, Interfaith Center on Corporate Responsibility, American Friends Service Committee, the American Committee on Africa, and the Washington Office on Africa. While differing on a variety of issues, they all agreed, for instance, on the policy of American disinvestment from South Africa that had first been espoused by American churches. None of them proposed boycotting Communist states like the USSR, Cuba, or East Germany. They maintained contact with international organizations such as the International Committee against Apartheid, Racism, and Colonialism in Southern Africa (a London-based organization that included SWAPO and ANC members in its secretariat and praesidium); the UN Center against Apartheid; the British anti-apartheid movement; and the Soviet Afro-Asian Solidarity Committee in Moscow – all organizations that also carried on a vigorous campaign against Western multinational corporations.

The reasons for this shift in emphasis were complex. The churches themselves became divided into several segments corresponding to the wider divisions of American society. The major Protestant churches – Episcopalians, Calvinists, Unitarians – were apt to become increasingly suburban in makeup and liberal in outlook, just like their congregations. In addition, the churches came to contain an increasing number of radicals, mainly teachers and students in ecclesiastical-training institutions and senior administrators, especially those concerned with international relations.

Within the Catholic Church, radical thought centered on members of certain orders, for instance, the Jesuits. The Maryknoll Fathers and Brothers, the largest of American Catholic Mission societies, took a particularly important part in restructuring missionary work and developing a kind of Christian Marxism. The fathers had originally concentrated their work in China. After the Communist takeover, they decided to diversify their work in other parts of the world, particularly Latin America, but also Africa. During the 1960s and 1970s, they had to contend with a striking decline in recruitment and with the increasing popularity of left-wing creeds on the campuses. The fathers tried to meet this difficulty by employing more lay brothers than before. The younger members of the order increasingly shifted to the left in politics; at the same time they tried to break down existing barriers between the clergy and their flock by encouraging their members to live among the poor. Many, though by no means all, of the Maryknollers enthusiastically took up the liberation theology developed during the 1960s. They came to stress what they called "conscientiation," by which they meant giving a sense of dignity to the poor and acquainting them with the identity and tactics of their wealthy oppressors.

According to their supporters, radical fathers thereby allied themselves with the oppressed masses of the Third World. According to their critics, the radical priests served a very different function. They overlooked the economic, religious, and social oppression customarily exercised by left-wing regimes. They aligned themselves with the new class of party functionaries, bureaucrats, and agitprops who have fastened a new tyranny on the Marxist–Leninist lands of the world. Worst of all, the radical priests distorted the very nature of Christianity by playing down (or even ignoring) the salvation of individual souls in favor of temporal issues of a social kind.

Whatever the merits or demerits of such controversies, the new breed of missionaries came to share the views of activist professors and students in prestigious secular institutions. The clergy in charge of parish work, by contrast, tended to be more conservative, as were their congregations – especially congregations in small towns, rural communities, and middle-class suburbs, who provide the NCC and kindred organizations with the requisite funds.

In the eyes of radical clergy, a radical policy seemed inevitable in the interests of justice and of a new realpolitik. The churches increasingly served a membership centered on the Third World. Moreover, they faced a dual challenge: They had to cope, on the one hand, with a multiplicity of independent African churches and, on the other, with Marxists. Marxism, to radical churchmen, seemed the wave of the future. The church, in their view, should not attempt to swim against the tide of history. There was also a sense of disappointment. After centuries of mission work in Africa, the churches had made limited progress: About one-third of Africa was Christian.

Radical politics, however, created new problems of its own. The radicals failed to win over most of the ordinary congregations. By the end of the 1970s some churches suspended their WCC affiliation; others cut down their financial support. The so-called establishment churches increasingly had to cope with opposition from evangelical Christians on the one hand and new dissident churches on the other – bodies such as the Church of Scientology (founded in 1954) that embarked upon new missionary efforts of their own. (The Church of Scientology subsequently established missions or groups in countries as far afield as South Africa, Zimbabwe, and Nigeria.) Christianity itself assumed indigenous African forms. By the early 1980s, for example, South Africa was the most heavily Christianized African country, measured by church membership, and the most numerous group of South African Christians consisted of about 3.5 million members of African independent churches, whose supporters professed a variety of orthodox, unorthodox, and sometimes bizarre doctrines and who were split into numerous organizations of varying size and cohesion. Over the continent as a whole, indigenous forms of animism, Islam, Marxism–Leninism, and Christianity in a variety of competing guises continued to vie for the soul of Africa.[21]

Africans in the United States

During the nineteenth century few free black Africans came to the United States – an estimated 30 a year. The number rose to 1,000 annually by 1914, but dropped significantly during the 1920s because of restrictive immigration legislation and the depression. After World War II the numbers of African immigrants rose again, but they represented white Africans, not black ones. Between 1951 and 1960 about 14,000 Africans entered the United States, and in the 1960s over 29,000 came; the collapse of colonial regimes after 1960 brought the great majority of the white African immigrants. In the 1970s the figure was 60,000, some of them Egyptians. The *Harvard Encyclopedia of American Ethnic Groups* claims that few of these immigrants were indigenous black Africans (previous censuses listed 89 percent as white). Most black Africans now in the United States are students; few have settled permanently. The number in the United States grew from 2,192 in 1960 to 13,442 in 1970; in 1980–81 there were 37,425 students from Africa enrolled in American schools.[22] Earlier censuses accounted for only 12 percent of African-born immigrants, but their share grew to 22 percent by 1970. (For an account of black African students in the United States, see Chapter 23.)

These newcomers came from a large number of independent countries; they derived from many different ethnic groups; and by the early 1980s there was no evidence that they considered themselves, or were likely to evolve into, a separate American ethnic group, distinct from the generality of black Americans. At the same time, white South Africans were coming to the United States in small but increasing numbers. By the late 1970s there were about 30,000 white South Africans in the United States; they entered at the rate of 1,000 a year, most of them young, English-speaking, professional people who had left South Africa for political reasons. Black South Africans numbered 793 in 1970; they tended to regard themselves as refugees in the United States, and were planning to return home.[23]

There was one exception to the pattern of immigrants from Africa – the Cape

Verdeans. Americans of Cape Verdean descent are the products of the only major "voluntary" migration of Africans to the United States. Their home, the Cape Verde Islands, lies in the Atlantic Ocean about four hundred miles west of Senegal. Formerly Portuguese, the islands became independent in 1975; their inhabitants are of mixed African and Portuguese descent, and though they are partly of slave origin, they took an active part in the slave trade. Cape Verdeans also signed on as sailors and cooks on American whalers who fished in the Atlantic waters. Cape Verdean seamen had an excellent reputation for their discipline, their capacity for hard work, and their willingness to work for less money than American mariners. Whaling was a particularly harsh and dangerous occupation, and during the second part of the nineteenth century, young white sailors increasingly switched to merchant ships or sought their fortunes ashore after their whaling experience. Cape Verdean crews came to dominate the whaling industry, for there was little racial discrimination aboard a whaler, where a man was recognized only for his ability and courage. In addition, Cape Verdeans are known to have come to New England as early as 1778, making homes for themselves in New Bedford, Massachusetts. During the nineteenth century they came as sailors; many more worked in the cordage plants and textile mills; others entered the cranberry and strawberry businesses as pickers (a regular shipping service between the islands and the United States was established by the 1870s to bring seasonal workers to labor in the cranberry bogs). They were also much appreciated as cooks.[24]

Until 1922 Cape Verdeans entered the United States freely, as did people from the Azores and the Madeiras.[25] The restrictive immigration laws of 1922 spelled the end of large-scale immigration. Not only could far fewer Cape Verdeans enter the United States than before, but those in the United States grew afraid to visit the islands unless their citizenship papers were in order. The harbor at Furna on Brava in the Cape Verde Islands became almost deserted, and migration to the United States receded to a trickle. At the same time, however, Cape Verdeans within America began to move to other parts of the United States. They settled in industrial cities in Connecticut and in New York; they found jobs in Pennsylvania steel towns, in Ohio's rubber-manufacturing centers, and in paper and clothing factories in Providence; others became longshoremen in San Francisco and Oakland, or farmers in Alameda County in California.

The new immigration laws of 1965 lifted existing barriers of a discriminatory kind, and a new wave of Cape Verdeans began to make its way to America. The newcomers made their homes in a country that they had known from childhood through letters of relatives and the visits of "Americanos" to Cape Verde. At the same time, Cape Verdeans established links to a worldwide community of countrymen settled as far afield as Lisbon, London, Rotterdam, and Dakar. Being a mixed people, the Cape Verdeans have their own problems of ethnic identity. European-looking Cape Verdeans were traditionally classed as whites by the immigration authorities; dark-skinned Cape Verdeans were known as black Portuguese, although they spoke a distinctive form of Portuguese known as Crioulo. By the late 1970s there were an estimated three hundred thousand persons of Cape Verdean descent in the United States. Substantial communities centered on New Bedford, Massachusetts's old whaling capital (about sixteen thousand), and on Boston (some ten thousand). There were also scattered settlements in cities such as Providence, Rhode Island (Rhode Island in fact formed a bilingual education department that also looked after the Cape Verdeans' needs); Nantucket Island; and Bridgeport and New Haven, Connecticut, and as far afield as Sacramento, California. Bleak economic conditions in Cape Verde and the long connections with the United States originally established through the whaling industry induced increasing numbers to migrate at this point. The newcomers were mainly of working-class origin, as educated Cape Verdeans preferred to look for jobs in Portugal, where their command of Portuguese as a first language was an advantage rather than a handicap. The bulk of the new immigrants to the United States found employment in unskilled and laboring jobs, though second- and third-generation Cape Verdeans commonly improved on their forebears' social position. In the face of American and Portuguese American prejudice, some Cape Verdeans attempted to retain their status as foreign ethnics; others sought to assimilate with black Americans.[26]

Overall, family links remained strong. The newcomers tried to assist family members in the old country by remittances of cash, clothes, and food, while helping them with loans and temporary accommodation after they had arrived in the United States. Like so many immigrants of other stock, many Cape Verdeans initially dreamed of returning with tidy bank balances; but because expenses in the new country commonly turned out to be higher than anticipated, stays insensibly grew longer, until the Cape Verdeans finally decided that America had become home.

What of the future? No one can be sure, but the number of immigrants from Africa to the United States will, in all likelihood, slowly increase. In earlier times Africa was geographically too remote to furnish great numbers of voluntary migrants and by the early 1980s transport by sea and air as yet remained expensive. But enforcement officials of the U.S. Immigration and Naturalization Service were beginning to cast a wary eye, not only toward Central America and the Caribbean, but also toward West Africa. A number of West Africans had settled in the United States; letters home and visits home from expatriates built an unofficial information network that served to attract more newcomers. A trickle of immigrants came into being, seeming to run from West Africa to Canada and then, illegally, to the United States.[27]

Africa's cultural impact on America in music and the arts also may well increase, but as already noted, the impact of any ethnic revival will be limited; ethnicity will remain more important as a badge of honor, a sign of upward social mobility within the American context, than as the distinguishing feature of separate nationalities. The African continent, by contrast, will continue to play a major part in American foreign policy by reason of its strategic and economic importance in the world at large. On this stage, Americans and Africans alike have vital parts to play. Much of the world's future will be shaped by the manner in which they meet the challenges to come.

Appendixes

Appendix A. The slave trade
Profits in the slave trade, 1861

In February 1861 the British consul-general Crawford, based in Cuba, estimated the costs and profit of a slaving expedition as follows (in dollars):

Cost of vessel and stores	25,000
Cost of 500 blacks at $50 each	25,000
Loss of 10 percent of the slaves at sea	2,500
Wages to crew	30,000
"Blood money" (bribes to Spanish officials) at $120 per slave, for 450 slaves	54,000
	136,500
12 months' interest on capital invested at 10 percent	13,650
Total cost of expedition	150,150
Sale of 450 slaves at $1,200	540,000
Profit	389,850

Warren S. Howard estimates the costs and profits as follows (in dollars):[a]

Cost of purchasing and fitting out a 300-ton vessel	12,000
Cost of port clearance	3,000
Cost of crew (advance wages)	1,500
Miscellaneous costs and services	3,500
Total cost of getting a slaver to sea	20,000
Half the slavers will be captured before embarking slaves; hence the average cost of each slaver actually shipping slaves will be	40,000
Cost of 600 slaves at $50 each	30,000
Cost of a laden slaver	70,000
Add 30 percent for slavers captured full of slaves	21,000
Cost of a shipload of slaves delivered to Cuba	91,000
Cost of permits to land 500 surviving slaves, identification cards, etc., at $85 per slave	42,500
Cost of paying off crew (captain, at $4,000; 15 seamen, at $800 each)	16,000
Total cost, delivered to slave vendor	149,500
Miscellaneous expenses	10,000
Total cost of expedition	159,500
Cost per delivered slave	320
Proceeds from sale of 500 slaves at $500 each	250,000
Net profit on an outlay of $159,500, or 56 percent	90,500

[a]Warren S. Howard, *American Slavers and the Federal Law, 1837–1862* (Berkeley: University of California Press, 1963), p. 236 (drawing on Crawford to Russell, February 5, 1861; and House of Commons, *Slave Trade Papers*, 1862, Class A, 7).

Estimated mortalities aboard slavers

Name	Date	No. shipped	No. died	No. landed[a]
Huntress	1864	750	250	500
John Bell	1861	482	82	400
Haidee	1858	1,100	200	900
W. D. Miller	1857	470	58	412
Julia Moulton	1854	665	165	500
Paez	1857	570	170	400
P. Soule	1855	479	12	467
Unknown slaver	1860	400	40	360
Herald	1848	1,150	40	1,110
Senator	1847	900	300	600
Fame	1847	530	3	527
Bogota	1860	418	7	411
Wildfire	1860	650	100	550
William	1860	744	174	570
Putnam	1858	450	130	320
Spitfire	1844	346	7	339
Brutus	1860	640	140	500
Total		10,744	1,878	8,866

[a]Number alive when captured by a warship in the West Indies, where applicable.
Source: Howard, *American Slavers,* p. 238.

Appendix B. American missions in Africa
Expenditures in Africa of the twenty-two principal American missionary organizations, 1963

Organization	Amount ($)
Southern Baptist Convention	3,391,742
Sudan Interior Mission (IFMA)	3,373,466
Methodist Church (DFM)	2,075,818
United Presbyterian Church (DFM)	1,569,251
Africa Inland Mission (IFMA)	1,255,162[a]
National Lutheran Council	1,239,567
American Lutheran Church (DFM)	1,155,489
United Church of Christ (DFM)	1,085,551
Christian Churches (Disciples of Christ)(DFM)	831,752
Assemblies of God (EFMA)	775,100[a]
Africa Evangelical Fellowship (IFMA)	729,242[a]
World Wide Evangelization Crusade (EFMA)	727,920[a]
Presbyterian Church in the U.S. (DFM)	675,447
Christian and Missionary Alliance (EFMA)	670,630[a]
Evangelical Alliance Mission (TEAM) (IFMA)	602,085[a]
Christian Missions in Many Lands	506,000[a]
Church of the Nazarene (EFMA)	475,170[a]
Evangelical United Brethren (DFM)	443,268
Christian Reformed Church (EFMA)	424,620[a]
Lutheran Church in America (DFM)	404,000
Protestant Episcopal Church (DFM)	398,410
Conservative Baptists (EFMA)	367,330[a]
Total	23,177,020[a]

Notes: DFM = Division of Foreign Missions; EFMA = Evangelical Foreign Missions Association; IFMA = Interdenominational Foreign Missions Association. This table does not include expenditures by such organizations as the American Bible Society, nor by numerous mission organizations which are known to be active in Africa but concerning which it was impossible to obtain information. Nor does it include Roman Catholic contributions and expenditures.
[a]Estimated.

Partial list of non-African personnel with American-sponsored missions in Africa

Organization	Number
Sudan Interior Mission	974
Africa Inland Mission	470
Southern Baptist Convention	428
Methodist Church	366
American Lutheran Church	267
Assemblies of God	230
United Presbyterian Church	223
World Wide Evangelization Crusade	216
Christian and Missionary Alliance	199
Africa Evangelical Fellowship	190
Christian Missions in Many Lands	150
Evangelical Alliance Mission	149
United Church of Christ	148
Lutheran Church in America	146
Church of the Nazarene	141
Seventh-Day Adventists	127
Christian Reformed Church	126
Presbyterian Church in the U.S.	117
Eastern Mennonites	117
Conservative Baptists	109
Total	4,893

Note: This list does not include many American churches that are known to have missions and missionaries in Africa; hence it is incomplete.

Partial list of hospitals maintained in Africa by American missionary organizations

Country	Number
Congo	51
Kenya	12
Nigeria	28
Cameroun	12
Angola	5
Rhodesia	12
Zambia	22
Malawi	3
Mozambique	2
Ghana	6
Madagascar	2
Tanzania	17
Liberia	6
Ruanda	2
Burundi	3
Uganda	2
Sudan	4
Bechuanaland	1
Central African Republic	2
Somalia	1
Swaziland	1
South Africa	14
Mali	1
Sierra Leone	4
Ethiopia	15
Total	228

Note: This list does not include hospitals in countries north of the Sahara, nor does it include the group of hospitals maintained by the African Methodist Episcopal Church, which were reported for several countries as a group.

Partial tabulation of educational institutions maintained in Africa by American missionary organizations

	Elementary	Secondary	College or university	Seminaries	Nursing or medical	Trade and vocational	Teacher training	Other
Congo	930	26	1	6	5	1	10	19
Nigeria	643	49	7	–	–	–	2	3
Sierra Leone	–	3	–	1	–	–	–	–
Kenya–Uganda	648	20	3	4	1	–	–	–
Cameroun	972	15	3	1	–	–	–	1
Malagasy Republic	356	12	1	–	–	–	–	1
Somalia	3	–	–	–	–	–	–	–
Togo	2	–	–	–	–	–	–	–
Tanzania	116	5	–	2	1	–	2	–
Liberia	23	5	–	–	1	–	–	–
Ghana	74	1	–	1	–	–	–	–
Rhodesia	24	2	–	–	–	–	–	1
Ethiopia	40	2	1	2	–	–	–	1
South Africa	17	5	–	3	–	–	–	2
Mozambique	2	1	–	–	–	–	–	–
Angola	250	2	–	2	–	6	1	–
Ruanda–Burundi	598	4	1	1	–	–	–	–
Malawi	3	–	–	–	–	–	–	–
Rio Muni	1	–	–	–	–	–	–	–
Sudan	6	4	–	–	–	–	–	1
Basutoland	–	–	–	1	–	–	–	–

Notes: This list is incomplete, including as it does only schools maintained by reporting organizations; information was not submitted about schools maintained by Roman Catholic missionary orders or by Jehovah's Witnesses, among others. Dashes indicate no data.

American Catholic missionaries in Africa, 1963

Country	Priests	Brothers	Sisters	Laymen
Algeria	–	–	1	–
Angola	–	–	2	–
Basutoland	3	22	12	4
Congo	3	1	3	2
Cameroun	–	–	8	–
Egypt	1	3	3	1
Ethiopia	1	8	6	–
Ghana	32	20	50	16
Kenya	4	36	6	7
Liberia	21	–	15	3
Malagasy	15	1	1	–
Morocco	1	–	–	–
Mozambique	–	–	1	–
Nigeria	18	10	28	14
Northern Rhodesia	14	26	8	4
Nyasaland	8	6	20	9
Ruanda-Burundi	–	–	1	1
Seychelles	–	2	–	–
Sierra Leone	1	–	–	–
Southern Rhodesia	8	3	9	17
South-West Africa	3	1	–	–
Sudan	3	–	–	3
Tanganyika	147	26	48	6
Uganda	20	35	10	14
South Africa	36	12	11	6
Total	339	212	243	107

Note: Dashes indicate no data.
Source: The 1963 National Catholic Almanac (Patterson, N.J.: St. Anthony's Guild), p. 519.

Notes

Preface

1. Peter Duignan and Clarence Clendenen, *The United States and the African Slave Trade, 1619–1862* (Stanford, Calif.: Hoover Institution Press, 1963); Clarence Clendenen and Peter Duignan, *Americans in Black Africa, up to 1865* (Stanford, Calif.: Hoover Institution Press, 1964); Clarence Clendenen, Robert Collins, and Peter Duignan, *Americans in Africa, 1865–1900* (Stanford, Calif.: Hoover Institution Press, 1966).

Chapter 1. The transatlantic slave trade: an overview

1. Ronald Cohen, "Slavery in Africa," *Trans-Action*, January–February 1967, p. 45.

2. J. C. Anene, "Slavery and the Slave Trade," in *Africa in the Nineteenth and Twentieth Centuries: A Handbook for Teachers and Students*, ed. Joseph C. Anene and Godfrey N. Brown (London: Nelson, 1966; Ibadon: Ibadon University press, 1967), p. 95.

3. Shepard Bancroft Clough and Charles Woolsey Cole, *Economic History of Europe* (Boston: Heath, 1952), pp. 259–62.

4. Philip D. Curtin, *The Atlantic Slave Trade: A Census* (Madison: University of Wisconsin Press, 1969).

5. Peter Duignan and Clarence Clendenen, *The United States and the African Slave Trade, 1619–1862* (Stanford, Calif.: Hoover Institution Press, 1963), pp. 1–5.

6. Will D. Weatherford and Charles S. Johnson, *Race Relations: Adjustment of Whites and Negroes in the United States* (Boston: Heath, 1934), pp. 124–5.

7. According to one estimate, the British in 1790 carried 38,000 slaves to America; the French, 20,000; the Portuguese, 10,000; the Dutch, 4,000; and the Danes, 2,000.

8. Kuczynski's estimates are as follows: sixteenth century, nearly 900,000; seventeenth century, 2.75 million; eighteenth century, 7 million; nineteenth century, over 4 million. See Robert Kuczynski, *Population Movements* (Oxford: Oxford University Press [Clarendon Press], 1936), pp. 8–15, quoted in *Problems in African History*, ed. Robert O. Collins (Englewood Cliffs, N.J.: Prentice-Hall, 1967), pp. 350–2.

9. Basil Davidson, *Black Mother: The Years of the African Slave Trade* (Boston: Little, Brown, 1961), p. 80.

10. See the important article by J. D. Fage, "Slavery and the Slave Trade in the Context of West African History," *Journal of African History* 10 (1969):394–404. This article discusses Curtin's *Atlantic Slave Trade*, now the major work on the subject. For more recent estimates see James A. Rawley, *The Transatlantic Slave Trade: A History* (New York: Norton, 1981); and J. Ade Ajayi and J. E. Inikori, "An Account of Research on the Slave Trade on Nigeria," in *The African Slave Trade from the Fifteenth to the Nineteenth Century* (Paris: UNESCO, 1979). Also see A. G. Hopkins, *An Economic History of West Africa* (London: Longmans, 1973), a pioneering work.

11. Duignan and Clendenen, *United States and the African Slave Trade*, p. 10.

12. Kenneth Gordon Davies, *The Royal African Company* (London: Longmans, Green, 1957), pp. 348–49.

13. S. Daniel Neumark, *Foreign Trade and the Economic Development in Africa: A Historical Perspective* (Stanford, Calif.: Stanford University, Food Research Institute, 1964), p. 57.

14. T. S. Ashton, *The Industrial Revolution, 1760–1830* (London: Oxford University Press, 1948), p. 47.

15. Rawley, *Transatlantic Slave Trade*, p. 19.

16. For a discussion of this phase of American economic development, see William Armstrong Fairburn, *Merchant Sail*, 6 vols. (Center Lovell, Me.: Fairburn Marine Educational Foundation, 1945–55), 1:142–51.

Chapter 2. The legal slave trade in North America

1. Governor John Winthrop noted in his journal on February 26, 1638: "Mr. Pierce in the Salem ship, the *Desire*, returned from the West Indies after seven months. He had been at Providence, and brought some cotton and tobacco and negroes, etc., from thence, and salt from Tortugas . . . Dry fish and strong liquors are the only commodities for those parts." John R. Spears, *The American Slave-Trade* (New York: Scribner, 1900), p. 7.

2. New Amsterdam, run by the Dutch Company, was the main North American slaving center in the first half of the seventeenth century.

3. Benjamin Brawley, *A Social History of the American Negro* (New York: Macmillan, 1921), p. 15.

4. "The Virginia Census, 1624–25," *Virginia Magazine of History and Biography* 7 (1900):364.

5. Brawley, *Social History*, pp. 14–15.

6. David Ramsay, *The History of South Carolina*, 2 vols. (Charleston, 1809) 1:19.

7. The increasing ratio of blacks to whites had occasioned some alarm. In 1698 the colonial assembly passed an act requiring slaveowners to preserve a proportion of at least one white servant to every six black men. Elizabeth Donnan, ed., *Documents Illustrative of the History of the Slave Trade to America*, 4 vols. (New York: Octagon Books, 1965), 4:250.

8. Elizabeth Donnan, "The Slave Trade in South Carolina before the Revolution," *American Historical Review* 33 (1928):805.

9. Donnan, *Documents Illustrative*, 4:415. Virginia tried again in 1761 to prevent the importation of slaves but was overruled by the crown.

10. New Englanders did, of course, sell captured Indians as slaves, and they kept a relatively large number of African slaves. In 1764–5 the census of Massachusetts showed 5,779 blacks. G. H. Moore, *Notes on the History of Slavery in Massachusetts* (New York, 1966), p. 51.

11. Donnan, *Documents Illustrative*, 3:108.

12. Ibid., p. 109. Governor Dudley of Massachusetts reported that two hundred slaves came into the colony between 1698 and 1707. Moore, *History of Slavery*, p. 50.

13. Donnan, *Documents Illustrative*, 3:117, 121, 139.

14. Lorenzo Johnston Greene, *The Negro in Colonial New England, 1620–1776* (New York: Columbia University Press, 1942), pp. 24–5.

15. The overwhelming majority of slaves came to North America in English rather than colonial ships. Virginia port records from 1727 to 1769 showed a total of 638 ships bringing African slaves into the colony. Of the larger slave ships, 176 were registered in Great Britain; not more than a dozen were shown as belonging to colonial ports. American ships were smaller and carried far fewer slaves. For example, between May 31 and July 23, 1736, 11 slave ships arrived in Virginia, 4 of English registry, 5 of Virginia registry; the English ships carried 754 slaves each, the Virginia ships had 12 slaves each.

16. In 1745, for example, Joseph Manesty, a Liverpool merchant who dealt in slaves on a large scale, wrote to Joseph Bannister, his Newport correspondent: "I desire you will order

Two Vessels built with the best white Oak Timber at Rhode Island . . . they are for the Affrican [*sic*] Trade." These solidly built, heavily armed vessels were specially designed "for messing Negroes on [the] lower deck." Donnan, *Documents Illustrative,* 3:137.

17. Ibid., p. 142.

18. Ibid., 3:143, 147–8.

19. Ibid., pp. 68–9.

20. Ibid., p. 205; Greene, *The Negro in Colonial New England,* p. 26.

21. Donnan, *Documents Illustrative,* 3:151.

22. Rum was also the medium by which the various African workers were paid. In the same year, 1767, Captain William Pinnegar noted in his account book that he had paid canoemen one and a half gallons for their services. Ibid., pp. 223–4.

23. Ibid., p. 188.

24. William B. Weeden, "The Early African Slave-Trade in New England," *Proceedings of the American Antiquarian Society,* n.s., 5 (1887–8):117.

25. Captain Peleg Clarke wrote to his ship's owner, John Fletcher, on February 20, 1776, that the men-of-war had orders to capture all property belonging to any American. They had already taken several ships and were in pursuit of a New York vessel in the Gaboon River. In April Clarke again wrote to Fletcher, to say that Captain Warren of HMS *Weasel* was determined to take all Americans he could find. In July, however, Clarke jubilantly told Fletcher that he had found a loophole in the law. Since he was bound for Jamaica, his vessel was excepted from the orders for the seizure of American-owned craft. Donnan, *Documents Illustrative,* 3:309, 311.

26. Ibid., p. 321.

27. Ibid., 2:471 n, 3:332 n.

28. Ships from the British Isles still ranged the African coast and, protected by the power of the British navy, voyaged without hindrance to places where ports were open and payments assured. Although figures are lacking, it is probable that the sale of slaves to the thirteen colonies represented only a fraction of the total slave trade at any time. The interruption of the traffic between Africa and Rhode Island, the Carolinas, and Virginia, therefore, did not give any respite to Africa.

29. A wealthy Quaker merchant, Moses Brown, led the fight. Soon after the war, on "26th, 8th mo. 1783," he wrote to two well-known merchant partners of Newport, protesting against their sending one of their vessels to Africa for slaves, as they were reported to be about to do. "You are men of feelings," he said, "and abilities to live without this Trade, why then should you be concerned in it against your own – against the feelings of your Friends? . . . Should you give orders to the Captn. not to Suffer any Negroes on Board, it would be grateful to many of your Connexions in Town, as well as your Friend." Donnan, *Documents Illustrative,* 3:334–5.

30. Daniel P. Mannix and Malcolm Cowley, *Black Cargoes: A History of the Atlantic Slave Trade, 1518–1865* (New York: Viking Press, 1962), p. 172.

31. Elizabeth Donnan, "The New England Slave Trade after the Revolution," *New England Quarterly* 3 (1930):253–4. For a fuller account of antislavery movements in the United States, see Mannix and Cowley, *Black Cargoes,* chap. 8; see also Thomas Edward Drake, *Quakers and Slavery in America* (New Haven, Conn.: Yale University Press, 1950).

32. Donnan, *Documents Illustrative,* 3:343–4.

33. William B. Weeden, *Economic and Social History of New England, 1620–1789,* 2 vols. (Boston: Houghton Mifflin, 1891), vol. 2, chaps. 19–20.

34. See the letter that William Fairfield of Salem wrote to his mother in 1789, telling her of his father's death in an uprising of the slaves on board the schooner *Felicity.* Fairfield's letter could have been composed only by a God-fearing, dutiful, Christian son, yet he felt no more qualms about the unfortunate Africans who had been killed in the uprising than if they had been so many dumb animals or inanimate pieces of merchandise. Nor did he seem to feel that

there was anything at all immoral in engaging in an occupation forbidden by law. James Duncan Phillips, *Salem and the Indies* (Boston: Houghton Mifflin, 1947), pp. 65–6; "A Strange Letter," *Essex Institute Historical Collections* 25 (1888):311–12.

35. Donnan, "New England Slave Trade," p. 275 n.

36. Charleston became one of the most active ports in the slave trade. From 1804 to 1807, 202 slave ships dropped anchor in Charleston and deposited 39,075 slaves. Mannix and Cowley, *Black Cargoes*, pp. 188–9.

Chapter 3. Ending the slave trade

1. Heinrich Heine, "Italien [1828]," in *Werke* (Hamburg: Hoffmann und Campe 1956), p. 315.

2. Both laws became effective on the same date: January 1, 1808. For the slave-trade debate see, for instance, Sir Reginald Coupland, *The British Anti-Slavery Movement* (London: Cass, 1964); Sir Eric Williams, *Capitalism and Slavery* (London: Deutsch, 1944); Roger Anstey, *Atlantic Slave Trade and British Abolition, 1760–1810* (New York: Humanities Press, 1975); and Seymour Drescher, *Anti-Slavery Religion and Reform* (Hamden, Conn.: Archon Books, 1980).

3. Similarly, the expansion of sugar and tobacco production in Cuba and of coffee in Brazil created an increased demand for slaves after 1808.

4. There is a wide difference of opinion about the number of slaves smuggled into the United States between 1808 and 1863. One estimate runs as high as 300,000 (Kenneth Onwuka Dike, *Trade and Politics in the Niger Delta, 1830–1885: An Introduction to the Economic and Political History of Nigeria* [Oxford: Oxford University Press (Clarendon Press), 1956], pp. 82–3), but Dike gives no source. Daniel P. Mannix and Malcolm Cowley (*Black Cargoes: A History of the Atlantic Slave Trade, 1518–1865* [New York: Viking Press, 1962], pp. 203–5) state that from 10,000 to 20,000 African slaves were imported into the South annually after 1810 for several years. These estimates differ widely from Frederic Bancroft's conclusions (*Slave Trading in the Old South* [Baltimore: J. H. Furst, 1931], pp. 358–61) that the number of Africans smuggled into the United States after abolition of the commerce was negligible.

The fact that in contemporary literature of the period, even the writings of the bitterest enemies of slavery, there is almost no reference to importation of large numbers of Africans seems to support Bancroft. Furthermore, the few slaves known to be recent arrivals from Africa attracted wide attention, which is evidence that they were a novelty rather than a commonplace. The 1870 census turned up only 1,984 blacks born in Africa.

For detailed consideration of this problem, see Philip D. Curtin, *The Atlantic Slave Trade: A Census* (Madison: University of Wisconsin Press, 1969); and Warren S. Howard, *American Slavers and the Federal Law, 1837–1862* (Berkeley: University of California Press, 1963).

5. For example, the *Amedie* case. See Elizabeth Donnan, ed., *Documents Illustrative, of the History of the Slave Trade to America,* 4 vols. (New York: Octagon Books, 1965), 4:531–50.

6. During the first restoration, the British offered to give France the island of Trinidad in return for abolishing the slave trade, but Louis XVIII wanted more. He got nothing, because it was Napoleon who ended the trade, during the Hundred Days.

7. William Law Mathieson, *British Slavery and Its Abolition* (London: Longmans, Green, 1926), p. 22.

8. Quoted in Samuel Flagg Bemis, *John Quincy Adams and the Foundations of American Foreign Policy* (New York: Knopf, 1949), p. 233 n.

9. *The Diary of John Quincy Adams,* ed. Allan Nevins (New York: Scribner, 1951), pp. 177–8.

10. Hugh G. Soulsby, *The Right of Search and the Slave Trade in Anglo-American Relations, 1814–1862* (Baltimore: Johns Hopkins Press, 1933), pp. 15–19.

11. Bemis, *John Quincy Adams*, p. 427.

12. Ibid., pp. 434–5.

13. The Portuguese agreed to limit their slave trade to the area south of the equator.

14. Soulsby, *The Right of Search*, p. 42.

15. "The Rhode Island Slave Trade in 1816," *Proceedings of the Rhode Island Historical Society* 6 (January 1899):226.

16. *Memoirs of John Quincy Adams, Comprising Portions of His Diary from 1795 to 1845*, ed. Charles Francis Adams, 12 vols. (Philadelphia: Lippincott, 1874–7), 5:416.

17. Ibid., pp. 472, 478–80.

18. Ibid., 6:28, 39–40.

19. Roy Olton, "Problems of American Foreign Relations in the African Area during the Nineteenth Century" (Ph.D. diss., Fletcher School of Law and Diplomacy, 1954), pp. 83–4.

20. Ibid., pp. 184–9. See also William A. Owens, *Slave Mutiny: The Story of the Revolt on the Schooner Amistad* (London: Davies, 1953).

21. Howard, *American Slavers*, pp. 153–63.

22. J. C. Furnas, "Patrolling the Middle Passage," *American Heritage*, 9 (October 1958):9.

23. Thomas Fowell Buxton, *The African Slave Trade and Its Remedy* (London: Murray, 1840), pp. 41–2.

24. Ibid., p. 43 n. An example of the abuse of the U.S. ensign of which the British complained was perpetrated by the *Venus*, a fast clipper that sailed from Baltimore in July 1838. It arrived at Havana in August and sailed from there for Mozambique in September under the American flag. After a quick voyage it returned to Havana in January 1839 under the Portuguese flag and landed almost nine hundred slaves. On the outward voyage it was well protected by the U.S. flag despite the fact that it was obviously equipped and supplied as a slave ship, the U.S. courts having previously decided that only the actual presence of slaves on board was acceptable proof of being a slaver.

25. Lawrence Cabot Howard, "American Involvement in Africa South of the Sahara, 1800–1860" (Ph.D. diss., Harvard University, 1956), p. 49. See also William Law Mathieson, *Great Britain and the Slave Trade, 1839–1865* (New York: Longmans, Green, 1929), pp. 67–9; and Frank B. Woodford, *Lewis Cass: The Last Jeffersonian* (New Brunswick, N.J.: Rutgers University Press, 1950), p. 212.

26. Curtin (*Atlantic Slave Trade*, pp. 72–5) estimates that about a thousand slaves a month came into the United States after 1808.

27. Howard Irving Chappelle, *The Baltimore Clipper: Its Origin and Development* (Salem, Mass.: Marine Research Society, 1930), pp. 137–40.

28. Howard, *American Slavers*, pp. 38–9.

Chapter 4. The U.S. Navy and the antislavery campaign

1. Henry Steele Commager, ed., *Documents of American History*, 2 vols. (New York: F. S. Croft, 1935), 2:300.

2. Perry later became famous for his role in opening Japan to Western trade and influence.

3. Secretary of the Navy John Y. Mason to Skinner, December 20, 1844, quoted in Lawrence Cabot Howard, "American Involvement in Africa South of the Sahara, 1800–1860" (Ph.D. diss., Harvard University, 1956), p. 118.

4. See, especially, W. E. B. Du Bois, *The Suppression of the African Slave-Trade to the United States of America, 1638–1870* (New York: Longmans, 1896; reprint, New York: Dover Publications, 1970); and Daniel P. Mannix and Malcolm Cowley, *Black Cargoes: A History of the Atlantic Slave Trade, 1518–1865* (New York: Viking Press, 1962).

5. Notably by John R. Spears in *The American Slave-Trade* (New York, Scribner, 1900) and by Mannix and Cowley in *Black Cargoes*.

6. Warren S. Howard (*American Slavers and the Federal Law, 1837–1862* [Berkeley: University of California Press, 1963], pp. 132–5) concludes that most officers were conscientious. Some, however, were too old or lazy. Flag Officer Conover, in the squadron from 1857 to 1859, patrolled only twenty-six days in twenty-six months. His successor, Inman, was not much better and was rebuked by the secretary of the navy.

7. Ibid., p. 41. Such absurdities as the incident of the *Mary Ann* in 1848 were unfortunate, but do not prove indifference on the part of the government or inefficiency or lack of zeal on the part of the navy. The crew of the *Mary Ann,* supposing that they had been enrolled for a legitimate trading voyage, mutinied on finding that they were committed to a slaving expedition. Putting the captain ashore, they cruised the coast hunting for a U.S. warship but could not find one. Under command of a mate, they returned to New York and surrendered themselves to the authorities – incidentally finding themselves in serious trouble for mutiny on the high seas and piracy!

8. Cf. Mannix and Cowley, *Black Cargoes*, pp. 219–20. They state that Americans had only a token force in 1843 and never had more than seven ships on patrol until 1857, whereas the British squadron averaged twenty ships. But the U.S. Navy was not as powerful as the Royal Navy, nor was its only mission to stop the slave trade. Whereas a united British public opinion made suppression of the trade a primary goal of British policy in Africa, the United States was not so concerned. And American zealousness to assert its independence by forbidding the British to stop Yankee ships admittedly hampered efforts to end the dealings in slaves.

9. Ibid., p. 223.

10. Of the twenty-six ships libeled between 1842 and 1853, sixteen were taken in African waters by the African squadron, six were seized off Brazil, and four were taken in U.S. harbors. See Howard, *American Slavers*, pp. 213–23.

11. Alan R. Booth, "The United States African Squadron, 1843–1861," in *Boston University Papers in African History*, ed. Jeffrey Butler, vol. 1 (Boston: Boston University Press, 1964), p. 100.

12. Department of the Navy, *Report of the Secretary of the Navy, November 25, 1843,* (Washington, D.C.: GPO, 1843), pp. 472–5.

13. House of Commons, *Session Papers*, December 3, 1857–August 2, 1858, 39:1–11.

14. "Correspondence with the United States' Government on the Question of the Right of Visit; Presented to Both Houses of Parliament by Command of Her Majesty," in ibid.

15. Although the U.S. Navy maintained as large a proportion of its ships on patrol as the Royal Navy, however, its effectiveness in catching slave ships was far less. The British averaged 19 ships on patrol for the American 4 or 5. They had better bases to operate from; they stayed on patrol longer; and they stopped all ships thought to be slavers. Between 1843 and 1861 the British captured 595 slave ships and liberated some 149,843 slaves. Christopher Lloyd, *The Navy and the Slave Trade: The Suppression of the African Slave Trade in the Nineteenth Century* (reprint, London: Cass, 1968), pp. 275–81.

16. See Howard, *American Slavers*, p. 141.

17. See Ronald Takaki, "The Movement to Reopen the African Slave Trade in South Carolina," *South Carolina Historical Magazine* 66 (1965):38–54.

18. Quoted in Howard, *American Slavers*, p. 124.

19. Notwithstanding the assertion by Mannix and Cowley (*Black Cargoes*, pp. 221, 264) that few American officers cooperated with the British.

20. See Andrew H. Foote, *Africa and the American Flag* (New York: Appleton, 1954; reprint, Folkestone, Eng.: Dawson, 1970), p. 248. "Captain" Theodore Canot (his real name probably was Theophile Conneau), in his readable *Captain Canot; or, Twenty Years of an African Slaver*, ed. Brantz Mayer (New York: Appleton, 1854), makes no mention of this

incident, although he tells at some length of being in that part of Africa at the time it occurred. It is, however, mentioned in the epilogue, of which he was not the author. Canot was finally captured by an American man-of-war in 1847 and was indicted at New York; released on bail, he went to Brazil.

21. Howard, *American Slavers*, pp. 190–1. See also ibid., pp. 213–23, for a list of slave ships captured by the American naval squadron and port officials.

22. Ibid., pp. 102–10.

23. Then, too, the seizure of suspected slavers was not without danger. In 1841, when HMS *Dolphin* sent a boarding party to a Brazilian craft, the bowmen of a gig and a cutter were both shot before they could board the vessel. After noting this, the commander of the *Dolphin* wrote: "Mr. Murray . . . was the first to board, though he was knocked back into the boat with the butt end of a musket, which broke his collarbone, but [he] immediately clambered up the side again, in the act of which his left hand was nearly severed at the wrist with the blow of a cutlass. Another cut was made at his head, which he fortunately parried, cutting the man down. This circumstance, together with Mr. Rees crossing over at the same moment and cutting down another of the party opposing the boarders on that side, was the occasion of her quick capture." "Capture of a Slaver," *Nautical Magazine and Naval Chronicle* (London), 1841, pp. 862–4.

So far as records indicate, no slaver captured by the Americans put up resistance comparable to this, but the danger was real enough not to be ignored by American sailors.

24. Howard, *American Slavers*, p. 78.

25. Ibid., p. 105.

26. W. E. F. Ward, *The Royal Navy and the Slavers: The Suppression of the Atlantic Slave Trade* (reprint, New York: Pantheon Books, 1969), p. 161.

27. Mannix and Cowley, *Black Cargoes*, p. 244.

28. The American ship *Incomprehensible* was captured in 1837 off Cape Town. Ibid., p. 246.

29. Ernest O. Moore, *Ivory, Scourge of Africa* (New York: Harper, 1931), pp. 54, 62. The use of slaves to carry ivory can be exaggerated; much of it was carried by Nyamwezi and other trading peoples.

30. See Mannix and Cowley, *Black Cargoes*, pp. 243–65, for fuller treatment of American slavers in East Africa.

31. British officials maintained that most of the ships engaged in the slave trade were built in shipyards in the United States and then transferred to Portuguese and Spanish registry for immunity. Since the American ships were much faster than the patrolling British frigates, no American ship was ever captured off Zanzibar, although several were taken while at anchor. Ibid., pp. 247, 254.

32. Mrs. Charles E. B. Russell, *General Rigby, Zanzibar, and the Slave Trade* (London: Allen & Unwin, 1935), pp. 195–8. A little earlier, in 1857, Commodore Wise of the British navy wrote angrily to his immediate superior, Rear Admiral Grey, of "the prostitution of the American flag," which "sets all our good efforts at defiance" (ibid.). American jealousy of possible revival of the right of search by the British made it almost impossible for the British navy to interfere with any vessel flying the American flag, except under most unusual and flagrant circumstances. American slavers could be captured lawfully only by American men-of-war, and there were none of these, normally, in the Indian Ocean.

33. Such incidents continued in spite of the well-known attitude of the U.S. government and most positive orders from the British government. For example, in 1854 Commander Thomas Miller of HMS *Crane* remarked that the British could do nothing without the right of search – the American slavers merely laughed at them. But after the appointment of an American consul in Angola, Miller said, a British officer who had grounds for suspicion and who "does not fear responsibility . . . may venture more than he could before." Miller evi-

dently was a man who did not fear responsibility, for he repeatedly boarded and investigated an American schooner, the *Gambriel,* of which he was suspicious, the last time just as the USS *Constitution* hove in sight. The *Constitution* seized the *Gambriel* a few days later off the mouth of the Congo with a full cargo of blacks. A short time later Miller found three suspicious vessels – English, Sardinian, and American – anchored at Appi Vista. The American ship's colors did not keep him from boarding and investigating it. Thomas Miller, "Western Africa: Its Coast, Resources, and Trade," *Nautical Magazine and Naval Chronicle* (London), June 1855, pp. 294–5.

34. Lewis Cass, *France, Its King, Court, and Government; and Three Hours at St. Cloud. By an American* (New York: Wiley & Putnam, 1841), p. 133.

35. In 1855 the bark *S. W. Nash* from New York was detained on the African coast because of the large number of empty casks it carried, although the ship's owners declared positively that the casks were for palm oil, not for water for slaves. In 1856 the British seized an American vessel, the *Panchita,* on the African coast, sending it to New York with a British prize crew aboard, as had been done in 1839.

36. Frank B. Woodford, *Lewis Cass: The Last Jeffersonian* (New Brunswick, N.J.: Rutgers University Press, 1950), pp. 317–19. " 'No change of name can change the illegal character of the assumption. Search or visit, it is equally an assault upon the independence of nations,' Cass said." Quoted from *Senate Executive Documents,* 35th Cong., 1st sess., 1858, no. 49, p. 48. See also Richard W. Van Alstyne, "British-American Diplomatic Relations, 1850–1860" (Ph.D. diss., Stanford University, 1928), pp. 217–49, for a discussion of the controversy.

37. Woodford, *Lewis Cass,* p. 320.

38. William Law Mathieson, *Great Britain and the Slave Trade, 1839–1865* (New York: Longmans, Green, 1920), p. 161; George Francis Dow, *Slave Ships and Slaving* (Salem, Mass.: Marine Research Society, 1927), p. 257, quoting Richard Drake, *Revelations of a Slave Smuggler; Being the Autobiography of Capt. Richard Drake, an African Trader for Fifty Years, from 1807 to 1857.* The authenticity of the latter account has been questioned by several authorities.

39. Mannix and Cowley, *Black Cargoes,* pp. 274–5.

40. "A Slave Trader's Letter Book," *North American Review* 143 (November 1886):454. See also Philip S. Foner, *Business and Slavery: The New York Merchants and the Irrepressible Conflict* (Chapel Hill: University of North Carolina Press, 1941). It was further alleged that a number of joint-stock corporations, masquerading under various false fronts of legitimate business, were formed, and that certain members of them came from the top ranks of New York's mercantile and financial aristocracy. See Appendix A for estimated profits of slaving expeditions.

41. Howard, *American Slavers,* pp. 218–23.

42. *Nautical Magazine and Naval Chronicle* (London), June 1858, p. 336.

43. Howard, *American Slavers,* p. 222. For British estimates of the extent of New York participation in the slave trade, see Mathieson, *Great Britain and the Slave Trade,* pp. 161–5.

44. Roy Olton, "Problems of American Foreign Relations in the African Area during the Nineteenth Century" (Ph.D. diss., Fletcher School of Law and Diplomacy, 1954), pp. 125–6. It is worthy of note, showing how completely U.S. policy was reversed because of the Civil War, that previous administrations had rejected British suggestions for mixed courts on the grounds that they were unconstitutional. No American citizen, it was held, could be subjected to the hazards of a court whose decisions would not be reviewed by the Supreme Court of the United States.

45. "The officers of the United States' Navy are extremely active and zealous in the cause." See "Papers Relative to the Suppression of the Slave Trade on the Coast of Africa," quoted in Elizabeth Donnan, ed., *Documents Illustrative of the History of the Slave Trade to America,* 4 vols. (New York: Octagon Books, 1965), 3:13.

46. See Howard, *American Slavers*, pp. 213–23.
47. American Colonization Society, *Memorial of the Semi-Centennial Anniversary of the American Colonization Society* (Washington: The Society, 1867), p. 190.
48. Mathieson, *Great Britain and the Slave Trade*, p. 165.

Chapter 5. The effects of the slave trade

1. See, for instance, Herbert S. Klein, *The Middle Passage: Comparative Studies on the Atlantic Slave Trade* (Princeton, N.J.: Princeton University Press, 1978). See also Appendix A.
2. The first New England slaver in Africa landed men and raided villages to capture slaves, but such methods seem to have been the exception: The raiding was usually done by African slave-hunters.
3. See Oliver MacDonagh, *A Pattern of Government Growth, 1800–1860* (London: Mac-Gibbon, 1961).
4. Oscar Handlin, *The Uprooted: The Epic Story of the Great Migrations That Made the American People* (New York, 1951, pp. 37–62).
5. The full list from which these items have been abstracted is printed in Eveline Martin, ed., *Nicholas Owen, Journal of a Slave Dealer: A View of Some Remarkable Axcedents in the Life of Nics. Owen on the Coast of Africa and America from the Year 1746 to the Year 1757* (London: Routledge, 1930).
6. A. W. Lawrence, *Trade Castles and Forts of West Africa* (Stanford, Calif.: Stanford University Press, 1964), p. 37.
7. Georg Nørregaard, *Danish Settlements in West Africa, 1658–1850* (Boston: Boston University Press, 1966).
8. Lawrence, *Trade Castles*, p. 38.
9. William O. Jones, *Manioc in Africa* (Stanford, Calif.: Stanford University Press, 1959), p. 60.
10. Anthony Benezet, *Some Historical Account of Guinea* ... (London: J. Phillips, 1788), p. 97.
11. Roland Oliver and J. D. Fage, *A Short History of Africa* (Baltimore: Penguin Books, 1962), p. 122.
12. J. D. Fage, "Slavery and the Slave Trade in the Context of West African History," *Journal of African History* 10 (1969):400.
13. J. Vansina, "Long-Distance Trade-Routes," *Journal of African History* 3 (1962):387.
14. See Oliver and Fage, *A Short History*, pp. 120–1; and L. H. Gann and Peter Duignan, *White Settlers in Tropical Africa* (Baltimore: Penguin Books, 1962), pp. 25–6.
15. See, for instance, Edward A. Alpers, "Trade, State and Society among the Yao in the Nineteenth Century," *Journal of African History* 10 (1969): 8–18.
16. Christopher Fyfe, "The Impact of the Slave Trade on West Africa," in Fyfe, *The Transatlantic Slave Trade from West Africa,* University of Edinburgh, Centre of African Studies (Edinburgh: The Center, 1965), pp. 81–8.
17. As in England, the profits of slave merchants helped provide the capital for industrial developments. For example, the De Wolf brothers of Bristol made their money in shipping and slaving and invested the profit in distilleries and textile mills. Daniel P. Mannix and Malcolm Cowley, *Black Cargoes: A History of the Atlantic Slave Trade, 1518–1865* (New York: Viking Press, 1962), pp. 165–6.
18. See L. H. Gann and Peter Duignan, *Africa and the World: An Introduction to the History of Sub-Saharan Africa from Antiquity to 1840* (San Francisco: Chandler, 1972), pp. 334–8.
19. Ira Berlin, "Time, Space, and the Evolution of Afro-American Society on British Mainland North America," *American Historical Review* 85 (1980):56.

20. Roger Bastide, *Les Amériques Noires: les civilisations africaines dans le nouveau monde* (Paris: Payot, 1967).

Chapter 6. American traders and whalers

1. Philip L. White, *The Beekmans of New York in Politics and Commerce, 1647–1877* (New York: New York Historical Society, 1956), pp. 309–11, 329–30.

2. See Paul Elmo Hohman, *The American Whaleman: A Study of Life and Labor in the Whaling Industry* (New York: Longmans, Green, 1928), p. 28. Between 1769 and 1774 the Browns of Providence, Rhode Island, sent whaling vessels regularly to the African coast. James B. Hedges, *The Browns of Providence Plantations: Colonial Years* (Cambridge, Mass.: Harvard University Press, 1952), pp. 87–8.

3. See Edouard A. Stackpole, *Whales and Destiny: The Rivalry between America, France, and Britain for Control of the Southern Whale Fishery, 1785–1825* (Amherst: University of Massachusetts Press, 1972).

4. St. Helena, a volcanic island in the South Atlantic nine hundred miles off the coast of Africa, became a great rendezvous point for whalers.

5. See Carl N. Haywood, "American Whalers and Africa" (Ph.D. diss. Boston University, 1966–7), passim. See also J. N. Tønnessen and A. O. Johnsen, *The History of Modern Whaling* (Berkeley: University of California Press, 1982).

6. See George E. Brooks, *Yankee Traders, Old Coasters, and African Middlemen: A History of American Legitimate Trade with West Africa in the Nineteenth Century* (Boston: Boston University Press, 1970), p. 30.

7. See Haywood, "American Whalers," passim.

8. Stackpole, *Whales and Destiny*, p. 372.

9. Mack Thompson, *Moses Brown, Reluctant Reformer* (Chapel Hill: University of North Carolina Press, 1962), p. 175. Unfortunately, there are very few sources or dependable secondary studies covering American commercial activities in West Africa before 1865. An exception to this general statement, and an authority upon which the present authors have drawn heavily, is Brooks, *Yankee Traders*.

For an exhaustive discussion of the fact that not all American ships on the African coast were slavers, see ibid. Legitimate U.S. trade is illustrated by one of the first captures made by the British in the war – that of the brig *Federal*, commanded by Captain Samuel Swan, Jr., bound from Africa to Boston and laden with "ivory, coffee, palm oil, old copper." Robert Greenhalgh Albion and Jennie Barnes Pope, *Sea Lanes in Wartime: The American Experience, 1775–1942* (London: Allen & Unwin, 1943), p. 114. Swan had made several voyages to Africa, all of them in legitimate trade.

10. See John Carroll Brent, "Leaves from an African Journal," parts 1, 2, *Knickerbocker Magazine* 33 (1849):41–8, 116–27, 206–15, 334–40, 399–409; 34 (1850):127–33, 227–34, 300–5; Thomas Edward Bowdich, *Excursions in Madeira and Porto Santo, during the Autumn of 1823, While on His Third Voyage to Africa* (London: G. B. Whittaker, 1825); Jacinto Pereira Carneiro, "Memoir on the Trade to the West Coast of Africa Northward of the Equator," *Nautical Magazine and Naval Chronicle* (London), 1855, pp. 407–15; Joshua A. Carnes, *Journal of a Voyage from Boston to the West Coast of Africa, with a Full Description of the Manner of Trading with the Natives on the Coast* (Boston: J. P. Jewett, 1852; reprint, New York: Johnson Reprint Co., 1970); Joseph Hawkins, *A History of a Voyage to the Coast of Africa and Travels into the Interior of That Country* (reprint, London: Cass, 1970); Charles W. Thomas, *Adventures and Observations on the West Coast of Africa and Its Islands* (New York: Derby & Jackson, 1860); and Thomas Miller, "Western Africa: Its Coast, Resources, and Trade," *Nautical Magazine and Naval Chronicle* (London), June 1855, pp. 291–6, 345–55.

11. Quoted in Brooks, *Yankee Traders*, pp. 61–2.

12. See Albion and Pope, *Sea Lanes in Wartime*, pp. 99–102; and Anna Cornelia Clauder, "American Commerce as Affected by the Wars of the French Revolution and Napoleon, 1793–1812" (Ph.D. diss., University of Pennsylvania, 1932), passim.

13. A very large number – possibly a majority – of the original colonists in Sierra Leone were American blacks who had escaped from their masters and fought on the British side in the Revolution. After the war the British took them to Nova Scotia, where they were completely destitute. It was then decided to transport them to Africa. See E. G. Ingham, *Sierra Leone after a Hundred Years* (London: Seeley, 1894), pp. 8–10; and Christopher Fyfe, *A History of Sierra Leone* (London: Oxford University Press, 1962), pp. 31–5.

14. Brooks, *Yankee Traders*, p. 245.

15. Fyfe, *History of Sierra Leone*, p. 132; Brooks, *Yankee Traders*, pp. 167–9. The thoroughness of MacCarthy's exclusion of American shipping is shown by the fact that between 1817 and 1824 only six American ships, two of which were in distress and one of which was seized, entered the colony's port.

16. Brooks, *Yankee Traders*, pp. 169–73.

17. Ibid., p. 76.

18. N. A. W. Cox-George, *Finance and Development in West Africa: The Sierra Leone Experience* (London: D. Dobson, 1961), p. 103. A shortage of currency forced Sierra Leone to allow other national coins to circulate as well.

19. Bella Sidney, Lady Southorn, *The Gambia: The Story of the Groundnut Colony* (London: Allen & Unwin, 1952), pp. 153–5.

20. Brooks, *Yankee Traders*, pp. 149–50.

21. E. J. Alagoa, "Preliminary Inventory of the Records of the United States Diplomatic and Consular Posts in West Africa, 1856–1935," *Journal of the Historical Society of Nigeria* 2, no. 1 (December 1960):78, 93; Lawrence Cabot Howard, "American Involvement in Africa South of the Sahara, 1800–1860" (Ph.D. diss., Harvard University, 1956), pp. 98–100. The share of American imports in the total of West African imports for selected years is given in Brooks, *Yankee Traders*, p. 6:

Year	Gambia	Sierra Leone	Gold Coast
1840	17%	5%	16% (1846)
1850	15	14	16
1860	28	12	41
1870	4	13	34

22. In French West Africa the peak years were 1865 to 1869. Brooks, *Yankee Traders*, pp. 298–9.

23. Carneiro, "Memoir on the Trade to the West Coast," pp. 412–13. It is safe to say that if there had been any serious losses because of trusting the Africans, the Yankee trader would soon have discontinued the practice. This form of trade is reminiscent of the silent trade of the western Sudan mentioned in E. W. Bovill, *The Golden Trade of the Moors* (London: Oxford University Press, 1968), p. 82.

24. Brooks, *Yankee Traders*, pp. 283–5.

25. Howard, "American Involvement in Africa," p. 102; Miller, "Western Africa," pp. 296, 347; Brent, "Leaves from an African Journal," 34 (1850):132; G. E. Metcalfe, *Maclean of the Gold Coast: The Life and Times of George Maclean, 1801–1847* (London: Oxford University Press, 1962), p. 115; *Missionary Herald* 41 (1845):157.

26. Howard, "American Involvement in Africa," p. 103.

27. Quoted in ibid., pp. 117–18.

28. Quoted in John R. Spears, *The American Slave-Trade* (New York: Scribner, 1900), pp. 42–3.

29. One of the founders of a pirate state called Libertalia in northern Madagascar was an American named Thomas Tew. After accumulating a dishonest fortune at sea, Tew returned to Rhode Island to live, but reverted to piracy and was killed somewhere in the Indian Ocean. A New York merchant named Frederic Phillips is said to have outfitted ships for slaving and for piratical voyages to East Africa and to Madagascar and other Indian Ocean coasts and islands during the later years of the seventeenth century and the early part of the eighteenth, while Philadelphia merchants were also seeking a share of the business. See John Biddulph, *The Pirates of Malabar and an Englishwoman in India Two Hundred Years Ago* (London: Smith & Elder, 1907), pp. 22–4; and A. Toussaint, "Early American Trade with Mauritius," *Essex Institute Historical Collections* 87 (1951):373.

30. Quoted in Foster Rhea Dulles, *The Old China Trade* (Boston: Houghton Mifflin, 1930), p. 4. See also Biddulph, *Pirates of Malabar,* pp. 38–68.

31. S. Pasfield Oliver, ed., *Memoirs and Travels of Mauritius Augustus Count de Benyowski* (London: Paul, Trench, Treubner, 1904) , pp. 456–620. Oliver (p.xix) says that Benyowski's objective was to establish a vast base for the slave trade. See also Abbé Rochon, "A Voyage to Madagascar and the East Indies," in *A General Collection of the Best and Most Interesting Voyages and Travels in All Parts of the World,* ed. John Pinkerton, 17 vols. (London: Longman, Hurst, Rees, & Orme, 1808–14), 16:779–96; and George A. Shaw, *Madagascar and France, with Some Account of the Island, Its People, Its Resources and Development* (London: Religious Tracts Society, 1885), pp. 67–78.

32. Quoted in Sydney Greenie and Marjorie Greenie, *Gold of Ophir; or, The Lure That Made America* (Garden City, N.Y.: Doubleday, Page, 1925), p. 29.

33. Massachusetts Historical Society, *The Commerce of Rhode Island, 1726–1880,* 2 vols. (Boston: The Society, 1914–15), 2:200–6; Richard H. McKey, Jr., "Elias Hasket Derby and the Founding of the Eastern Trade," *Essex Institute Historical Collections* 98 (1962):1–25, 65–83. All of these ships were heavily armed and sailed prepared for trouble. For instance, Derby's ship, the *Grand Turk,* carried twenty-two guns, an armament calculated to discourage pirates and ensure a friendly reception from Africans. Derby's ships, incidentally, never engaged in the slave trade, in spite of voyaging to Guinea.

34. Toussaint, "Early American Trade," passim. See also Edwin B. Hewes, "Nathaniel Bowditch, Supercargo and Mariner," *Essex Institute Historical Collections* 70 (1934):210–17; and Jonathan Tucker, "The First Voyage to India from Salem, 1786–1787," ibid. 75 (1939):44–5.

35. Quoted in Holden Furber, "The Beginnings of American Trade with India, 1784–1812," *New England Quarterly* 11 (1938):241–2. See also William Milburn, *Oriental Commerce,* 2 vols. (London: Murray, 1813), 2:136. Milburn, who was an official of the East India Company, credits the *Chesapeake* with being the first American ship to reach India, but it appears that the *United States* preceded it by several months.

36. Americans were willing and ready to purchase prizes taken by the British as well as those taken by the French.

37. Eric Rosenthal, *Stars and Stripes in Africa* (London: Routledge, 1938), p. 57.

38. Milburn, *Oriental Commerce,* 2:48. In August 1789 Hasket Derby, son of Elias Hasket Derby, stopped at Cape Town on a return voyage from Calcutta, sold $1,500 worth of Calcutta cloth, and purchased 253 ostrich feathers. McKey, "Elias Hasket Derby," p. 24.

39. Nathaniel Isaacs, *Travels and Adventures in Eastern Africa [1836],* ed. L. Herrman, 2 vols. (Cape Town: Van Riebeek Society, 1935–6), 2:322.

40. Ibid., pp. 5; 329–30 (emphasis added).

41. Hohmann, *American Whaleman,* pp. 150, 230.

42. Milburn, *Oriental Commerce,* 1:34; Alexander Starbuck, *History of the American Whale Fishery . . . to the Year 1876* (Waltham, Mass.: The Author, 1878), p. 90.

43. Quoted in Rosenthal, *Stars and Stripes*, p. 68.

44. Isaacs, *Travels and Adventures*, 2:283.

45. Quoted in Rosenthal, *Stars and Stripes*, p. 92; see also J. N. Reynolds, *Voyage of the United States Frigate Potomac, under the Command of Commodore John Downes, during the Circumnavigation of the Globe, in the Years 1831, 1832, 1833, and 1834* (New York: Harper & Bros., 1835), pp. 82–3. Stout praised the Africans highly for the hospitality and help they extended to him and his crew after the wreck.

46. Quotation from Rosenthal, *Stars and Stripes*, p. 93. See also Edgar Stanton Maclay, *A History of the United States Navy from 1775 to 1893*, 2 vols. (New York: Appleton, 1894–5), 1:192; and Maclay, "Extract of Capt. E. Preble's Journal on Board the Essex," *Essex Institute Historical Collections* 10, part 3 (1869):66–9.

47. Quotations from Rosenthal, *Stars and Stripes*, pp. 93–4.

48. The title was an honorary degree from Columbia University.

49. Quoted in Rosenthal, *Stars and Stripes*, p. 97.

50. Quoted in Harold Graham Mackeurtan, *The Cradle Days of Natal (1497–1845)* (London: Longmans, Green, 1930), p. 329. Smith's prediction seemed partly fulfilled by the arrival in 1835 of a group of American missionaries who came in response to an invitation from the Dr. Philip who, ten years earlier, had been in terror of the American peril. The earnest, devoted men of the missionary group, who were destined to achieve an honorable place in South African history, would have been shocked if they had known that they were feared as political agents – as spies and what were later called fifth columnists. The warship mentioned was the USS *Peacock*, carrying an envoy from President Andrew Jackson to negotiate commercial treaties with the sultan of Muscat and other Eastern potentates.

51. Quoted in John S. Galbraith, *Reluctant Empire: British Policy on the South African Frontier, 1834–1854* (Berkeley: University of California Press, 1963), p. 182.

52. Herbert M. Bratter, "Jonathan Lambert of Salem, the Yankee Who Would Be King," *Essex Institute Historical Collections* 88 (1952):150–62; Edwin B. Hewes, "Jonathan Lambert of Salem, King of Tristan D'Acunha," ibid. 71 (1935):1–6; Captain Benjamin Morrell, *A Narrative of Four Voyages* (Upper Saddle River, N.J.: Gregg Press, 1970), pp. 354–5; Benjamin Seaver, "Mr. Seaver's Letter Concerning the Islands of Tristan D'Acunha," *Historical Collections of the Massachusetts Historical Society*, 2d. ser., 2 (1814):125–8. Seaver, the British visitor referred to in the text, said that there were three Americans on the island, although he named only Lambert.

53. Norman Robert Bennett, "Americans in Zanzibar, 1825–1845," *Essex Institute Historical Collections* 95 (1959):240–2.

54. C. T. Brady, *Commerce and Conquest in East Africa* (Salem, Mass.: Essex Institute, 1950), pp. 89–90; W. S. W. Ruschenberger, *A Voyage Round the World, Including an Embassy to Muscat and Siam in 1835, 1836, and 1837* (Philadelphia: Carey, Lea & Blanchard, 1838), pp. 10–11.

55. Ruschenberger, *Voyage Round the World*, pp. 89–94.

56. Ibid., p. 96.

57. Ibid., p. 97.

58. Brady, *Commerce and Conquest*, p. 98.

59. Bennett, "Americans in Zanzibar, 1825–1845," p. 250.

60. Ibid., pp. 254–5. The first British consul, Captain Atkins Hamerton, complained that at his initial audience with the sultan the latter was flanked on each side by a picture of a British warship surrendering to an American.

61. Hermann Frederick Eilts, "Ahmad bin Na'aman's Mission to the United States in 1840: The Voyage of Al-Sultanah to New York City," *Essex Institute Historical Collections* 98 (1962):219–77.

62. Ibid., pp. 234–5.

63. Winthrop L. Marvin, *The American Merchant Marine: Its History and Romance from 1620 to 1902* (New York: Scribner, 1902), p. 202.

64. Bennett, "Americans in Zanzibar, 1825–1845," pp. 260–2.

65. Howard, "American Involvement in Africa," p. 102.

66. David Livingstone, "Letters from David Livingstone, the Distinguished African Explorer, Written in 1856," *Essex Institute Historical Collections* 12 (1874):285.

67. Samuel Eliot Morison, *The Maritime History of Massachusetts, 1783–1860* (Boston: Houghton Mifflin, 1921), p. 377; Robert Greenhalgh Albion, "From Sails to Spindles: Essex County in Transition," *Essex Institute Historical Collections* 95 (1959):119.

68. Charles E. Cartwright, *The Tale of Our Merchant Ships* (New York: Dutton, 1924), p. 123. Ships drawing more than twelve feet could not dock there.

69. Kenneth Ingham, *A History of East Africa* (London: Longmans, 1962), pp. 71–3.

70. Ernest O. Moore, *Ivory, Scourge of Africa* (New York: Harper, 1931), pp. 211–12.

71. Ibid., passim.

72. Miller, "Western Africa," p. 296.

73. Department of the Treasury, *Report of the Secretary of the Treasury, Transmitting a Report from the Register of the Treasury, of the Commerce and Navigation of the United States for the Year Ending June 30, 1855* (Washington, D.C.: GPO, 1855), pp. 223, 241. It may be recalled that the brig *Pilgrim*, on the voyage immortalized by Richard Henry Dana, Jr., in *Two Years before the Mast*, sailed around the Horn to California to obtain a cargo of hides.

74. Brooks, *Yankee Traders*, pp. 216–17.

75. Howard, "American Involvement in Africa," p. 166.

76. This change hurt American trade with West Africa, for rum and tobacco were the main U.S. trade goods. Duties on U.S. rum from 1875 to 1885 averaged over 50 percent of all revenues collected by the Gold Coast government. Brooks, *Yankee Traders*, pp. 273–85.

77. Numerous examples show that steamships were cutting deeply into the business of sailing-ship owners during the 1870s and 1880s; see Norman R. Bennett, "William H. Hathorne, Merchant and Consul in Zanzibar," *Essex Institute Historical Collections* 99 (1963):125, 132, 134.

Chapter 7. Missionaries and colonization societies

1. Walter L. Williams, *Black Americans and the Evangelization of Africa, 1877–1900* (Madison: University of Wisconsin Press, 1982).

2. Reginald Coupland, *Wilberforce: A Narrative*, 2d ed. (London: Collins, 1945), p. 282.

3. See Ellen Gibson Wilson, *The Loyal Blacks* (New York: Putnam, 1976).

4. Ibid., pp. 405–6.

5. Wilson (ibid., p. 406) quotes one official report: "By their idleness and turbulence [they] had kept the settlement in constant danger of dissolution."

6. Ibid., pp. 361–82, 405–7. See also John Peterson, *Province of Freedom: A History of Sierra Leone, 1787–1870* (London: Faber & Faber, 1969).

7. When Cuffee visited Freetown in 1811 it contained 1,917 non-African inhabitants, of whom 982 were black Americans who had gone to Nova Scotia during the American Revolution. See Sheldon H. Harris, "An American's Impression of Sierra Leone in 1811," *Journal of Negro History*, 47 (1923):35–41.

8. Benjamin Griffith Brawley, *Negro Builders and Heroes* (Chapel Hill: University of North Carolina Press, 1937), pp. 35–9; Henry Noble Sherwood, "Paul Cuffe," *Journal of Negro History* 8 (1923):153–229; Sheldon H. Harris, *Paul Cuffe, Black Americans and the African Return* (New York: Simon & Schuster, 1972).

9. Early Lee Fox, *The American Colonization Society, 1817–1840* (Baltimore: Johns Hop-

kins Press, 1919), p. 46; P. J. Staudenraus, *The African Colonization Movement, 1816–1865* (New York: Columbia University Press, 1961), pp. 27–30.

10. Fox, *American Colonization Society*, p. 61.

11. Ibid., pp. 52–3; Staudenraus, *African Colonization Movement*, pp. 37, 41.

12. They were aided by John Kizell (or Kizzell), a former slave in South Carolina. Kizell was one of the blacks who joined the British in the Revolution; he had been taken to Nova Scotia and from there, finally, to Sierra Leone. He was a trader on Sherbro Island.

13. Robert Earle Anderson, *Liberia, America's African Friend* (Chapel Hill: University of North Carolina Press, 1952), pp. 64–5.

14. Ibid., pp. 65–8.

15. Staudenraus, *African Colonization Movement*, pp. 63–5. Cape Mesurado is the site of the present city of Monrovia.

16. It seems to have been the only organization with which the government dealt directly. Between 1820 and 1843, 4,571 emigrants went to Liberia; by 1843 only 1,819 remained, owing to a high death rate (20 percent), especially in the first two years after arrival. Their race did not give blacks any protection, as was commonly assumed, and they died in as high proportions as whites had done in West Africa. The American Colonization Society worried that high death rates might hurt recruitment. See Tom W. Shick, "A Quantitative Analysis of Liberian Colonization from 1820–1843, with Special Reference to Mortality," *Journal of African History* 12 (1971):45–59.

17. Samuel W. Langhorn, "Administrative Problems in Maryland in Liberia – 1836–1851," *Journal of Negro History* 26 (1941):325–64.

18. Fox, *American Colonization Society*, pp. 61–3; A. Doris Banks Henries, *The Liberian Nation: A Short History* (New York, 1954), p. 65.

19. Henries, *The Liberian Nation*, pp. 67–9.

20. The terms "tribe" or "tribal" have been widely unpopular among American Africanists as demeaning to Africans. But African militants such as Kwame Nkrumah or the Marxist–Leninist theoreticians of the Popular Movement for the Liberation of Angola (MPLA) and Frente de Libertação de Moçambique (FRELIMO) have themselves no inhibitions about using such terms. We mean by a "tribal" society one in which there is no individual land ownership, in which every recognized member of the community is entitled to a share in the available land by virtue of membership in the group.

21. Staudenraus, *African Colonization Movement*, pp. 240–50. The American Colonization Society was officially dissolved in 1912. A vestigial body was still in nominal existence in 1959 – with six members.

22. Senate, "Report of the Secretary of the Interior," *Senate Executive Documents*, 37th Cong., 2d sess., 1861, no. 1, p. 453.

23. Senate, "Message of the President, December 3, 1861," *Senate Executive Documents*, 37th Cong., 2d sess., 1861, no. 1, p. 6.

24. House of Representatives, "Message of the President, December 1, 1862," *House Executive Documents*, 37th Cong., 3d sess., 1863, no. 1, p. 5; House of Representatives, "Letter of the Secretary of State Transmitting a Report on the Commercial Relations of the United States, January 6, 1863," *House Executive Documents*, 37th Cong., 3d sess., 1863, no. 28, p. 1.

25. Wade Crawford Barclay, *History of Methodist Missions*, part 1, *Early American Methodism, 1769–1844*, 2 vols. (New York: Methodist Church Mission Board, 1949–50), 1:285, 301, 310, 338, 340–3, 344; 2:147.

26. Mr. Herman Kahn, assistant archivist for civil archives, National Archives, Washington, D.C., to the authors, July 11, 1962. It is not clear why the first representatives to Liberia (and Haiti as well) were designated commissioners instead of ministers. Seys was the first to hold the title of minister.

27. See L. R. Mehlinger, "The Attitude of the Free Negro toward African Colonization," *Journal of Negro History*, 1 (1916):276–301.

28. Quoted in A. H. M. Kirk-Greene, "America in the Niger Valley: A Colonization Centenary," *Phylon* 23 (1962):230–1.

29. Ibid., p. 235.

30. Robert Campbell, *A Pilgrimage to My Motherland: An Account of a Journey among the Egbas and Yorubas of Central Africa, in 1859–60* (New York, 1861), pp. 109–10.

31. For a scholarly discussion of Delany and his projects, see Kirk-Greene, "America in the Niger Valley," pp. 225–39. Other sources are Martin Robinson Delany, *Official Report of the Niger Valley Exploring Party* (1861; reprint, Philadelphia: Historic Publications, 1969); F. A. Rollin, *Life and Public Services of Martin R. Delany* (Boston, 1868); Robert Campbell, *A Few Facts Relating to Lagos, Abeokuta, and Other Sections of Central Africa* (Philadelphia, 1860); and Campbell, *Pilgrimage to My Motherland*. See also Cyril E. Griffith, *The African Dream: Martin R. Delany and the Emergence of Pan-Africanism* (University Park: Pennsylvania State University Press, 1975).

32. Howard H. Bell, "Negro Nationalism: A Factor in Emigration Projects, 1858–1861," *Journal of Negro History* 47 (1962):42–57.

33. Olaudah Equiano, *The Interesting Narrative of the Life of Olaudah Equiano, or Gustavus Vassa, the African, Written by Himself* (London, 1789), pp. 3–25, cited in Thomas L. Hodgkin, *Nigerian Perspectives: An Historical Anthology* (London: Oxford University Press, 1960), p. 155.

34. Wilber Christian Harr, "The Negro as an American Protestant Missionary in Africa" (D.D. diss., University of Chicago Divinity School, 1945), pp. 12–13; Williams D. Johnston, "Slavery in Rhode Island, 1755–1776," *Publications of the Rhode Island Historical Society* 2 (1894): 154–5.

35. Christopher Fyfe, "The West African Methodists in the Nineteenth Century," *Sierra Leone Bulletin of Religion* 3, no. 1 (1961):22–3; Fyfe, "The Countess of Huntingdon's Connexion in Nineteenth Century Sierra Leone," ibid. 4, no. 2 (1962):53–4; see also Fyfe, *A History of Sierra Leone* (London: Oxford University Press, 1962), p. 38.

36. Fyfe, "Countess of Huntingdon's Connexion," pp. 54–5, credits Cato Perkins with having inspired one of the founders of the London Missionary Society to consider missions in Africa.

37. Charles Pelham Groves, *The Planting of Christianity in Africa*, 4 vols. (London: Butterworth, 1948–58), 1:216.

38. Harold R. Isaacs, *The New World of Negro Americans* (New York: John Day, 1963), p. 124.

39. Harr, "Negro as an American Protestant Missionary," pp. 20, 50–3; see also Charles W. Thomas, *Adventures and Observations on the West Coast of Africa and its Islands* (New York: Derby & Jackson, 1860), pp. 99–100; and William H. Sheppard, *Presbyterian Pioneers in Congo* (Louisville, Ky: Pentecostal Publishing Co., n.d.). When the Ethiopian and Zionist churches sprang up after 1900, the colonial powers sought to discourage black missionaries. Fears engendered by Chilembwe in Nyasaland, Kitawala in the Congo, and the Watch Tower movement in Northern Rhodesia made it difficult for black American missionaries to gain entrance into colonial territories. White Christian churches may be blamed for accommodating themselves to colonial governments in East and South Africa and not sending black Americans, but it is hard to see what else they could have done. For further discussion, see the final section of Chapter 18.

40. Barclay, *Early American Methodism*, 1:327–8; Fyfe, *History of Sierra Leone*, p. 132–3, 181, 257.

41. Information on Carey is found in Miles Mark Fisher, "Lott Cary, the Colonizing Missionary," *Journal of Negro History* 7 (1922): 380–418; Edward A. Freeman, *The Epoch*

of Negro Baptists and the Foreign Mission Board (Kansas City, Kans.: Foreign Mission Board, 1953), pp. 107–9; William Gammell, *A History of American Baptist Missions in Asia, Africa, Europe, and North America, under the Care of the American Baptist Missionary Union* (Boston, 1854), pp. 244–8; and Harr, "Negro as an American Protestant Missionary," pp. 46–7. Black Baptists later sent their own missionaries to Africa, and a Lott Carey Missionary Society was established in 1897. Information supplied by Dr. St. Clair Drake when on the faculty of Roosevelt University; see also his article on Carey in *The American Negro Reference Book* (1966).

42. Cox died uttering the words, "Though a thousand fall, let not Africa be given up." See Johannes Du Plessis, *The Evangelisation of Pagan Africa* (Cape Town: J. C. Juta, 1930), p. 100.

43. Groves, *Planting of Christianity*, 1:296.

44. Ibid., pp. 296–7.

45. *Missionary Herald* 29 (1833):19. The "Committee" was the Prudential Committee, the ABCFM's governing body.

46. Ibid., p. 401.

47. Ibid. In addition, it was the board's hope that its missions would ultimately extend from the base that Wilson would establish to the depths of the unknown Niger Valley and the slopes of the Mountains of the Moon: "An object of primary importance in respect to the inland parts of western Africa, and the central portions of the continent eastward of the Niger, is the *exploration of the country with a view to missionary operations*." Ibid., p. 402 (emphasis in original).

48. Ibid. 30 (1834):212–10; ibid. 32 (1836):4, 64–6, 409–14.

49. Wilson informed the board in September 1840 that he was printing a Bassa spelling book and a hymnbook for the Baptist mission at Bassa. Since the Baptists were "very much straitened from want of funds," this work was being done gratis. James later serves in Gabon for several years before resigning from the mission and returning to Liberia. See ibid. 37 (1841):138–9.

50. Ibid. 32 (1836):413. See also Du Plessis, *Evangelisation of Pagan Africa*, pp. 100–2.

51. *Missionary Herald* 30 (1834):187; Philip D. Curtin, *The Image of Africa: British Ideas and Action, 1780–1850* (Madison: University of Wisconsin Press, 1964), p. 484.

52. See *Missionary Herald* 33 (1837):219–20, 269, 364–7; ibid. 38 (1842):172, 177–9, 412–13.

53. Du Plessis, *Evangelisation of Pagan Africa*, pp. 103–4.

54. See Schomburg Collection, "Biographical Index," in *Calendar of the Manuscripts in the Schomburg Collection of Negro Literature* (Ann Arbor, Mich.: University Microfilms, 1952); *Appleton's Cyclopedia of American Biography* (1888–9), 4:685.

55. Karl David Pattersen, "The Mpongwe and the Orungu of the Gabon Coast, 1815–1875: The Transition to Colored Rule" (Ph.D. diss., Stanford University, 1971), pp. 181–3. See also *Missionary Herald* 33 (1837):219–20, 269, 364–7; ibid. 38 (1842):172, 177–9, 381, 412–13, 497–500.

56. Pattersen, "The Mpongwe and the Orungu," p. 185.

57. *Missionary Herald* 39 (1843):404.

58. Ibid. 40 (1844):349–51.

59. The use of the American flag may have appeared to be a provocation to the French, who felt, with some reason, that the missionaries were encouraging Mpongwe resistance.

60. *Missionary Herald* 42 (1846):25–31. The bombardment occurred in July 1845.

61. Ibid., 42:104, 157–8, 210–11, 316.

62. Ibid., 43 (1847):257.

63. Groves, *Planting of Christianity*, 2:67–70; *Missionary Herald* 48 (1852):58; Clifton Jackson Phillips, *Protestant America and the Pagan World: The First Half Century of the*

American Board of Commissioners for Foreign Missions, 1810–1860 (Cambridge, Mass.: Harvard University Press, 1969), p. 224.

64. Pattersen, "The Mpongwe and the Orungu," p. 221.

65. Ibid., pp. 222–3.

66. Robert H. Nassau, *My Ogowe, Being a Narrative of Daily Incidents during Sixteen Years in Equatorial West Africa* (New York: Neale, 1914), pp. 18, 44–8.

67. *Missionary Herald* 46 (1850):38.

68. Du Plessis, *Evangelisation of Pagan Africa*, p. 174.

69. This was the case despite two carefully organized exploring expeditions in 1832 and 1842, both of which ended in disaster.

70. Du Plessis, *Evangelisation of Pagan Africa*, pp. 134–7. Samuel Adjai Crowther was a native African rescued from slavery by the Royal Navy and converted to Christianity at Sierra Leone. He proved to be an apt scholar. Crowther was later a member of the disastrous exploring expedition of 1842. Shortly afterward he was ordained by the bishop of London, and he became the first Anglican bishop of Nigeria – the first African to hold such an ecclesiastical office.

71. E. C. Routh, "Thomas Jefferson Bowen," *Encyclopedia of Southern Baptists*, 3 vols. (Nashville, Tenn.: Broadman Press, 1958–71), 1:183.

72. He wrote to a friend on May 16, 1851, from Iketu: "Some of these Episcopalians were laboring in Africa when I was a wicked young man in the Texas cavalry, ranging the prairies of the western frontier with my sword and yager." Bowen Papers, Southern Baptist Convention Historical Commission, Nashville, Tenn.

73. Thomas Jefferson Bowen, *Central Africa: Adventures and Missionary Labors in Several Countries in the Interior of Africa, from 1849 to 1856* (Charleston, S.C., 1857).

74. Bowen makes no mention of this episode in any of his surviving letters, but Biobaku says that the Texas cavalryman virtually directed the defense of the walls. S. O. Biobaku, *The Egba and Their Neighbours, 1842–1872* (Oxford: Oxford University Press [Clarendon Press] 1957), p. 44. See also Michael Crowder, *The Story of Nigeria* (London: Faber & Faber, 1962), pp. 126–30.

75. See Thomas Jefferson Bowen, *Grammar and Dictionary of the Yoruba Language, with an Introductory Description of the Country and People of Yoruba* (Washington, D.C., 1858); and *Meroke; or, Missionary Life in Africa* (Philadelphia, 1858), an anonymous work revised by Bowen that gives a biographical sketch of Henry Townsend, one of the Church of England missionaries whom Bowen particularly admired.

76. Bowen Papers.

77. Bowen to the Reverend A. M. Pointdexter, October 10, 1859, ibid. In this letter Bowen speaks of his visit to New York City to promote "emigration among the Blacks." It is possible that there was some connection between this scheme and Martin Robison Delany's Niger Valley exploration of 1859.

In 1858 Bowen attempted unsuccessfully to found a Southern Baptist mission in Brazil. He served briefly as a chaplain in the Confederate army in the Civil War, and spent most of the remainder of his life preaching and trying to regain his health. Although his intense physical suffering caused periods of near insanity, he was sustained by his religious faith. His interest in Africa continued, and he hoped someday to return. In 1859, when the church was considering the abandonment of the Nigeria mission because of missionary mortality, he wrote to Pointdexter: "Shall we abandon sixty millions of people to heathenism, and to eternal perdition, because they live in a sickly climate?" Ibid.

78. St. Clair Drake, *The Redemption of Africa and Black Religion* (Chicago: Third World Press, 1970).

79. Ralph M. Wiltgen, *Gold Coast Mission History, 1471–1880* (Techny, Ill.: Divine Word Publications, 1956), pp. 115–19; Du Plessis, *Evangelisation of Pagan Africa*, p. 334.

80. D. J. Kotzé, ed., *Letters of the American Missionaries, 1835–1838* (Cape Town: Van Riebeeck Society, 1950), pp. 8–15; *Missionary Herald* 29 (1833):414–20; Phillips, *Protestant America and the Pagan World*, p. 212. The names of the two Zulu chiefs are spelled in various ways by different authors; here we follow the forms used by Philip in his letter to Purney.

81. *Missionary Herald* 33 (1837):337–9, 416–21.

82. Ibid. 34 (1838):307–14. See also Alan R. Booth, ed., *Journal of the Reverend George Champion, American Missionary in Zululand, 1835–1839* (Cape Town: C. Struik, 1967).

83. Eric Anderson Walker, *The Great Trek* (London: A. & C. Black, 1938), p. 216.

84. Sir George E. Cory, *The Rise of South Africa*, 5 vols. (London: Longmans, Green, 1926), 4:190; see also Edwin William Smith, *The Life and Times of Daniel Lindley (1801–1880), Missionary to the Zulus, Pastor of the Voortrekkers Ubebe Umhlope* (London: Epworth Press, 1949), pp. 225, 250–1.

85. *Missionary Herald* 34 (1840):247–8; ibid. 44 (1848):196–8.

86. Eleanor S. Reuling, *First Saint to the Zulus* (Boston, 1960). The Bryant article was published in the *Journal of the American Oriental Society* 1 (1849):385–96; it is interesting to note that this volume also includes linguistic articles by John Leighton Wilson and Lewis Grout.

87. Reuling, *First Saint*, p. 38.

Chapter 8. Explorers and frontiersmen

1. Mabel V. Jackson, *European Powers and South-east Africa: A Study of International Relations on the South-east Coast of Africa, 1796–1856* (London: Longmans, Green, 1942), pp. 24–5.

2. See Robin Hallet, *The Penetration of Africa: European Exploration in North and West Africa to 1815* (New York: Praeger, 1965), pp. 200–3.

3. Archibald Robbins, *A Journal, Compromising an Account of the Loss of the Brig Commerce, of Hartford* . . . (Hartford, Conn., 1836).

4. George E. Ellis, "Memoir of Jared Sparks, LL.D.," *Proceedings of the Massachusetts Historical Society* 10 (1867–9):226–7.

5. Paul du Chaillu, *Explorations and Adventures in Equatorial Africa* (New York, 1861), pp. 27, 226, 260, 478. Du Chaillu's career is sketched later. Tribes in the interior, too, frequently tried to monopolize trade with tribes beyond them; the Matabele of southern Africa, for example, tried hard to keep the Europeans from passing through Matabeleland.

6. For additional examples of Africans' opposition to European commercial penetration of the interior, see Kenneth Onwuka Dike, *Trade and Politics in the Niger Delta, 1830–1885: An Introduction to the Economic and Political History of Nigeria* (Oxford: Oxford University Press [Clarendon Press], 1956), pp. 206–7.

7. Andrew H. Foote, *Africa and the American Flag* (New York: Appleton, 1954; reprint, Folkestone, Eng.: Dawson, 1970), pp. 235–8.

8. Du Chaillu, *Explorations and Adventures*, p. 268.

9. The episode is discussed and Walker's report is published in K. D. Patterson, "Early Knowledge of the Ogowe River and the American Explorations of 1854," *African Historical Studies* 5, nos. 1–4 (1972): 75–90.

10. Du Chaillu, *Explorations and Adventures*, passim. See Alfred H. Guernsey, "Paul du Chaillu," parts 1–3, *Harper's Magazine* 36 (1867–8):582–94; 38 (1868–9):164–74; 40 (1869–70):201–13. See also Michel Vaucaire, *Paul de Chaillu: Gorilla Hunter* (New York, 1930), pp. 1–11.

11. Paul du Chaillu, *The Country of the Dwarfs* (New York, 1872).

Chapter 9. The vanishing flag

1. Department of State, Bureau of Statistics, *Commercial Relations of the United States with Foreign Countries during the Years 1894 and 1895* (Washington, D.C.: GPO, 1865–1900), 1:17.

2. Ibid., *1895 and 1896*, pp. 58, 59, 62, 71, 98, 109–11. In the period 1895–6 the total value of imports and exports between the United States and Hawaii was $33,831,815; the total trade with all of Africa amounted to $25,027,679.

3. Senate, "Letter of the Secretary of State, Transmitting a Report on the Commercial Relations of the United States with Foreign Countries for the Year Ended September 30, 1862," *Senate Executive Documents*, 37th Cong., 3d sess., 1863, p. 155.

4. George E. Brooks, *Yankee Traders, Old Coasters, and African Middlemen: A History of American Legitimate Trade with West Africa in the Nineteenth Century* (Boston: Boston University Press, 1970), pp. 126–8.

5. Ibid., p. 127.

6. Ibid., pp. 272–3.

7. In 1883 goods from the United States constituted only about 9 percent of Sierra Leone's imports. See Department of State, *Commercial Relations . . . 1882 and 1883*, pp. 90–3.

8. Brooks, *Yankee Traders*, pp. 292–3. See also Department of State, *Commercial Relations . . . 1894 and 1895*, 1:19.

9. Department of State, *Commercial Relations . . . 1894 and 1895*, 1:23–4. See also House of Representatives, "Report on Commercial Relations of the United States with All Foreign Nations," *House Executive Documents*, 34th Cong., 1st sess., 1857, no. 47, p. 476.

Chapter 10. Liberia: the lamb and the wolves

1. Department of State, *Papers Relating to the Foreign Relations of the United States, 1867–1868* (Washington, D.C.: GPO, 1865–1900), pp. 318–19, 326–31.

2. Benjamin J. K. Anderson, *Narrative of a Journey to Musardu, the Capital of the Western Mandingoes* (New York, 1870). It has not been possible to identify "Musardu" positively, but it seems to have been close to, or identical with, the city now called N'Zérékoré in Guinea, near the Liberian border.

3. Department of State, *Foreign Relations, 1872–1873*, pp. 330–7; ibid., *1879*, pp. 699–701. Turner believed that Liberian coffee was the best in the world.

4. Ibid., *1878–1879*, pp. 523–5.

5. Ibid., *1872–1873*, p. 323.

6. Ibid., *1875*, pp. 832–5.

7. Ibid., p. 836.

8. Ibid., *1878–1879*, pp. 520–3.

9. Ibid., *1880*, pp. 704–5.

10. Ibid., *1879*, pp. 718. At this time Liberia, like other small countries, appointed its consular officers from among citizens of the countries where the consulates were located. Such officials were compensated by occasional consular fees and by the prestige of such titles as "consul general." In 1879 the two Liberian consular officers in France – a consul general at Bordeaux and a consul in Paris – were both Frenchmen.

11. Ibid., pp. 341–2. Nothing has ever come to light to gainsay the conclusion that the French government was not officially involved, but it is possible that without prompt American diplomatic intervention Carrance's scheme might have developed into something serious. See John D. Hargreaves, *Prelude to the Partition of West Africa* (New York: St. Martin's Press, 1963), p. 294.

12. Department of State, *Foreign Relations, 1880*, pp. 692–3, 705–6.

13. Ibid., pp. 693–700, 705–6.

14. Ibid., *1882*, p. 734.

15. Ibid., pp. 734–6.

16. Ibid., *1882–1883*, p. 380.

17. Ibid., *1878–1879*, pp. 256–66; ibid., *1879*, p. 717; Hargreaves, *Prelude to the Partition*, p. 242.

18. Nathaniel R. Richardson, *Liberia's Past and Present* (London: Diplomatic Press, 1959), p. 110; Charles Morrow Wilson, *Liberia* (New York: W. Sloane, 1947), pp. 17–18.

19. Department of State, *Foreign Relations, 1883*, pp. viii–ix.

20. See Richardson, *Liberia's Past and Present*, p. 110; and Hargreaves, *Prelude to the Partition*, p. 243.

21. Department of State, *Foreign Relations, 1886*, pp. 298–9.

22. Ibid.

23. Ibid., pp. 305–9.

24. Ibid., pp. 271–2, 307.

25. Ibid., p. vii.

26. Ibid., *1888*, pp. 1084–6.

27. Ibid., pp. 1081–3.

28. Ibid., *1892*, pp. 231–2.

29. Ibid.

30. Judson M. Lyon, "Edward Blyden: Liberian Independence and African Nationalism, 1903–1909," *Phylon* 17 (1980):36–49.

Chapter 11. Bula Matari and the Congo

1. Henry M. Stanley, *How I Found Livingstone: Travels, Adventures, and Discoveries in Central Africa, Including Four Months' Residence with Dr. Livingstone* (London, 1873), pp. 2–5, 11.

2. Ibid., pp. 31, 39–40.

3. Several years later he replied to the question, "Are you an American citizen?" in this way: "I am undoubtedly a citizen of the United States. I travel under an American passport and always have. I claim and possess all rights of an American citizen . . . I always have with me the emblem of nationality – in civilized countries the passport – in savage countries the flag of the United States of America, and I have never sought the protection, aid, or counsel of any foreign agent, resident, minister or consul. . . . I have sacrificed honours and distinctions for having done deeds worthy of honour because I am an American citizen." Quoted in Frank Hird, *H. M. Stanley: The Authorized Life* (London: Macmillan, 1935), p. 202.

4. Henry M. Stanley, *Through the Dark Continent; or, The Sources of the Nile, around the Great Lakes of Equatorial Africa, and down the Livingstone River to the Atlantic Ocean*, 2 vols. (New York, 1878), 2:2–3.

5. Byron Farwell, *The Man Who Presumed: A Biography of Henry M. Stanley* (New York: Holt, 1957), pp. 169–70.

6. Henry M. Stanley, *The Congo and the Founding of Its Free State: A Story of Work and Exploration*, 2 vols. (New York, 1885), 2:33–8; Henry Wellington Wack, *The Story of the Congo Free State: Social, Political, and Economic Aspects of the Belgian System of Government in Central Africa* (New York: Putnam, 1905), pp. 8–13.

Sanford is usually referred to as General Sanford, and one writer has described him as "a grizzled American soldier." He was not, however, a soldier at all but a career diplomat in days when U.S. diplomatic appointments were usually awarded as prizes in the spoils system. He held diplomatic posts at St. Petersburg, Frankfurt, and Paris before becoming the U.S minister to Belgium in 1861. In Brussels he was active in watching and thwarting Confederate efforts in Europe. He also assisted the state of Minnesota in obtaining cannon in Europe to arm its artillery for the Civil War, and for this action he was made a major general in the Minnesota militia – hence the title "General." Sanford represented the United States at international conferences in Berlin in 1885 and in Brussels in 1890. Late in life he was the founder and promoter of the city of Sanford, Florida, where his papers are preserved in the Sanford Memorial Library (see the account of his life in the *Dictionary of American Biography* [1928 ff.]).

7. Stanley, *The Congo*, 1:21.

8. Emory Ross, *Out of Africa* (New York: Friendship Press, 1936), p. 8; Farwell, *Man Who Presumed*, pp. 85–6.

9. Although the Comité d'Etudes du Haut Congo was nominally separate and distinct from the International Association, for all practical purposes it shortly became no more than an extension of the association.

10. Jesse Siddall Reeves, *The International Beginnings of the Congo Free State*, Johns Hopkins University Studies in Historical and Political Science, ser. 12, XI–XII (Baltimore: Johns Hopkins University, 1894), p. 18.

11. Count Savorgnan de Brazza, the French explorer and empire builder, seems to have shared this suspicion. See Albert Maurice, ed., *H. M. Stanley: Unpublished Letters* (New York: Philosophical Library, 1957), p. 149.

12. Roger Anstey, *Britain and the Congo in the Nineteenth Century* (Oxford: Oxford University Press [Clarendon Press], 1962), pp. 112–67; Sybil E. Crowe, *The Berlin West African Conference, 1884–1885* (London: Longmans, Green, 1942), pp. 11–22; H. R. Fox Bourne, *Civilization in Congoland: A Story of International Wrong-Doing* (London: P. S. King, 1903), pp. 158–9. Most of the writers who have discussed the Anglo-Portuguese treaty and the resulting Berlin conference seem to be intent upon proving that Great Britain was motivated solely by philanthropic and humanitarian purposes. Fox Bourne, for example, says that Great Britain insisted upon recognizing the interests acquired by the association and the trading rights of all nations, and that the treaty was "subject to its being approved by the other Powers." Nothing in the text of the treaty indicates any such reservations. Crowe's work is so biased that her statements and conclusions can be accepted only in part and with modifications.

13. Anstey, *Britain and the Congo*, pp. 113–38; Demetrius C. de K. Boulger, *The Reign of Leopold II, King of the Belgians and Founder of the Congo State, 1865–1909*, 2 vols. (London: Ardenne, 1925), 1:146.

14. Quoted in Anstey, *Britain and the Congo*, p. 169.

15. Department of State, *Papers Relating to the Foreign Relations of the United States, 1883* (Washington, D.C.: GPO, 1886), p. ix.

16. Senate, "Report of the Secretary of State Relative to Affairs of the Independent State of the Congo," *Senate Executive Documents*, 49th Cong., 1st sess., 1886, no. 196, p. 348.

Chapter 12. Neutrality and philanthropy

1. Senate, "Report of the Secretary of State Relative to Affairs of the Independent State of the Congo," *Senate Executive Documents*, 49th Cong., 1st sess., 1886, no. 196, p. 7. To infer or assume, as some writers have done, that Bismarck was a cat's-paw for Leopold or that the conference resulted from conniving by Henry Shelton Sanford is to ascribe to Bismarck a weakness that has never been detected, even by his enemies. For reasons of his own, Bismarck saw advantages for Germany in such a conference.

2. *U.S. Congressional Directory*, 48th Cong., 1st sess., 1884, pp. 27–8. Kasson's record proves that there is little justification for Sybil Crowe's statement that he was "distinguished more by verbosity than by brains" or for the idea that he was merely a puppet in the hands of

Sanford. See Sybil E. Crowe, *The Berlin West African Conference, 1884–1885* (New York: Longmans, Green, 1942), p. 97. See also Edward Younger, *John A. Kasson: Politics and Diplomacy from Lincoln to McKinley* (Iowa City, Iowa: 1955), pp. 141–52, 210–28, 278–95, 322–43.

3. Senate, "Report of the Secretary of State Relative to . . . the Congo," pp. 16–17.

4. Ibid., pp. 19–20. Many – possibly all – of the charges and allegations of deception, double dealing, and general villainy laid against Sanford and Stanley seem to have originated with Tisdale. There was an obvious clash of personalities from the start, especially since Tisdale, who maintained that he knew as much about Africa as Stanley did, disagreed with Stanley's conclusions on the economic potential of the Congo. This disagreement did not come out until later, for Tisdale left Berlin without attending any of the sessions of the conference (see ibid., pp. 21, 346–87).

5. Ibid., p. 34.

6. Ibid., p. 42.

7. Stanley died in London in 1904. He wanted to be buried in Westminster Abbey next to Livingstone, but the dean of the abbey refused; Stanley's achievements, the dean felt, did not warrant such national recognition.

8. Quoted in Perry Belmont, *An American Democrat: The Recollections of Perry Belmont,* 2d ed. (New York: Columbia University Press, 1941), p. 314.

9. Ibid., p. 329.

10. Department of State, *Papers Relating to the Foreign Relations of the United States, 1886* (Washington, D.C.: GPO, 1865–1900), pp. viii–ix. This remark was interpreted by Kasson as an unwarranted reprimand. He replied in a lengthy article in the *North American Review* (February 1886) in which he refuted, point by point, all the arguments that had been adduced by Belmont and other traditionalists. For the full antitreaty argument, written by Belmont, see House of Representatives, *Participation of the United States in the Congo Conference: H. Rep. 2655,* 48th Cong., 2d sess., 1885. One may suspect an underlying element of partisanship: President Arthur's administration was Republican; Cleveland and Belmont were Democrats.

11. Department of the Navy, *Annual Report of the Secretary of the Navy for the Fiscal Year Ending June 30, 1880* (Washington, D.C.: GPO, 1880), p. 27.

12. See Shufeldt's reports to the secretary of the navy – May 21, June 3, June 19, June 20, 1879 – in the Robert W. Shufeldt Papers, 1864–1884, Naval Historical Foundation Collection, Library of Congress. See also "The Congo Commission," *Bradstreet's* 10 (1884):146.

13. James P. White, "The Sanford Exploring Expedition," *Journal of African History* 7 (1967):291–302.

14. Ruth M. Slade, *English-speaking Missions in the Congo Independent State (1878–1908)* (Brussels: Académie Royale des Sciences Coloniales, 1959), pp. 32–77.

15. Shortly after taking over, the American Baptists closed one remote station and turned another over to a Swedish missionary organization. A few years later still another detached station, at Balenge on the equator seven hundred miles from the mouth of the Congo, was turned over to a Disciples of Christ mission from the United States.

16. William H. Sheppard, *Pioneers in Congo* (Louisville, Ky.: Pentecostal Publishing Co., n.d.), pp. 11–15.

17. Ibid., pp. 91–157; Johannes Du Plessis, *The Evangelisation of Pagan Africa* (Cape Town: J. C. Juta, 1930), pp. 216–21.

18. Mohun to the State Department, December 23, 1892, quoted in C. T. Brady, *Commerce and Conquest in East Africa* (Salem, Mass.: Essex Institute, 1950), pp. 200–1.

19. The Richard Dorsey Mohun Papers, National Archives, Washington, D.C. See also Richard Dorsey Mohun, "The Death of Emin Pasha," *Century Magazine,* no. 49, 1894–5, pp. 591–8.

20. Mohun Papers, passim; Brady, *Commerce and Conquest,* pp. 113, 209–10; Isaac F.

Marcosson, *An African Adventure* (New York: Lane, 1921), pp. 245–6; Demetrius C. de K. Boulger, *The Congo State; or, The Growth of Civilization in Central Africa* (London: W. Thacker, 1898), pp. 316–17. Leopold made Mohun a chevalier of the Royal Order of the Lion of the Congo for his services in the Arab war, an honor that he accepted subject to the approval of his own government.

Chapter 13. Traders and soldiers of misfortune

1. F. B. Pearce, *Zanzibar, the Island Metropolis of Eastern Africa* (London: Unwin, 1920), pp. 133–4.
2. R. O. Hume, "Letter to the American Board, July 3, 1839," *Missionary Herald* 36 (1840):60; Hermann Frederick Eilts, "Ahman bin Na'aman's Mission to the United States in 1840: The Voyage of Al-Sultanah to New York City," *Essex Institute Historical Collections* 98 (1962):219–77.
3. The decline is evident in the shipping statistics. In 1859 American shipping entering Zanzibar amounted to 10,890 tons – more than the combined tonnage of all other countries – and in 1866, before the postwar recovery began, it was only 2,515 tons. See Reginal Coupland, *The Exploitation of East Africa, 1856–1890* (London, 1939), pp. 78–9.
4. Robert S. Rantoul, "The Port of Salem," *Essex Institute Historical Collections* 10 (1869):72; see also Norman Robert Bennett, "Americans in Zanzibar, 1865–1915," *Essex Institute Historical Collections* 98 (1962):36.
5. Ernest O. Moore, *Ivory, Scourge of Africa* (New York: Harper, 1931), pp. 116–17.
6. C. T. Brady, *Commerce and Conquest in East Africa* (Salem, Mass.: Essex Institute, 1950), p. 113; National Archives to the authors, January 31, 1964.
7. Bennett, "Americans in Zanzibar, 1865–1915," p. 37.
8. Ibid., p. 38.
9. Department of State, *Papers Relating to the Foreign Relations of the United States, 1872–1873* (Washington, D.C.: GPO, 1865–1900), pp. 208–10.
10. Ibid., pp. 210–11.
11. Ibid., pp. 214–15.
12. Quoted in Coupland, *Exploitation of East Africa*, p. 193.
13. Bennett, "Americans in Zanzibar, 1865–1915," pp. 41–4.
14. Ibid., pp. 45–7.
15. Quoted in ibid., p. 59.
16. William B. Hesseltine and Hazel C. Wolf, *The Blue and the Gray on the Nile* (Chicago: University of Chicago Press, 1961), p. 2. Although the U.S. government officially had nothing to do with the presence of the Americans in Egypt, General Sherman was deeply interested and gave his personal recommendation to many of them, Confederate as well as Union. The Americans in Ismail's service were not the first of their nationality to wear the uniform of an Egyptian ruler's army. In 1820 and 1821 George Bethune English of Massachusetts, graduate of Harvard and former officer of the U.S. Marine Corps, was chief of artillery in an Egyptian expedition dispatched by Mohammed Ali to destroy the remnants of the Mamelukes and bring the upper valley of the Nile into subjection. English held the rank of general officer in the Egyptian forces and had among his soldiers two Americans who had apostatized and become Moslems – as, indeed, English himself had done, at least outwardly. See George Bethune English, *A Narrative of the Expedition to Dongola and Sennar under the Command of His Excellence Ismael Pasha, Undertaken by Order of His Highness Mehemmed Ali Pasha, Viceroy of Egypt* (Boston, 1823), pp. 15–16, 158; and Walter L. Wright, Jr., "George Bethune English," *Dictionary of American Biography* (1931). English did not consider himself an explorer, yet his description of much of the country through which the army moved was the first modern eyewitness account by an American or European. One of the American

soldiers, identified only by his assumed name of Khalil Aga, was reported by English to be the first person to travel the entire length of the Nile from Rosetta to Sennar.

17. Edward Dicey, in *The Story of the Khedivate* (New York: Scribner, 1902), p. 257, erroneously credits Stone with having been "an officer of distinction in the Confederate army." Other writers have supposed that several of these Americans were Englishmen.

18. George Birkbeck Hill, ed., *Colonel Gordon in Central Africa, 1874–1879*, 2d ed. (London, 1884), p. 205.

19. Thomas D. Johnson, "The Egyptian Campaign in Abyssinia, from the Notes of a Staff Officer," *Blackwoods' Edinburgh Magazine* 122 (1877):26–39.

20. Pierre Crabitès, *Americans in the Egyptian Army* (London: Routledge, 1938), p. 20.

21. William Wing Loring, *A Confederate Soldier in Egypt* (New York, 1884), p. 298.

22. See Crabitès, *Americans in the Egyptian Army*, pp. 64–90; and Hesseltine and Wolf, *The Blue and the Gray*, pp. 120–48.

Raleigh Colston's *Rapport sur les régions centrales et nordiques du Kordofàn* was published in 1875 and Henry G. Prout's *General Report on the Province of Kordofan* in 1877, both at Cairo. Colston, a brigadier general in the Confederate army during the war, was primarily an educator, having been a professor at the Virginia Military Institute (VMI). He had come to Egypt to organize an Egyptian military academy along lines similar to those of West Point and VMI, but he was instead given the role of field geologist, botanist, and explorer. The Colston Papers are at the University of North Carolina Library, which also has the papers of other Americans who served in Egypt.

23. Crabitès, *Americans in the Egyptian Army*, pp. 214–27. Oscar Eugene Fechet's *Journal of the March of an Expedition in Nubia between Assouan and Abouhamed . . . 1873* was published in Cairo in 1878. Alexander McComb Mason's *Report on a Reconnaissance of Lake Albert* was published in 1878 as vol. 22 of the *Proceedings of the Royal Geographical Society, London*. Mason was a descendant of a signer of the Declaration of Independence and was closely related to several men distinguished in the affairs of the United States, particularly in the armed forces.

24. Charles Chaillé-Long, *My Life in Four Continents*, 2 vols. (London: Hutchinson, 1912), 1:65–7. There was some opposition by British officials in Egypt to Chaillé-Long's initial appointment on the grounds that such a position should be held by an Englishman, but Gordon himself insisted upon an American. (The hyphen that Chaillé-Long habitually inserted in his name has led some writers to assume that he *was* an Englishman.)

25. Quoted in Hill, *Colonel Gordon*, pp. 54–5; see also Chaillé-Long, *My Life in Four Continents*, 1:90–111.

26. Chaillé-Long, *My Life in Four Continents*, pp. 146–7.

27. Ibid., pp. 173–95.

28. Chaillé-Long's achievements in Africa remained unrecognized until recent years, perhaps because of his egotism, arrogance, and belligerence. The Chaillé-Long Papers, held by the Library of Congress, provide further details of his career.

29. See Thomas Stevens, *Scouting for Stanley in East Africa* (New York, 1890), pp. 210–71; and Stevens, *Africa as Seen by Thomas Stevens and the Hawk-Eye* (Boston, 1890), passim (the Hawk-Eye was a camera). See also Henry M. Stanley, *In Darkest Africa; or, The Quest, Rescue, and Retreat of Emin, Governor of Equatoria*, 2 vols. (New York, Scribner, 1890), 2:410.

30. Arthur Donaldson Smith, *Through Unknown African Countries: The First Expedition from Somaliland to Lake Lamu* (London, 1897), p. 1.

31. Ibid., pp. 368–74.

32. Shufeldt refers to the queen and her government as *Hovas*, a term now taken to mean the middle class rather than a tribal designation.

33. See Mason A. Shufeldt, "To, about, and across Madagascar," parts 1–5, *United*

Service 12 (January–June 1885):1, 506, 691; 13 (July–December 1885):79, 203. It is not certain whether Shufeldt's expedition was the first crossing of Madagascar by a white man. References to the area are difficult to find. James Sibree, who was a missionary there for more than half a century, says in *Fifty Years in Madagascar: Personal Experience of Mission Life and Work* (London: Allen & Unwin, 1924), p. 64, that in the early times of his missionary work in the 1860s the interior was "unexplored and unknown."

Chapter 14. Miners and adventurers

1. Quoted in James Gray, *Payable Gold: An Intimate Record of the History of the Discovery of the Payable Witwatersrand Goldfields and of Johannesburg in 1886 and 1887* ([Johannesburg]): Central News Agency, 1937), pp. 17–18.

2. Alpheus F. Williams, *Some Dreams Come True: Being a Sheaf of Stories Leading up to the Discovery of Copper, Diamonds and Gold in Southern Africa, and of the Pioneers Who Took Part in the Excitement of Those Early Days* (Cape Town: H. B. Timmins, 1948), pp. 57–71.

3. John Angove, *In the Early Days: The Reminiscences of Pioneer Life on the South African Diamond Fields* (Kimberley: Handel House, 1910), pp. 9–10. Angove does not identify this Irishman.

4. Jerome L. Babe, *The South African Diamond Fields* (New York, 1872), pp. 27, 32, 56, 105. The inference in Eric Rosenthal, *Stars and Stripes in Africa* (London: Routledge, 1938), pp. 206, 208, that Babe was associated with Thomas Baines and others in opening the Mashonaland gold fields is not substantiated by Babe's account. He seems to have been in the diamond fields for only about five months and then to have returned to the United States.

5. In a letter he wrote to a friend on October 3, 1886, J. X. Merriman said, "Your picture of the old Californian panning gold on your stoop is idyllic." See Phyllis Lewsen, ed., *Selections from the Correspondence of J. X. Merriman, 1870–1890* (Cape Town: Van Riebeeck Society, 1960), p. 220.

6. See John Hays Hammond, *Autobiography*, 2 vols. (New York: Farrar & Rinehart, 1935), vol. 1.

7. Patrick Manning, "A Draft: Notes toward a History of American Technical Assistance in Southern Africa, from 1870–1950" (mimeograph, California Institute of Technology, 1963), pp. 10–11. Woodford was one of the few Americans in South Africa who sided with the Boers during their war with Great Britain. He held a commission from President Steyn of the Orange Free State to enlist American support, though he failed to get that support.

8. For other names and a more detailed treatment, see ibid., pp. 4–18.

9. See Thomas T. Read, "Hamilton Smith," *Dictionary of American Biography* (1935).

10. Industrial Commission of Enquiry, *Evidence and Report of the Industrial Commission of Enquiry* (Johannesburg, 1897). Several other Americans also testified before the commission.

11. Williams, *Some Dreams Come True*, pp. 217–38. See also Thomas T. Read, "Gardner Williams," *Dictionary of American Biography* (1936); Gardner F. Williams, "The Genesis of the Diamond," in *Annual Report of the Board of Regents of the Smithsonian Institute . . . 1905* (Washington, D.C.: The Institution, 1906); Williams, *The Diamond Mines of South Africa: Some Account of Their Rise and Development* (New York: Macmillan, 1902).

12. Hammond, *Autobiography*, 1:85–6.

13. John Hays Hammond, *The Truth about the Jameson Raid* (Boston: Marshall Jones, 1918), pp. 2–4.

14. Ibid., pp. 13–31; Hammond, *Autobiography*, 1:325–7. See also his wife's account – Natalie Hammond, *A Woman's Part in a Revolution* (London: 1897), passim – and "John Hays Hammond," *National Cyclopaedia of American Biography* (1901).

15. For a recent summary of the American technological and scientific impact on South

Africa during this period see *Lantern: Journal of Knowledge and Culture* (published by the Foundation for Education, Science and Technology in Pretoria, South Africa), special ed., June 1983, especially pp. 75–116.

16. Hammond, *Autobiography*, 1:242; see also L. Sprague de Camp and Catherine C. de Camp, *Ancient Ruins and Archaeology* (Garden City, N.Y.: Doubleday, 1964), p. 118.

17. Guillermo Antonio Farini, *Through the Kalahari Desert: A Narrative of a Journey with Gun, Camera, and Note-book to Lake N'Gami and Back* (London, 1886). Most authorities on the Kalahari are convinced of the actual existence of the prehistoric city he claimed to have discovered. Several recent attempts have been made to locate it, but without success. See Fay Goldie, *Lost City of the Kalahari: The Farini Story and Reports on Other Expeditions* (Cape Town: Balkema, 1963).

18. Ian D. Colvin, *The Life of Jameson* (London, 1923), 1:121–5. See also Frank W. F. Johnson, *Great Days: The Autobiography of an Empire Pioneer* (London: Bell, 1940).

19. Heany is called a West Pointer in Reginald Ivan Lovell, *The Struggle for South Africa, 1875–1899: A Study in Economic Imperialism* (New York: Macmillan, 1934), pp. 332–3, but he never attended the U.S Military Academy. Further, the authors have been informed by the adjutant general, Washington, D.C., that there is no record of Heany's ever having served in the U.S. Army. For additional information on Heany, see William Harvey Brown, *On the South Africa Frontier: The Adventures and Observations of an American in Mashonaland and Matabeleland* (New York, 1899), p. 67; and A. S. Hickman, *Men Who Made Rhodesia: A Register of Those Who Served in the British South Africa Company's Police* (Salisbury: British South Africa Company, 1960), pp. 30–1.

20. See the Heany File in the Southern Rhodesia Archives, Salisbury; and Colvin, *Life of Jameson*, 2:51–4, 60, 67, 92–3, 118, 162.

21. Brown, *On the South Africa Frontier*, pp. 44–9. It is interesting to note that enlistment in the Pioneer Corps was a private contract. The corps was a modern revival of an ancient practice, the private army.

22. Frederick Russell Burnham, *Scouting on Two Continents* (Garden City, N.Y.: Doubleday, Page, 1928); Burnham, *Taking Chances* (Los Angeles: Haynes Corporation, 1944); Burnham, "Remarks," *Annual Publications of the Historical Society of Southern California* 13, no. 4 (1927):334–52. See also Hammond, *Autobiography*, 1:251–3; Robert S. S. Baden-Powell, *The Matabele Campaign: Being a Narrative of the Campaign in Suppressing the Native Rising in Matabeleland and Mashonaland, 1896*, 4th ed. (London: Methuen, 1901), pp. 70–1, 81–2.

23. Hammond, *Autobiography*, 1:273–4. Burnham, in his published writings, makes no mention at all of his exploration of the copper areas.

24. Cf. Julian Ralph, *An American with Lord Roberts* (New York: Stokes, 1901).

25. John Frederick Maurice, *History of the War in South Africa, 1899–1902*, 4 vols. (London: Hurst & Blackett, 1907), 2:49–50. This is the British official history of the war. See also Louis Creswicke, *South Africa and the Transvaal War*, 7 vols. (Edinburgh: T. C. & E. Jack, n.d.), 4:21; and Lewis Michell, *The Life of the Rt. Hon. Cecil John Rhodes, 1853–1902*, 2 vols. (London: Arnold, 1910), 2:271–2. According to Michell, Labram's gun was a surprise to the Boers, who retaliated by hauling a six-inch Creusot gun nicknamed "Long Tom" into position to shell Kimberley. Other writers have stated that Long Cecil was built as a reply to Long Tom – a more probable version. Labram was killed on February 9, 1900, by a hundred-pound shell from the Boer gun.

26. John Y. Fillmore Blake, *A West Pointer with the Boers: Personal Narrative of Col. J. Y. F. Blake, Commander of the Irish Brigade* (Boston: Angel Guardian Press, 1903); Michael Davitt, *The Boers' Fight for Freedom, from the Beginning of Hostilities to the Peace of Pretoria* (New York, 1902), pp. 318–27; Charles D. Pierce, *The South African Republics: Souvenir Published for and in Behalf of the Boer Relief Fund* (New York, 1900), pp. 30–1.

Blake graduated from West Point in the class of 1880 and spent several years on the frontier as an officer of the U.S. Sixth Cavalry. Upon resigning from the service he went into the railroad business and wound up in South Africa, where he sympathized with the desire of the Boers to preserve their independence from British rule. After the war he returned to the United States; he died in 1907 at the age of fifty-one.

The term "brigade," as used in the Boer forces, bears no reference to a brigade in other armies; Blake's "Irish Brigade" was actually a commando force of about two hundred men.

27. Davitt, *Boer's Fight for Freedom,* p. 325; *New York Evening Post,* quoted by Pierce, *South African Republics,* p. 37.

28. Davitt, *Boers' Fight for Freedom,* p. 327; Pierce, *South African Republics,* p. 22.

29. Henry Houghton Beck, *History of South Africa and the Boer-British War* (Philadelphia: Globe Bible Publishing Co., 1900), pp. 430–1. It should be noted that the SS *Maine* was a converted merchant ship and was unconnected in any way with the USS *Maine,* destroyed in Havana harbor.

30. Rees Alfred Davis, *Citrus-Growing in South Africa: Oranges, Lemons, Naartjes, etc.* (Pretoria: Government Printing Press, 1919); Davis, *Citrus-Growing in South Africa* (Cape Town: Specialty Press, 1924); Davis, *Fruit-Growing in South Africa* (Johannesburg: Central News Agency, 1928). Davis uses many illustrations and examples of California orchards and fruit processing.

31. The Farrell Shipping Lines of Boston (about which see the end of Chapter 17) pioneered the sale of South African fruit in the United States.

32. Frank Clements and Edward Harben, *Leaf of Gold: The Story of Rhodesian Tobacco* (London: Methuen, 1962), pp. 50–3.

Chapter 15. Capitalists and missionaries

1. Department of State, *Papers Relating to the Foreign Relations of the United States, 1890* (Washington: D.C.: GPO, 1865–1900), p. viii.

2. J. Scott Keltie, "British Interests in Africa," *Contemporary Review* 54 (1888):121–2.

3. Malcolm McIlwraith, "The Delagoa Bay Arbitration," *Fortnightly Review* 74 (1900):413–16, 421–3. See also Philip R. Warhurst, *Anglo-Portuguese Relations in South-Central Africa, 1890–1900* (London, 1962), pp. 113–14.

4. Johannes Du Plessis, *A History of Christian Missions in South Africa* (London: Longmans, Green, 1911), pp. 303–6. The board was originally an interdenominational organization, but it soon became – as it remains today – exclusively an agency of the Congregational Church.

For the part played by black Americans in missionary ventures and for their views concerning the partition of Africa see Sylvia M. Jacobs, *The African Nexus: Black American Perspectives on the European Partitioning of Africa, 1880–1920* (Westport, Conn.: Greenwood Press, 1981).

For the links between black American education and missionary education in Africa see Kenneth James King, *Pan-Africanism and Education: A Study of Race, Philanthropy and Education in the Southern States of America and East Africa* (Oxford: Oxford University Press [Clarendon Press], 1971).

5. James B. McCord with John S. Douglas, *My Patients Were Zulus* (London: Mueller, 1951), pp. 41–5. Bridgeman and his successors were handicapped by well-meant opposition from a fellow ABCFM missionary, a man of dynamic personality who believed in faith healing and succeeded in convincing not only Africans but some missionaries that disease was a punishment for sin and that taking medicine was a sin in itself.

6. Du Plessis, *A History of Christian Missions,* p. 306.

7. See Levi Jenkins Coppin, *Observations of Persons and Things in South Africa, 1900–1904* (Philadelphia: A.M.E. Book Concern, [1905?]).

8. Department of State, *Foreign Relations, 1884*, pp. 637–40; ibid., *1885* (18), pp. 646–7. See also Eduardo Moreira, *Portuguese East Africa: A Study of Its Religious Needs* (London: World Dominion Press, 1936), pp. 20–1.

9. The Free Methodist Church should not be confused with the African Methodist Episcopal Church or with the Methodist Episcopal Church. The last-named is the denomination usually referred to simply as Methodist, a usage that is followed here.

10. Moreira, *Portuguese East Africa*, pp. 21–2, 81; Erwin H. Richards, "Notes from Inhambane, East Africa," in *The Gospel in All Lands* (New York, 1898), p. 415.

11. Du Plessis, *A History of Christian Missions*, p. 307.

12. *Missionary Herald* 89 (1893):25–6, 304.

13. Ibid. 89 (1893):410.

14. Ibid. 91 (1895):190.

15. Ibid.

16. Ibid., pp. 240–1. He reported that in 1894 he responded to no less than 590 professional calls, many of them at a considerable distance.

17. Charles Pelham Groves, *The Planting of Christianity in Africa*, 4 vols. (London: Butterworth, 1948–58), 3:102.

18. Ibid., p. 103.

19. The ABCFM received nearly thirty-one thousand acres, the Methodists about ten thousand acres, and the Brethren in Christ a little over three thousand. See Per S. Hassing, "The Christian Missions and the British Expansion in Southern Rhodesia, 1888–1923" (Ph.D. diss., American University, 1960), p. 234.

20. See Dr. W. J. van der Merwe to Per Schioldberg Hassing, August 30, 1958, in ibid., p. 237.

21. See Robert I. Rotberg, ed., *Strike a Blow and Die: A Narrative of Race Relations in Colonial Africa by George Simeon Mwase* (Cambridge, Mass.: Harvard University Press, 1967). For the definitive work on the rebellion, see George Shepperson and Thomas Price, *Independent African: John Chilembwe and the Origins, Setting, and Significance of the Nyasaland Native Rising of 1915* (Edinburgh: Edinburgh University Press, 1958). Chilembwe and the rebellion of 1915 are discussed in more detail in Chapter 18.

22. James Duffy, *Portuguese Africa* (Cambridge, Mass.: Harvard University Press, 1959), p. 124; Kenneth Scott Latourette, *The Great Century in the Americas, Australia, and Africa, A.D. 1800–A.D. 1914: A History of the Expansion of Christianity*, 5 vols. (New York: Harper, 1943), 5:399.

23. Department of State, *Foreign Affairs, 1884*, pp. 634–6; ibid., *1885*, pp. 631–4, 641, 643–8.

24. Taylor was an enthusiast, a natural evangelist, who had been a street-corner preacher in San Francisco and had spent several years on leave of absence from his conference as a voluntary missionary in Canada and Australia in the 1850s and 1860s. The illness of his son led him to the climate of South Africa, and his attention focused on the missionary needs of the continent. He felt that his sojourn in Africa because of his child's illness was a call from God to evangelical service in that region. See William Taylor, *Christian Adventures in South Africa* (New York, 1879), pp. 1–11.

25. Quoted in Héli Chatelaine, "Bishop Taylor's Missions in Angola," in *The Gospel in All Lands* (1888), pp. 216–18. See also Johannes Du Plessis, *The Evangelisation of Pagan Africa* (Cape Town: J. C. Juta, 1930), pp. 232–3.

26. Du Plessis, *Evangelisation of Pagan Africa*, pp. 234–5.

27. Quoted in Chatelaine, "Bishop Turner's Missions," p. 219.

28. Du Plessis, *Evangelisation of Pagan Africa*, p. 233. See also Taylor's statement in *The Gospel in All Lands* (1889), pp. 478–9.

29. James Bertin Webster, *The African Church and the Yoruba, 1888–1922* (Oxford:

Oxford University Press [Clarendon Press], 1964); see also A. I. Asiwaju, *Western Yoruba-land under European Rule, 1889–1945* (Atlantic Highlands, N.J.: Humanities Press, 1976), p. 216, especially for the social consequences of Christianity.

30. Edwin S. Redkey, "The Meaning of Africa to Afro-Americans, 1890–1914," *Black Academy Review*, 3, nos. 1–2 (1972):16–17.

31. Quoted in ibid., p. 17.

32. See John W. E. Bowen, ed., *Africa and the American Negro: Addresses and Proceedings of the Congress on Africa* (Atlanta: Gammon Theological Seminary, 1896), for speeches at the conference.

33. The definitive study for back-to-Africa movements for the period is Edwin S. Redkey, *Black Exodus: Black Nationalists and Back to Africa Movements, 1890–1910* (New Haven, Conn.: Yale University Press, 1969).

34. Ibid., p. 11.

35. Quoted in ibid., p. 13.

36. Quoted in ibid., p. 32.

37. For Du Bois's views, see for instance William Edward Burghardt DuBois, *Dusk of Dawn; An Essay toward an Autobiography of a Race Concept* (New York: Schocken Books, 1968), and his *The World and Africa: An Inquiry into the Part Which Africa Has Played in World History* (1947; reprint, Millwood, N.Y.: Kraus Reprint Co., 1965).

Chapter 16. Official America

1. Sir Harry Johnston, *The Story of My Life* (London: Chatto & Windus, 1923), pp. 377, 383–9.

2. Joseph Bucklin Bishop, *Theodore Roosevelt and His Time, Shown in His Own Letters*, 2 vols. (New York: Scribner, 1920), 1:467–505. See also Alfred L. Dennis, *Adventures in American Diplomacy, 1896–1906* (New York: Dutton, 1928), pp. 485–517.

3. George West Van Siclen, *American Sentiment: A Plebiscite upon the Boer War* (New York, 1900).

4. *Outlook* 68 (May–October 1901):8–9.

5. See ibid.; see also *North American* 171 (1900):135–44. These are illustrative examples; they by no means exhaust the evidence of pro-Boer sympathy.

6. Frank Schell Ballentine, "A Visit to the Boers in Bermuda," *Outlook* 69 (September–December 1901):633–7. Edward Everett Hale was president of a society that sent numerous packages of comforts for the Boers in Bermuda. See p. 849 of the same volume of *Outlook*.

7. Department of State, *Papers Relating to the Foreign Relations of the United States, 1902* (Washington, D.C.: GPO, 1865–1900), pp. 469–70. The correspondent did not state why Versluis was in danger of execution, but apparently the fear was based upon rumors of the barbarity of the British. A drumhead court-martial is a device completely unknown in British and American military law.

8. Ibid., pp. 477–8, 482.

9. Ibid., pp. 485–6.

10. Presidents McKinley and Roosevelt were determined not to risk their newfound friendship with Great Britain; they remained neutral. Roosevelt at least thought the world balance of power was better served if Britain dominated South Africa. For a detailed assessment, see Frederick W. Marks, *The Diplomacy of Theodore Roosevelt* (Lincoln: University of Nebraska Press, 1979).

11. Marie D. Gorgas and Burton J. Hendrick, *William Crawford Gorgas – His Life and Work* (Garden City, N.Y.: Garden City Publication Co., 1924), pp. 264–99.

12. René Lemarchand, *Political Awakening in the Belgian Congo* (Berkeley: University of California Press, 1964), pp. 33–4.

13. Robert Howard Russell, "Glave's Career," *Century Magazine* 28, no. 50 (1895):865–8. Glave's journal and records of his journey and adventures were published posthumously by the magazine.

14. "Cruelty in the Congo Free State. Concluding Extracts from the Journals of the Late E. J. Glave," *Century Magazine* 32, no. 54 (1897):699.

15. Ibid., pp. 705–6.

16. Ibid.

17. Edmund Dene Morel, *Affairs of West Africa* (London: Heinemann, 1902), pp. 327–42; Morel, *King Leopold's Rule in Africa* (London: Heinemann, 1904); Morel, *Red Rubber: The Story of the Rubber Slave Trade Which Flourished on the Congo for Twenty Years, 1890–1910*, rev. ed. (Manchester, 1920). Morel's objectivity suffers from the fact that he was emotionally an almost professional sympathizer with the underdog. This tendency led him frequently to accept at face value, without corroborating evidence, the most lurid reports.

18. Frederick Starr, *The Truth about the Congo* (Chicago: Forbes, 1907). See also L. H. Gann and Peter Duignan, *The Rulers of Belgian Africa, 1884–1914* (Princeton, N.J.: Princeton University Press, 1979).

19. Edgar Wallace, *People: The Autobiography of a Mystery Writer* (Garden City, N.Y.: Doubleday, 1929), pp. 189–95.

20. Henry Wellington Wack, *The Story of the Congo Free State: Social, Political, and Economic Aspects of the Belgian System of Government in Central Africa* (New York: Putnam, 1905), p. 16.

21. Senate, "Memorial concerning Conditions in the Independent State of the Congo," *Senate Executive Documents*, 58th Cong., 2d sess., 1904, no. 282.

22. *The Letters of Theodore Roosevelt*, ed. Eltinge Morison, 8 vols. (Cambridge, Mass.: Harvard University Press, 1951), 4:958, 5:439.

23. There were rumors that the British government was planning to send gunboats to Monrovia. The rumor was unfounded, but Liberians had not forgotten that on a previous occasion British gunboats had suddenly appeared at Monrovia and their country had suffered territorial losses as a result. Cf. Nathaniel R. Richardson, *Liberia's Past and Present* (London: Diplomatic Press, 1959), p. 116.

24. Johnston, *The Story of My Life*, pp. 383–4.

25. Department of State, *Foreign Relations, 1910*, pp. 694–5. See also Richardson, *Liberia's Past and Present*, pp. 123–4.

26. Department of State, *Foreign Relations, 1910*, pp. 699–707.

27. Senate, "Affairs in Liberia," *Senate Executive Documents*, 61st Cong., 2d sess., 1909, no. 457, pp. 14–19. This is the commission's official report to the president of the United States.

28. Department of State, *Foreign Relations, 1911*, pp. 342–7. Clark, a native of New Hampshire, had served as secretary to Senator Burnham of his state and also had been a clerk of various committees of the U.S. Senate. He held a law degree and had been admitted to the bar, but apparently had never practiced law as a profession. Before entering politics he had been a professor of modern languages at George Washington University.

29. Ibid., *1912*, pp. xxi, 664–7.

30. Ibid., p. 667.

31. Ibid., *1913*, pp. 681–2.

32. Ibid., *1912*, p. 672.

33. Ibid., pp. 674–5, 683–4, 688–90.

34. Ibid., pp. 697–700.

35. Ibid., pp. 654–62.

36. Ibid., p. 665. See also Judson M. Lyon, "Informal Imperialism: The United States in

Liberia," *Diplomatic History,* 5, no. 3 (1981): 22–243. The author interprets U.S.–Liberian relations as a neocolonial relationship.

37. Department of State, *Foreign Relations, 1914,* pp. 440–2.

38. For details, see Ronald W. Davis, "The Liberian Struggle for Authority on the Kru Coast," *International Journal of African Historical Studies* 8, no. 2 (1975):222–65, which indicates the way Liberians were able to use British – and, to a lesser extent, American – influence to preserve their authority.

39. Department of State, *Foreign Relations, 1915,* pp. 626–35. It is not clear whether or not landing parties from the *Chester* took part in the fighting. The rebels charged that they did – an assertion that Bundy, the American chargé d'affaires, denied.

40. See I. K. Sundiata, *Black Scandal: America and the Liberian Labor Crisis, 1929–1936* (Philadelphia: Institute for the Study of Human Issues, 1980).

41. A Liberian writer, A. Doris Banks Henries, remarks (in *The Liberian Nation: A Short History* [New York: St. Martin's Press, 1966], p. 120) that this was an expensive rejection for Liberia, but may have saved the country from further international humiliation.

42. Faulkner's letter, addressed to Sir Eric Drummond, secretary-general of the League of Nations, was published in full in the *New Republic* 130 (February 26, 1930):256.

43. Henries, *The Liberian Nation,* pp. 122–3.

44. James C. Young, *Liberia Rediscovered* (Garden City, N.Y.: Doubleday, 1934), pp. 73–4.

45. Raymond Leslie Buell, *The Native Problem in Africa,* 2 vols. (New York: Macmillan, 1928), 2:779–80.

46. Department of State, *Report of the International Commission of Inquiry into the Existence of Slavery and Forced Labor in the Republic of Liberia,* State Department Publication no. 147 (Washington, D.C.: GPO, 1931), pp. 4–5. See also Department of State, *Foreign Relations, 1929,* 3:274–5.

47. Department of State, *Foreign Relations, 1929,* 3:282.

48. Ibid., p. 278.

49. Department of State, *International Commission,* p. 5.

50. Ibid., pp. 134–5.

51. Ibid.

52. Raymond Leslie Buell, "The New Deal and Liberia," *New Republic* 74 (August 16, 1933):17–19.

53. Editorial, *New Republic* 70 (March 30, 1932):2.

54. Clarence Lorenzo Simpson, *Memoirs* (London: Diplomatic Press, 1961), pp. 198–9.

55. Richard B. Moore, "Africa Conscious Harlem," in *Black Brotherhood: Afro-Americans and Africa,* ed. Okon Edet Uya (Lexington, Mass.: Heath, 1971), p. 248.

56. See Edward H. McKinley, *The Lure of Africa: American Interests in Tropical Africa, 1919–1939* (Indianapolis: Bobbs-Merrill, 1974), pp. 92–102.

57. Ibid., p. 105.

58. Claude McKay, *A Long Way from Home* (New York: L. Furman, 1937), p. 7.

59. W. D. Hambly, *Source Book for African Anthropology,* 2 vols. (Chicago: Natural History Museum, 1937). See McKinley, *The Lure of Africa,* chap. 5.

60. Brice Harris, Jr., *The United States and the Italo-Ethiopian Crisis* (Stanford, Calif.: Stanford University Press, 1964). See also George W. Baer, *The Coming of the Italian-Ethiopian War* (Cambridge, Mass.: Harvard University Press, 1964); and Baer, *Test Case: Italy, Ethiopia, and the League of Nations* (Stanford, Calif.: Hoover Institution Press, 1976).

61. For an excellent study of the period as a whole, see Edward Harvey McKinley, "American Relations with Tropical Africa, 1919–1939" (Ph.D. diss., University of Wisconsin, 1971). On the role of Pan-Africanism in education, see Kenneth James King, *Pan-Africanism and Education: A Study of Race, Philanthropy and Education in the Southern States of*

America and East Africa (Oxford: Oxford University Press [Clarendon Press], 1971). For the impact of the Ethiopian war on Pan-African opinion throughout the world, see J. Ayodele Langley, *Pan-Africanism and Nationalism in West Africa, 1900–1945: A Study in Ideology and Social Class* (Oxford: Oxford University Press [Clarendon Press], 1973).

Chapter 17. Private interest groups

1. William Astor Chanler, *Through Jungle and Desert: Travels in Eastern Africa* (London, 1896), p. 1.

2. See Marius Maxwell, *Stalking Big Game with a Camera in Equatorial Africa, with a Monograph on the African Elephant* (New York: Century Co., 1924), pp. 183–4n. Writing only thirty years after Chanler's attempt at the Lorian Swamps, Maxwell remarked that the country Chanler and von Höhnel had found completely impenetrable was now easily entered, so much had Africa changed in a few years.

3. William Edgar Geil, *A Yankee in Pygmyland* (London: Hodden & Stoughton, 1905). Geil, visiting the Congo at the time when atrocities were supposed to be at their worst, made no mention of them.

4. See Theodore Roosevelt, *African Game Trails: An Account of the African Wanderings of an American Hunter-Naturalist* (London: Syndicate Publishing Co., 1910), for a full narrative of Roosevelt's African safari. The book immediately became a best seller in both the United States and Great Britain.

5. It was Akeley who first interested Roosevelt in a hunting trip to Africa, and they had conferred before either left the United States.

6. Carl E. Akeley, *In Brightest Africa* (Garden City, N.Y.: Doubleday, 1920), pp. 3–6. Akeley lists eight notable men (modestly omitting himself) who got their start in Ward's museum during the four years in which he himself was employed there, among them William M. Wheeler, E. N. Gueret, J. William Critchley, Henry L. Ward, and William T. Hornaday. He mentions that there was a "long list" of others who were not his contemporaries at Ward's. One wonders if the undergraduate students in Ward's classes at the University of Rochester (he was not much older than they themselves) knew that he had already fought Bedouins in the Sinai desert; penetrated the interior of unknown Africa (alone); almost died of the dread African fever; suppressed a mutiny, revolver in hand; and been marooned on an African beach. Few could have foreseen that at an age when most men retire from activity Ward still would have the vitality and spark to explore Patagonia, the deserts of Australia, and the Great Barrier Reef.

7. Ibid., p. 248.

8. Mary L. Jobe Akeley, *Congo Eden: A Comprehensive Portrayal of the Historical Background and Scientific Aspects of the Great Game Sanctuaries of the Belgian Congo, etc.* (London: Gollancz, 1951), p. ix. After Akeley's death, his second wife, Mary L. Jobe Akeley, continued and completed the work of the safari and later made several additional trips to Africa, becoming herself an acknowledged authority on Africa. Carl Akeley, in addition to being an artist, explorer, and scientist, was also an inventor. Dissatisfied with the photographs and motion pictures he obtained on his first trips to Africa, he developed an improved motion-picture camera for the purpose of taking animal pictures. His experiments in using concrete as a foundation for mounting specimens made him an authority on reinforced concrete, a capacity in which he was employed as a consultant by the U.S. government during World War I.

9. Mary Hastings Bradley, *On the Gorilla Trail* (New York: Appleton, 1922); Bradley, *Caravans and Cannibals* (New York: Appleton, 1926). See also Akeley, *In Brightest Africa*, p. 189; and Mary L. Jobe Akeley, *Carl Akeley's Africa* (New York: Dodd, Mead, 1930), p. 3.

10. James L. Clark, *Good Hunting: Fifty Years of Collecting and Preparing Habitat Groups for the American Museum* (Norman: University of Oklahoma Press, 1966), p. 151.

11. Paul J. Rainey, "The Royal Sport of Hounding Lions," *Outing Magazine* 59 (1911):131–52. See also George Fortiss, "Paul Rainey, Sportsman," *Outing Magazine* 58 (1911):746–9. Upon Rainey's death, his sister presented his Louisiana game preserve – over twenty-five thousand acres – to the Audubon Society as a wildlife refuge.

12. Guy H. Scull, "Lassoing Wild Animals in Africa," *Everybody's Mazagine* 23 (191):309–22, 526–38, 609–21. See also Theodore Roosevelt and Edmund Heller, *Life Histories of African Game Animals*, 2 vols. (New York: Appleton, 1914), 1:204, 209, 363, 383. Scull was Jones's manager and was an eyewitness to and active participant in the scenes he described.

13. Stewart Edward White, *African Camp Fires* (Garden City, N.Y.: Doubleday, Page, 1913); see also White, "In Back of Beyond," parts 1, 2, *Outing Magazine* 64 (1914): 65 (1914–15).

14. Robert P. Skinner, *Abyssinia To-day: An Account of the First Mission Sent by the American Government to the Court of the King of Kings (1903–1904)* (London: Longmans, Green, 1906), pp. 35–6.

15. See Roosevelt, *African Game Trails*, pp. 41, 104, 223, 225; Osa Johnson, *Four Years in Paradise* (Philadelphia: Lippincott, 1941), pp. 170–4; and Akeley, *Carl Akeley's Africa*, p. 35.

16. Nairobi Town Council, *The McMillan Memorial Library* (Nairobi: n.d.).

17. Osa Johnson, *I Married Adventure: The Lives and Adventures of Martin and Osa Johnson* (Garden City, N.Y.: Halcyon House, 1942), p. 190.

18. Martin Johnson, *Camera Trails in Africa* (New York: Century Co., 1924).

19. George Eastman, *Chronicles of an African Trip* (Rochester, N.Y.: privately printed, 1927), p. 15.

20. See Edward H. McKinley, *The Lure of Africa: American Interests in Tropical Africa, 1919–1939* (Indianapolis: Bobbs-Merrill, 1974), chap. 4.

21. Robert O. Collins, "Ivory Poaching in the Lado Enclave," *Uganda Journal* 24 (1960):220.

22. Ibid., pp. 224–6. Apparently Rogers was shot by one of his own men during the melee. It may or may not have been accidental. While dying, he specified that he did not want any religious services when buried, but services of a sort were conducted by his sole white companion, who seems to have been a renegade missionary.

23. Herbert Hoover, *Memoirs*, 2 vols. (New York: Macmillan, 1952), 2:83. See also Charles R. Whittlesey, *Government Control of Crude Rubber: The Stevenson Plan* (Princeton, N.J.: Princeton University Press, 1931), pp. 30–5. The driving force behind the Stevenson Plan seems to have been Winston Churchill, then secretary of state for the colonies.

24. Hoover, *Memoirs*, 2:82; Joseph Brandes, *Herbert Hoover and Economic Diplomacy: Department of Commerce Policy, 1921–1928* (Pittsburg: University of Pittsburg Press, 1962), pp. 84–128; Alfred Lief, *The Firestone Story: A History of the Firestone Tire and Rubber Company* (New York: Whittlesey House, 1951), pp. 144–5.

25. Lief, *The Firestone Story*, p. 151.

26. Ibid., pp. 137–8. See also Richard P. Strong, ed., *The African Republic of Liberia and the Belgian Congo, Based on Observations Made and Material Collected during the Harvard African Expedition, 1926–1927*, 2 vols. (Cambridge, Mass.: Harvard University Press, 1930), vol. 1.

27. *Outlook* 149 (August 1928):607.

28. Harvey O'Connor, *The Guggenheims: The Making of an American Dynasty* (New York: Covici, Friede, 1937), pp. 178–9.

29. Isaac F. Marcosson, *An African Adventure* (New York: Lane, 1921), pp. 264–7.

30. Bruce Fetter, *The Creation of Elisabethville, 1910–1940* (Stanford, Calif.: Hoover Institution Press, 1976), pp. 57–71.

31. The reader who is interested in the details of the financing arrangements is referred to

L. H. Gann, *A History of Northern Rhodesia: Early Days to 1953* (London: Chatto & Windus, 1964), pp. 204–7.

32. Kenneth Bradley, *Copper Venture: The Discovery and Development of Roan Antelope and Mufulira* (London: Mufulira Copper Mines, 1952), p. 95.

33. Ibid., p. 97.

34. H. Maclean Bate, *Report from the Rhodesians* (London: Melrose, 1953), pp. 140–1.

35. Robert Greenhalgh Albion, *Seaports South of Sahara: The Achievements of an American Steamship Service* (New York: Appleton-Century-Crofts, 1959), p. 65.

36. Ibid., p. 249.

37. Edward W. Chester, *Clash of Titans: Africa and U.S. Foreign Policy* (Maryknoll, N.Y.: Orbis Books, 1974), p. 57.

Chapter 18. Preachers and teachers in Africa

1. *Missionary Herald* 91 (1895):240–1.

2. James S. Dennis, *Centennial Survey of Foreign Missions: A Statistical Supplement to "Christian Missions and Social Progress," Being a Conspectus of the Achievements and Results of Evangelical Missions in All Lands at the Close of the Nineteenth Century* (New York: Revell, 1902), pp. 193–5.

3. Victor W. Macy, "A History of the Free Methodist Mission in Portuguese East Africa" (master's thesis, Biblical Seminary, New York, 1946), pp. 268–72.

4. Wilber Christian Harr, "The Negro as an American Protestant Missionary in Africa" (D.D. diss., University of Chicago Divinity School, 1945), pp. 53–5. See also Linton Wells, "Jungle Doctor," *Reader's Digest* 40 (May 1942):103–6.

5. Charles Pelham Groves, *The Planting of Christianity in Africa*, 4 vols. (London: Butterworth, 1948–58), 4:170; Alfred B. Stonelake, *Congo, Past and Present* (London: World Dominion Press, 1937), pp. 47, 118.

6. Stonelake, *Congo, Past and Present*, p. 118.

7. James B. McCord with John S. Douglas, *My Patients Were Zulus* (London, 1951).

8. Martin Flavin, *Black and White—from the Cape to the Congo* (New York: Harper, 1949), p. 233.

9. Charles W. Thomas, *Adventures and Observations on the West Coast of Africa and Its Islands* (New York: Derby & Jackson, 1860), pp. 139–40.

10. Department of State, *Papers Relating to the Foreign Relations of the United States, 1878–1879* (Washington, D.C.: GPO, 1865–1900), p. 524.

11. Ibid., *1885*, p. 648.

12. Dennis, *Centennial Survey*, pp. 69, 73, 84, 107–8, 115.

13. Adolphus C. Good, "The Church in Cameroun" (uncompleted manuscript in A. C. Good Papers, Hoover Institution, Stanford University), p. 59.

14. Harry R. Rudin, *Germans in the Cameroons, 1884–1914: A Case Study in Modern Imperialism* (London: Cape, 1938), pp. 356–8, 360, 374–5. See also Ellen C. Parsons, *A Life for Africa: Rev. Adolphus Good, Ph.D., American Missionary in Equatorial West Africa* (New York, 1898).

15. W. Reginald Wheeler, *The Words of God in an African Forest: The Story of an American Mission in West Africa* (New York: Revell, 1931), pp. 121–2.

16. Ibid., pp. 128–30.

17. Dr. James B. McCord, the American medical missionary in South Africa, found that many of the Zulus whom he treated were suffering from malnutrition. See McCord and Douglas, *My Patients Were Zulus*, p. 53.

18. Information furnished by E. D. Hanson, Field Secretary, General Conference of Seventh-Day Adventists, Highland, Salisbury, Rhodesia.

19. George Arthur Roberts, *Let Me Tell You a Story* (Bulawayo: Rhodesian Christian Press, 1964).

20. Keigwin visited the American South in 1925–6 and studied what was being done at Hampton Institute.

21. The arguments were that Alvord was a foreigner and a missionary and had not been in the country long enough to know anything about it. Moreover, "everyone knows what American colleges are like. They are no higher than a second-rate technical high school in England." Emory D. Alvord, "The Development of Native Agriculture and Land Tenure in Southern Rhodesia" (mimeograph, Federal Extension Service, U.S. Department of Agriculture, FR&T-224, November 1959), p. 16.

22. Ibid., p. 39.

23. The foregoing outline of Aggrey's career is condensed from Edwin W. Smith, *Aggrey of Africa: A Study in Black and White* (New York: Doubleday, Doran, 1929).

24. Samuel B. Coles, *Preacher with a Plow* (Boston: Houghton Mifflin, 1957), p. 241.

25. Coles attended Snow Hill and Talladega College, the former of which was modeled after the Tuskegee and Hampton institutes to teach farming and industrial arts skills.

26. Coles, *Preacher with a Plow*, p. 48.

27. Ibid.

28. John Merle David, ed., *Modern Industry and the African* (London: Macmillan, 1933).

29. SAIRA was modeled to some extent, on the Southern Commission on Interracial Cooperation in the American South, formed by the Reverend W. W. Alexander, a Methodist minister in Atlanta, Georgia. Information from Professor St. Clair Drake.

30. Ray E. Phillips, *The Bantu Are Coming: Phases of South Africa's Race Problems* (London: S.C.M. Press, 1930).

31. Thomas Jesse Jones, *Education in Africa: A Study of West, South and Equatorial Africa by the African Education Commission, under the Auspices of the Phelps-Stokes Fund and Foreign Mission Societies of North America and Europe* (New York: Phelps-Stokes Fund, 1922), p. 10.

32. Ibid., p. 11.

33. Ibid., p. 133.

34. Thomas Jesse Jones, *Education in East Africa: A Study of East, Central and South Africa by the Second African Education Commission under the Auspices of the Phelps-Stokes Fund, in Cooperation with the International Education Board* (New York: Phelps-Stokes Fund, 1924), p. 3.

35. Jones, *Education in Africa*, p. 16.

36. Bengt G. M. Sundkler, *Bantu Prophets in South Africa*, 2d ed. (London: Oxford University Press, 1962), p. 39. See also Levi Jenkins Coppin, *Observations of Persons and Things in South Africa, 1900–1904* (Philadelphia: A.M.E. Book Concern, [1905?]), pp. 8–11.

37. See Sundkler, *Bantu Prophets*, pp. 40–1; and Coppin, *Observations of Persons and Things*, pp. 12–13.

38. Cited in Josephus Roosevelt Coen, "The Expansion of the Missions of the African Methodist Episcopal Church in South Africa" (D.D. diss., Hartford Seminary, 1961), p. 173.

39. George Shepperson, "Ethiopianism and African Nationalism," *Phylon* 14 (1953):9. As the only independent African state other than Liberia, Ethiopia also had strong appeal on political grounds.

40. Sundkler, *Bantu Prophets*, pp. 53–6.

41. Ibid. See also Mia Brandel-Syrier, *Black Woman in Search of God* (London: Lutterworth Press, 1962), pp. 31, 235.

42. Sundkler, *Bantu Prophets*, p. 59.

43. Rolvix Harlan, "John Alexander Dowie and the Christian Catholic Apostolic Church in Zion" (D.D. diss., Graduate Divinity School, University of Chicago, 1906), p. 142.

44. Sundkler, *Bantu Prophets,* p. 48.

45. George Shepperson and Thomas Price, *Independent African: John Chilembwe and the Origins, Setting, and Significance of the Nyasaland Native Rising of 1915* (Edinburgh: Edinburgh University Press, 1958), pp. 18–36. See also Shepperson, "Ethiopianism," pp. 13–14; and Shepperson, "The Politics of African Church Separatist Movements in British Central Africa," *Africa* 24 (1954):234–5.

46. Shepperson, "Ethiopianism," p. 13.

47. See Shepperson and Price, *Independent African,* for a scholarly and exhaustive treatment of this confused episode in African religious and political history.

48. Ibid., p. 340.

49. Smith, *Aggrey of Africa,* p. 181.

50. Sundkler, *Bantu Prophets,* pp. 72–3. The student of nineteenth-century American history cannot help noting the close similarity between Mgjima's affair and the "Ghost Dance" troubles with the American Indians in 1890, culminating in the winter battle of Wounded Knee, in which hundreds of red men, believing themselves immune to the white man's bullets, were killed. Another striking parallel occurred early in the century when the Shawnee prophet spurred his warriors to the attack on General W. H. Harrison's army at the battle of Tippecanoe, promising them that his magic would protect them from the white man's bullets.

51. See Marley Cole, *Jehovah's Witness: The New World Society* (New York: Vantage Press, 1955), p. 220. To illustrate the church's mushroom growth, in Northern Rhodesia the number of Jehovah's Witnesses ministers rose from 939 in 1938 to 20,373 in 1953.

52. Sundkler, *Bantu Prophets,* pp. 354–74.

53. John V. Taylor and Dorothea A. Lehmann, *Christians of the Copper-belt: The Growth of the Church in Northern Rhodesia* (London: S.C.M. Press, 1961), pp. 227–46; Hortense Powdermaker, *Coppertown: Changing Africa. The Human Situation on the Rhodesian Copperbelt* (New York: Harper & Row, 1962), pp. 54–5; Andrew Roberts, *A History of Zambia* (New York: Africana Publishing Co., 1976), p. 250.

54. Robert T. Parsons, *The Churches and Ghana Society, 1918–1955: A Survey of Three Protestant Mission Societies and the African Churches Which They Established in Their Assistance to Societary Development* (Leiden: Brill, 1963), pp. 34–52.

55. Ibid., p. 167.

56. Ibid., p. 166.

57. E. G. Parrinder, "The Religious Situation in West Africa," *African Affairs* 59 (1960):41–2.

58. Roland Oliver, *The Missionary Factor in East Africa* (London: Longmans, 1952), p. 291.

59. See A. Jacques Garvey, *Garvey and Garveyism* (Kingston, Jamaica, 1963).

60. Ibid., pp. 77–110; see also John V. Taylor, *The Growth of the Church in Buganda: An Attempt at Understanding* (London: S.C.M. Press, 1958), p. 98.

61. Monica Wilson, *Communal Rites of the Nyakyusa* (London, 1959), pp. 167, 171–3.

62. Ibid., p. 167; Cole, *Jehovah's Witnesses, pp.* 220–8.

63. Shepperson and Price, *Independent African,* pp. 154–6.

64. For a discussion of Ngunzism, see Efraim Andersson, "Messianic Popular Movements in the Lower Congo," *Studia Ethnographica Upsalienta* (Upsala, Sweden) 14 (1958):48–67.

65. Ibid., p. 71.

66. Ibid., p. 69.

67. Cecil Northcott, *Christianity in Africa* (London: S.C.M. Press, 1962), p. 77.

68. K. J. King, "The American Negro as Missionary to East Africa: A Critical Aspect of African Evangelism," *African Historical Studies* 3 (1970):5–22.

69. Ibid., pp. 11, 16.

70. Ibid., p. 12.
71. Ibid., p. 14.
72. Ibid., p. 16.
73. The agreement was that the "best type of negro missionary as the Tuskegee type could be entertained for Kenya." Ibid., p. 17. In fact, none were accepted into Kenya.
74. Andersson, "Messianic Popular Movements," p. 247.
75. Shepperson and Price, *Independent African*, p. 135.
76. Ibid., p. 137.
77. Harr, *Negro as an American Protestant Missionary*, pp. 39, 41.
78. Emory Ross, *Out of Africa* (New York, 1936), p. 158.
79. Amos Jerome White and Luella Graham White, *Dawn in Bantuland: An African Experiment, or an Account of Missionary Experience and Observations in South Africa* (Boston, 1953).
80. John T. Stewart, *The Deacon Wore Spats: Profiles from America's Changing Religious Scene* (New York, 1965), p. 53.

Chapter 19. Black nationalism and the search for an African past

1. George Shepperson, "Notes on Negro American Influences on the Emergence of African Nationalism," *Journal of African History* 1 (1960):299.
2. During the first three decades of the twentieth century, well over 100,000 West Indians entered the United States. The influx diminished during the depression and World War II, but after the end of hostilities, immigration resumed. The McCarran-Walter Act of 1952, however, entirely changed the situation. Allowed hitherto to make use of the unfilled portion of the large British quota, the West Indians were thereafter allocated a tiny quota of their own. The movement to the United States diminished; henceforth West Indians migrated in increasingly large number to London, Birmingham, and other British cities. See Maldwyn Allen Jones, *American Immigration* (Chicago: University of Chicago Press, 1960), pp. 293–5. West Indians, however, continued to occupy a major place in black American politics: Malcolm X, Stokely Carmichael, Shirley Chisholm, Roy Innes, and many other civil rights leaders of the 1960s and 1970s were of West Indian origin.
3. See Hollis Lynch, *Edward Wilmot Blyden: Pan-Negro Patriot, 1832–1912* (New York: Oxford University Press, 1970).
4. See Edmund D. Cronon, *Black Moses: The Story of Marcus Garvey and the Universal Negro Improvement Association* (Madison: University of Wisconsin Press, 1968); and Robert A. Hill, ed., *The Marcus Garvey and Universal Negro Improvement Association Papers*, 2 vols. (Berkeley: University of California Press, 1983). Unfortunately, we can only cite Hill's excellent work, as it appeared when our study was in press.
5. Shepperson, "Notes on Negro American Influences," p. 300.
6. Ibid.
7. Ibid., p. 301.
8. This section is based on Edwin S. Redkey, *Black Exodus: Black Nationalists and Back to Africa Movements, 1890–1910* (New Haven, Conn.: Yale University Press, 1969).
9. Alexander Crummell was a leading exponent of this movement (see Shepperson, "Notes on Negro American Influences," p. 302).
10. St. Clair Drake, "Negro Americans and the African Interest," *The American Negro Reference Book* (1966), p. 669.
11. The schools most attended were Hampton, Howard, Lincoln, Tuskegee, Wilberforce, and Fisk.
12. William H. Sheppard went to the Belgian Congo in 1890 with a white minister, S. N. Lapsley, to set up a mission, and remained for twenty years. Sheppard, who was born in

Waynesboro, Va., had dreamed from childhood of being a missionary to Africa. In 1880 he entered Hampton Normal and Industrial Institute and later was sent by the Presbyterian church to Tuscaloosa Theological Institute. While at Tuscaloosa, he agreed to go to Africa as a missionary, and he was appointed to the Belgian Congo after serving as a minister in Georgia and Alabama. See William H. Sheppard, *Pioneers in Congo* (Louisville, Ky.: Pentecostal Publication Co., n.d.).

13. See C. C. Boone, *Congo As I Saw It* (New York: Little & Ives, 1927).

14. Quoted in Drake, "Negro Americans and the African Interest," p. 674.

15. Shepperson, "Notes on Negro American Influences," pp. 303–4.

16. Ibid.

17. Ibid., p. 306; see also K. J. King, "The American Negro as Missionary to East Africa: A Critical Aspect of African Evangelism," *African Historical Studies* 3 (1970):5–22.

18. As Redkey demonstrates convincingly in his *Black Exodus*, black nationalism at the turn of the twentieth century was a lower-class movement among blacks who had considerable interest in back-to-Africa undertakings.

19. The paper was banned as dangerous by many colonial governments. Cronon, *Black Moses*, p. 46.

20. Ibid., passim.

21. Shepperson, "Notes on American Negro Influences," p. 303.

22. Benjamin Quarles, *The Negro in the Making of America* (New York: Collier Books, 1964), pp. 195–7.

23. Ibid., p. 196.

24. Quoted in David Cronon, "Black Moses: Marcus Garvey and Garveyism," in *Black Brotherhood: Afro-Americans and Africa*, ed. Okon Edet Uya (Lexington, Mass.: Heath, 1971), p. 172.

25. Quoted in Drake, "Negro Americans and the African Interest," p. 676.

26. Kwame Nkrumah, *Ghana: The Autobiogaphy of Kwame Nkrumah* (Edinburgh, 1957), p. 45.

27. Cronon, *Black Moses,* 39.

28. See Edward W. Blyden, *Christianity, Islam and the Negro Race* (1887; reprint, Edinburgh: Edinburgh University Press, 1967).

29. Shepperson, "Notes on Negro American Influences," p. 308.

30. *Negro Culture in West Africa* (New York: Neale Publishing Co., 1914), by George Ellis, the black American secretary of the U.S. legation in Liberia from 1901 to 1910, is only one example of this newly stimulated interest in black history and culture.

31. *Horizon,* the *Crisis* (discussed in the next section), and the *Southern Workman* previously had carried news and articles on Africa for a popular audience.

32. European scholars have been late to discover and use this valuable source. See Ulysses Lee, "The ASNL, the *Journal of Negro History* and Ameri-Scholarly Interest in Africa," in *Africa from the Point of View of American Negro Scholars* (Paris, 1958), pp. 401–18. In the same publication, see also the important "Bibliographical Checklist of American Negro Writers about Africa," by Dorothy B. Porter, pp. 379–99.

33. Shepperson, "Notes on Negro American Influences," p. 312.

34. Drake, "Negro Americans and the African Interest," p. 673.

35. George Padmore, *Pan-Africanism or Communism? The Coming Struggle for Africa* (New York: Ray, 1956), p. 463. Padmore's book was until 1962 the standard history of Pan-Africanism.

36. Immanuel Wallerstein, "Pan-Africanism as Protest," in *The Revolution in World Politics,* ed. Morton A. Kaplan (New York: Wiley, 1962). This is an excellent survey of the Pan-African movement.

37. Alexander Walters, *My Life and Work* (New York, 1917), p. 253.

38. Elliot M. Rudwick, *W. E. B. Du Bois: A Study in Minority Leadership* (Philadelphia: University of Pennvania Press, 1960); see also Colin Legum, *Pan-Africanism: A Short Political Guide* (New York: Praeger, 1962).

39. Francis L. Broderick, *W. E. B. Du Bois, Negro Leader in a Time of Crisis* (Stanford, Calif.: Stanford University Press, 1959), p. 3.

40. An active political role distinguished the NAACP from Booker T. Washington's more accommodationist line, which stressed economic opportunity at the expense of racial equality and political power. Du Bois and Washington were to remain divided on the question how black Americans could best achieve success in the United States.

41. James W. Ivy, "Traditional N.A.A.C.P. Interest in Africa as Reflected in the Pages of *The Crisis*," in *Africa from the Point of View of American Negro Scholars*, pp. 239–40. The readership grew until in 1919 more than 104,000 people subscribed to the publication. See Broderick, *W. E. B. Du Bois*, p. 116.

42. W. E. B. Du Bois, "The First Universal Races Congress," *Independent* 71 (August 24, 1911):401–3; Eliot M. Rudwick, "W. E. B. Du Bois and the Universal Races Congress of 1911," *Phylon* 20 (1959):372–8.

43. W. E. B. Du Bois, "The Negro's Fatherland," *Survey* 39 (November 10, 1917):141.

44. W. E. B. Du Bois, *The World and Africa: An Inquiry into the Part Which Africa Has Played in World History* (1947; reprint, Millwood, N.Y.: Kraus Reprint Co., 1965), p. 11.

45. The 1921 Pan-African sessions produced one major achievement: The International Bureau of Labor of the League of Nations agreed to set up a section on black labor.

46. W. E. B. Du Bois, "A Second Journey to Pan-Africa," *New Republic* 29 (December 7, 1921):40.

47. Ibid., p. 41.

48. The defeat of Ethiopia stimulated some black concern once again.

49. Louis R. Harlan, "Booker T. Washington and the White Man's Burden," *American Historical Review* 81 (1966):460. We have drawn freely upon this article, in which Harlan has brought to light a mass of primary material (in the Booker T. Washington Papers held at the Library of Congress) previously unused by students of African relations. Louis R. Harlan, *Booker T. Washington: The Makings of a Black Leader, 1856–1901* (New York: Oxford University Press, 1972), and Harlan, *Booker T. Washington: The Wizard of Tuskegee, 1901–1915* (New York: Oxford University Press, 1983).

50. Drake, "Negro Americans and the Africa Interest," p. 680. See also John W. E. Bowen, ed., *Africa and the American Negro: Addresses and Proceedings of the Congress on Africa* (Atlanta: Gammon Theological Seminary, 1896).

51. Harlan, "Booker T. Washington," pp. 450–2.

52. The operations, report, and results of the commission's findings are discussed in Chapter 16. See also ibid., p. 459.

53. Emmett J. Scott, "Tuskegee in Africa and Africa at Tuskegee" (manuscript in the Washington Papers, Container 334). See also John W. Robinson, "Cotton-Growing in Africa," in *Tuskegee and Its People*, ed. Booker T. Washington (New York: Appleton, 1905), pp. 164–9. The *Tuskegee Student* of October (?) 1900 includes a short note on the farewell to Calloway and his party when they left; see also "From Africa Party," ibid., March 23, 1901; "New Cotton Fields," ibid., August 24, 1901; and "Tuskegee Institute Graduates in Africa," ibid., March 30, 1907. The writers are indebted to Paul L. Puryear, director of Social Science Research, Tuskegee Institute, for copies of these items.

54. *Tuskegee Student*, 1901. The harvest result later in the year was the first shipment of twenty-five bales of cotton to Germany. Harlan, "Booker T. Washington," p. 444.

55. Robinson, "Cotton-Growing in Africa," p. 196.

56. See George Arthur Roberts, *Let Me Tell You a Story* (Bulawayo: Rhodesian Christian Press, 1964).

57. Booker T. Washington, *The Story of the Negro: The Rise of the Race from Slavery,* 2 vols. (New York: Doubleday, Page, 1909), 1:38.

58. Ibid., p. 39.

59. Harlan, "Booker T. Washington," p. 445.

60. *Tuskegee Student,* March 30, 1907.

61. Harlan, "Booker T. Washington," p. 446.

62. Ibid.

63. The French scholar Robert Cornevin takes an opposite view. He maintains that the "colonial Americans" were used to richer land and large plantations and were unable to cope with the land and its people, although they found a few types of cotton that worked. See Robert Cornevin, *Histoire du Togo* (Paris: Berger-Levrault, 1962), pp. 85–7.

64. Harlan, "Booker T. Washington," p. 447; Arthur Gaitskell, *Gezira: A Story of Development in the Sudan* (London: Faber & Faber, 1959), pp. 51–2.

65. Washington, *The Story of the Negro,* 2:285.

66. Information provided by Paul Puryear, director of Social Science Research, Tuskegee Institute.

67. See Drake, "Negro Americans and the Africa Interest," pp. 679–85. See also *Educational Adaptions: Report of Ten Years Work of the Phelps-Stokes Fund, 1910–1920* (New York: Phelps-Stokes Fund, 1920); *Twenty-Year Report of the Phelps-Stokes Fund, 1911–1931* (New York: Phelps-Stokes Fund, 1931). Also see Nuffield Foundation and Colonial Office, *African Education: A Study of Educational Policy and Practice in British Tropical Africa* (London: Crown Agent for the Colonies, [1952]). For a survey of Washington and the Hampton–Tuskegee approach, see August Meier, *Negro Thought in America, 1890–1915: Racial Ideology in the Age of Booker T. Washington* (Ann Arbor: University of Michigan Press, 1963).

68. The fund also sponsored the major *Bibliography of the Negro in Africa and America* (New York: Phelps-Stokes Fund, 1938), compiled by Monroe Work. A project for an Encyclopedia Africana, to be edited by Du Bois, was supported, as were the *Dictionary of Negro Biography* (New York: Phelps-Stokes Fund, 1938) and Douglas Varley's *African Native Music* (New York: Phelps-Stokes Fund, 1936), a bibliography.

69. Kenneth J. King, "Africa and the Southern States of the U.S.A.: Notes on J. H. Oldham and American Negro Education for Africans," *Journal of African History* 10 (1969):659–77. The opposite kind of education, the Atlanta–Fisk style favoring liberal arts, was not approved by many, for blacks either in Africa or in the United States. Du Bois, of course, championed the liberal arts education to produce an educated elite, "the talented Tenth."

70. King, "Africa and the Southern States," p. 659.

71. The adviser to the English Board of Education, Michael Sadler, came in 1901; the governor of the Gold Coast, J. P. Rodger, in 1902; the great colonial administrator-scholar Sir Harry Johnston, in 1908. See ibid., p. 600.

72. "The value of industrial and agricultural training for the negro race is abundantly proved by the experience of the Normal and Industrial Institute at Hampton, Virginia, and the Normal and Industrial School at Tuskegee, Alabama." Quoted in King, "Africa and the Southern States," p. 661.

73. King, "Africa and the Southern States," p. 664.

74. Ibid.

75. Oldham visited the United States in 1921 and brought the president of Tuskegee, Robert Moton, to the International Missionary Council Meeting of 1921 to preach Tuskegee's potential in African education.

76. The Tuskegee–Hampton tradition did seem to keep American blacks "in their place." And the use of the Tuskegee approach appealed to colonial and missionary authorities as a way of ensuring control. The Atlanta tradition of liberal education appeared more threaten-

ing to whites. Washington was lionized by whites (even presidents sought his advice); Du Bois was feared and mistrusted.

77. King, "Africa and the Southern States," p. 665.

78. Ibid., p. 667.

79. Ibid., pp. 670–1.

80. Ibid., p. 673.

81. Ibid., p. 676.

82. For an excellent account of Lincoln University's interest in Africa see Horace Mann Bond, "Forming African Youth: A Philosophy of Education," in *Africa from the Point of View of American Negro Scholars*, pp. 247–61.

83. The break came when Edward W. Blyden, the Liberian scholar, renounced his Christian religion. No more Liberian students attended Lincoln until 1949, when the grandson of Blyden enrolled. Ibid.

84. Ibid., p. 254.

85. Schools like Tuskegee, where "practical education" was the policy, were to prosper while Lincoln was ignored by philanthropists.

86. Bond, "Forming African Youth," p. 260.

Chapter 20. Africa between East and West

1. See, for example, William Roger Louis, *Imperialism at Bay: The United States and the Decolonization of the British Empire, 1941–1945* (New York: Oxford University Press, 1978); and Richard O. Mahoney, *Ordeal in Africa* (New York: Oxford University Press, 1983).

2. For a detailed assessment that emphasizes ideological change in the Soviet Union, see Helen Desfosses Cohn, *Soviet Policy toward Black Africa: The Focus on National Integration* (New York: Praeger, 1972).

3. For a detailed discussion, see Vernon McKay, *Africa in World Politics* (New York: Harper & Row, 1963), especially pp. 313–15.

4. Speech to the Senate on June 14, 1960, cited in ibid., p. 27.

5. Department of State, *The United States and Africa*, Publication 7710 (Washington, D.C.: GPO, 1964), p. 3. It was from such considerations that the U.S. government, through its Economic Cooperation Administration, advanced, for instance, $3 million toward opening the Chibuluma mine in what was then Northern Rhodesia, a mine expected at the time to yield annually sixteen thousand tons of copper and half a million pounds of cobalt. See Kenneth Bradley, *Copper Venture: The Discovery and Development of Roan Antelope and Mufulira* (London: Mufulira Copper Mines, 1952), p. 100.

6. Walter Goldschmidt, ed., *The United States and Africa* (New York: Columbia University, American Assembly, 1958), pp. 3–4.

7. For a detailed breakdown of American agencies concerned with African affairs and American expenditure, see "A Survey of the United States Investment in Africa," in *Issue 8*, nos. 2–3 (1978): 22–8 (*Issue* is the journal of the African Studies Association of the United States). See L. H. Gann and Peter Duignan, *Why South Africa Will Survive: A Historical Analysis* (New York: St. Martin's Press, 1981), pp. 251–67, for a discussion of U.S. lobbies and bureaucratic pressure groups. For a similar discussion written from the liberal viewpoint, see Anthony Lake, *The "Tar Baby" Option: American Policy Toward Southern Rhodesia* (New York: Columbia University Press, 1978). For Roosevelt's earlier policy, see Louis, *Imperialism at Bay*.

8. Conservative lobbies, apt to take a stand in favor of conservative causes such as South Africa and Rhodesia, included the American Legion as well as conservative Christian groups and some, though by no means all, of the business firms with interests in South Africa and

Rhodesia. Liberal groups were drawn from the ranks of the prestige media, academe, the trade unions, the churches, black organizations, and a great variety of professional groups composed of men and women with academic or semiacademic backgrounds. The following, for example, backed sanctions against Rhodesia (now Zimbabwe) and South Africa: American Committee on Africa; American Ethical Union; American Humanist Association; Episcopal Church General Convention; Friends Committee on National Legislation; National Office of Black Catholics; The Sisters Network; Unitarian Universalist Association; United Church of Christ General Synod; United Methodist Church (Board of Church and Society, Board of Global Ministries); United Presbyterian Church General Assembly; United States Catholic Conference; AFL–CIO; Amalgamated Meatcutters and Butcher Workmen of North America; American Federation of Teachers (AFL–CIO); Communication Workers of America (AFL–CIO); International Longshoremen's and Warehousemen's Union; Oil, Chemical and Atomic Workers; United Auto Workers; United Steelworkers of America; Black Political Convention (International Policy Commission); Congress on Racial Equality; IFCO-Action; National Association for the Advancement of Colored People; National Association of Colored Women's Clubs; National Council of Negro Women; Pan African Congress USA; Transafrica; American Bar Association; Americans for Democratic Action; International League for Peace and Freedom; National Student Association; National Student Lobby; Women's International League for Peace and Freedom; World Federalists USA; Young Women's Christian Association; African Liberation Support Committee; American Committee on Africa; Committee for a Free Mozambique; Gulf Boycott Coalition; Southern Africa Committee; Youth Organization for Black Unity. Even more important were the National Council of Churches and, above all, the congressional Black Caucus.

9. See David E. Albright, "The USSR, Its Communist Allies and Southern Africa," in *Munger Africana Library Notes* (Pasadena: California Institute of Technology, 1980), pp. 11–17; and L. H. Gann and Peter Duignan, *Africa South of the Sahara: The Challenge to Western Security* (Stanford, Calif.: Hoover Institution Press, 1981).

10. See Gann and Duignan, *Why South Africa Will Survive.* For an opposing interpretation, see Foreign Policy Study Foundation, *South Africa: Time Running Out: The Report of the Study Commission of U.S. Policy toward Southern Africa* (Berkeley: University of California Press, 1981).

Chapter 21. Economic activities: the private sector

1. Department of Commerce, Bureau of the Census, *Statistical Abstract of the United States* (Washington, D.C.: GPO, 1963), pp. 878–82.

2. Ibid. (1975), tab. 8.

3. Edward W. Chester, *Clash of Titans: Africa and U.S. Foreign Policy* (Maryknoll, N.Y.: Orbis Books, 1974), pp. 57–9. For greater detail, see Robert Greenhalgh Albion, *Seaports South of the Sahara: The Achievements of an American Steamship Service* (New York: Appleton-Century-Crofts, 1959).

4. See Rupert Emerson, "The Character of American Interests in Africa," in *The United States in Africa,* ed. Walter Goldschmidt (New York: American Assembly, 1958), pp. 20–1; and Department of Commerce, *Historical Statistics of the United States* (Washington, D.C.: GPO, 1960), pp. 557–66.

5. Department of Commerce, Bureau of the Census, *Survey of Current Business* (Washington, D.C.: GPO, 1970).

6. See L. H. Gann, "Neo-Colonialism, Imperialism, and the New Class," *Survey* (London) 19, no. 1 (1973).

7. See Rayford W. Logan, "Liberia in the Family of Nations," *Phylon* 7 (1971):5–6; and Smith Hempstone, *Africa – Angry Young Giant* (New York: Praeger, 1961), p. 463. At one

time during the war as many as seventeen thousand aircraft per month landed at Roberts Field.

8. Clarence Lorenzo Simpson, *Memoirs* (London, 1961), pp. 231–2; Albion, *Seaports South of the Sahara*, pp. 203–5. See also Philip Wayland Porter, "Monrovia," in *Encyclopaedia Britannica* (1965).

9. *New York Times* 31 (June 23, 1951):8.

10. *Minerals Year Book*, 4:972.

11. Ibid., pp. 972–3; Liberian Iron Ore, Ltd., *Annual Report, 1964* (New York, 1964), pp. 4–5.

12. Olin Mathieson financed 48.5 percent; Pechiney-Uginey of France, 26.5 percent; British Aluminum Company, Ltd., 10 percent; Aluminum Industrie Aktiengesellschaft of Switzerland, 10 percent; and Vereinigte Aluminum-Werke A.G. of Germany, 5 percent.

13. Statement of Stanley De J. Osborne, president of Olin Mathieson Chemical Corporation, in House of Representatives, *Hearings before the Subcommittee on Africa of the Committee on Foreign Affairs*, 87th Cong., 1st sess., May 8, 1961, pp. 6–7.

14. Department of the Interior, Bureau of Mines, *Minerals Year Book* (Washington, D.C.: GPO, 1963), 4:932. Hereafter referred to as *Minerals Year Book*.

15. Ibid.

16. Official trade statistics in 1973 (in thousands of escudos) were as follows for Angola: total exports, 19,158,291; exports to the United States, 5,380,294; total imports, 13,268,823; imports from the United States, 1,262,112.

17. See L. H. Gann and Peter Duignan, *Why South Africa Will Survive: A Historical Analysis* (New York: St. Martin's Press, 1981).

18. Ibid., pp. 248–50.

19. Alexander Campbell, *The Heart of Africa* (New York: Longmans, Green, 1954), pp. 169–71, gives a firsthand account of the Tsumeb project while early construction was still under way. For a later picture, see Frank Haythornthwaite, *All the Way to Abenab* (London: Faber & Faber, 1956), pp. 222–46; and Haythornthwaite, "The Mine at Tsumeb," *Amax Journal* 2 (Summer 1964):2–8. See also Newmont Mining Corporation, *Annual Reports* (New York: The Corporation, 1961–4).

20. For a detailed discussion, see Daan Prinsloo, *United States Foreign Policy and the Republic of South Africa* (Pretoria: Foreign Affairs Association, 1978), pp. 64–70; and Ann W. Seidman, *Outposts of Monopoly Capitalism* (Westport, Conn: L. Hill, 1980), pp. 22–38.

21. In 1979 U.S. investments generated $360 million in profits, an 18 percent average rate of return. Of this amount, $130 million was repatriated to the United States in 1979; $230 million was reinvested in South Africa. American trade with South Africa was on an equally modest scale. By the end of 1980 U.S. exports to South Africa totaled $2.2 billion, and the United States imported $3 billion in goods and services. For more details, see Investor Responsibility Research Center, *Analysis C 1981* (Washington, D.C.: The Center, 1981).

Chapter 22. Economic activities: the public sector

1. Rupert Emerson, *Africa and United States Policy* (Englewood Cliffs, N.J.: Prentice-Hall, 1967), pp. 35–42; Vernon McKay, *Africa in World Politics* (New York: Harper & Row, 1963), pp. 364–8.

2. Department of State, *The Foreign Assistance Program: Annual Report to Congress: Fiscal Year 1965* (Washington, D.C.: GPO, 1965), pp. 61–2.

3. According to Department of Commerce, Bureau of the Census, *Statistical Abstract of the United States* (Washington, D.C.: GPO, 1980), pp. 868–9, foreign aid to Africa increased as follows: 1945–55: $0.143 billion; 1956–65: $2.096 billion; 1966–74: $2.949 billion; 1975–9: $2.858 billion.

In 1980 total U.S. aid to Africa amounted to $1.862 billion; bilateral aid stood at $624,000 million; and multilateral aid, at $460,000 million. (The estimated gross national product of Senegal in 1977 was $1.700 billion.) To administer these funds, AID required (1978) a total of 159 officials in Washington and 437 stationed throughout Africa – not an excessive number of civil servants, given the extent of the sums disbursed.

4. For a detailed survey, see *Issue* (the organ of the African Studies Association) 8, nos. 2–3 (1978).

5. This line included the Economic Cooperation Association, the Mutual Security Administration, the Technical Cooperation Administration, the Foreign Operations Administration, and the International Cooperation Administration. AID also took over the operation of the Development Loan Fund and certain local currency dealings of the Export–Import Bank. For a summary of U.S. agencies working in Africa, see ibid.

6. U.S. Agency for International Development, *Fiscal Submission to the Congress: Africa Programs, 1978* (Washington, D.C.: The Agency, 1978).

7. For an intelligent defense of Liberia, however, see Martin Lowenkopf, *Politics in Liberia: The Conservative Road to Development* (Stanford, Calif.: Hoover Institution Press, 1976).

8. See for instance Lloyd B. Baker, "United States Economic Aid to Africa," *African Studies Bulletin* 8, no. 1 (1965).

9. Between 1945 and 1979 the United States supplied a total of $8.045 billion to Africa. The largest African receivers, in order of magnitude, were Morocco, $1.066 billion; Zaire, $0.883 billion; Algeria, $0.769 billion; Ethiopia, $0.365 billion; Nigeria, $0.357 billion; Ghana, $0.331 billion; Liberia, $0.273 billion; Tanzania, $0.266 billion; Kenya, $0.233 billion; Libya, $0.206 billion.

10. By 1976 food and nutrition accounted for 48.03 percent of AID's African budget; about 12.00 percent went to education and "human resources." Population planning and health planning came next, with 10.63 percent of the African budget. The remainder went into varied fields; one example is Security Supporting Assistance to Southern Africa (that is to say, assistance for training Africans from countries under white rule, such as Rhodesia, South-West Africa, and South Africa, to prepare them for filling manpower needs upon majority rule).

11. See Emerson, *Africa and United States Policy*, pp. 38–41. Between 1948 and 1965 U.S. aid was distributed as follows: Congo, $207.9 million; Nigeria, $136.8 million; Ethiopia, $104.7 million; Liberia, $103.6 million; Ghana, $91.0 million.

12. Rhodesian Ministry of Finance, *Economic Survey of Rhodesia* (Salisbury: Government Printer, 1976), tab. 3.

13. Nigeria, Africa's most populous country, put its faith in private enterprise. Yet even the Nigerian Development Plan for 1975–80 provided for a public sector investment of 20,000 million naira, an investment in state governments of 6,500 million naira, and a private sector investment of only 10,000 naira. Of the public sector investment of 20,000 million naira, only 1,400 million were directly devoted to agriculture. See the section on Nigeria in *Africa South of the Sahara, 1980–81* (London: Europa Publications, 1980). (1 naira ψ U.S. $0.56 in 1980.)

14. P. T. Bauer, "Foreign Aid and the Third World," in *The United States in the 1980s*, ed. Peter Duignan and Alvin Rabushka (Stanford, Calif.: Hoover Institution Press, 1980), p. 567. See also Bauer, *Dissent on Development* (Cambridge, Mass.: Harvard University Press, 1976). The literature in favor of foreign aid is enormous; see, for instance, Gunnar Myrdal, *Economic Theory and Underdeveloped Regions* (London: Duckworth, 1957).

15. See, for instance, Agency for International Development, *A Report to Congress on Development Needs and Opportunities for Cooperation in Southern Africa* (Washington, D.C.: GPO, 1979). This work faithfully reflected all the beliefs held sacred by liberal acade-

mia. As regards Zimbabwe, for instance, the AID officials assumed that the white settlers were overpaid – a surprising assumption, since white specialists in Rhodesia received salaries considerably below those paid to their opposite numbers in U.S. and international aid agencies. The white farmers' rapid departure was held to be undesirable; after all, they had made Zimbabwe self-sufficient in food, and even provided a surplus of comestibles for export. Yet land redistribution at their expense was held to be essential. Any "short-term supply crisis" in its wake should be met by Western taxpayers (pp. 146–7). More surprising still, AID actually made itself into a spokesman for the Marxist–Leninist republics of Angola and Mozambique. According to AID, there was "a convergence of interests between the United States, Angola, and Mozambique in several key areas" (p. 21). Angola supposedly looked to "an African blend of socialism" (p. 28); hence AID called upon Congress to give more aid to Angola – all this at a time when Angola had strengthened its ties to the Soviet Union, when the ruling MPLA had liquidated its "Africanist" faction, when the MPLA had frequently avowed its hostility to the United States and its social system, and when the MPLA had consistently proclaimed its loyalty to "scientific socialism" of the Soviet variety and had unswervingly backed Moscow in international politics. For a detailed breakdown of AID expenditure in the 1970s, see *Issue* 8, nos. 2–3 (1978):28–72.

Chapter 23: American interests in Africa, 1945–1983

1. Sir Charles Wentworth Dilke, *Greater Britain: A Record of Travel in English-Speaking Countries during 1866–7* (Philadelphia: Lippincott, 1867), pp. 71–2.

2. See Adelaide C. Hill, "African Studies in the United States," in *Africa in the United States,* ed. Vernon McKay (New York: Macfodder Student Edition, 1967), chap. 4.

3. E. Jefferson Murphy, *Creative Philanthropy: Carnegie Corporation and Africa, 1953–1973* (New York: Teachers College Press, 1976).

4. Ibid., pp. 28–9.

5. Ford Foundation, *Annual Report, 1982* (Washington, D.C., 1982), pp. 19–26.

6. On private foreign aid and foundations, see Landrum R. Bolling, *Private Foreign Aid: U.S. Philanthropy for Relief and Development* (Boulder, Colo.: Westview Press, 1982).

7. See Joint Committee on the Foreign Area Fellowship Program of the American Council of Learned Societies and the Social Science Research Council, *Directory of Foreign Area Fellows, 1952–1971,* ed. Dorothy Soderlund (New York: Foreign Area Fellowship Program, 1973); and Department of State, Office of External Research, *Directory of University Centers of Foreign Affairs Research* (Washington, D.C.: GPO, 1968). See also African Studies Association, Research Liaison Committee, *Directory of African Studies in the United States* (Waltham, Mass.: The Association, 1971), which listed more than 100 African studies programs, ranging from prestigious centers of the kind found at UCLA to minuscule programs at small schools. During the same period, the Ford Foundation created an Africa section in its organization, and the Carnegie Corporation, the Rockefeller Foundation, and the Rockefeller Brothers Fund began to take an active interest in many aspects of Africa; the Phelps-Stokes Fund had already made its name among the foremost in promoting African studies and in research on Africa. In addition, scores of other philanthropic organizations took a direct part in the U.S. effort in Africa. (The State Department at the time listed 176 organizations, exclusive of religious bodies, concerned in and with Africa.)

8. For a survey of scholarship on colonialism, see Peter Duignan and L. H. Gann, *Colonialism in Africa, 1870–1960,* vol. 5, *A Bibliographical Guide to Colonialism in Sub-Saharan Africa* (Cambridge: Cambridge University Press, 1973). For a general review of Africa-centered works, see Peter Duignan, ed., *Guide to Research and Reference Works in Sub-Saharan Africa* (Stanford, Calif.: Hoover Institution Press, 1971).

9. For instance, the prestigious report issued by the Foreign Study Foundation, *South*

Africa: Time Running Out: The Report of the Study Commission on U.S. Policy toward Southern Africa (Berkeley: University of California Press, 1981), called for a variety of restrictions on U.S.–South Africa trade as one of various means to alter the South African power structure. The commission included Franklin A. Thomas, president of the Ford Foundation: Alan Pifer, president of the Carnegie Corporation; a senior AFL–CIO official; a number of academicians, all of them drawn from the liberal left; and two business members previously concerned with the cause of expanding U.S. trade: Charles P. McColough, chairman of the Xerox Corporation, who had held a directorship of the Joint U.S.–U.S.S.R. Trade and Economic Council, and J. Irwin Miller of the Cummins Engine Company and other prestigious concerns, who had been a member of Lyndon B. Johnson's President's Commission on Trade Relations with the Soviet Union and Eastern European Nations.

10. In November 1977 Accuracy in Media, a Washington-based organization, published a survey of the coverage given by the *New York Times,* the *Washington Post,* and the three major television networks – CBS, NBC, and ABC – on human rights in five selected countries under authoritarian rule. They found for 1976 1 story on North Korea, a hard-line Stalinist country; 1 on Cuba, despite Cuba's proximity to the United States and its thousands of political prisoners; and a few on Cambodia, where the Cambodian government had been slaughtering hundreds of thousands of people. Against this, there were 90 columns, stories, and editorials on South Korea and 137 on Chile, both pro-Western countries. During the same year, the South Africa Foundation, a South African body, calculated that the *New York Times* and the *Washington Post* alone had published 513 stories, editorials, and columns about civil rights in South Africa, hardly a contender for the crown of brutality when compared with Cambodia, North Korea, or – for that matter – Uganda or Burundi.

11. House of Representatives, Committee on Foreign Affairs, "African Students and Study Programs in the United States," *Report and Hearings of the Subcommittee on Africa: H. Rep. 809,* 89th Cong., 1st sess., 1965, pp. 14–17.

12. African-American Institute, *Annual Report, 1971* (New York, 1971), pp. 1–11.

13. African-American Institute, Women's Committee, *The Role of Women in Africa,* ed. Mary Craig, et al. (New York: The Committee, 1959).

14. We are indebted to personal information from the organization. See also USSALEP, Study Team, *Education, Race, and Social Change in South Africa,* ed. John A. Marcum (Berkeley: University of California Press, 1982).

15. For a critique of AAI, see *The African-American Institute* (Washington, D.C.: Heritage Foundation, 1983), no. 23.

16. African-American Institute, *1980 Annual Report* (New York, 1981).

17. Sir Eric Ashby, *African Universities and Western Tradition* (London: Oxford University Press, 1964), pp. 46, 65–7, 79–80. See also *Ethiopia: The Handbook for Ethiopia* (Nairobi: University Press of Africa, 1980), pp. 110–14; Harold D. Nelson and Irving Kaplan, eds., *Ethiopia: A Country Study* (Washington, D.C.: American University, 1981), p. 130.

18. See Joseph E. Harris, ed., *Global Dimensions of the African Diaspora* (Washington, D.C.: Howard University Press, 1982), especially the articles by Adell Paton, "Howard University and Meharry Medical Schools in the Training of African Physicians, 1868–1978," pp. 142–61, and Kings M. Phiri, "Afro-American Influence on Colonial Malawi, 1891–1945: A Case Study of the Interaction between Africa and the Diaspora," pp. 250–67. For the Chilembwe rising also see the standard work, George Shepperson and Thomas Price, *Independent African: John Chilembwe and the Origins, Setting and Significance of the Nyasaland Native Rising of 1915* (Edinburgh: Edinburgh University Press, 1958).

19. For the period, see James Hooker, "Negro American Press and Africa in the 1930s," *Canadian Journal of African Studies,* no. 1, 1967, pp. 43–50; and Hooker, "The Impact of African History on Afro-Americans, 1930–1945," *Black Academy Review* 3, nos. 1–2 (1972):46–7.

20. George Padmore, ed., *History of the Pan-African Congress* (London: Hammersmith Bookshop, 1963), pp. 24–6.

21. Immanuel Geiss, *Panafrikanismus: Zur Geschichte der Dekolonisation* (Franfurt am Main: Europaïsche Verlagsanstalt, 1968).

22. Hollis R. Lynch, *Black American Radicals and the Liberation of Africa: The Council on African Affairs, 1937–1955*, Monograph Series, no. 5 (Ithaca, N.Y.: Cornell University, Africana Studies and Research Center, 1978).

23. See John Hendrik Clarke, "The African Heritage Studies Association (AHSA): Some Notes on the Conflict with the African Studies Association (ASA) and the Fight to Reclaim African History," *Issue* 6, nos. 2–3 (1976):5–11.

24. I. K. Sundiata, *Black Scandal: America and the Liberian Labor Crisis, 1929–1936* (Philadelphia: Institute for the Study of Human Issues, 1980), p. 161.

25. See, for instance, J. K. Obalata, "U.S. 'Soul' Music in Africa," *African Communist* 41 (1970):80–9.

26. See Clayborne Carson, *In Struggle: SNCC and the Black Awakening of the 1960s* (Cambridge, Mass.: Harvard University Press, 1981), p. 22.

27. *Public Opinion* (published by the American Enterprise Institute), June–July 1981, pp. 21–40.

28. Between 1966 and 1982 the percentage of black voters who indicated that they had voted in congressional elections went up from 41.7 to 43.0 (corresponding figures for whites were respectively 57.0 and 49.9). The percentage of black voters who reported having taken part in the presidential elections of 1968 and 1980 actually declined, from 57.6 to 50.5 (corresponding figures for whites were 69.1 and 60.9 respectively). In 1971 President Nixon had obtained a 30 percent job approval figure from blacks; by 1983 President Reagan commanded a job approval figure of no more than 10 percent of blacks (corresponding figures for whites were 55 percent and 42 percent). According to a *Los Angeles Times* poll in 1983, 30 percent of eligible black voters supported Jesse Jackson, 24 percent Mondale, and 9 percent Glenn. See Margaret Roberts, "This Could Be the Election in Which Black Voters Hold the Key to the Presidential Races," *National Journal,* October 29, 1983, pp. 2208–9. For a general discussion see Michael B. Preston et al., eds., *The New Black Politics: The Search for Political Power* (New York: Longmans, 1982), especially the article by Marguerite Ross Barnett, "The Congressional Black Caucus: Illusions and Realities of Power," pp. 28–54.

29. For the history of anti-apartheid movements, see George W. Shepherd, Jr., *Anti-Apartheid: Transnational Conflict and Western Policy in the Liberation of South Africa* (Westport, Conn.: Greenwood Press, 1977).

30. For a more detailed breakdown, see Harold Soref and Ian Greig, *The Puppeteers: An Examination of Those Organizations and Bodies Concerned with the Elimination of the White Man in Africa* (London: Tandem Books, 1965); and Ronald Segal, *Political Africa: A Who's Who of Personalities and Parties* (New York: Praeger, 1961).

31. For a list of some U.S. anti-apartheid groups see n. 8, Chapter 20.

32. Washington Office on Africa, *African Future* (Washington, D.C.: The Office, n.d.), p. 2.

33. On U.S. fronts, see *Red Locusts: Soviet Support for Terrorism in South Africa* (Alexandria, Va.: Western Books, 1981); Richard Edward Lapchick, "South Africa: Sport and Apartheid Policies," *Annals of the American Academy,* no. 445, September 1979, pp. 155–65; and Lapchick, *The Politics of Race and International Sport: The Case of South Africa* (Westport, Conn.: Greenwood Press, 1975).

Chapter 24. Americans in Africa, and Africans in America

1. Kwane Nkrumah, *Neo-Colonialism: The Last Stage of Imperialism* (London: Nelson, 1965), pp. 247–9.

2. Rupert Emerson, *Africa and United States Policy* (Englewood Cliffs, N.J.: Prentice-Hall, 1967), p. 43.

3. *New Encyclopaedia Britannica,* 15th ed., s.v. "Peace Corps."

4. Rudyard Kipling, "The White Man's Burden," in Kipling, *Collected Verse* (New York: Doubleday, Page, 1910), pp. 215–17. Kipling's poem, though often derided, by no means called for colonial repression, but for a moderately reformist program; the colonial rulers and their gods would ultimately be judged by their subjects.

5. Peace Corps, *The Toughest Job You'll Ever Love* (Washington, D.C.: GPO, 1981), p. 2.

6. The Peace Corps accepts U.S. citizens at least eighteen years old and in good health; there is no upper age limit. Married couples are accepted, provided both want to be volunteers. Volunteers receive a brief initial training to acquaint them with local languages and customs. Their pay overseas provides for essential food, housing, and a little spending money; it averaged about $300 a month at the end of 1980. At the end of that year volunteers leaving the Peace Corps received $125 for every month of completed service to enable them to adjust once more to life in the United States.

7. *Peace Corps in Africa* (Washington, D.C.: GPO, 1966), p. 8. For a critical discussion see David Hapgood, *Agents of Change: A Close Look at the Peace Corps* (Boston: Little, Brown, 1968).

8. *Peace Corps in Africa.*

9. "Cross Roads Africa," *Africa Special Report* 3, no. 6 (1958): 3–4, 14.

10. Quoted in R. Freeman Butts, *American Education in International Development* (New York: Harper & Row, 1983), p. 26.

11. Information provided by R. Freeman Butts, formerly of Teachers College, Columbia University.

12. Vernon McKay, ed., *Africa in the United States* (New York: Macfodder Student Edition, 1967), pp. 30–1.

13. *The 1963 National Catholic Almanac* (Patterson, N.J.: St. Anthony's Guild, 1963); *The Encyclopedia of Modern Christian Missions: The Agencies,* ed. W. N. Kerr (Camden, N.J.: Nelson, 1967). For detailed statistics on American missionaries in Africa and their work, see Appendix B.

14. American Protestant missionaries at the end of 1960 numbered about twenty-seven thousand men and women scattered throughout the world, compared with some seven thousand from Great Britain. For more details, see "Missions gesellschaften," *Brockhaus Encyclopädie* (1971).

15. The Nyasaland Protectorate's revenue in 1963 was $7,699,006. *Whitaker's Almanac* (London, 1964), p. 782.

16. L. H. Gann, *The Birth of a Plural Society: The Development of Northern Rhodesia under the British South Africa Company, 1894–1914* (Manchester: Manchester University Press, 1958), pp. 37–8.

17. Bengt Sundkler, *The Christian Ministry in Africa* (Uppsala: Swedish Institute of Missionary Research, 1960); *Encyclical Letter of . . . John XXIII, by Divine Providence Pope, on the Mission, Known as Princeps Pastorum . . . , 28 November 1960* (Rome, 1960).

18. See L. H. Gann, *A History of Northern Rhodesia: Early Days to 1953* (London: Chatto & Windus, 1964), pp. 114–15, 317–19.

19. The NCC in 1971 comprised some 62 missions with about 10,000 missionaries. In addition, the Interdenominational Foreign Mission had 44 missions and 6,500 missionaries not tied to particular churches, and the Evangelical Foreign Mission Association had 58 missions and 6,000 missionaries. The NCC itself was affiliated with the World Council of Churches.

20. Ernest W. Lefever, *Amsterdam to Nairobi: The World Council of Churches and the*

Third World (Washington, D.C.: Georgetown University Press, 1979). Equally important was the Conference of Theologians of the Third World, held at Dar-es-Salaam in 1976, which helped to elaborate the new liberation theology.

21. See Edward Norman, *Christianity in the Southern Hemisphere: The Churches in Latin America and South Africa* (London: Oxford University Press, 1980).

22. See Stephen Thernstrom, ed., *Harvard Encyclopedia of American Ethnic Groups* (Cambridge, Mass.: Harvard University Press [Belknap Press], 1980), s.v. "Africans," "Afro-Americans," and "Cape Verdeans."

23. Thernstrom, *Harvard Encyclopedia,* s.v. "South Africans."

24. Raymond Anthony Almeida, ed., *Cape Verdeans in America: Our Story* (Boston: American Committee for Cape Verde, 1978).

25. Most Cape Verde immigrants come from the Fogo and Brava islands. Remittances from the United States were important in the local economy, and returnees introduced English words and evangelical Protestantism to the islands. Between 1870 and 1930 the "Americanos" had "transformed the face of Brava and Fogo and replaced the grass-roofed cabins of old by neat white houses, embowered in flowers and fruit-trees." Archibald Lyall, *Black and White Make Brown: An Account of a Journey to the Cape Verde Islands and Portuguese Guinea* (London: Heinemann, 1938), p. 86.

26. Leo Pap, *The Portuguese-Americans* (Boston: Twayne, 1981), pp. 159–62.

27. Paul R. Ehrlich, Roy Bilderback, and Anne Ehrlich, *The Golden Door: Internal Migration, Mexico and the United States* (New York: Wideview Books, 1981), pp. xiv–xv.

Selected bibliography

Here are listed only books published or reprinted in English in the last twenty-five years or so. For fuller listings, see the Notes.

Africa Seen by American Negroes. Paris: Presénce Africaine, 1958.

Albion, Robert Greenhalgh. *Seaports South of Sahara: The Achievements of an American Steamship Service.* New York: Appleton-Century-Crofts, 1959.

Albright, David E. *Communism in Africa.* Bloomington: Indiana University Press, 1980.

Almeida, Raymond Anthony, ed. *Cape Verdeans in America: Our Story.* Boston: American Committee for Cape Verde, 1978.

Ambrose, Stephen. *Rise to Globalism: American Foreign Policy, 1938–1980.* New York: Viking/Penguin, 1980.

Anene, Joseph C., and Brown, Godfrey N. *Africa in the Nineteenth and Twentieth Centuries: A Handbook for Teachers and Students.* London: Nelson, 1966; Ibadan: Ibadan University Press, 1967.

Archdeacon, Thomas J. *Becoming an American: An Ethnic History.* New York: Free Press, 1983.

Arnove, Robert F., ed. *Philanthropy and Cultural Imperialism: The Foundations at Home and Abroad.* Bloomington: Indiana University Press, 1982.

Attwood, William. *The Reds and the Blacks: A Personal Adventure.* New York: Harper & Row, 1967.

Austin, Dennis. *Politics in Africa.* Hanover, N.H.: University Press of New England, 1980.

Baer, George W. *Test Case: Italy, Ethiopia, and the League of Nations.* Stanford, Calif.: Hoover Institute Press, 1976.

Bailey, Thomas A. *A Diplomatic History of the American People.* 10th ed. Englewood Cliffs, N.J.: Prentice-Hall, 1980.

Bailey, Thomas A., and Kennedy, David M. *The American Pageant: A History of the Republic.* 7th ed. 2 vols. Lexington, Mass.: Heath, 1983.

Barnett, Marguerite Ross, and Wilkinson, Doris. *Images of Blacks in American Popular Culture: 1865–1955.* New York: Holmes & Meier, 1983.

Berman, Ronald. *America in the Sixties: An Intellectual History.* New York: Free Press, 1968.

Blyden, Edward W. *Christianity, Islam and the Negro Race.* Edinburgh: Edinburgh University Press, 1967.

Boorstin, Daniel J. *The Americans: The Democratic Experience.* New York: Random House, 1973.

Booth, Alan, R. *The United States Experiences in South Africa, 1784–1870.* Cape Town: Balkema, 1976.

Broderick, Francis L. *W. E. B. Du Bois, Negro Leader in a Time of Crisis.* Stanford, Calif.: Stanford University Press, 1959.

Brooks, George E. *Yankee Traders, Old Coasters, and African Middlemen: A History of American Legitimate Trade with West Africa in the Nineteenth Century.* Boston: Boston University Press, 1970.

Burton, Robert. *The Life and Death of Whales.* London: Deutsch, 1973.

Butler, Jeffrey, ed. *Boston University Papers in African History.* 2 vols. Boston: Boston University Press, 1964.

Carter, Gwendolen. *Which Way Is South Africa Going?* Bloomington: Indiana University Press, 1983.

Carter, Gwendolen, and O'Meara, Patrick, eds. *International Politics in South Africa.* Bloomington: Indiana University Press, 1983.

  Southern Africa: The Continuing Crisis. 2d ed. Bloomington: Indiana University Press, 1982.

Carter, Wilfred, and Kilson, Martin, eds. *The African Reader: Independent Africa.* New York: Vintage Books, 1970.

Casada, James A., ed. *African and Afro-American History.* Buffalo: Conch Magazine, 1978.

Chester, Edward W. *Clash of Titans: Africa and U.S. Foreign Policy.* Maryknoll: N.Y.: Orbis Books, 1974.

Clark, James L. *Good Hunting: Fifty Years of Collecting and Preparing Habitat Groups for the American Museum.* Norman: University of Oklahoma Press, 1966.

Clements, Frank, and Harben, Edward. *Leaf of Gold: The Story of Rhodesian Tobacco.* London: Methuen, 1962.

Clendenen, Clarence; Collins, Robert; and Duignan, Peter. *Americans in Africa, 1855–1900.* Stanford, Calif.: Hoover Institution Press, 1966.

Clendenen, Clarence, and Duignan, Peter. *Americans in Black Africa, up to 1865.* Stanford, Calif.: Hoover Institution Press, 1964.

Cohn, Helen Desfosses. *Soviet Policy toward Black Africa: The Focus on National Integration.* New York: Praeger, 1972.

Coles, Samuel B. *Preacher with a Plow.* Boston: Houghton Mifflin, 1957.

Coughtry, Jay. *The Notorious Triangle: Rhode Island and the African Slave Trade, 1700–1807.* Philadelphia: Temple University Press, 1981.

Council on Foreign Relations, *The United States in World Affairs.* New York: Harper & Row, annual.

Cronon, Edmund. *Black Moses: The Story of Marcus Garvey and the Universal Negro Improvement Association.* Madison: University of Wisconsin Press, 1968.

Cunningham, Simon. *The Copper Industry in Zambia: Foreign Mining Companies in a Developing Country.* New York: Praeger, 1981.

Curti, Merle. *American Philanthropy Abroad: A History.* New Brunswick, N.J.: Rutgers University Press, 1963.

Curtin, Philip D. *The Atlantic Slave Trade: A Census.* Madison: University of Wisconsin Press, 1969.

Davis, John Presten, ed. *The American Negro Reference Book.* Englewood Cliffs, N.J.: Prentice-Hall, 1966.

Degler, Carl N. *Out of Our Past: The Forces That Shaped Modern America.* 3d ed. New York: Harper & Row, 1983.

Donnan, Elizabeth, ed. *Documents Illustrative of the History of the Slave Trade to America.* 4 vols. New York: Octagon Books, 1965.

Dowling, Harry F. *Fighting Infection: Conquests of the Twentieth Century.* Cambridge, Mass.: Harvard University Press, 1977.

Draper, Theodore. *The Rediscovery of Black Nationalism.* New York: Viking Press, 1970.

Du Bois, W. E. B. *Color and Democracy: Colonies and Peace.* 1945. Reprint. Millwood, N.J.: Kraus Reprint Co., 1975.

  The Correspondence of W. E. B. Du Bois. Edited by Herbert Aptheker. 3 vols. Amherst: University of Massachusetts Press, 1973–8.

The Suppression of the African Slave-Trade to the United States of America, 1638–1870. 1896. Reprint. New York: Dover Publications, 1970.

The World and Africa: An Inquiry into the Part Which Africa Has Played in World History. 1947. Reprint. Millwood, N.Y.: Kraus Reprint Co., 1965.

Duffy, James. *Portuguese Africa.* Cambridge, Mass.: Harvard University Press, 1959.

Duignan, Peter, ed. *Guide to Research and Reference Works in Sub-Saharan Africa.* Stanford, Calif.: Hoover Institution Press, 1971.

Duignan, Peter, and Clendenen, Clarence. *The United States and the African Slave Trade, 1619–1862.* Stanford, Calif.: Hoover Institution Press, 1963.

Edinburgh, University of, Center of African Studies. *The Transatlantic Slave Trade from West Africa.* Edinburgh: University of Edinburgh Press, 1965.

Ellis, David, and Walvin, James, eds. *The Abolition of the Atlantic Slave Trade: Origins, and Effects in Europe, Africa, and the Americas.* Madison: University of Wisconsin Press, 1981.

Ellis, Richard. The Book of Whales. New York: Knopf, 1980.

Emerson, Rupert. *Africa and United States Policy.* Englewood Cliffs, N.J.: Prentice-Hall, 1967.

Farer, Tom J. *War Clouds on the Horn of Africa: The Widening Storm.* New York: Carnegie Endowment for International Peace, 1979.

Farwell, Byron. *The Man Who Presumed: A Biography of Henry M. Stanley.* New York: Holt, 1957.

Fetter, Bruce. *The Creation of Elisabethville, 1910–1940.* Stanford, Calif.: Hoover Institution Press, 1976.

Foote, Andrew H. *Africa and the American Flag.* New York: Appleton, 1954. Reprint. Folkstone, Eng.: Dawson, 1970.

Franck, Thomas M., and Weisband, Edward. *Foreign Policy by Congress.* New York: Oxford University Press, 1979.

Franklin, John Hope, and Meier, August, eds. *Black Leaders of the Twentieth Century.* Champaign: University of Illinois Press, 1983.

Fry, Joseph A. *Henry S. Sanford: Diplomacy and Business in Nineteenth Century America.* Reno: University of Nevada Press, 1982.

Gann, L. H. *A History of Northern Rhodesia: Early Days to 1953.* London: Chatto & Windus, 1964.

Gann, L. H., and Duignan, Peter. *Africa and the World: An Introduction to the History of Sub-Saharan Africa from Antiquity to 1840.* San Francisco: Chandler, 1972.

Africa South of the Sahara: The Challenge to Western Security. Stanford, Calif.: Hoover Institution Press, 1981.

Why South Africa Will Survive: A Historical Analysis. New York: St. Martin's Press, 1981.

Garvey, A. Jacques. *Garvey and Garveyism.* Kingston, Jamaica, 1963.

Geiss, Imanuel. *The Pan-African Movement: A History of Pan-Africanism in America, Europe and Africa.* New York: Africana, 1974.

Girling, John L. S. *America and the Third World: Revolution and Intervention.* London: Routledge & Kegan Paul, 1980.

Goldschmidt, Walter, ed. *The United States and Africa.* New York: Columbia University, American Assembly, 1958.

Goode, Robert C. *U.D.I.: The International Politics of the Rhodesian Rebellion.* London: Faber & Faber, 1973.

Griffith, Cyril E. *The African Dream: Martin R. Delany and the Emergence of Pan-Africanism.* University Park: Pennsylvania State University Press, 1975.

Groves, Charles Pelham. *The Planting of Christianity in Africa.* 4 vols. London: Butterworth, 1948–58.

Hallett, Robin. *Africa to 1875: A Modern History.* Ann Arbor: University of Michigan Press, 1970.

The Penetration of Africa: European Exploration in North and West Africa to 1815. New York: Praeger, 1965.

Hargreaves, John D. *Prelude to the Partition of West Africa.* New York: St. Martin's Press, 1963.

Harlan, Louis R. *Booker T. Washington.* 2 vols. New York: Oxford University Press, 1972, 1983.

Harlan, Louis R., and Smock, Raymond W., eds. *The Booker T. Washington Papers.* 11 vols. Chicago: University of Illinois Press, 1972–81.

Harris, Brice, Jr. *The United States and the Italo-Ethiopian Crisis.* Stanford, Calif.: Stanford University Press, 1964.

Harris, Sheldon H. *Paul Cuffe, Black Americans and the African Return.* New York: Simon & Schuster, 1972.

Henriksen, Thomas H., ed. *Communist Powers and Sub-Saharan Africa.* Stanford, Calif.: Hoover Institution Press, 1981.

Hesseltine, William B., and Wolf, Hazel C. *The Blue and the Gray on the Nile.* Chicago: University of Chicago Press, 1961.

Hill, Adelaide Cromwell, and Kilson, Martin, comps. *Apropos of Africa: Sentiments of Negro Leaders on Africa from the 1800's to the 1950's.* London: Cass, 1969.

Hill, Robert A., ed. *The Marcus Garvey and Universal Negro Improvement Association Papers.* 2 vols. Berkeley: University of California Press, 1983.

Holloway, Joseph E. *Liberian Diplomacy in Africa: A Study of Inter-African Relations.* Washington, D.C.: University Press of America, 1981.

Hooker, James R. *Black Revolutionary: George Padmore's Path from Communism to Pan-Africanism.* London: Pall Mall Press, 1967.

Howard, Warren S. *American Slavers and the Federal Law, 1837–1862.* Berkeley: University of California Press, 1963.

Huggins, Nathan. *Black Odyssey: The Afro-American Experience in Slavery.* New York: Vintage Books, 1979.

Huggins, Nathan I., et al, eds. *Key Issues in the Afro-American Experience.* 2 vols. New York: Harcourt, Brace, 1971.

Hull, Galen Spencer. *Pawns on a Chessboard: The Resource War in Southern Africa.* Washington, D.C.: University Press of America, 1982.

Isaacs, Harold R. *The New World of Negro Americans.* New York: John Day, 1963.

Jacobs, Sylvia M. *The African Nexus: Black American Perspectives on the European Partitioning of Africa, 1880–1920.* Westport, Conn.: Greenwood Press, 1981.

July, Robert W. *The Origins of Modern African Thought.* New York: Praeger, 1967.

Kaplan, Marion. *Focus Africa.* New York: Doubleday, 1983.

Kilson, Martin, and Rotberg, R., eds. *The African Diaspora: Interpretative Essays.* Cambridge, Mass: Harvard University Press, 1976.

King, Kenneth James. *Pan-Africanism and Education: A Study of Race, Philanthropy and Education in the Southern States of America and East Africa.* Oxford: Oxford University Press (Clarendon Press), 1971.

The Kissinger Study of Southern Africa: National Security Study Memorandum 39. Edited and introduced by Mohammed H. El Khawas and Barry Cohen. Westport, Conn: Lawrence Hill, 1976.

Kitchen, Helen. *U.S. Interests in Africa.* New York: Praeger, 1983.

Kitchen, Helen, ed. *Africa: From Mystery to Maze.* Critical Choices for Americans Series, vol. 11. Lexington, Mass.: Lexington Books, 1976.

Klein, Herbert S. *The Middle Passage: Comparative Studies on the Atlantic Slave Trade.* Princeton, N.J.: Princeton University Press, 1978.

Lake, Anthony. *The "Tar Baby" Option: American Policy toward Southern Rhodesia.* New York: Columbia University Press, 1978.

Lamb, David. *The Africans.* New York: Random House, 1982.

Langley, J. Adoyele. *Pan-Africanism and Nationalism in West Africa, 1900–1945: A Study in Ideology and Social Class.* Oxford: Oxford University Press (Clarendon Press), 1973.

Latourette, Kenneth Scott. *A History of Christianity.* 2 vols. New York: Harper & Row, 1975.

Lefever, Ernest W. *Amsterdam to Nairobi: The World Council of Churches and the Third World.* Washington, D.C.: Georgetown University Press, 1979.

Legum, Colin. *Pan-Africanism: A Short Political Guide.* New York: Praeger, 1962.

Lemarchand, René, ed. *American Policy in Southern Africa: The Stakes and the Stance.* Washington, D.C.: University Press of America, 1978.

Liebenow, J. Gus. *Liberia: The Evolution of Privilege.* Ithaca: Cornell University Press, 1969.

Lloyd, Christopher. *The Navy and the Slave Trade: The Suppression of the African Slave Trade in the Nineteenth Century.* Reprint. London: Cass, 1968.

Logan, Rayford W., and Winston, Michael R., eds. *The Dictionary of American Negro Biography.* New York: Norton, 1983.

Louis, Roger William. *Imperialism at Bay: The United States and the Decolonization of the British Empire, 1941–1945.* New York: Oxford University Press, 1978.

Lowenkopf, Martin. *Politics in Liberia: The Conservative Road to Development.* Stanford, Calif.: Hoover Institution Press, 1976.

Lynch, Hollis R. *Black American Radicals and the Liberation of Africa: The Council on African Affairs, 1935–1955.* Monograph Series, no. 5. Ithaca, N.Y.: Cornell University, Africana Studies and Research Center, 1978.

Edward Wilmot Blyden: Pan-Negro Patriot, 1832–1912. New York: Oxford University Press, 1970.

McKay, Vernon. *Africa in World Politics.* New York: Harper & Row, 1963.

McKinley, Edward H. *The Lure of Africa: American Interests in Tropical Africa, 1919–1939.* Indianapolis: Bobbs-Merrill, 1974.

Mahoney, Richard D. *J.F.K.: Ordeal in Africa.* New York: Oxford University Press, 1983.

Mannix, Daniel P., and Cowley, Malcolm. *Black Cargoes: A History of the Atlantic Slave Trade, 1518–1865.* New York: Viking Press, 1962.

Marcus, Harold G. *Ethiopia, Great Britain, and the United States, 1941–1974: The Politics of Empire.* Berkeley: University of California Press, 1983.

Marcus, Robert D., and Burner, David, eds. *America since 1945.* New York: St. Martin's Press, 1981.

Marita, Golden. *Migrations of the Heart: A Personal Odyssey.* New York: Anchor Press, 1983.

Marnham, Patrick. *Fantastic Invasion: Notes on Contemporary Africa.* New York: Harcourt Brace Jovanovich, 1980.

Martin, Tony. *Race First: The Ideological and Organizational Struggles of Marcus Garvey and the Universal Negro Improvement Association.* Westport, Conn.: Greenwood Press, 1976.

Meier, August. *Negro Thought in America, 1890–1915: Racial Ideology in the Age of Booker T. Washington.* Ann Arbor: University of Michigan Press, 1963.

Moikobu, Josephine M. *Blood and Flesh: Black American and African Identification.* Westport, Conn.: Greenwood Press, 1981.

Morison, Samuel Eliot. *The Oxford History of the American People.* London: Oxford University Press, 1965.

Morris, Charles R. *Times of Passion: America, 1960–1980.* New York: Harper & Row, 1983.

Mower, A. Glenn, Jr. *The United Nations and Human Rights: The Eleanor Roosevelt and Jimmy Carter Eras.* Westport, Conn.: Greenwood Press, 1979.

Munger, Edwin S. *Touched by Africa.* Pasadena, Calif: Castle Press, 1983.

Myers, Desaix B., et al. *U.S. Business in South Africa: The Economic, Political and Moral Issues.* Bloomington: Indiana University Press, 1983.

Neumark, S. Daniel. *Foreign Trade and the Economic Development in Africa: A Historical Perspective.* Stanford, Calif.: Stanford University, Food Research Institute, 1964.

Nielsen, Waldemar. *The Great Powers and Africa.* New York: Praeger, 1969.

Norman, Edward. *Christianity in the Southern Hemisphere: The Churches in Latin America and South Africa.* London: Oxford University Press, 1980.

Padmore, George. *Pan-Africanism or Communism? The Coming Struggle for Africa.* New York: Ray, 1956.

Padmore, George, ed. *History of the Pan-African Congress.* London: Hammersmith Bookshop, 1963.

Pastor, Robert A. *Congress and the Politics of U.S. Foreign Economic Policy, 1929–1976.* Berkeley: University of California Press, 1980.

Paterson, Thomas G. *Major Problems in American Foreign Policy.* 2d ed. 2 vols. Lexington, Mass.: Lexington Books, 1983.

Peterson, John. *Province of Freedom: A History of Sierra Leone, 1787–1870.* London: Faber & Faber, 1969.

Phillips, Clifton Jackson. *Protestant America and the Pagan World: The First Half Century of the American Board of Commissioners for Foreign Missions, 1810–1860.* Cambridge, Mass.: Harvard University Press, 1969.

Price, Robert M. *U.S. Foreign Policy in Sub-Saharan Africa: National Interests and Global Strategy.* Berkeley, Calif.: Institute of International Studies, 1979.

Quarles, Benjamin. *The Negro in the Making of America.* New York: Collier Books, 1964.

Redkey, Edwin S. *Black Exodus: Black Nationalists and Back to Africa Movements, 1890–1910.* New Haven, Conn.: Yale University Press, 1969.

Roberts, George Arthur. *Let Me Tell You a Story.* Bulawayo: Rhodesian Christian Press, 1964.

Rudwick, Elliot M. *W. E. B. Du Bois: A Study in Minority Leadership.* Philadelphia: University of Pennsylvania Press, 1960.

Seidman, Ann, and Seidman, Neva. *South Africa and U.S. Multinational Corporations.* Westport, Conn.: Lawrence Hill, 1978.

Shepperson, George, and Price, Thomas. *Independent African: John Chilembwe and the Origins, Setting, and Significance of the Nyasaland Native Rising of 1915.* Edinburgh: Edinburgh University Press, 1958.

Slade, Ruth M. *English-speaking Missions in the Congo Independent State (1878–1908).* Brussels: Académie Royal des Sciences Coloniales, 1959.

Stackpole, Edouard A. *Whales and Destiny: The Rivalry between America, France, and Britain for Control of the Southern Whale Fishery, 1785–1825.* Amherst: University of Massachusetts Press, 1972.

Staudenraus, P. J. *The African Colonization Movement, 1816–1865.* New York: Columbia University Press, 1961.

Stockwell, John. *In Search of Enemies: A C.I.A. Story.* New York: Norton, 1978.

Sundiata, I. K. *Black Scandal: America and the Liberian Labor Crisis, 1929–1936.* Philadelphia: Institute for the Study of Human Issues, 1980.

Sundkler, Bengt G. M. *Bantu Prophets in South Africa.* 2d ed. London: Oxford University Press, 1962.

Selected bibliography

The Christian Ministry in Africa. Uppsala: Swedish Institute of Missionary Research, 1960.

Thernstrom, Stephen, ed. *Harvard Encyclopedia of American Ethnic Groups.* Cambridge, Mass.: Harvard University Press (Belknap Press), 1980.

Unger, Irwin. *The Movement: A History of the American New Left, 1959–1972.* New York: Dodd, Mead, 1974.

Uya, Okon Edet. *Black Brotherhood: Afro-Americans and Africa.* Lexington, Mass.: Heath, 1971.

Walker, James W. St. G. *The Black Loyalists: The Search for a Promised Land in Nova Scotia and Sierra Leone, 1783–1870.* New York: Africana, 1976.

Ward, W. E. F. *The Royal Navy and the Slavers: The Suppression of the Atlantic Slave Trade.* Reprint. New York: Pantheon Books, 1969.

Weissman, Stephen R. *American Foreign Policy in the Congo, 1960–1964.* Ithaca, N.Y.: Cornell University Press, 1974.

Whitaker, Jennifer Seymour. *Conflict in Southern Africa.* New York: Foreign Policy Association, 1978.

Whitaker, Jennifer Seymour, ed. *Africa and the United States: Vital Interests.* New York: New York University Press, 1978.

Williams, Lorraine A., ed. *Africa and the Afro-American Experience: Eight Essays.* Washington, D.C.: Howard University Press, 1977.

Wilson, Ellen Gibson. *The Loyal Blacks.* New York: Putnam, 1976.

Witherell, Julien W., comp. *The United States and Africa: Guide to U.S. Official Documents and Government-Sponsored Publications on Africa, 1785–1975.* Washington, D.C.: Library of Congress, 1978.

Index

American African Affairs Association, 333
American Baptist Board, 227
American Baptist Missionary Union, 137, 171, 227
American Board of Commissioners for Foreign Missions (ABCFM), 389n47, n49, 400n4; in Angola, 168; in Gabon, 65, 96–8; in Liberia, 93–5; in Mozambique, 165, 166, 226; in Rhodesia, 226, 401n19; in South Africa, 101, 103, 164, 227, 235
American Colonization Society, 25, 81–95 passim, 123, 172, 254, 263; dissolution of, 387n21; and Latrobe as president of, 130; and Liberian death rates, 95, 387n16; MacCarthy and, 62
American Committee on Africa (ACOA), 350–1, 352, 261
American Council of Learned Societies, 331
American Friends Service Committee, 361
American Lutheran Missionary Society, 171
American Metal Climax, 310
American Metal Company, 223, 224
American Missionary Association, 171
American Mission for Lepers, 227
American Museum of Natural History, 211, 213, 216
American Negro Leadership Conference on Africa (ANLCA), 341–2
American Red Cross, 330
American Society of African Culture (AMSAC), 341
American South African Line, 224–5
American West African Line, 206
Amin, Idi, 322
Amistad, 28–9, 30
Anderson, Benjamin J. K., 117–18
Andersson, Efraim, 248
Anglo-American Corporation, 223, 303–4
Anglo-American Expedition for the Discovery of the Nile and Congo Sources, 127
Angola, 44, 49, 298, 322; missionaries in, 168–9, 227–34 passim, 277, 360; oil industry in, 303, 309, 313; trade with, 77, 116, 301, 416n16; U.S. policy toward, 291–9 passim, 351, 418n15
annexationism (*see also* imperialism), 65, 71, 110, 119–20
anticolonialism/antiimperialism, 164, 288, 290, 339, 361
anti-Europeanism, 240, 245
antimony trade, 300
apartheid, 290–1, 297–8, 311–13, 245, 249–52, 361
Arabs, 6, 36–7, 41, 107, 139, 193
Ardent, HMS, 35
armed forces, *see* military forces
arms embargoes: in Italo-Ethiopian war, 209; against South Africa, 294–5, 352
arms transfers, U.S., 295–6
Army Research Branch, U.S., 325–6
Aroux, P., 121–3
Arthur, Chester A., 121, 131, 135, 395n10
arts, African influences in, 207
Ash, William 91–2
Ashanti expeditions, 127, 233
Ashburn, Percy M., 196

Ashmun, Jehudi, 84, 278
Association for Promoting the Discovery of the Interior Parts of Africa, 80, 107
Association for the Study of Negro Life and History (ASNL), 261
Association of Concerned African Scholars (ACAS), 350, 352
Aswan, 146
Atlanta, 108
"Atlanta Compromise" speech, 270
Atlantic Monthly, 266
Aulick, John, 76
automobiles, 206–7, 218–19, 222, 310
Ayres, Eli, 83–4
Azikiwe, Nnamdi, 262, 278, 336, 339, 341
Azores, 59, 60, 291, 364

Babe, Jerome L., 152, 398n4
back-to-Africa movements (*see also* colonization societies; emigrationism), 252–8 passim, 344, 411n18; Bowen and, 99–100; Delany and Campbell and, 88–90, 253; Garvey and, 254, 257, 268
Bacon, Samuel, 83, 84
Bailey, Thomas, 334
Bailundu, Benguela, 168
Baines, Thomas, 398n4
Bakwena people, 297
Balenge, 138, 395n15
Ballard, Major, 197, 198
Baltimore, 29, 31
Baltimore Afro-American, 278
Ba Mogopa people, 297
Bancroft, Frederic, 376n4
Banda, Hastings Kamuzu, 262, 284, 338
bank loans, *see* loans
Bank Loans to South Africa, 312
Banks, Sir Joseph, 107
Bankson, John B., 83
Bantu Are Coming, The, 235
Bantu speakers, 235, 243, 256
Baptists, 249, 255, 389n41, 390n77; in Congo, 137, 138, 227, 246, 256, 395n15; in Liberia, 93, 227, 389n49; in Nigeria, 92, 98–9, 101, 169–71, 390n77; in Nyasaland, 241, 242
Barber Lines, 206
Barclay, Arthur, 204
Barclay, Edwin J., 204, 305
Barnato, Barney, 154–5
Barotseland, 44, 360
Barron, Edward W., 100
Barth, Heinrich, 109
Bassa Cove, Liberia, 85
Bastide, Roger, 50
Bates, Francis, 166
Bathurst, Gambia, 64
Bauer, P. T., 323
bauxite deposits, 308, 318
Bauxites du Midi, 308
Bayard, Thomas F., 123, 124
Beatty, Alfred Chester, 221, 223
Beekman family, 58
Beit, Alfred, 302
Belgian residents, in Katanga, 222

Index

New York World, 148
Ngunzism, 245–6
Niagara Movement, 260
Niger Dam, 319, 321
Nigeria, 290, 334, 341; aid to, 317, 319, 417n9; back-to-Africa movement and, 89–90, 253; civil war in, 99, 309, 343; Communist Party in, 285–6; cotton crops in, 274; economy of, 308–9, 417n13; education in, 336–7, 357; investments in, 301, 308–9; religion in, 98–9, 101, 169–71, 246–7, 359, 363, 390n77; slavery in, 6; trade with, 300, 301
Niger Valley, 89–90, 98–9, 389n47, 390n77
Nile River, 144–7, 211, 215
Nimba range, Liberia, 306
Nixon, Richard M., 291, 293, 420n28
Nkosi, Lewis, 341
Nkrumah, Kwame, 262, 278, 339–40, 342, 343; and aid, 319; at Fifth Pan-African Congress, 284, 340; and Garvey, 259; and Peace Corps, 354; Stalin on, 285; and "tribe" (term), 387n20; and Volta River project, 306
North Atlantic Treaty Organization (NATO), 285, 286, 291
North Carolina, 19, 20, 233
Northern Rhodesia, 262, 286, 288n39; mining/minerals in, 158, 222, 223–4, 234–5, 300, 303–4, 414n5
northern United States (*see also* New England): black migration to, 257, 268; NAACP and, 260; slave trade of, 47
Northwestern Christian Advocate, 169
Northwestern University, 326
Nova Scotia, 91, 383n13, 386n7, 387n12
Noyes, Edward F., 119
Nsukka University, 327, 336–7
Nsumba, Gordon, 245
Nubia, S., 91
Nubia, 6, 146
Nujoma, Sam, 341
nurses' training, 226–7
Nyakyusa people, 245
Nyasaland, 286, 304, 338; agriculture in, 230; education in, 167–8, 328, 336, 338; missionaries in, 167–8, 230, 241–2, 245, 338, 388n39; revenue of, 421n15
Nye, Gerald P., 208

Odlum, G. M., 161
Office of Education, U.S., 331
Office of International Security Affairs, U.S. Defense Department, 289
Ogbomosho, Nigeria, 99, 169, 170
Ogowe River, 98, 109, 110
oil, 209, 300, 308–9, 310, 311, 313
Oklahoma State University, 337
Oldham, J. H., 247, 275–7, 413n75
Old Umtali, Southern Rhodesia, 167, 230
Olduvai Gorge, Tanzania, 217, 329
Olin Mathieson Chemical Corporation, 307–8
Oliver, Roland, 244
Open Door policy, 185, 266
Oppenheimer, Ernest, 223

Orange Free State, 155, 189
Order of Ethiopia, 239
Organization of African Unity, 342, 349
Outlook, 189
Overland cars, 206
Overseas Private Investment Corporation, 316
Ovimbundu people, 168, 234
Owen, William T., 69, 70

Pacific Ocean, 185
pacifism, 85, 220, 242
Padmore, George, 252, 262, 338–40, 411n35
Paine, John S., 35
palladium trade, 311
Palmerton, Lord, 71, 74
palm oil trade, 7, 61, 78
Pan-African congresses, 208, 264–7 passim, 284, 339, 340, 412n45
Pan-African Federation, 252, 339, 340
Pan-Africanism, 249, 253, 261–8, 340–1; defined, 262–3; Du Bois and, 208, 259, 260, 263, 264–8, 275, 340, 341; missionary, 256, 275; Padmore and, 252, 262, 411n35; Washington and, 262, 263, 270
Pan-Africanism or Communism? 252, 411n35
Panama, 191
Panama Canal, 185, 191
Pan American Airways, 304–5
pan concept, 262–3
Panther, 199
Paris Peace Conference, 267
partition, of Africa (*see also* imperialism), 79, 101, 147, 164, 300, 360
patriotism, American, 348
Payne, John, 96
Peabody Museum, 207–8, 217
Peace Corps, 330, 337, 354–6, 357, 358, 421n6
Peacock, USS, 72, 73–4, 385n50
peanuts, 43, 61, 63
Pennsylvania, 20, 67, 384n29
Perkins, Cato, 91–2, 388n36
Perry, Matthew C., 2, 32, 33, 65–6, 108, 377n2
personality, African, 261
Peter, king of Cape Mesurado, 84
pharmaceuticals, donation of, 308
Phelps, Caroline, 235
Phelps Dodge, 310
Phelps Hall Bible Training school, 275
Phelps-Stokes Commission, 235–7, 247, 275, 276; Aggrey as representative of, 233, 242, 246, 247, 262, 275, 276; reports of, 236–7, 276, 277
Phelps-Stokes Fund, 235, 237, 276, 418n7
Philadelphia, 67, 384n29
Philadelphia Negro, The, 260
philanthropy, 235–7, 314, 321, 414n85, 418n7; *see also* aid, U.S.; foundations
Philbin, Eugene A., 194
Philip, John, 70, 101, 385n50, 391n80
Philippines, 164, 185, 187, 189, 220
Phillips, Frederic, 384n29
Phillips, Ray E., 235
Phillips Petroleum, 309
Philosophy and Opinions of Marcus Garvey, 259

444